A HANDBOOK OF
PERSONNEL
MANAGEMENT
PRACTICE

A HANDBOOK OF

PERSONNEL MANAGEMENT PRACTICE

FOURTH EDITION

MICHAEL ARMSTRONG

**KOGAN
PAGE**

First published in 1977
Second edition published in 1984
Third edition published in 1988
Fourth edition published in 1991

Kogan Page Limited
120 Pentonville Road
London N1 9JN

British Library Cataloguing in Publication Data

A CIP record for this book is available from the British Library.

ISBN 0 7494 0226 1

Typeset by DP Photosetting, Aylesbury, Bucks
Printed in England by Clays Ltd, St Ives plc

Dedication

To Stan Remington, Chief Executive Book Club Associates 1976–1987,
with whom I worked productively and enjoyably throughout this time,
and from whom I learnt so much about the reality of management in a
competitive world. His positive, entrepreneurial and, at the same time,
human approach to management has strongly influenced the views I
express in this book.

Thank you Stan.

Contents

7

management is about 82; The constituents of human resource strategies 83; Developing human resource strategies 84; Setting out the HR strategic plan 87; Case studies in HR strategic planning 87; Making HR strategy work 89

Commitment and performance 182; The significance of
commitment 182; Creating commitment 183

Process consultancy 262; Performance management 262; Culture management 262; An integrated approach to improving organizational effectiveness 264; Managing change 266; Mission statements 271; Value statements 272; Motivation strategy 275; Commitment strategy 275; Teamwork 276; Communications and involvement 279; Conflict management 279; Managing stress 280; Quality and customer care 281

11

13

Appendices

List of Figures

17

List of Figures

List of Tables

Foreword

Since the third edition of this handbook was published in 1988, we have moved from the hard-nosed and greedy 1980s to the softer and more socially conscious '90s. Much has happened in the world of personnel management during this period. It has become recognized at last that the personnel function can make a major contribution to bottom-line performance, especially if it is built into the fabric of the business. This means that the personnel director is, or should be, a business partner, sharing responsibility with his or her fellow board members for the success of the organization.

The debate on human resource management versus personnel management has largely died down. HRM is more an attitude of mind than a totally different system. Its concepts have always been applied by effective personnel departments. It is, however, still a useful term for an approach to personnel management which emphasizes the need for strategic thinking, for treating people as *the* key resource, and for developing 'mutuality' by concentrating on increasing commitment and identification with the organization through communications and involvement.

The last three years have seen a greater emphasis on competences, total quality management, decentralized collective bargaining and harmonization of terms and conditions. There has been pressure for greater flexibility on all aspects of human resource management, organization and job design. This has involved the creation of 'flexible' firms which rely on a core of key staff who are multiskilled, who work flexible hours, and whose efforts are supplemented by part-timers, temporary staff and subcontracted workers.

Another important development has been the increased importance attached to teamwork in all its forms to enable people in flatter and more flexible organizations to operate more effectively together in dealing with the challenge of change.

The Institute of Personnel Management has identified four key issues which have affected personnel management in the last two or three years and will continue to be significant in the 1990s. These are:

1. competition and the need for competitiveness;
2. the need to adapt to the single European market and, indeed, to the global market;
3. social and environmental pressures and requirements;
4. changing employee and employee expectations, which include the recognition that long-term security, careers and deferred benefits are no longer very relevant under the present climate of company and labour market insecurity and job change.

Employers want immediate performance and employees are no longer as interested in 'cradle-to-grave' careers.

Finally, personnel management has recently gone through a period of major concern about the so-called demographic time bomb, referring to impending acute shortages of young people entering the labour market. The recession of the early 1990s has taken the heat off this problem, but it has not gone away, and the need to concentrate more on strategies for attracting and retaining high-quality staff is just as pressing.

This fourth edition reflects all these developments and concerns. It has also been updated and extended in line with the recent changes to the Institute of Personnel Management's syllabus for its professional qualification.

Plan of the book

The plan of the book is as follows:

- The *Introduction* summarizes the basic concepts of personnel management and human resource management and traces the development of this function over the years.
- *Part I* presents an overview of the context in which the personnel function exists and the main activities and roles of the function.
- *Part II* provides a framework for the practice of personnel management, which is best carried out on the basis of individual and group behaviour in organizations. It includes an entirely new chapter on the individual at work.
- *Parts III to VI* cover the major personnel management activities, organization and job design, forecasting human resource requirements, recruiting people, developing their skills and rewarding them appropriately. These parts contain much new material on job design,

improving organizational effectiveness, job analysis, assessment centres, performance management and human resource development.

- *Part VII* includes a largely rewritten chapter on industrial relations in order to clarify the considerable changes which have taken place in these areas recently.
- *Parts VIII and IX* deal with the important areas of health, safety, and welfare, and contain a new chapter dealing with the legal framework. The chapter on employment practices has been extended to deal with a number of important issues, such as attendance management, ageing, substance abuse, and AIDS, not covered in the previous edition. Part IX also includes an updated review of computerized personnel information systems, covering, for example, new job evaluation applications.
- *Part X* concludes the handbook with a review of key issues and trends.

Introduction: Personnel and human resource management — concepts and development

What personnel management is about

The Institute of Personnel Management defines the profession of personnel management as follows:

> The profession of personnel management has as its principal aim the task of ensuring the optimum use of human resources to the mutual benefit of the enterprise, each person and the community at large.

Personnel management, however, is not the sole preserve of professional personnel managers. It is, or should be, a major preoccupation of the top management of the organization and of all its individual managers who depend on people as a key resource to achieve their objectives. For them, as well as for personnel specialists, personnel management is concerned with:

- obtaining, developing and motivating the human resources required by the organization;
- developing a positive corporate culture as manifested in values, norms, and management style which combine to promote commitment to excellence and quality throughout the organization;
- creating a climate of employee relations which develops feelings of mutuality and encourages cooperation;
- making the best use of the skills and capacities of all those employed in the organization;
- ensuring that the organization meets its social and legal responsibilities toward its employees, with particular regard to the conditions of employment and quality of working life provided for them and the need to promote occupational health and safety and equal opportunities for all.

Stages in the development of personnel management

Personnel management has, broadly, gone through the following stages:

1. *Welfare* — providing employees with facilities such as canteens and looking after their personal interests. Welfare officers first appeared on the scene in any numbers in the munition factories of World War I.
2. *Personnel administration* — providing, in addition to welfare, personnel administrative support to management in the form of recruitment, basic training, and record keeping. This function grew between the wars.
3. *Personnel management — the developing phase*, in which the whole range of personnel services was provided, including salary administration, craft and supervisory training, and advice on industrial relations. But these operated primarily at the tactical level and with relatively little involvement in strategic issues. This phase developed during World War II and through the 1950s.
4. *Personnel management — the mature phase*, which extended during the 1960s and '70s the services provided in the previous phase into organization and management development, systematic training (under the influence of the training boards), performance appraisal and manpower planning. This included the use of more sophisticated training, salary administration and appraisal (management by objectives) techniques. It also included the application of behavioural science knowledge to job design and motivation. There was increased involvement by personnel managers in strategic issues, especially those concerned with industrial relations, a major concern during this period, which saw productivity bargaining come and go. Personnel directors began to appear more frequently on boards although the extent to which they took a full part in strategic decision making was limited in many cases. The introduction of an elaborate system of employment legislation during this period placed more onus on personnel specialists to provide guidance on relevant policies and procedures, and deal with any problems that arose.
5. *Personnel management — the entrepreneurial phase*. The 1980s saw the personnel function adjusting to the enterprise culture and the market economy. The 'entrepreneurial personnel director' who emerged was very much concerned with strategic issues and promoting the achievement of business objectives by making a direct and measurable contribution to the bottom line. US writers such as Peters, Kanter and

Walton emphasized the need to develop positive corporate cultures, to manage and, indeed, thrive on change, and to develop commitment and 'mutuality'. The Japanese phenomenon influenced ways of managing people and industrial relations (single-union agreements). Additionally, the major economic, social and business environmental changes taking place during the decade, as discussed in Chapter 1, resulted in different approaches to organizing and handling people. The human resource management (HRM) concept, as described below, also became prominent in the 1980s.

6. *Personnel management — the post-entrepreneurial phase.* The 1990s began with a reaction to the more egregious features of the enterprise culture, with its emphasis on greed and individualism. The virtues of teamwork and a 'climate of consent' are now being emphasized. At the same time, the contribution of the strategic approach to human resource management to organizational success appeared on a number of agendas, although doubts have been expressed about the capacity of some personnel directors and managers to respond to this challenge. The 1990s also is seeing managers and personnel specialists forced to take a European view in the light of the implications of the single European market and the Social Charter.

Influences on personnel management

The brief history of personnel management set out above referred to a number of influences on its development, especially over the last three decades. These influences, which also contributed to the rise of HRM, can be classified into five groups of writers and researchers: the pioneers, the behavioural science movement, the organization development movement, the corporate culture analysts and the commitment movement.

The pioneers

Current thinking has been strongly influenced by the pioneering work of Drucker and McGregor in the1950s. Drucker[1], in *The Practice of Management*, virtually invented management by objectives. He wrote: 'An effective management must direct the vision and effort of all managers towards a common goal.' This concept of visionary, goal-directed leadership is fundamental to HRM.

McGregor[2] advocated management by integration and self-control, partly as a form of management by objectives, but more importantly as a strategy for managing people which affects the whole business. He believed that a management philosophy needed to be built up, based on attitudes and beliefs about people and the managerial role of achieving integration. He did not see this process as simply one of deploying personnel techniques, manuals and forms. A key role of the personnel function, as he saw it, was 'to devise means of getting management to examine its assumptions, to consider the consequences of its present strategy and to compare it with others'.

He, like Drucker, therefore, paved the way to the HRM philosophy that human resource policies and programmes must be built into the strategic objectives and plans of the business and must also aim to get every one involved in the achievement of these objectives and plans.

The behavioural science movement

The behavioural science movement came into prominence in the 1960s. It was founded by writers such as Maslow[3] whose hierarchy of human needs places self-fulfilment or self-actualization at the top of the pyramid, and Likert[4] who developed his integrating principle of supportive relationships. This stated that organization members should, in the light of their values and expectations, view their work as supportive and as contributing to the building and maintenance of their sense of personal worth and importance.

Another important figure in the behavioural science movement was Argyris[5] who believed that organization design should plan for integration and involvement, and that individuals should feel that they have a high degree of self-control over setting their own goals and over the paths to defining those goals.

The most influential member of the behavioural science school, however, was Herzberg,[6] who advocated job enrichment as a means of increasing organizational effectiveness, claiming that such improvements should centre on the work itself as a source of motivation — if people feel that the job is stretching them, they will be moved to perform it well.

The behavioural science movement had a somewhat idealistic flavour about it, but it did make two useful contributions to HRM. First, it underlined the importance of integration and involvement, and, second, it highlighted the idea that management should accept as a basic value the need consciously and continuously to improve the quality of working life as a means to obtaining increased motivation and improved results.

The organization development movement

The concepts of the behavioural scientists provided the impetus for the

Introduction

organizational development (OD) movement of the 1960s and 1970s, whose philosophy was summarized by Bennis[7] as follows:

1. A new concept of man based on increased knowledge of his complex and shifting needs, which replaces an oversimplified, innocent, push-button idea of man.
2. A new concept of power, based on collaboration and reason, which replaces a model of power based on coercion and threat.
3. A new concept of organization values, based on humanistic-democratic ideas, which replaces the mechanistic value system of bureaucracy.

The OD movement advocated the implementation of programmes designed to improve the effectiveness with which an organization functions and responds to change, with particular emphasis on how people carry out their work and interact with one another. The management of change and team development are often important parts of an organization development programme.

Like the behavioural scientists they usually were, OD practitioners tended to be idealistic, but the good ones saw the organization as a whole and based their plans on a systematic analysis of its circumstances and the changes and problems affecting it. This total approach to organizational behaviour exerted a strong influence on many of those who, in the late 1970s and early 1980s, began to concentrate on corporate culture as a central issue in the management of human resources.

The corporate culture analysts

The interest in corporate culture has derived partly from the organizational behaviour specialists but, importantly, the main thrust behind the cult of culture has come from empirical studies of the ingredients that make for corporate success.

One of the seminal works was *The Art of Japanese Management* by Pascale and Athos.[8] This study of the secrets of Japanese business success attributed much of it to the creation of powerful organizational cultures, from which are derived the shared values between management and workers which emphasize 'mutality' — a common interest in corporate excellence.

Another influential work was *In Search of Excellence* by Peters and Waterman.[9] They found that companies whose only articulated goals were financial did not do nearly as well as companies that had broader sets of values. They quoted with approval Pettigrew,[10] who saw the process of

31

shaping culture as the prime management role. He said: 'The [leader] not only creates the rational and tangible aspects of organizations, such as structure and technology, but also is the creator of ideologies, language, beliefs, rituals and myths', and found that the value sets of the excellent companies integrate the 'notions of economic health, serving customers and making meanings down the line'. Peters and Waterman also noted that the excellent companies were people orientated, by a wide range of 'people programmes'. Like Drucker, they warned against the 'gimmick trap' (for example, quality circles) if it is not part of an overall approach which has the absolute backing of top management and is truly representative of the corporate culture and its values.

The commitment movement

An important concept associated with the corporate culture movement is the emphasis on commitment. Walton[11] expressed this well in his seminal *Harvard Business Review* article 'From control to commitment', in which he wrote that the traditional model for management is to 'establish order and achieve efficiency in the application of the workforce'. This is replaced by the commitment strategy, which, as he defined it, has three major features:

1. 'Teams, not individuals, often are the organizational units responsible for performance.'
2. 'With management hierarchies relatively flat and differences in status minimised, control and lateral coordination depend on shared goals, and expertise, rather than formal position, determines influence.'
3. 'Performance standards are high and serve not to define minimum standards but to provide "stretch objectives", emphasise continuous improvement and reflect the requirements of the marketplace'.

Shifts in assumptions about how people should be managed

The cumulative impact of these influences and the major changes in the business, economic, and social environment combined to produce a number of major shifts in assumptions about how people should be managed and how relationships with employees should be developed and maintained. As defined by Beer and Spector[12], these are as follows:

1. Organizations are viewed as systems, whose effectiveness in terms of transforming inputs to outputs is achieved by developing a fit between the various components in the system (functions and people) and between the system and its environment.

2. There is a long-term coincidence of interest among all the stake-holders in an organization.
3. Power equalization is a key to encouraging openness and collaboration among stakeholders.
4. People are capable of growth in terms of skills, values and commitment if and when the work environment encourages it.
5. Employees will be motivated and the organization more effective if the workforce considers the objectives to be legitimate.
6. Open communication builds trust and commitment.
7. People who participate in defining problems and solutions will become committed to the new directions that result from the process of participation.

What is emerging from these shifts is an overriding principle, that of mutuality, which may be defined as a common interest in corporate excellence. This means unleashing the latent creativity and energies of people throughout the business by emphasizing common interests, gaining understanding and acceptance of the mission and core values of the organization, and increasing commitment by involving people in its affairs. It requires the creation of mutual influence mechanisms which facilitate change, encourage flexibility, and lead to improvements in performance and better bottom-line results.

It is these principles, together with the belief that personnel management strategy should be more fully integrated with the business strategy, that have exerted considerable influence on the development of the human resource management, or 'HRM', approach to personnel management.

Human resource management

As mentioned above, the HRM movement emerged during the 1980s and was promoted by its advocates as a major new departure in the management of people. It is now generally agreed that human resource management does not replace personnel management, but it does look at the processes involved from a different perspective. Its basic philosophies may also differ significantly from traditional concepts of personnel management. Certain approaches to personnel management and employee relations can usefully be described as HRM approaches because they are in line with its basic philosophy as described below.

Definition of human resource management

Human resource management can be defined as a strategic approach to

33

acquiring, developing, managing, motivating and gaining the commitment of the organization's key resource — the people who work in and for it.

Philosophy of human resource management

Human resource management (HRM) is an approach to the management of people which is based on four fundamental principles:

1. Human resources are the most important assets an organization has and their effective management is the key to its success.
2. Organizational success is most likely to be achieved if the personnel policies and procedures of the enterprise are closely linked with, and make a major contribution to, the achievement of corporate objectives and strategic plans.
3. The corporate culture and the values, organizational climate and managerial behaviour that emanate from that culture will exert a major influence on the achievement of excellence. This culture must be managed, which means the continuous effort, starting from the top, will be required to get the values accepted and acted upon.
4. Continuous effort is required to achieve integration — getting all the members of the organization involved and working together with a sense of common purpose. This point was originally made by McGregor[2] when he defined his principle of integration as 'the creation of conditions such that the members of the organization can achieve their own goals best by directing their efforts towards the success of the enterprise.'

HRM policy goals

Guest[13] suggests four policy goals for HRM:

1. *Strategic integration* is concerned with fully integrating HRM into strategic planning, with developing coherent policies throughout the organization, and with getting HRM practices accepted and used by line managers as part of their everyday work.
2. *Commitment* is concerned with binding employees to the organization and getting them to dedicate their efforts to high performance.
3. *Flexibility* is concerned with developing an organization structure which is adaptive and receptive to innovation, and, in the phrase used by Atkinson and Meager[14] offers 'functional flexibility'. This implies job design based on job enrichment or autonomous work groups and

multiskilling of the workforce to meet the requirements of this type of design.

4. *Quality* is concerned with obtaining and developing the high quality of staff required to produce high-quality goods and services in the flexible organization

Approaches to HRM

Two approaches to HRM can be identified. First the 'hard HRM' approach, which has been adopted by a number of US organizations, and which means dealing with employees as just another factor in the input–output equation, to be managed as efficiently and tightly as any other resource. HRM strategies are concerned with improving employee utilization (the cost-effective approach) and, in effect, getting them to accept that their interests coincide with those of the organization — the principles of mutuality and commitment. An HRM industrial relations strategy, as described in Chapter 31 (pages 674–679), will develop direct links with individuals and groups of workers, and may by-pass the trade unions and their representatives. Employees will be involved in the improvement of quality and productivity but are unlikely to participate in business decision making.

The 'soft HRM' approach pays more attention to the fact that employees cannot be treated just like any of the other resources because, unlike them, people think and react. There is more emphasis on strategies for gaining commitment by informing employees about the company's mission, values, plans, and trading conditions; involving them in deciding how tasks should be carried out; and grouping them in teams which work without strict supervision. But it stops short of advocating worker participation in corporate decision making. HRM is therefore a distinctively Anglo-American package of ideas which sits uneasily with the traditions of worker participation in Europe.

Reservations about HRM

Some people dismiss HRM as being no more than 'old wine in new bottles', and, although it can be argued that HRM does present certain new perspectives on personnel management, it does not stand up to any claims that it constitutes a totally different approach. Indeed, the concept of HRM has been embraced with so much enthusiasm in some quarters that it has been disparaged as a fad or no more than a 'flavour of the month' like other management nostrums such as organizational development, job enrichment and similar implications of the behavioural sciences. Overenthusiasm can kill or at least maim a fundamentally good idea.

In an article in *Personnel Management*, Fowler,[15] while approving of much of the HRM approach, said that the message tends to be beguilingly simple: 'Don't bother too much about the techniques or content of personnel management, it says. Just manage the context. Get out from behind your desk, bypass the hierarchy, and go and talk to people. That way you will unlock an enormous potential for improved performance.' But Fowler points out that commitment needs competence, and this includes the use of the skills of marketing, financial, production, data processing, *and* personnel professionals. He also says, quite rightly, that there is a danger of implying that the HRM culture, as prescribed, is right for all organizations; but there is ample evidence that different situations can call for different organizations and different management styles. There is no one simple way of doing anything when dealing with organizations and people.

Some people also express reservations about the manipulative aspects of HRM. They say that, adapting the principle of 'what is good for General Motors is good for America', chief executives with a mission for HRM believe that 'what is good for the business must be good for everyone in it'. Such executives could be right, but not always, and all the forces of internal persuasion and propaganda may be deployed to get people to accept values with which they are not in accord and which may in any case be against their interests.

As Fowler pointed out, HRM also seems to ignore the existence of trade unions. As a system of management, it starts at the top and cascades to all levels of management and staff through various processes of communication, backed by specific devices such as team briefing. The emphasis is rightly on participation, but it takes two to play at that game. However hard management tries to get its message across about identification and commitment, there may still be the belief in the offices and on the shop floor that the collective interests of the workforce need to be protected by trade unions or staff associations.

This could be correct: in some ways an organization is a plural society, containing many related but separate interests and objectives which must be maintained in some kind of equilibrium. Management has to work with trade unions to build harmonious relationships and to develop agreed systems of rules and procedures which will facilitate this process and resolve, with the minimum amount of damage to either party, the conflicts that will almost inevitably arise. HRM in some of its forms does not seem to recognize that this need exists.

All these are valid points, but they do not destroy the basic principles of HRM. What the reservations do tell you is that you have to be cautious about applying the HRM message too simplistically; you must avoid trying to impose an HRM-type culture which is not relevant to the circumstances of the organization, or does not take sufficient account of the possibility that the values of management and employees are too far apart to be integrated with ease.

HRM and personnel management

HRM is a total approach to the strategic management of a key resource and as such has to be the responsibility of the board and senior management. But personnel directors should be involved in developing those strategies as part of their contribution to the strategic management of the business. And personnel managers provide the advice and support required to implement the strategies.

Human resource management implies that personnel managers identify themselves more clearly with the business interest and the senior management team, but, as Sir Pat Lowry[16] has pointed out:

> Personnel work has always included strategic matters and the present emphasis on business issues merely represents another change in environment in which the personnel manager adapts by strengthening competences needed for the new situation. Human resource management is just the continuing process of personnel management — it is not different.

Of course, Sir Pat is right in stating that HRM is not significantly different from personnel management. But it can be argued that the awareness of the required strategic and business competences might not have become so prevalent without the promotion of the HRM concept.

It can also be said that HRM represents not only a business-like approach to personnel management but also a particular approach to employee relations, with its emphasis on commitment and mutuality as things which concern all managers and not just those who happen to be employed in the personnel department.

HRM is therefore best regarded as a particular concept of personnel management which will embrace many if not all of the approaches used by strategically minded personnel directors and managers who:

* recognize the need to integrate business and human resource strategies in order to achieve strategic fit;
* are concerned with creating conditions conducive to commitment, flexibility, high performance and high quality;

- see themselves as business partners working alongside their colleagues and making an equal contribution with them to the achievement of organizational goals.

References

1. Drucker, P *The Practice of Management*. Heinemann, London, 1955.
2. McGregor, D 2*The Human Side of Enterprise*. McGraw-Hill, New York, 1966.
3. Maslow, A *Motivation and Personality*. Harper & Row, New York, 1954
4. Likert, R *New Patterns of Management*. McGraw-Hill, New York, 1966.
5. Argyris, C *Personality and Organization*. Harper & Row, New York, 1957.
6. Herzberg, F *et al The Motivation to Work*. Wiley, New York, 1959.
7. Bennis, W *Organizational Development*. Addison-Wesley, Reading, MA, 1960.
8. Pascale, R and Athos, A *The Art of Japanese Management*. Simon and Schuster, New York, 1981.
9. Peters, T and Waterman, R *In Search of Excellence*. Harper & Row, New York, 1982.
10. Pettigrew, A 'The creation of corporate culture'. Paper given in Copenhagen, 1976.
11. Walton, R 'From control to commitment in the workplace'. *Harvard Business Review*, March–April 1985.
12. Beer, M and Spector, B 'Transformations in HR management' *HRM Trends and Challenges*. (ed. Walton, R and Lawrence, P) Harvard University Press, Boston, MA, 1985.
13. Guest, D 'Personnel and HRM: can you tell the difference?', *Personnel Management*, January 1989.
14. Atkinson, J and Meager, N *Changing Patterns of Work*, IMS/OECD, London, 1986.
15. Fowler, A 'When chief executives discover HRM'. *Personnel Management*, January 1987.
16. Lowry, P as reported in *Personnel Management Plus*, December 1990.

Part I
Personnel Management —
An Overview

This part starts with an analysis of the context within which personnel management takes place — the environment which, from a contingency point of view, will strongly influence the role and activities of the personnel function and its place in the organization.

Personnel management is considered as an integral part of the overall process of management for which all managers as well as personnel specialists are responsible. Personnel management processes are then analysed from the point of view of the objectives, activities, strategies and policies needed to meet organizational requirements.

1

The Context of Personnel Management

Fundamental approaches to personnel management

The following are the three fundamental approaches to personnel management which underpin everything that personnel managers do as described in this book.

The strategic approach

The strategic approach to personnel management links it firmly to the long-term strategies of the organization and ensures that personnel staff provide the guidance and expert support needed to accomplish the strategies.

The systems approach

The systems approach recognizes that personnel management policies and procedures have to take account of the fact that the organization is an open system in which social and technological processes must be combined in order to convert inputs into outputs within the organization's external environment.

The contingency approach

The contingency approach to personnel management is a function of the strategic and systems approaches and is based on contingency theory as described below. It means that all personnel policies and activities will be dependent on the situation in which the organization operates.

Contingency theory

Contingency theory was developed originally in sociology under the name of structural functionalism. It emphasized the interdependence of organizations with their environment (cf Gluckman[1]). The empirical studies of Woodward,[2] Burns and Stalker,[3] and Lawrence and Lorsch[4] applied the theory to work organizations.

In its crude, deterministic form, contingency theory implies that the internal structure and its system are a direct function of the environment, as illustrated in Figure 1.1. This model has been criticized as being simplistic, and Silverman[5] has developed his more sophisticated 'action theory' approach. This suggests a much more complex set of relationships between the contingent factors, which might be external (market, economic) or internal (technical, cultural) and management plans and actions. This is illustrated in Figure 1.2.

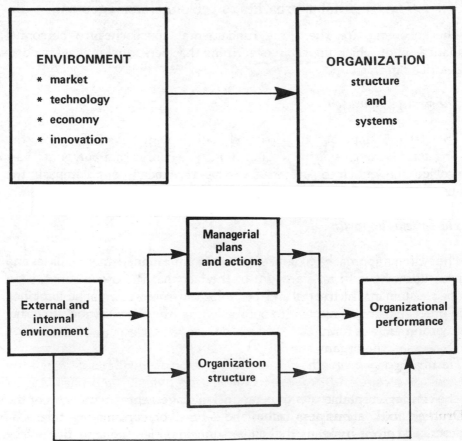

Contingency theory tells us that definitions of aims, policies and strategies; lists of activities; and analyses of the role of the personnel department are valid only if they are related to the circumstances of the organization. Descriptions in textbooks such as this can be only generalizations which suggest approaches and provide guidelines for action; they cannot be prescriptive in the sense of laying down what should be done.

Key contextual elements

The strategic, systems and contingency approaches to personnel management are best carried out on the basis of an understanding of the following key elements of the context within which personnel managers work:

- The organization as an entity with its own culture and structure.
- The external economic, political, business and social environment.
- The process of strategic planning.
- The process of management.
- The social system.
- The technological system.
- The European connection.
- The global connection.
- The phenomena of change, turbulence and ambiguity.

The organization as an entity

A systems approach to personnel management means that the organization has to be seen as an entity, with a purpose, corporate objectives, a culture of its own, various organizational processes or methods of working, and a structure.

Purpose

Organizations exist to achieve a purpose. In the public sector or in a non-profit-making organization, the purpose may be defined as the provision of certain services for national or local government, the community, or the members of the organization.

The purpose of a business is to create and satisfy customer demands for goods or services, to provide customers with value for money and to generate an acceptable rate of return on the investment of its owners. As Drucker[6] said, 'a business cannot be defined or explained in terms of profit', and profit-making is not the sole purpose of a company. But unless shareholders are satisfied that they are getting a reasonable return on their investment and unless sufficient cash is generated to finance trading and development, the business will not survive or grow.

The steps taken to achieve the purposes of the organization may conflict with the needs of its employees. McGregor[7] has pointed out that the biggest challenge to personnel managers is to integrate the needs of the organization with the needs of those who work in it. It is not an impossible challenge, and there are a number of ways in which it can be met, as described later in this book. But none of these approaches will work unless personnel managers understand what the organization is setting out to achieve just as clearly as they understand what individuals need and want.

Corporate objectives

Corporate objectives in public sector or non-profit-making organizations will be related to the implementation of political programmes, the provision of services, the achievement of the overall purpose of the organization, and the achievement of cost-effectiveness in the management of operations and their administration.

In the private sector, corporate objectives are developed under four headings:

1. The purpose or mission of the company
According to Levitt,[8] there are four prime business purposes:

(a)   To create and keep customers.
(b)   To produce and deliver goods and services that people want and value at prices and under conditions that are reasonably attractive relative to those offered by others.
(c)   To produce revenue in excess of costs in sufficient regularity to attract and hold investors in the enterprise.
(d)   To keep at least abreast and sometimes ahead of competitive targets.

2. Economic or financial targets
Overall corporate economic or financial objectives may be set as one fundamental goal, for example: 'Increase the return on shareholders' capital (ROSC) by x per cent within the next five years.'

3. Ownership
Ownership objectives are set in terms of whether or not the company should remain private or go public, remain independent and resist strongly a takeover bid or merger proposal, or accept the logic of the right sort of merger.

4. What business are we in?

'What business are we in?' is Drucker's[6] famous question. It leads to a definition of the markets and customers for which the company should be providing goods or services. It is answered by looking at the business from the point of view of the customer and then relating the particular strengths and weaknesses of the company to market opportunities. The internal and external appraisals carried out as part of the corporate planning process provide information which will help to define what the business should be at a future date. This definition will lead to strategies for product innovation, diversification, acquisition, and expansion to increase market share. The personnel strategy of the organization will be integrated with these strategies.

Organization structure and size

The structure of an organization is related to its technology and size, which will influence the degree of formality in defining roles and relationships, the extent to which the organization is decentralized and the numbers of levels of management or supervision that exist. In turn, these factors will influence the procedural aspects of personnel management (eg the use of formal job descriptions) and the ways in which people are managed and communications take place.

On the whole, large organizations are more formalized, and specialist functions such as personnel departments are more likely to exist. Size, however, brings with it problems of integration and communication with which personnel managers have to contend. Schumacher's[9] proposition 'small is beautiful' has its attractions to anyone concerned with managing and motivating people.

The external environment

Organizations are affected by factors in their external environment such as competition, changes in markets, economic forces, government policies, public opinion and trade unions. Turbulence in the environment can create conditions which significantly alter personnel policies and practices, the most obvious example being shortage of work leading to cutbacks and redundancies. Perhaps the most important environmental factors affecting firms are the single European market and the globalization of business. These are discussed later in this chapter.

How organizations function

The basis upon which an organization functions, as described in Chapter 9, is related to its culture, its structure and its processes such as leadership, teamwork, power and conflict. All these are affected by its external environment, its purpose and its internal technology, and will in turn affect personnel policies and practices.

Corporate culture

The corporate culture is the system of assumptions about what is important to the organization, and what it should do and how it should do it. As Katz and Kahn[10] put it:

> Every organization develops its own culture and climate; with its own taboos, folkways and mores. The climate or culture of the system reflects both the norms and values of the formal system and their reinterpretation in the informal system. Organizational climate reflects also the history of internal and external struggles, the types of people the organization attracts, its work processes and physical layout, the modes of communication, and the exercise of authority within the system.

The impact of culture on human behaviour in organizations and, therefore, on personnel management is considerable and is discussed fully in Chapter 10.

Strategic planning

Definition of strategy

A strategy can be defined as a broad statement of where the organization as a whole, or a significant part of it, is going in the longer term to achieve its objectives. It defines overall means to achieve ends and is a declaration of intent which provides for the development and implementation of action plans and programmes.

This definition assumes that the ends or goals have been defined and that strategy is evolved to achieve them. But the process of formulating strategy may in itself include the definition of long-term objectives.

Chandler,[11] for example, defines strategy as follows:

> Strategy is the determination of the basic long-term goals and objectives of the enterprise and the adoption of courses of action and allocation of resources necessary for carrying out these goals.

In practice, the creation of strategy takes place within the framework of the mission, overall objectives, values and policies of the firm. But the process of formulating strategy is a continuous one, and it produces more specific medium and long-term objectives and therefore influences the overall aims.

Business strategy

Business strategies exist to create value. They are declarations of intent. The aim is to look ahead as far as one can see and define in broad terms what needs to be done in order to:

- achieve the mission of the organisation;
- meet the expectations of its owners or whoever has the overall responsibility for the organization;
- manage changes imposed by the external and internal environment;
- capitalize on the distinctive competences of the organization (what it is best at doing);
- add value through the effective use of resources.

Strategies are not plans — these are the product, not the essence, of strategy, but strategies are expressed in the strategic plans of the organization.

Strategic planning

Strategic planning is a systematic, analytical approach which reviews the business as a whole in relation to its environment. It has two major functions:

1. To develop an integrated, coordinated and consistent view of the route the company wishes to follow.
2. To facilitate the adaptation of the organization to environmental change.

Porter[12] has suggested that strategic planning takes place to enable a business to achieve 'sustainable competitive advantage'. He has also stated that 'corporate strategy is what makes the corporate whole add up to more than the sum of its business unit parts' (the concept of synergy).

The aim of strategic planning is to create a viable link between the organization's objectives and resources and its environmental opportunities. It will therefore determine the future posture of the enterprise with specific reference to its product–market scope (the products it can produce and the markets it can be in), its profitability, its size, its rate of innovation, its distinctive competences and its relationships both with its stakeholders (shareholders, suppliers, employees, customers and the public) and the external environment generally. Thus, in Ansoff's[13] words:

> Strategy and objectives together describe the concept of the firm's business. They specify the amount of growth, the area of growth, the directions for growth, the leading strengths, and the profitability target. Furthermore, they are stated operationally, in a form usable for guiding management decisions and actions.

Formulating strategic plans

Strategic planning is concerned with the formulation of strategies within the framework of company policies. It involves processes of strategic management, as described in Chapter 14, which, through various operational and project plans, will lead to action and the achievement of goals.

Strategy formulation, however, is not always a rational and continuous process, as was pointed out by Mintzberg.[14] He believes that, rather than being consciously and systematically developed, strategy re-orientations happen in brief quantum loops. He also suggests that, paradoxically:

> The very concept of strategy is rooted in stability not change. . . . Organizations pursue strategies to set directions, lay out courses of action and elicit cooperation from their members around common, established guidelines. By any definition, strategy imposes stability on an organization. No stability means no strategy (no concern for the future, no pattern from the past). Indeed the mere fact of having a strategy, and especially of making it explicit . . . creates resistance to change.

Mintzberg goes on to state that, most of the time, management pursues a given strategic orientation: 'Change may seem continuous, but it occurs in the context of that orientation.'

Strategies, according to Mintzberg, are not always deliberate. In theory, he says, the formulation of strategies is a systematic process. 'First we think, then we act. We formulate; then we implement.' In practice, 'a realized strategy can emerge in response to an evolving situation.' The strategist can often be 'a pattern organizer, a learner if you like, who manages a process in which strategies (and visions) can emerge as well as be deliberately conceived. . . . To manage strategy . . . is not so much to promote change as to *know* when to do so.'

But the fact that strategies do evolve in this way does not mean that organizations can afford to ignore the value of deliberately taking a view

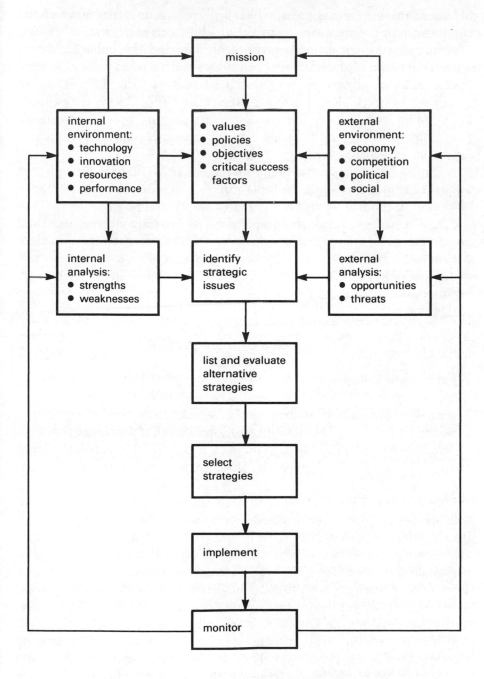

Figure 1.3 The process of strategic planning

of where the business is going which will include an assessment of the significance of the 'quantum leaps' to which Mintzberg refers.

A formal, strategic planning process, as illustrated in Figure 1.3, starts with the mission of the business from which is derived its values, policies, overall aims or objectives and the critical success factors applicable to achieving its stated aims. These are interrelated and, ideally, they should be updated regularly in response to changes in the organization's environment, which will include its markets, competitors, technology and any other external factors.

A continuous process of strategic management, as described in Chapter 14 (pages 255–256), and the formulation of corporate plans can now take place within the framework of the firm's values and policies.

These activities lead to the preparation of operational, resource, and project plans and related budgets. Action is thus initiated which takes place within budgets and aims to achieve targets, complete projects, or meet standards of performance as laid down in the statement of objectives. Feedback loops are built into the system to monitor progress and performance.

The process of management

What is management?

Essentially, management is about deciding what to do and then getting it done through people. This definition emphasizes that people are the most important resource available to managers. It is through this resource that all the other resources — knowledge, finance, materials, plant, equipment, etc — are managed.

However, managers are there to get results. To do this, they have to deal with events and eventualities. They may do this primarily through people, but an overemphasis on the people content of management diverts attention from the fact that in managing events managers have to be personally involved. They manage themselves as well as other people. They cannot delegate everything. They frequently have to rely on their own resources to get things done. These resources consist of experience, know-how, skill and, importantly, time — all of which have to be deployed, not only in directing and motivating people but also in understanding situations and issues, problem analysis and definition, decision making and in taking direct action, themselves, as well as through other people. They will get support, advice and assistance from their staff, but in the last analysis they are on their own. They have to make the decisions and they have to initiate and sometimes take the action. A chairman fighting a takeover bid will get lots of advice, but he or she will personally manage the crisis, talking directly to the financial institutions, merchant banks, financial analysts, City editors and the mass of shareholders.

The basic definition of management should therefore be extended to read 'deciding what to do and then getting it done through the effective use of resources'. The most important part of management will indeed be getting things done through people, but managers will be concerned directly or indirectly with all other resources, including their own.

The nature of managerial work

Over the years many attempts have been made to define the nature of managerial work as a model consisting of a number of well-defined and interrelated activities which together provide a framework for the analysis and conduct of the managerial task. Typically, management is described in terms of the following four functions:

- Planning
- Organizing
- Directing
- Controlling.

This analytical model, which could be described as the classical approach, has been challenged by those who take an empirical view of management as a much more fragmented activity, the nature of which depends more on the demands of the situation and the people concerned than on any theoretical division of the task into clearly differentiated elements. These empiricists observe that the work of manager is fragmented, varied, subjected to continual adjustment and governed to a large degree by events over which the manager has little control, and by a dynamic network of interrelationships with other people. Managers exist to control their environment but sometimes it controls them. They may consciously or unconsciously seek to plan, organize, direct and control, but their days almost inevitably become a jumbled sequence of events. Managers have to cope with ambiguity and turbulence, indeed chaos. The ordered world within which the classical theorists developed their model has vanished.

To the empiricists, management is a process involving a mix of rational, logical, problem-solving, decision-making activities and intuitive, judge-mental activities. It is therefore both art and science. The activities of managers are characterized by brevity, variety and fragmentation. Because of the open-ended nature of the work, managers feel compelled to perform a great variety of work at an unrelenting pace. As Mintzberg[15] comments:

> The manager actually appears to prefer brevity and interruption to his work. He becomes conditioned by his workload; he develops an appreciation of the opportunity cost of his own time; and he lives continuously with an awareness of what else might or must be done at any time. Superficiality is an occupational hazard of the manager's job. . . . The manager gravitates to the more active elements of his world — the current, the specific, the well-defined, the non-routine activities.

And Burgoyne[16] has suggested that:

> Managerial work is always at the boundary between order and chaos, between what has not been done and what has already been done. Management is literally a creative activity, and like any creative activity its successful execution moves forward its boundary or future.

When establishing policies and procedures, providing advice, or devising management development and training programmes, personnel managers have to bear in mind the fragmented nature of management. It is no use preaching the virtues of order, structure and total compliance to rules if managers are compelled to operate flexibly in order to respond to the constantly changing demands made upon them.

In carrying out their own work, personnel managers should also remember that they are subject to the same pressures as other managers and that, because of the ambiguity that often surrounds their role, they may find it even more difficult to act in the orderly manner which they would prefer.

The social system

An organization has been defined by Duncan[17] as 'A collection of interacting and interdependent individuals who work toward common goals and whose relationships are determined according to a common structure.'

This social system as analysed by Argyle,[18] involves three types of relationships:

1. Cooperation over a task.
2. Managerial or supervisory relationships.
3. Social relationships which involve conveying information, discussion, negotiation, or providing expert advice without authority.

Personnel managers must always remember that, while many of their dealings will be with individual employees on matters such as their selection, promotion, motivation, training, development, remuneration and personal problems or grievances, these individuals are usually working in formal or informal groups. These groups set their own norms and standards of behaviour, provide social benefits to their members, and, through their cohesiveness, can exert strong influence on individual behaviour, often stronger than the influence exerted by management.

The technological system

The significance of technology

The managerial task varies according to the technology of the business. This was demonstrated in a pioneering study by Woodward[2] of a number of Essex firms, from which she concluded that variations between firms in organizational requirements are nearly always linked with differences in their techniques of production. She stated that:

> The following features can be traced to the technology of each system of production: a coordination of functions and centralisation of authority in unit production; an extensive specialisation and delegation of authority in mass production; and in process industry a specialisation between development, marketing and production, combined with integration within each function and the co-operative character of decision-making.

As Burns and Stalker[3] found out in another pioneering study of Scottish industry, the type of organizations, the tasks of managers, and the way managers manage (management style) was clearly dependent on the technology of the firm. They also emphasized that the rate of change in the firm's environment was a key factor in determining how it could operate.

In a firm processing rayon filament yarn, for example:

> The whole concern can be seen as a three-sided pyramid of power, technical expertise and knowledge of circumstances. At every step down from the top there was less authority, less technical expertise and less information. Each person's task was clearly laid down and defined by his superior. He knew just what he could do in normal circumstances without consulting anyone else; just what point of deviation from the norm he should regard as the limit of his competence; and just what he should do when this limit was reached, ie report to his superior. The whole system was designed to preserve normality and stability ... the outstanding characteristic of the structure was that it was mechanical and authoritarian. And it worked very well.

Burns and Stalker contrasted this 'mechanistic' organization with the much more flexible and free-flowing one which had evolved in an electronics firm which was mainly involved in high-technology development. In the volatile environment in which this form of operation exists, a rigid system of ranks and routines would inhibit the organization's speed and sensitivity of response. According to Burns and Stalker, the structure and methods of working need to be 'organic' in the sense that they are a function of the situation in which the enterprise finds itself, rather than conforming to any rigid view of how it should operate. Individual managerial responsibilities are less clear cut and managers must constantly relate what they are doing to their organization's general situation and specific problems.

These and other studies, such as those carried out by Tom Lupton,[19] indicate that the technology or technical system is closely interrelated with the social system — the ways in which work groups are organized and the processes of interaction that take place in the firm. This 'socio-technical' model, as evolved by the Tavistock Institute, was based on research within industry and, as stated by Trist,[20] it revealed that:

> The technological system and the effectiveness of the total production system will depend upon the adequacy with which the social system is able to cope with these requirements.

The significance of this to personnel managers is that they must be aware that they are involved with both the social and the technical systems. And when conditions are unstable and the reactions of individuals are likely to be unpredictable (which is more often than not the case), the task of personnel management becomes correspondingly more complex and difficult.

Introducing new technology

The introduction of new technology requires the use of different skills and methods of working and may result in a reduction of the number of jobs (downsizing). This can present a considerable threat to employees, and one of the key responsibilities of personnel managers in these circumstances is to advise on the management of change.

The impact of information technology

Drucker[21] wrote in 1988: 'Information is data endowed with relevance and purpose.' He also suggested that the impact of information technology will mean that

> The typical large business 20 years hence will have fewer than half the levels of management of its counterpart today, and no more than a third the managers. . . . Businesses, especially large ones, have little choice but to become information-based. Demographics, for one, demands the shift. The centre of gravity in employment is moving fast from manual and clerical workers to knowledge workers who resist the command-and-control model that business took from the military 100 years ago.

The European connection

The single European market means that UK companies will have to adapt to new legal requirements and to follow the principles expressed in the European Community's (EC) Social Charter. They will have to develop flexible and skilled workforces capable of competing with the best in Europe and beyond. These twin — and often conflicting — demands must be managed in the context of demographic shortfalls and the free movement of people across national boundaries.

Companies are increasingly aware of the need to be multinational, multidisciplinary and multilocational if they are to operate successfully in the rapidly changing business environment. This section explores the European context under the following headings:

- EC employment legislation;
- The European labour market;
- Involvement;
- Recruitment;
- Remuneration;
- Training.

EC employment legislation

The Treaty of Rome, which set up the EC and the Single European Act, contains binding provisions covering:

- Freedom of movement for workers.
- Social security cover for migrant workers.
- Freedom of establishment, including the right to take up and pursue activities as self-employed persons.
- Equal pay for men and women.
- The European Social Fund, which provides financial support to

organizations in member states which run schemes of vocational training, retraining and job creation for specific jobs.
● The working environment.
● Economic and social cohesion in the Community.

The Social Charter

The latest proposal from the Commission is to establish a Social Charter of individual and collective rights. Supported by all EC countries except (as of August 1991) the UK, this provides for EC standards and conditions to be determined through Community or national legislation, or through collective bargaining.

The Social Charter is a political declaration of intent. It broadly covers the following areas:

● Improvement of living and working conditions.
● Right to freedom of movement.
● Employment and remuneration — right to a fair wage.
● Right to social protection.
● Right to freedom of association and collective bargaining.
● Right to vocational training.
● Right of men and women to equal treatment.
● Right to information, consultation and worker participation.
● Right to health protection and safety at the workplace.

An Action Programme has been presented by the Commission to implement the main provisions of the Social Charter. Whether or not the UK finally accepts it, the Charter will become a major influence on personnel management in the many UK companies which operate now, or will operate, elsewhere in Europe.

The European labour market

The European labour market will be an increasingly mobile one. There will be a greater flow of semi-skilled, unskilled and service sector workers from the poorer regions of Greece, Italy, Spain and Portugal to the northern member states. Individuals in the UK are likely to have a broader view of the labour market and of the opportunities that are open to them. Young and mobile professionals may seek the European sun. In Spain, for example, there is a severe shortage of skilled staff, especially in information technology, and good job opportunities at attractive salaries are to be found.

More people from the UK will be transferred abroad by their companies, who should not overlook the fact that the performance of staff overseas can depend on the support which they obtain from their partners and families. Their views and needs should be taken into account when selecting staff for assignments overseas.

Another factor which UK personnel managers will have to bear in mind are the requirements of local employment law. In the Netherlands, for example, companies that are profitable are not allowed to make employees redundant after a merger. In Germany, when a company reaches a certain size, it is required to set up a works council.

Involvement

One of the most important factors that UK managements will have to take into account is the emphasis in Europe on communications and employee involvement and the likelihood that this will be reinforced by Community law.

Recruitment

The CBI[22] has stated that the competition for those with scarce skills will increase in the single market, and companies will need to become more aggressive in recruitment policy. Job specifications and the method of recruitment will have to become more focused. Line management is likely to become more involved in defining requirements and assessing candidates.

Whether companies use local or expatriate staff will depend on a number of factors such as the type of operation and its scale. In start-up situations expatriate staff will have a greater knowledge of the company and its products. Local managers, however, know more about market conditions — both the commercial and the labour markets. Employing local staff in production, operational and selling activities is usually essential, but it is also evidence of a depth of commitment and may make it easier to attract a higher calibre of local employees as the business grows.

Remuneration

Remuneration packages should reflect the realistic costs of living and working in a particular location to the categories of staff concerned. Estimates and assumptions of living costs should be reviewed periodically. It is often easier and fairer to encourage staff to take a high proportion of their total remuneration in the form of cash. Each individual can then determine whether or not to adjust a consumption pattern to local practice. This approach can also have the advantage of reducing employment costs in that some benefits can be expensive to operate overseas at the same level as in the UK.

One feature which is apparent in Europe (and is increasingly becoming the case in the UK) is the widening spectrum of earnings between the high-flyer and the average executive or professional. This recognizes that some individuals can make a very special contribution and are aware of that fact. They have to be remunerated accordingly.

Training

At management level, training will have to concentrate more on developing an international perspective. Conventional management training will not prepare executives for the special demands and pressures which occur in an international setting.

The CBI[22] suggests that areas of expertise which will become more important in management education and development include:

- Identifying and anticipating change in the global environment.
- An awareness of contemporary international economics and financial and trade issues.
- An appreciation of international risk analysis.
- An assessment of the sources of corporate power and influence.
- An understanding of crisis decision making.
- International bargaining and negotiation skills.
- Relevant area and political studies.
- Guidance on corporate planning in a regional and international context.

In other areas, training will have to concentrate more on widening the range of skills people possess (multiskilling) and increasing their capacity to develop and apply new technologies.

The global connection

According to the CBI,[22] the principal trends towards interdependence in a global economy are as follows:

- An increase in world trade which is ahead of the rate of economic growth.

- Changes in the structure of world trade as 'new entrant' economies develop outside the traditional industrialized world.
- The development of new technologies which facilitate international operation.
- Rising aspirations and standards around the globe.
- The international spread and global reach of a more innovative and enterprising culture.

A noticeable trend in the 1980s, which is gathering force in the 1990s, is the increasing global nature of competition. This is not just the result of developments in the European Community. In South-East Asia, the Far East and the rapidly growing Pacific Rim region, competitive economies are emerging with high annual rates of growth and strong export performance.

One of the most important effects of globalization has been the rise of the multinationals. They have existed for a long time, of course, but the accelerating processes of global expansion, takeovers and mergers mean that they have become an increasingly important feature in the industrial and commercial scene as international companies move into the UK and UK firms expand overseas.

These events affect the personnel manager in two ways. First, a larger proportion of managers and professional and technical staff will become internationally mobile, which means paying special attention to their career development, remuneration and personal circumstances. Secondly, more international companies will be opening plants or financial service operations in the UK. US and Japanese firms are already well established. More will follow. This means a higher proportion of personnel managers working for corporations whose culture and methods of management are fundamentally different (not better or worse) from those in the UK. Success in these situations requires a process of mutual adjustment even though the internationals generally recognize the need to adjust to local cultures. The best analysis of this process is Wickens'[23] description in *The Road to Nissan* of how Nissan established and developed its motor manufacturing plant in Washington, Tyne and Wear.

Change, turbulence and ambiguity

The economic and business environment has become much more turbulent, uncertain and demanding. Peters[24] has referred to 'an era of unprecedented change' and suggested that 'predictability is a thing of the past'.

Environmental change

Environmental change has taken place in a number of ways, as described below:

- Economic and political change saw a rise in the 1990s of the so-called enterprise culture and its associated phenomenon, the market economy. In the 1990s, softer values to do with social and environmental responsibility have emerged, and greed as a motivating force is not so evident.
- Social change has produced a trend towards individualism and away from collectivism.
- Consumer expectations are higher than ever before. They want value for money, as always, but they are now demanding, quite rightly, higher standards of quality and service.
- The business environment in the 1980s was characterized by an emphasis on growth and a rash of takeovers and acquisitions. Recession in the early 1990s in producing business failures, disinvestments, cutbacks and a general climate of uncertainty. Conditions of growth and prosperity may return but uncertainty will persist.
- The 'demographic time bomb' was identified in the 1980s and caused alarm and despondency about skill shortages as the supply of young people coming into the labour market dwindled. In times of recession when 'downsizing' rather than expansion is the order of the day, not so much concern is expressed about these shortages. 'Short-termism' prevails and companies are unwilling to think ahead about their human resource requirements. Training programmes suffer, as they always do in recessions, thus creating skill shortages for the future and not coping with the shortages that still exist.
- Changing patterns of work have emerged — the development of a core of key full-time and permanent workers surrounded by part-timers, contract workers, and 'teleworkers' who sit by their terminals and fax machines and operate their computers in the new electronic cottage industry.
- Increased competition is coming from Europe, Japan and multinational corporations.
- Product life cycles are shorter and leading-edge firms must innovate to remain competitive and to establish and maintain their position in increasingly segmented markets.
- New technology is playing a much greater part in the management process in so far as that process is largely concerned with information flows.

The impact of change on the firm

Environmental and technological developments have resulted in fundamental changes to the ways in which firms are structured and managed. We now have:

- *The responsive firm*, which has to react quickly to changes in the marketplace and in customer needs and preferences.
- *The proactive firm*, which has to make markets as well as adapt itself to them.
- *The flexible firm*, which has to adjust its structure, its product range, its marketing strategies and its manufacturing facilities quickly to respond to and, more importantly, anticipate change. The flexible firm needs flexible people; hence the emphasis on multiskilling (providing employees with the breadth of experience and training which will extend their range of skills and ensuring that education and training programmes are not overspecialized).
- *The information-based firm*, which is knowledge-orientated and composed largely of specialists who direct and discipline their own performance through organized feedback from colleagues, customers, and the strategic business units into which the organization is divided in accordance with the markets it serves.
- *The compact firm*, which has a flatter organization structure as superfluous layers of management are stripped out. This is because, as Drucker[21] points out, organizations have established through the development of new technology and the extended use of knowledge workers, that 'whole layers of management neither make decisions nor lead. Instead, their main, if not their only, function is to serve as "relays" — human boosters for the faint, unfocused signals that pass for communications in the traditional pre-information organization.'
- *The decentralized firm* which consists of strategic business units placed firmly in their market niches and capable of responding quickly to opportunities. These units are tightly managed to achieve well-defined goals with the minimum of interference from above. Handy[25] has suggested that the extension to this approach is the 'federal' firm in which the centre, as its name implies, is in the middle of things (not at the top) and is mainly concerned with strategy, the provision of resources, coordinating, influencing and providing advice. The centre maintains a fairly low profile — initiative, energy and drive are supplied by the federated units.

The impact of change on people

People have to learn to exist with change, like the organizations in which they work. They have to be more flexible and more responsible to new and challenging demands. In the decentralized organization of today, managers must be able to operate independently — the very essence of effective managers is that they achieve the goals they set themselves. But in the flatter organization they also have to be good team workers able to deploy a wider range of skills in working with others across organizational boundaries.

Change can result in role conflict and role ambiguity, a result which can produce stress. People generally prefer to work in an orderly structure which provides a framework within which they have a fair degree of autonomy. They like a certain amount of predictability, and although they welcome variety, it has to be within reasonable bounds. But life in organizations is not like that. Uncertainty and ambiguity are ever present. Organizations are supposed to behave rationally, progressing steadily from A to B — this is the philosophy of strategic planning. But they don't. They consist of webs of power and politics and proceed by fits and starts.

All managers will have to learn how to reconcile the need for order and continuity and the demands of the situation, which involve flexibility and discontinuity. Organizations suffer too. Kanter[26] points out that businesses are trying at one and the same time to conserve resources and be entrepreneurial: 'This constitutes the ultimate balancing act. Cut back and grow. Trim down and build. Accomplish more, and do it in new areas, with fewer resources.'

Change as an organizational process is discussed in Chapter 9, and techniques of change management are considered in Chapter 14.

Turbulence

Personnel managers, like their colleagues, have to manage most of their time in turbulent conditions. Turbulence is usually imposed on the organization by its environment although it can be self-generated on the basis of what entrepreneurial and driving managements think needs to be done. As Kanter[27] writes: 'Organizational change is stimulated not by pressures from the environment but by the *perceptions* of that environment and the pressures held by key actors.'

And as Peters[24] writes: 'Violent and accelerating change, now commonplace, will become the grist of the opportunistic winner's mill. The losers will view such confusion as a problem to be "dealt" with.'

Turbulence, however, although often sparked off by external events, can be internally generated. A driving, visionary top management team can impose change. Innovation also creates turbulence. New products, new markets, new technology, and new organization structures and systems all require people to abandon their present steady state and learn new ways. And it is happening all the time. Managers have to adopt variety as a way of life.

Ambiguity

Peters[24] has said that 'predictability is a thing of the past'. Uncertainty among people about the future coupled, often, with uncertainty about exactly what they are supposed to do, adds up to ambiguity. As noted above, people, on the whole, prefer structure. They like to know where they are, where they are going and what is expected of them. But such structured existences are seldom possible in today's conditions.

It is not only turbulence and the difficulty of knowing what is going to happen next which creates this situation. Organizations are becoming more fluid. Responsibilities overlap. Information technology means that top managers can get instant data on their desktop screen about anything that is happening anywhere in their organization. They can and do skip layers of management to go straight to the data source to ask what is happening and why. Middle managers feel superfluous. They do not know how they fit into what used to be called 'the chain of command'.

Confusion and ambiguity can, paradoxically enough, be caused by the emphasis on end results. Managers are told what they have to achieve but are often left in the dark about how to achieve it. This is not because they are being deliberately starved of information; it is rather because in turbulent and rapidly changing conditions there are often alternative means available to achieve the ends. One of the modern principles of management to have emerged from the conditions under which managers now have to operate is 'constancy towards ends but flexibility about means'. This is a necessary approach in turbulent times, but managers can often be left asking forlornly, 'Where do I go from here?' And, increasingly, they will be expected to answer that question themselves.

Ambiguity is also created by the often fragmented, variable and diversified nature of managerial work in fluid and rapidly changing organizations. Managers can learn to cope with it simply by recognizing its inevitability on a day-to-day basis and concentrating on clarifying the main goals they are expected to achieve, together with the critical success factors which determine whether these goals have been accomplished. So far as possible, they must take a strategic view of their work, which means defining the broader issues with which they are concerned. Tactics or the things they have to deal with on the spot can be flexed according to the situation, as long as they are conducted within the broad framework of a strategy which provides a sense of direction. In these circumstances, ambiguity is a short-term state and can be managed accordingly.

The impact of turbulence and ambiguity

As a result of fluidity and turbulence, the days of elaborate job descriptions, spelling out in great detail exactly how people should perform their work, are disappearing. Instead we find a one-sentence definition of the overall purpose or objectives of the job, followed by a list of seven or eight 'principal accountabilities', each setting out, again in one sentence, a main area of the job for which the individual will be expected to deliver results. The key words today are performance and delivery, not task or duty. This is appropriate to the prevailing conditions in most organizations, but managers and other people have to learn to cope with ambiguity about means if not about ends. Self-reliance and self-determination are therefore very important qualities for them to possess.

Williamson and Ouchi[28] have distinguished between 'hard' and 'soft' contracting in organizational life. In 'hard-contracting', relationships are formalized, jobs are task-specific and legalistic interpretations are made of the employment contract. A more authoritative or 'macho' approach to management is likely in these circumstances. In contrast, 'soft-contracting' aims to create harmonious units based on tacit understanding and a reciprocal sense of obligation. Any managers who believe in a soft-contracting approach could find themselves in a hard-contracting situation with a feeling of ambiguity about their role and how they perform it. They may have to choose between going along with it, getting out, or quietly working against the grain (not easy).

Ambiguity can be bad enough in the so-called line jobs — that is, those such as production or sales which are dealing directly with the end product, either making it or selling it. It can be even worse in what used to be termed 'staff' jobs — that is, those jobs which exist to provide support services such as finance, data processing, and, notably, personnel management. (Line and staff are old military terms which are not used so much nowadays, perhaps because the distinction between them has become more blurred.) There will always be some jobs — and personnel management is one of them — where it is more difficult to measure the direct contribution of job holders to achieving organizational objectives.

Conclusions

Pascale in *Managing on the Edge*[29] suggests that to cope with the challenging environment described in this chapter it is necessary to 'anchor the corporation in transcendent human and social purposes in order to make meaning for its employees'. He also suggests that the genius of the Japanese methodology is in 'constructing organizations that motivated and then harvested tiny improvements in a thousand places'. He attaches great importance to developing new paradigms — perceptions of patterns developed over time, which form a mental infrastructure or mind-set. The problem with paradigms or mind-sets is that we tend to see through them and therefore they filter our understanding of what is really happening. 'As life goes on, we increasingly live in our perception of what's "right", "wrong" or "impossible" etc. instead of what's real.' Change and transformation can be achieved properly only if attention is given to the four factors which drive renewal in organizations:

1. *Fit* — consistency and coherence of the organization's structure and processes.
2. *Split* — techniques used to sustain autonomy and diversity such as decentralized profit centres and human networks.
3. *Contend* — the presence and value of constructive conflict. Some tensions, such as those between a tight inventory control and high levels of services are inescapable and can be used productively.
4. *Transcend* — managing the complexity in orchestrating fit, split, and contend. Transformation 'looks to the tension (or dynamic synthesis) between contradicting opposites as the engine of self-renewal. It is predicated on the notion that disequilibrium is a better strategy for adaptation and survival than order and equilibrium. This process of transformation requires attacks on many fronts which display the characteristic of not just 'having-the-answers' but of 'living-in-the-question'. In other words, transformation relies upon constant questioning of assumptions to reveal what is possible and to create opportunities.

This is where personnel managers come in. They are well placed to observe and question what is going on in the organization and make suggestions about what needs to be done about the management and development of its human resources in conditions of change and uncertainty.

References

1. Gluckman, M (ed.) *Closed Systems and Open Minds*. Oliver and Boyd, London, 1964.

2. Woodward, J *Industrial Organization*. Oxford University Press, Oxford, 1965.
3. Burns, T and Stalker, G *The Management of Innovation*. Tavistock, London 1961.
4. Lawrence, P and Lorsch, J *Organization and Environment*. Harvard University Press, Cambridge, MA, 1976.
5. Silverman, D *The Theory of Organizations: A Sociological Framework*. Heinemann, London, 1970.
6. Drucker, P *The Practice of Management*. Heinemann, London, 1955.
7. McGregor, D *The Human Side of Enterprise*. McGraw-Hill, New York, 1966.
8. Levitt, T *The Marketing Imagination*. Free Press, New York, 1983.
9. Schumacher, E F *Small is Beautiful*. Blond & Briggs, London, 1973.
10. Katz, D and Kahn, R *The Social Psychology of Organizations*, Wiley, New York, 1964.
11. Chandler, A *Strategy and Structure*. MIT Press, Cambridge, MA, 1962.
12. Porter, M E 'From competitive advantage to corporate strategy'. *Harvard Business Review*, May–June 1987.
13. Ansoff, H I *Corporate Strategy*. McGraw-Hill, New York, 1965.
14. Mintzberg, H 'Crafting strategy'. *Harvard Business Review*, July–August 1987.
15. Mintzberg, H *The Nature of Managerial Work*. Harper & Row, New York, 1973.
16. Burgoyne, J *Competency Approaches to Management Development*. Centre for the Study of Management Learning, University of Lancaster, 1988.
17. Duncan, W J *Organizational Behaviour*. Houghton Mifflin, New York, 1981.
18. Argyle, M *The Social Psychology of Work*. Penguin, Harmondsworth, 1989.
19. Lupton, T 'Best fit in the design of organizations'. *Personnel Review*. Vol 4, No. 1, 1975.
20. Trist, E L *Organizational Choice*. Tavistock, London, 1963.
21. Drucker, P 'The coming of the new organizations'. *Harvard Business Review*, January–February 1988.
22. CBI *Employment and Training*. Mercury Books, London, 1990.
23. Wickens, P *The Road to Nissan*. Macmillan, London, 1987.
24. Peters, T *Thriving on Chaos*. Macmillan, London, 1988.
25. Handy, C *The Age of Unreason*. Business Books, London, 1989.
26. Kanter, R M *When Giants Learn to Dance*. Simon & Schuster, London, 1989.
27. Kanter, R M *The Change Masters*. Allen & Unwin, London, 1984.
28. Williamson, E E and Ouchi, W C 'The markets and hierarchical programmes of research, origins, implications and prospects'. In Francis, A, Turk, J and Willmar, P, eds, *Power, Efficiency and Institutions*. Heinemann, London, 1983.
29. Pascale, R *Managing on the Edge*. Viking, London, 1990.

2

The Basis of Personnel Management

This chapter contains definitions of personnel management and its overall aims and objectives. It describes the main personnel management activities and concludes with a description of how they develop over time — the personnel management life cycle.

Definition of personnel management

Personnel management is concerned with:

- obtaining, developing and motivating the human resources required by the organization to achieve its objectives;
- developing an organization structure and climate and evolving a management style which will promote co-operation and commitment throughout the organization;
- making the best use of the skills and capacities of all those employed in the organization;
- ensuring that the organization meets its social and legal responsibilities towards its employees, with particular regard to the conditions of employment and quality of working life provided for them.

Aim of personnel management

The overall aim of personnel management is to make an effective contribution to the objectives of the organization and to the fulfilment of its social responsibilities.

Personnel objectives

Definition

Personnel objectives are the aims, goals and targets that have been set for the way in which an organization manages its human resources. They are developed within the framework of corporate objectives.

The role of personnel objectives

The role of personnel objectives is to further the achievement of corporate objectives. But in formulating the latter, human resource considerations should exert a major influence — the organization cannot afford to get its programmes for human resource planning, management and development wrong.

Personnel objectives need to be formulated as a means of shaping corporate strategies in so far as they involve the utilization of human resources, on which, of course, effective organization entirely depends. Finance is required as well but this is obtained and used and generated by people.

Personnel objectives also provide the basis for the formulation of personnel strategies and policies.

Formulating personnel objectives

The formulation of personnel objectives is, or should be, an analytical process. The factors which should be considered are:

- *Corporate objectives* under the four headings mentioned earlier: purpose, targets, ownership and the business the company is in.
- *Core values* — the accepted beliefs on what is best or good for the organization and what should or ought to happen. They define how management intends to conduct the business and to treat the people who work in it.
- *The nature of the business* — the type of work carried out, its technology and the sort of people it employs.
- *The climate of employee relationships in the organization.*

Context of personnel objectives

Personnel objectives and the means for achieving them will depend on their context. There are no universal objectives, just as there are no absolute principles governing personnel policies and practices. There are only certain basic headings and guidelines which provide a framework within which the organization does what it needs to do in the way which best suits itself.

The Basis of Personnel Management

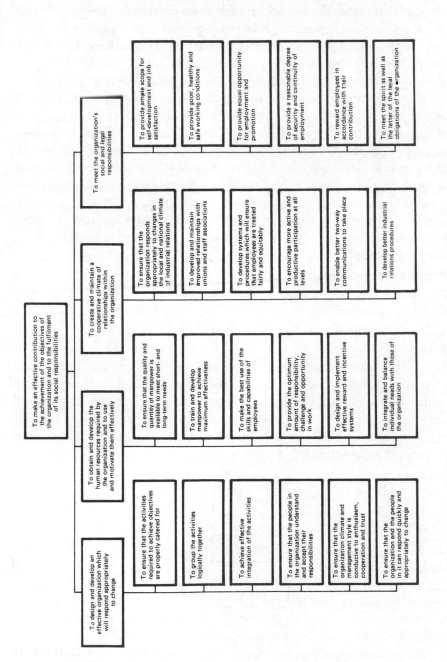

To make an effective contribution to the achievement of the objectives of the organization and to the fulfilment of its social responsibilities

To design and develop an effective organization which will respond appropriately to change

- To ensure that the activities required to achieve objectives are properly catered for
- To group the activities logically together
- To achieve effective integration of the activities
- To ensure that the people in the organization understand and accept their responsibilities
- To ensure that the organization climate and management style is conducive to enthusiasm, cooperation and trust
- To ensure that the organization and the people in it can respond quickly and appropriately to change

To obtain and develop the human resources required by the organization and to use and motivate them effectively

- To ensure that the quality and quantity of manpower is available to meet short- and long-term needs
- To train and develop manpower to achieve maximum effectiveness
- To make the best use of the skills and capabilities of employees
- To provide the optimum amount of responsibility, challenge and opportunity in work
- To design and implement effective reward and incentive systems
- To integrate and balance individual needs with those of the organization

To create and maintain a cooperative climate of relationships within the organization

- To ensure that the organization responds appropriately to changes in the local and national climate of industrial relations
- To develop and maintain improved relationships with unions and staff associations
- To develop systems and procedures which will ensure that employees are treated fairly and equitably
- To encourage more active and productive participation at all levels
- To enable better two-way communications to take place
- To develop better industrial relations procedures

To meet the organization's social and legal responsibilities

- To provide ample scope for self-development and job satisfaction
- To provide good, healthy and safe working conditions
- To provide equal opportunity for employment and promotion
- To provide a reasonable degree of security and continuity of employment
- To reward employees in accordance with their contribution
- To meet the spirit as well as the letter of the legal obligations of the organization

Hierarchy of personnel objectives

Personnel objectives can be set out in the form of a hierarchy as in Figure 2.1. This states the overall and the main objectives concerned with organization, human resources, relationships and responsibility. Beneath each of these main objectives are listed possible subobjectives. This is not a universally applicable list. It begs a number of questions; for example: What is an 'effective organization'? What is 'effective effort'? To what extent is it appropriate to pursue the objective of achieving a 'cooperative climate of relationships'?

Effectiveness has to be defined, and it may be necessary and even desirable to accept a degree of conflict in working through problems of relationships. A bland and, on the surface, smooth-running organization is not necessarily an effective one in achieving the objectives of its owners, its management, its workpeople and the unions.

A hierarchy such as the one illustrated in Figure 2.1 has its uses, however, as an indication of the main areas for concern in developing appropriate personnel strategies, policies and programmes.

Personnel activities

Fundamental activities

Organizations can survive and thrive only if they obtain, retain and develop the quantity and quality of human resources they need. The fundamental activities of personnel management are therefore to plan and implement programmes to achieve objectives in those areas. The programmes constitute the basic personnel strategy; Figure 2.2 is a model of these fundamental activities.

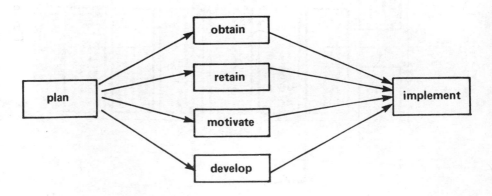

Figure 2.2 Personnel activities — basic model

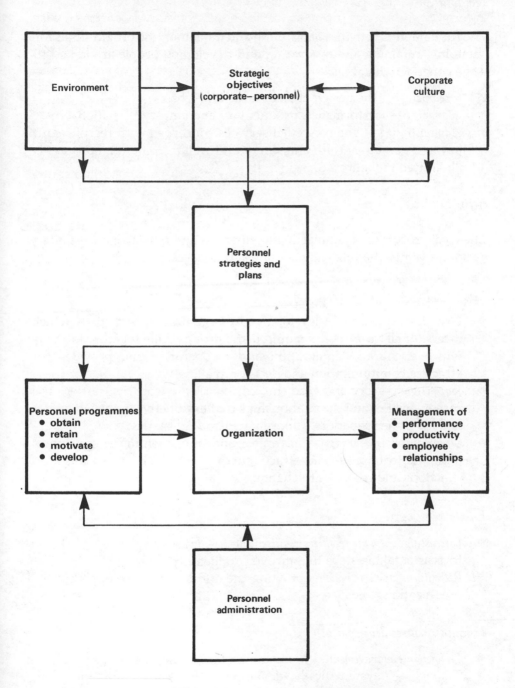

The process of personnel management

The total process

The fundamental activities of planning and implementing programmes for obtaining, retaining and motivating and developing people are linked to three other activity areas:

1. *Organizing* — the design of structures and jobs.
2. *Managing* — performance, productivity and employee relationships.
3. *Administrating* — the personnel services concerned with recruitment, pay and benefits, health and safety and welfare. The total process is illustrated in Figure 2.3.

Activity areas

The total process of personnel management as described in Figure 2.3 can be analysed into the following specific activity areas:

Organization

- *Organization design* — developing an organization structure which caters for all the activities required and groups them together in a way which encourages integration and co-operation and provides for effective communication and decision making.
- *Job design* — deciding on the content of a job: its duties and responsibilities and the relationships that exist between the job holder and his or her superiors, subordinates and colleagues.
- *Organization effectiveness* — planning and implementing programmes designed to improve the effectiveness with which an organization functions and responds to change.

Employee resourcing

- *Forecasting human resource requirements* — making plans to achieve forecasts, taking steps to improve productivity.
- *Recruitment and selection* — obtaining the number and type of people the organization needs.

Human resource development

- *Performance management* — assessing and improving performance.
- *Training* — systematically developing the knowledge and skills required to perform adequately a given job or task.

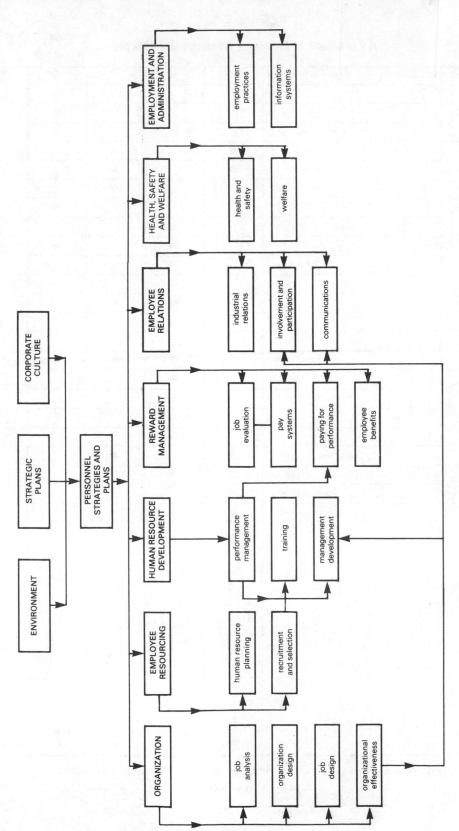

Figure 2.4 Personnel activities — interrelationships

A Handbook of Personnel Management Practice

Category	Activity	Organization	Human resources	Relationships	Responsibilities
Employment and administration	Information systems		●		●
	Welfare				●
	Health and safety				●
	Employment practices		●		●
Employee relations	Communications	●		●	
	Involvement and participation	●		●	
	Industrial relations			●	
Reward management	Employee benefits				●
	Paying for performance		●		
	Pay systems		●		●
	Job evaluation		●		
Human resource development	Management development		●		
	Training	●	●	●	
	Performance management		●		
Employee resourcing	Recruitment and selection		●		
Human resource planning	Productivity plan		●		
	Retention plan		●		
	Acquisition plan		●		
	Supply forecasting		●		
	Demand forecasting		●		
Organization	Organization development	●		●	
	Job design	●			
	Organization design	●			
	Job analysis	●	●		
		Organization	Human resources	Relationships	Responsibilities
		To design and develop an effective organization which will respond appropriately to change	To obtain, retain and develop the human resources needed by the organization and to use and motivate them effectively.	To maintain a corporate culture which creates a co-operative climate of relationships within the organization.	To meet the organization's legal and social responsibilities

Figure 2.5 How personnel activities contribute to the achievement of personnel objectives

- *Management development* — ensuring that the organization has the effective managers it requires to meet its present and future needs.
- *Career management* — planning the careers of people with potential.

Reward management

- *Job evaluation* — establishing the relative value of jobs in a pay structure.
- *Pay* — developing and administering pay structures and systems.
- *Paying for performance* — relating rewards to effort and results.
- *Employee benefits* — pensions, sick pay, etc.

Employee relations

- *Industrial relations* — co-operating and negotiating with trade unions and staff associations.
- *Participation* — jointly involving management and employees in making decisions on matters of mutual interest.
- *Communications* — creating and transmitting information of interest to employees.

Health, safety and welare

- *Health and safety* — administering health and safety programmes.
- *Welfare* — providing welfare services and helping with personnel problems.

Employment and personnel administration

- *The legal framework* within which personnel policies, practices and procedures operate.
- *Employment practices and procedures* — conditions of service; dealing with promotions, transfers, discipline, grievances and redundancy; implementing policies on such matters as equal opportunity, sexual harassment, racial relations (including ethnic monitoring), age, substance abuse, smoking and AIDS; generally ensuring that the legal and social obligations of the organization are fulfilled.
- *Personnel information systems* — provision of computerized information systems and other records to provide a database and to assist in decision making.

Relationships between activities and objectives

The considerable degree of interdependence among those activities is illustrated in Figure 2.4 and the contribution personnel activities make to achieving personnel objectives is shown in Figure 2.5.

The personnel management life cycle

While there can be no standard pattern for the development of personnel management in organizations — it depends so much on the circumstances — it is possible to identify certain trends which are linked to the business cycle as described below.

The business cycle

- *Growth* — start-up, increasingly successful development and marketing of a product or service in a particular market niche; emphasis on entrepreneurship — administration relegated to the provision of basic services.
- *Maturity* — diversification into new products or services and markets; divisionalization, administration and tight central control increasingly important.
- *Decline* — overambition leading to involvement in doubtful enterprises and overstretched financial and human resources; inability to cope with change; complacency — 'nothing fails like success'; a tendency towards organizational extremes — too much decentralization leading to loss of control or overcentralization involving tight control and oppressive, bureaucratic-type management; fierce and high levels of competition for which management is unprepared.
- *Regeneration* — achieved through trauma (a takeover or merger), or transformational leadership from a new chief executive with a mission to 'turn round' the business in the shortest possible time; or a realization at the top that major changes have to be made, accompanied by a well-planned campaign to accomplish them.

Relationships between the personnel and business cycles

Personnel management always takes place within the context of the business cycle. Personnel policies and practices grow, mature, decline and are regenerated alongside similar developments in the business although not necessarily at the same rate. There is a danger that personnel managers lose touch with what is happening to the organization and carry on regardless of its changing needs. Awareness of and sensitivity to business trends is a key requirement for effective personnel management.

The main areas in which the personnel life cycle operates are:

- organization
- resourcing
- performance management
- rewards
- employee relations.

Organization

- *Growth* — flexible, responsive, fluid, informal; people work well together in the common cause.
- *Maturity* — structured, clear job definitions and lines of communication and control; devolution to strategic business units (SBUs); integration achieved successfully through project teams, task forces, and committees.
- *Decline* — pulling back authority from SBUs and developing overcentralized and bureaucratic control mechanisms; or, allowing SBUs to go their own sweet way without adequate guidance or control; meetings become a way of life without enhancing cooperation; teamwork is no longer regarded as important and political means are used to achieve goals.
- *Regeneration* — a search for a new mission and a changed set of values; a belief in leadership from the centre accompanied by a move towards a federal organization; the development of a more flexible approach to the organization, recognizing that it has to be both tight and loose as circumstances demand; not imposing any academic or management consultant's prescriptions without ensuring they fit the mission, strategies and culture of the organization; effective teamwork is promoted and recognized as one of the key values of the organization.

Resourcing

- *Growth* — bringing in talented people and giving them scope to use their abilities; managing rapid internal movements.
- *Maturity* — emphasis on 'make' rather than 'buy', ie the establishment of well-developed policies and procedures for satisfying human resource requirements from within; encouraging mobility; recognizing, however, that new blood is often needed and therefore injecting high-quality people into the organization as a matter of policy; removing dead wood as necessary, but in a planned and sensitive

manner; well-conceived training and management development programmes are available to meet ascertained needs.

- *Decline* — a rigid approach to finding and developing people from within the organization which is not related to sensible human resource plans; panic buying of people from outside who may not fit the organization's needs; unplanned redundancies and layoffs, ruining morale and creating dissent; training and management development programmes are bureaucratic and largely irrelevant.
- *Regeneration* — a total reconsideration of the sort of people the organization needs and of where they can be obtained; targeted campaigns to recruit people with the specific abilities required; communication, education and training programmes designed to develop the corporate culture and, as required, gain acceptance to new values and behaviours or reinforce existing ones; training is performance related, ensuring that the required new skills are developed and that the workforce can operate much more flexibly.

Performance management

- *Growth* — as a result of continuous interaction, people understand what is expected of them and know just how well, or badly, they are doing; successes or failures are rewarded or penalized quickly.
- *Maturity* — a performance appraisal system involving merit ratings and, possibly, based on management by objectives is operating; people are clear about their goals and formal reviews are used to tell them how they are getting on and discuss how they can make better use of their strengths or overcome their weaknesses.
- *Decline* — the performance appraisal system has become a bureaucratic, form-filling exercise; managers are largely incapable of conducting satisfactory performance review meetings and dislike doing it; as a rule, such meetings demotivate rather than motivate staff.
- *Regeneration* — a performance management system is developed which does not rely on form-filling and is only introduced after an intensive training and briefing programme; the system is based on the joint agreement of objectives, standards, action plans and development needs; it is emphasized that performance management is a continuous process, not an annual event.

Rewards

- *Growth* — there is no formal pay structure; employees are paid individual 'spot' rates very much dependent upon market trends; basic benefits such as pension and company cars are provided.

- *Maturity* — a fully-developed, graded pay structure is in operation based upon job evaluation and market rate analysis; performance-related pay and incentive pay schemes may be used for a large proportion of employees, both salaried and wage earners; a full range of employee benefits which meet people's needs are provided.
- *Decline* — the pay structure is rigid and unresponsive to changes in market rates and organizational requirements; wage and grade drift (increases in pay or upgradings which are unrelated to performance or responsibility) abound; job evaluation has become a cottage industry; rates of pay are no longer competitive; increases consist of an across-the-board, inflation-related sum and a largely undiscriminating (and for high-level performers, inadequate) merit award; there is no clear policy on how to treat market pressures; the benefits package is no longer cost-effective; people have no choice in what benefits they get.
- *Regeneration* — a much more flexible approach to reward management is adopted; pay curve structures and skills-based schemes relate pay to competence and level of skill; increases are related both to market rate movements and performance — there is no automatic increase to cover inflation and a much wider range of merit awards can be made; there is a move towards a 'clean cash' policy rather than a top-heavy benefit package, and employees are allowed some choice in what benefits they want; there is a strong drive towards the harmonization of the pay and benefits system.

Employee relations

- *Growth* — no unions; largely informal systems for communication and involvement.
- *Maturity* — unions are recognized; there are formal procedure agreements and joint consultation arrangements which minimize disputes and grievances; methods of communication and involvement such as team briefing and quality circles are introduced successfully.
- *Decline* — overcentralized and multiunion bargaining leads to the organization's losing a measure of control over industrial relations; disputes on pay, demarcation, and other employment issues are frequent and not easily resolved; joint consultation is dominated by the trade union side and does not address the real issues; communication and involvement systems have 'withered on the vine' and manage-

ment is unable or disinclined to talk directly to members of the work-force.

- *Regeneration* — decentralized and single union/single table bargaining enables the organization to manage employee relations in harmony with the trade unions; 'new style' agreements are concluded which provide for flexibility, harmonization and strike avoidance procedures such as pendulum bargaining; HRM approaches involving direct communication with employees to develop mutuality are introduced; the organization does not have to rely absolutely on formal systems, such as team briefing on quality circles, but uses them judiciously.

3

Strategic Human Resource Management

Definition

Strategic human resource management is concerned with the development and implementation of people strategies which are integrated with corporate strategies and ensure that the culture, values and structure of the organization and the quality, motivation and commitment of its members contribute fully to the achievement of its goals.

Aims

Strategic human resource management is based on the principle that it is people who implement the corporate plan. It takes a broader, more integrated view of the personnel function, ensuring that it is built into the fabric of the business, linking it firmly to the attainment of the long-term strategies of the organization, and ensuring that personnel people provide the guidance and expert support needed to accomplish these strategies.

In particular, human resource strategies aim to:

- ensure that from the outset corporate planning processes recognize that the ultimate source of value is people;
- see that all concerned in strategic planning appreciate the human resource implications of their proposals and understand the potential human resource constraints if appropriate action is not taken;
- achieve a close match between corporate objectives and the objectives of the personnel function;
- provide guidance on the design and management of the organizational processes and culture of the organization to ensure that they help

everyone to do their jobs better and assist in getting and keeping high-calibre people;
* identify the organization's distinctive competences and the types of people who will be wanted to build and maintain them;
* assess the performance requirements needed to reach the organization's goals and decide the lines along which these requirements should be satisfied;
* review the levels of motivation and commitment throughout the organization and plan ways to improve them where necessary.

What strategic human resource management is about

Human resource strategy as an integral part of the corporate plan

Strategic human resource management is not simply an add-on to the corporate plan. It is, or should be, an integral part of it, ie there must be 'strategic fit'. Business strategies must take into account the human implications of the plans as they are being formulated.

The corporate plan should be based on a strategic vision of where it is believed the company should be going. Turning that vision into reality is a matter of defining the mission of the company and then setting its goals and developing strategic plans for their achievement.

The goals will refer to growth by expansion from the present base and/ or acquisition, market development, product development, the introduction of new technology, and, perhaps, the preservation of the business from external threats. Strategies will be concerned not only with plans but also with the capability of the business to accomplish its goals. Capability will be related to the supply of financial and technical systems and physical resources, but, equally importantly, it will depend on the availability of the human resource and how that resource is organized, developed and motivated.

Key factors affecting human resource (HR) strategy

Guest[1] has suggested that strategic human resource management is largely about integration. Its concern is to ensure that human resource management (HRM) 'is fully integrated into strategic planning; that HRM policies cohere both across policy areas and across hierarchies; and that HRM practices are accepted and used by line managers as part of their everyday work'. Miller[2] emphasizes that the key to effective HR strategy is 'the concept of fit — the fit of human resource management with the strategic thrust of the organisation'. Wickens[3] believes that the difficulty is 'not so much in trying to define strategies but in trying to separate personnel decisions from the business strategy'.

One of the difficulties facing those involved in the formulation of HR strategies is distinguishing the two levels of strategy: corporate level and the level of the business unit.

Corporate-level and unit strategies

Corporate-level strategies relate to the corporate portfolio and its cohesiveness, mergers and acquisitions, the image and imagination of the company and the ethos of how business should be conducted.

At business-unit level, strategies are mainly concerned with answering the question: 'Where and how are we going to compete to earn sustained high returns?' This means making decisions on how, in the longer term, the business can develop and maintain superior effectiveness, a superior cost position and superior quality coupled with the ability to meet customers' real needs.

Cooke and Armstrong[4] have established that, although relatively few strategic HR issues arise at corporate level, those that do may be decisive. They include the organization's mission; its values, culture and style; management as a corporate resource; and the management of change.

The constituents of human resource strategies

HR strategies generally have to be broad-brush affairs which point the way to go in the form of declarations of intent, but do not spell out in fine detail how to get there. The latter process is a matter of personnel planning and programming, which, however, is made more coherent by being carried out within the framework of the strategic plan.

The areas in which human resource strategies are applicable comprise:

- *culture change* — developing a more positive and appropriate corporate culture;
- *organization design* — redesigning the organization in the light of new requirements;
- *organizational effectiveness* — improving the effectiveness of the organization in such areas as teamwork, communications, productivity and customer service, and increasing the ability to manage change;
- *resourcing* — providing the human resources required by the planning and implementation of recruitment, retention, training and human resource development programmes;

- *performance management* -- improving the performance of individuals and therefore the organization by such means as performance appraisal and performance-related training;
- *reward management* — evolving strategies which underpin the organization's values of excellence, performance, teamwork and quality; convey messages to employees that the organization will satisfy their reward expectations; and indicate what type of performance will be rewarded and how;
- *motiviation* — redesigning jobs and designing reward systems (financial and non-financial) which provide for both intrinsic and extrinsic motivation (see Chapter 7 for a definition of these terms and Chapter 14 for a description of motivation strategies);
- *commitment* — developing communication, involvement, people management and training programmes designed to create a feeling of 'mutuality' — the integration of the needs of the individual with those of the organization (see also Chapters 8 and 14);
- *employee relations* — establishing policies, plans and procedures which maximize the degree to which management and employees cooperate to their mutual benefit and which minimize the causes and effects of conflict and restrictive practices;
- *flexibility* — developing a structure, climate, systems and organization which enable the organization to respond flexibly to change. This will include programmes for multiskilling, redesigning jobs and creating autonomous work groups;
- *quality* — establishing total quality management (TQM) as a way of life.

Developing human resource strategies

The overall approach

Human resource strategies should be formulated by a continuous process of analysing what is happening to the organization and where it is going. They generally have to be broad-brush affairs which point the way to go but do not spell out in fine detail how to get there. The latter process is achieved by action planning — creating programmes which spell out how defined objectives are to be achieved and which define both the costs and the benefits of attaining those objectives.

The approach requires, first, an overall assessment of the business; secondly, an analysis of the business plan; and, finally, a review of the specific areas in which strategies need to be developed.

Business assessment

An overall analysis of the business should aim to provide answers to the questions set out in Figure 3.1.

Business	Human resources
What business are we in?	What sort of people do we need in the business?
Where are we going?	What sort of organization do we need to get there?
What are our strengths, weaknesses, opportunities, and threats?	To what extent are those strengths and weaknesses related to our human resource capability? What opportunities have we got to develop and motivate our staff? What are the threats in such areas as skill shortages and the retention of key staff?
What are the main strategic issues facing the business?	To what extent do these issues involve organizational and HR considerations?
What are the critical success factors which determine how well we achieve our mission?	How far will business success be helped or hindered by the quality, motivation, commitment, and attitudes of our employees?

Figure 3.1 Analysis of business and human resource requirements

Business plan analysis

The business plan analysis extends the overall assessment of the business to deal with the specific human resource requirements implied by the strategy. For example, the chosen business strategy of an engineering company involved the acquisition of two businesses, a major capital investment in new product technology, the continuing development of a cellular manufacturing strategy designed to simplify the business, the closure of one site and relocation to a second site and the reorganization of one business unit.

In the light of this business strategy, the main elements of the HR strategy were to:

- integrate the organization and management teams of the acquired businesses into the division;
- provide the thrust for successful investment in new technologies

through targeted programmes for developing skills and competence and maximizing productivity;
● manage downsizing and restructuring humanely and responsibly;
● establish a clear ethos and culture for the division based on values relevant to the business strategy.

These elements could then be translated into programmes for organizational restructuring; management training; high-performance work design incorporating multiskilling and autonomous working groups; new performance management systems at all sites; and reaffirmation of total quality management and customer-care initiatives across the division as a basis for integrating the new businesses within the value system of the company.

The link between business and human resource strategies can be explored analytically by relating each strategic heading with an HR strategy area on a matrix, as illustrated in Figure 3.2.

HR strategy formulation matrix					
	Market development	Product development	New technology	Diversification	Other
Organization					
Resourcing					
Training					
Performance Management					
Other					

Figure 3.2 HR strategy formulation matrix

Specific strategic areas

In the light of the assessments of the business and its strategy, the formulation of HR strategy should proceed by answering the following basic questions:

● What are the implications for HR strategy of the overall business assessment?

- In what areas does the business plan indicate that personnel strategies need to be formulated?

These can be supplemented by providing answers to the following general questions:

- What is the nature of the corporate culture? Is it supportive or dysfunctional?
- Will the organization be able to cope with future challenges in its present form?
- What kind of people and how many will be required?
- Are performance levels high enough to meet demands for increased profitability, innovation, higher productivity, better quality and improved customer service?
- What is the level of commitment towards the company?
- Are there any potential constraints such as skill shortages or industrial relations problems?

Setting out the HR strategic plan

There is no standard format for setting out a strategic plan. The following is an example of a framework used by the writer when he was responsible at Book Club Associates for both corporate planning for the business as a whole and for HR planning.

1. Overall assessment of the HR implications of the present situation of the business and its prospects.
2. Analysis of the specific HR implications of each aspect of the business plan.
3. Proposed HR strategies in each of the following areas to meet business requirements:
   (a) Organization development — teamwork and flexibility;
   (b) Resourcing — recruitment and development;
   (c) Performance management — improving results and productivity;
   (d) Reward management — improving motivation and commitment;
   (e) Employee relations — communications and involvement;
   (f) Customer care and quality.

Case studies in HR strategic planning

The following is the approach to HR strategic planning adopted by two organizations, as described by Armstrong.[5]

Ford Motor Company

The Director of Personnel for the Ford Motor Company, John Hougham, describes how personnel strategies fit into the business strategy at Ford.

> We fully participate in a regular planning process which takes into account all the major components of the company. We start with contributions to the strategic review. There may be special contributions on issues which we believe are of particular importance in the year we are looking at, like the growth of information technology or any acquisitions. But more importantly, we are looking ahead and asking 'What is the outlook for the market?' Because after all that's what we are all here for. We are all here to make motor cars, and trucks and tractors and whatever, and sell them. So there is a tremendous amount of input from the sales and marketing people.
>
> Then we get contributions from the manufacturing people. What kind of impact is new technology going to have on the business? What is the plan this year to continue improving quality? (This is paramount.) What do they see as being achievable in terms of further productivity improvements? And this process runs right through each facet of the business. When it comes to us the kind of things we are saying, they are about quality, the human dimension of quality — what we are doing to inculcate quality thinking into people, to make them more responsible for quality? We talk about our plans for improving the calibre of the workforce, our recruitment plans, what we are going to do about shortfalls, the demographic problem — there aren't going to be so many good people around, so what are we going to do about it? We discuss the need to interchange people more between the various parts of our business, manufacturing and engineering, to grow more rounded managers. We have started to talk about developing people much more between national companies, to grow good European managers.
>
> We talk also on the issues that manufacturing, sales and marketing have highlighted, because none of these things stands in isolation. We say what we think we in personnel should be doing to respond to those requirements and, by the way, here are some ideas of our own. We talk about compensation strategy — 'Ford-speak' for how you pay people and what benefits they have — bringing the executive up to date on what's going on in the outside world, profit-sharing, relating pay to performance, for example.
>
> And then we look at labour strategy — recognizing that what we are really after is increasing labour flexibility, with less demarcation. What is the likely union reaction going to be to that?

Thorn EMI

Thorn EMI's integrated business and HR strategy defined the following five main characteristics of the group:

1. Its capacity to manage businesses in different national markets and exploit its creative/marketing, technological and management skills internationally.
2. Its ability to give real opportunity and authority for strong managers to be enterprising in their own businesses, while exercising strong strategic control through the willingness of its top management to behave interdependently.
3. Its ability to coordinate its approaches fast and responsively to market opportunities which require integrated action by more than one business area.
4. Having a strong balance between demanding excellence of performance from its managers and investing skill and time into helping managers to improve their performance and potential.
5. Its ability to manage its research and technologies in a market-sensitive manner across all its business units.

In Thorn EMI, as elsewhere, corporate strategy sets the agenda for HR strategy in the areas of culture, values, organization, performance and the management of change. It should not in itself be overinfluenced by HR factors (HR strategies are about making business strategies work), but it must take account of key HR opportunities and constraints. And it is the task of human resource directors to ensure that this is exactly what the board and senior managers do.

At the business unit level, strategic HR may be more closely involved in the cultural, organizational and resourcing implications of the business strategy.

Making HR strategy work

Human resource strategy is justified by the corporate strategy. It should be business driven, imaginative, bold, clear and action orientated. It must also be selective, focusing on priorities, and flexible, rapidly adjusting to change. The head of the personnel or HR function has the prime responsibility for making HR strategy work and his or her role in this area is discussed in Chapter 4.

Because strategies tend to be expressed as abstractions, they must be translated into programmes with clearly stated objectives and deliverables. The personnel function must demonstrate that it is responding directly to the needs of the business and that its proposals are realistic and cost-effective.

But getting strategies into action is not easy. In many ways the concept of HR strategy is an elusive one. The term has been devalued in some quarters; sometimes to mean no more than a few generalized ideas about personnel policies; at other times to describe a short-term plan; for example, to increase the retention rate of graduates. It must be emphasized that HR strategies are not just programmes, policies, or plans concerning personnel issues which the personnel department happens to think are important. Piecemeal initiatives do not constitute strategy.

HR strategy, if it is to make any impact at all, *must* be integrated with business strategy and must address the real business issues which affect human resource management — and these are likely to be most, if not all of them. The impact of HR strategy depends on commitment at the top supported by powerful guidance and support from the personnel director or head of the HR function, who must have a say in corporate strategy equal to that of any other member of the top management team.

Making HR strategy work requires sustained effort from all concerned. The effort, however, is worthwhile. The important thing is to give an overall sense of purpose to HR activities which can provide the people the organization needs and help them to understand where they are going, how they are going to get there, why certain things are happening, and, most important, the contribution they are expected to make towards achieving the company's projected future growth and prosperity.

References

1. Guest, D 'Personnel and HRM: can you tell the difference?' *Personnel Management*, January 1989.
2. Miller, P 'Strategic HRM: what it is and what it isn't', *Personnel Management*, February 1989.
3. Wickens, P 'A strategic role for personnel', *Personnel Management*, January 1990.
4. Cooke, R and Armstrong, M 'The search for strategic HRM', *Personnel Management*, December 1990.
5. Armstrong, M *Personnel and the Bottom Line*. Institute of Personnel Management, London, 1989.

4

Personnel Policies

What are personnel policies?

Personnel policies are continuing guidelines on the approach the organization intends to adopt in managing its human resources. They define the philosophies and values of the organization on how people should be treated, and from these are derived the principles upon which managers are expected to act when dealing with personnel matters. Personnel policies therefore serve as reference points when human resource management programmes are being developed and when decisions are being made about people. They help to define 'how things are done around here'.

Relationships of personnel policies to personnel objectives, strategies and procedures

Personnel policies should be distinguished from objectives, strategies and procedures. In essence:

- *personnel objectives* define ends;
- *personnel strategies* lay down the direction to be followed in achieving ends;
- *personnel policies* control the means of achieving ends;
- *personnel procedures* implement the policies.

Objectives lead both to strategies and policies, but guidelines on how these strategies should be achieved are needed in the shape of personnel policies. In turn, agreed policies are extended into personnel procedures which enable them to be implemented. The interconnections between objectives, strategies, policies and procedures are shown in Figure 4.1.

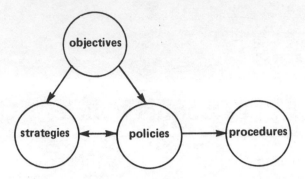

Interconnections between personnel objectives, strategies, policies and procedures

Why have personnel policies?

It is necessary to develop a coherent approach to managing people which binds together the various personnel strategies of the organization. This is the main function of personnel policies, or employment policies, as they are sometimes described.

Company personnel or employment policies are frameworks within which actions take place. They promote consistency and equity in the way in which people are treated. Because they provide guidance on what managers should do in particular circumstances they facilitate decentralization and delegation. And, while they should fit the corporate culture, they can also help to shape it.

Do policies need to be formalized?

All organizations have personnel policies. Some, however, exist implicitly as a philosophy of management and an attitude to employees that is expressed in the way in which personnel issues are handled; for example, the introduction of new technology. The advantage of explicit policies in terms of consistency and understanding may appear to be obvious, but there are disadvantages: written policies can be inflexible, platitudinous, or both. To a degree, policies have often to be expressed in abstract terms and managers do not care for abstractions. But they do prefer to know where they stand — people like structure — and formalized personnel policies can provide the guidelines they need.

Formalized personnel policies can be used as the basis for induction, supervisory and management training which help those undergoing it to understand the philosophies and values of the company and how they are expected to behave within that context.

Personnel policy areas

Personnel policies can be expressed as overall statements of the philosophy of the organization and of its values. The specific policy areas, which may be contained in the overall statement or issued as separate documents, are:

- employment
- equal opportunity
- pay
- development and training
- participation
- employee relations
- new technology
- health and safety.

The main points that could be covered in each of these policies are summarized below. Examples of company policy statements are given in Appendix A.

Overall policy

The overall policy defines how the organization fulfils its social responsibilities for its employees and sets out its attitudes towards them. It is an expression of its values or beliefs about how people should be treated. In *In Search of Excellence*, Peters and Waterman wrote that if they were asked for one all-purpose bit of advice for management, one truth that they could distil from all their research on what makes a company excellent, it would be: 'Figure out your value system. Decide what the company *stands* for.'[1] In *Leadership and Administration*, Selznick[2] emphasized the key role of values in organizations, when he wrote: 'The formation of an institution is marked by the making of value commitments, that is, choices which fix the assumptions of policy makers as to the nature of the enterprise, its distinctive aims, methods and roles.'

The values expressed in an overall statement of personnel policies may explicitly or implicitly refer to the following concepts:

1. *Equity* — treating employees fairly and justly by adopting an 'even-handed' approach. This includes protecting individuals from any unfair decisions made by their superiors, providing equal opportunities for

employment and promotion and operating an equitable payment system.

2. *Consideration* — taking account of individual circumstances when making decisions which affect the prospects, security or self-respect of employees.

3. *Quality of working life* — consciously and continually aiming to improve the quality of working life as a means of increasing motivation and improving results. This involves increasing the sense of satisfaction people obtain from their work by, so far as possible, reducing monotony, increasing variety and responsibility and avoiding placing people under too much stress.

4. *Working conditions* — providing healthy, safe and, so far as practicable, pleasant working conditions.

It may be difficult to express these policies in anything but generalized terms and, although ideals of social justice and welfare are important, it should be remembered that, as Sadler and Barry[3] expressed it: 'Organizations in general and business enterprises in particular, are established to achieve specific sets of objectives and not to satisfy the needs of their members'.

Increasingly, however, organizations are having to recognize that they are subject to external as well as internal pressures which act as constraints on the extent to which they can disregard the higher standards of behaviour that are expected of employers.

Employment policies

Employment policies cover the following areas:

1. *Human resource planning* — a commitment by the company to planning ahead in order to maximize the opportunities for employees to develop their careers within the organization and to minimize the possibility of compulsory redundancy.

2. *Quality of employees* — an organization may deliberately set out in its policy statement that, as a company which is dedicated to the pursuit of excellence and professionalism in all it does, it believes in recruiting people who have the ability or potential to meet the high standards of performance that will be expected of them.

3. *Promotion* — the policy would state the company's wish to promote from within wherever this is appropriate as a means of satisfying its requirements for high-quality staff. The policy would, however, recognize that there will be occasions when the organization's present and future needs can only be met by recruitment from

outside. The point could be made that a vigorous organization needs infusions of fresh blood from time to time if it is not to stagnate. In addition, the policy might state that employees will be encouraged to apply for internally advertised jobs and will not be held back from promotion by their managers, however reluctant the latter may be to lose them.

4. *Equal opportunity* — a reference should be made in the general employment policy statement to the fact that 'this is an equal opportunity company'.

5. *Redundancy* — the redundancy policy could state that it is the company's intention to use its best endeavours to avoid involuntary redundancy through its human resource redeployment and retraining procedures. However, if redundancy is unavoidable those affected will be given fair and equitable treatment, the maximum amount of warning, and every help that can be provided by the company to obtain suitable alternative work.

6. *Discipline* — the disciplinary policy should state that employees have the right to know what is expected of them and what could happen if they infringe the company's rules. It would also make the point that, in handling disciplinary cases, the company will treat employees in accordance with the principles of natural justice.

7. *Grievances* — the policy should state that employees have the right to raise their grievances with their manager, to be accompanied by a representative if they so wish, and to appeal to a higher level if they feel that their grievance has not been resolved satisfactorily.

8. *Age and employment* — the policy would define the approach the company adopts to engaging, training and promoting older employees.

9. *Ethnic monitoring* — how the company deals with monitoring the employment of ethnic minorities.

10. *Sexual harassment* — the policy would express the company's strong disapproval of sexual harassment and outline the measures taken to eliminate it.

11. *Smoking* — the policy would define no-smoking rules.

12. *Substance abuse* — how the company treats employees with drink or drug problems.

13. *AIDS* — how the company approaches the employment of people who are HIV positive or are actually suffering from AIDS.

Equal opportunity policy

The equal opportunity policy should spell out the company's

determination to give equal opportunities to all, irrespective of sex, race, creed, or marital status. It could also state that the company will use its best endeavours to provide equal opportunities to disabled people.

Pay policy

The pay policy could cover such matters as:

- paying market rates;
- paying for performance;
- gain-sharing — sharing in the gains (added value) or profits of the company;
- providing an equitable pay system;
- equal pay for work of equal value, subject to overriding market considerations.

Development and training policy

The development and training policy should express the company's commitment to the continuous development of the skills and abilities of employees in order to maximize their contribution and to give them the opportunity to advance their careers.

Involvement and participation policy

The involvement and participation policy should spell out the company's belief in involvement and participation as a means of generating the commitment of all employees to the success of the enterprise. This policy could also refer to the basis upon which the company intends to communicate information to employees.

Employee relations policy

The employee relations policy will set out the company's approach to the rights of employees to represent their interests to management through trade unions, staff associations or some other form of representative system.

New technology policy

A new technology policy could be incorporated in the employment policy, but in most organizations these days the introduction of new technology is so significant that it justifies a separate policy statement. Such a statement would refer to consultation about the introduction of new technology and to the steps that would be taken by the company to minimize the risk of compulsory redundancy.

Health and safety policy

Health and safety policies cover how the company intends to provide healthy and safe places and systems of work.

Formulating policies

Personnel policies are based on the values held in the company about how its human resources should be treated. These shared values act as an informal control system that tells people what is expected of them. They need, however, to be expressed in the form of personnel policies which provide more explicit guidance to the approach required to specific areas of human resource management.

The core values are a function of the corporate culture and it is therefore the culture that will ultimately determine the scope of personnel policies.

All corporate values are different. They are contingent on the culture and they have to match it. An example of a statement of core values is given in Appendix B.

The following steps should be taken when formulating or revising personnel policies:

1. *Gain understanding of the corporate culture and its shared values.* This is an analytical process and is discussed in Chapter 5.
2. *Analyse existing policies — written and unwritten.* Personnel policies will exist in any organization, even if they are implicit rather than expressed formally.
3. *Analyse external influences.* Company personnel policies are subject to the influence of employment legislation and the official codes of practice issued by bodies in the UK, such as ACAS (The Advisory, Conciliation and Arbitration Service), the EOC (Equal Opportunities Commission), the CRR (Commission on Racial Relations) or the Health and Safety Executive. The codes of practice issued by the professional institutions, especially the Institute of Personnel Management, should also be consulted.
4. *Seek managers' views.* Check with managers, preferably starting at the

top, on their views about personnel policies. This goes hand-in-hand with the analysis of corporate culture and values.

5. *Seek the views of employees.* Conduct an attitude survey to obtain the views of employees about the company's existing personnel policies.
6. *Seek the views of union representatives.* Find out from unions or staff representatives what they think about policies.
7. *Prepare draft policies.* Analyse the information obtained in the first six steps and prepare draft policies.
8. *Consult.* Discuss and agree policies with management and union representatives.

References

1. Peters, T and Waterman, R *In Search of Excellence.* Harper & Row, New York, 1987.
2. Selznick, P *Leadership and Administration.* Row, Evanston, IL, 1957.
3. Sadler, P and Barry, B *Organizational Development.* Longman, London, 1970.

5

Role of the Personnel Function

Overall role

The role of the personnel function is to provide guidance and support which will enable management to deal effectively with all matters concerning the employment of people and the relationships between the management of the organization and the people it employs.

Sir Leonard Peach,[1] Director of Personnel and Corporate Affairs at IBM and formerly President of the Institute of Personnel Management and Chief Executive of the National Health Service Management Board, defined the role as follows:

> Personnel management is concerned with creating an environment which enables line management to recruit, train and motivate the people they need for today's and tomorrow's jobs. In other words, personnel management is an enabling function which creates a particular set of policies, but line managers are directly responsible for the people they control.

Sir Leonard's point must be emphasized — the personnel function does not exist to usurp the basic responsibility of management and supervision for the human resources that they have to lead, motivate, develop, direct and control.

This chapter examines the role of the personnel function under the following headings:

- the specific roles of the function;
- models of personnel management;
- the contingency approach to personnel management;
- what personnel managers do;
- how the personnel function can be evaluated;
- the constraints upon personnel management;
- the ambiguous nature of personnel management;

- values and professionalism;
- the organization of the personnel function;
- how to be an effective personnel manager.

Specific roles of the personnel function

Personnel managers have a number of roles within the overall framework described at the beginning of this chapter. They are, as Sir Leonard Peach says, *enablers*, and in this capacity they provide guidance and support. They are *facilitators* who help the organization to manage change — in fact they can often provide important levers for change (see Chapter 14, page 270). The personnel function can also *empower* people by helping them to acquire the expertise and confidence they need to perform more effectively in their jobs. But personnel people can and should be *interventionists* as required, speaking out on what needs to be done.

The enabling role

As Peter Hobbs,[1] Group Personnel Director of the Wellcome Foundation Ltd, has said of personnel people:

> We are enablers. We may often present managers with some of the stars in the firmament and say 'Hey, isn't that nice?' and get people to reach for them. But we are enabling other people to do things rather than doing things ourselves.

Enabling in a personnel context means ensuring that management is able to exercise its responsibility for human resources effectively. Enabling involves the provision of guidance and support.

The guidance role

Personnel directors and managers guide and advise management as a whole on:

- the human resource implications of business strategies;
- the human resource strategies organizations should adopt concerning resourcing, human resource development, reward management and employee relations;
- the tactics which should be used in dealing with short-term problems related, for example, to shortages or surpluses of employees, the impact of a merger or acquisition, the need to acquire or develop new skills, how to deal with a trade union pay claim or handle a dispute, or health and safety issues.

Individual managers, supervisors or team leaders will be provided with guidance on the interpretation and application of personnel policies and on dealing with problems such as obtaining the right quality and quantity of staff, training, pay, health and safety, handling disputes and grievances, and generally meeting the requirements of employment legislation on such matters as equal opportunity.

The support role

The provision of practical and effective guidance is the prime means of supporting line management. Specifically, however, the support services provided by the personnel function cover the following areas:

- assisting with organization and job design;
- generally helping to improve organizational effectiveness;
- preparing demand and supply forecasts for future manpower requirements;
- advising on means of improving productivity and the cost-effective use of human resources;
- recruitment and selection — job analysis, tapping the various resources of recruits, sifting applications, advising on selection procedures, conducting filter interviews, assisting with final interviews, administering tests and making arrangements for offers, employment contracts, references and induction training;
- developing and administering performance management (performance review) and development schemes;
- identifying and satisfying training needs;
- administering management development and career management programmes;
- monitoring market rates;
- developing and administering job evaluation schemes;
- developing pay structures and systems and advising on rates of pay and pay increases (general or individual);
- administering the pay system (this can sometimes include the payroll);
- advising on and administering employee benefits, including pensions, sick pay, maternity benefits, leave, company loans, relocation expenses and company cars;
- taking part in pay negotiations and the handling of disputes and grievances;
- administering communications systems;
- dealing with health and safety requirements and problems;
- administering personnel record systems.

The facilitating role

Personnel managers also act as change agents or managers. They help to facilitate change by advising on the implications of new technology, restructuring, new systems of work, new procedures, and mergers or acquisitions.

Personnel directors and managers can be instrumental in developing 'agendas for change' such as the one developed by Geoff Armstrong[1] for the MB group. This set out a plan for a campaign for change based on:

- a shared agenda against which progress can be measured;
- a communications programme aimed at internal and external audiences;
- an increased investment in training so that managers develop both the skills and the vision to manage the change process.

The key issues in this campaign to accelerate the pace of change were:

- the need for an explicit agenda;
- the description of the desired behaviour so that the agenda is more than a collection of 'buzz words';
- ways of setting agreed objectives and of measuring performance and progress towards them, both short and long term;
- an environment of support in which recognition of achievement to date will reinforce confidence to do more;
- executive group leadership which encourages managers to be bold and innovative and to harness the ideas and talents of all employees in the search for better ways of doing things;
- collaboration and partnership between business and corporate resources;
- the generation of a widespread attitude among all employees that encourages change and innovation.

The empowering role

In the context of human resource management, empowering means ensuring that people are able to use and develop their skills and knowledge in ways which help to achieve both their own goals and those of the organization. Empowerment is achieved by organization and job design approaches which place responsibility fairly and squarely on individuals and teams, by recognizing the contribution people can make, by providing mechanisms such as improvement groups to enable them to make this contribution, and by training and development programmes which increase both competences and confidence.

The interventionist role

As facilitators, catalysts, enablers, change agents and creators of environments conducive to successful accomplishment, personnel managers have to intervene. They cannot contribute from a supine position.

Tony Vineall,[1] Deputy Head of Personnel, Unilever, sees personnel managers as being concerned with the implementation and monitoring of policies but also with 'selective intervention': 'You need to dive in and get really involved.'

> As well as defining policies you need to monitor what's going on with as little paperwork as you can. You must try very hard to keep down the bureaucracy. On the basis of that, you intervene selectively. First you find methods of monitoring what's happening in a simple way, then you act.
>
> You intervene in different ways in different situations, and it's an opportunistic business. You have to start with an overview of where the pressure points are in an organization and where you can make a useful intervention. But the opportunity to intervene can come at the most unexpected times.

Models of personnel management

The Tyson and Fell models

Tyson and Fell[2] evolved three models of personnel management from their research:

1. *The 'clerk of works' model.* In this model all authority for action is vested in line managers. 'Personnel policies are formed or created after the actions which created the need.' Policies are not integral to the business and are short term and *ad hoc*. Authority is vested in line managers and personnel activities are largely routine — employment and day-to-day administration.
2. *The 'contracts manager' model.* In this model policies are well established, often implicit, with a heavy industrial relations emphasis, possibly derived from an employers' association. The personnel department will use fairly sophisticated systems, especially in the field of employee relations. The personnel manager is likely to be a professional or very experienced in industrial relations. He or she will not be on the board, and, although having some authority to 'police' the implementation of

policies, acts mainly in an interpretive, not a creative or innovative, role.
3.   *The 'architect' model.* In this model explicit personnel policies exist as part of the corporate strategy. Human resource planning and development are important concepts and a long-term view is taken. Systems tend to be sophisticated. The head of the personnel function is probably on the board and his or her power is derived from professionalism and perceived contribution to the business.

Of course, these roles overlap in many organizations and exist in different ways in different parts of large or diversified companies. Whether a personnel department, at one end of the scale, is carrying out relatively routine recruitment, employment and administrative functions in an entirely reactive way, or, at the other end, is sophisticated, high-powered and proactive, will depend on a number of factors. These will include the size and sophistication of the organization, its traditional approach to personnel management, and the extent to which those at the top believe in a 'human resource management' approach which recognizes that people are the most important resource and act accordingly. It also depends on the professionalism, ability and credibility of whoever heads up the personnel function.

The David Guest model

At the London School of Economics, Guest[3] and his colleagues asked a number of personnel managers to identify the UK personnel department they most admired or looked to as a model of excellence. From their answers it was possible to identify the following four distinct models:

- A *paternalist welfare model* where the emphasis was on looking after employees as a path to ensuring that they in turn looked after customers. Marks and Spencer provided the stereotype of this model.
- A *production model* where the central role of the personnel department was to support continuity of production by ensuring that staff were in place and that a clear and consistent set of industrial relations guidelines operated. Ford provided the typical example of this model.
- A *professional model* reflecting demonstrated and acknowledged competence displayed by high-quality personnel department staff in the core areas of selection, training and development, pay, and industrial relations. Companies such as Shell and ICI were seen as falling into this category.
- A *human resource model* reflecting a people orientated focus throughout the organization, including respect for the individual, full utilization of

individual abilities, and sophisticated policies for employee involvement. The stereotypical company in this category was IBM.

The HRM model

The HRM model emphasizes what Guest terms 'strategic integration' — the achievement of strategic fit between business and human resource plans and policies. This accords with Miller's[4] criteria for strategic HR management:

> HRM cannot be a stand-alone corporate issue. Strategically speaking, it must flow from and be dependent on the organization's (market-orientated) corporate strategy.

The HRM model requires personnel managers to avoid, in Guest's[3] words, the 'piecemeal introduction of techniques without the strategic integration to ensure their impact'. And, as Michael Armstrong[5] put it:

> Personnel directors who remain in their corner nursing their knowledge of the behavioural sciences, industrial relations tactics and personnel techniques, while other directors get on with running the business, cannot make a fully effective contribution to achieving the company's goals for growth, competitive gain and the improvement of the bottom-line performance. It is not enough for personnel directors just to understand the business and its strategy; their role must be built into the fabric of the business.

The HRM model does, of course, incorporate the characteristics of the human resource model mentioned above and broadly corresponds to the 'architect' model of Tyson and Fell. But it also focuses on strategy, commitment, flexibility and quality, as described in the introduction to this book.

The contingency approach to personnel management

The model appropriate to an organization is dependent or contingent upon the type of business it is and the environment in which it exists. A paternalist welfare approach works well for Marks and Spencer but would not necessarily be appropriate elsewhere. This equally applies to the Ford production, ICI professional and IBM human resource models. These have been developed and applied successfully because they fit the culture and technology of their organizations. They cannot be applied elsewhere in their entirety and even the most sophisticated and effective personnel practices and techniques will not necessarily transfer comfortably to other cultures and environments.

As Legge[6] comments:

> Different organizational and environmental circumstances will necessitate a transformation of general prescription into concrete strategy adapted to the situation in which it is to operate.

A contingency approach to developing and introducing personnel policies, systems and procedures is therefore desirable. This requires a careful analysis of the culture of the organization (see Chapter 10); its strategies; its technology; the business, social and political environment in which it operates; its employee (labour) market; and the attitudes, opinions and needs of its management and staff.

What personnel managers do

Personnel managers:

- *Innovate* — they formulate strategies and devise and propose new or amended policies, techniques and procedures.
- *Solve problems* — they solve general problems relating to the implementation of corporate and human resource strategies and specific problems concerning disputes, grievances and disagreements with colleagues and superiors.
- *Administrate* — they manage the activities for which the personnel department is responsible.

As *innovators*, they are expected to be proactive, to anticipate problems and to exploit opportunities. As *problem solvers*, personnel managers use consultancy skills in the following ways:

- They *define* the nature of the problem or conceptualize it — becoming aware of the difficulty or need for improvement and analysing the circumstances leading to and surrounding the situation.
- They *diagnose* the cause(s) of the problem or the reason(s) for the situation's arising. This process of diagnosis accompanies the process of definition, and it is often iterative; ie possible explanations may highlight the need for further analysis which will lead to a different diagnosis which may indicate that more data is required, and so on.
- They *decide* on a course of action to take or recommend, having weighed up the relative merits of a number of alternatives.

As *administrators*, they manage the activities for which the personnel department is responsible such as recruitment, training, pay administration, health and safety and record keeping.

Activity sample

It is not possible, for the reasons given above, to describe the typical activities of a personnel department. The following, however, is a sample of what happened in a busy personnel department in a fairly typical week, in addition to the routine functions of recruitment, welfare and record keeping, using a computerized system.

1. A vacancy for a cost accountant has been outstanding for six months. Two offers have been rejected and one appointee has resigned after six weeks for personal reasons. The agencies have no more applicants on their books and the manager doing the recruiting has come to the Personnel Department in a state of distress and frustration.

2. The senior financial manager has approached Personnel about two other vacancies for qualified accountants (circa £20,000). One has been outstanding for six months; the other has just arisen. They are difficult to fill as salaries are below market rate.

3. A senior manager complains that a manager appointed in his department about two months ago is not proving to be satisfactory.

4. Mrs Smith complains that she was held up by Personnel and was too late in applying to the DSS for full National Insurance deductions. She claims, therefore, that she will be delayed 12 months in obtaining sick pay because of the company's inefficiency.

5. Four months ago a redundancy was avoided (embarrassing for a growing company) by redeploying a member of staff. Her manager is now complaining that she is not suited to the new job and wants to know what arrangements Personnel will make.

6. The senior representative of the union has confirmed with you that it is company policy for staff to see their own job descriptions on request. She has now told you that several people have been refused by their managers.

7. An employee with six weeks' service goes to the agency who placed her to complain that she is being persecuted by colleagues because of her colour. The agency staff telephone to warn us.

8. Following an urgent set of regrading applications, jobs in the Finance Department have been graded higher when a £20,000 professionally qualified accountant is required. This caused some concern with line management, who eventually accepted the need for the qualification. Finance has now submitted a further job description which says this job could be carried out by someone who is not professionally qualified but who has the experience of a qualified accountant. The job is organizational at the same level as that of qualified accountants.

9. The company has an agreement with the union to consult prior to altering prices of food to employees. Two incidents upset the staff representatives:

    (a) A letter from the catering company to the office manager was opened in the wrong office; it refers to an agreement to raise drink prices by 5p per cup.

    (b) Rolls and sandwiches were increased in price by the catering company's restaurant manager because he thought, wrongly, that consultations had been carried out.

10. The distribution director has run into problems with the union in changing rates in the bonus scheme and wants advice on how to force the changes through without causing serious unrest.

11. The operations director wants to 'front-load' staff time to the earlier part of the week when the pressure of work is greatest. He seeks advice on how hours can be flexed to achieve this and so reduce overtime costs.

12. The managing director has 'discovered' quality circles and wants to know what the company should do about them.

Evaluating the personnel function

The nature of personnel management as an enabling and support function makes it difficult to evaluate its effectiveness by reference to quantifiable outputs. Tyson and Fell[2] got a group of personnel specialists to describe from their experience how they were evaluated by their board, by line managers and by themselves. They produced the following criteria:

1. *Board* — Personnel specialists should:

    - be able to sell themselves to management;
    - have an appreciation of the business;
    - control personnel costs;
    - create high-quality manpower resources.

2. *Line Managers* — Personnel specialists should:

    - have the ability to solve line managers' personnel problems;
    - be judged by the speed of their communications;
    - be available;
    - be visible;
    - be judged on the accuracy of their advice.

3. *Personnel specialists* should judge themselves by:

- their satisfaction of client demands;
- achievement of specific objectives;
- involvement in central policy-making;
- their ability to anticipate the needs of their clients.

These are largely behavioural, but this does not mean that the evaluations should not be as objective as possible — against agreed standards — and should not relate to the achievement of specified objectives wherever possible. An example of an 'accountability statement' for a personnel manager which sets out the headings under which performance will be assessed is given in Appendix C.

Overall evaluation

The best overall approach to evaluating the personnel function is to identify its objectives or critical success factors and measure the degree to which they have been achieved. Peach[7] advocates the IBM approach of agreeing critical success factors with senior management to provide the contract 'which makes our future action comprehensible, acceptable and "excellent"'.

The examples of objectives given in Chapter 2 could also serve as a basis for evaluating performance in broad terms. It is also necessary to consider more specifically how the principal guidance and support roles of the function can be evaluated.

Evaluating the guidance role

In their guidance role, personnel specialists can be evaluated qualitatively only on the extent to which:

- they show that they understand the real needs of the business;
- they anticipate problems and come up with realistic answers to them;
- advice on strategies, policies and solutions to problems is practical and made in a positive, persuasive and straightforward manner;
- proposals are succinct and well argued — they must define the need or problem, explain why it should be dealt with, describe how it should be tackled, set out the costs involved, and end with a clear statement of the benefits which should result from the proposal;
- their guidance or advice works — this assessment, however, may largely be subjective in the personnel field except where advice is given on dealing with a specific problem.

The problem of evaluating the guidance role of a personnel manager is that, as Legge[6] says: 'Useful advice has a habit of becoming the property of the recipient and, unlike bad advice, its origins lost in the allocation of praise.'

Evaluating the support role

The support role should in theory be the easiest to evaluate. Standards can be set and the personnel department can be required to operate within a defined budget in meeting these standards. In this way cost-effectiveness can be measured, in theory at least. The difficulty is in selecting areas where realistic standards can be defined.

Some of the possible areas where quantitative standards or targets can be determined include:

- recruitment — speed in filling vacancies, advertising costs, recruitment cost per head, number of unfilled vacancies;
- employment — reduction in wastage rates and absenteeism;
- training — throughput of training schemes, time taken to develop and introduce new courses, impact of training on performance;
- management development — availability of trained managers to provide for management succession;
- industrial relations — number of disputes, extent to which disputes are resolved, time taken to progress a grievance through the procedure at each stage;
- communications — speed with which briefing groups are convened; speed with which information is generally disseminated among employees;
- personnel costs — expenditure in relation to budget, cost of personnel function per employee.

In all or any of these areas, however, quantification may be impossible. In these circumstances, evaluation is inevitably carried out in qualitative terms. As Tyson and Fell[2] suggest, 'There is a strong agreement in favour of assessing the performance of personnel managers by assessing their interpersonal behaviour. Personnel managers, often without formal authority, have a need to influence management colleagues and work-people in order to sustain personnel policies and to control personnel systems.

To be regarded as successful, personnel managers have to persuade top management and their own management that they are providing them with good support. This success is more likely to be achieved if personnel managers can demonstrate that they are able to help.

A further aspect of personnel management support activities which can be evaluated is in specific projects set up to develop and introduce personnel systems as procedures. If a cost/benefit analysis has been agreed at the start of the project, this will provide a good basis for assessing the results achieved.

Constraints on personnel management

As Thurley[8] has said, personnel managers, in the UK at least, are often 'working against the grain of British culture and values' and it is judged that attempts to break out of this situation by developing overall strategies are difficult due to the constraints under which organizations have to work.'

A hostile or turbulent environment or a recession, as in the early 1990s, may restrict the positive things that personnel managers can do. What some managements regard as fringe activities, eg training, are the first in troubled times to be cut. Personnel departments go into reverse, removing rather than recruiting people. General and line managers become more hard-nosed.

There are, however, more fundamental and permanent constraints on what personnel departments can do. Legge wrote that it is easy to state that good personnel management should aim for 'the optimum utilization of the organization'.[6] In reality, however, this aim is difficult to define for the following reasons:

1. The goals and objectives of organizations are often hard to pin down and the targets for personnel aims and policies are therefore less clear.
2. Even when primary organizational goals can be defined (eg maximize profit), the secondary goals required to achieve them may not be obvious. In other words, while it is sometimes relatively easy to define ends, there is often conflict over the best means to achieve these ends.
3. The concept of 'optimization' is not as clear as it seems. There are many interests in organizations, eg management and workers, not to speak of the state, the owners and the public. These groups may legitimately have different interests which are incompatible with one another and consequently difficult, if not impossible, to reconcile (the concept of the plurality of legitimate groups in organizations).
4. Although managers profess to aim for optimization, in practice they are often forced into choosing the just adequate or 'good enough' course of action. This is because choice is limited by constraints operating in or on the organization, limited knowledge, and the perceived need to avoid uncertainty and make decisions that will at least work even if they are not necessarily the 'best' decisions.

5. The ends (primary goals) and the means (secondary goals) will be influenced by the context of the organization — its environment, role, structure, management style, technology, etc. What is required and works well in one organization will not necessarily be appropriate or work in another setting.
6. The power of the personnel function to influence policies may be constrained by the values of the organization and the part the function is allowed to play in the decision-making process.

Variations in the organizational context and its values and environmental changes mean that there is no fixed pattern for what personnel managers do or how they do it. This and a number of other factors contribute to the ambiguity inherent in the role of personnel management.

The ambiguous nature of personnel management

Personnel managers, in Thurley's[8] words, are 'specialists in ambiguity'. This arises partly because of the equivocal nature of the attitudes of line managers to personnel specialists, but also because the latter are often unsure about where they stand. Ambiguity in the role of the personnel function can result in confusion between ideals and reality. Tyson and Fell[2] see a contrast between the ideologies and actual realities of organizational life to which personnel managers, as 'organization men or women', have to conform.

This ambiguity is reflected in the comments about the role of the personnel function made by writers on personnel management. For example, Mackay and Torrington[9] suggest that:

> Personnel management is never identified with management interests, as it becomes ineffective when not able to understand and articulate the aspirations of the work force.

In complete contrast, Tyson and Fell[2] believe that:

> Classical personnel management has not been granted a position in decision making circles because it has frequently not earned one. It has not been concerned with the totality of the organization but often with issues which have not only been parochial but esoteric to boot:

Legge,[6] recognizing the ambiguity inherent in the personnel role distinguishes between two types of personnel professionals: the convergent innovators who seek to introduce changes congruent with senior managers' value systems, and the divergent innovators who would establish the relevance of different values and try to convert managers to them. The debate on human resource management (HRM) versus personnel management has been generated by, but has also contributed to, this ambiguity. HRM is management-orientated, and sees people as a key resource to be used to further the organization's objectives. Traditional personnel management, however, is more people-orientated, taking the view that if their needs are satisfied, the organization as well as its members will benefit. Personnel managers can sometimes find themselves being pulled in both directions. It does not make their life any easier.

Values and professionalism

Personnel managers are clearly most effective if they work within the framework of an understood set of values and adopt a professional approach to their work. These approaches are easier said than done, however, as is explained below.

Values

Personnel managers often find themselves acting as a support function in a hard-nosed, entrepreneurial environment, but this does not mean that they can remain unconcerned about developing and helping to uphold the core values of the organization in line with their own values on the approach to human resource management. These may not always be reconcilable and if this is strongly the case, the personnel manager may have to make a choice on whether he or she can remain with the organization.

Professionalism

If the term is used loosely, personnel managers are *professional* because they display expertise in doing their work. A professional occupation such as medicine or law could, however, be defined as one which gives members of its association exclusive rights to practise their profession. A profession is not so much an occupation as a means of controlling an occupation. Personnel management is not in this category.

A 'profession' may alternatively be identified, using the following less rigid criteria:

- skills based on theoretical knowledge; the provision of training and education;
- a test of the competence of members administered by a professional body;
- a formal professional organization which has the power to regulate entry to the profession;

- a professional code of conduct.

By these standards personnel management could be regarded as a profession, especially in the UK where the Institute of Personnel Management carries out all the functions of a professional body.

A third approach to the definition of a profession is to emphasize the service ethic — the professional person is there to serve others. This, however, leads to confusion when applied to personnel managers. Whom are they trying to serve? The organization and its values, or the people in the organization and their needs (organizational values and personal needs do not necessarily coincide)? As Tyson and Fell have commented: 'In recent years the personnel manager seems to be encouraged to make the line manager his client, while trying simultaneously to represent wider social standards, and to possess a sense of service to employees. This results in confusion and difficulty for the personnel executive.'[2] In the face of this difficulty, the question has to be asked, why bother? The answer was suggested by Watson,[10] who asserted that the adoption of a professional image by personnel managers is a strategic response by personnel specialists to their felt lack of authority. They are in an ambiguous situation and sometimes feel they need all the help they can get to clarify and, indeed, strengthen their authority and influence.

If a profession is defined rigidly as a body of people who possess a particular area of competence, who control entry so that only members of the association can practise in that area, who unequivocally adopt the 'service ethic' and who are recognized by themselves and others as belonging to a profession, then personnel management is not a profession. This is the case even when a professional institution like the Institute of Personnel Management exists with the objective of acting as a professional body in the full sense of the word, an aim which it does its best to fulfil.

On the basis of their research, Guest and Horwood[11] expressed their doubts about the professional model of personnel management as follows:

> The [research] data also highlights the range of career types in personnel management. Given the diversity of personnel roles and organizational contexts, this is surely something to be welcomed. It is tempting but wrong to view personnel managers as homogeneous. Their different backgrounds and fields of operations raise doubts about the value of a professional model and of any attempt to view personnel problems as amenable to solution through a primary focus on professionalism.

However, a broader definition of professionalism as the practice of specific skills based upon a defined body of knowledge in accordance with recognized standards of behaviour would entitle personnel management to be regarded as a profession. Sir Peter Parker,[12] Chairman of British Rail for many years, had no doubts on this subject: 'I am an ardent advocate of professionalism in personnel management. There must be a core of disciplined expertise at the heart of its effectiveness.' But he was not saying that personnel management is a 'profession'.

The debate continues, but it is an academic one. What matters is that personnel managers need expertise and have to use it responsibly. In other words, they should act professionally but do not *have* to be members of a professional association to do that. Such associations, however, have an important part to play in setting and improving professional standards.

Organization of the personnel function

The organization and staffing of the personnel department clearly depends on the size of the company, the extent to which operations are decentralized, the type of work carried out, the kind of people employed and the role assigned to the personnel function.

There is no standard ratio for the number of personnel specialists to the number of employees. It can vary from 1 to 80, to 1 to 1000 or more. This ratio is affected by all the factors mentioned above and can be decided only empirically by analysing what personnel services are required and then deciding on the extent to which they are provided by full-time professional staff or can be subcontracted to external agencies or consultants. The degree to which the organization believes that the management of human resources is the prime responsibility of line managers and team leaders affects not only the numbers of personnel staff but also the nature of the guidance and support services they provide.

There are, therefore, no absolute rules for organizing the personnel function, but current practice suggests that the following guidelines should be taken into account:

- The head of the function should report directly to the chief executive and should be on the board, or at least on the management committee, in order to play a full part in the formulation and integration of personnel strategies and policies.
- In a decentralized organization, subsidiary companies, divisions, or operational units should be responsible for their own personnel management affairs within the framework of broad strategic and policy guidelines from the centre.
- The central personnel function in a decentralized organization should be slimmmed down to the minimum required to develop group human resource strategies and policies. It will probably be concerned with

resourcing throughout the group at senior management level and advising on both recruitment and career development. It may also control remuneration and benefits policies for senior management. The centre may coordinate industrial-relations negotiating if bargaining has been decentralized, especially where bargaining is related to terms and conditions such as hours of work, holidays and employee benefits. Although rates of pay may vary among subsidiaries, it is generally desirable to develop a consistent approach to benefit provision.

- Within the personnel department the ability to provide advice and support in the major personnel management fields has to be catered for. This covers resourcing, management development, training, reward management, employee relations and personnel services in such areas as health and safety, welfare, personnel information, systems and employment matters generally. In a large department, each of these areas may be provided for separately, but they can be combined in various ways.

The most important principle to bear in mind about the organization of the personnel function is that it should fit the needs of the business. Against that background, there will always be choice about the best structure to adopt, but this choice should be made on the basis of an analysis of what the organization wants in the way of personnel management guidance and services.

Examples of job descriptions for personnel specialists are given in Appendices C, D and E.

How to be an effective personnel manager

There is a host of things which personnel managers have to do and administer. They recruit, they train, they run the pay system, they ensure that the social and legal obligations of the organization are met, they deal with day-to-day employee relations issues and grievances, they help to solve personal problems at work, and they maintain a personnel database.

If they do these things efficiently, they make a contribution to the 'bottom line' or whatever criterion the results achieved by the organization are measured by.

There is, however, always a danger in personnel management, if it is perceived mainly as an administrative function, of spending too much time making ineffective organizations efficient. Progress, development, growth and added value from the use of human resources are achieved by positive drives to improve all-round effectiveness rather than pursuing the narrower aims of achieving efficiency.

Effective personnel managers:

1. *Operate strategically* — they have the ability to take, and implement, a strategic view of the whole range of personnel practices in relation to business activity as a whole.
2. *Understand the culture of the organization* and have the capability to facilitate change and help to create a culture of success.
3. *Understand organizational and individual needs* — against the background of an understanding of organizational behaviour, how organizations function and the factors affecting individual motivation and commitment, they are capable of analysing and diagnosing the human resource management requirements of the organization and proposing and implementing appropriate action.
4. *Understand personnel systems and techniques* — if they are specialists, they have a thorough knowledge of relevant personnel systems and techniques. If they are generalists, their knowledge may be more broadly based, but they will be capable of identifying the need for a specific approach and, with expert help, of putting it to use. In either case, they are careful to ensure that the system or technique fits the organization's particular circumstances and needs.
5. *Are value driven* — they have a well-developed set of values relating to the management of people, and measure what they propose to do against these values. But they have to be able to cope with the possibility that some of the values they espouse, such as equal opportunity, may not be seen as so important by the managers they advise.
6. *Are business-like* — if they are in the private sector, they are fully aware of the needs of the business as a commercial, market-orientated and profit-making enterprise and are equally aware of the contribution they can make to fulfilling these needs. In the public or not-for-profit sectors, personnel managers have to adopt an equally business-like approach, but this is directed towards cost-effectiveness in the sense of ensuring that what they do produces benefits, in the shape of improved performance, which more than justify the costs involved. In any sector, personnel managers have to demonstrate their efficiency as administrators as well as their effectiveness in their enabling role.
7. *Get involved* — they get involved in the business and with the people who run the business. They must know what is going on. Perhaps the most practical of all personnel techniques is PMBWA: personnel management by walking about. Thus they can find out what people

117

as well as the business need and want. Using their antennae, they can spot symptoms and, using their diagnostic skills (an important attribute), they can identify causes and solutions to the problems. If they want to get anything done they know that managers must 'own' both the problem and its solution. Close involvement means that personnel people can become adept at transferring ownership.

8. *Intervene effectively* — personnel managers have to use their knowledge and awareness of business needs to select the right place and time to intervene.

9. *Are persuasive* — they present the proposals and recommendations emerging from their interventions persuasively. Davis[13] has emphasized the need for personnel managers to take a broad overall view of the business. They need to know about the 'correlation between business success and progressive personnel policies'; above all, they have to show that

> Personnel managers who do not recognize that they are in the persuasion business are doomed to carry on being seen in the traditional bureaucratic image.

According to Davis, personnel managers are too often the 'harbingers of doom', telling everyone what will go wrong if they don't follow their advice and in effect training their managements to think of them as talking only of disasters. The answer to this problem is that personnel people must persuade management to invest in systems where they have demonstrated that there is a pay-off. As Davis says:

> Instead of being the 'harbingers of doom', personnel managers can become the innovators of excellence and the accelerators of productivity.

10. *Are realistic* — they recognize the law of the situation — the logic of facts and events. This means that:

- ideas for improvement or innovation are thoroughly tested against an analysis of the characteristics and true needs of the organization;
- ideas are sold to management on the basis of the practical and, wherever possible, measurable benefits that will result from their implementation (it is not the idea itself that is saleable but the result it can achieve);
- new procedures or techniques are pilot-tested to make sure they work in practice and to provide evidence of the benefits they produce;

- the procedures or techniques are presented with great care to managers as providing direct help to them in running the organization or their department more effectively than before;
- unobtrusive assistance, guidance and encouragement is provided in implementing new techniques — not from the stance of a would-be professional who knows it all, but from the point of view of a colleague who can give practical help in achieving something worthwhile.

Personnel directors

Personnel directors or heads of personnel functions need to be able to do all the things mentioned above. But there is a particular need for them to be:

- very much part of the top management team;
- involved in business planning and the integration of human resource plans with business plans;
- well placed to exert influence on the way in which the business is organized, managed and staffed — all with a view to helping it achieve its strategic objectives;
- dependent more on business awareness and skills and credibility as effective than on professional competence in personnel techniques;
- involved heavily in resourcing at top and senior levels and in so doing be in a strong position to improve organizational effectiveness and, therefore, bottom-line performance;
- concerned with the management of change and with shaping corporate culture and values;
- fully aware of the needs to develop a vision of what the personnel function exists to do, to define its mission, to provide leadership and guidance to the members of the function (without getting involved in day-to-day personnel matters) and to maintain the quality of the support the function provides to line managers;
- essentially enablers but ones who are well placed to make a significant contribution to end results.

The changing role of personnel

There is increasing pressure to devolve personnel responsibility to line management. In fact, the basis of HRM philosophy is that people as a key resource *must* be the line manager's responsibility, with personnel managers concentrating on their enabling, supporting and service roles.

These pressures for line managers to take on more direct responsibility arise from the following factors:

- the move towards the consumer;
- total quality management;
- employees' expectations of what managers can and should do for them;
- the demand for a more participative management style;
- the emphasis on performance management systems in which it is the responsibility of managers to develop their staff and improve their performance.

Increasingly, line managers are expected to manage their own reward systems, although always within policy guidelines and budgets. Managers need all the power they can be given to manage their resources, human and otherwise, in these difficult times.

Of course, the extent to which responsibility is devolved to line management varies considerably, depending on the situation. Wareing[14] has used the matrix illustrated in Figure 5.1 (originally developed by John Purcell of Templeton College, Oxford) to demonstrate how, at different stages in an organization's development, the role of the personnel function changes.

In this matrix, the horizontal axis — collectivism — involves recognition

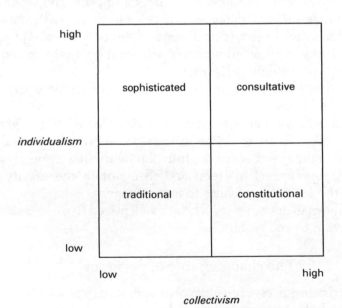

Figure 5.1 Employee relations matrix
(adapted from the grid developed by John Purcell)

that employees have a collective or group interest in the operation of the organization and in decision making at various levels. The vertical axis — individualism — relates to policies for managing people based on a belief in the value of individuals and their contribution to the enterprise. Where individualism is high, the personal relationship between individuals and their managers is emphasized.

The characteristics of each quadrant in the matrix are as follows:

- *Traditional* — personnel functions operating in this environment are likely to be weak. Managers have power in a traditional master/servant relationship and the role of personnel is to service this. Recruitment, terms and conditions and welfare are likely to be the key tasks.
- *Constitutional* — personnel functions in this quadrant may well have great power as holders and interpreters of the rule book. This is the classic industrial relations environment, with wide ranging collective agreements. Precedent and institutionalized arrangements for fairness predominate.
- *Consultative* — life becomes harder for personnel functions operating in this area. They have to balance collective arrangements with freedom for the individual. Managers want the scope to solve individual problems, but a strong collective framework still exists. There are, however, many dilemmas.
- *Sophisticated* — a large part of the personnel role in this type of organization is concerned in the joint formulation with management of human resource management strategies and policies. Personnel directors and managers concentrate on their enabling roles and spend much of the time 'coaching' line managers and supervisors and providing support to their management activities. Personnel specialists monitor employee opinion through attitude surveys and advise management on any policy changes required in response to the information the surveys provide. They are very much concerned with providing levers for change and with developing teamwork and flexibility in the use of skills, working terms and conditions and reward management systems.

The last role is, of course, the most rewarding one for personnel specialists, but they have to earn it. As John Skae[15], Group Director (Resources), Legal and General, has said: 'Human resource expertise alone does not merit a place at the top table.' Personnel directors must demonstrate that they are capable of fitting in as fully contributing members of the top management team.

References

1. Quoted in Armstrong, M *Personnel and the Bottom Line*. Institute of Personnel Management, London, 1989.
2. Tyson, S and Fell, A *Evaluating the Personnel Function*. Hutchinson, London, 1986.
3. Guest, D 'Personnel and HRM: can you tell the difference?' *Personnel Management*, January 1989.
4. Miller, P 'Strategic HRM: what it is and what it isn't'. *Personnel Management*, February 1989.
5. Armstrong, M 'Personnel directors' view from the bridge'. *Personnel Management*, October 1989.
6. Legge, K *Power, Innovation and Problem Solving in Personnel Management*. McGraw-Hill, Maidenhead, 1978.
7. Peach, L 'A practitioner's view of personnel excellence'. *Personnel Management*, September 1989.
8. Thurley, K 'Personnel management in the UK: a case for urgent treatment'. *Personnel Management*, February 1983.
9. Mackay, L and Torrington, D *The Changing Nature of Personnel Management*. Institute of Personnel Management, London, 1986.
10. Watson, A *The Personnel Managers*. Routledge and Kegan Paul, London, 1977.
11. Guest, D and Horwood, R 'Perceptions of effectiveness in personnel management'. *Personnel Management*, May 1981.
12. Parker, P 'How I see the personnel function'. *Personnel Management*, January 1981.
13. Davis, T 'How personnel can lose its Cinderella image'. *Personnel Management*, December 1987.
14. Wareing, A 'How to devolve personnel management to line management'. Presentation at 'The Changing Role of Personnel'. Conference organized by H R Limited, April 1991.
15. Skae, J 'A future for personnel'. Presentation at 'The Changing Role of Personnel'. Conference organized by H R Limited, April 1991.

Part II
Organizational Behaviour

The study of organizational behaviour is the study of how organizations function, in terms of their structure and processes, and how the people within organizations act, individually or in groups.

Personnel managers perform their jobs within complex systems called organizations. Managers in general, and personnel managers in particular, exist to influence behaviour in a desired direction. Skills in the analysis and diagnosis of patterns of organizational behaviour are therefore important. They help in the definition or organizational context, and, as Nadler and Tushman[1] have said:

> *The manager needs to be able to understand the patterns of behaviour that are observed to predict in what direction behaviour will move (particularly in the light of managerial action), and to use this knowledge to control behaviour over the course of time. Effective managerial action requires that the manager be able to diagnose the system he or she is working in.*

The purpose of this part of the book is to outline a basic set of concepts and to provide analytical tools which will enable the personnel manager to diagnose organizational behaviour and to take appropriate actions. The actions will include the use of techniques to design organizations and jobs, to develop more effective organizations and people, to manage change and conflict, to motivate people to work and to deal with problems concerning individuals or groups. These techniques should be developed and operated in the knowledge of the processes at work in the organization as they affect and are affected by the behaviour of the people in it.

The framework for this part is provided by a general analysis of individuals at work — individual differences, the nature of skill and competence, what happens to people over time, the sources of social influence, how we make judgements about people and the factors affecting behaviour, including orientation to work and roles.

The concepts of individual motivation and commitment are then explored in Chapters 7 and 8 before reviewing generally the ways in which organizations function — formal and informal structures and how people work together in groups. The particular factors of culture and structure which affect organizational behaviour are examined in Chapters 9 and 10.

Reference

1. Nadler, D A and Tushman, M L *A Congruence Model for Diagnosing Organizational Behaviour*. Resource Book in Macro-Organizational Behaviour, R H Miles (ed.), Goodyear Publishing, Santa Monica, CA, 1980.

6

The Individual at Work

To manage human resources effectively, we must understand the factors that affect how people behave at work and influence their motivation and commitment, as discussed in Chapters 7 and 8. This chapter reviews these factors under the following headings:

- Individual differences — how people differ in terms of their abilities, aptitudes, intelligence and personality.
- The nature of skilled performance and competence.
- What happens to people over time — the processes of maturation, development and ageing.
- The sources of social influence on individuals.
- How we perceive and make judgements about people at work.
- Behaviour at work — the factors that affect behaviour and its manifestation in attitudes, frustration and aggression, stress, and resistance to change.
- The approaches or orientation adopted by people towards work.
- The roles people play at work.

Individual differences

Personal management would be much easier if everyone were the same, but they are, of course, hugely different because of their background (the environment in which they were brought up) and their needs and wants, as described in Chapter 7. Differences can also be explained by reference to the factors discussed below; ability, intelligence and personality.

Ability

Ability is the quality that makes an action possible. Abilities have been analysed by UK psychologists such as Burt[1] and Vernon.[2] They classified abilities into two major groups:

- V:ed — standing for verbal, numerical, memory and reasoning abilities.
- K:m — standing for spatial and mechanical abilities, as well as perceptual (memory) and motor skills relating to physical operations such as eye–hand co-ordination and mental dexterity.

It has been suggested that overriding these abilities there is a 'g' or general intelligence factor which accounts for most variations in performance.

An alternative classification was produced by a US psychologist, Thurstone,[3] as follows:

S — spatial ability
P — perceptual speed
N — numerical ability
V — verbal meaning
M — memory
F — verbal fluency
I/R — inductive reasoning

An additional three ability headings were identified by Argyle:[4]

- *Judgement* — the capacity to make realistic assessments of practical solutions to particular problems.
- *Creativity* — the ability to see situations from a new point of view and to propose original solutions.
- *Social skills* — the capacity to persuade, to carry out various kinds of conversation effectively and to sustain good relationships with others.

Intelligence

Intelligence has been defined as:

- 'the capacity to solve problems, apply principles, make inferences and perceive relationships' — Argyle;[4]
- 'the capacity for abstract thinking and reasoning with a range of different contents and media — Toplis, Dulewicz and Fletcher;[5]
- 'what is measured by intelligence tests' — Wright and Taylor.[6]

The last, tautological definition is not facetious. It expresses the difficulty many writers have had in producing a universal definition. An operational definition of this kind can at least be related to the specific aspects of reasoning, inference, cognition (ie knowing, conceiving) and perception (ie understanding, recognition) which intelligence tests attempt to measure.

General intelligence, as noted above, consists of a number of mental abilities which enable a person to succeed at a wide variety of intellectual tasks which use the faculties of knowing and reasoning. The mathematical technique of factor analysis has been used to identify the constituents of intelligence, such as Thurstone's multiple factors listed above. There is no general agreement among psychologists as to what these factors are or, indeed, whether there is such a thing as general intelligence.

An alternative approach to the analysis of intelligence was put forward by Guilford,[7] who distinguished five types of mental operation:

- thinking;
- remembering;
- divergent production (problem solving which leads to unexpected and original solutions);
- convergent production (problem solving which leads to the one, correct solution);
- evaluating.

He then suggested that there are six types of products of these operations (units, classes, relations, systems, transformations and implications), and he finally defined four types of content upon which operations are performed (figural, symbolic, semantic and behavioural). These classifications generate 120 distinguishable abilities, a number which suggests a much more complex (and probably realistic) concept of intelligence.

Implications for the personnel manager

Personnel managers need not bother too much about the subtleties of the definitions listed above of ability and intelligence. It is, however, useful to understand the broad concept and the definitions in order to use psychometric tests properly (see Chapter 17) and to analyse performance and competences (see below).

Personality

Personality can be defined as the relatively stable and enduring aspects of individuals which distinguish them from other people. This can be described as the 'trait' concept of personality, traits being predispositions to behave in certain ways in a variety of different situations. The assumption that people are consistent in the ways they express these traits is the basis for making predictions about their future behaviour. We all attribute traits to people in an attempt to understand why they behave in the way they do. As Chell[8] says: 'This cognitive process gives a sense of order to what might otherwise appear to be senseless uncoordinated behaviours. Traits may therefore be thought of as classification systems, used by individuals to understand other people's *and their own* behaviour.'

Perhaps the best-known classification of traits is that produced by Cattell.[9] It forms the basis for the Sixteen Personality Factor Questionnaire (the 16PF personality test). Cattell's extensive empirical work used factor analysis to produce the following 16 dimensions or factors:

Factor	High-score description	Low-score description
A	Outgoing	Reserved
B	More intelligent	Less intelligent
C	Emotionally stable	Affected by feelings
E	Assertive	Humble
F	Happy-go-lucky	Sober
G	Conscientious	Expedient
H	Venturesome	Shy
I	Tender-minded	Tough-minded
L	Suspicious	Trusting
M	Imaginative	Practical
N	Shrewd	Forthright
O	Apprehensive	Placid
Q1	Experimenting	Conservative
Q2	Self-sufficient	Group-dependent
Q3	Controlled	Casual
Q4	Tense	Relaxed

Other classifications of traits form the basis for the following personality tests:

- *Myers-Briggs Type Indicator*, which contains four scales: introversion–extroversion; sensing–intuition; thinking–feeling; judging–perspective.
- *Saville and Holdsworth's Occupational Personality Questionnaire (OPQ)*, which covers three domains of personality: relationships with people; thinking style; feelings and emotions.
- *Gordon Personal Profile and Inventory*, in which the profile measures ascendancy, responsibility, emotional stability and sociability, and the inventory measures cautiousness, original thinking, personal relations and vigour.

The use of personality tests as selection aids is discussed in Chapter 17.

Another factor analysis study by Eysenck[10] identified three structural dimensions of personality: extroversion/introversion, neuroticism and psychoticism. He developed a hierarchical model of personality structure in which, for example, under the type level of introversion, trait levels were placed consisting of persistence, rigidity, subjectivity, shyness and irritability. These are expressed first in an habitual response level and finally in a specific response level.

But the trait theory of personality has been attacked by people such as Mischel,[11] Chell,[12] and Harre.[13] The main criticisms have been as follows:

- People do not necessarily express the same trait across different situations or even the same trait in the same situation.
- Different people may exhibit consistency on some traits and considerable variability on others.
- Classical trait theory (as typified by Eysenck and Cattell) assumes that the manifestation of trait behaviour is independent of the situations and the persons with whom the individual is interacting — this assumption is questionable, given that trait behaviour usually manifests itself in respone to specific situations.
- Trait attributions are a product of language — they are devices for speaking about people and are not described as objective features of action.

It is also noticeable that, as Chell[8] points out:

> When people account for their own behaviour they point to some feature of the situation; when they account for other people's behaviour, they tend to make reference to traits. This is especially true when behaviour might be thought to be reprehensible in some way. This suggests that trait ascriptions are part of a moral commentary upon oneself and others; in general, they lead to the disapproval of others and credit for oneself.

These criticisms suggest that, while it is inevitable that we attribute certain dispositions (eg extroversion/introversion) to people, we should be careful to avoid assuming that they are fixed traits and that they will be displayed consistently in all situations. And, for this purpose, it may be best to adopt the following definition of personality produced by Toplis, Dulewicz and Fletcher,[5] which incorporates interaction with the environment and avoids the assertion that there are stable and enduring traits that can be used to predict future behavour. 'The term personality is all-embracing in terms of the individual's behaviour and the way it is organised and co-ordinated when he or she interacts with the environment.'

The nature of skilled performance and competence

Skilled performance

Skilled performance is achieved when a worker reaches defined standards in the accomplishment of specified tasks. It can be described as an 'experienced worker's standard' (EWS) but must always be measured in terms of what the individual can actually do. The achievement of skilled performance levels is recorded by profiling, which assesses performance in specified competences, such as using a micrometer or word processing, by reference to predetermined standards or criteria (sometimes called 'criterion-referenced' assessment).

Competence

Competence is defined as the ability and willingness to perform a task. It is a term which has become increasingly fashionable in recent years, especially in connection with management development programmes (see Chaper 21). In one sense, competence is synonymous with skilled performance, but competence assessment concentrates more specifically on:

- *Job analysis* — the analysis of job requirements to determine units of competence from which specific elements can be clearly defined.
- *Performance criteria* — the establishment of performance criteria which enable standards of performance to be assessed accurately.

What happens to people over time

Personnel management is continually concerned not only with what people are doing now but also with how they develop over time. These considerations affect employment policies and practices for older workers and the way in which career management programmes are structured (see Chapter 22). The three processes which need to be considered are maturation, development and ageing.

Maturation

Maturation can be defined as progress towards the achievement of maturity, which means possessing fully developed powers of body and mind. The implication of this definition is that maturation ceases when the optimal development level of a characteristic or trait is reached. Maturation is both physiological and behavioural and occurs through growth and ageing. It is sometimes distinguished from learning, which can be defined as changes due to environment (nurture rather than nature). But the processes of maturing and learning are not independent — the development of behaviour should be regarded as a single, continuous process.

There is, in fact, considerable overlap between the concepts of maturity and development. Maturity can be regarded as a state which people reach because of what they are — their innate and endogenous (ie growing from within) characteristics — and because of what happens to them (their environment). A mature person could therefore be regarded as someone who has reached this state. Development, however, could be described as a continuous process which does not stop when a condition of physical or emotional maturity is reached. Development relies more on experience (or training) and is concerned with abilities and aptitudes as well as personality.

Maturation can also be described as the achievement of full potential through a process of self-actualization. As Argyris[14] describes it, from the individual's point of view, self-actualization is achieved when the person is attempting to:

- develop from a state of passivity to one of increased activity as an adult;
- develop from a state of dependence to one of independence;
- increase his or her skills, abilities and repertoire of behaviours;
- develop from having merely short-term perspectives to much longer-term perspectives;
- develop from being in a subordinate position to aspiring to be in an equal or superordinate position;
- develop from a lack of awareness of self to an awareness and control over oneself as an adult.

This assumes a concept of personality which can mature and develop throughout life — people do not reach a certain level of maturity and then stop. They continue to grow, given the right environment.

Development

Development is a continuous process of change in behaviour and personality which can take place as people get older. It involves maturation, but other changes may occur which could not be regarded as an increase in maturity. Sheehy[15] has suggested the following stages of 'passages' of adult development:

1. *Pulling up roots* — this occurs in the later teens when the adolescent is

striving for independence and freedom. This stage is often character-ized by a brash show of confidence and the hiding of fears. It usually involves an identity crisis.

2. *The trying 20s* — this is a period of exploration of one's identity. It is characterized by two strong urges, first, to build up a safe and secure base and second, to experiment and take advantage of opportunities.

3. *Catch-30* — this is a period of reassessment in the early 30s and is characterized by an urge to burst out of the routine which had been established in the 20s. It is a time for reassessing one's career and moving into a more down-to-earth, realistic stage.

4. *The deadline decade* — this starts at about the age of 35 and involves a re-evaluation of the self. This might be described as an authenticity crisis. The earlier sense of independence gives way to a sense of isolation and awful responsibility for one's actions and one's destiny. There is a feeling that 'last chances must be taken now' and the individual may become more self-assertive.

5. *Renewal or resignation* — in the mid-40s stability may eventually be gained either by a process of renewal arising from the previous stage, or by one of resignation because the renewal has not been achieved.

Another model of adult development was conceived by Levinson,[16] who suggested that the 'individual life structure' is shaped by three types of external event:

1. The socio-cultural environment.
2. The roles one plays and the relationships one has.
3. The constraints and opportunities that enable or inhibit people in expressing and developing their personality.

Ageing

It is commonly believed that, as people age, apart from any physical deteriorations, there is a tendency for them to become less flexible, less willing to take on extra responsibilities and slower in learning. But it would be wrong to assume that these changes are inevitable during a person's working life or that every worker will deteriorate (if they deteriorate at all) at the same rate. And even if, for example, the speed of learning has declined, it is quite conceivable that older people will be just as conscien-tious and determined to learn as their younger colleagues, if not more so. Again, it would be rash to assume that maturity in judgement always increases with age, but there is no reason to suppose that it will inevitaby decline.

It is usually found that older people are more satisfied with their jobs —
as established by research conducted by Kalleberg and Loscocco[17] and
others. This could be because older people tend to have more rewarding
and higher-status jobs. But it is more likely to be because they become
more adjusted to their work and more ready to accept the level they have
reached. In other words, their attainments and aspirations have come
closer together.

A study of job satisfaction carried out in Manchester, as reported by
Robertson and Smith[18] showed that satisfaction with work tended to
increase with age, but that there is a dip in satisfaction in the 40–50 years
age group, suggesting that this group is the most difficult to motivate. In
particular, satisfaction with promotion prospects falls to very low levels
during the ages of 40–50 before rising again, possibly because people over
the age of 50 become resigned to the status quo. As Robertson and Smith
comment: 'The age distribution within an organisation forms an implicit
career timetable and people use this timetable to decide whether their own
careers are on or off schedule. In one study, managers who saw
themselves as "behind time" had more negative attitudes to work than
other managers.'

Sources of social influences on individuals

The sources of influence on individuals are the family, social contacts
outside work and the work group. The last-named is likely to make the
most immediate impact. Socially, people have a strong need to conform to
the norms of the group to which they belong. Norms are shared ways of
behaving, shared attitudes and beliefs, and shared ways of feeling and
perceiving, particularly in relation to the central tasks or activities of the
group.

Acceptance of group norms commonly goes through two stages —
compliance and internalization. Initially, a group member complies in
order not to be rejected by the group, although he or she may behave
differently when away from the group. Progressively, however, the
individual accepts the norm whether with the group or not — the group
norm has been internalized. As noted by Chell,[8] pressure on members to
conform can cause problems when:

- there is incompatibility between a member's personal goals and those
  of the group;
- there is no sense of pride from being a member of the group;
- the member is not fully integrated with the group;
- the price of conformity is too high.

How we make judgements about people

The ways in which we perceive and make judgements about people at work are explained by attribution theory, which concerns the assignment of causes to events. We make an attribution when we perceive and describe other people's actions and try to discover why they behaved in the way they did. We can also make attributions about our own behaviour. Heider[19] has pointed out: 'In everyday life we form ideas about other people and about social situations. We interpret other people's actions and we predict what they will do under certain circumstances.'

In attributing causes to people's actions we distinguish between what is in the person's power to achieve and the effect of environmental influence. A personal cause, whether someone does well or badly, may, for example, be the amount of effort displayed, while a situational cause may be the extreme difficulty of the task. Kelley[20] has suggested that there are four criteria which we apply to decided whether behaviour is attributable to personal rather than external (situational) causes:

1. Distinctiveness — the behaviour can be distinguished from the behaviour of other people in similar situations.
2. Consensus — if other people agree that the behaviour is governed by some personal characteristic.
3. Consistency over time — whether the behaviour is repeated.
4. Consistency over modality (ie the manner in which things are done) — whether the behaviour is repeated in different situations.

Attribution theory is also concerned with the way in which people attribute success or failure to themselves. Research by Weiner[21] and others has indicated that when people with high achievement needs have been successful they ascribe this to internal factors such as ability and effort. High achievers tend to attribute failure to lack of effort and not lack of ability. Low achievers tend not to link success with effort but to ascribe their failures to lack of ability.

Behaviour at work

Factors affecting behaviour

Behaviour at work is dependent on both the personal characteristics of individuals and the situation in which they are working. These factors interact, and this theory of behaviour is sometimes called interactionism. It is because of this process of interaction and because there are so many variables in personal characteristics and situations that behaviour is difficult to analyse and predict.

The headings under which personal characteristics can vary have been classified by Mischel[22] as follows:

- *Competences* — abilities and skills.
- *Constructs* — the conceptual framework which governs how people perceive their environment.
- *Expectations* — what people have learned to expect about their own and others' behaviour.
- *Values* — what people believe to be important.
- *Self-regulatory plans* — the goals people set themselves and the plans they make to achieve them.

Environmental or situational variables include the type of work individuals carry out; the culture, climate and management style of the organization (these organizational features are discussed in Chapter 9); the social group within which individuals work; and the 'reference groups' which individuals use for comparative purposes (eg comparing conditions of work between one category of employee and another).

The behaviour of individuals at work also manifests itself and is affected by the following factors as discussed below: attitudes, frustration and aggression, stress and resistance to change.

Attitudes

An attitude can broadly be defined as a settled mode of thinking. The following is a more detailed definition produced by Newcomb:[23]

> An attitude is an individual's organisation of psychological processes, as inferred from his behaviour, with respect to some aspect of the world which he distinguishes from other aspects. It represents the residue of his experience with which he approaches any subsequent situation including that aspect and, together with the contemporary influences in such a situation, determines his behaviour in it. Attitudes are enduring in the sense that such residues are carried over to new situations, but they change in so far as new residues are acquired through experience in new situations.

Thus, attitudes are developed through experience and then influence behaviour. But they can change as new experiences are gained. Attitude surveys can be used to measure attitudes but, because attitudes vary as a result of situational changes, such measurements cannot be used accurately to predict behaviour. They can indicate, however, where changes to personnel policies and practices may be necessary and can also suggest areas where measures need to be taken by the organization in order to attempt to change attitudes.

Frustration and aggression

Frustration occurs when individuals find that they are prevented from achieving their goals, meaning that their wants and needs are unlikely to be satisfied. Frustration can produce three types of reaction:

1. *Aggression* (fight) as discussed below;
2. *Regression* (flight) — a return to earlier habits;
3. *Fixation* of habits — continuing mechanically and unthinkingly to do the same thing.

According to Lorenz,[24] aggression is a natural instinct. But it is generally held by psychologists that even if there is some instinctive tendency to be aggressive, it is usual for aggression to be either stimulated or learned as an appropriate mode of behaviour.

Aggressive responses to frustrating situations are, in the first place, directed towards whoever causes the frustration. But the aggression may be displaced. Instead of attacking the boss, an individual may take it out on his wife. Aggression, however, is often whipped up by the individual as it occurs rather than being discharged elsewhere. Aggressive behaviour can be learned. If individuals find that aggression succeeds, they will use it to gain their ends on later occasions.

Stress

Unfortunately, stress is a feature of organizational life associated with getting work done, relating to other people, and being subjected to change, supervision and the exercise of power.

Causes of stress
The main causes of stress are:

- the work itself — overpressurized; actual or perceived failure;
- role in the organization — ambiguity in what is expected of the individual or conflict between what he or she wants to do and can do (role ambiguity);
- poor relationships within the organization — lack of information, little effective consultation, restrictions on behaviour, office politics;

- feelings about job or career — lack of job security, overpromotion, or underpromotion;
- external pressures — clash between demands made by the organization and those made by the family or other external interests. Home interface problems of excessive hours (why should people be expected by means of cultural pressures to start early and stay late?), lots of travelling, company moves, etc can be extremely stressful and organizations tend to ignore these problems.

Coping with stress

How people deal with stress depends on their personality, tolerance for ambiguity and ability to live with change. Some people revel in highly pressurized jobs. Others cannot cope. Motivation also comes into it. Motivation is a form of pressure. People can be too highly motivated and pressure becomes stress when they cannot achieve what they set out or are expected to do.

Stress can be coped with through adaptive behaviour. An overworked manager may adapt successfully by delegating some work, but someone else may accept the overload with the result that his performance deteriorates. And, as Torrington and Cooper[25] point out, a manager who adapts successfully to role ambiguity will seek clarification with his superior or colleagues, but a manager who cannot adapt will withdraw from some aspect of his work role. Organizational approaches to managing stress are discussed in Chapter 14 (pages 280–281).

Resistance to change

People resist change because it is seen as a threat to familiar patterns of behaviour as well as to status and financial rewards. Woodward[26] made this point clearly:

> When we talk about resistance to change we tend to imply that management is always rational in changing its direction, and that employees are stupid, emotional or irrational in not responding in the way they should. But if an individual is going to be worse off, explicitly or implicitly, when the proposed changes have been made, any resistance is entirely rational in terms of his own best interest. The interests of the organization and the individual do not always coincide.

Specifically, the main reasons for resisting charge are as follows:

- *The shock of the new* — people are suspicious of anything which they perceive will upset their established routines, methods of working, or conditions of employment. They do not want to lose the security of the familiar. They may not believe statements by management that the change is for their benefit as well as that of the organization; sometimes with good reason. They may feel that management has ulterior motives and sometimes, the louder the protestations of management, the less they will be believed.

- *Economic fears* — loss of money, threats to job security.
- *Inconvenience* — the change will make life more difficult.
- *Uncertainty* — change can be worrying because of uncertainty about its likely impact.
- *Symbolic fears* — a small change which may affect some treasured symbol, such as a separate office or a reserved parking space, may symbolize big ones, especially when employees are uncertain about how extensive the programme of change will be.
- *Threat to interpersonal relationships* — anything that disrupts the customary social relationships and standards of the group will be resisted.
- *Threat to status or skill* — the change is perceived as reducing the status of individuals or as deskilling them.
- *Competence fears* — concern about the ability to cope with new demands or to acquire new skills.

Techniques of managing change and overcoming resistance to it are discussed in Chapter 14 (pages 266–271).

Orientation to work

Orientation theory examines the factors which are instrumental, ie serve as a means, in directing people's choices about work. An orientation is a central organizing principle which underlies people's attempts to make sense of their lives. In relation to work, as defined by Guest[27]: 'An orientation is a persisting tendancy to seek certain goals and rewards from work which exists independently of the nature of the work and the work content.' The orientation approach stresses the role of the social environment factor as a key factor affecting motivation

Orientation theory is primarily developed from fieldwork carried out by sociologists rather than from laboratory work conducted by psychologists. Goldthorpe and his colleagues studied skilled and semi-skilled workers in Luton, and, in *The Affluent Worker*,[28] they stressed the importance of instrumental orientation, that is, a view of work as a means to an end, a context in which to earn money to purchase goods and leisure. According to Goldthorpe, the 'affluent' worker interviewed by the research team valued work largely for extrinsic reasons:

Considerations of pay and security appear most powerful in binding men to their present job... Workers in all groups within our sample tend to be particularly motivated to increase their power as consumers and their domestic standard of living, rather than their satisfaction as producers and the degree of their self-fulfilment in work.

He went on to emphasize the economic returns as the key factor:

The workers have in effect chosen in favour of work which enables them to achieve a higher level of economic return... a decision has been made to give more weight to the *instrumental* at the expense of the expressive aspects of work.

However, it should be recognized that while pay may be the dominant factor in the choice of employer, there is no evidence that the level of pay determined the degree of satisfaction with the work itself.

In their research carried out with blue-collar workers in Peterborough, Blackburn and Mann[29] found a wider range of orientations. They suggested that different ones could come into play with varying degrees of force in different situations. The fact that workers, in practice, had little choice about what they did contributed to this diversity — their orientations were affected by the choice or lack of choice presented to them and this meant that they might be forced to accept alternative orientations.

But Blackburn and Mann confirmed that pay was a key preference area, the top preferences being:

1. pay
2. security
3. workmates
4. intrinsic job
5. autonomy.

And they commented: 'An obsession with wages clearly emerged... A concern to minimise unpleasant work was also widespread.' Surprisingly, perhaps, they also revealed that 'the most persistent preference of all was for outside work', a fairly clear desire for a combination of 'fresh air and freedom'.

Roles

When faced with any situation, eg carrying out a job, people have to enact a *role* in order to manage that situation. This is sometimes called the 'situation-act model'. As decribed by Chell,[8] this indicates that 'The person must act within situations: situations are rule-governed and how a person behaves is often prescribed by these socially acquired rules. The person thus adopts a suitable role in order to perform effectively within the situation.'

At work, the term *role* describes the part to be played by individuals in fulfilling their job requirements. Roles therefore indicate the specific forms of behaviour required to carry out a particular task or the group of tasks contained in a *position* or job. Work roles primarily define the requirements in terms of the ways they are done but may also refer to broader aspects of behaviour, especially with regard to working with others and styles of management or performance.

The role individuals occupy at work — and elsewhere — exists in relation to other people — their 'role set'. These people have expectations about the individuals' role, and if they live up to these expectations they will have successfully performed the role. Performance in a role is a product of the situation individuals are in and their personality. Situational factors are important, but the role they perform can both shape and reflect their personalities. Stress and inadequate performance result when roles are ambiguous, incompatible, or in conflict with one another.

Role ambiguity

When individuals are unclear about what their role is, what is expected of them, or how they are getting on, they may become insecure or lose confidence in themselves.

Role incompatibility

Stress and poor performance may be caused by roles having incompatible elements, as when there is a clash between what other people expect from the role and what individuals believe it is.

Role conflict

Role conflict results when even if roles are clearly defined and there is no incompatibility between expectations, individuals have to carry out two antagonistic roles. For example, conflict can exist between the roles of individuals at work and their roles at home.

Implications for personnel managers

The main implications for personnel managers of the factors described above which affect individuals at work are as follows:

- *Individual differences* — when designing jobs, preparing training programmes, appraising and counselling staff, developing reward systems
and dealing with grievances and disciplinary problems, it is necessary
to remember that all people are different. What fulfils one person may
not fulfil another. Abilities, aptitudes and intelligence differ widely and
it is necessary to take particular care in fitting the right people in the
right jobs and giving them the right training. The definitions contained
in the section on individual differences in this chapter provide useful
points of reference when preparing person specifications (see also
Chapter 16).

  Personalities should not be judged simplistically in terms of
stereotyped traits. People are complex and they change, and account
has to be taken of this. The problem for personnel managers and
managers in general is that, while they have to accept and understand
these differences and take full account of them, they have ultimately
to proceed on the basis of fitting them to the requirements of the
situation, which are essentially what the organization needs to
achieve. There is always a limit to the extent to which an organization
which relies on collective effort to achieve its goals can adjust itself to
the specific needs of individuals. But the organization has to appreciate
that the pressures it makes on people can result in stress and therefore
can become counterproductive. Stress management is discussed in
Chapter 14.

- *Skilled performance and competence* — the need is for personnel managers to
be capable, first, of defining and measuring standards of performance
and competence and then, of preparing recruitment, employment,
training and development programmes which take account of these
definitions and measures. These issues are taken further in Chapters
13, 17, 20 and 21.

- *What happens to people over time* — in structuring employment policies and
career development programmes, it is necessary to bear in mind the
impacts of the processes of maturation, development and ageing
described earlier in this chapter. Employment policies related to age are
described in Chapter 37.

- *Social influences* — it is always necessary to remember that at work, and
elsewhere, no man is an island. Whatever plans we make to motivate
or influence individuals, they are always under pressure to conform to
the norms of the group to which they belong. And the more cohesive
the group, the more powerful the pressure.

- *Judgements about people (attribution theory)* — we all ascribe motives to other
people and attempt to establish the causes of their behaviour. We must

be careful, however, not to make simplistic judgements about causality — for ourselves as well as in respect of others — especially when we are assessing performance.

- *Behaviour at work* — it is helpful to analyse attitudes by the use of some form of attitude survey. We must be aware, however, that we cannot predict what the attitudes are likely to be in the future and we should bear in mind that, although it is possible to change attitudes, this can be a difficult and long haul, especially when they are deep-seated, as they often are. An understanding of the causes of aggression and the effects of frustration should help us to deal with conflict and misbehaviour at work. Resistance to change as a natural phenomenon should be recognized and anticipated in change management programmes

- *Orientation theory* — the significance of orientation theory is that it stresses the importance of the effect of environmental factors on the motivation to work.

- *Role theory* — role theory helps us to understand the need to clarify with individuals what is expected of them and to ensure when designing jobs that they do not contain any incompatible elements (job design is considered in Chapter 13). We must also be aware of the potential for role conflict in order that steps can be taken to alleviate stress.

References

1. Burt, C 'The Differentiation of Intellectual Ability'. *British Journal of Educational Psychology*, Vol. 24, 1954.
2. Vernon, P E *The Structure of Human Abilities*. Methuen, London, 1961.
3. Thurstone, L L 'Current Issues in Factor Analysis'. *Psychological Bulletin*, Vol. 30, 1940.
4. Argyle, M *The Social Psychology of Work*. Penguin, Harmondsworth, 1989 (2nd edn).
5. Toplis, J. Dulewicz, V, and Fletcher, C *Psychological Testing*. Institute of Personnel Management, London, 1987.
6. Wright, D S and Taylor, A *Introducing Psychology*. Penguin, Harmondsworth, 1970.
7. Guilford, J P *The Nature of Human Intelligence*. McGraw-Hill, New York, 1967.
8. Chell, E *The Psychology of Behaviour in Organisations*. Macmillan, London, 1987.
9. Cattell, R B *The Sixteen Personality Factor Questionnaire*. Institute for Personality and Ability Training, Illinois, 1963.
10. Eysenck, H J *The Structure of Human Personality*, Methuen, London, 1953.
11. Mischel, W *Introduction to Personality*. Holt, Rinehart and Winston, New York, 1981 (3rd edn).

12. Chell, E *Participation and Organisation*. Macmillan, London, 1985.
13. Harre, R *Social Being*. Blackwell, Oxford, 1979.
14. Argyris, C *Personality and Organization*. Harper & Row, New York, 1957.
15. Sheehy, G *Passages: Predictable Crises of Adult Life*. Dutton, New York, 1976.
16. Levinson, D *The Seasons of Man's Life*. Knopf, New York, 1978.
17. Kalleberg, A L and Loscocco, K A 'Aging, Values and Rewards: Explaining Age Differences in Job Satisfaction'. *American Sociological Review*, **48**, 1983.
18. Robertson, I T and Smith, M *Motivation and Job Design*. Institute of Personnel Management, London, 1985.
19. Heider, F *The Psychology of Interpersonal Relationships*. Wiley, New York, 1958.
20. Kelley, H H 'Attribution Theory in Social Psychology'.In D Levine (ed), *Nebraska Symposium on Motivation*. University of Nebraska Press, Lincoln, NB, 1967.
21. Weiner, B *Achievement Motivation and Attribution Theory*. General Learning Press, New Jersey, 1974.
22. Mischel, W *Personality and Assessment*. Wiley, New York, 1968.
23. Newcomb, T M 'On the Definition of Attitudes'. In M Jahoda and N Warren (eds), *Attitudes*, Penguin, Harmondsworth, 1966.
24. Lorenz, K *On Aggression*. Methuen, London, 1966.
25. Torrington, D P and Cooper, C L 'The Management of Stress in Organisations and the Personnel Initiative'. *Personnel Review*, Summer 1977.
26. Woodward, J 'Resistance to change.' *Management International Review*, Vol. 8, 1968.
27. Guest, D 'What's new in Motivation?' *Personnel Management*, May 1984.
28. Goldthorpe, J H, Lockwood, D C, Bechofer, F and Platt, J *The Affluent Worker: Industrial Attitudes and Behaviour*. Cambridge University Press, 1968.
29. Blackburn, R M and Mann, R *The Working Class in the Labour Market*. Macmillan, London, 1979.

7

Motivation

Introduction

Behaviour at work

The way in which people behave at work depends upon three factors:

1. *Their personal characteristics:*

   (a) their abilities, aptitudes and personality, including the state of maturity or development they have achieved;
   (b) their needs, goals and drives, i.e. their motivation to work;
   (c) their commitment to the organization and its values.

2. *The situation or environment in which they work:*

   (a) the organization context, which includes its technology, culture, values, norms, climate, structure, management style and quality of leadership;
   (b) the influence of the group on individual behaviour.

3. *How, in the light of all the above factors, they adjust to their roles at work,* taking into account any efforts made by the organization to increase motivation and commitment and to provide a good working environment.

The basic personal characteristics of individuals (abilities, personality, etc) were discussed in Chapter 6 as was the significance of role theory and the influence of the group on individual behaviour. The factors affecting commitment will be considered in Chapter 8, and the organizational context will be dealt with in Chapters 9 to 11. This chapter is concerned entirely with the motivation to work.

Plan of the chapter

There are a multiplicity of motivation theories. To thread our way through these complexities, we shall in this chapter:

1. Discuss the nature of motivation, which will include considering the processes involved (the needs–goal–action model and the supporting theories relating to reinforcement, homeostasis and open systems), and distinguishing between extrinsic and intrinsic motivation.
2. Describe the main models of motivation as classified by Schein:[1] rational-economic model, social model, self-actualizing model and complex model.
3. Study in more detail the various motivation theories which have contributed to the development of the concept of motivation as described earlier. The theories include those relating to need or content (need hierarchies, the two-factor model, ERG theory, McClelland's classification of needs) and those relating to process (expectancy, goal, reactance and equity theory).
4. Examine the relationships between satisfaction, performance and motivation.
5. Examine the role of money as a motivator.
6. Describe methods of measuring motivation.
7. Summarize through the presentation of a general theory of motivation.

The nature of motivation

Definition

Motivation is concerned with the strength and direction of behaviour. A well-motivated person is someone with clearly defined goals who takes action which he or she expects will achieve those goals.

The process of motivation

Motivation is inferred from or defined by goal-directed behaviour. It is anchored in two basic concepts: (a) the *needs* that operate within the individual and (b) the *goals* in the environment toward or away from which the individual moves. In its simplest form, the process of motivation is initiated by the conscious or unconscious recognition of an unsatisfied need. A goal is then established which, it is thought, will satisfy that need, and a course of action is determined that will lead towards the attainment of the goal. But, as goals are satisfied, new needs emerge and the cycle continues.

This basic model is illustrated in Figure 7.1.

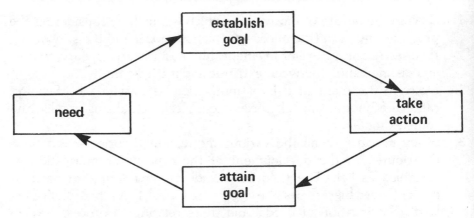

Figure 7.1 Basic motivation model

The concepts of reinforcement, homeostasis and open systems have each exercised strong influence over motivation theory and are described below.

Reinforcement

As experience is gained in taking action to satisfy needs, people perceive that certain actions help to achieve their goals while others are less successful. Some actions bring rewards; others result in failure or even punishment. Reinforcement theory as developed by Hull[2] suggests that successes in achieving goals and rewards act as positive incentives and reinforce the successful behaviour which is repeated the next time a similar need emerges. The more powerful, obvious and frequent the reinforcement, the more likely it is that the behaviour will be repeated until, eventually, it can become a more or less unconscious reaction to an event. Conversely, failures or punishments provide negative reinforcement, suggesting that it is necessary to seek alternative means of achieving goals. This process has been called the law of effect.

The degree to which experience shapes future behaviour does, of course, depend, first, on the extent to which an individual correctly perceives the connection between the behaviour and its outcome and, second, on the extent to which he is able to recognize the resemblance between the previous situation and the one that now confronts him. Perceptive ability varies between people as does the ability to identify correlations between events. For these reasons, some people are better at learning from experience than others, just as some people are more easily motivated than others.

It has been suggested that theories based on the law of effect or the principle of reinforcement are limited because they imply, in Allport's phrase, a 'hedonism of the past'.[3] They assume that the explanation of the present choices of an individual is to be found in an examination of the consequences of his or her past choices. Insufficient attention is paid in the theories to the influence of expectations, and no indication is given of any means of distinguishing in advance the class of outcomes which would strengthen responses and those which would weaken them.

Homeostasis

The human organism, like all other living organisms, is constantly in a state of disequilibrium. It expends energy to stay alive and must replenish this energy. Automatic mechanisms exist to maintain a normal body temperature. This is called the homeostatic principle and it underlies all behaviour and motivation. The drive to satisfy unsatisfied needs is actuated by the constant move towards equilibrium.

Another concept which has some affinity with the principle of homeostasis is the desire to master one's immediate environment. Individuals subjectively organize their environment by reference to past experience, present needs and future expectations. This develops into a pattern which is taken for granted until some external influence affects it. The individual then engages in interpretative or problem-solving activity in an attempt to absorb or resist the change.

Open-system theory

Open-system theory was originally formulated by Von Bertalanffy,[4] who wrote:

> A living organism is an open-system which continually gives up matter to the outer world and takes in matter from it, but which maintains itself in the continuous exchange in a steady state.

Allport[5] further developed this definition by setting out the following features of an open system:

- Intake and output of both matter and energy.
- Achievement and maintenance of steady (homeostatic) states so that

the intrusion of outer energy will not seriously disrupt internal form and order.
● Increase in order over time owing to an increase in complexity and differentiation of parts.
● Extensive transactional commerce with the environment.

The concept was developed by Lawrence and Lorsch,[6] who suggested that an individual can usefully be conceived as a system of biological needs, psychological motives, values and perceptions. The individual's system operates so as to maintain its internal balance in the face of the demands placed upon it by external forces and it develops in response to his or her basic needs to solve the problems presented by the external environment. But each individual system will have unique characteristics because, as Lawrence and Lorsch say:

1. Different individual systems develop with different patterns of needs, values and perceptions.
2. Individual systems are not static, but continue to develop as they encounter new problems and experiences.

Motivating forces

Needs and wants and the processes of reinforcement and homeostasis all operate within an open system and the complexities involved indicate why simplistic approaches to motivation are seldom effective. These complexities are compounded by the existence of two motivating forces — intrinsic and extrinsic motivation — as described below.

Intrinsic and extrinsic motivation

Motivation at work can take place in two ways. First, people can motivate themselves by seeking, finding and carrying out work (or being given work) which satisfies their needs or at least leads them to expect that their goals will be achieved. Secondly, people can be motivated by management through such methods as pay, promotion, praise, etc.

These two types of motivation can be described as:

● *Intrinsic motivation* — the self-generated factors which influence people to behave in a particular way or to move in a particular direction. These factors include responsibility (feeling that the work is important and having control over one's own resources), freedom to act, scope to use and develop skills and abilities, interesting and challenging work and opportunities for advancement.

- *Extrinsic motivation* — what is done to or for people to motivate them. This includes rewards, such as increased pay, praise, or promotion, and punishments, such as disciplinary action, withholding pay, or criticism.

The extrinsic motivators can have an immediate and powerful effect, but it will not necessarily last long. The intrinsic motivators, which are concerned with the quality of working life, are likely to have a deeper and longer-term effect because they are inherent in individuals and not imposed from outside. The concept of intrinsic motivation has influenced the principles of job design, as described in Chapter 13. The effectiveness of pay as an extrinsic motivator is a matter for continuing debate, as discussed later in this chapter and in Chapter 23.

Motivation Models

The theory of motivation is an eclectic one, derived from a number of schools of thought. To obtain an initial perspective of this complicated subject, we may summarize the main approaches that have been developed, adopting the four classifications used by Schein:[1]

1. Rational-economic man.
2. Social man.
3. Self-actualizing man.
4. Complex man.

Since Schein developed these classifications, a fifth has emerged which may be described as the Japanese model.

Rational-economic model

According to this view, people are primarily motivated by economic rewards. It assumes that a person will be motivated to work if rewards and penalties are tied directly to his or her performance; thus the awards are contingent upon effective performance. This approach has its roots in the scientific management methods of Taylor,[7] who wrote: 'It is impossible, through any long period of time, to get workmen to work much harder than the average men around them unless they are assured a large and permanent increase in their pay.'

This approach is based upon the law of effect, as mentioned on page 146 of this chapter. This states that if a person undertakes an action and this action is followed by a reward, the probability that the action will be repeated is increased. On the other hand, if the person undertakes an action which is ignored or followed by a punishment, that behaviour is less likely to be repeated.

Motivation using this approach has been and still is widely adopted and can be successful in some circumstances. But it is based exclusively on a system of external controls and fails to recognize a number of other human needs. It also fails to appreciate the fact that the formal control system can be seriously affected by the informal relationship existing between workers.

This rational motivation model is illustrated in Figure 7.2.

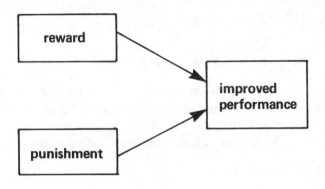

Figure 7.2 The rational motivation model

Social human relations model

Mayo[8] and his colleagues observed this shortcoming and developed an approach which emphasized people's social needs. The need for belonging was seen as providing the basic motivation for individuals to work. The social controls set up by cohesive work groups can be a powerful countervailing force to management's efforts to use financial rewards and organizational controls to achieve what it wants. This concept rapidly developed into the human relations school, which believed that productivity was directly related to job satisfaction and that individuals' output will be high if they like their co-workers and are given pleasant supervision.

To a certain extent, this approach is akin to paternalism, where it is assumed that people can be induced to work out of a feeling of gratitude for the system.

This human relations model is illustrated in Figure 7.3.

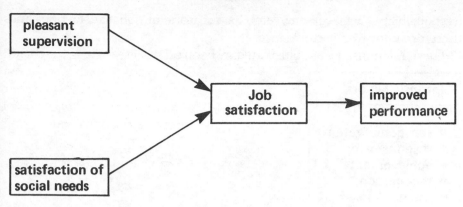

Figure 7.3 The human relations model

Self-actualizing model

The social man/human relations school was seen by many psychologists as somewhat naive, especially in its apparent assumption that a contented individual is necessarily highly productive. It was considered by Maslow, Alderfer, McGregor, Argyris, and Herzberg that people are motivated by a number of different needs. The most important of these needs from the point of view of long-term motivation are the higher order needs for self-fulfilment, self-actualization, and growth. These needs are linked to the work people do and are not subject to an external control system. The key point in McGregor's[9] Theory Y, 'that people will exercise self-direction and self-control in the achievement of organizational objectives to the degree that they are committed to those objectives', is fundamental to this concept. Argyris[10] also sees each person as having a potential which can be fully realized, and believes that such self-realization or self-actualization benefits not only individuals but also those around them and the organization in which they work.

The other significant contributor to this model was Herzberg,[11] whose basic theme is that opportunities for self-actualization are the essential requirements of both job satisfaction and high performance.

The behavioural scientists who developed the self-actualizing model tended to belittle the importance of the extrinsic motivators (rewards and punishments) although they accepted, with some reluctance, that they could have a direct, albeit short-lived, effect on motivation and performance. Instead, they emphasized the role of the intrinsic motivators (responsibility, achievement, etc) as creators of job satisfaction and therefore improved performance.

These relationships are illustrated in Figure 7.4.

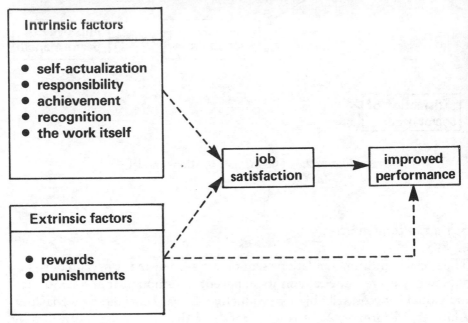

Figure 7.4 The self-actualizing motivation model

These concepts provide the rationale for job enrichment. But a number of researchers, as quoted in Chapter 13 (page 245–246), have questioned the generalized statement that workers need to find fulfilment from work. They have instead postulated that the majority of workers seek fulfilment *outside* work.

Complex man

None of the models described before is completely wrong; their only fault is that they oversimplify. Motivation is a complex affair, first, because people are complicated, having a multitude of needs and expectations; secondly, because the situations in which people work vary and affect motivation in different ways; and thirdly, because these situations are in a constant state of change. The models make the assumption that satisfaction always increases motivation, which cannot be sustained, and they do not take sufficient account of expectations, ability loads, the perceived

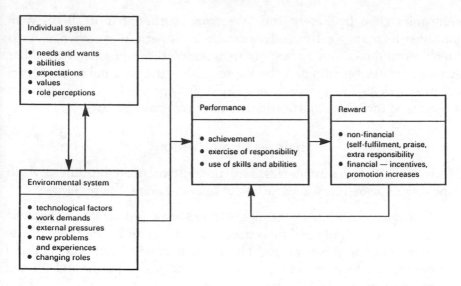

Figure 7.5 'Complex man' open system motivation model

value of the reward and what is called role perception — feelings about what individuals want to do or think they are required to do.

The complex model was developed by Schein[1] and is based on open-system theory, as described earlier in this chapter (page 147). The complexity arises because of the interactions between the various aspects of the individual's system and the environmental system, as shown in Figure 7.5. In combination, they motivate performance, which in turn is the means of creating a non-financial or financial reward which feeds back to influence performance. This model therefore suggests that performance is primarily affected by the factors contained within the two systems. Rewards follow performance and can influence performance, but they are not instrumental in creating the conditions for high performance.

The Japanese model

Attempts made to explain the secret of Japanese business success by such writers as Ouchi,[12] and Pascale and Athos[13] have led to the belief that the best way to motivate people is to get their full commitment to the values of the organization by leadership and involvement. This might be called the 'hearts and minds' approach to motivation and, among other things, it popularized such devices as quality circles.

The baton was taken up by Peters and Waterman[14] and their many imitators in the 1980s. It seems to work in Japan and in the 'excellent' companies cited by Peters and Waterman (although not all of them managed to maintain themselves on their pinnacle of excellence). It is much more direct and obvious than some of those produced by other schools. But it oversimplifies the issues. Unless the national or corporate culture supports this approach, employees may passively or actively resist attempts to force togetherness down their collective throats.

Theories of motivation

Motivation theory can be classified under two main headings which provide complementary approaches to understanding the process:

1. *Needs theory*, which is sometimes referred to as content theory because it focuses explicitly on the content of motivation in the form of the fundamental human needs. These needs create wants (generalized desires to achieve or obtain something) and goals (specific and defined requirements) which shape behaviour.
2. *Process theory*, which attempts to develop understanding of the psychological processes involved in motivation.

Under each of these headings a number of theories have been evolved, and these are described below. These will then be summarized in a general theory of motivation at the end of this chapter.

Needs (content) theory

An unsatisfied need creates tension and a state of disequilibrium. To restore the balance a goal is identified which will satisfy the need, and a behaviour pathway is selected which will lead to the achievement of the goal. All behaviour is therefore motivated by unsatisfied needs.

Not all needs are equally important for a person at any one time — some may provide a much more powerful drive towards a goal than others, depending on the individual's background and present situation. Complexity is further increased because there is no simple relationship between needs and goals. The same need can be satisfied by a number of different goals and the stronger the need and the longer its duration, the broader the range of possible goals. At the same time, one goal may satisfy a number of needs — a new car provides transport as well as an opportunity to impress the neighbours.

Needs theory has been developed by:

- *Maslow*,[15] who developed the concept of a hierarchy of needs which he believed were fundamental to the personality.

- *Alderfer*,[16] who produced a simpler and more flexible model of three basic needs (ERG theory).
- *Herzberg*,[11] who postulated a two-factor model of needs in order to identify those aspects of the work environment which motivate people.
- *McClelland*,[17] who identified three needs which motivate managers, and who, while agreeing with Maslow that needs motives are part of the personality, believed they are triggered off by environmental factors.

Maslow's hierarchy of needs

The most famous classification of needs is the one formulated by Maslow.[15] He suggested that there are five major need categories which apply to people in general, starting from the fundamental physiological needs and leading through a hierarchy of safety, social and esteem needs to the need for self-fulfilment, the highest need of all. Maslow's hierarchy is as follows:

1. *Physiological* — the need for oxygen, food, water and sex.
2. *Safety* — the need for protection against danger and the deprivation of physiological needs.
3. *Social* — the need for love, affection and acceptance as belonging to a group.
4. *Esteem* — the need to have a stable, firmly based, high evaluation of oneself (self-esteem) and to have the respect of others (prestige). These needs may be classified into two subsidiary sets: first, 'the desire for achievement, for adequacy, for confidence in the face of the world, and for independence and freedom', and, second, the desire for reputation or status defined as respect or esteem from other people, and manifested by recognition, attention, importance, or appreciation.
5. *Self-fulfilment* (self-actualization) — the need to develop potentialities and skills, to become what one believes one is capable of becoming.

Maslow's theory of motivation states that when a lower need is satisfied the next highest becomes dominant and the individual's attention is turned to satisfying this higher need. The need for self-fulfilment, however, can never be satisfied. He said that man is a 'wanting animal'; only an unsatisfied need can motivate behaviour and the dominant need is the prime motivator of behaviour. Psychological development takes place as people move up the hierarchy of needs, but this is not necessarily a straightforward progression. The lower needs still exist, even if temporarily dormant as motivators, and individuals constantly return to previously

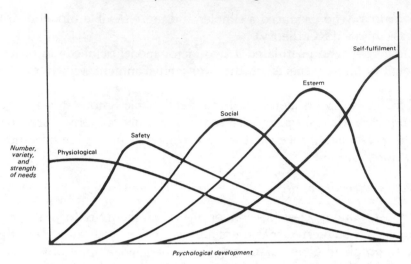

Figure 7.6 Progressive development of needs (Maslow)[15]

satisfied needs. The schematic representation of the progressive development of needs is shown in Figure 7.6.

One of the implications of Maslow's theory is that the higher order needs for esteem and self-fulfilment provide the greatest impetus to motivation — they grow in strength on satisfaction, while the lower needs decline in strength on satisfaction. But the jobs people do will not necessarily satisfy their needs, especially when they are routine or deskilled.

Maslow's needs hierarchy has an intuitive appeal and has been very influential. But it has not been verified by empirical research and it has been criticized for its apparent rigidity — different people may have different priorities and it is difficult to accept that people's needs progress steadily up the hierarchy. In fact, Maslow himself expressed doubts about the validity of a strictly ordered hierarchy.

Alderfer's ERG theory

ERG theory (the needs for existence, relatedness and growth) as formulated by Alderfer[16] is about the subjective states of satisfaction and desire. Satisfaction concerns the outcome of events between people and their environment. It is a subjective reaction which refers to the internal state of people who have obtained what they are seeking and is synonymous with getting and fulfilling. Desire is even more subjective because it refers exclusively to the internal state of a person related to needs, wants, preferences and motives. ERG theory adopts an 'open system' approach to understanding the human personality. This approach suggests that human beings are open systems which are constantly engaging in transactions with their environment which inevitably affect their behaviour.

From this basis, Alderfer devised a theory of human needs which postulated three primary categories:

1. *Existence needs*, which reflect the requirement people have for material and energy exchange and the need to reach and maintain a homeo-static equilibrium with regard to the provision of certain material substances. Hunger and thirst represent deficiencies and are existence needs. Pay, fringe benefits and working conditions are other types of existence needs.
2. *Relatedness needs*, which acknowledge that people are not self-contained units but must engage in transactions with their human environment. The basic characteristic of relatedness needs is that their satisfaction depends on a process of sharing or mutuality. Acceptance, under-standing, confirmation and influence are elements of the relatedness process.
3. *Growth needs* emerge from the tendency of open systems to increase in internal order and differentiation over time as a consequence of going beyond the environment. Growth needs impel people to make creative or productive efforts for themselves: 'Satisfaction of growth needs depends on a person finding the opportunities to be what he is most fully and to become what he can.'

Herzberg's two-factor model

The two-factor model of satisfiers and dissatisfiers was developed by Herzberg[11] following an investigation into the sources of job satisfaction and dissatisfaction of accountants and engineers. It was assumed that people have the ability and the motivation to report accurately the conditions which made them satisfied and dissatisfied with their jobs. Accordingly, the subjects were asked to tell their interviewers about the times during which they felt exceptionally good and exceptionally bad about their jobs and how long their feelings persisted. It was found that the accounts of 'good' periods most frequently concerned the content of the job. Achievement, recognition, advancement, responsibility, and the work itself were the most frequently coded themes in such accounts. On the other hand, accounts of 'bad' periods most frequently concerned the context of the job. Company policy and administration, supervision, salary and working conditions more frequently appeared in these accounts than in those told about 'good' periods. The main implications of this research, according to Herzberg, are that:

> The wants of employees divide into two groups. One group revolves around the need to develop in one's occupation as a source of personal growth. The second group operates as an essential base to the first and is associated with fair treatment in compensation, supervision, working conditions and administrative practices. The fulfilment of the needs of the second group does not motivate the individual to high levels of job satisfaction and to extra performance on the job. All we can expect from satisfying [this second group of needs] is the prevention of dissatisfaction and poor job performance.

These groups form the two factors in Herzberg's model: one consists of the *satisfiers* or motivators, because they are seen to be effective in motivating the individual to superior performance and effort. The other consists of the *dissatisfiers*, which essentially describe the environment and serve primarily to prevent job dissatisfaction, while having little effect on positive job attitudes. These were named the *hygiene* factors in the medical use of the term, meaning preventive and environmental.

Herzberg's theory has been strongly attacked. The research method has been criticized because no attempt was made to measure the relationship between satisfaction and performance. It has been suggested that the two-factor nature of the theory is an inevitable result of the questioning method used by the interviewers. It has also been suggested that wide and unwarranted inferences have been drawn from small and specialized samples and that there is no evidence to suggest that the satisfiers do improve productivity. In an extended critique of the theory, Opsahl and Dunnette[18] stated that the data on feelings about salary 'seem inconsistent with the interpretations and lend no substantial support to hypotheses of a so-called differential role for money in leading to job satisfaction or job dissatisfaction.'

In spite of these criticisms (or perhaps because of them, as they are all from academics), the Herzberg theory continues to thrive; partly because for the layman it is easy to understand and seems to be based on 'real-life' rather than academic abstractions, and partly because it fits in well with the highly respected ideas of Maslow and McGregor in its emphasis on the positive value of the intrinsic motivating factors. It is also in accord with a fundamental belief in the dignity of labour and the Protestant ethic — that work is good in itself. As a result, Herzberg has had immense influence on the job enrichment movement, which seeks to design jobs in a way which will maximize the opportunities to obtain intrinsic satisfaction from work and thus improve the quality of working life.

McClelland's achievement — affiliation — power needs

An alternative way of classifying needs was developed by McClelland,[17] who based it mainly on studies of managerial staff. He identified three needs as being most important:

1. *The need for achievement*, defined as the need for competitive success measured against a personal standard of excellence.
2. *The need for affiliation*, defined as the need for warm, friendly, compassionate relationships with others.
3. *The need for power*, defined as the need to control or influence others.

Different individuals have different levels of these needs. Some have a greater need for achievement, others a stronger need for affiliation, and still others a stronger need for power. While one need may be dominant, however, this does not mean that the others are non-existent.

These needs may be given different priorities at different levels of management. High need for achievement is particularly important for success in many junior- and middle-management jobs where it is possible to feel direct responsibility for task accomplishment. But in senior-management positions a concern for institutionalized as opposed to personal power becomes more important. A strong need for affiliation is not helpful at any level. However, as Guest remarks[19]: 'Those making a bid for power should take note of one of McClelland's findings. In a 20-year follow-up of Harvard graduates who had scored high on the need for power, 58 per cent had high blood pressure or had died of heart failure.'

A general theory of needs

People have a wide range of needs, many of which are latent until stimulated by the environment. Maslow and Herzberg have produced simple classifications which have become enormously popular. But in their different ways they are flawed, and they have not been supported by research.

Alderfer also presents a simplified model of needs, but it is more realistic than Maslow's and has been supported by research, although caution in interpretation of research is necessary because of the difficulty of providing acceptable measures of needs.

As Guest[19] points out, the four needs which have potentially important implications in work settings are the needs for achievement, power, affiliation and autonomy. These embrace two of the ERG (relatedness and growth), and McClelland's extensive research concentrated on the first

Table 7.1 Comparison of needs theories

Maslow Needs hierarchy	Alderfer ERG theory	Herzberg Two-factor model	McClelland Three-factor model	Integrated Five-factor model
• *Physiological*	• *Existence*	• *Dissatisfiers* — company policy — supervision — pay — working conditions		• *Existence*
• *Safety*				
• *Social*	• *Relatedness*	• *Satisfiers* — recognition — responsibility — advancement — achievement	• *Affiliation*	• *Affiliation*
• *Esteem*			• *Power*	• *Power*
				• *Autonomy*
• *Self-fulfilment* (self-actualization)	• *Growth*		• *Achievement*	• *Achievement*

three. They are, of course, included in the other classifications, but this formulation is more useful as a guide to motivation strategy. An integrated, five-factor model of human needs can be developed which incorporates Guest's four factors but adds Alderfer's existence needs in recognition that these are fundamental. A comparison between the various needs theories is shown in Table 7.1.

Process theory

In process theory, the emphasis is on the psychological processes or forces which affect motivation, as well as on basic needs. Process theory can be more useful to managers than needs theory because it provides better guidance on motivation techniques. The processes are:

- expectations (expectancy theory);
- goal achievement (goal theory);
- behavioural choice (reactance theory);
- feelings about equity (equity theory).

Expectancy theory

The concept of expectancy was originally developed in the valency-instrumentality-expectancy (VIE) theory which was formulated by Vroom.[20] Valency stands for value, instrumentality is the belief that if we do one thing it will lead to another, and expectancy is the probability that action or effort will lead to an outcome. This concept of expectancy was defined in more detail by Vroom as follows:

> Whenever an individual chooses between alternatives which involve uncertain outcomes, it seems clear that his behaviour is affected not only by his preferences among these outcomes but also by the degree to which he believes these outcomes to be possible. An expectancy is defined as a momentary belief concerning the likelihood that a particular act will be followed by a particular outcome. Expectancies may be described in terms of their strength. Maximal strength is indicated by subjective certainty that the act *will* be followed by the outcome, while minimal (or zero) strength is indicated by subjective certainty that the act *will not* be followed by the outcome.

The strength of expectations may be based on past experiences (reinforcement), but individuals are frequently presented with new situations — a change in job, payment system, or working conditions imposed by management — where past experience is an inadequate guide to the implications of the change. In these circumstances, motivation may be reduced.

Motivation is only likely when a clearly perceived and usable relationship exists between performance and outcome, and the outcome is seen as a means of satisfying needs. This explains why extrinsic motivation — for example, an incentive or bonus scheme — works only if the link between effort and reward is clear and the value of the reward is worth the effort. It also explains why intrinsic motivation arising from the work itself can be more powerful than extrinsic motivation; intrinsic motivation outcomes are more under the control of the individual, who can place greater reliance on his past experiences to indicate the extent to which positive and advantageous results are likely to be obtained by his or her behaviour.

This theory was developed by Porter and Lawler[21] into the model shown in Figure 7.7. This suggests that there are two factors determining the effort people put into their jobs:

1. The values of the rewards to individuals in so far as they satisfy their needs for security, social esteem, autonomy, and self-actualization.
2. The probability that rewards depend on effort, as perceived by the individual — in other words, his or her expectations about the relationships between effort and reward.

Thus, the greater the value of a set of awards and the higher the probability that receiving each of these rewards depends upon effort, the greater the effort that will be put forth in a given situation.

But mere effort is not enough. It has to be effective effort if it is to produce the desired performance. The two variables additional to effort which affect task achievement are:

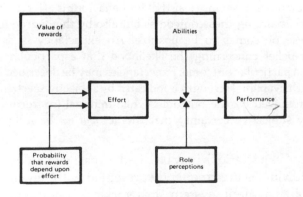

Figure 7.7 Motivation model (Porter and Lawler)

- ability — individual characteristics such as intelligence, manual skills, know-how;
- role perceptions — what the individual wants to do or thinks he or she is required to do. These are good from the viewpoint of the organization if they correspond with what it thinks the individual ought to be doing. They are poor if the views of the individual and the organization do not coincide.

Goal theory

Goal theory as developed by Latham and Locke[22] states that motivation and performance are higher when individuals are set specific goals, when goals are difficult but accepted, and when there is feedback on performance. Participation in goal setting is important as a means of getting agreement to the setting of higher goals. Difficult goals must be agreed and their achievement reinforced by guidance and advice. Finally, feedback is vital in maintaining motivation, particularly towards the achievement of even higher goals.

Goal theory is in line with the concept of management by objectives. The latter approach, however, has often failed because it has been tackled bureaucratically without gaining the real support of those involved and, importantly, without ensuring that managers are aware of the importance of the processes of agreement, reinforcement and feedback, and are skilled in practising them.

Goal theory, however, is the basis for the performance management systems which have evolved from the largely discredited management-by-objectives approaches first introduced in the 1960s. Performance management systems are described in Chapter 19.

Reactance theory

Reactance theory as formulated by Brehm[23] starts from the premise that 'to the extent a person is aware of his needs and the behaviour necessary to satisfy these needs, and providing he has the appropriate freedom, he can choose behaviour so as to maximize need satisfaction.'

If, however, this freedom to act is threatened, people will react, that is, they will, in accordance with the principle of homeostasis, be motivationally aroused to the avoidance of any further loss of freedom. In essence, as Brehm says:

> Given that a person has a set of free behaviours, he will experience reactance whenever any of these behaviours is eliminated or threatened with

elimination, and when a free behaviour of an individual is eliminated (or threatened) his desire for that behaviour or for the object of it will increase.

In other words, individuals are not passive receivers and responders. Instead, they actively strive to make sense of their environment and to reduce uncertainty by seeking to control factors influencing rewards. Management may have all sorts of wonderful ideas about motivating employees, but they will not necessarily work unless they make sense to the people concerned in terms of their own values and orientations.

Equity theory

Equity theory is concerned with the perceptions people have about how they are being treated as compared with others. To be dealt with equitably is to be treated fairly in comparison with another group of people (a reference group) or a relevant other person. Equity involves feelings and perceptions and it is always a comparative process. It is not synonymous with equality, which means treating everyone the same, since this would be inequitable if they deserve to be treated differently.

Equity theory states, in effect, that people will be better motivated if they are treated equitably and demotivated if they are treated inequitably. But it explains only one aspect of the processes of motivation and job satisfaction, although it may be significant in terms of morale.

Relationships between satisfaction, performance and motivation

Job satisfaction

The term 'job satisfaction' refers to the attitudes and feelings people have about their work. Positive and favourable attitudes towards the job indicate job satisfaction, and negative and unfavourable attitudes towards the job indicate job dissatisfaction.

Morale is often defined as being equivalent to job satisfaction. Thus, Guion[24] defines morale as 'the extent to which the individual's needs are satisfied and the extent to which the individual perceives that satisfaction as stemming from his total work situation'. Other definitions stress the group aspects of morale; for example, Gilmer[25] suggests that morale 'is a feeling of being accepted by and belonging to a group of employees through adherence to common goals'. And he, like others, distinguishes between morale as a group variable, related to the degree to which group members feel attracted to their group and desire to remain a member of it, and as an individual variable, related to the feeling employees have about their jobs.

Factors affecting job satisfaction

The following factors affect job satisfaction:

1. *The intrinsic motivating factors.* These relate to job content, especially variety, challenge, responsibility, control over work methods, control over work pace, the opportunity to use skills and abilities and influence in decision-making.
2. *The extrinsic factors.* These relate to pay and the context in which the work is carried out.
3. *The quality of supervision.* The Hawthorne studies[26] resulted in the claim that supervision is the most important determinant of worker attitudes. The Ohio State University Leadership Studies[27] later identified two major independent dimensions of leadership behaviour (while other studies distinguished between employee orientation and production orientation). The first dimension was called 'consideration' and includes supervisory behaviour 'indicative of friendship, mutual trust, respect and warmth'. The second dimension was termed initiating structure, which includes behaviour in which the supervisor organizes and defines group activities and his relation to the group. A number of subsequent studies have suggested that the display of consideration of supervisors has increased employee satisfaction and resulted in lower labour turnover, less absenteeism and fewer grievances. But they have not shown that there is a direct relationship between consideration, satisfaction and productivity. Herzberg,[11] however, claimed that the importance of supervision has been overrated and it seems clear that considerate supervision is only one out of many factors that can affect attitudes and satisfaction.
4. *The work group.* Mayo[8] believed that 'a man's desire to be continuously associated in work with his fellows is a strong, if not the strongest, human characteristic'. And it is true that social interaction can be highly rewarding to most people, and that experiences with one's fellow workers can be a major satisfaction at work. Research has shown that larger groups where less interaction is possible have lower cohesiveness or morale than smaller groups. The social isolation which exists on assembly lines is a known cause of dissatisfaction.
5. *Success or failure.* Success obviously creates satisfaction, especially if it enables individuals to prove to themselves that they are using their

skills effectively. And it is equally obvious that the reverse is true of failure.

Job satisfaction and performance

It is a commonly held and apparently not unreasonable belief that an increase in job satisfaction results in improved performance. The whole human relations movement was based on the belief that productivity could be increased by making workers more satisfied. The first real blow to this view came from the Survey Research Centre studies in an insurance company[28] and a railway.[29] No differences were found in either study between the satisfaction with wages, satisfaction with job status, or satisfaction with fellow workers in high and low productivity sections.

A review of the extensive literature on this subject by Brayfield and Crockett[30] concluded that there was little evidence of any simple or appreciable relationship between employee attitudes and the effectiveness of their performance. An updated version of their analysis by Vroom[20] covered 20 studies, in each of which one or more measures of job satisfaction or employee attitudes was correlated with one or more criteria of performance. The median correlation of all these studies was 0.14, which is not high enough to suggest any marked relationship between satisfaction and performance. Our own observations confirm the results of this analysis. We are constantly coming across people who are perfectly content to do the minimum that will keep them in employment.

It has been suggested that it is not increases in satisfaction that produce improved performance but improved performance that increases satisfaction. This is certainly true in the sense that individuals are motivated to reach certain goals and will be satisfied if they achieve those goals through improved performance. But individual goals can be satisfied in other ways besides working harder or better. Improved performance is not a necessary or the only factor in improving satisfaction. As Brayfield and Crockett suggested:

> Productivity is seldom a goal in itself but is more commonly a means to goal attainment. Therefore .... we might expect high satisfaction and high productivity to occur together when productivity is perceived as a path to certain important goals and when these goals are achieved. Under other conditions, satisfaction and productivity might be unrelated or even negatively related.[30]

Increases in satisfaction may therefore reduce staff turnover, absenteeism, and grievances, but they do not necessarily result in increases in productivity. Satisfaction and performance are often related, but the precise effect on each other depends upon the working situation and the people in it. Motivation is not simply a matter of increasing job satisfaction. The common-sense view that people are motivated only when they have something to strive for accords with Maslow's suggestion that only an unsatisfied need motivates behaviour. A measure of dissatisfaction and a desire for more achievement or power may be the best motivator for some people. But it will all depend on the people concerned and the environment in which they are working.

Motivation and performance

Although there is some doubt about the relationship between performance and satisfaction, it seems obvious that the link between motivation and performance is a positive one: increased motivation should result in more effort and improved performance. But there are two qualifications to this point of view. First, there is the effect of ability, and, second, there are the possible detrimental effects of too much motivation. There is also the whole question of the impact of such factors as rewards and individuals' understanding of the kinds of activities and behaviour they should engage in to perform their job successfully (role perceptions).

Motivation and ability

However keen people are to do something, they will not be able to do it unless they have the required abilities. Vroom[20] suggested on the basis of a number of experiments that:

> The effects of motivation on performance are dependent on the level of ability of the worker, and the relationship of ability to performance is dependent on the motivation of the worker. The effects of ability and motivation on performance are not additive but interactive. The data presently available on this question suggest something more closely resembling the multiplicative relationship depicted in the following formula:

$$\text{Performance} = \text{Ability} \times \text{Motivation}$$

This formula expresses more than the truism that you cannot perform a task without some ability *and* some motivation. The emphasis is on the multiplicative relationship between the two factors, from which it follows that when ability is low, increases in motivation result in smaller increases in performance than when ability is high. Similarly, when motivation is low, increases in ability result in smaller increases in performance than when motivation is high.

The implication is that it is as necessary to concentrate on improving ability by means of good selection and training as it is to concentrate on improving motivation by some manipulation of the extrinsic and intrinsic factors affecting it. At the same time, more is to be gained from increasing the motivation of those who are high in ability than of those who are low in ability, and more is to be gained from increasing the ability of those who are highly motivated than of those who are relatively less well motivated.

Effects of high motivation

There is a second qualification to the concept that higher motivation always results in greater productivity. It is possible for someone to be too highly motivated; to want something so much that he becomes over-anxious and therefore prone to indecision and error or to ignoring relevant information. Vroom proposed three hypothetical relationships between the amount of motivation and performance, as shown in Figure 7.8. He suggests that while it is possible for performance to improve steadily, as in the straight line on Figure 7.8, it is equally possible that the rate at which performance increases diminishes until there is no further increase, as in the dotted line. Another plausible relationship is shown by the broken line, where performance reaches its maximum point under moderate levels of motivation and then drops off under high levels of motivation. The latter view is supported by a number of research studies.

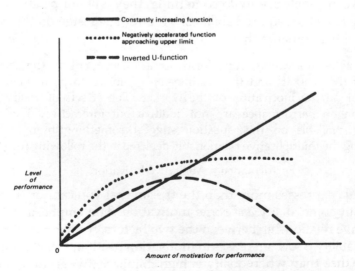

Figure 7.8 Hypothetical relationships between motivation and performance

Motivation/performance/satisfaction model

A model of the relationships between motivation, performance and satisfaction is shown in Figure 7.9 on page 170.

The role of money as a motivator

Money, in the form of pay or some other sort of remuneration, is the most obvious extrinsic reward. Money provides the carrot which most, if not all, people want.

Doubts have been cast on the effectiveness of money by Herzberg because, while the lack of it can cause dissatisfaction, its provision does not result in lasting satisfaction. There is something in this, especially for people on fixed salaries or rates of pay who do not benefit directly from an incentive scheme. They may feel good when they get an increase — apart from the extra money, it is about as tangible a form of recognition as you can find — but this feeling of euphoria can rapidly die away. Other dissatisfactions from Herzberg's list of hygiene factors, such as working conditions or the quality of management, loom larger in their minds, when they fail to get the satisfaction they need from the work itself.

Nevertheless, money provides the means to achieve a number of different ends. It is a powerful force because it is linked directly or indirectly to the satisfaction of many needs. In Maslow's hierarchy, it clearly satisfies the basic needs for survival and security, if it is coming in regularly. It can also satisfy the need for self-esteem (as noted above, it is a visible mark of appreciation) and status — money can set you in a grade apart from your fellows and can buy you things they can't to build up your prestige. Money satisfies the less desirable but still prevalent drives of acquisitiveness and cupidity.

Money may in itself have no intrinsic meaning, but it acquires significant motivating power because it comes to symbolize so many intangible goals. It acts as a symbol in different ways for different people, and for the same person at different times. And, as noted by Goldthorpe[31] and Blackburn and Mann[32], pay is the dominant factor in the choice of employer and considerations of pay seem most powerful in binding people to their present job. In other words, pay is an important factor in attracting and retaining people to and at work. But do financial rewards motivate people?

Financial rewards can work well for some people because their expectations that they will receive them are high. But these people will tend to be well motivated anyway, and less confident employees may not respond to incentives which they do not expect to achieve. It can also be

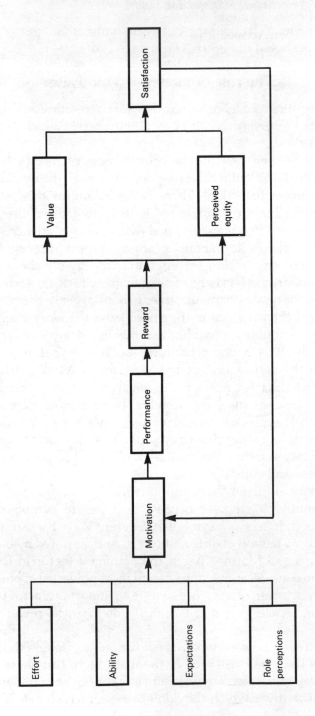

Figure 7.9 Motivation/performance/satisfaction model

argued that extrinsic rewards may erode intrins   ?rest — people who work just for money could find their tasks less pleasurable and may not, therefore, do them so well. What we do know, as discussed in the previous section of this chapter, is that a multiplicity of factors is involved in performance improvements and many of those factors are interdependent.

Money can therefore provide positive motivation in the right circumstances, but Herzberg is correct in pointing out that pay systems can demotivate. Another researcher in this area was Jaques, who emphasized the need for such systems to be perceived as being fair and equitable. In other words, the reward should be clearly related to effort or level of responsibility and people should not receive less money than they deserve compared with their fellow workers. Jaques[33] called this the 'felt-fair' principle.

Attitude surveys

Attitude surveys can provide general information on attitudes and feelings as a basis for formulating policies. Attitude surveys can also be used to:

- provide particular information on the preferences of employees, for example, on a union recognition issue;
- give warning on potential trouble spots;
- diagnose the cause of particular troubles;
- compare morale in different parts of the organization;
- evaluate training;
- assess how organizational and other policy changes have been received;
- observe the effects of policies and actions over a period of time;
- provide people with the opportunity to express their views — attitude surveys are therefore in themselves a means of increasing job satisfaction as long as feelings of frustration do not arise because of lack of action on the part of management after the survey;
- provide an additional means of communication, especially if the survey includes some discussions with employees on their attitudes and what actions they would like management to take.

Approach

The approach is first to identify the individual's needs and then to assess the extent to which these needs are being met. This means using two questionnaires. The first questionnaire would ask people how they feel about various things for *any* job they might do, not just their present job. Thus, against the heading of 'good wages', they would be asked to indicate how they feel by ticking the appropriate heading — absolutely top priority, very important, fairly important, and not very important. The second questionnaire would ask them to express their feelings about different aspects of their present job, for example, indicating against 'pay' whether their feelings about it are very good, good, neither good nor bad, bad, or very bad.

Methods of conducting attitude surveys

There are three methods of conducting attitude surveys:

1. By the use of *structured questionnaires* issued to all or a sample of employees. The questionnaires may be standardized ones, such as the Brayfield and Rothe Index of Job Satisfaction, or they may be developed specially for the organization. The advantage of using standardized questionnaires is that they have been thoroughly tested and in many cases norms are available against which results can be compared. Additional questions specially relevant to the company can be added to the standard list. A tailor-made questionnaire can be used to highlight particular issues, but it may be advisable to obtain professional help from an experienced psychologist, who can carry out the skilled work of drafting and pilot-testing the questionnaire and interpreting the results. Questionnaires have the advantage of being relatively cheap to administer and analyse, especially when there are large numbers involved.

2. By the use of *interviews*. These may be 'open-ended' or depth interviews in which the discussion is allowed to range quite freely. Or they may be semi-structured in that there is a check-list of points to be covered, although the aim of the interviewer is to allow discussion to flow around the points so that the frank and open views of the individual are obtained. Alternatively, and more rarely, interviews can be highly structured so that they become no more than the spoken application of a questionnaire. Individual interviews are to be preferred because they are more likely to be revealing and are easier to analyse. But they are expensive and time-consuming. Group discussions are a quicker way of reaching a large number of people, but the results are not so easy to quantify and some people may have difficulty in expressing their views in public.

3. By a combination of *questionnaire and interview*. This is the ideal approach because it combines the quantitative data from the questionnaire with

the qualitative data from the interviews. It is always advisable to accompany questionnaires with some depth interviews, even if time permits only a limited sample. An alternative approach is to administer the questionnaire to a group of people and then discuss the reactions to each question with the group. This ensures that a quantified analysis is possible but enables the group, or at least some members of it, to express their feelings more fully.

4. By the use of *focus groups*. A focus group is a representative sample of employees whose attitudes and opinions are sought on issues concerning the organization and their work. The essential features of a focus group are that it is structured, informed, constructive and confidential.

The steps to take when planning focus groups are to:

1. establish objectives;
2. define the points to be covered and the time allowed (not too many points and not more than two hours or so);
3. agree group membership (a representative sample of no more than 10 employees);
4. set up and convene groups;
5. feed back data to groups.

The steps to be taken in conducting an attitude survey by means of a structured questionnaire are illustrated in Figure 7.10 on page 174.

Assessing results

It is an interesting fact that when people are asked directly if they are satisfied with their job, most of them (70 to 90 per cent) will say they are. This is regardless of the work being done and often in spite of strongly held grievances. The probable reason for this phenomenon is that while most people are willing to admit to having grievances — in fact, if invited to complain, they will complain — they may be reluctant to admit, even to themselves, to being dissatisfied with a job which they have no immediate intention of leaving. Many employees have become reconciled to their work, even if they do not like some aspects of it, and have no real desire to do anything else. So they are, in a sense, satisfied enough to continue, even if they have complaints. Finally, many people *are* satisfied with their job overall, although they grumbled about many aspects of it.

Overall measures of satisfaction do not, therefore, always reveal anything interesting. It is more important to look at particular aspects of satisfaction or dissatisfaction to decide whether or not anything needs to

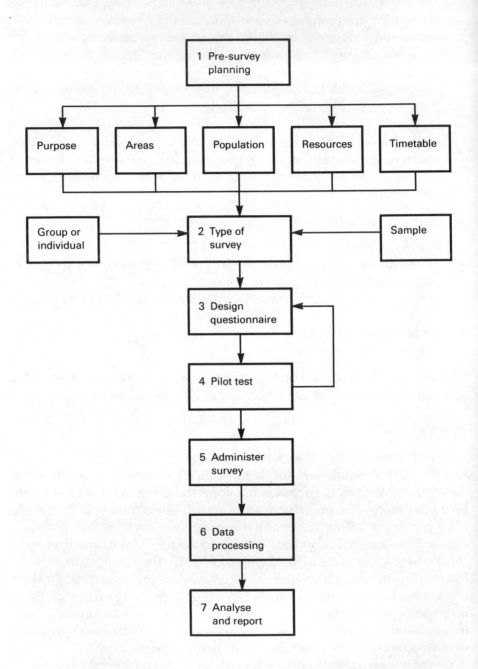

Figure 7.10 Designing and running an attitude survey

be done. In these circumstances, the questionnaire will indicate only a line to be followed up. It will not provide the answers. Hence the advantage of individual meetings or focus group discussions to explore in depth any issue raised.

A general theory of motivation

A general theory of motivation can be derived from the various schools and theories described above. This general theory covers the following areas:

- the process of motivation, involving homeostasis, reinforcement and the needs-goals model;
- the specific influences of needs, goals and wants on motivation;
- the relevance of the extrinsic and intrinsic factors on motivation;
- the importance of expectations as motivating forces;
- the influence of orientations and reactions on motivation;
- the relationship between motivation and performance;
- the key factors to consider when motivating people.

The process of motivation

- *Basis* — the basis of motivation is the process of recognizing a need and taking action to satisfy it by reaching a goal.
- *Complexity* — motivation is a complex process because people have different needs and varied perceptions about them.
- *Homeostasis* — individuals are in essence open systems constantly interacting with their environment and at the same time striving for equilibrium. Consequently, they have a wide variety of goals and of perceptions about the actions which are likely to help them achieve those goals. Motivation is very much a matter of perceptions which will be influenced by past experiences and the present environment.
- *Reinforcement* — success in achieving goals and rewards acts as an incentive and reinforces the successful behaviour, which is repeated as similar needs arise.

The influence of needs

In response to stimuli from the environment, needs emerge which upset equilibrium. If equilibrium is to be restored in accordance with the principle of homeostasis, these needs must be satisfied.

The basic needs are related to existence — survival, security and maintaining a reasonable standard of living in relation to expectations. Another powerful need is for relationships or affiliations with others. But the key motivating needs are for growth and freedom, that is:

- achievement
- power
- autonomy.

Money, however, may be a dominant motivating force because it can be instrumental in satisfying a multitude of needs, especially those concerned with existence, growth, achievement, power and autonomy.

The significance of wants

Needs can create wants, which are broad expressions of what people like to get out of work. What is wanted can be established by attitude surveys such as the one carried out by the Henley Forecasting Centre in 1988, which covered 2000 people. Things employees wanted out of work were ranked in the following order:

1. having control over what to do;
2. using knowledge and experience to make decisions;
3. having a variety of things to do;
4. amount you earn;
5. being with and making friends;
6. doing a job that you know people respect.

It is important to establish what individuals or groups want in operational terms, such as those mentioned above, as the basis for formulating motivation strategies and agreeing specific goals. Generalized lists of needs are not so helpful because, although they may indicate the strength of motivation, they are not so clear about its direction.

The influence of goals

Individuals at work are motivated by having specific goals, and they perform better when they are aiming for difficult goals which they have accepted and when they receive feedback on performance.

Extrinsic and intrinsic motivating factors

Motivation at work can be either extrinsic — provided by the employer in the context of the job, or intrinsic — derived from the content of the job.

Extrinsic rewards provided by the employer, including pay, can be important in attracting and retaining employees and, in the short term, increasing effort and minimizing dissatisfaction. Intrinsic rewards related to responsibility, achievement and the work itself may have a longer-term and deeper effect in creating and increasing satisfaction.

The importance of expectations

The degree to which people are motivated will depend not only upon the perceived value of the outcome of their actions — the goal or reward — but also upon their perceptions of the likelihood of obtaining the reward, ie their expectations. They will be highly motivated if they can control the means to attain their goals.

Higher effort or motivation therefore exists when employees perceive a link between effort, performance and rewards. The extent to which better performance is achieved depends partly on the strength of the need and the attractiveness of the goal but, also, and to a large extent, on their expectation of reaching the goal. In addition, employees must have the necessary knowledge and skills and an understanding of the requirements of their job or role.

The influence of orientations and reactions

Organizations may have expectations about how their motivating strategies will improve performance as well as helping to attract and retain employees. But the situation may not be under as much control as they would wish because of the influence of:

- *Orientations* — independently of what the company attempts to do in the way of motivating its employees, people have orientations or preferences for what they want to get out of work which are influenced by their environment and the choice of activities or work that is available to them.
- *Reactance* — individuals are not passive receivers and responders; they attempt to control their own environment irrespective of what the organization wants them to do, and react against any threat to whatever autonomy they possess or think they possess.

The relationship between motivation and performance

The basic requirements for job satisfaction may include comparatively higher pay, an equitable payment system, real opportunities for promotion, considerate and participative supervision, a reasonable degree of social interaction at work, interesting and varied tasks and a high degree of control over work pace and work methods. The degree of satisfaction obtained by individuals, however, depends largely upon their own needs and expectations and the environment in which they work.

But research has not established any strongly positive connection between satisfaction and performance. A satisfied worker is not necessarily a high producer, and a high producer is not necessarily a satisfied worker. Some people claim that good performance produces satisfaction rather than the other way round, but their case has not been proved.

The key motivating factors

The overriding consideration in motivation is that the members of an organization contribute to the organization in return for the inducements that the organization offers them. In the words of Simon: 'Individuals are willing to accept organization membership when their activity in the organization contributes, directly or indirectly, to their own personal goals.[34] The task of the organization is to analyse its own circumstances and the particular needs and requirements of its employees to determine the mix of extrinsic and intrinsic motivating factors needed to attract and retain good-quality staff and to obtain consistently high standards of performance from them.

If management wishes to increase productivity it has to bear in mind that, in the words of Georgopoulos:[35]

> Individual productivity is, among other things, a function of one's motivation to produce at any given level; in turn such motivation depends upon (a) the particular needs of the individual as reflected in the goals towards which he is moving, and (b) his perception regarding the relative usefulness of productivity behaviour as an instrumentality, or as a path to the attainment of these goals.

Thus the individual's main concern is to assess the benefits that will accrue to him from doing what the organization wants him to do, and the penalties that may result from a failure to act as the organization requires. The organization has to make assumptions about what people want in deciding how they should be motivated. This is the problem of motivation. Many such assumptions are invalid because they are based on generalizations and an inadequate understanding of the process of motivation. Even if attitude surveys are used to assess needs and wants, they can easily produce misleading results because of the difficulties of administration and interpretation. Finally, there is the problem that all managers meet — it is easy to observe behaviour; it is much more difficult to interpret and attach reasons for that behaviour when it has been motivated by a set of hidden needs and goals.

Implications of motivation theory

Motivation theory helps us to understand why people behave in the way they do and what we can do about it. There are, however, no easy answers. Motivation is a complex process. The relationship between satisfaction and performance is not as clear as some people would have us believe. Motivation can be extrinsic or intrinsic but the relative importance of these to individuals depends on their personality and expectations, and the latter are not always predictable. Motivation theory does not, therefore, provide us with all the answers. But it does give us a set of analytical tools which we can use to assess the situation and consider what actions are most likely to be appropriate in the circumstances. Motivation strategies are considered in Chapter 14.

References

1. Schein, E H *Organizational Psychology*. Prentice-Hall, Englewood Cliffs, NJ, 1965.
2. Hull, C *Essentials of Behaviour*. Yale University Press, New Haven, CT, 1951.
3. Allport, G 'The historical background of modern social psychology'. In G Lindzey (ed.) *Handbook of Social Psychology*. Addison-Wesley, Cambridge, MA, 1954.
4. Von Bertalanffy, L 'Theoretical models in biology and psychology'. In Krech, D and Klein, G S (eds) *Theoretical Models and Personality Theory*. Duke University Press, Durham, NC, 1952.
5. Allport, G 'The open system in personality theory', *Journal of Abnormal and Social Psychology*, 1960, **61**, pp. 301–11.
6. Lawrence, P R and Lorsch, J W *Developing Organizations*. Addison-Wesley, Reading, MA, 1969.
7. Taylor, F W 'The Principles of Scientific Management', *Scientific Management*, Harper, New York, 1947.
8. Mayo, E *The Human Problems of an Industrial Civilization*. Macmillan, London, 1933.
9. McGregor, D *The Human Side of Enterprise*. McGraw-Hill, New York, 1960.
10. Argyris, C *Personality and Organization*. Harper & Row, New York, 1957.
11. Herzberg, F W, Mausner, B and Snyderman, B *The Motivation to Work*. John Wiley, New York, 1957.
12. Ouchi, W G *Theory Z*. Addison-Wesley, Reading, MA, 1981.

13. Pascale, R T and Athos, A G *The Art of Japanese Management*. Simon & Schuster, New York, 1981.
14. Peters, T J and Waterman, R H *In Search of Excellence*. Harper & Row, New York, 1982.
15. Maslow, A H *Motivation and Personality*. Harper & Row, New York, 1954
16. Alderfer, C P *Existence, Relatedness and Growth*. Free Press, New York, 1972.
17. McClelland, D C *Power, The Inner Experience*. Irvington, New York, 1975.
18. Opsahl, R C and Dunnette, M D 'The role of financial compensation in industrial motivation', *Psychological Bulletin*, Vol. 56, 1966, pp. 94–118.
19. Guest, D 'What's new in motivation?', *Personnel Management*, May, 1984.
20. Vroom, V H *Work and Motivation*, John Wiley & Sons, New York, 1964.
21. Porter, L W and Lawler, E E *Managerial Attitudes and Performance*. Irwin-Dorsey, Homewood, IL, 1968.
22. Latham, G P and Locke, F A 'Goal setting — a motivating technique that works', *Organizational Dynamics*, **8**, 1979.
23. Brehm, J W *A Theory of Psychological Reactance*. Academic Press, New York, 1966.
24. Guion, R M 'Industrial morale (a symposium) — The problems of terminology', *Personnel Psychology*, Vol. 11, 1958, pp. 59–64.
25. Gilmer, B *Industrial Psychology*. McGraw-Hill, New York, 1961.
26. Roethlisberger, F J and Dickson, W J *Management and the Worker*, Harvard University Press, Cambridge, MA, 1939.
27. Halpin, A W and Winer, B J 'A factorial study of the leader behavioural description'. In R M Stogdill and A E Coons (eds) *Leader Behaviour: Its Description and Measurement*. Ohio State University, Columbus, OH, 1957.
28. Katz, D, Maccoby, N, and Morse, N C *Productivity, Supervision and Morale in an Office Situation*. Survey Research Centre, University of Michigan, Ann Arbor, MI, 1950.
29. Katz, D, Maccoby, N, Gurin, G and Floor, L G *Productivity, Supervision and Morale Among Railroad Workers*. Survey Research Centre, University of Michigan, Ann Arbor, MI, 1951.
30. Brayfield, A H and Crockett, W H 'Employee attitudes and employee performance', *Psychological Bulletin*, Vol. 52, 1955, pp. 346–424.
31. Goldthorpe, J H, Lockwood, D C, Bechoter, F, and Platt, J *The Affluent Worker: Industrial Attitudes and Behaviour*. Cambridge University Press, 1968.
32. Blackburn, R M and Mann, R *The Working Class in the Labour Market*. Macmillan, London, 1979.
33. Jaques, E *Equitable Payment*. Heinemann, London, 1961.
34. Simon, H A *Administrative Behaviour*. Macmillan, New York, 1957.
35. Georgopoulos, B S, Mahoney, G M and Jones, N W 'A path-goal approach to productivity', *Journal of Applied Psychology*, Vol. 41, pp. 345–353.

8

Commitment

Definition of commitment

Commitment, as defined by White,[1] denotes three areas of feeling or behaviour related to the company in which a person works:

1. Belief in, and acceptance of, the organization itself and/or its goals and values.
2. Willingness to exert effort on behalf of the organization beyond what is contracted for. This might include giving private time to work, postponing a holiday, or making some other personal sacrifice for the organization without the expectation of immediate personal gain.
3. Desire to maintain membership of the organization.

It is possible to distinguish between passive (intention to stay) and active (desire to achieve) commitment. White suggests four possible groups, as shown in Figure 8.1.

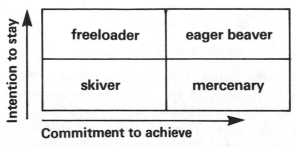

Figure 8.1 Commitment psychology

Commitment and motivation

Commitment is a wider concept than motivation and tends to be more stable over a period of time. It is less responsive to transitory aspects of an employee's job. It is possible to be dissatisfied with a particular feature of a job while retaining a reasonably high level of commitment to the organization as a whole.

In relating commitment to motivation it is useful to distinguish, as do Buchanan and Huczynski,[2] three perspectives.

1. The goals towards which people aim. From this perspective, goals such as the good of the company, or effective performance at work, may provide a degree of motivation for some employees, who could be regarded as committed in so far as they feel they own the goals.
2. The process by which goals and objectives at work are selected, which is quite distinct from the way in which commitment arises within individuals.
3. The social process of motivating others, usually, in a working context, to perform effectively. From this viewpoint, strategies aimed at increasing motivation also affect commitment. It may be true to say that, where commitment is evident, motivation is likely to be strong, particularly if a long-term view is taken of effective performance.

Commitment and performance

The link between commitment and performance, like that between job satisfaction and performance, is not always clear. Strong commitment to the work should in theory result in conscientious and self-directed application to do the job, regular attendance, and a high level of effort, but this has not been proved by research. Commitment to the organization is also thought to be related to the intention to stay, in other words, loyalty to the company.

The significance of commitment

The significance of commitment has been emphasized by such writers as:

*   *McGregor*,[3] who stated that the greatest challenge to personnel managers is to integrate the needs of the organization with the personal needs of its members.
*   *Pascale and Athos*[4] — their study of the reasons for Japanese success attributed much of it to the creation of powerful organizational cultures, from which are derived the shared values between management and workers which emphasize mutuality.
*   *Peters and Austin*,[5] who advised organizations: 'Trust people and treat them like adults, enthuse them by lively and imaginative leadership, develop and demonstrate an obsession for quality, make them feel

they own the business, and your workforce will respond with total commitment.'

- *Walton,[6]* who wrote that the basis of commitment strategy should be 'a management philosophy that acknowledges the legitimate claims of the company's multiple stakeholders — owners, employees, customers and the public. At the centre of this philosophy is a belief that eliciting employee commitment will lead to enhanced performance.'

Creating commitment

As suggested by Martin and Nicholls,[7] there are three major 'pillars' of commitment:

1. a sense of belonging to the organization;
2. a sense of excitement in the job;
3. confidence in management.

A sense of belonging

Creating a sense of belonging
To create a sense of belonging, one must get people to identify with the organization; to believe that it is worth working for; to feel comfortable with, indeed to support, its mission (what it is setting out to do), its values (what management believes to be important) and its norms (the accepted ways of behaving in the organization).

The importance of 'ownership'
A sense of belonging is enhanced if there is a feeling of 'ownership' among employees. Not just in the literal sense of owning shares (although this can help) but in the sense of believing that they are genuinely accepted by management as a key part of the organization. This important concept of 'ownership' extends to participating in decisions on new developments and changes in working practices which affect the individuals concerned. If they can be involved in making those decisions and if they feel that their ideas have been listened to and that they have contributed to the outcome, then they are more likely to accept the decision or change because it is owned by them rather than being imposed by management.

A sense of excitement in the job

A sense of excitement in the job can be created by concentrating on the intrinsic motivating factors as listed in Chapter 7 and using these principles to govern the way in which jobs are designed (see Chapter 13). Excitement in the job is also created by the quality of leadership and the willingness of managers and supervisors to recognize that they will get increased motivation and commitment if they pay continuous attention to the way in which they delegate responsibility and give their staff the scope to use their skills and abilities.

Confidence in management

Confidence in management is most likely to be created and sustained if the organization is successful and appears likely to maintain its success. Management has to demonstrate that it knows where it is going, that it knows how it is going to get there and that it is capable of turning these intentions and plans into reality. This cannot, however, be left to chance. It is necessary to inform everyone concerned of the company's achievements or, in harder times, of the determination of management to overcome the problems and how they intend to act.

Commitment strategies are discussed in Chapter 14, page 275–276.

References

1. White, G *Employee Commitment*. Advisory, Conciliation and Arbitration Service, Work Research Unit Occasional Paper 38, October 1987.
2. Buchanan, D A and Huczynski, A A *Organizational Behaviour*. Prentice-Hall, New York, 1985.
3. McGregor, D *The Human Side of Enterprise*. McGraw-Hill, New York, 1960.
4. Pascale, R and Athos, A *The Art of Japanese Management*. Simon and Schuster, New York, 1981.
5. Peters, T and Austin, N *A Passion for Excellence*. London, Collins, 1985.
6. Walton, R 'From control to commitment in the work-place', *Harvard Business Review* March–April 1985.
7. Martin, P and Nicholls, J *Creating a Committed Workforce*. Institute of Personnel Management, London 1987.

9

How Organizations Function

The basis upon which organizations function

Organizations are best regarded as systems which exist within an ever-changing and often turbulent environment in order to transform inputs (human, financial and physical resources) into outputs (goods or services). This transformation is achieved by the use of technology and operational and administrative systems. The key factors affecting this are structure, culture and processes.

Structure — formal and informal organization

The structure of an organization consists of units and functions. These contain positions in which job holders are accountable for achieving results. Between these positions relationships exist which require the exercise of authority and the exchange of information. In the traditional 'command and control' structure there is, therefore, what used to be called a 'chain of command', starting at the top, defining a hierarchy of positions and indicating who is accountable to whom for what. A defined organization structure attempts to describe how the overall management task has been divided into a number of activities and to indicate how these activities are directed, coordinated and controlled. The structure may be presented in organization charts and manuals which set out the formal organization of relationships and describe who is supposed to do what.

The command and control structure as described above is, however, not a satisfactory model for the way in which organizations actually function. First, many organizations find that they have to operate more flexibly and recognize that it is *collective* effort which achieves organizational ends. In this type of fluid and responsive organization, authoritarianism no longer works. What has to be developed is a teamwork approach which involves devolving responsibility to largely autonomous work groups and recognizing that the organization has to develop a culture of consent.

Secondly, the formal organization, as so described, may usefully define the theoretical framework for getting things done, but it cannot convey *how* that work is done. There is, in fact, a powerful informal organization, as was first suggested in 1938 by a businessman, Chester Barnard.[1] He believed that organizations are cooperative systems, not the products of mechanical engineering or of paperwork bureaucracies. He advocated natural groups within the organization, upward communication and leaders who function as cohesive forces. He emphasized the significance of the informal roles and relationships which strongly influence the way the formal structure operates.

Organization theory related to structures is considered in Chapter 11, and approaches to the design of organizations are described in Chapter 12.

How the organization functions is also determined by its culture and by the processes which affect its informal operations.

Culture

Corporate culture manifests itself as 'the way things are done around here'. It is founded on well-established beliefs and assumptions and, as described in Chapter 10, can make a significant impact on the performance of the organization.

Processes

The organizational processes which affect the way the organization functions are those related to group behaviour, team roles, leadership, conflict, power and politics. These are discussed below.

Group behaviour

Organizations consist of groups of people working together. Interactions take place within and between groups and the degree to which these processes are formalized varies according to the organizational context. To understand and influence organizational behaviour, one must understand how groups behave. In particular, this means considering the nature of:

- formal groups
- informal groups
- the processes that take place within groups

- group cohesion
- the factors that make for group effectiveness.

Formal groups

Formal groups are set up by organizations to achieve a defined purpose. People are brought together with the necessary skills to carry out the tasks and a system exists for directing, co-ordinating and controlling the group's activities. The structure, composition and size of the group will depend largely on the nature of the task; although tradition, organizational culture and management style may exert considerable influence. The more routine or clearly defined the task is the more structured the group will be. In a highly structured group the leader will have a positive role and may well adopt an authoritarian style. The role of each member of the group will be precise and a hierarchy of authority is likely to exist. The more ambiguous the task the more difficult it will be to structure the group. The leader's role is more likely to be supportive — he will tend to concentrate on encouragement and co-ordination rather than on issuing orders. The group will operate in a more democratic way and individual roles will be fluid and less clearly defined.

Informal groups

Informal groups are set up by people in organizations who have some affinity for one another. It could be said that formal groups satisfy the needs of the organization while informal groups satisfy the needs of their members. One of the main aims of organization design and development should be to ensure, so far as possible, that the basis upon which activities are grouped together and the way in which groups are allowed or encouraged to behave satisfy both these needs. The values and norms established by informal groups can work against the organization. This was first clearly established in the Hawthorne studies which revealed that groups could regulate their own behaviour and output levels irrespective of what management wanted. An understanding of the processes that take place within groups can, however, help to make them work for, rather than against, what the organization needs.

Group processes

As mentioned above, the way in which groups function is affected by the task and by the norms in the organization. An additional factor is size.

There is a greater diversity of talent, skills and knowledge in a large group, but individuals find it more difficult to make their presence felt. According to Handy,[2] for best participation and for highest all-round involvement, the optimum size is between five and seven. But to achieve the requisite breadth of knowledge the group may have to be considerably larger, and this makes greater demands on the skills of the leader in getting participation.

The main processes that take place within groups are:

Interaction

There are three basic channels of communication within groups, as illustrated below:

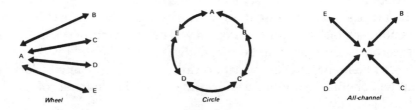

These patterns were defined by Leavitt,[3] and he and subsequent researchers found the following to be true:

● Wheel groups, where the task is straightforward, work faster, need fewer messages to solve problems and make fewer errors than circle groups, but they are inflexible if the task changes.
● Circle groups are faster in solving complex problems than wheel groups.
● All-channel groups are the most flexible and function well in complex, open-ended situations.

The level of satisfaction for individuals is lowest in the circle, fairly high in the all-channel and mixed in the wheel, where the leader is more satisfied than the outlying members.

Task and maintenance functions

The following functions need to be carried out in groups:

● task — initiating, information seeking, diagnosing, opinion-seeking, evaluating, decision-managing;
● maintenance — encouraging, compromising, peace-keeping, clarifying, summarizing, standard-setting.

It is the job of the group leader or leaders to ensure that these functions operate effectively. Leaderless groups can work, but only in special circumstances. A leader is almost essential — whether official or self-appointed. The style adopted by the leader affects the way the group operates. If he is respected, this will increase the group's cohesiveness and its ability to get things done. An inappropriately authoritarian style creates tension and resentment. An overpermissive style means that respect for the leader diminishes and the group does not function so effectively.

Group ideology
In the course of interacting and carrying out its task and maintenance functions, the group develops an ideology which affects the attitudes and actions of its members and the degree of satisfaction which they feel.

Identification
An individual will identify with his group if he likes the other members, approves of the purpose and work of the group and wishes to be associated with the standing of the group in the organization. Identification will be more complex if the standing of the group is good.

Group cohesion
If the group ideology is strong and individual members identify closely with the group, it will become increasingly cohesive. Group norms or implicit rules will be evolved which define what is acceptable behaviour and what is not. The impact of group cohesion can, however, result in negative as well as positive results. Janis's[4] study of the decision making of US foreign policy groups established that a cohesive group of individuals, sharing a common fate, exerts a strong pressure towards conformity. He coined the term 'group think' to describe the exaggeration of irrational tendencies which appears to occur in groups. He argued that a group setting can magnify weakness of judgement. To be 'one of us' is not always a good thing in management (or political) circles. A sturdy spirit of independence, even a maverick tendency, may be more conducive to correct decision making. Although team working is a good thing, so is flexibility. These need not be incompatible, but could be if there is too much emphasis on cohesion and loyalty to the group.

Group development

Tuckman[5] has identified four stages of group development:

1. *Forming* when there is anxiety, dependence on the leader and testing to

find out the nature of the situation and the task, and what behaviour is acceptable.

2. *Storming* where there is conflict, emotional resistance to the demands of the task, resistance to control and even rebellion against the leader.
3. *Norming* when group cohesion is developed, norms emerge, views are exchanged openly, mutual support and cooperation increase and the group acquires a sense of its identity.
4. *Performing* when interpersonal problems are resolved, roles are flexible and functional, there are constructive attempts to complete tasks and energy is available for effective work.

Group effectiveness

An effective group is likely to be one in which the structure, leadership and methods of operation are relevant to the requirements of the task. The Tavistock Institute, Longwall, and Ahmedabad studies referred to in Chapter 11 emphasized the importance of commitment to the whole group task and the need to group people in a way which ensures that they are related to each other by way of the requirements of task performance and task interdependence.

In an effective group, its purpose is clear and its members feel that the task is important both to them and the organization (the concept of saliency). According to McGregor,[6] the main features of a well-functioning, creative group are as follows:

1. The atmosphere tends to be informal, comfortable, and relaxed.
2. There is a lot of discussion in which initially everyone participates, but it remains pertinent to the task of the group.
3. The task or objective of the group is well understood and accepted by the members. There will have been free discussion of the objective at some point until it was formulated in such a way that the members of the group could commit themselves to it.
4. The members listen to each other. Every idea is given a hearing. People do not appear to be afraid of being considered foolish by putting forth a creative thought even if it seems fairly extreme.
5. There is disagreement. Disagreements are not suppressed or overridden by premature group action. The reasons are carefully examined, and the group seeks to resolve them rather than to dominate the dissenter.
6. Most decisions are reached by a kind of consensus in which it is clear that everybody is in general agreement and willing to go along.

Formal voting is at a minimum; the group does not accept a simple majority as a proper basis for action.

7. Criticism is frequent, frank and relatively comfortable. There is little evidence of personal attack, either openly or in a hidden fashion.
8. People are free in expressing their feelings as well as their ideas both on the problem and on the group's operation.
9. When action is taken, clear assignments are made and accepted.
10. The leader of the group does not dominate it, nor does the group defer unduly to him. There is little evidence of a struggle for power as the group operates. The issue is not who controls, but how to get the job done.

These characteristics together present an ideal which might be striven for but is seldom attained. The extent to which it is possible or even desirable for them to be achieved depends on the situation. A mechanistic or bureaucratic type of enterprise — where this is appropriate to the technology — cannot allow its formal organizational units to function just like this, although it should try to ensure that any committees, task forces, or project teams that are set up do exhibit these forms of behaviour.

Team roles

Bales[7] found that effective teams need people who help to get things done. They also need people who are concerned with the social side of working in a group. Task-orientated team members are most influential but socially inclined members are most liked. Belbin[8] identified eight different roles played by management team members.

1. *Chairmen* — control the way in which a team moves towards the group objectives by making the best use of team resources; recognizing where the team's strengths and weaknesses lie and ensuring that the best use is made of each team member's role.
2. *Shapers* — specify the ways in which team effort is applied, directing attention generally to the setting of objectives and priorities and seeking to impose some shape or pattern on group discussion and on the outcome of group activities.
3. *Company workers* — turn concepts and plans into practical working procedures and carry out agreed plans systematically and efficiently.
4. *Plants* — specify new ideas and strategies, with special attention to major issues. Look for possible breaks in approaches to the problems with which the group is confronted.
5. *Resource investigators* — explore and report on ideas, developments and

resources outside the group, creating external contacts that might be useful to the team and conducting any subsequent negotiations.

6. *Monitor-evaluators* — analyse problems and evaluate ideas and suggestions so that the team is better placed to take better decisions.

7. *Team workers* — support members in their strengths (ie building on their suggestions), underpin members in their shortcomings, improve communications between members and foster team spirit generously.

8. *Completer-finishers* — ensure that the team is protected from mistakes, actively search for work which needs more than a usual degree of attention, and maintain a sense of urgency in the team.

Belbin suggests that although the main roles of team members can be slotted into one or other of these categories, most people have an alternative, back-up role which they use as necessary.

Leadership

The function of the leader is to achieve the task set for him or her with the help of the group. The leader and the group are therefore interdependent.

Main roles

The leader has two main roles. First he or she must achieve the task. Secondly, he or she has to maintain effective relationships between themselves and the group and the individuals in it — effective in the sense that they are conducive to achieving the task. These two roles were first identified by the Ohio State University researchers (Halpin and Winer),[9] who identified the two dimensions of leadership behaviour:

- Initiating structure — specifying ways and means of accomplishing the goals of the group and co-ordinating the activities of its members.
- Consideration — motivating the members of the group to accept the group goals and to work at the group task while at the same time maintaining internal harmony and satisfaction.

In fulfilling his or her role, the leader has to satisfy the following needs:

1. *Task needs.* The group exists to achieve a common purpose or task. The leader's role is to ensure that this purpose is fulfilled. If it is not, he or she will lose the confidence of the group and the result will be frustration, disenchantment, criticism and, possibly, the ultimate disintegration of the group.

2. *Group maintenance needs.* To achieve its objectives, the group needs to be

held together. The leader's job is to build up and maintain team spirit and morale.

3. *Individual needs.* Individuals have their own needs which they expect to be satisfied at work. The leader's task is to be aware of these needs so that where necessary he or she can take steps to harmonize them with the needs of the task and the group.

As John Adair[10] pointed out, these three needs are interdependent. The leader's actions in one area affect both the others; thus successful achievement of the task is essential if the group is to be held together or the individual is to be motivated to give his or her best effort to the job. Action directed at meeting group or individual needs must be related to the needs of the task. It is impossible to consider individuals in isolation from the group or to consider the group without referring to the individuals within it. If any need is neglected, one of the others will suffer and the leader will be less successful.

Exercising leadership

The kind of leadership exercised will be related to the nature of the task and the people being led. It will also depend on the environment and, of course, on the actual leader. Analysing the qualities of leadership in terms of intelligence, initiative, self-assurance and so on has only limited value. The qualities required may be different in different situations. It is more useful to adopt a contingency approach and take account of the variables the leader has to deal with; especially the task, the group and his or her own position in the group.

Fiedler,[11] in particular, concentrated upon the relationship between the leader and the group and the structure of the task as determinants in the choice of the most effective style of leadership. His research indicated that the leaders of the most effective groups tended to maintain greater distance between themselves and their subordinates than the leaders of less effective groups. He found that an 'initiating structure' approach was most effective when the situation was either very favourable or unfavourable to the leader, while 'consideration' was more appropriate when the situation was only moderately favourable. Fiedler also emphasized the 'situational' aspects of leadership:

> Leadership performance then depends as much on the organization as on the leader's own attributes. Except perhaps for the unusual case, it is simply not meaningful to speak of an effective leader and an ineffective leader; we

can only speak of a leader who tends to be effective in one situation and ineffective in another.

Leadership style

The most effective leaders fit their style to the situation, which includes their own preferred style of operating and personal characteristics as well as the nature of the task and the group.

Leadership style is the way in which managers exercise their leadership role — it characterizes their approach to managing people. Leadership styles tend to be defined in terms of extremes:

authoritarian	—	democratic
autocratic	—	participative
job-centred	—	people-centred
close, directive	—	general, permissive

In fact, most managers develop an approach somewhere between the two extremes. There is no one style appropriate to all situations. Managers must be prepared to adjust their style according to the circumstances. This does not imply inconsistency. Effective managers adopt the same approach in similar situations.

A continuum of leadership behaviour based on the work of Tannenbaum and Schmidt[12] (Figure 9.1) suggests that there are five basic styles: tell, sell, consult, join and delegate. These styles move from the authoritarian to the democratic, but it is not suggested that one is better than the other. There will be circumstances when a manager has to *tell* someone to do something; in other circumstances he may have to sell the idea or consult his subordinates in one way or another. The job of the leader is to analyse the situation and apply the most appropriate style in accordance with their knowledge of their capabilities and limitations.

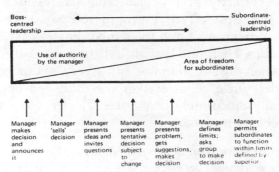

Figure 9.1 Continuum of leadership behaviour

Conflict

Conflict is inevitable in organizations because they function by means of adjustments and compromises among competitive elements in their structure and membership. These elements produce conflict of two kinds: horizontal conflict between functions, departments and groups, and vertical conflict between different levels in the hierarchy.

Conflict also arises when there is change, because it may be seen as a threat to be challenged or resisted, or when there is frustration — this may produce an aggressive reaction; fight rather than flight. Conflict is not to be deplored. It is an inevitable result of progress and change and it can and should be used constructively.

Conflict between individuals raises fewer problems than conflict between groups. Individuals can act independently and resolve their differences. Members of groups may have to accept the norms, goals, and values of their group. The individual's loyalty will usually be to his own group if it is in conflict with others.

Techniques of conflict management are discussed in Chapter 14 (pages 279–280).

Power

Organizations exist to get things done and in the process of doing this people or groups exercise power. Directly or indirectly, the use of power in influencing behaviour is a pervading feature of organizations, whether it is exerted by managers, specialists, informal groups or trade union officials.

Sources of power

Power is clearly linked to position and rank. But to a certain degree it has to be earned. Managers give orders to their subordinates but they will get more out of them if they obtain their willing cooperation rather than their grudging submission. Power is bestowed upon managers, but they also have to justify their use of it. There are, however, other sources of power, namely:

- *Access to people with power.* Proximity or a direct line obviously gives people more scope to exert influence, actual or perceived. That is why secretaries are important.
- *Control over information.* 'Knowledge is power' or, alternatively, 'authority goes to the one who knows'. If people are in the know, they are in

a better position to control events or, if they want to play politics, to put a spoke in other people's wheels.

- *Control over results.* Power goes to those who can control what the organization achieves. When trade unions strike, they are exercising this sort of power.
- *Control over resources.* If control is exercised over resources, such as money, manpower, equipment or services that anyone else needs, the person in that position will have power.
- *Control over rewards and punishments.* People have power if they can give rewards or punishments or influence others who control them.
- *Expertise.* People gain and keep power if they can convince others that they are the experts.
- *Identification.* Power can be achieved over others if they identify with what is being done or with the individual concerned. This is what charismatic leaders do by enthusiasm, dedication, getting people involved and sheer force of personality.

Politics

Power and politics are inextricably mixed, and in any organization there will inevitably be people who want to achieve their satisfaction by acquiring power, legitimately or illegitimately.

Organizations consist of individuals who, while they are ostensibly there to achieve a common purpose, are, at the same time, driven by their own needs to achieve their own goals. Effective management is the process of harmonizing individual endeavour and ambition to the common good. Some individuals genuinely believe that using political means to achieve their goals will benefit the organization as well as themselves. Others rationalize this belief. Yet others unashamedly pursue their own ends.

It can be argued that a political approach to management is inevitable and even desirable in any organization where the clarity of goals is not absolute, where the decision-making process is not clear cut and where the authority to make decisions is not evenly or appropriately distributed. And there can be few organizations where one or more of these conditions do not apply. Kakabadse[13] recognizes this point when he says: 'Politics is a process, that of influencing individuals and groups of people to your point of view, where you cannot rely on authority.' In this sense, a political approach can be legitimate as long as the ends are justifiable from the viewpoint of the organization. He identifies seven approaches that organizational politicians adopt:

1. Identify the stakeholders, ie those who have a commitment to act in a particular way.
2. Keep the stakeholders comfortable, concentrating on behaviour, values, attitudes, fears and drives that the individuals will accept, tolerate and manage (comfort zones).
3. Fit the image — work on the comfort zones and align their image to that of the people with power.
4. Use the network — identify the interest groups and people of influence.
5. Enter the network — identify the gatekeepers; adhere to the norms.
6. Make deals — agree to support other people where this is a mutual benefit.
7. Withhold and withdraw — withhold information as appropriate and withdraw judiciously when the going gets rough.

References

1. Barnard, C *Functions of the Executive*. Harvard University Press, Cambridge, MA, 1938.
2. Handy, C *Understanding Organizations*. Penguin, Harmondsworth, 1981.
3. Leavitt, H 'Some effects of certain communication patterns on group performance', *Journal of Abnormal Psychology*, 1951.
4. Janis, I *Victims of Groupthink*, Houghton Mifflin, Boston MA, 1972.
5. Tuckman, B. 'Development sequences in small groups', *Psychological Bulletin*, **63**, 1965.
6. McGregor, D *The Human Side of Enterprise*. McGraw-Hill, New York, 1966.
7. Bales, R *Interaction Process Analysis*, Addison-Wesley, Reading, MA, 1950.
8. Belbin, M *Management Teams: Why They Succeed or Fail*. Heinemann, London, 1981.
9. Halpin, A and Winer, B *A Factorial Study of the Leader Behaviour Descriptions*. Ohio State University, 1957.
10. Adair, J *The Action-Centred Leader*. McGraw-Hill, London, 1973.
11. Fiedler, F *A Theory of Leadership Effectiveness*, McGraw-Hill, New York, 1967.
12. Tannenbaum, R and Schmidt, W 'How to choose a leadership pattern', *Harvard Business Review*, May–June 1973.
13. Kakabadse, A *The Politics of Management*. Gower, Aldershot, 1983.

10

Corporate Culture

Definition of corporate culture

Corporate culture is the pattern of shared beliefs, attitudes, assumptions and values which, although they may not have been articulated, in the absence of direct instructions, shape the way people act and interact and strongly influence the way that things get done. This culture encompasses the organization's goals, behavioural norms and dominant ideologies. Culture can be expressed through the organization's myths, heroes, legends, stories, jargon, rites and rituals. It is manifested in norms and values which strongly influence organizational behaviour.

The importance of culture to organizations

Corporate culture is a key component in the achievement of an organization's mission and strategies, the improvement of organizational effectiveness and the management of change. The significance of culture arises because it is rooted in deeply held beliefs. It reflects what has worked in the past, being composed of responses which have been accepted because they have met with success. Culture is manifested in norms and values which largely determine organizational behaviour — 'the way things are done around here'.

Corporate culture can work for an organization by creating an environment which is conducive to performance improvement and the management of change. It can work against an organization by erecting barriers which prevent the attainment of corporate strategies. These barriers include resistance to change and lack of commitment.

The impact of culture can include:

- conveying a sense of identity and unity of purpose to members of the organization;

- facilitating the generation of commitment;
- shaping behaviour by providing guidance on what is expected.

Personnel managers have to live within the corporate culture. They must understand it as a basis for diagnosing and solving problems and for developing new policies or procedures. And they may well be involved in managing the culture in times of change or during crises.

The constituents of corporate culture

Corporate culture contains assumptions about the nature of the business and its markets and customers, the way in which business should be carried out, how work should be organized, the sort of people the organization needs and how they should be treated.

A corporate culture can be strong or weak, and a strong culture is not necessarily a good one — it could be the wrong culture and it could be difficult to change. A weak culture, even a practically non-existent culture, may be acceptable if the organization functions well. Within one organization there may be a dominant culture, but there will certainly be many subcultures in different departments or locations.

Corporate cultures are different: that at Mars is totally different from that at Cadbury's; IBM and ICL are quite unalike; no one could have anything to do with Allied Dunbar or the Prudential and not become quickly aware that they are fundamentally different. But you would be hard put to it to attribute the relative levels of success achieved by each of these pairs to particular cultural attributes.

To an extent, the interest in the concept of corporate culture has been encouraged by attempts to uncover the secrets of Japanese success. Pascale and Athos in *The Art of Japanese Management*[1] emphasized the advantages of the Japanese culture in the shape of its ability to help Japanese executives manage ambiguity, uncertainty and imperfection, and in its emphasis on interdependence as the most approved mode of relationship. Although there may be many good things about Japanese corporate culture which we could usefully apply in our own organizations, it is not necessarily a model which we should slavishly copy.

Manifestations of culture

Culture is manifested in the form of:

- *norms* — the unwritten rules of behaviour.
- *values* — what is regarded as important, expressed as beliefs on what is best or good for the organization and what ought to happen. Values

can be implicit or articulated in value statements. The value set of an organization may only be recognized at the top level, or the values may be shared so that the enterprise could be described as value driven. Values can be espoused but not put into practice. They may be supported by statements describing general principles of behaviour.

- *artefacts* — the tangible aspects of an organization that people hear, see or feel.
- *organization climate* — the working atmosphere of the enterprise. This can be described as the explicit culture and was defined by Payne and Pugh[2] as a concept 'reflecting the content and strength of the prevalent values, norms, attitudes, behaviours and feelings of a social system'.
- *management style* — the way in which managers behave and exercise leadership and authority.
- *organization behaviour* — the ways in which people act and interact in the organization.
- *the structure of the organization.*
- *the processes and systems* used in the organization.

Varieties of culture

The strength of a culture clearly influences its impact on corporate behaviour. Strong cultures have more widely shared and more clearly expressed beliefs and values than do weak ones. These values will probably have been developed over a considerable period of time and they will be perceived as functional in the sense that they help the organization achieve its purpose.

How corporate culture is formed

Culture is learned. Schein[3] suggests that there are two ways in which this learning takes place. First, there is the trauma model, in which members of the organization learn to cope with some threat by the erection of defence mechanisms. Second, there is the 'positive reinforcement' model, where things which seem to work become embedded and entrenched. Learning takes place as people adapt to and cope with external pressures, and as they develop successful approaches and mechanisms to handle the technologies of their organization.

Environmental influences make a strong impact on the corporate culture. The type of activity the organization carries out largely determines the way it goes about its business, and this in turn affects the way the corporate culture develops and is manifested within the organization.

Against this background, corporate culture is created by organizational members, with the values, philosophy, beliefs, assumptions and norms of top management playing a dominant role.

Development of culture

Corporate culture can be described as a system, as illustrated in Figure 10.1 below, which is continuously affected by events and influences over time. These derive from the organization's external environment and from its internal processes, systems and technology.

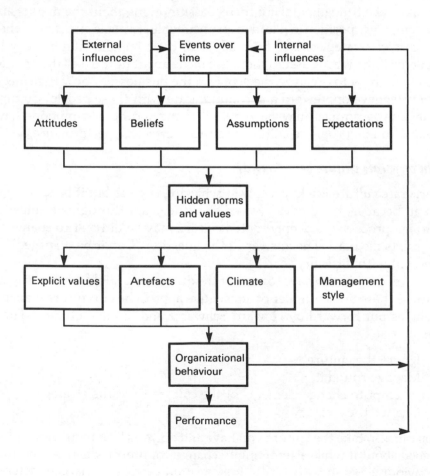

Figure 10.1 Corporate culture as a system

Culture management

Because corporate culture is based on taken-for-granted assumptions and beliefs about what is good and not good for the organization, it is a somewhat elusive concept. There may not be a single culture but a number of cultures spread throughout the organization; and this does not make 'managing' the culture any easier. In any case, there is no such thing as a 'good' or 'bad' culture, but only cultures which are appropriate or inappropriate. If you have an appropriate culture, its management consists of no more than maintaining the existing values, climate and management style; change is not necessary.

Corporate cultures can, however, have significant effects on behaviour. These can be fundamental if incorrect assumptions about the market and the company's position in it lead to an unsuitable strategic plan. Even when the correct strategies have been adopted, their implementation may be hindered if the wrong assumptions are made about how to sell the product or service; how to organize the people in the business; or how to manage, motivate, develop, reward and communicate with these people. Cultural change programmes may be required if the wrong assumptions have created an inappropriate culture and this is affecting performance.

Can corporate culture be managed?

Corporate culture is a key factor in achieving success but it is not easy to get at. Because it will have evolved over the years through a number of learning processes, a deeply rooted culture may be difficult to change — old habits die hard. The answer to the question, 'Can it be managed?' is, 'Yes, but with difficulty'.

However, you also have to answer the question, 'Should it be managed?' because there are a number of alternative approaches to culture management, as put forward by Howard Schwartz and Stanley Davies.[4] These are:

- Ignore the culture.
- Manage round it.
- Attempt to change elements of the culture to fit the strategy.
- Change the strategy.

You can also take the culture you have and do your best to maintain what is good about it while attempting to change counterproductive aspects of behaviour.

Deal and Kennedy[5] said that there are only five reasons to justify large-scale cultural change:

1. if your company has strong values that do not fit a changing environment;
2. if the industry is very competitive and moves with lightning speed;
3. if your company is mediocre or worse;
4. if your company is about to join the ranks of the very largest companies;
5. if your company is small but growing rapidly.

Deal and Kennedy say that if none of these reasons apply, don't do it. Their analysis of 10 cases of attempted cultural change indicated that it will cost between 5 and 10 per cent of what you already spend on the people whose behaviour is supposed to change and even then you are likely to get only half the improvement you want. They warn that it costs a lot (in time, effort and money) and will take a long time.

How should corporate culture be managed?

A culture management programme involves the following steps, which are described in more detail later in this section:

1. Identify basic assumptions and beliefs and challenge them if necessary.
2. Define or redefine the core values — stated or unstated.
3. Analyse the organizational climate.
4. Analyse the management style.
5. Plan and implement on the basis of steps 1 to 4 what aspects of the culture (as defined by assumptions, values, climate and management style) need to be changed and what aspects should be maintained or reinforced.

A key part is played in this process by the chief executive who, with the support of his team, achieves excellence by defining the organization's mission, getting his vision of what needs to be done across to everyone (visioning), defining and promulgating what he believes to be the right organizational values, exercising leadership in order to motivate the members of the organization, and ensuring that they are involved in and committed to achieving its objectives.

Personnel specialists should be closely involved in the analytical work. They should also play a major part in the culture management programme, as described below.

The approaches that can be adopted to manage corporate culture and help to achieve cultural change are:

1. *Reorganization* to facilitate integration, to create departments or jobs

which are responsible for new activities or to eliminate unnecessary layers of management.

2. *Organization development* to improve the effectiveness with which an organization functions and responds to change.

3. *Communications* to get the message across about the values and to achieve objectives for a communications change programme such as the following:

   (a) increase the identification of staff with the firm and therefore enhance their commitment;

   (b) provide the opportunity for all levels of staff to become more involved in the firm's affairs;

   (c) generate ideas from staff to develop the business, improve the levels of customer service and increase productivity.

4. *Training* to help form new attitudes to such matters as customer service, quality, managing and motivating people or productivity; to increase commitment to the firm and its values; to review and challenge assumptions; and to improve skills or teach new skills.

5. *Recruitment* to set out deliberately to change the type of people recruited to fit the desired culture or to reinforce the existing culture by drawing up related job specifications and finding candidates who meet those specifications.

6. *Performance management* to ensure that managers, supervisors and staff are aware of their objectives and are assessed on the basis of the results they achieve, and that performance improvement programmes consisting of self-development, coaching, counselling and training are used to capitalize on strengths or overcome weaknesses.

7. *Reward management* to enhance the cultural assumption that rewards should be related to achievement.

References

1. Pascale, R and Athos, A *The Art of Japanese Management*. Simon & Schuster, New York, 1981.
2. Payne, R and Pugh, D 'Organisational Structure and Climate' in Handbook of Industrial and Organisational Psychology, ed by Dumette, M, Rand-McNally, New York, 1976.
3. Schein, E *Organizational Dynamics*, Summer 1983.
4. Schwartz, H and Davis, D *Matching Corporate Culture and Strategy*. MAP Concept Paper, Cambridge, MA, 1983.
5. Deal, T and Kennedy, A *Corporate Cultures*. Addison-Wesley, Reading, MA, 1982.

Part III
Organization Design and Effectiveness

This part deals with the analyses which have to be carried out and the plans that must be made to design and develop an effective organization.

Organizational design is concerned with the overall structure: the allocation of responsibilities, the grouping of activities and the definition of lines of communication and control. Within this structure, attention has to be paid to the design of individual jobs so that they make sense in terms of the work that has to be carried out and, importantly, provide, so far as possible, for the motivation of job holders through giving them opportunities for achievement, responsibility and the utilization of the skills they possess or can be helped to acquire.

Organizational effectiveness is discussed as a matter which is very much the concern of personnel managers as well as line management. The various approaches to improving organizational effectiveness are discussed at length in Chapter 14. These include change management (a vital concern for personnel managers who can provide and apply pressure to many of the levers for change within organizations), motivation and commitment strategies, teambuilding, conflict and stress management and the important areas of total quality management and customer service.

11

Organization Structure

Organizations exist to get work done. The organization itself is an entity which is there for a purpose. This determines what it sets out to do, but *what* it actually does and *how* it does it will be influenced by a number of external and internal forces, including the environment and the history of the organization.

The process of organizing can be described as the design, development and maintenance of a system of co-ordinated activities in which individuals and groups of people work co-operatively under authority and leadership towards commonly understood and accepted goals. The key word in that definition is 'system'. Organizations are systems which, as affected by their environment, have a structure which has both formal and informal elements.

All organizations have some form of structure, which has been defined by Child[1] as comprising 'all the tangible and regularly occurring features which help to shape its members' behaviour'. This chapter deals with the considerations that affect the structure of the organizations. It does this by reviewing the various organization 'models' developed by the theorists on this subject. These concepts are intended to provide a background against which the design of organizations and jobs, as discussed in Part III of this book, can be carried out.

Organization models

Organizations vary in their complexity, but in every case it is necessary to divide the overall management task into a variety of activities and to establish means of co-ordinating and controlling these activities. This design process leads to the development of a formal organization structure consisting of units and positions between which there are relationships involving the exercise of authority and the communication and exchange of information.

The structure must be appropriate to the organization's purpose and to the situation in which it exists. As Lupton[2] says: 'Organizations are seen as patterns of human tasks and relationships, shaped so as to allow at least survival, at most growth and development, in environments which constrain, but which also offer opportunities.'

Personnel managers are, or should be, involved in the design and development of organizations. They should base their contribution on an understanding of the forces shaping their own organization. To do this, they need tools which will help them to analyse and appreciate what is happening. These tools are provided in the form of 'models' developed by a number of writers and researchers on organization.

The original model derived from the work of the *classical school* of organization theorists, who believed that the design of the structure should conform to certain general principles. The *human relations school*, however, emphasized that the way organizations function and how, therefore, they should be structured, is primarily dependent on how people behave, interact and create the informal organization. The *bureaucratic model* developed by Weber suggested that there were circumstances in which organizations did require formal hierarchies and clear definitions of responsibilities. The *systems* and *contingency schools* stressed correctly that the way organizations functioned and were structured was closely related to their environment, technology and the amount of change and differentiation to which they were subjected. More recently, new organization models emphasizing the importance of *flexibility* and *teamwork* have evolved.

It should be remembered, however, that while these models either contribute to our understanding of the different forms of organization or provide a basis for tackling organizational problems they do not add up to a universal theory of organization. As Perrow[3] wrote: 'We know enough about organizations now to recognize that most generalizations that are applicable to all organizations are too obvious or too general to be of much use for specific predictions.' And the earliest models produced by the scientific management or 'classical' school fell into this trap, which is why, as will emerge later, the contingency approach seems to have most to offer.

The classical school

The classical or scientific management school, as represented by Fayol, Taylor and Urwick believed in control, order and formality. Organizations need to minimize the opportunity for unfortunate and uncontrollable informal relations, leaving room only for the formal ones. From these overriding principles the following concepts are derived:

1. *Structure.* Formal structures are required to provide orderly relationships between functions. The basic structure contains the line organization, which exercises delegated authority in performing the functions of the enterprise, and the staff organization which offers advice and provides services required by the line organization. Structural considerations include the span of control, which relates to the number of subordinates an executive can manage and the number of levels in the hierarchy.

2. *Specialization.* As the human organization grows, work must be broken down along lines as natural as possible to provide well-defined areas of specialization. This is the classical economic theory of the division of labour and all other scientific-management principles are derived from it.

3. *Co-ordination.* The need for specialization creates the need for co-ordination. The many different functions performed by the members of an organization must be co-ordinated or tied together in order that they contribute jointly to the end result. To achieve this, members have to carry out their work as and when required so that each contribution fits the contribution of others.

4. *Authority.* Organizations achieve order and regularity by the use of authority implemented through a defined hierarchy or chain of command.

5. *Continuity.* Organizations should be designed to achieve continuity, stability and predictability. This must be done by minimizing disruptions caused by personality and individual idiosyncrasy. The organization consists of replaceable members, and its design should not be affected by the people who happen to be employed in it.

The classical or scientific management model has been attacked vigorously because it is too rigid and because it makes no allowance for situational factors such as the environment or technology. Neither does it take account of change or human factors, including the informal organization. But this approach, with its emphasis on organization charts and manuals, job descriptions, clear definitions of responsibility and authority and limited spans of control, still thrives. As Lupton[2] pointed out: 'The attraction of the classical design from the point of view of top management is that it seems to offer them control.' Managers like to think they are rational and this has all the appearance of a rational approach. Many line managers when asked to describe their organizations will draw hierarchical charts, produce job descriptions and use such expressions as chain of command, levels of authority, line and staff and span of control. This is the language of classical theory and it is not inherently wrong — most people prefer some structure and find it difficult to tolerate ambiguity. But it must not be applied too rigidly. There are other considerations.

The human relations school

The classical school reigned supreme until the late 1930s and still holds sway in the 1990s, as mentioned above. But in 1938 Barnard[4] emphasized the importance of the informal organization — the network of informal roles and relationships which, for better or worse, strongly influences the way the formal structure operates. He wrote: 'Formal organizations come out of and are necessary to informal organization: but when formal organizations come into operation, they create and require informal organizations.' Much more recently, Child[1] has pointed out that it is misleading to talk about a clear distinction between the formal and the informal organization. Formality *and* informality can be designed into structure. Unofficial policies do exist in organizations but they are not to be confused with informality. Organization designers recognize the relevance of informal relationships but do not implement unofficial structures.

In 1938 Roethlisberger and Dickson[5] reported on the Hawthorne Studies — the first large-scale investigation of productivity and industrial relations, which took place at the Hawthorne plant at Western Electric. This highlighted the importance of informal groups, work restriction norms and decent, humane leadership.

It was widely, if unfairly, believed that supporters of the human relations school approach only wanted organizations to be nice to people. But by appearing to ignore business needs, that is the impression they often made.

The behavioural science school

In the 1960s a number of behavioural scientists emerged who would not like to be described as part of the human relations school, but did in fact subscribe to some of the fundamental beliefs of that school, although these beliefs were refined and re-presented on the basis of further study and research. The most notable contributors to this postwar development were McGregor, Likert and Argyris.

Douglas McGregor

The central principle of organizations that McGregor[6] derived from his Theory Y, as described in Chapter 7, is that of integration — the process of recognizing the needs of both the organization and the individual and creating conditions which will reconcile their needs so that members of the organization can work together for its success and share in its rewards: 'Man will exercise self-direction and self-control in the service of objectives to which he is committed'.

Rensis Likert

Likert[7] derived his concept of organizations based on supportive relationships from his research at the University of Michigan. The initial studies distinguished between job-centred and employee-centred supervisors, and established that employee-centred supervisors were higher producers than the job-centred ones. The studies also distinguished between general and close supervision and showed that general rather than close supervision is more often associated with a high rather than a low level of productivity.

From his analysis of high-producing managers, Likert found that their operations were characterized by attitudes of identification with the organization and its objectives and a high sense of involvement in achieving them. This situation was created by 'harnessing effectively all the major motivational forces which can exercise significant influence in an organizational setting and which, potentially, can be accompanied by co-operative and favourable attitudes.'

The integrating principle of supportive relationships was derived from this analysis. This principle states that:

> The leadership and other processes of the organization must be such as to ensure a maximum probability that in all interactions and all relationships with the organization each member will, in the light of his background, values and expectations, view the experience as supportive and one which builds and maintains his sense of personel worth and importance.

Chrys Argyris

The research carried out by Argyris[8] into personality development in organizations suggested to him 'that the formal organization creates in a healthy individual feelings of failure and frustration, short time perspective and conflict'. He further concluded that the formal work organization requires many members to act in immature rather than adult ways: 'At all levels there is behaviour that is not productive in the sense of helping the organization achieve its objectives. For example, at the lower levels we found apathy, indifference and non-involvement. At the upper levels we found conformity, mistrust, inability to accept new ideas, and fear of risk taking.'

To overcome this problem, Argyris wants individuals to feel that they have a high degree of control over setting their own goals and over defining the paths to these goals. The strategy should be to 'develop a climate in which the difficulties can be openly discussed, the employee's hostility understood and accepted, and a programme defined in which everyone can participate in attempting to develop new designs. Wherever this is impossible, the attempt will be made to design new work worlds that can be integrated with the old and that help the employee obtain more opportunity for psychological success.'[9] Lest this seem too idealistic (a tendency shared by all members of the human relations school), Argyris stresses the need for some structure to provide 'the firm ground on which to anchor one's security'. Organization design has therefore to plan for integration and involvement, although these processes will probably have to take place within the traditional pyramidal structure.

Other contributions to the behavioural science movement

The behavioural science movement, pioneered by the writers mentioned above, but furthered by people such as Herzberg and Blake, continued to emphasize that in organizations the proper study of mankind is man. The research conducted by Herzberg and his colleagues[10] suggests that improvements in organization design must centre on the individual job as the positive source of motivation. If individuals feel that the job is stretching them, they will be moved to perform it well. (Herzberg's theories are dealt with in more detail in Chapter 7.)

Blake and Mouton[11] concentrates on management style — the way in which managers manage, based on their beliefs and values. He suggests that there are two factors: 'concern for people' and 'concern for production' (this is in line with the distinction made by the Ohio State University researchers Halpin and Winer[12] between leadership styles based on 'consideration' or 'initiating' structure). Blake's managerial grid presents a matrix of 81 styles based on nine degrees of concern for people and nine degrees of concern for production. A manager scoring 9 for people and 1 for production would be a 9/1 manager — the softy who lets production slide to avoid offending anyone; someone who scores 1 for people and 9 for production would be too tough, the no-nonsense person who gets the staff out of the door and doesn't care who is hurt in the process. Ideally, one should be 9/9 but most people are probably 5/5 or thereabouts. Blake believes that the process of analysing managerial style along the lines of discussing how to progress to 9/9 is the best way to seek organizational efficiency.

The concepts of these and other behavioural scientists provided the impetus for the organization development movement, whose beliefs were summarized by Bennis[13] as follows:

(a) a new concept of man based on increased knowledge of his complex and shifting needs which replaces an oversimplified, innocent, push-button idea of man;

(b) a new concept of power, based on collaboration and reason, which replaces a model of power based on coercion and threat;

(c) a new concept of organization values, based on humanistic-democratic ideals, which replaces the mechanistic value system of bureaucracy.

Views on the behavioural science school

No one can quarrel with the values expressed by the human relations school and those behavioural scientists associated with it — we are all in favour of virtue. But there are a number of grounds on which the more extreme beliefs of the school can be criticized:

1. It claims that its concepts are universally applicable, yet organizations come in all shapes and sizes, types of activity and context.

2. It ignores the real commercial and technological constraints of industrial life. Instead, it reflects more of an ideological concern for personal development and the rights of the individual rather than a scientific curiosity about the factors affecting organizational efficiency.

3. It overreacts against the excessive formality of the classical or scientific management school by largely ignoring the formal organization.

4. Its emphasis on the need to minimize conflict overlooks the point that conflict is not necessarily undesirable, and may rather be an essential concomitant of change and development.

To be fair, not all behavioural scientists were so naive. Although McGregor's Theory Y was somewhat idealistic, he at least recognized that 'industrial health does not flow automatically from the elimination of dissatisfaction, disagreement, or even open conflict. Peace is not synonymous with organizational health; socially responsible management is not co-extensive with permissive management.'[6]

The bureaucratic model

Meanwhile, as Perrow[14] put it:

> In another part of the management forest, the mechanistic school was gathering its forces and preparing to outflank the forces of light. First came the numbers men — the linear programmers, the budget experts, the financial analysts. . . . Armed with emerging systems concepts, they carried the 'mechanistic' analogy to its fullest — and it was very productive. Their work still goes on, largely untroubled by organizational theory; the theory, it seems clear, will have to adjust to them, rather than the other way around. . . . Then the works of Max Weber, not translated until the 1940s . . . began to find their way into social science thought.

Max Weber coined the term 'bureaucracy' as a label for a type of formal organization in which impersonality and rationality are developed to the highest degree. Bureaucracy, as he conceived it, was the most efficient form of organization because it is coldly logical and because personalized relationships and non-rational, emotional considerations do not get in its way. The ideal bureaucracy, according to Weber, has the following features:

- maximum specialization;
- close job definition as to duties, privileges and boundaries;
- vertical authority patterns;
- decisions based on expert judgement, resting on technical knowledge and on disciplined compliance with the directives of superiors;
- policy and administration are separate;
- maximum use of rules;
- impersonal administration of staff.

At first, with his celebrations of the efficiency of bureaucracy, Weber was received with only reluctant respect, even hostility. Most writers were against bureaucracy. But it turned out, surprisingly, that managers are not. They prefer clear lines of communication, clear specifications of authority and responsibility and clear knowledge of whom they are responsible to. Admittedly, in some situations, as Burns and Stalker[15] point out, they might want absolute clarity but they can't get it. On the other hand there are circumstances when the type of work carried out in an organization requires a bureaucratic approach in the Weberian, not the pejorative 'red tape', sense. The apparently conflicting views of the human relations and bureaucratic schools of thought had to be reconciled. Much of what they said was right, but it was insufficiently related to context. The first step was to look at how organizations worked as systems related to their environment — this was taken by the systems school. At the same time a number of researchers were looking at organizations primarily in relation to their environment; they constitute what may be termed the contingency school.

The systems school

The systems approach to organizations as formulated by Miller and Rice[16] states that organizations should be treated as open systems which are continually dependent upon and influenced by their environments. The basic characteristic of the enterprise as an open system is that it transforms inputs into outputs within its environment.

As Katz and Kahn[17] wrote: 'Systems theory is basically concerned with problems of relationship, of structure and of interdependence.' As a result there is a considerable emphasis on the concept of transactions across boundaries — between the system and its environment and between the different parts of the system. This open and dynamic approach avoided the error of the classical and human relations theorists, who thought of organizations as closed systems and analysed their problems with reference to their internal structures and processes of interaction, without taking account of external influences and the changes they impose or of the technology in the organization.

The socio-technical model

The basic idea of the organization as a system was extended by the Tavistock Institute researchers into the socio-technical model of organizations. The basic principle of this model is that in any system of organization, technical or task aspects are interrelated with the human or social aspects. The emphasis is on interrelationships between, on the one hand, the technical processes of transformation carried out within the organization, and, on the other hand, the organization of work groups and the management structures of the enterprise.

The socio-technical model originated from two major studies carried out by members of the Tavistock Institute: first, the Longwall study in the mines of Durham; and, second, the study of the textile mills in Ahmedabad, India. In the mining study it was found that two very different forms of organization were operated in the same seam and with identical technology. The conventional Longwall system combined a complex formal structure with simple work roles. The miner was committed to only one task and entered into a very limited number of unvarying social relations that were sharply divided between those within the particular task group and those who were outside. With those 'outside' he shared no sense of belongingness and recognized no responsibility to them for the consequences of his actions. The composite Longwall system, in contrast, combined a simple formal structure with complex work roles. The miner in this system had a commitment to the whole group task and consequently found himself drawn into a variety of tasks in co-operation with different members of the work group. As Trist[18] wrote:

> That two such contrasting social systems can effectively operate the same technology is clear enough evidence that there exists an element of choice in designing a work organization. However, it is far from a matter of indifference which form of organization is selected. . . . The technological system and the effectiveness of the total production system will depend upon the adequacy with which the social system is able to cope with these requirements.

The research demonstrated that the composite system showed superiority over the conventional in terms of production and costs. It enabled miners to operate more flexibly and thereby cope better with changing conditions. It made better provision for the personnel needs of miners and reduced stress as measured by absenteeism.

The analysis of the Longwall study suggested that when changes are being made in technology, it is necessary to choose carefully from among the alternatives available for the division in labour, the working practices and the reward system. While the aim should be to exploit the new technology, care should be taken not to threaten the existing social system.

The textile studies in India conducted by Rice were concerned with the redesign of an organization and based upon the socio-technical model. The reorganization was based on the following principles:

1. There is an optimum level of grouping activities, which can be determined only by an analysis of the requirements of the technological system.
2. Grouping should be such that the workers are primarily related to each other by way of the requirements of task performance and task interdependence.
3. Supervisory roles should be designed after analysing the system's

requirements for control and co-ordination. The aim should be to create unified commands which correspond to natural task groupings. This should free the supervisor for his tasks of planning, co-ordinating and controlling; first, by enabling him to detect and to manage the boundary conditions which relate his individual commands to the larger system, and second, by maximizing the autonomous responsibility of the work groups for internal control and co-ordination.

The contingency school

The contingency school consists of writers, such as Burns and Stalker; Woodward; Lawrence and Lorsch; and Perrow, who have analysed a variety of organizations and concluded that their structures and methods of operation are a function of the circumstances in which they exist. They do not subscribe to the view that there is one best way of designing an organization or that simplistic classifications of organizations as formal or informal, bureaucratic or non-bureaucratic are helpful. They are against those who see organizations as mutually opposed social systems (what Burns and Stalker refer to as the 'Manichean world of the Hawthorne studies') which set up formal against informal organizations and against those who impose rigid principles of organization irrespective of the technology or environmental conditions.

Burns and Stalker

Burns and Stalker[15] based their concept of mechanistic and organic organizations on research into a number of Scottish firms in the electronics industry. They emphasized the rate of change in the environment of the organization as being the key factor in determining how it could operate.

In stable conditions a highly structured or 'mechanistic' organization emerges with specialized functions, clearly defined roles, strict administrative routines and a hierarchical system of exercising authoritarian control. In effect, this is the bureaucratic system. However, when the environment is volatile, a rigid system of ranks and routines inhibits the organization's speed and sensitivity of response. In these circumstances the structure is, or should be, 'organic' in the sense that it is a function of the situation in which the enterprise finds itself rather than conforming to any predetermined and rigid view of how it should operate. Individual responsibilities are less clear cut and members of the organization must constantly relate what they are doing to its general situation and specific problems.

Perhaps the most important contribution made by Burns and Stalker was the stress they placed on the suitability of each system to its own specific set of conditions. They concluded their analysis by writing:

> We desire to avoid the suggestion that either system is superior under all circumstances to the other. In particular, nothing in our experience justifies the assumption that mechanistic systems should be superseded by organic in conditions of stability. The beginning of administrative wisdom is the awareness that there is no one optimum type of management system.

Woodward

Woodward's[19] ideas about organization derived from a research project carried out in Essex designed to discover whether the principles of organization laid down by the classical theorists correlate with business success when put into practice. She found considerable variations in patterns of organization which could not be related to size of firm, type of industry or business success. She also found that there was no significant correlation between adherence to the classical principles relating to matters such as span of control or number of levels in the hierarchy, and business success. After further analysis, she concluded:

> When, however, the firms were grouped according to similarity of objectives and techniques of production, and classified in order of the technical complexity of their production systems, each production system was found to be associated with a characteristic pattern of organization. It appeared that technical methods were the most important factor in determining organizational structure and in setting the tone of human relationships inside the firms. The widely accepted assumptions that there are principles of management valid for all types of production systems seemed very doubtful.

Woodward's main contribution to organization theory is, therefore, her belief that different technologies demand different structures and procedures and create different types of relationships.

Lawrence and Lorsch

Lawrence and Lorsch[20] developed their contingency model on the basis of a study of six firms in the plastics industry. Organization, as they define it, is the process of co-ordinating different activities to carry out planned transactions with the environment. The three aspects of environment upon which the design of the organization is contingent are the market, the technology (ie the tasks carried out) and research and development. These may be differentiated along such dimensions as rate of change and uncertainty. This process of reacting to complexity and change by *differentiation* creates a demand for effective *integration* if the organization as a whole is to adapt efficiently to the environment. This concept of differentiation and integration is, in fact, the greatest contribution of Lawrence and Lorsch to organization theory.

They suggested that:

> As organizations deal with their external environments, they become segmented into units, each of which has as its major task the problem of dealing with a part of the conditions outside the firm. . . . These parts of the system need to be linked together towards the accomplishment of the organization's overall purpose.

Their research showed that the two organizations with the most successful records had, in fact, achieved the highest degree of integration of the six, and were also among the most highly differentiated. The differentiation of the various units was more in line with the demands of the environment for those two organizations than for the others.

One of the most important implications of the Lawrence and Lorsch model for organization designers is that, although differentiation demands effective integration, this must not be achieved by minimizing differences and producing a common bland outlook. Instead, integration should be achieved by allowing each department to be as different in its outlook and its structure as its tasks demand — that is, to be highly distinctive — but to use mediating devices such as committees, *ad hoc* project groups and assigned 'integrators' who stand midway between the functions with which they are concerned and are not dominated by any of them. Integration can therefore be achieved by structural means as well as by organizational development interventions designed to increase trust and understanding between groups and to confront conflict.

Perrow

The model developed by Perrow[3] recognizes the importance of structure and the inevitable tendency towards routinization, standardization and bureaucracy in organizations. In accordance with the views of other members of the contingency school, he suggests that different structures can exist within the same firm and that a bureaucratic structure is as appropriate for some tasks as a non-bureaucratic structure is for other tasks.

Charles Handy

Handy[21] describes two types of organization; the 'shamrock' and the federal.

The shamrock organization

The shamrock organization consists of three elements:

- the core workers (the central leaf of the shamrock) — professionals, technicians and managers;
- the contractual fringe — contract workers;
- the flexible labour force consisting of temporary staff.

The federal organization

The federal organization takes the process of decentralization one stage further by establishing each key operational, manufacturing or service provision activity as a distinct, federated unit. Each federal entity runs its own affairs although they are linked together by the overall strategy of the organization and, if it is a public company, are expected to make an appropriate contribution to corporate profitability in order to provide the required return on their shareholders' investments and to keep external predators at bay.

The centre in a federal organization maintains a low profile. The federated activities are expected to provide the required initiative, drive and energy. The centre is at the middle of things, not at the top. It is not just a banker but it does provide resources. Its main role is to coordinate, advise, influence, suggest and help to develop integrated corporate strategies.

New organization models — flexibility and teamwork

Developments in organization theory and structures during the 1980s and early '90s have been mainly empirical. The visible presence of 'new, flexible competitors', as Peters[22] put it; the need to respond to change, challenge and uncertainty; and the impact of new technology, have combined to emphasize the need for flexibility and teamwork. The processes of federalizing and flattening organizations (stripping out layers of middle management) have added to this emphasis.

Kanter[23] has described this as the 'post-entrepreneurial corporation'. This represents a triumph of process over structure; 'relationships and communication and the flexibility to temporarily combine resources are more important than the "formal" channels and reporting relationships represented in an organizational chart . . . What is important is not how responsibilities are divided but how people can pull together to pursue new opportunities.'

Peters[22] suggests that new flexible manufacturing systems and the decentralized availability of the information needed for fast product changeover are leading to the wholesale adoption of cellular manufacturing, 'which eventually concentrates all the physical assets needed for making a product in a self-contained configuration which is tailor-made for team organization'. His prescription for the new model organization is:

- the creation of self-managing teams, responsible for their own support activities such as budgeting and planning;
- managers who act as 'on call' experts, spending most of their time helping teams;
- managers who encourage constant front-line contact among functions;
- no more than five layers of structure;
- the use of small units; 'small within big' configurations everywhere.

Organizations such as British Petroleum (BP) are replacing large, formal hierarchical departments with small, flexible teams, many of them cross-functional, and some of them temporary. The emphasis is on 'networking', in which a broad group of people communicate openly and informally as the need arises. Each team does have a leader, but, in the words of a BP 'Project 1990' document: 'Managers are there to support and empower their staff, not to monitor or control their activities.' The BP head office organization chart has been dubbed The Egg because the various functions such as finance, human resources, corporate strategy, research and IT (information technology) strategy are depicted as a number of elements which network together within an overall context (expressed in an oval shape) but are not linked by formal control and communication channels.

Application of organization theory

The different schools of organization theory provide a number of ways of analysing organizations from the point of view of the formal structure, individual behaviour, the organization as a system and the environmental influences which affect the shape and climate of an organization. The most pragmatic approach is provided by the contingency school. They say: first ensure that you understand the environment, the technology and the existing systems of social relationships, and then design an organization which is *contingent* upon the circumstances of the particular case. There is always some choice, but designers should try to achieve the best fit they can. And in making their choice, they should be aware of the structural, human and systems factors which will influence the design, and of the context within which the organization operates. They must also take into account the culture of the organization, the processes that take place in it, namely change and the exercise of leadership and power, and the effect all this has on relationships (conflict), on individuals (stress) and on groups within the organization. This empirical approach will be largely influenced by environmental and cultural factors and it will have to take particular note of the needs for flexibility and good teamwork.

References

1. Child, J *Organization, A Guide to Problems and Practice*. Harper and Row, London, 1977.
2. Lupton, T '"Best Fit" in the design of organizations', *Personnel Review*, **4**, 1, 1975.
3. Perrow, C *Organizational Analysis. A Sociological View*. Tavistock, London, 1970.
4. Barnard, C *Functions of the Executive*. Harvard University Press, Cambridge, MA, 1938.
5. Roethlisberger, F and Dickson, W *Management and the Worker*. Harvard University Press, Cambridge, MA, 1939.
6. McGregor, D *The Human Side of Enterprise*. McGraw-Hill, New York, 1966.
7. Likert, R *New Patterns of Management*. McGraw-Hill, New York, 1961.
8. Argyris, C *Personality and Organization*. Harper, New York, 1957.
9. Argyris, C *Integrating the Individual and the Organization*. John Wiley, New York, 1964.
10. Herzberg, F *et al, The Motivations to Work*. John Wiley, New York, 1959.
11. Blake, R and Mouton, J *The Managerial Grid*. Gulf Publishing, Houston, TX, 1964.
12. Halpin, A and Winer, B *A Factorial Study of the Leader Behaviour Description*. Ohio State University, 1957.
13. Bennis, W *Organization Department*. Addison-Wesley, Reading, MA, 1969.
14. Perrow, C *The Short and Glorious History of Organizational Theory*. Resource Book in Macro-Organizational Behaviour, R H Miles (ed.), Goodyear Publishing, Santa Monica, CA, 1980.
15. Burns, T and Stalker, G *The Management of Innovation*. Tavistock, London, 1961.
16. Miller, E and Rice, A *Systems of Organization*. Tavistock, London, 1967.
17. Katz, D and Kahn, R *The Social Psychology of Organizations*. John Wiley, New York, 1964.

18. Trist, E *et al*, *Organizational Choice*. Tavistock, London, 1963.
19. Woodward, J *Industrial Organization*. Oxford University Press, 1965.
20. Lawrence, P and Lorsch, J *Organization and Environment*. Harvard University Press, Cambridge, MA, 1967.
21. Handy, C *The Age of Unreason*. Business Books, London, 1989.
22. Peters, T *Thriving on Chaos*. Macmillan, London, 1988.
23. Kanter, R *When Giants Learn to Dance* Simon & Schuster, London, 1989.

12

Organization Design

Much of personnel management in its broadest sense is concerned with providing answers to questions such as 'Who does what?', 'How should functions and people be grouped together?', 'What lines and means of communication need to be established?' and 'How should people be helped to understand their roles in relation to the objectives of the organization and the roles of their colleagues?'

Organization design deals with the structural aspects of organizations; it aims to analyse roles and relationships so that collective effort can be explicitly organized to achieve specific ends. It is necessary to divide the overall management task into a variety of activities and to establish means of co-ordinating and controlling these activities. This design process leads to the development of an organization structure consisting of units and positions between which there are relationships involving the exercise of authority and communication and exchange of information. Organization design may thus lead to the definition and description of a more or less formal structure but it cannot ignore the existence of the informal organization — the network of informal social roles and relationships, as described in Chapter 9.

It may be appropriate to think in terms of organization redesign or modification. Organizations are in a constant state of change and anyone with responsibilities for organization has to be able to move fast. But action should be based upon an understanding of the objectives, activities, decision-making processes and relationships within the organization. And this must be developed against the background of an understanding of the historical background to the organization — how it got to where it is; the personalities involved — who exerts influence, how and why; the power relationships between people; the reward system; the economic and

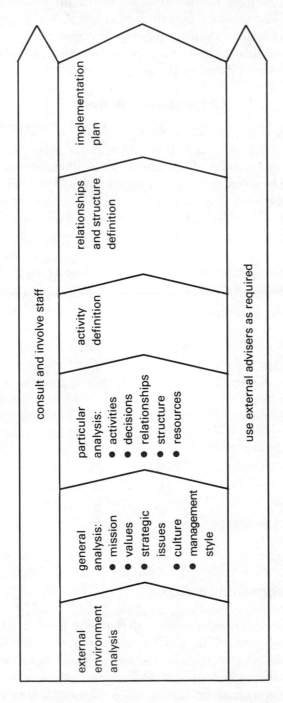

Figure 12.1 Organization analysis and design programme

cultural environment; and the dynamics of the organization — what is happening to it and where it is going.

The first stage in an organization design review is therefore an analysis of the present and future circumstances of the enterprise. This is followed by the detailed planning and implementation stages.

Organization analysis

Organization analysis is the process of defining the mission, values, strategic issues, objectives, activities and required structure of an enterprise in the light of a study of its external and internal environment. The analysis should be carried out by management in full consultation with staff and with the help, as necessary, of external advisers who can take an independent view and help to facilitate change. The sequence of activities in an organization design or redesign programme is illustrated in Figure 12.1.

The design programme should move from the general to the particular. In general, it should examine the organization's:

- external environment
- mission
- values
- strategic issues
- objectives
- corporate culture
- management style.

In particular, it should analyse:

- activities
- decisions
- relationships
- organization structure
- job structure
- human resources.

Analysing the external environment

The external environment consists of the economic, market, financial, legislative, social and cultural climate within which the enterprise operates. The analysis of the environment should determine, first, the extent to which it is turbulent or stable, and second, the rate and direction of any changes that may be taking place. The constraints, threats and opportunities imposed or presented by the environment should then be assessed. For the whole enterprise, this means looking at economic and market indicators as well as considering the implications of legislation and social change. For individual functions within the enterprise, it will mean looking at particular external influences.

Defining the mission

The mission of the organization should be examined in the light of the environmental analysis. This will establish the extent to which it is relevant and also the degree to which a sense of identity and purpose is defined and understood throughout the organization. In examining overall aims and purpose, this means answering Drucker's famous question: 'What business are we in?'

Defining values

The values of the organization (what is believed to be important about the ways in which it operates) should be studied to indicate the extent to which they are appropriate and understood. As necessary, steps should be taken to define or redefine values in such areas as teamwork, quality, customer service, performance expectations, innovation, respect for the individual and community relationships.

Identifying strategic issues

The strategic issues facing the organization should be identified under such headings as growth, profitability, competition, market position and standing, organizational effectiveness and the availability of the required human, financial and physical resources.

Analysing objectives

Objectives are the specific aims or targets to be achieved if the organization is to fulfil its purpose. In a profit-making concern these would be set out under such headings as profits, level of investment, future ownership, product development, market standing, manufacturing facilities, personnel policies and social responsibilities. The objectives of departments or individuals would then be determined by reference to their function or role. These could be expressed quantitatively (eg profit, volume), or qualitatively (eg level of service, quality of advice).

In a non-profit-making organization the objectives would be defined by reference to the areas in which services are provided for the government, for members of the organization or for the public. Thus a professional institution might set out its objectives under such headings as developing and maintaining high professional standards, improving the technical competence of its members, providing information and other services for its members and representing the interests of the profession to the government and the public at large.

The analysis of objectives should concentrate on establishing the extent to which they are clearly defined, understood and relevant.

Analysing corporate culture

The analysis of corporate culture should refer to the initial assessment of values and go on to assess the norms, beliefs and assumptions that affect organization climate and behaviour. A check-list for the analysis of corporate culture is given in Appendix F.

Analysing management style

Management style in the sense of the degree to which management is autocratic, democratic or permissive is one of the manifestations of corporate culture, but it is significant enough for organizational design purposes to be the subject of a separate analysis.

Analysing activities

Activity analysis establishes what work is done and what needs to be done if the enterprise is to achieve its objectives. The analysis should start with a broad look at the basic functions and technologies of the enterprise. Is it profit-making or non-profit-making? Is it primarily an administrative service, a manufacturing company, or a selling organization? To what extent does the work involve planning, research and development, administration, selling or production? Is the work continuous or subject to constant changes, as in project or case work? What type of production system is used: unit, mass, process, batch or flow? To what extent is the work routine or innovative? How much numerical analysis is used? To what extent are systems computerized?

The analysis of activities should establish what is and what is not being done, who is doing it, where it is being done and how much is being done. The most important points to be established are that everything is being done that needs to be done and nothing is being done that does not need to be done. Whether or not the activities are being done in the right place and by the right people can be established when looking at the structure of the organization.

Analysing decisions

The analysis of activities and tasks leads naturally into the analysis of decisions. This will establish how work is being delegated or decentralized and how and where interrelated decisions are being made.

Decision analysis is most helpful when it cuts across vertical and horizontal boundaries: vertical between levels of management in the hierarchy; horizontal between individuals in different functions who jointly contribute to making corporate decisions.

Decision analysis moves horizontally across functions but may also incorporate some vertical analysis of the division of responsibility between managers and their subordinates. The aim is to establish who ultimately has the authority to make the operating decision. The analysis should also show who is responsible for formulating the policy guidelines which determine the boundaries within which the decision is made, and who is contributing to the decision by providing information and advice. It should help, therefore, to identify information flows and areas where co-operation is required as well as clarifying the responsibilities and authorities for decision taking.

Questions on decisions should concentrate on the extent to which decisions are being made in the right place and on the degree to which there is adequate information, communications and consultation during the process of decision-making.

Analysing relationships

Relationships should be analysed from the point of view of the communications that take place between people and units in the organization and the contacts that are regularly made by individuals inside and outside the company with colleagues, customers and outside bodies. The analysis should provide information which can be used to assess whether the grouping of activities, lines of communication, information system and organization climate generally are conducive to effective management, teamwork and decision making. The relationship analysis should also cover the power structure of the organization — who exerts influence; who gets things done.

Analysing the organization structure

The structural aspects of the organization that should be analysed are:

- how activities are grouped together;
- the span of control of managers and supervision;
- the number of levels in the hierarchy.

Grouping activities

The analysis should establish which activities are carried out by the different functions and in the different organizational units. The two main points to be covered are: first, the extent to which the activities are grouped logically together and, second, whether or not there is any unnecessary duplication of activities.

The analysis of how activities are grouped should also consider the need to integrate closely related activities to avoid problems of co-ordination and communication and to enable those responsible for the function or group of activities to have adequate control of all the resources they require.

Span of control

Spans of control should be analysed in order to find out if they are too wide or too narrow. However, the organization designer must avoid falling into easy assumptions about what is an optimum span. It is an almost instinctive reaction to say that more means worse. But there have been many instances where what might appear to be overextended spans of control have worked perfectly well because the manager was a good delegator.

Very small spans of control can work badly. In one instance, the chief executive had only two direct subordinates. But they formed themselves into armed camps and because the chief executive identified himself with the operational wing of the enterprise (there is a tendency towards polarization in these situations), the administrative and financial wing was left out in the cold. As a result, operational decisions were made without proper regard to their financial implications and the enterprise rapidly became insolvent.

The organization designer must also beware of imposing mechanistic span-of-control assumptions. If work alters rapidly or if it is carried out by frequently changing project teams, span of control in the classical sense may no longer be a valid concept when analysing structures. In these circumstances, the analyst must concentrate more on establishing that the project teams or task forces are set up properly in the sense that they know what they are there to do and are in a position to do it — because they have the resources they need and, when necessary, are able to integrate their work with that of others.

Management levels

The number of management levels in the hierarchy should be studied to establish whether communications are being affected by the existence of too many barriers or whether unnecessary layers of management have been inserted in the structure.

Analysing job structure

The analysis of the organization structure concentrates on the grouping of activities into units and on the relationships between these units. The next stage is to look at the structure of the individual jobs within those units in terms of the range of tasks to be carried out, the demands made on the job holders, the amount of authority and responsibility they are given and their relationship with other people.

The analyst should find out whether tasks have been grouped logically together into jobs, whether job holders have been given sufficient responsibility and authority and whether they understand what they are expected to do. The design of individual jobs is dealt with in Chapter 13.

Analysing human resources

Management and resources need to be analysed from two points of view: first, the extent to which the existing structure has been built round the personalities and strengths or weaknesses of the key people in the organization; second, the availability of the quality and quantity of people required to enable any necessary changes in organization structure to take place.

All but the most bureaucratic or mechanistic type of organizations allow the structure to adapt itself to the people available — to a certain degree. This may be unavoidable and it could be desirable in the more organic type of organization where room has to be provided for entrepreneurs, innovators and others with special administrative and technical skills. But it can go too far, and the analyst must try to assess whether the structure has been unnecessarily distorted by empire-building or by weakly accommodating people whose skills are by no means unique. This information is required because the designer may have to accept that pure logic has to bow to necessity. But he should not accept it too readily. The case has to be made.

Organization design guidelines

The design of the organization should be based on this analysis. A contingency, informal, non-bureaucratic and organic (form following function) approach should be followed. Although there are no rigid principles of design, such as those expounded by the classical school of organization theorists, there are certain guidelines which should be taken into account. These are:

- *Allocation of work.* The work that has to be done should be defined and allocated to functions, units, departments, work teams, project groups and individual positions. Related activities should be grouped together. There will be a choice between dividing work by product, process, market or geographical area.
- *Differentiation and integration.* It is necessary to differentiate between the different activities that have to be carried out, but it is equally necessary to ensure that these activities are integrated so that everyone in the organization is working towards the same goals.
- *Teamwork.* Jobs should be defined and roles described in ways which facilitate and underline the importance of teamwork. Areas where cooperation is required should be emphasized. The organization should be designed and operated in such a way as to facilitate cooperation across departmental or functional boundaries. Wherever possible, self-managing teams and autonomous work groups should be set up and given the maximum amount of responsibility to run their own affairs, including planning, budgeting and exercising quality control. Networking should be encouraged in the sense of people communicating openly and informally with one another as the need arises. It is recognized that these informal processes can be more productive than rigidly working through 'channels' as set out in the organization chart.
- *Flexibility.* The organization structure should be flexible enough to respond quickly to change, challenge and uncertainty. Flexibility should be enhanced by the creation of core groups, using temporary and contract workers to handle extra demands. At top management level and elsewhere, a 'collegiate' approach to team operation should be considered in which people share responsibility and are expected to work with their colleagues in areas outside their primary function or skill.

- *Role clarification.* People should be clear about their roles as individuals and as members of a team. They should know what they will be held accountable for and be given every opportunity to use their abilities in achieving objectives which they have agreed to and are committed to. Job descriptions should define key result areas but should not act as strait-jackets, restricting initiative and unduly limiting responsibility.
- *Decentralization.* Authority to make decisions should be delegated as close to the scene of action as possible. Profit centres should be set up as strategic business units which operate close to their markets and with a considerable degree of autonomy. A multiproduct or market business should develop a federal organization with each federated entity running its own affairs, although they will be linked together by the overall business strategy.
- *De-layering.* Organizations should be 'flattened' by stripping out superfluous layers of management and supervision in order to promote flexibility, facilitate swifter communication, increase responsiveness, enable people to be given more responsibility as individuals or teams and reduce costs.

Organization design leads into organization planning — assessing implications of structural changes on future manpower requirements and taking steps to meet those requirements.

Organization planning

Organization planning is the process of converting the analysis into the design. It determines structure, relationships, roles, manpower requirements and the lines along which changes should be implemented. There is no one best design. There is always a choice between alternatives. Logical analysis will help in the evaluation of the alternatives but the law of the situation will have to prevail. The final choice will depend upon the present and future circumstances of the organization. It will be strongly influenced by personal and human considerations — the inclinations of top management, the strengths and weaknesses of management generally, the availability of people to man the new organization and the need to take account of the feelings of those who will be exposed to change. Cold logic may sometimes have to override these considerations. If it does, then it must be deliberate and the consequences must be appreciated and allowed for when planning the implementation of the new organization.

It may have to be accepted that a logical regrouping of activities cannot be introduced in the short term because no one with the experience is available to manage the new activities, or because capable individuals are so firmly entrenched in one area that to uproot them would cause serious damage to their morale and would reduce the overall effectiveness of the new organization. This frequently happens when planning a highly structured organization, where one of the most difficult tasks facing the designer is that of reconciling ideal requirements with the practical realities of the situation. But it can also happen in non-structured situations, although the problem may not be so well recognized. The designer may wish to develop a more loosely defined organic type of organization, but he could find that many people like structure and feel threatened if the well-defined framework within which they live their lives is taken away from them. The organic concept may have to be modified and some structure left behind.

The worst sin that organization designers can commit is that of imposing their own ideology on the organization. Their job is to be eclectic in their knowledge, sensitive in their analysis of the situation and deliberate in their approach to the evaluation of alternatives.

Having planned the organization and defined structures, relationships and rules, one must consider how the new organization should be implemented. It may be advisable to stage an implementation over a number of phases, especially if new people have to be found and trained. It will be even more necessary to address the often significant problems of introducing organizational change.

Introducing organizational change

Management may feel that it has perfectly valid reasons for introducing organizational change; for example, to:

- respond to changes in the environment — market or technological;
- deal with the new arrangements required following an acquisition, merger or takeover;
- eliminate overlapping areas of activity;
- cater for the introduction of new activities or the elimination of old ones;
- gain economies of scale by amalgamating activities;
- facilitate better co-ordination, control or communications;
- decentralize or de-layer operations to place decision making closer to the point of action, to reduce the size of an unwieldy head office and/ or to cut down on bureaucracy;
- centralize operations to provide for better control from the top;
- accommodate management changes;
- 'shake up the business a bit' — managements have been known to

articulate a belief that change is a stimulus in itself. There could be some truth in this in a stagnant organization, but 'change for change's sake' is a dangerous doctrine.

The problem of organizational change

Those affected by organizational change may not perceive it the same way. They have seen it all happen before. They may call it organization by whim not by design. They will have seen fashions for centralization and decentralization come and go. And they may quote wisely among themselves the old saying: 'organize — reorganize — disorganize'. If they are classicists, they may even be able to quote someone else who felt about reorganizations as they do — Gaius Petronius Arbiter, a Roman general of Nero's time, who was said to have complained:

> We trained hard, but it seemed that every time we were beginning to form up into teams, we would be reorganized. I was to learn later in life that we tend to meet any new situation by reorganizing, and a wonderful method it can be for creating the illusion of progress while producing confusion, inefficiency and demoralization.

These fears and reactions may seem to management to be unreasonable, but they can seriously prejudice the success of a reorganization, however carefully it has been planned and executed.

Reasons for adverse reactions to organizational change

Adverse reactions to reorganization from the point of view of those affected by it are not unreasonable. It constitutes change, about which most people are wary, if not overtly hostile. The reasons for resistance to change are quite clear: it is a combination of a fear of the unknown, a reluctance to change familiar and comfortable working habits, a belief in general that change is always for the worse, and a feeling in particular that the individuals affected by it are going to lose out in a number of specified ways.

The most frequently expressed or felt fears about organizational change are:

- loss of job;
- reduction of career prospects;
- downgrading of work and possible reduction in present or future rates of pay;

- loss or erosion of carefully built up empires;
- loss of status;
- reduction in responsibility and job interest;
- need to learn new skills, which could be difficult;
- new and unknown bosses, or even new and *known* bosses if their bad reputations come before them;
- break-up of well-established work groups and friendships;
- transfer to new, unknown (or known and disliked) locations or departments.

The list is formidable but not exhaustive. There are plenty of other adverse reactions people can have to organizational change, and, whether or not they are justified, every attempt must be made to prevent them happening before they arise or, if this is impossible, at least to deal with them swiftly if they emerge.

Gaining acceptance for organizational change

Prevention is always better than cure and the following ten preventive steps should be taken to minimize hostility, although, people being what they are, some fears will probably remain in their minds, whatever is done to eliminate them.

1. Base the change on a thorough organizational analysis.
2. Involve those concerned in the analysis — explain why it is being carried out and seek their views on what improvements are required.
3. If the change is forced on the company, explain why it is happening and, if at all possible, allay fears at this stage about adverse effects.
4. Consult people on alternative methods of dealing with the situation. Try to get them to 'own' the solution as theirs, and not something imposed upon them by an unfeeling management.
5. Accentuate the positive benefits — if they exist — to those affected by change. They could include increased responsibility, more clearly defined duties, the removal of barriers to communication, new challenges and opportunities, greater security in a more effective or prosperous organization, or the chance to learn new skills.
6. If the changes may adversely affect individuals or groups of people, attempt to mitigate them in advance by offering, if the worst comes to the worst, generous redundancy settlements involving voluntary redundancy where possible; 'outplacement' benefits, ie redundancy counselling and help to find alternative work; generous relocation allowances, retraining facilities; guarantees, if feasible, on loss of pay

or status; and a measure of choice about relocations or transfers.

7. Be prepared to modify the ideal solution in response to any reasonable fears expressed by those concerned — show willingness to listen and to act accordingly.

8. Take particular care in defining the new organization and the responsibilities of those concerned. Involve everyone affected in drawing up job descriptions. Set up training schemes to develop new skills and communications programmes to get the message across about changes.

9. Get groups together with their existing or new bosses to discuss the changes and their implications and agree jointly on how they are going to be managed.

10. Consider the use of third parties or 'change agents' to facilitate change and get involved in discussions on what is happening, why it is happening and what everyone should do about it.

Who does the work?

Organization design may be carried out by line management with or without the help of members of the personnel function or internal consultants, or it may be done by outside consultants. Personnel management should always be involved because organization design is essentially about people and the work they do — subjects on which personnel managers should be capable of giving sound advice. The advantage of using outside consultants is that an entirely independent and dispassionate view is obtained. They can cut through internal organizational pressures, politics and constraints and bring experience of other organizational problems they have dealt with. Sometimes, regrettably, major changes can be obtained only by outside intervention. But there is a danger of consultants suggesting theoretically ideal organizations which do not take sufficient account of the problems of making them work with existing people. They do not have to live with their solutions as do line and personnel managers. If outside consultants are used, it is essential to involve people from within the organization so they can ensure that they are able to implement the proposals smoothly.

13

Job Design

What is job design?

Job design has been defined by Davis[1] as 'The specification of the contents, methods, and relationships of jobs in order to satisfy technological and organizational requirements as well as the social and personal requirements of the job holder.'

Job design has two aims: first, to satisfy the requirements of the organization for productivity, operational efficiency and quality of product or service, and second, to satisfy the needs of the individual for interest, challenge and accomplishment. Clearly, these aims are interrelated and the overall objective of job design is to integrate the needs of the individual with those in the organization.

The process of job design must start from an analysis of what work needs to be done — the tasks that have to be carried out if the purpose of the organization or an organizational unit is to be achieved. This is where the techniques of work study, process planning, organization and methods and organizational analysis are used. Inevitably, these techniques are directed to the first aim of job design: the improvement of organizational performance. They concentrate on the work to be done, not the worker. They may lead to a high degree of task specialization and assembly line processing; of paper work as well as physical products. This in turn can lead to the maximization of individual responsibilty and the opportunity to use personal skills.

It is necessary, however, to follow Drucker and distinguish between efficiency and effectiveness. The most efficient method may maximize outputs in relation to inputs in the short run, but it may not be effective in the longer term in that it fails to achieve the overall objectives of the activity. Short-term profits may be achieved by efficient stock control which minimizes inventory levels; in the long run, however, customer dissatisfaction because of delays in providing spares may have a detrimental effect on sales which wipes out the initial profits. Similarly, in job design, the pursuit of short-term efficiency by imposing the maximum degree of task specialization may reduce longer-term effectiveness by demotivating job holders and increasing labour turnover and absenteeism.

Job design has therefore to start from work requirements because that is why the job exists — too many writers on job design seem to imply that job design is *only* concerned with human needs. When the tasks to be done have been determined it should then be the function of the job designer to consider how the jobs can be set up to provide the maximum degree of intrinsic motivation for those who have to carry them out. Consideration has also to be given to the third implied aim of job design: to fulfil the social responsibilities of the organization to the people who work in it by improving the quality of working life, an aim which, as stated in Wilson's[2] report on this subject, 'depends upon both efficiency of performance and satisfaction of the worker'.

Factors affecting job design

Job design is fundamentally affected by the technology of the organization, the changes that are taking place in that technology and the environment in which the organization operates. Job design has therefore to be considered within the context of organizational design, as described in Chapter 12, but it must also take into account the following factors:

- the process of intrinsic motivation;
- the characteristics of task structure;
- the motivating characteristics of jobs;
- the implications of group activities.

The process of intrinsic motivation

The case for using job design techniques is based on the premise that effective performance and genuine satisfaction in work follow mainly from the intrinsic content of the job. This is related to the fundamental concept that people are motivated when they are provided with the means to achieve their goals. Work provides the means to earn money, which as an extrinsic reward satisfies basic needs and is instrumental in providing ways of satisfying higher-level needs. But work also provides intrinsic rewards which are under the direct control of the worker himself.

Characteristics of task structure

Job design requires the assembly of a number of tasks into a job or a group of jobs. An individual may carry out one main task which consists of a number of interrelated elements or funtions. Or task functions may be split between a team working closely together or strung along an assembly line. In more complex jobs, individuals may carry out a variety of connected tasks, each with a number of functions, or these tasks may be allocated to a group of workers or divided between them. Complexity in a job may be a reflection of the number and variety of tasks to be carried out, or the range and scope of the decisions that have to be made, or the difficulty of predicting the outcome of decisions.

The internal structure of each task consists of three elements: *planning* (deciding on the course of action, its timing and the resources required), *executing* (carrying out the plan), and *controlling* (monitoring performance and progress and taking corrective action when required). A completely integrated job includes all these elements for each of the tasks involved. The worker, or group of workers, having been given objectives in terms of output, quality and cost targets, decides on how the work is to be done, assembles the resources, performs the work, and monitors output, quality and cost standards. Responsibility in a job is measured by the amount of authority someone has to do all these things.

The ideal arrangement from the point of view of intrinsic motivation is to provide for fully integrated jobs containing all three task elements. In practice, management and supervisors are concerned with planning and control, leaving the worker responsible for execution. To a degree, this is inevitable, but one of the aims of job design is often to extend the responsibility of workers into the functions of planning and control.

Motivating characteristics of jobs

Three characteristics have been distinguished by Lawler[3] as being required in jobs if they are to be intrinsically motivating.

1. *Feedback*. Individuals must receive meaningful feedback about their performance, preferably by evaluating their own performance and defining the feedback. This implies that they should ideally work on a complete product, or a significant part of it which can be seen as a whole.
2. *Use of abilities*. The job must be perceived by individuals as requiring them to use abilities they value in order to perform the job effectively.

3. *Self-control*. Individuals must feel that they have a high degree of self-control over setting their own goals and over defining the paths to these goals.

Approaches to job design

Job design should start with an analysis of task requirements, using the job analysis techniques described in Chapter 16. These requirements will be a function of the purpose of the organization, its technology, and its structure. The analysis has also to take into account the decision-making process — where and how it is exercised and the extent to which responsibility is devolved to individuals and work groups.

Robertson and Smith[4] suggest the following five approaches to job design:

1. To influence *skill variety*:

    (a) provide opportunities for people to do several tasks;
    (b) combine tasks;

2. To influence *task identity*:

    (a) combine tasks;
    (b) form natural work units;

3. To influence *task significance*:

    (a) form natural work units;
    (b) inform people of the importance of their work;

4. To influence *autonomy*: give people responsibility for determining their own working systems;

5. To influence *feedback*:

    (a) establish good relationships;
    (b) open feedback channels.

Turner and Lawrence[5] identified six important characteristics which they called 'requisite task characteristics', namely: variety, autonomy, required interactions, optional interactions, knowledge and skill and responsibility. And Cooper[6] outlined four conceptually distinct job dimensions: variety, discretion, contribution and goal characteristics.

An integrated view suggests that the following motivating characteristics are of prime importance in job design:

*   autonomy, discretion, self-control and responsibility;
*   variety;

- use of abilities;
- feedback;
- belief that the task is significant.

These are the bases of the characteristics approach which is used in job enrichment, as described later in this chapter.

Techniques of job design

The five job design techniques are as follows:

1. *Job rotation*, which comprises the movement of employees from one task to another to reduce monotony by increasing variety.
2. *Job enlargement*, which means combining previously fragmented tasks into one job, again to increase the variety and meaning of repetitive work.
3. *Job enrichment*, which goes beyond job enlargement to add greater autonomy and responsibility to a job and is based on the job characteristics approach.
4. *Autonomous work groups*, which means creating self-regulating groups who work largely without direct supervision. The philosophy on which this technique is based is a logical extension of job enrichment but is strongly influenced by socio-technical systems theory (see Chapter 10).
5. *High performance work design*, which concentrates on setting up working groups in environments where high levels of performance are required.

Of these five techniques, it is generally recognized that, although job rotation and job enlargement have their uses in developing skills and relieving monotony, they do not go to the root of the requirements for intrinsic motivation and for meeting the various motivating characteristics of jobs as described above. These are best satisfied by using, as appropriate, job enrichment, autonomous work groups, or high-performance work design.

Job enrichment

Job enrichment aims to maximize the interest and challenge of work by providing the employee with a job that has these characteristics:

- It is a complete piece of work in the sense that the worker can identify a series of tasks or activities that end in a recognizable and definable product.

- It affords the employee as much variety, decision-making responsibility and control as possible in carrying out the work.
- It provides direct feedback through the work itself on how well the employee is doing his job.

Job enrichment is not just increasing the number or variety of tasks; nor is it the provision of opportunities for job rotation. It is claimed by advocates of job enrichment that these approaches may relieve boredom, but they do not result in positive increases in motivation.

Job enrichment techniques

There is no one way of enriching a job. The technology and the circumstances will dictate which of the following techniques or combination of techniques is appropriate:

- increasing the responsibility of individuals for their own work;
- giving employees more scope to vary the methods, sequence and pace of their work;
- giving a person or a work group a complete natural unit of work — ie reducing task specialization;
- removing some controls from above while ensuring that individuals or groups are clearly accountable for achieving defined targets or standards;
- allowing employees more influence in setting targets and standards of performance;
- giving employees the control information they need to monitor their own performance;
- encouraging the participation of employees in planning work, innovating new techniques and reviewing results;
- introducing new and more difficult tasks not previously handled;
- assigning individuals or groups specific projects which give them more responsibility and help them to increase their expertise.

Steps to job enrichment

In the development of job enrichment, the following steps are usually recommended:

- Select those jobs where better motivation is most likely to improve performance.
- Set up a controlled pilot scheme before launching the full programme of job enrichment — do not try to do too much too quickly.

- Approach these jobs with a conviction that they can be changed — it is necessary to challenge assumptions at this stage, especially about the ability of people to take on responsibility and the scope for changing established work methods.
- Brainstorm a list of changes that may enrich the jobs, without concern at this stage for their practicability.
- Screen the list to concentrate on motivation factors such as achievement, responsibility and self-control.
- Ensure that the changes are not just generalities such as 'Increase responsibility'; list specific differences in the way in which the jobs are designed and carried out.
- Do not be too concerned about achieving a high degree of participation from employees in changing their jobs. Improvement is to be achieved by changing the *content* of jobs, not making employees feel happier because they have been consulted.
- Make the maximum use of line management and supervision in enriching jobs, but make sure that they have the training, guidance, encouragement and help they need.
- Bear in mind that job enrichment may develop into a major change programme and appreciate that change may be resisted and will have to be introduced with care.
- Set precise objectives and criteria for measuring success and a timetable for each project, and ensure that control information is available to monitor progress and results.

Impact of job enrichment

The advocates of job enrichment have been so dedicated to their cause that one cannot help feeling sometimes that their enthusiasm for the philosophy of their movement has clouded their judgement of its real benefits to the organization, let alone to the individuals who are supposed to have been 'enriched'.

There have been plenty of case studies which have indicated success, although this has often been measured in subjective terms. Volvo is the famous example, although ICI has carried out a number of job enrichment programmes in the UK, and the US there are the well-known examples of American Telephone and Telegraph and Texas Instruments. Ford's[7] report on the AT & T programme said that 'of the 19 studies, nine were rated outstandingly successful'. Ford goes on to admit:

No claim is made that these 19 trials cover a representative sample of jobs and people within the Bell system. For example, there were no trials among the manufacturing or laboratory employees, nor were all operating companies involved. There are more than a thousand different jobs in the Bell system, not just the nine in these studies.

McGregor[8] has said that 'unless there is opportunity *at work* to satisfy these higher level needs (esteem and self-actualization) people will be deprived, and their behaviour will reflect this deprivation'. But extensive research into the effects of job enrichment has not found this belief to be universally applicable. For example, Reif and Schoderbek's[9] study of 19 US companies who had introduced job enrichment revealed that only four thought their experience was very successful. They found that only 15 per cent of the companies had attempted to enrich unskilled jobs, and in follow-up interviews three major reasons emerged why it was more difficult to get unskilled workers to accept job enrichment: (a) the unskilled preferred the *status quo*; (b) the unskilled seemed to prefer highly specialized work, and (c) the unskilled showed a lack of interest in improvements in job design which require learning new skills or assuming greater responsibility. A representative comment was: 'Most unskilled workers prefer the routine nature of their jobs, and it has been my experience that they are not eager to accept responsibility or learn new skills.' Numerous studies quoted by Reif and Luthans[10] have pointed out that repetitive work can have positively motivating characteristics for some workers. Kilbridge[11] found that assembly line workers in television factories did not necessarily regard repetitive tasks as dissatisfying or frustrating.

A study by Hulin and Blood[12] of all relevant research on job enrichment concluded that the effects of job enrichment on job satisfaction or worker motivation are generally overstated and in some cases unfounded. They argue convincingly that many shop-floor workers are not alienated from the work environment but are alienated from the work norms and values of the middle class, especially its belief in the work-related elements of the Protestant ethic and in the virtue of striving for the attainment of responsible positions.

Fein's[13] study of worker motivation reached essentially the same conclusion. He states:

Workers do not look upon their work as fulfilling their existence. Their reaction to their work is the opposite of what the behaviouralists predict. It is only because workers *choose* not to find fulfilment in their work that they are able to function as healthy human beings. By rejecting involvement in their work which simply cannot be fulfilling, workers save their sanity . . . The concepts of McGregor and Herzberg regarding workers' needs to find fulfilment through their work are sound *only for those workers who choose to find fulfilment through their work* . . . Contrary to their postulates, the majority of workers seek fulfilment outside their work.

Autonomous work groups

An autonomous work group is allocated an overall task and given discretion over how the work is done. This provides for intrinsic motivation by giving people autonomy and the means to control their work, which will include feedback information. The basis of the autonomous work group approach to job design is socio-technical systems theory, which suggests that the best results are obtained if grouping is such that workers are primarily related to each other by way of task performance and task interdependence. As Emery[14] has stated:

> In designing a social system to efficiently operate a modern capital intensive plant the key problem is that of creating self-managing groups to man the interface with the technical system.

An autonomous work group:

- enlarges individual jobs to include a wider range of operative skills;
- decides on methods of work and the planning, scheduling and control of work;
- distributes tasks itself among its members;
- decides on work pace and when to work.

The advocates of autonomous work groups claim that this approach offers a more comprehensive view of organizations than the rather simplistic individual motivation theories which underpin job rotation, enlargement and enrichment. Be that as it may, the strength of this system is that it does take account of the social or group factors and the technology as well as the individual motivators.

High performance work design

High-performance work design, as described by Buchanan[15], requires the following steps:

1. Management clearly defines what it needs in the form of new technology or methods of production and the results expected from its introduction.
2. Multiskilling is encouraged — that is, job demarcation lines are eliminated as far as possible and encouragement and training are provided for employees to acquire new skills.

3. Equipment is selected which can be used flexibly and is laid out to allow freedom of movement and vision.
4. Autonomous working groups are established, each with around a dozen members and with full 'back-to-back' responsibility for product assembly and testing, fault-finding and some maintenance.
5. Managers adopt a supportive rather than an autocratic style with groups and group leaders (this is the most difficult part of the system to introduce).
6. Support systems are provided for kit-marshalling and material supply, which help the groups to function effectively as productive units.
7. Management sets goals and standards for success.
8. The new system is introduced with great care by means of involvement and communication programmes.
9. Thorough training is carried out on the basis of an assessment of training needs.
10. The payment system is specially designed with staff participation to fit their needs as well as those of management.

In the case quoted by Buchanan (Digital Equipment Corporation), management felt that the autonomous work groups had demonstrated, among other things:

- an ability to change;
- communication helped by layout changes;
- product identification and 'ownership' for actions;
- greater flexibility through multiskilling;
- better priority setting.

References

1. Davis, L E 'The design of jobs', *Industrial Relations*, Vol. 6, 1966.
2. Wilson, N A B *On the Quality of Working Life*. Her Majesty's Stationery Office, London, 1973.
3. Lawler, E E 'Job Design and Employee Motivation', *Personnel Psychology*, Vol. 22, 1969, pp. 426–35.
4. Robertson, I T, and Smith, M *Motivation and Job Design*. Institute of Personnel Management, London, 1985.
5. Turner, A N and Lawrence, P R *Industrial Jobs and the Worker: An Investigation of Response to Task Attributes*. Harvard University Graduate School of Business Administration, Boston, MA, 1965.
6. Cooper, R 'Task characteristics and intrinsic motivation', *Human Relations*, August 1973.

7. Ford, R *Motivation Through the Work Itself*. American Management Association, New York, 1969.
8. McGregor, D *Leadership and Motivation*. MIT Press, Cambridge, MA, 1966.
9. Reif, W E and Schoderbek, P F *Job Enlargement*. University of Michigan, Ann Arbor, 1969.
10. Reif, W E and Luthans, F 'Does Job Enrichment Pay Off?', *California Management Review*, Vol. XV, No. 1, 1973.
11. Kilbridge, M D 'Do Workers Prefer Larger Jobs?', *Personnel*, Sept–Oct 1960.
12. Hulin, C L and Blood, M R 'Job Enlargement, Individual Differences and Worker Responses', *Psychological Bulletin*, Vol. 69, No. 1, 1968.
13. Fein, M *Approaches to Motivation*, Hillsdale, NJ, 1970.
14. Emery, F F 'Designing socio-technical systems for "greenfield" sites', *Journal of Occupational Behaviour*. Vol. 1, No. 1, 1980.
15. Buchanan, D 'Job enrichment is dead: long live high performance work design!', *Personnel Management*, May 1987.

14

Improving Organizational Effectiveness

Definition of organizational effectiveness

An effective organization can broadly be defined as one that successfully achieves its objectives while also meeting its responsibilities to its stakeholders. These stakeholders consist of:

1. The owners, shareholders, public authorities or trustees who direct or fund the organization.
2. The employees who run the organization.
3. The customers, clients or members of the public for whom the organization provides goods or services.
4. The third parties through whom the organization does business.
5. The community in which the organization operates.

This chapter is concerned with what can be done to create and develop an effective organization. In this process, the personnel function should make a major contribution, which will largely be concerned with the quality of the organization's human resources, the ways in which they are managed and how they interact.

Improving organizational effectiveness will be considered in this chapter under the following headings:

1. What makes an organization effective?
2. The various approaches to improving organizational effectiveness;
3. An integrated approach;
4. Change management;
5. The preparation of mission and value statements;
6. Motivation strategies;
7. Commitment strategies;

8. Team building and improving interpersonal relationships;
9. Communications and involvement;
10. Conflict management;
11. Stress management;
12. Total quality management and customer service.

What makes an organization effective?

There are a number of formulas for organizational effectiveness and some of the better-known ones are summarized below.

Pascale and Athos

From their analysis of the art of Japanese management, Pascale and Athos[1] defined the seven *S*'s for success, which are:

1. *Strategy* — the plan to reach identified goals;
2. *Structure* — the characteristics of the organization's structure — functional, decentralized, etc;
3. *Systems* — the routines for processing and communicating information;
4. *Staff* — the categories of people employed;
5. *Style* — how managers behave in achieving the organization's goals;
6. *Skills* — the capabilities of key people;
7. *Superordinate goals* — the significant meanings of guiding concepts with which an organization imbues its members (ie its values).

Peters and Waterman

From their research into 75 highly regarded companies, Peters and Waterman[2] identified the following eight attributes which characterize the excellent innovation companies:

1. *A bias for action.* The excellent companies get on with it. They are analytical in their decision making but this does not paralyse them, as it does some companies.
2. *Close to the customer.* They get to know their customers and provide them with quality, reliability and service.
3. *Autonomy and entrepreneurship.* Leaders and innovators are fostered and given scope.
4. *Productivity through people.* They really believe that the basis for quality and productivity gain is the rank and file. They do not just pay lip service to the slogan, 'people are our most important asset'. They do something about it by encouraging commitment and getting everyone involved.

5. *Hands-on, value-driven.* The people who run the organization get close to those who work for them and ensure that the organization's values are understood and acted upon.
6. *Stick to the knitting.* The successful organizations stay reasonably close to the businesses they know.
7. *Simple form, lean staff.* The organization structure is simple and corporate staff are kept to a minimum.
8. *Simultaneous loose-tight properties.* They are both decentralized and centralized. They push decisions and autonomy as far down the organization as they can get into individual units and profit centres. But, as Peters and Waterman say, 'they are fanatic centralists around the few core values they hold dear'.

Some of the 'excellent' companies included in this study, however, have not done so well subsequently.

Peters

In his study of how managers can deal with chaos, Peters[3] produced the following prescriptions for a 'world turned upside down':

- create total customer responsiveness;
- pursue fast-paced innovation;
- achieve flexibility by empowering people;
- learn to love change by a new view of leadership at all levels.

Kanter

Kanter[4] has emphasized the importance of managing change. She believes that managers must become: 'change masters, helping and guiding the organization, its management and all who work in it to manage and, indeed, to exploit and triumph over change'. Kanter[5] has also recorded how Apple Computer devised a three-pronged approach to improving organizational effectiveness as follows:

1. Develop an organizational structure that produces synergies, not conflict.
2. Create more cooperative alliances with suppliers and customers.
3. Find ways to maintain a flow of new ideas toward new products and new ventures.

Beckhard

Beckhard[6] defined a healthy organization, from the point of view of a behavioural scientist, as having the following characteristics:

1. The total organization, the significant subparts, and individuals manage their work against goals and plans for the achievement of these goals.
2. Form follows function (the problem, or task or project, determines how the human resources are organized).
3. Decisions are made by and near the source of information, regardless of where these sources are located on the organization chart.
4. The reward system is such that managers and supervisors are rewarded (and punished) comparably for:

    (a) short-term profit or production performance;
    (b) growth and development of their subordinates;
    (c) creating a viable working group.

5. Communication laterally and vertically is relatively undistorted. People are generally open and confronting. They share all the relevant facts, including feelings.
6. There is a minimum amount of inappropriate win/lose activity between individuals and groups. Constant effort exists at all levels to treat conflict and conflict situations as problems subject to problem-solving methods.
7. There is a high 'conflict' (clash of ideas) about tasks and projects, and relatively little energy spent in clashing over interpersonal difficulties because they have been generally worked through.
8. The organization and its parts see themselves as interacting with each other *and* with a *larger* environment. The organization is an 'open system'.
9. There is a shared value, and management strategy to support it, of trying to help each person (or unit) in the organization to maintain his or her (or its) integrity and uniqueness in an interdependent environment.
10. The organization and its members operate in an 'action research' way. General practice is to build in feedback mechanisms so that individuals and groups can learn from their own experience.

This is a somewhat idealistic view of how organizations should behave, and represents the philosophy adopted by most organization development practitioners. But there is some danger in adopting these values as ends in themselves and neglecting the fact that organizations exist to serve a purpose.

Harvey-Jones

Harvey-Jones[7] has made the following suggestions on the approaches adopted by successful businesses:

- 'Nothing will happen unless everyone down the line knows what they are trying to achieve and gives of their best to achieve it.'
- 'The whole of business is about taking an acceptable risk.'
- 'The process of deciding where you are taking the business is the opportunity to get the involvement of others, which actually forms the motive power that at the end of the day will make it happen.'
- 'The business must continually strive to achieve better ways of doing more with less.'

Handy

Handy[8] has suggested that an effective organization is a learning organization, which has a formal way of asking questions, seeking out theories, testing them and reflecting upon them. The questions include:

- What are its strengths, talents and weaknesses?
- What sort of organization does it want to be?
- What does it want to be known for?
- How does it plan to achieve it?

He has also suggested that the formula for success is $AV = I$, where AV stands for added value and I stands for intelligence, information and ideas.

Child

Child[9] has identified three organizational attributes which are linked to superior economic performance:

1. An emphasis on methods to communicate key values and objectives and to ensure that action is directed towards them.
2. The delegation of identifiable areas of responsibility to relatively small units, including work groups.
3. The use of a lean, simple structure of management which is intended to avoid the rigidities of bureaucracy, the complexities of matrix, and the overheads of both.

Nissan

As quoted by Wickens,[10] the Nissan 'tripod' for achieving success the Japanese way is:

- flexibility
- quality consciousness
- teamwork.

Pascale

In *Managing on the Edge*, Pascale[11] revisited his findings in his earlier book, *The Art of Japanese Management*,[1] which he wrote with Athos. He also looked at the views of some of the other writers on management such as Peters. From this analysis he noted that 'nothing fails like success', the point of this paradox being that businesses and people can too easily become complacent. He supports the idea of creative tension as a means of breaking away from paradigms or mind-sets which imprison people in the past. His main theme is that:

> Managerial behaviour is predicated on the assumption that we should rationally order the behaviour of those we manage. That mind-set needs to be challenged . . . a system requires 'internal variety' to cope with external change. . . . Internal difference can widen the spectrum of an organization's options by generating new points of view. This, in turn, can promote disequilibrium; under the conditions self-renewal and adaptation occur.

Ten factors contributing to organizational effectiveness

From the above statements and the writer's own experience and observations, the following ten factors appear to be relevant:

1. strong visionary leadership from the top;
2. a powerful management team;
3. a well-motivated, committed, skilled and flexible workforce;
4. effective teamwork throughout the organization, with win/lose conflict well under control;
5. a continuous pressure to innovate, coupled with the ability to manage and thrive on change;
6. clearly defined goals and strategies to accomplish them;
7. a positive corporate culture;
8. a value system which emphasizes performance, quality and the responsibilities of the organization to its stakeholders;

254

9. an ability to get into action fast and make things happen;
10. a sound financial base and good systems for management accounting and cost control.

Approaches to improving organizational effectiveness

A number of approaches have been adopted to improving organizational effectiveness. Some of the most significant are:

- strategic management;
- the behavioural science approach;
- organization development (OD);
- process consultancy;
- performance management;
- culture management.

Strategic management

Strategic management is the process by which an organization formulates objectives and long-range plans and is managed to achieve them. It requires:

- the determination of medium- and long-term objectives — the strategic intent;
- the selection of a coherent strategy to achieve these objectives;
- the direction of the organization so that it moves constantly towards their achievement.

Strategic management is concerned with both ends and means. As an end, it describes a vision of what something will look like in a few years' time. As means, it shows how it is expected that the vision will be realized. Strategic management is therefore visionary management, concerned with creating and conceptualizing ideas of where the organization should be going. But it is also empirical management, which decides how, in practice, it is going to get there.

The focus is on identifying the organization's mission and strategies, but attention is also given to the resource base required to make it succeed. It is always necessary to remember that strategy is the means to create value. Managers who think strategically have a broad and long-term view of where they are going. But they are also aware that they are responsible, first, for planning how to allocate resources to opportunities which contribute to the implementation of strategy, and secondly, for managing these opportunities in ways which significantly add value to the results achieved by the firm.

Key concepts in strategic management

The key concepts used in strategic management are:

1. *Distinctive competence* — working out what the organization is best at and what its special or unique capabilities or attributes are, and planning to carry out or utilize these things.
2. *Focus* — concentrating on the key strategic issues.
3. *Competitive advantage* — selecting markets where the organization can excel and where its distinctive competences give it a competitive edge. Markets are selected where the business can either beat competitors or avoid them. Without competitive edge, there is no ability to earn a true economic profit.
4. *Synergy* — developing a product-market posture with a combined performance that is greater than the sum of its parts (ie 2 + 2 = 5). Synergy in sales takes place when products use common distribution channels, common salesforces and administration, or common warehousing. In operational terms, synergy occurs when there is higher utilization of facilities and personnel, spreading of overheads, and bulk purchasing. Management synergy happens if the abilities and skills of individual managers can be used to solve problems and develop strategies better or more comprehensively than they would have been able to do on their own.
5. *Environmental scanning* — strategic thinking and management involves scanning the internal and external environment of the firm to ensure that full awareness is gained of strengths and weaknesses, or of threats and opportunities.
6. *Resource allocation* — understanding the resource requirements of the strategy (human, financial, plant, and equipment) and ensuring that the resources are made available and that their use is optimized.

The process of strategic planning was described in Chapter 1 (pages 47–50).

The behavioural science approach

The behavioural science movement was founded by individual theorists or schools such as those described below.

Argyris

Argyris[12] believed that organization design should plan for integration and involvement and that individuals should feel that they have a high degree of self-control over setting their own goals and defining the paths to achieving those goals.

The group relations/dynamics/processes schools

In general, the social psychologists who concentrated on studying group behaviour identified the following four characteristics of groups:

- activity toward a common goal;
- maintaining themselves;
- meeting the needs of individual members;
- establishing group norms which strongly influence behaviour.

They also worked out methods of analysing and describing group 'processes' (patterns of behaviour) and of helping people to observe and understand these processes and act appropriately. The three schools were:

1. *The group relations school*, consisting of social psychologists such as Mayo[13] and Whyte,[14] who emphasized the importance of the informal group and group norms and who demonstrated, as Brown[15] put it, that 'the unit of observation is the social relationship rather than the individual'.
2. *The group dynamics school*, the members of which derived their approach mainly from Lewin's[16] concept of 'action research' (ie collecting data and feeding them back to those who generated them in order to identify problems and possible causes so that possible actions can be tested). This led to the development of group-dynamics training methods, as described in Appendix P.
3. *The group processes school*, the members of which studied group processes and evolved methods of analysing group interactions and diagnosing problems which were called 'process consulting'. Bales[17] analysed the ways in which groups solved problems and demonstrated that groups developed certain patterns of behaviour which were quite predictable.

Schein[18] also evolved methods of analysing group processes and developed methodologies for process consulting, as described later in this chapter (page 262).

Herzberg

Herzberg[19] advocated job enrichment (see Chapter 13) as a means of improving organizational effectiveness, arguing that such improvements should centre on the work itself as a source of motivation. If people feel that the job is stretching them, they will be moved to perform it well. This provided the impetus for the 'quality of working life' movement, which emphasized the idea that management should accept as a basic value the need consciously and continuously to improve the quality of working life as a means of obtaining increased motivation and improved results.

Likert

Likert[20] developed his integrating principle of supportive relationships. This stated that the members of the organization should, in the light of their values and expectations, view their work as supportive and as contributing to the building and maintenance of their sense of personal wealth and importance.

Maslow

Maslow[21] contributed the concept of self-fulfilment or self-actualization, which he placed at the top of his hierarchy of human needs.

McGregor

McGregor[22] developed his theory X and theory Y to distinguish between the different assumptions which managers make about human nature and human behaviour.

1. *Theory* X is the traditional view of direction; its assumptions are as follows:

    (a) Average workers have an inherent dislike of work and will avoid it if they can.
    (b) Because of this human characteristic of dislike of work, most people must be coerced, controlled, directed and threatened with punishment to get them to put forth adequate effort towards achievement of organizational objectives.
    (c) The average human being prefers to be directed, wishes to avoid responsibility, has relatively little ambition and wants security above all.

2. *Theory* Y is concerned with the integration of individual and organizational goals. Its assumptions are as follows:

    (a) The expenditure of physical and mental effort in work is as natural as play or rest.

(b) External control and the threat of punishment are not the only means for bringing about effort towards organizational objectives. People will exercise self-direction and self-control in the service of objectives to which they are committed.

(c) Commitment to objectives is a function of the rewards associated with their achievement. The most significant of such rewards, eg the satisfaction of ego and self-actualization needs, can be direct products of efforts directed towards organizational objectives.

(d) The average human being learns, under proper conditions, not only to accept but also to seek responsibility.

(e) The capacity to exercise a relatively high degree of imagination, ingenuity, and creativity in the solution of organizational problems is widely, not narrowly, distributed in the population.

(f) Under the conditions of modern industrial life, the intellectual potentialities of the average human being are only partially utilized.

This somewhat Manichean view of managerial assumptions is not based on research and most managers, in practice, probably subscribe to parts of theories X and Y simultaneously. But these theories have been highly influential, not least on the quality of working life movement. McGregor's message was clear: 'Management must assume the onus of developing conditions of employment for their people so that they feel free to exploit their self-fulfilment needs. This is an ambitious and optimistic hope.'

The Tavistock school

The research workers of the Tavistock Institute of Human Relations, such as Trist *et al*,[23] described the way work is organized as a 'socio-technical system' (see also Chapter 10) which links the work organization with its technical element. They refer to the organization as an 'open' system (one affected by outside factors, particularly economic ones) and as 'organic' (adaptable to change).

The humanistic school

The humanistic school consists of a number of the behavioural scientists mentioned above, including Maslow, Herzberg and others. As described by Weightman,[24] 'This school of thought is really about ideas. It is more a description of what could and should be than an analysis of what is. The central belief is that each of us has within ourselves and capacity to develop in a healthy and creative way.' Rogers[25] has defined four stages people go through in becoming fully functional:

1. the need to be open to experience;
2. a tendency to live each moment more fully;
3. increased trust in themselves;
4. taking responsibility for themselves and their actions.

This philosophy has exerted considerable influence on consultants and others working in the fields of organization development, process consulting and culture change. It has encouraged the pursuit of approaches such as participation in decision making, 'ownership' of ideas, autonomous work groups (see Chapter 13) and the emphasis on self-development in management training.

Comments on the behavioural science approach

The behavioural science movement has an idealistic flavour about it, but it has been very influential. First, it emphasized the importance of integration and involvement. Secondly, it promulgated the idea that management should accept as a basic value the need consciously and continuously to improve the quality of working life as a means to increase motivation and commitment. And thirdly, it stressed the importance of handling interpersonal relations and the significance of informal groups. But it encouraged the naive belief that the application of the behavioural sciences was the only way to increase organizational effectiveness, a view which has bedevilled the organization development enthusiasts.

Organization development

What is organization development?

Organization development is usually defined as being concerned with the planning and implementation of programmes designed to improve the effectiveness with which an organization functions and responds to change. The programmes are based on a variety of behavioural science concepts and techniques, and the aim of organization development is to integrate them in order that a coherent approach is used to change for the better the ways in which people carry out their work and interact with others.

Organization development, as described above, should be distinguished from management development, although the two often overlap. Management development (discussed in Chapter 21) is mainly aimed at the improvement of the performance and potential of individuals, while organization development is more concerned with improving the overall effectiveness of the organization — in particular, the way its various processes function and its people work together.

Methods of organization development

Organization development programmes in their original form were usually characterized by three main features;

1. They were managed, or at least strongly supported, from the top but often made use of third parties or 'change agents' to diagnose problems and to manage change by various kinds of planned activity or 'intervention'.
2. The plans for organization development were based upon a systematic analysis and diagnosis of the circumstances of the organization and the changes and problems affecting it.
3. They used behavioural science knowledge and aimed to improve the way the organization copes in times of change through such processes as interaction, communications, participation, planning and conflict.

Organization development programmes have consisted of any one or a mix of these activities, and this is why it is difficult to describe 'OD', as it is familiarly known, in a satisfactorily comprehensive way. In some companies an OD programme is no more than a glorified management development package, using a few team-building exercises and informal training courses and, perhaps, dabbling in some interactive skills training such as transactional analysis. In others the programme embraces a number of different but related activities, all designed to achieve a measurable improvement in the performance of the organization.

The role of the OD practitioner

OD programmes have generally been 'facilitated' by consultants because external interventions are likely to be more effective than internal ones. Argyris[26] summarized the primary tasks of the OD practitioner or interventionist as being to:

- generate and help clients to generate valid information which they can understand about their problems;
- create opportunities for the clients to search effectively for solutions to their problems and to make free choices;

● create conditions for internal commitment to these choices and apparatus for the continual monitoring of the action taken.

Process consultancy

Process consultancy, as described by Schein,[18] is a technique used in OD assignments but it is equally valid in culture management and other approaches used in improving organizational effectiveness. Process consulting involves helping clients to generate information which they can understand about their projects and problems and creating conditions for clients to own the solutions to the problems by gaining internal commitment to their choice.

The process consultant is usually someone from outside the organization but it is possible for people from within the company to operate in this capacity as long as they can preserve their objectivity and a measure of independence. Suitably qualified and experienced members of the personnel function can do this but it is not an easy task to fulfil the following ten roles that a process consultant plays as a facilitator of change:

1. sharer
2. challenger
3. interventionist
4. catalyst
5. provider of insight
6. process analyst
7. listener/observer
8. provider of structure
9. developer of ownership
10. action stimulator.

Performance management

Performance management, as described in Chapter 19, is a means of getting better results by managing performance within an agreed framework of planned goals, objectives and standards.

Culture management

Definition

Culture management is the process of maintaining and increasing organizational effectiveness by reinforcing the existing culture or, when necessary, developing a more positive culture. Culture management uses many of the organization development and process consulting techniques described above. But it focuses more clearly on organizational strategies and performance. It is very much concerned with the mission of the organization and the extent to which its norms and values either support the achievement of that mission or are dysfunctional. It is an enabling process to help the organization obtain the maximum added value from its use of resources and, for business enterprises, to achieve competitive advantage. It is often associated with human resource management and development programmes.

Aims

The three aims of culture management are to:

1. Enable, empower and energize the members of the organization.
2. Create, in Kanter's[4] words a 'culture of pride and a climate of success'.
3. Provide leverage for change.

Culture management programmes

Culture management programmes consist of the following stages:

1. *Analysis* of the current situation in terms of

    (a) mission, objective, strategies and performance;
    (b) culture — norms, values, climate and management style;
    (c) structure;
    (d) systems and processes;
    (e) availability and quality of resources — human, financial and material.

2. *Diagnosis* of the steps which need to be taken to reinforce or change the culture; to change structures, systems or processes; or to improve the availability and quality of resources.
3. *Action Planning* — the development of reinforcement or change programmes, making use of change management techniques. These may deal with primarily cultural or human resource aspects, such as creating and disseminating mission and value statements, formulating motivation and commitment strategies, team building and developing interpersonal relations, improving communication and involvement processes, achieving better integration and managing conflict and stress (these are all discussed below). The action plans may also be concerned with job design (see Chapter 13), total quality management

and customer service development programmes (see later in this chapter) and improvements in systems or processes such as strategic, financial and market planning; performance management; reward management, or budgetary control. A description of the last-named systems or processes is outside the scope of this book, but they all have an impact on what sort of people are required, how they should be managed and how the work should be structured. The personnel function needs to be aware of proposals in each of these areas so that steps can be taken to deal with the human issues and problems that may arise.

4. *Implementation* Again the personnel function needs to be involved in, or at least fully aware of, what is happening in any aspect of implementing the culture management programme in order that advice and help can be made available as required.

An integrated approach to improving organizational effectiveness

Each of the approaches described above can contribute to a programme for improving organizational effectiveness.

- *Strategic management* provides the marketing, innovatory and operational framework into which all the other activities fit. It first defines what the organization is to achieve (its mission and goals) and then indicates the direction in which it is going and how it intends to get there.
- *Behavioural science theories* emphasize the human aspects of organizational behaviour and how integration can be achieved between individual and corporate goals. They provide a conceptual, as distinct from a strategic, framework for OD, process consulting, performance management and culture management activities.
- *Organization development (OD) approaches* are derived directly from behavioural science knowledge and concentrate on team building, interpersonal relations, education and training and 'techno-structural' (ie task organization, structure definition and change) activities.
- *Process consulting techniques* are used in diagnosing and handling process issues (group behaviour, problem solving and leadership). They are closely associated with OD approaches but are also deployed in culture management programmes.
- *Performance management* focuses on outputs and how people achieve agreed objectives. Greater emphasis is placed on the needs of the business as defined in its strategic and operational plans than in organizational development, without neglecting the key aspects of

organization and human behaviour which are covered in OD programmes and analysed by the use of process consulting techniques.

* *Culture management* can incorporate all the approaches adopted in OD and
  uses process consulting techniques. But, like performance management, it is also concerned more explicitly with the achievement of the
  organization's mission and does not fall into the same trap as those
  exponents of behavioural science theory who seem to believe that being
  nice and maintaining cosy relationships inevitably produce improvements in organizational performance. Culture management also deals
  with the broader aspects of how the organization behaves (its norms
  and values) and is linked explicitly to many of the concepts of human
  resource management described in the introduction to this book.

In a sense, culture management, as defined above, forms an integrated
approach in that it uses concepts and techniques from behavioural science,
OD, process consulting and performance management. Complete integration, however, can be achieved only if these are deployed within the context
of corporate strategies and by reference to the particular circumstances of
the organization.

An integrated approach is necessarily a systems approach, linking the
organization's function with its internal technologies and resources and
with the external environment. It is also a contingency approach, relating
what needs to be done to the needs of organizations, and not prescribing
nostrums on the basis of theoretical and generalized beliefs about what is
good for employees. The integrated approach will therefore be based on a
thorough analysis of the organization — its plans, systems, structures and
circumstances — followed by a diagnosis of its problems and their likely
causes and the development of plans to overcome the problems and to
manage the changes required.

The programmes that follow from this analysis and diagnosis will include
reviews of organizational strategies and the plans required to achieve them.
They may include the introduction of new technology, the development of
improved planning and operational processes, organizational restructuring
and the introduction of better performance management and budgetary
control procedures. They will also consider the human, financial and
material resource implications.

An integrated approach is very much concerned with change management, as discussed in the next section. It also deals, selectively and as
appropriate, with other areas of human resource management and development as considered later in this chapter, namely:

* the preparation of mission and value statements;

- motivation strategy;
- commitment strategy;
- promoting teamwork;
- communications and involvement processes;
- conflict management;
- stress management;
- total quality management.

It is also concerned with the other key aspects of organizational performance — total quality management (TQM) and customer care. These are areas in which the achievement of high standards of quality and customer service depend very much on the attitudes, skills and behaviour of everyone in the organization. They are therefore firmly in the domain of the human resource management function.

Managing change

All organizations are, to a greater or lesser extent, in a perpetual state of change. To survive and thrive, businesses have to grow. They must innovate, develop new products, expand into new markets, reorganize, introduce new technology, and change working methods and practices. Even if this does not happen voluntarily, change may be forced upon them by competition and changes in the business, political and social environment. Managers have to be able to introduce and to manage change and gain the commitment of their teams to it. Members of the personnel function have a key role as 'facilitators' or 'change agents' in ensuring that change can be managed effectively in the organization.

To manage change, we must first understand why people resist change; this was explained in Chapter 6. The following aspects of change management should then be considered.

1. the impact of change;
2. change management;
3. programming change;
4. the approaches that can be used to overcome resistance and obtain commitment to change;
5. the steps that can be taken to accelerate change.

The impact of change

Change can create instability and ambiguity and replace order and predictability with disharmony and surprise. The corporate culture, as discussed in Chapter 9, can create solidarity and meaning and can inspire commitment and productivity. But the culture can actively and forcefully work against an organization when change becomes necessary. If not properly managed, change can decrease morale, motivation and commitment and create conditions of conflict within an organization.

Change mechanisms

The basic mechanisms for managing change, according to Lewin,[27] are as follows:

1. *Unfreezing* — altering the present stable equilibrium which supports existing behaviours and attitudes. This process must take account of the inherent threats change presents to people and the need to motivate those affected to attain the natural state of equilibrium by accepting change.
2. *Changing* — developing new responses based on new information.
3. *Refreezing* — stabilizing the change by introducing the new responses into the personalities of those concerned.

Programming change

A change programme should incorporate the following processes, according to Beckhard:[6]

1. setting goals and defining the future state or organizational conditions desired after the change;
2. diagnosing the present condition in relation to these goals;
3. defining the transition state activities and commitments required to meet the future state;
4. developing strategies and action plans for managing this transition in the light of an analysis of the factors likely to affect the introduction of change.

Those wanting change should be constant about the ends, but they may have to be flexible about the means. This requires them to come to an understanding of the forces likely to resist change as well as those creating the need for change.

Lewin[27] called this process 'field force analysis', and it involves:

1. Analysing the restraining or driving forces which will affect the transition to the future state. These restraining forces will include the reactions of those who see change as unnecessary or as constituting a threat.
2. Assessing which of the driving or restraining forces are critical.

3.   Taking steps both to increase the critical driving forces and to decrease the critical restraining forces.

When analysing the potential impact of change in one part of the organization, it is necessary not only to consider how it directly affects the people in that area but also to take a view of how the proposed changes will affect the organization as a whole. In making this analysis, the individual introducing the change, who is often called the 'change agent' should recognize that new ideas are likely to be misunderstood and should make ample provision for the discussion of reactions to proposals to ensure complete understanding of them. It is also necessary to try to gain an understanding of the feelings and fears of those affected so that unnecessary worries can be relieved and, as far as possible, ambiguities can be resolved.

Overcoming resistance to change

Resistance to change is likely to be less if:

*   The change is perceived as being consistent with the norms of the organization and in accordance with its existing values.
*   The programme for change offers the kind of new experience which interests participants.
*   The change is seen as reducing rather than increasing present burdens.
*   Those affected feel that their autonomy and security are not threatened, as far as this is possible.
*   It can be demonstrated that the change meets the needs of those affected, ie 'there is something in it for them'.
*   The outcome of change is reasonably certain.
*   There is a compelling and fully understood reason for change.
*   The organization is familiar with change.
*   It can be demonstrated that the organization will take steps to reduce, if not eliminate, any potentially detrimental results of change. These steps could include retraining, guarantees of employment elsewhere in the organization, protection of existing status and pay (if possible) or comprehensive outplacement for those unavoidably made redundant.

Gaining commitment to change

'People support what they help create.' Commitment to change is improved if those affected by change are allowed to participate as fully as possible in planning and implementing it. The aim should be to get them to 'own' the change as something they want and will be glad to live with. Getting involvement in the introduction of change will be effective in gaining commitment only if management is prepared to listen and to change its plans if there is a clear message that they are unworkable, or could be made more acceptable without impairing the achievement of the objectives of the change programme.

Accelerating change

The steps outlined above are an essential part of a change management programme. If they are carried out properly, the further actions required to accelerate the pace of change are as follows:

1. Agree firm objectives, ie an 'agenda for change'.
2. Determine success criteria and define methods of measuring performance and progress towards achieving the objectives, both short- and long-term.
3. Provide, in Kanter's[4] words, 'An environment of support in which recognition of achievements to date will reinforce confidence to do more.'
4. Deliver visionary leadership which encourages people to be bold and innovative and harnesses the ideas and talents of employees in the search for better ways of doing things.
5. Ensure the full collaboration and partnership of all resources in the business.
6. Generate a widespread attitude among all employees that encourages commitment to innovation and change by:

   (a) Personal briefings on the proposed changes cascading down through each level in the organization to cover all employees. This is better than simply issuing memos, a step which may generate only a 'so what?' reaction.
   (b) Workshops in which groups get together to discuss, analyse and interpret the proposed changes. These should be treated as opportunities for employees to get involved in planning change as well as implementing it.
   (c) Various forms of educational and training programmes which allow plenty of time to get the various messages across and to discuss their meaning and applications fully.

Levers for change

A number of levers for change are available, as illustrated in Figure 14.1. All these levers can and should be actuated by top management but the

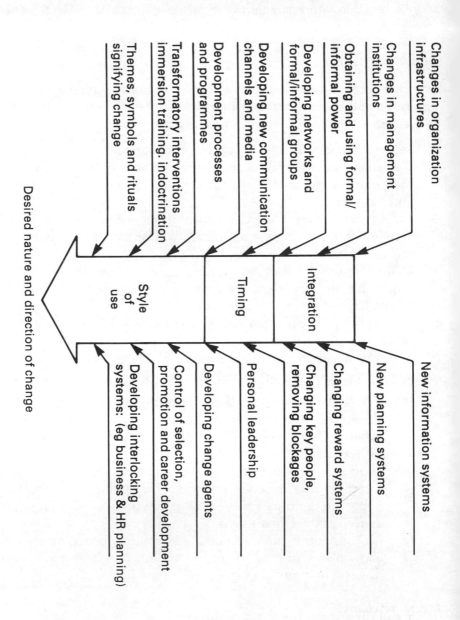

Changes in organization infrastructures

Changes in management institutions

Obtaining and using formal/informal power

Developing networks and formal/informal groups

Developing new communication channels and media

Development processes and programmes

Transformatory interventions immersion training; indoctrination

Themes, symbols and rituals signifying change

New information systems

New planning systems

Changing reward systems

Changing key people, removing blockages

Personal leadership

Developing change agents

Control of selection, promotion and career development

Developing interlocking systems: (eg business & HR planning)

Integration

Timing

Style of use

Desired nature and direction of change

Figure 14.1 Some levers for change

personnel director and his or her staff can exert much influence as change agents in helping to develop and implement the policies, procedures and processes involved.

Mission statements

Definition

A mission statement defines the purpose of the organization, where it is going and the guiding principles it is following to get there.

Use

Mission statements can:

- Focus attention on purpose — what the organization exists to do.
- Convey top management's vision about the future of the organization.
- Provide a foundation upon which strategic plans can be built.
- Lead to the development of explicit statements defining the core values of the organization.
- Be used as levers for change by acting as the starting point for programmes designed to develop new structures and systems or achieve other innovations and improved performance.

Preparation

A mission statement is best prepared at a top management workshop in which plenty of time — a whole day is not too long — is spent in thoroughly examining the issues and their implications.

The mission statement should be prepared as follows:

- It should have 'personality'. In other words, it should reflect what the organization and its top management are really like and should not contain bland pieces of prose reached down from the shelf.
- There should be top management consensus about the statement and commitment to its message.
- The formulation of a mission statement should go hand in hand with the definition of strategies, core values and critical success factors — what the business intends to do, the way it intends to go about doing it and the criteria for accomplishment.
- The mission statement should take account of the external environment and the corporate culture.

271

- Management behaviour must be consistent with its declared mission; otherwise, the statement is devalued and loses credibility.
- Specific action in the shape of briefings, discussions and workshops should be taken to ensure that the mission statement and its supporting strategies, core values and critical success factors are disseminated and discussed throughout the organization.

Value statements

Definition

A value statement expresses basic beliefs on the behaviour which is believed to be good for the organization and on what the organization considers important.

Use

The purpose of a value statement is to develop a value-driven and committed organization which conducts its business successfully by reference to shared beliefs and an understanding of what is best for the business.

Value statements are closely associated with mission statements and, like them, can be used as levers for change — getting people to behave differently in ways which will support the attainment of the organization's objectives. And it is only by changing behaviour that fundamental changes in the culture can be achieved.

Content

A value statement defines core values in areas such as:

- care for customers;
- concern for people (creating what Handy[8] calls a 'concern culture');
- competitiveness;
- enterprise;
- excellence;
- flexibility;
- growth as a major objective;
- innovation;
- market/customer orientation;
- performance orientation;
- productivity;
- quality;
- teamwork.

The individual statements may be backed up by lists of general principles on how they should be applied. For example, one of ICL's core values is commitment to teamwork. This commitment is defined as follows. Teamwork is vital to ICL because it improves our performance in two ways:

1. It helps to raise our individual standards by sharing talent and by improving each other's creative performance.
2. It enables everyone in our highly integrated business to work closely with others in order to harness all the skills the job requires.

The guiding principles in developing teamwork are:

*   Teamwork must be based on the need to heighten the capabilities, competences and contributions of each individual.
*   Even when formal team structures do not exist, we have to get into the way of talking to each other and working together whenever it would improve performance to do so.
*   ICL accepts its obligations as a company to provide individuals with a high degree of freedom to do their job and to develop their own individuality and contribution to the full, within the context of real achievement through teamwork and cooperation.

Preparation of value statements

Value statements should be prepared as follows:

*   The statement should be based on a thorough analysis of existing core values. This analysis should be carried out by means of individual and group meetings (workshops) starting at the top and covering all areas and levels of the organization.
*   Functional, ie acceptable values can then be reaffirmed.
*   If, however, values need to be restated, they should be expressed in a form which represents either reality, what is happening, or an intention to make it happen — a definition of what can realistically be achieved in a way acceptable to all concerned.
*   There is no point in top management's preparing a statement and then simply issuing it. The statement should be produced in draft form following the initial analysis of core values. It should then be discussed at all levels and modified as necessary.

Follow-up

Follow-up action should take five forms:

1. top management's demonstrating by its behaviour that the values are real;
2. workshops;
3. process development;
4. systems development;
5. performance management.

These are described below.

Top management support

Top management should not merely make pronouncements. Exhortation is not enough. It should visibly be acting in accordance with the values. If, for example, one of the values is encouraging partnership or mutuality, top managers should be involved in workshops and project teams, should walk about, and should respond positively to proposals emerging from improvement groups or productivity task forces.

Workshops .

Workshops (see Appendix P, pages 935–936) should be used not only to devise and present the value statement but also to explore its implications at each level. Their aim should be to gain commitment to the values. Participants can be encouraged to restate the values in their own language and to suit their own circumstances. Action plans can emerge from these discussions. Workshops should be held within every division, function and level to cater for the fact that there will be a number of subcultures in the organization.

Process development

Values associated with processes such as teamwork, quality and customer care can be supported by further training, which should be highly participative (workshops). Process consulting techniques should also be used.

Systems development

Each value should be analysed to determine the extent to which existing systems need to be developed or new systems introduced which will underpin the value and help to make it a way of life. For example:

- Planning and budgetary control;
- Total quality assurance;
- Customer care;
- Performance appraisal using goal setting techniques;
- Performance related training programme;
- Performance related pay;

- Human resource planning;
- Career development.

Performance management
Values can be incorporated into a performance management system (see Chapter 19) as factors to be taken into account when setting performance standards and reviewing results.

Motivation strategy

The following ten-point motivation strategy is based on the combined messages of expectancy and goal theory, as described in Chapter 7.

1. Set demanding goals.
2. Provide feedback on performance.
3. Create expectations that certain behaviours and outputs will produce worthwhile rewards.
4. Design jobs which enable people to feel a sense of accomplishment, to use their abilities and to exercise their own decision-making powers.
5. Provide appropriate financial rewards for achievement.
6. Provide non-financial rewards, such as praise and recognition for work well done.
7. Communicate the links between performance and reward.
8. Appoint managers and team leaders who will be able to motivate, and provide them with training in leadership skills as necessary.
9. Give people the guidance and training which will help them to use their abilities to the full.
10. Help individuals to understand what they have to do to satisfy their career aspirations.

Commitment strategy

The ten components of commitment strategy are as follows:

1. Define and disseminate the mission and values of the organization.
2. Develop shared objectives by ensuring that everyone understands the strategies of the organization and participates in setting his or her own objectives within the framework of those strategies.
3. Get people involved in defining problems and working out solutions in order that they 'own' any changes that emerge from this process.
4. Provide transformational leadership from the top which can inspire people with a vision for the future.

5.   Use every medium of communication available to ensure that messages about the organization's mission, values and strategies get across.
6.   Ensure by example and training that the prevailing management style in the organization encourages involvement and teamwork.
7.   Develop processes and an organizational climate which encourages people's growth in terms of skill and higher levels of achievement.
8.   Introduce company-wide profit or gain-sharing plans which encourage people to identify with the organization.
9.   Use induction training programmes to ensure that new employees form a good impression of the company from the outset.
10. Use workshops and other types of training to get people together to discuss the issues facing the company and give them the opportunity to contribute their own ideas. Take action on any good ideas that emerge from this process.

Teamwork

Significance of effective teamwork

The importance of improving the effectiveness of teamwork arises because the flatter organizations of today rely much more on people working well together to get results, especially on complex projects and under pressure.

Approach to achieving good teamwork

Walton[28] has commented that in the new commitment-based organization:

> Jobs are designed to be broader than before, to combine planning and implementation and to include efforts to upgrade operations, not just maintain them. Individual responsibilities are expected to change as conditions change, and often teams, not individuals, are the organizational units accountable for performance.

However, teamwork, as Wickens[10] has said, 'is not dependent on people working in groups but upon everyone working towards the same objectives'. The Nissan concept of teamwork is expressed in its General Principles as quoted by Wickens which emphasize the need to:

*   promote mutual trust and cooperation between the company, its employees and the union;
*   recognize that all employees, at whatever level, have a valued part to play in the success of the company;

- seek actively the contributions of all employees in furthering these goals.

Waterman[29] has noted that teamwork 'is a tricky business; it requires people to pull together toward a set of shared goals or values. It does not mean that they always agree on the best way to get there. When they don't agree they should discuss, even argue these differences.' Pascale[11] underlined this point when he wrote that successful companies can use conflict to stay ahead: 'We are almost always better served when conflict is surfaced and channelled, not suppressed.' The pursuit of teamwork should not lead to a 'bland' climate in the organization in which nothing new or challenging ever happens. It is all very well to be 'one big happy family' but this could be disastrous if it breeds complacency and a cosy feeling that the family spirit comes first, whatever is happening in the outside world.

Things to do to improve teamwork

- Pick people who will fit the culture and work well with others but who are still capable of taking their own line when necessary.
- Keep on emphasizing that constructive teamwork is a key core value in the organization.
- Assess people's performance not only on the results they achieve but also on the degree to which they uphold this value of teamwork.
- Encourage people to build networks — things get done in organizations, as in the outside world, on the basis of whom you know as well as what you know. It is no good being right if you cannot carry other people along with you. And this is best done through informal channels rather than relying on reports, memoranda or committees. This, incidentally, is an approach that people without a strong power base in the organization, such as some personnel managers, can use to good effect.
- Set up interdepartmental project teams with a brief to get on with it.
- Clamp down on unproductive politics.
- Describe and think of the organization as a system of interlocking teams united by a common purpose. Don't emphasize hierarchies. Abolish departmental boundaries if they are getting in the way, but do not be alarmed if there is disagreement — remember the value of *constructive* conflict.
- Devise and implement commitment and communications strategies which develop mutuality and identification.
- Hold 'away days' and conferences for work teams so that they can get together and explore some of the real issues without the pressures of their day-to-day jobs.

- Use training programmes to build relationships. This can often be a far more beneficial result of a course than the increase in skills or knowledge which was its ostensible purpose.
- Use team-building and interactive skills training to supplement all the other approaches.
- Set overlapping objectives for managers and their teams.

Team-building and interactive skills development

Team-building training aims to:

- increase awareness of the social processes that take place within groups;
- develop the interactive or interpersonal skills which enable individuals to function effectively as team members;
- increase the overall effectiveness with which groups operate in the organization.

The ways in which team building can influence attitudes and behaviour are illustrated in Figure 14.2. Interactive or interpersonal skills training aims to increase the effectiveness with which individuals interact, not only with fellow team members but also with anyone else with whom they come into contact.

To be effective, team building and other interpersonal development programmes should:

- be directly relevant to the responsibilities of the participants;

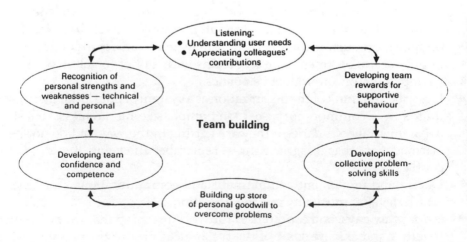

Figure 14.2 Team building as an influence on attitudes and behaviour

- be seen as relevant by participants, their managers, subordinates and colleagues;
- support business objectives;
- fit in with practical working arrangements;
- reflect the values the organization wishes to promote.

More information on team building and interactive skills training is given in Appendix P.

Communications and involvement

Communications and involvement programmes aim to increase the identification of people with the organization and therefore their commitment. This is provided by giving employees at all levels the opportunity to become more involved in the organization's affairs. These programmes also aim to generate ideas from people to improve overall organizational effectiveness, especially in the areas of quality, customer service and productivity.

Methods of developing communications and involvement include:

- joint consultation;
- quality circles or improvement groups;
- briefing groups;
- better use of media such as company magazines.

These are described in Chapters 31 and 32.

Conflict management

The basic assumptions about conflict made by Blake, Shepart and Mouton[30] are that:

- Conflict is inevitable; agreement is impossible.
- Conflict is not inevitable, yet agreement is not possible.
- Although there is conflict, agreement is possible.

The third assumption is clearly the most hopeful. Three approaches can be adopted if this assumption is held:

1. *Peaceful co-existence.* People are encouraged to work happily with one another. There is the maximum amount of information, contact and exchange of views, and people move freely between groups. This is a pleasant ideal but it may lead to smoothing over real differences and is not practicable in all circumstances.
2. *Problem solving.* The joint development of solutions to the problem and the sharing of responsibility to see that the solutions work. This is

clearly the best approach. It emphasizes the need to find a genuine solution to the problem, rather than simply accommodating different points of view.

3. *Compromise.* Splitting the difference by negotiation or bargaining. This approach assumes that there is no right or best answer and is essentially pessimistic, although it may be inevitable if the other two approaches are tried and do not work.

The problem-solving approach may involve some form of confrontation. According to Walton,[31] the confrontation is most likely to be successful if:

1. Both parties have incentives to resolve the dispute.
2. Equal power is established between the two parties.
3. Adequate time is allowed for the 'differentiation' phase before moving into the 'integration' phase when the aim is to identify common ground.
4. Conditions are created which favour openness.
5. Mutual understanding is increased through effective communication.
6. Stress and tension in the situation is, as far as possible, kept at a moderate level.

A third party, who could be a member of the personnel department or a consultant, can help to achieve successful integration.

Managing stress

There are two main reasons why organizations should take account of stress and do something about it; first, because they have the social responsibility to provide a reasonable quality of working life and, secondly, because excessive stress among managers and other staff can reduce organizational effectiveness.

The ways in which stress can be managed by an organization include:

- *Job design* — clarifying roles, reducing the danger of role ambiguity and conflict and giving people more autonomy within a defined structure to manage their responsibilities;
- *Placement* — taking care to place people in jobs which are within their capabilities;
- *Career development* — planning careers and promoting staff in accordance with their capabilities, taking care not to over- or under-promote;
- *Performance reviews*, which allow a dialogue to take place between managers and their subordinates about the latters' problems and ambitions;
- *Counselling* — giving individuals the opportunity to talk about their

problems with a member of the personnel department or the company medical officer;

- *Management training* in performance review and counselling techniques and in what managers can do to alleviate their own stress and reduce it in others;
- *Motivation* — encouraging methods of leadership and motivation which do not place excessive demands on people.

Quality and customer care

The need for total quality and customer care

Competitive edge is built and sustained in many ways: by innovation; by aggressive marketing; by efficiency in manufacturing, distribution or the provision of a service; by top-level, inspirational leadership; by effective performance management; and by developing a highly competent and fully involved workforce. Transcending all these, however, is the need for everyone in the organization to pursue excellence in all they do. This means the generation of total commitment to quality and a determination to achieve high levels of customer service.

The president and chief executive officer of Hewlett-Packard, John Young, has said:

> In today's competitive environment, ignoring the quality issue is tantamount to corporate suicide.

Wickens has noted that the Japanese have no word for quality. Instead, they use the word 'kaizen', meaning 'continuous improvement by all the staff at all times'.[10]

Production rather than market orientation was perhaps inevitable in the middle years of this century when the determinants of commercial success were mainly price and availability in the marketplace. But markets became saturated, consumerism emerged as a living and powerful force, and buying points in many markets reduced in number with a resulting shift of influence to the retailer. In global markets, the provision of maximum choice to customers became a favoured weapon in the fight for competitive advantage.

Product life cycles are shrinking. Businesses had to become market driven, to recognize that 'the customer is king'. And what customers demand is quality, in terms of both the product itself and the services provided by the organization. Businesses have had to recognize that they can thrive and survive only by delivering quality to their customers.

Quality assurance and BS 5750

BS 5750, as summarized in Appendix G, provides the national standards which tell suppliers and manufacturers what is required of a quality system. It sets out, in the words of Collard,[32] 'how an organization can establish, document and maintain an effective quality system which will demonstrate to customers that the organization is committed to quality and is able to meet their quality needs'. It therefore provides for quality assurance standards, but these are not ends in themselves. They are only a basis for a total quality management (TQM) approach, as described below.

Total quality management (TQM)

What it is

Total quality management is an intensive, long-term effort directed at the creation and maintenance of the high standards of product quality and services expected by customers. The object is significantly to increase the awareness of all employees that quality is vital to the organization's success and their future. The business must be transformed into a unit which exists to deliver value to customers by satisfying their needs. The steps to successful total quality management (TQM) are the following:

- measure quality;
- determine the cost of quality;
- incorporate quality objectives into strategic plans;
- build TQM into accountabilities of every job and into all related systems (eg performance appraisal);
- form quality teams which are integrated, top to bottom and bottom to top, as well as laterally to include suppliers and customers;
- obtain demonstrable commitment from top management;
- build skills through training;
- recognize and reward quality improvement.

What it isn't

Total quality management is not a 'programme', a term which implies a finite beginning and end. It is, in fact, a continuous performance.

However, although the emphasis on quality can never be relaxed, quality management is not simply a matter of demanding ever-increasing quality target levels, thus implying that acceptable quality is unattainable. This is a defeatist approach. Neither is it a matter of using quality control and inspection systems and expecting that these alone will improve quality, although they have their uses as monitoring and measuring devices. Total quality is not achieved by techniques, such as quality circles, which, as Wickens[10] says, are no more than 'a fine tuning mechanism for companies whose quality is already good'.

Quality is an attitude of mind which leads to appropriate behaviours and actions. It has to be, as at Nissan, 'the centrepiece of the company's philosophy, with commitment *at every level* to a zero-defect product'.

The approach to TQM

Giles and Williams[33] have suggested that quality management should be achieved

> by the application of basic principles of motivation throughout the organization. Top management sets the priorities and initial goals and allocates responsibility. Those made responsible then say what they need in the way of resources and top management back-up to achieve these. The process continues down through the hierarchy until all those on the shopfloor have negotiated what their priorities are and the resources needed to achieve these. Goals are thus set in a way that everyone's work fits in with the organization's priorities and each person knows what they have to do, in measurable terms.

And Collard[32] suggests: 'Quality improvement should always be at the forefront of *everything* that is done, continuously reinforced and developed by management through the systems, processes and organizations which make each improvement possible.'

Customer care programmes

Total quality management processes aim to improve all aspects of quality, although the focus is always on satisfying customer needs. Customer care programmes concentrate on the levels of service provided by the organization as an important aspect of total quality. This covers the services provided to customers at the order-processing or fulfilment (selling) stage, which includes all personal contacts with customers, as well as after-sales service. Customer service is a continuous process and although it is usually described as a programme, this is misleading if it implies that it consists of a limited campaign.

Customer care programmes recognize that customer choice is increasingly being determined by the perceived level of service the business provides for them. They are also based on the understanding that quality and service are the main factors which generate customer loyalty — to the product or to the brand. An enterprise wants to obtain good business from its customers but it also wants repeat business.

The general principles governing the improvement of levels of customer care and service are similar to those for total quality improvement, namely:

1. The drive for customer care must be led from the top.
2. Customer care must be accepted and 'owned' by management at all levels as something which will lead to specific and measurable improvements in organizational performance and the bottom line.
3. Actions speak louder than words. Anything that management does which affects customer service, however remotely (and this means just about everything), should be seen by all concerned as part of a continuous improvement process.
4. The concept of customer care and all that it implies must be spread to all levels of the organization. A 'cascade' approach is usually best if it generates commitment and action at each level which can be passed on down the organization.
5. The approach to developing constructive, positive and profitable attitudes towards customer care must make the customer come alive for all employees. This involves making the points as strongly as possible that 'real people are counting on us to do our jobs well' and that 'every contact with a customer is an opportunity to add value and quality'.
6. Explicitly identify and strengthen all customer connections.
7. Bear in mind that all employees are also customers, so that messages about customer service can be presented to them as real concerns which they have to live with, rather than abstractions such as productivity and profitability. They know when they are getting value as customers and the concept of added value can therefore easily be made real to them.
8. Establish direct links between what every function does and its impact on the customer. This includes those which are not in direct contact with customers. In fact, particular care should be taken to include them. Having established the links, analyse the attitudes and skills required to provide better customer care and assess the degree to which the attitudes exist and the skills are practised. Any gaps identified between actual and desired behaviour define a training need.
9. Remember that doing things better generally means doing things differently. Improving levels of customer service involves cultural change. This is not achieved easily or quickly. One- or two-day seminars and a lot of sloganizing are not enough. Continuing effort is required to produce commitment to customer care and to make

significant changes for the better in attitudes and behaviour.

10. The impact of customer care on performance and on customer attitudes and buying behaviour must be measured. Success criteria should be set and results monitored against these criteria in direct bottom-line terms or by means of customer research and attitude surveys.

The contribution of the personnel function

The personnel function is ideally placed to make a major contribution to total quality and customer care. Improvements in these areas mean influencing the attitudes and behaviour of employees. Cultural change is involved.

To achieve this requires research and analysis of present attitudes, beliefs and competences and the development and implementation of relevant education, training, communication and performance appraisal programmes. All these are within the remit of the personnel function, which has, or should have, the skills and the independence required to support and help implement top management's total quality improvement mission.

As Cowan[34] put it:

When you get into customer care you get into the whole culture of the organization. This means that personnel directors are riding into the basic philosophy of the company. And this is inevitable when you think it's about people — their selection, training, career progression and organization. In this area the personnel director can contribute directly to the bottom line by providing what Karen Legge[35] calls 'unique, non-substitutable expertise'.

References

1. Pascale, R and Athos, A *The Art of Japanese Management.* Sidgwick & Jackson, London, 1986.
2. Peters, T and Waterman, R *In Search of Excellence.* Harper & Row, New York, 1982.
3. Peters, T *Thriving on Chaos.* Macmillan, London, 1988.
4. Kanter, R M *The Change Masters.* Allen & Unwin, London, 1984.
5. Kanter, R M *When Giants Learn to Dance.* Simon & Schuster, London, 1989.
6. Beckhard, R *Organization Development: Strategy and Models.* Addison-Wesley, Reading, MA, 1969.
7. Harvey-Jones, J *Making it Happen.* Collins, London, 1988.
8. Handy, C *The Age of Unreason.* Business Books, London, 1989.
9. Child, J 'What determines organization performance?' In Magnusen, K M (ed.), *Organization Design, Development and Behaviour: A Situational View.* Scott Foreman, Glenview, IL, 1977.

10. Wickens, P *The Road to Nissan*. Macmillan, London, 1987.
11. Pascale, R *Managing on the Edge*. Viking, London, 1990.
12. Argyris, C *Personality and Organization*. Harper, New York, 1961.
13. Mayo, E *The Human Problem of an Industrial Civilization*. Macmillan, London, 1933.
14. Whyte. W F *Human Relations in the Restaurant Industry*. McGraw-Hill, New York, 1948.
15. Brown, J A C *The Social Psychology of Industry*. Penguin, Harmondsworth, 1954.
16. Lewin, K 'Frontiers in group dynamics', *Human Relations*, 1947.
17. Bales, R F 'A set of categories for the analysis of small group interaction', *American Sociological Review*, 1954.
18. Schein, E H *Process Consultation*. Addison-Wesley, Reading, MA, 1969.
19. Herzberg, F 'One more time: how do you motivate employees', *Harvard Business Review*, September–October 1987.
20. Likert, R *New Patterns of Management*. McGraw-Hill, New York, 1969.
21. Maslow, A H *Motivation and Personality*. Harper & Row, New York, 1954.
22. McGregor, D *The Human Side of Enterprise*. McGraw-Hill, New York, 1966.
23. Trist, E *et al Organizational Choice*. Tavistock, London, 1963.
24. Weightman, J *Managing Human Resources*. Institute of Personnel Management, London, 1990.
25. Rogers, C *On Becoming a Person*. Constable, London, 1967.
26. Argyris, C *Intervention Theory and Method*. Addison-Wesley, Reading, MA, 1970.
27. Lewin, K *Field Theory in Social Science*. Harper & Row, New York, 1951.
28. Walton, R 'From control to commitment in the work place', *Harvard Business Review*. March–April 1985.
29. Waterman, R *The Renewal Factor*. Bantam, New York, 1988.
30. Blake, R, Shepart, H, and Mouton, J *Managing Intergroup Conflict in Industry*. Gulf Publishing, Houston, TX, 1964.
31. Walton, R *Interpersonal Peacemaking: Confrontations and Third Party Consultation*. Addison-Wesley, Reading, MA, 1969.
32. Collard, R *Total Quality: Success Through People*. Institute of Personnel Management, London, 1989.
33. Giles, E and Williams, R, 'Can the personnel department survive quality management?' *Personnel Management*, April, 1991.
34. Cowan, N, quoted in Armstrong, M *Personnel and the Bottom Line*. Institute of Personnel Management, London, 1989.
35. Legge, K *Power, Innovation and Problem-Solving in Personnel Management*. McGraw-Hill, Maidenhead, 1978.

Part IV
Employee Resourcing

Employee resourcing means ensuring that the organization knows and gets what it wants in the way of the people needed to run the business now and in the future. It starts from an initial analysis of the strategic objective of the company and continues with an analysis of the human resources required to achieve them.

Human resource planning uses demand and supply forecasting techniques to set out needs in both quantitative (how many people) and qualitative (what sort of people) terms. It provides the basis for resourcing programmes which use recruitment procedures and selection techniques to ensure that requirements are met in accordance with quality, quantity and time specifications.

15

Human Resource Planning

Definition

Human resource planning has been defined by the Institute of Personnel Management as

> The systematic and continuing process of analysing an organization's human resource needs under changing conditions and developing personnel policies appropriate to the longer-term effectiveness of the organization. It is an integral part of corporate planning and budgeting procedures since human resource costs and forecasts both affect and are affected by longer-term corporate plans.

Aims

The aims of human resource planning are to ensure that the organization:

- obtains and retains the quantity and quality of people it needs;
- makes the best use of its human resources;
- is able to anticipate the problems of potential surpluses or deficits of people;
- can develop a well-trained and flexible workforce, thus contributing to the organization's ability to adapt to an uncertain and changing environment;
- reduces its dependence on external recruitment when key skills are in short supply — this means formulating retention, as well as human resource development strategies.

Resourcing strategy

Resourcing strategy contributes both to the formulation and the implementation of business strategies.

Formulation of business strategies

Resourcing strategy contributes to the formulation of business strategy by identifying opportunities to utilize human resources more effectively and pointing out how human resource constraints may affect the implementation of the proposed strategies unless action is taken. Those constraints might include skill shortages; high recruitment, training and employment costs; or insufficient flexibility.

Implementation strategies

These consist of:

- *acquisition strategies*, which define how the resources required to meet forecast needs will be obtained;
- *retention strategies*, which indicate how the organization intends to keep the people it wants;
- *development strategies*, which describe what needs to be done to extend and increase skills (multiskilling) to fit people for greater responsibility, and also define the outputs required from training programmes;
- *utilization strategies*, which indicate intentions to improve productivity and cost-effectiveness;
- *flexibility strategies*, which show how the organization can develop more flexible work arrangements;
- *downsizing strategies*, which define what needs to be done to streamline the labour force.

The basis of human resourcing strategies

The basis for human resourcing strategies is longer-term business plans and shorter-term budgets and programmes. These define demand requirements. But the strategy must also deal with the supply side, from within and outside the organization. Internal supply-side planning means forecasting the output of training schemes and losses through labour turnover. The impact of absenteeism would also have to be considered.

External supply-side planning means looking at demographics — the likely supply of school-leavers, professionally qualified staff and university graduates entering the local and national labour market. The 'demographic time bomb' which was identified in the 1980s highlighted and accelerated decline in the number of young people entering the labour market in the early 1990s while noting that the numbers will slowly increase in the second half of the decade.

A further key factor is the increasing demand from employers for 'knowledge workers' and other highly skilled craftsmen, coupled with their requirement for workers with a wider range of skills in the core of the new, flexible firm.

Turning broad strategies into action plans

Resourcing strategies show the way forward through the analysis of business strategies and demographic trends. They are converted into action plans based on the outcome of the following interrelated planning activities:

1. *Demand forecasting* — estimating future manpower needs by reference to corporate and functional plans and forecasts of future activity levels.
2. *Supply forecasting* — estimating the supply of manpower by reference to analyses of current resources and future availability, after allowing for wastage.

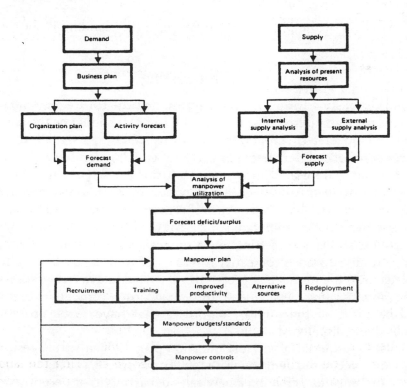

Figure 15.1 The process of human resource planning

3. *Forecasting requirements* — analysing the demand and supply forecasts to identify future deficits or surpluses with the help of models, where appropriate.
4. *Productivity and cost analysis* — analysing productivity, capacity, utilization and costs in order to identify the need for improvements in productivity or reductions in cost.
5. *Action planning* — preparing plans to deal with forecast deficits or surpluses of manpower, to improve utilization and productivity or to reduce costs.
6. *Budgeting and control* — setting human resource budgets and standards and monitoring the implementation of the plans against them.

Although these are described as six separate areas, and are analysed as such in later sections of this chapter, they are, in fact, closely interrelated and often overlap. For example, demand forecasts are estimates of future requirements, and these can be prepared only on the basis of assumptions about the productivity of employees. But the supply forecast will also have to consider productivity trends and how they might affect the supply of people.

A flow chart of the process of human resource planning is shown in Figure 15.1.

Demand forecasting

Demand forecasting is the process of estimating the future quantity and quality of people required. The basis of the forecast should be the annual budget and longer-term corporate plan, translated into activity levels for each function and department. In a manufacturing company the sales budget would be translated into a manufacturing plan giving the numbers and types of products to be made in each period. From this information the number of hours to be worked by each skill category to make the quota for each period would be computed. A plan for a van sales operation would start from the sales plan setting out a programme for establishing new rounds. In an insurance company, forecasts of new business would be translated into the number of proposals that would have to be processed by the underwriting department. In a mail order company, forecasts would be made of the number of orders that have to be processed, assembled and dispatched.

Details are required of any organization plans which would result in increased or decreased demands for staff. For example, setting up a new regional organization, creating a new sales department, or decentralizing a head office function to the regions.

The planning data would refer to expected changes in productivity or manpower levels arising from changes in working methods or procedures, automation or mechanization. These could be set out as a crude percentage increase in productivity which could be used to adjst the required hours for a given level of output. Or they might give specific instances of cases where the manning for a machine, a production line, a clerical section or a sales office is to be increased or decreased.

Demand forecasting methods

There are four basic demand forecasting methods:

1. managerial judgement;
2. ratio-trend analysis;
3. work study techniques;
4. modelling.

These are described separately below, although in many cases a combination of, say, managerial judgement and statistical techniques would be used.

Managerial judgement

The most typical method of forecasting used in smaller companies is managerial judgement. This simply requires managers to sit down, think about their future workloads, and decide how many people they need. It might be done on a 'bottom-up' basis with line managers submitting proposals for agreement by senior management.

Alternatively, a 'top-down' approach can be used, in which company and departmental forecasts are prepared by top management, possibly acting on advice from the personnel departments. These forecasts are reviewed and agreed with departmental managers. A less directive approach is for top management to prepare planning guidelines for departmental managers setting out the planning assumptions and the targets they should try to meet.

Perhaps the best way of using managerial judgement is to adopt both the 'bottom-up' and 'top-down' approach. Guidelines for departmental managers should be prepared which indicate broad company assumptions about future activity levels which will affect their departments. Targets are also set where necessary. Armed with these guidelines, departmental managers prepare their forecasts to a laid-down format. They are encouraged to seek help at this stage from personnel or work study.

Meanwhile, the personnel department, in conjunction as necessary with planning and work study departments, prepares a company human resource forecast. The two sets of forecasts can then be reviewed by a human resource planning committee consisting of functional heads. This committee reconciles with departmental managers any discrepancies between the two forecasts and submits the final amended forecast to top management for approval. This is sometimes called the 'right-angle method'.

An example of a staff forecast form using managerial judgement is shown in Figure 15.2.

Ratio-trend analysis

In its crudest form, ratio-trend analysis is carried out by studying past ratios between, say, the number of direct and indirect workers in a manufacturing plant, and forecasting future ratios, having made some allowance for changes in organization or methods. Activity level forecasts are then used to determine direct labour requirements and the forecast ratio of indirects to directs is used to calculate the number of indirect workers needed. For example, Table 15.1 shows how ratio-trend analysis could be used to forecast the number of inspectors required in an assembly plant. Similar techniques could be used to develop fairly crude ratios between activity levels and numbers of staff.

Table 15.1 Demand forecast — inspectors

	Year	No. of Employees		Ratio Inspector : Production
		Production	*Inspector*	
Actual	–3	1500	150	1 : 10
	–2	1800	180	1 : 10
	Last year	2000	180	1 : 11
Forecast	Next year	2200*	200†	1 : 11
	+2	2500*	210†	1 : 12
	+3	2750	230†	1 : 12

* calculated by reference to forecast activity levels
† calculated by applying forecast ratio to forecast activity levels

Category of staff .... Year		
Staff members and movements	*No. of staff to be provided*	*Remarks*
1. Number of staff at 1.1 ..... (excluding known resignations) 75	—	Age groups: Under 25 30 25–34 20 35–44 15 45 and over 10
2.(a) Expected retirements, transfers out, and promotions during year 8 (b) Less expected transfers in, promotions, and new appointments already made 3	 5	(dates to be specified) Increase in number to be substantiated by O&M report
3.(a) Number of staff required at 1 January, next year 80 (b) Less present staff 75	5	
4. Expected staff losses due to normal wastage of existing staff 15	15	Estimated by age groups: Under 25 12 25–34 2 35–44 1 45 and over —
5. Expected losses of staff to be recruited in the period 5	5	Short service staff turnover at 20% of 25 (events 2. + 3. + 4 above)
6. Total staff to be provided during period	30	5 to be recruited by 1 February — others to be programmed later

Figure 15.2 Staff forecast form

Table 15.2 shows how an analysis of actual and forecast ratios between the number of routine proposals to be processed by an insurance company underwriting department and the number of underwriters employed could be used to forecast future requirements.

These techniques, although crude, are easy to understand and use. Their value depends upon accurate records and realistic estimates of future activity levels and effect of improved performance or changed methods.

Table 15.2 Demand forecast — underwriters

	Year	No. of underwriters	No. of proposals per week	Ratio Underwriters : Proposals
	–3	10	2000	1 : 200
Actual	–2	10	2500	1 : 250
	Last Year	12	3600	1 : 300
	Next Year	14	4200	1 : 300
Forecast	+2	16	4800	1 : 300
	+3	18	5400	1 : 300

Work study techniques

Work study techniques can be used when it is possible to apply work measurement to calculate how long operations should take and the amount of labour required. The starting point in a manufacturing company is the production budget prepared in terms of volumes of saleable products for the company as a whole, or volumes of output for individual departments. The budgets of productive hours are then compiled by the use of standard hours for direct labour, if standard labour times have been established by work measurement. The standard hours per unit of output are then multiplied by the planned volume of units to be produced to give the total planned hours for the period. This is divided by the number of actual working hours for an individual operator to show the number of operators required. Allowance may have to be made for absenteeism and forecast levels of idle time. The following is a highly simplified example of this procedure:

(a)	Planned output for year	20,000 units
(b)	Standard hours per unit	5 hours
(c)	Planned hours for year	100,000 hours
(d)	Productive hours per man/year (allowing normal overtime, absenteeism and down time)	2000 hours
(e)	Number of direct workers required (c/d)	50

Work study techniques for direct workers can be combined with ratio-trend analysis to calculate the number of indirect workers needed. Clerical staff requirements may also be estimated by these methods if clerical work measurement techniques can be used.

Modelling

Mathematical modelling techniques using computers can help in the preparation of demand forecasts. These are discussed later in this chapter (pages 307-10).

Supply forecasting

Human resources comprise the total effective effort that can be put to work as shown by the number of people and hours of work available, the capacity of employees to do the work and their productivity. Supply forecasting measures the number of people likely to be available from within and outside the organization, having allowed for absenteeism, internal movements and promotions, wastage and changes in hours and other conditions of work. The supply analysis covers:

- existing human resources;
- potential losses to existing resources through labour wastage;
- potential changes to existing resources through internal promotions;
- effect of changing conditions of work and absenteeism;
- sources of supply from within the firm.

The information required and the methods of analysis that can be used are considered below. As in the case of demand forecasting, the process of supply forecasting can be greatly facilitated by the use of human resource modelling techniques.

Analysing existing human resources

The basic analysis should classify employees by function or department, occupation, level of skill and status.

The aim should be to identify from this analysis 'resource centres' consisting of broadly homogenous groups for which forecasts of supply need to be made. There is endless scope for cross analysis in preparing human resource inventories, but beware of collecting useless data; it is necessary to subject the analytical scheme to rigorous analysis, and for each category to ask the questions: 'Why do we need this information?' and 'What are we going to do with it when we get it?'

Some detailed analysis may be essential. For example, the review of current resources may need to cut across organizational and occupational boundaries to provide inventories of skills and potential. It may be important to know how many people the organization has with special skills or abilities; for example, chemists, physicists, mathematicians, economists or linguists. From the point of view of management succession planning and the preparation of management development programmes, it may be equally important to know how many people with potential for promotion exist and where they can be found.

An analysis of staff by age helps to identify problems arising from a sudden rush of retirements, a block in promotion prospects, or a preponderance of older employees. Age distribution can be illustrated graphically, as in Figure 15.3, which shows that a large number of staff will retire shortly and that the proportion of employees in the older age brackets is unduly high.

Length of service analysis may be even more important because it will provide evidence of survival rates, which, as discussed later, are a necessary tool for use by planners in predicting future resources.

The analysis of current resources should look at the existing ratios between different categories of staff; for example, supervisors to employees, skilled to semi-skilled, direct to indirect, or clerical to production. Recent movements in these ratios should be studied to provide guidance on trends and to highlight areas where rapid changes may result in manpower supply problems.

Wastage or staff turnover

Employee wastage should be analysed in order to forecast future losses and to identify the reasons that people leave the organization. Plans can

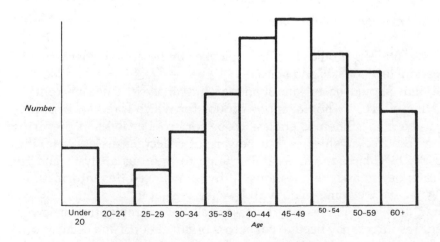

Figure 15.3 Analysis of age distribution

then be made to attack the problems causing unnecessary wastage and to replace uncontrollable losses. The human resource planner therefore has to know how to measure wastage and how to analyse its causes.

Measuring turnover or wastage
This can be done in various ways:

Turnover Index.   This is the traditional formula for measuring wastage:

$$\frac{\text{Number of leavers in a specified period (usually 1 year)}}{\text{Average number of employees during the same period}} \times 100$$

This method is in common use because it is easy to calculate and to understand. It is a simple matter to work out that if last year 30 out of an average force of 150 skilled fitters left (20 per cent turnover), and this trend continues, then the company will have to recruit 110 fitters during the following year, in order to increase and to hold the labour force at 200 in that year (50 extra fitters, plus 40 to replace the 20 per cent wastage of the average 200 fitters employed, plus 20 to replace wastage of the 90 recruits).

This wastage formula is simple to use. But it can be positively misleading. The main objection to the measurement of turnover in terms of the proportion of those who leave in a given period is that the figure may be inflated by the high turnover of a relatively small proportion of the work-force, especially in times of heavy recruitment. Thus, a company employing 1000 people might have had an annual wastage rate of 20 per cent, meaning that 200 jobs had become vacant during the year. But this could have been spread throughout the company, covering all occupations and long- as well as short-service employees. Alternatively, it could have been restricted to a small sector of the workforce — only 20 jobs might have been affected although each of these had to be filled ten times during the year. These are totally different situations, and unless they are appreciated, inaccurate forecasts would be made of future requirements and inappropriate actions would be taken to deal with the problem. The turnover index is also suspect if the average number of employees upon which the percentage is based is unrepresentative of recent trends because of considerable increases or decreases during the period in the numbers employed.

Stability Index.   This measure is considered by many to be an improvement:

$$\frac{\text{Number with 1 year's service or more}}{\text{Number employed 1 year ago}} \times 100$$

Table 15.3 Analysis of leavers by length of service

| Occupation | Leavers by Length of Service 19...... | | | | | | Total no. leaving | Average no. employed | Index of labour turnover |
	less than 3 months	3–6 months	6 months– 1 year	1–2 years	3–5 years	5 or more years			%
Skilled	5	4	3	3	2	3	20	200	10
Semi-skilled	15	12	10	6	3	4	50	250	20
Unskilled	20	10	5	3	1	1	40	100	40
Totals	**40**	**26**	**18**	**12**	**6**	**8**	**100**	**550**	**20**

This index provides an indication of the tendency for longer-service employees to remain with the company, and therefore shows the degree to which there is a continuity of employment. But this too can be misleading because the index will not reveal the vastly different situations that exist in a company or department with a high proportion of long-serving employees in comparison with one where the majority of employees are short service.

Length of Service Analysis. This disadvantage of the stability index may be partly overcome if an analysis is also made of the average length of service of people who leave, as in Table 15.3.

This analysis is still fairly crude, because it deals only with those who leave. A more refined analysis would compare for each service category the numbers leaving with the numbers employed. If, in the example shown, the total numbers employed with fewer than three months' service was 80 and the total with more than five years was 80, the proportion of leavers in each category would be, respectively, 50 per cent and 10 per cent — much more revealing figures, especially if previous periods could be analysed to reveal adverse trends.

Survival Rate. Another method of analysing turnover which is particularly useful for human resource planners is the survival rate: the proportion of employees who are engaged within a certain period who remain with the firm after so many months or years of service. Thus, an analysis of trainees who have completed their training might show that after two years, ten of the original cohort of 20 trainees were still with the company, a survival rate of 50 per cent.

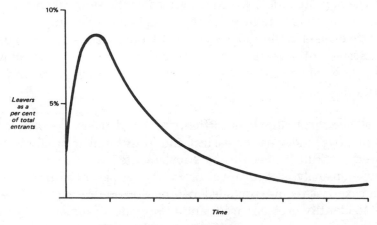

Figure 15.4 A survival curve

The distribution of losses for each entry group, or cohort, can be plotted in the form of a 'survival curve' as shown in Figure 15.4.

The basic shape of this curve has been found to be similar in many situations, although it has been observed that the peak of the curve may occur further along the time scale and/or may be lower when it relates to more highly skilled or trained entry cohorts. Table 15.4 would tell human resource planners that they have to allow for half the number of recruits in any one year to be lost over the next five years, unless something can be done about the factors causing wastage. Thus, to achieve a requirement of 50 trained staff in five years' time, 100 people would have to be engaged this year.

Table 15.4 Survival rate analysis

Entry cohort	Original strength	No. surviving to end of year after engagement				
		Year 1	Year 2	Year 3	Year 4	Year 5
A	40	35	28	26	22	20
B	32	25	24	19	18	17
C	48	39	33	30	25	23
D	38	32	27	24	22	19
E	42	36	30	26	23	21
Average survival rate	100%	83%	71%	62%	55%	50%

Half-Life Index. A simpler concept derived from survival rate analysis is that of the half-life index, which is defined as the time taken for a group or cohort of starters to reduce to half its original size through the wastage process (five years in the above example). Comparisons can then be made for successive entry years or between different groups of employees in order to show where action may have to be taken to counter undesirable wastage trends.

Choice of Measurement. It is difficult to avoid using the conventional labour turnover index as the easiest and most familiar of all methods of measurement. But it needs to be supplemented with some measure of stability — an analysis of turnover or wastage as part of a human resource planning exercise requires detailed information on the length of service of leavers to identify problem areas and to provide a foundation for supply forecasts.

Analysing the effect of promotions and transfers

The supply forecast should indicate the number of vacancies that will have to be filled to meet the demand forecast. Vacancies arise because people leave, but the exit of a senior manager may produce a chain reaction of replacements. Transfers between departments and divisions may also have to be allowed for.

In a large organization, persistent patterns of promotion or transer may develop and it may be possible to predict the proportions of employees in particular categories who are likely to be promoted or moved in the future by starting with a forecast of the chain reaction factor, to give a broad indication of the number of displacements that may occur. For example, where there are three levels of management:

3rd line management	:	1 promotion	=	3 moves
2nd line management	:	5 promotions	=	10 moves
1st line management	:	25 promotions	=	25 moves
Total promotions/moves		**31**		**38**

But this is very crude, and in most companies, management succession planning has to be worked out specifically by reference to known retirements and transfers.

Assessing changes in conditions of work and absenteeism

This assessment should cover factors operating within the firm such as changes in all of the following: normal weekly hours of work; overtime policies; the length and timing of holidays; retirement policy; the policy for employing part-timers; and shift systems.

The effect of absenteeism on the future supply of employees should also be allowed for, and trends in absenteeism should be analysed to trace causes and identify possible remedial actions.

Analysing sources of supply

Internal sources include the output from established training schemes or management development programmes and the reservoirs of skill and potential that exist within the organization. But the availability of people from the local and national labour markets is also a vital factor when preparing development plans. Too often, corporate or functional plans make assumptions about the availability of people locally or nationally which could easily be proved wrong after a brief investigation. It is particularly necessary to identify at an early stage any categories of employees where there might be difficulties in recruiting the numbers required, in order that action can be taken in good time to prepare a recruiting campaign, to tap alternative sources, or to develop training or retraining programmes to convert available staff to meet the company's needs. The factors which can have an important bearing on the supply of manpower are listed below.

Local labour market

1. population densities within reach of the company;
2. current and future competition for staff from other employers;
3. local unemployment levels;
4. the traditional pattern of employment locally, and the availability of people with the required qualifications and skills;
5. the output from the local educational system and government or other training establishments;
6. the pattern of immigration and emigration within the area;
7. the attractiveness of the area as a place to live;
8. the attractiveness of the company as a place to work in;
9. the availability of part-time employees;
10. local housing, shopping and transport facilities.

National labour market

1. trends in the growth of the working population;
2. national demands for special categories of employees — graduates, professional staff, technologists, technicians, craftsmen, secretaries;
3. the output of the universities, polytechnics, and professional institutions;
4. the effect of changing educational patterns — children staying longer at school, or different emphases in university or school curriculae;
5. the impact of national government training schemes;
6. the impact of government employment regulations such as, in the UK, the Employment Protection Act, the Sex Discrimination Act or the Equal Pay Act.

Forecasting human resource requirements

Human resource requirements are forecast by relating the supply to the demand forecasts and establishing any deficits or surpluses of employees that will exist in the future. Table 15.5 shows how demand and supply

Table 15.5 Forecast of recruitment needs for fitters

		Year 1	Year 2	Year 3	Year 4	Year 5
Demand	1. Numbers required at beginning of year	120	140	140	120	120
	2. Changes to requirements forecast during year	+20	Nil	−20	Nil	Nil
	3. Total requirements at end of year (1+2)	140	140	120	120	120
Supply	4. Numbers available at beginning of year	120	140	140	120	120
	5. Gains from transfers and promotions in	5	5	—	—	—
	6. Losses through:					
	(a) retirements	3	6	4	1	3
	(b) wastage	15	17	18	15	14
	(c) transfers and promotions out	2	4	6	3	—
	(d) total losses	20	27	28	19	17
	7. Total available at end of year (4+5−6)	105	118	112	101	103
Requirement	8. Deficit (d), or surplus (s): (3−7)	25(d)	22(d)	8(d)	19(d)	17(d)
	9. Losses of those recruited during year	3	6	2	4	3
	10. Additional numbers required during year (8+9)	28	28	10	23	20

forecasts can be scheduled over a period of five years to indicate the number of fitters to be recruited.

The first year of the forecast could be the labour budget for the year, and the forecast would be updated annually, or more frequently if there are rapid changes in demand. In some situations it might be impossible to forecast as far ahead as five years, and in others there might be no point in doing so because no action could be taken by the company more than one or two years in advance.

An example of a more detailed one-year staff budget for a sales organization is shown in Table 15.6.

The reconciliation of demand and supply forecasts shows how many people may have to be recruited or made redundant and this forms the

Table 15.6 Sales staff budget: year commencing —

	Current establishment	New appointments during year	Forecast losses of existing staff during year				Requirements during year			Losses of staff recruited during year	Number to be recruited during year
			Retirement	Wastage	Promotion out	Total	Total (2+6)	By promotion	By recruitment		
	(1)	(2)	(3)	(4)	(5)	(6)	(7)	(8)	(9)	(10)	(11)
General sales manager	1	—	1	—	—	1	1	1	—	—	—
Regional sales managers	6	1	1	—	1	2	3	3	—	—	—
Area sales managers	18	2	—	2	3	5	7	6	1	—	1
Sales representatives	165	10	1	15	6	22	32	—	32	3	35

basis for the manpower plan proper — drawing up recruitment campaigns and training programmes or preparing for redundancy.

In situations where a considerable number of demand and supply data have to be analysed and a number of assumptions about the future need to be evaluated, use of human resource modelling techniques is advisable.

Human resource modelling

Definition

A model is a representation of a real situation. It depicts interrelationships between the relevant factors in that situation and, by structuring and formalizing any information about these factors, presents reality in a simplified form.

Use of modelling — in general

Models can help to:

- increase the decision maker's understanding of the situation in which a decision has to be made and the possible outcomes of that decision;
- stimulate new thinking about problems by, among other things, providing answers to 'what if?' questions (sensitivity analysis);
- evaluate alternative courses of action.

Application of human resource models

Human resource modelling techniques can be used to prepare general human resource forecasts; to understand, predict and measure wastage; and to assist in career evaluation. If a computerized personnel information system exists, as described in Chapter 38, the information contained on the database can be exploited swiftly to provide detailed analyses of great numbers of data which can be turned into projections of future demand and supply flows and forecasts of staff requirements.

The 'what if?' questions that can be answered by a model include the impact on human resource requirements of alternative activity level forecasts or variations in assumptions about wastage rates, promotions and transfers, or changing patterns in the use of skills arising from the introduction of new technology or changes in marketing strategy.

Data required

The data required for setting up and operating human resource models are essentially the same as those used for demand and supply forecasting. But they may have to be organized on a more systematic basis to fit the modelling process.

The main headings under which data need to be assembled are:

1. *The human resource system.* This describes how people move into and out of the organization or any of its units and how they progress between the various organizational levels or grades. A highly simplified representation of the system is illustrated in Figure 15.5.

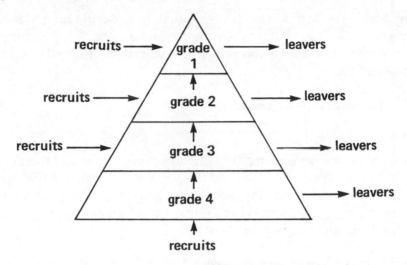

Figure 15.5 A human resource system

2. *Stocks.* Stocks — the number of people employed in each grade — are analysed in age or length of service bands.
3. *Flows.* Leavers, recruits and promotion flows are also analysed by grade and age or length of service.
4. *Assumptions.* Alternative assumptions can be made about the future behaviour of the system so that the implication of the different outcomes can be evaluated. These assumptions might include a 'push' analysis of flows where the organization 'pushes' people through the system as their career progresses without having fixed grade sizes (this type of system uses salary progression curves rather than salary ranges, as discussed in Chapter 26). In a graded system the assumptions will be concerned with targets for grade sizes expressed as a growth or shrinkage percentage rate per grade, or target numbers from the operational plan.
5. *Careers analysis.* A 'careers prospectus' can be built up by analysing data

on promotions between grade and career progression curves, and by projecting trends. The model can link this data to information on the database about the potential of current employees in order that future stocks for promotion can be estimated.

The data on stocks and flows can be recorded on a form such as the one illustrated in Figure 15.6.

Grade	Age ranges			
Grade 4	16–24	25–34	35–44	45–65
Stocks at beginning of year				
Recruits during year				
Recruits leaving during year				
Leavers during year				
Promotions to grade 3				
Promotions from grade 5				
Stocks at end of year				

Figure 15.6 Stocks and flows data schedule

Using models

Models such as those produced by the Institute of Manpower Studies (Microprospect, IMS-Monitor, IMS-WASP, IMS-CAMPLAN) can be obtained to use on a computerized personnel information system, as described in Chapter 38. The advice given by the Institute of Manpower Studies in operating its models includes the following points:

● Understand why a model is being used, what outputs are required and what assumptions have to be included.

- In making assumptions about the manpower system, flows and targets, start by asking what happens if current practices continue to be operated and then consider possible changes in market conditions, the use of new technologies, etc.
- Use time series data, ie trend analysis, wherever possible to provide the basis for extrapolations.
- Although disaggregation, ie splitting mass data into subdivisions, can apparently lead to greater accuracy, this could be spurious if it involves manipulating very small numbers.
- Do not push the data further than they will go. When dealing with small or doubtful numbers, smooth or aggregate where necessary or sensible.
- Cross-check assumptions about wastage rates with other companies to ensure they are reasonable.
- Carry out sensitivity analysis, ie the study of assumptions in order to predict alternative outcomes, depending on the assumption.
- Look first for significant results in the model's output, especially changes in workforce composition and unusually large or small flows.

Productivity and costs

Planning is just as concerned with making the best use of people as with forecasting and getting the numbers required. An increase in activity levels can be catered for by improving productivity as well as by recruiting more staff. This means looking at productivity and employment costs as well as the possibility of treating human resources as assets rather than liabilities, to be invested in, maintained and allocated on the same rational basis that is used for all other assets.

Productivity

Fundamentally, productivity represents the output of goods and services which can be obtained from a given input of employees. Within the firm, productivity should be monitored by using such measures as employment costs per unit of output, employment costs at a ratio of sales value, added value per employee, sales value per employee, tons of product handled per man hour, or labour costs as a percentage of added value (the difference being production costs and sales value). Internal and external comparisons may then reveal areas where improvement is required by mechanization, automation, improved management, a more flexible approach to resourcing (see pages 317–322) or other means.

Employment costs

Employment costs can be grouped under seven headings as follows:

1. *Remuneration costs:*

    (a) pay — basic, bonuses, profit-sharing, overtime and shift payments, merit pay, other supplementary pay;
    (b) direct fringe benefits — pensions, life insurance, holidays, car, luncheon vouchers/subsidized meals, share ownership schemes, housing schemes, housing assistance, education loans;
    (c) statutory costs — national insurance and pension fund contributions, training board levies (offset by grants), employer's liability insurance.

2. *Recruitment costs:*

    (a) preparation of job specifications and advertisements;
    (b) advertising and general promotional activities;
    (c) sifting applications, interviewing and corresponding with applicants;
    (d) selection testing;
    (e) medical examinations;
    (f) induction.

3. *Training costs:*

    (a) remuneration and expenses of trainees and trainers;
    (b) preparing and maintaining training programmes;
    (c) training materials, equipment and premises;
    (d) lower efficiency of trainees until fully trained.

4. *Relocation costs:*

    (a) travel, accommodation and disturbance allowances;
    (b) housing assistance;
    (c) hostel charges.

5. *Leaving costs:*

    (a) loss of production between leaving and replacement;
    (b) statutory redundancy payments, less rebates;
    (c) *ex gratia* payments.

6. *Support costs:*

    (a) indirect fringe benefits — social and sports facilities; medical,

    welfare, rehabilitation and convalescent schemes; canteens;
    preferential purchase schemes; house magazines, music-while-
    you-work; library;

(b)   long-service awards;

(c)   suggestion schemes;

(d)   safety facilities;

(b)   car parking.

7.   *Personnel administration costs:* personnel department costs, other than
those allocated under other headings.

It may be difficult to collect and allocate expenses under all these headings,
but the more detailed the analysis the better the control that can be
exercised over manpower costs.

Action planning

Action plans are derived from the broad resourcing strategies and the
more detailed analysis of demand and supply factors. However, the plans
often have to be short-term and flexible because of the difficulty of making
firm predictions about human resource requirements in times of rapid
change. The 'demographic time bomb' rightly gained much attention in
the 1980s but was defused in the many companies suffering from the
effects of the recession in the early '90s. But skill shortages remain in
certain sectors and they will almost certainly return elsewhere as the
economy regains its vitality, as fewer young people enter the job market,
and as the cut-backs in training during the recession have their effect.

    Action plans should be made in the following areas:

- an overall plan as required to deal with shortages arising from
  demographic pressures;
- a human resource development plan;
- a recruitment and retention plan;
- a plan to achieve greater flexibility;
- a productivity plan;
- a downsizing plan, if required.

Overall plan

The overall human resource plan should consider the following measures
to counteract skill shortages and reductions in the number of young
people entering the labour market:

- improving methods of identifying the sort of young people the
  organization wants to recruit;

- establishing links with schools and colleges to gain their interest in the organization;
- developing career programmes and training packages to attract young people;
- widening the recruitment net to include, for example, more women re-entering the labour market;
- finding ways of tapping alternative pools of suitable workers;
- adapting working hours and arrangements to the needs of new employees;
- providing more attractive benefit packages; for example, child-care facilities;
- developing the talents and making better use of existing employees;
- providing retraining for existing and new employees to develop different skills;
- making every effort to retain new recruits and existing staff.

The human resource development plan

The human resource development plan will show:

- The number of trainees required and the programme for recruiting and training them;
- the number of existing staff who need training or retraining and the training programmes required;
- the new courses to be developed or the changes to be made to existing courses;
- how the flow of promotable managers can be increased.

The recruitment and retention plans

Recruitment plan

The recruitment plan will take account of the flow of trainees or retrained staff and set out:

- the numbers and types of employees required to make up any deficits and when they are needed;
- the likely sources of recruits;
- methods of attracting good candidates; these may include training and development programmes, attractive pay and benefit packages, 'golden hellos' (sums of money paid upfront to recruits), flexible working arrangements, generous relocation payments, child-care

facilities and, generally, improving the image of the company as an employer;
- how any special problems in the supply of recruits will be dealt with;
- the recruitment programmes.

Retention plan

The retention plan should be based on an analysis of why people leave. Exit interviews may provide some information but they are unreliable — people rarely give the full reasons why they are leaving. A better method is to conduct attitude surveys at regular intervals. The retention plan should address each of the areas in which lack of commitment and dissatisfaction can arise. The actions to be considered under each heading are listed below.

1. *Pay* — problems arise because of uncompetitive, inequitable or unfair pay systems. Possible actions include:

    (a) reviewing pay levels on the basis of market surveys;
    (b) introducing job evaluation or improving an existing scheme to provide for equitable grading decisions;
    (c) ensuring that employees understand the link between performance and reward;
    (d) reviewing performance-related pay schemes to ensure that they operate fairly (criteria for such schemes are set out in Chapter 27, page 573);
    (e) adapting payment-by-results systems to ensure that employees are not penalized when they are engaged only on short runs;
    (f) tailoring benefits to individual requirements and preference;
    (g) involving employees in developing and operating job evaluation and performance-related pay systems.

2. *Jobs* — dissatisfaction results if jobs are unrewarding in themselves. Jobs should be designed to maximize skill variety, task significance, autonomy and feedback, and they should provide opportunities for learning and growth.

3. *Performance* — employees can be demotivated if they are unclear about their responsibilities or performance standards, are uninformed about how well they are doing, or feel that their performance appraisals are unfair. The following actions can be taken:

    (a) express performance requirements in terms of hard but attainable goals;

314

(b)   get employees and managers to agree on those goals and the steps required to achieve them;

(c)   encourage managers to praise employees for good performance but also get them to provide regular, informative and easily interpreted feedback — performance problems should be discussed as they happen in order that immediate corrective action can be taken;

(d)   train managers in performance review techniques such as counselling; brief employees on how the performance management system works and obtain feedback from them on how it has been applied.

4.   *Training* — resignations and turnover can increase if people are not trained properly, or feel that demands are being made upon them which they cannot reasonably be expected to fulfil without proper training. New employees can go through an 'induction crisis' if they are not given adequate training when they join the organization. Training schemes should be developed and introduced which:

(a)   give employees the competence and confidence to achieve expected performance standards;

(b)   enhance existing skills;

(c)   help people to acquire new skills so that they can undertake a greater variety of tasks and earn more under skill-based pay schemes;

(d)   ensure that new employees quickly acquire and learn the basic skills and knowledge needed to make a good start in their jobs.

5.   *Career development* — dissatisfaction with career prospects is a major cause of turnover. To a certain extent, this has to be accepted. More and more people recognize that to develop their careers they need to move on, and there is little their employers can do about it. These are the individuals who acquire a 'portfolio' of skills and may consciously change direction several times during their career. To a certain degree, employers should welcome this tendency. The idea of providing 'cradle to grave' careers is no longer as relevant in the more changeable job markets of today, and this self-planned, multiskilling process provides for the availability of a greater number of qualified people. But this does not mean that employers should neglect to provide career opportunities by:

(a)   providing employees with wider experience within the organization;

(b)   introducing more systematic processes for identifying potential, such as assessment centres;

(c)   encouraging promotion from within;

(d)   developing more equitable promotion procedures;

(e)   providing advice and guidance from managers and management development specialists in career paths.

Employers may also have to bear in mind that career prospects are limited in some jobs and should make that clear when recruiting or promoting employees. It is also advisable to take care in placing people in such jobs. It is clearly pointless to appoint ambitious men and women to posts which cannot possibly fulfil their aspirations. However, the scope for providing horizontal moves which enlarge experience should always be considered.

6.   *Commitment* — lack of commitment to the organization and its values is a major underlying cause of high turnover. Commitment can be increased by:

(a)   explaining the organization's mission, values and strategies and encouraging employees to discuss and comment on them;

(b)   communicating with employees in a timely and candid way, with the emphasis on face-to-face communications through such means as briefing groups;

(c)   constantly seeking and taking into account the views of people at work;

(d)   providing opportunities for employees to contribute their ideas on improving work systems;

(e)   introducing organization and job changes only after consultation and discussion.

7.   *Lack of group cohesion* — employees can feel isolated and unhappy if they are not part of a cohesive team or if they are bedevilled by disruptive power politics. Steps can be taken to tackle this problem through:

(a)   teamwork — setting up autonomous work groups or project teams;

(b)   team building — emphasizing the importance of teamwork as a key value, rewarding people for working effectively as members of teams and developing teamwork skills.

8.   *Dissatisfaction and conflict with managers and supervision* — a common reason for resignations is the feeling that management in general, or individual managers and supervisors in particular, are not providing

the leadership they should and/or are treating people unfairly. This problem should be remedied by:

(a)   selecting managers and supervisors with leadership qualities;
(b)   training them in leadership skills and in methods of resolving conflict and dealing with grievances;
(c)   introducing better procedures for handling grievances and disciplinary problems, and training everyone in how to use them.

9.   *Recruitment, selection, and promotion* — rapid turnover can result simply from poor selection or promotion decisions. It is essential to ensure that selection and promotion procedures match the capacities of individuals to the demands of the work they have to do.
10. *Overmarketing* — creating expectations about career development opportunities, tailored training programmes and varied and interesting work can, if not matched with reality, lead directly to dissatisfaction and early resignation. Care should be taken not to oversell the firm.

The flexibility plan

The aims of the flexibility plan should be to:

- provide for greater operational flexibility;
- improve the utilization of employees;
- reduce employment costs;
- help to achieve downsizing smoothly and in a way which avoids the need for compulsory redundancies;
- generally increase productivity.

In preparing the plan, the possibility of introducing more flexible patterns of work, as described below, should be explored.

Flexible patterns of work

A survey by the Institute of Manpower Studies in 1984 identified the following characteristics underpinning employers' strategies following the recession in the early 1980s:

- a priority for achieving a permanent reduction in unit labour costs against a background of market uncertainty and growing international competition;
- a reluctance of firms to commit themselves to any increase in

317

permanent, full-time employees even in the event of an upturn in business;

- a need to look for novel patterns of working against a background of pressure for shorter basic hours which would otherwise drive up unit labour costs.

In 1986, an Institute of Personnel Management survey established that many firms were developing three kinds of flexibility:

- *functional flexibility* in order that employees with the appropriate training or retraining can be redeployed quickly to different activities and crafts. Examples include the multiskilled craftsman or career changes among management and professional staff.
- *numerical flexibility*, which enables the organization to increase or decrease employee numbers quickly in response to short-term changes in the demand for labour. Examples include temporary employment, subcontracting and part-time staff.
- *financial flexibility*, which involves the establishment of payment systems which reinforces the organization's greater requirement for flexibility. Thus, for example, there have been a greater emphasis on the market rate for the job, rather than 'across the board' increases in pay, and a shift towards rewarding performance or rewarding on the basis of the range of skills possessed and individual performance.

Since that date, the pressure for more flexibility along these lines to reduce unit labour costs has increased and the recession in the early 1990s has accelerated this process.

The steps to be considered when formulating a flexibility plan are as follows:

- a radical look at traditional employment patterns to find alternatives to full-time, permanent staff — this may take the form of segregating the labour force into a 'core group' and one or more peripheral groups;
- new arrangements for flexible hours;
- new overtime arrangements;
- new shift-working arrangements.

Arrangements for introducing financial flexibility in reward management systems are described in Part VI of this book.

Alternatives to full-time permanent staff

The first step in reducing the number of full-time, permanent staff is to identify the 'core' of permanent, full-time employees who are essential to the direction, coordination and development of the firm's activities. The core may include:

- *managers*, but in reduced numbers because of flattened hierarchies and more decentralization;
- *team leaders*, ie those needed to lead teams of core workers or peripherals — the term 'team leader' is being increasingly used as an alternative to supervisor to emphasize the importance of team work in the new organizations and to remove connotations of autocratic control.
- *professional staff* in fields such as finance, legal and personnel who are involved continually and at high level in providing professional advice and services;
- *knowledge workers* who are involved in the development and management of new technology, including information technology;
- *technicians and highly skilled workers* in laboratories, drawing offices, toolrooms, etc, who need to be continuously available as the core element in project or work teams.

Employees in the core group are likely to be highly flexible and adaptable.

Having identified the core group, one's next step is to consider how, where, and to what extent peripherel workers can be used. The choice lies between:

- temporary workers;
- part-time workers;
- job sharing;
- new technology — homeworking and teleworking;
- subcontracting.

Temporary workers

Temporary workers can be used as part of a flexibility plan to reduce the company's commitment to the cost of employing people on a permanent basis. Their numbers can easily be increased or reduced to match fluctuations in the level of business activity. Temporary workers are also employed for the traditional reasons of providing cover for staff shortages, sickness or holidays.

The two main new trends in temporary working are:

1. To establish permanent staffing levels to meet minimum or normal levels of demand and rely on temporary staff to cover peaks.
2. To develop a 'two-tier' workforce in order to provide greater job security for the core workers by employing a certain percentage of temporary staff at the periphery.

Part-time workers

Part time work currently accounts for about 20 per cent of total employment in the UK. The advantages to employers of part-time workers include:

- more scope for flexing hours worked;
- better utilization of plant and equipment by, for example, the introduction of a 'twilight shift';
- lower unit labour costs because overtime levels for full-time workers are reduced;
- higher productivity on repetitive work because part-time workers can give more attention to their work during their shorter working day.

The disadvantages include the following points:

- Part-timers are generally less willing to undertake afternoon or evening work, may find it more difficult to vary their hours of work, and may be less mobile.
- Rates of labour turnover may be higher among part-timers.
- Part-timers may be less committed than full-time employees.

Job-sharing

Job-sharing is an arrangement whereby two employees share the work of one full-time position, dividing pay and benefits between them according to the time each works. Job-sharing can involve splitting days or weeks or, less frequently, working alternate weeks. The advantages of job-sharing include reduced labour turnover and absenteeism because it suits the needs of individuals. Greater continuity results because if one-half of the job-sharing team is ill or leaves, the sharer will continue working on at least half the job. Job-sharing also means that a wider employment pool can be tapped for those who cannot work full-time but want permanent employment. The disadvantages are the administrative costs involved and the risk of responsibility being divided.

New technology — homeworking and teleworking

Home-based employees, as in F International, a leading software house, can be recruited to work as consultants, analysts, designers or programmers. The advantages of these arrangements are:

- flexibility to respond rapidly to fluctuations in demand;
- reduced overheads;
- lower employment costs if the homeworkers are self-employed (care, however, has to be taken to ensure that they are regarded as self-

employed for income tax and national insurance purposes);
- higher productivity and lower absenteeism.

Teleworking involves people working at home with a terminal which is linked to the main company or networked with other outworkers.

The Rank Xerox teleworking system was introduced to achieve greater flexibility, rapid access to skills and the retention of skilled employees who would otherwise be lost to the company. Teleworkers are used in a number of functions such as marketing, finance, personnel and management services. The arrangement does, however, depend for its success on the involvement and education of all employees (full-time and teleworkers), the careful selection and training of teleworkers, allocating adequate resources to the teleworkers and monitoring the operation of the system.

Subcontracting
Subcontracting enables:

- resources to be concentrated on core business activities;
- costs to be reduced;
- flexibility and productivity to be increased;
- job security for core employees to be enhanced.

The potential drawbacks include:

- the legal status of subcontractors — this has to be clarified for income tax, national insurance and employment legislation purpose;
- the degree to which subcontractors will be able to meet delivery and quality requirements;
- negative reactions from employees and trade unions who prefer work to be kept within the firm.

The decision on how much work can be subcontracted is mainly an operational one, but the flexibility plan should cover the implications of subcontracting on employment levels and employee relations.

Flexible hour arrangements

Flexible hour arrangements can be included in the flexibility plan in one or more of the following ways:

- *Flexible daily hours* — these may follow an agreed pattern day by day according to typical or expected work loads (eg flexitime systems).
- *Flexible weekly hours* — providing for longer weekly hours to be worked at certain peak periods during the year.

- *Flexible daily and weekly hours* — varying daily or weekly hours or a combination of both to match the input of hours to achieve the required output. Such working times, unlike daily or weekly arrangements, may fluctuate between a minimum and a maximum of hours.
- *Compressed working weeks* in which employees work fewer than the five standard days.
- *Annual hours* — scheduling employee hours on the basis of the number of hours to be worked, with provisions for the increase or reduction of hours in any given period, according to the demand for goods or services.

Overtime arrangements

A flexibility plan can contain proposals to reduce overtime costs by the use of flexible hours, new shift arrangements (eg twilight shifts), time off in lieu and overtime limitation agreements. The reduction of overtime is often catered for in formal productivity deals which include a *quid pro quo* in the form of increased pay for the elimination of overtime payments and the introduction of flexible work patterns.

Shift-working arrangements

These can be introduced or modified to meet demand requirements, reduce overtime or provide for better plant or equipment utilization.

The productivity plan

The productivity plan sets out programmes for improving productivity or reducing employment costs in such areas as

- improving or streamlining methods, procedures and systems
- mechanization, automation or computerization
- the use of financial and non-financial incentives.

These will be additional to any proposals contained in the flexibility plan.

The productivity plan should also set productivity or efficiency targets such as:

- payroll or total employment costs as a percentage of sales revenue or added value;
- profit as a percentage of employment costs;
- sales or profit per employee;
- added value per employee;
- labour costs per unit of output;
- standard hours as a percentage of actual hours worked.

The downsizing plan

If all else fails, it may be necessary to deal with surplus numbers of employees by 'downsizing'. The downsizing plan should be based on the timing of reductions and forecasts of the extent to which these can be achieved by natural wastage or voluntary redundancy. The plan should set out:

- the total number of people who have to go and when and where this needs to take place;
- arrangements for informing and consulting with employees and their trade unions or staff associations;
- a forecast of the number of losses which can be taken up by natural wastage;
- any financial or other inducements to encourage voluntary redundancy;
- a forecast of the likely numbers who will volunteer to leave;
- a forecast of the balance of employees, if any, who will have to be made redundant (the plan should, of course, aim to avoid this through natural wastage and voluntary redundancy);
- the redundancy terms;
- any financial inducements to be offered to key employees whom the company wishes to retain;
- any arrangements for retraining employees and finding them work elsewhere in the organization;
- the steps to be taken to help redundant employees find new jobs by counselling, contacting other employers or offering the services of outplacement consultants;
- the arrangements for telling individual employees about the redundancies and how they are affected, and for keeping the trade unions informed.

Control

The human resource plan should include budgets, targets, and standards. It should also clarify responsibilities for implementation and control, and establish reporting procedures which will enable achievements to be monitored against the plan. These may simply report on the numbers employed against establishment (identifying both those who are in post and those who are in the pipeline) and on the numbers recruited against the recruitment targets. But they should also report employment costs against budget and trends in wastage and employment ratios. Procedures and forms for preparing and presenting personnel statistics are dicussed in Chapter 18 on personnel records.

Job Analysis and Job Descriptions

Job analysis is one of the most important techniques in personnel management. It provides the information required to produce personnel and training specifications and job descriptions and these are of fundamental importance in organization and job design, recruitment and selection, performance management, training, management development, career management, job evaluation and the design of pay structures. These constitute most of the key processes of personnel management.

This chapter deals with the subject under the following headings:

- Definitions;
- The approach to job analysis;
- Data collection — the basic steps;
- Job analysis techniques;
- Skills analysis;
- Competence analysis;
- Job descriptions — their purpose and format, and how to write them.

Definitions

Job analysis

Job analysis is the process of collecting, analysing and setting out the following information about a job:

- *Overall purpose* — why the job exists and, in essence, what the job holder is expected to contribute.
- *Content* — the nature and scope of the job in terms of the tasks and operations to be performed and duties to be carried out — ie the processes of converting inputs (knowledge, skills and abilities) into outputs (results).

- *Accountabilities* — the results or outputs for which the job holder is accountable.
- *Performance criteria* — the criteria, measures or indicators which enable an assessment to be carried out to ascertain the degree to which the job is being performed satisfactorily.
- *Competences* — the knowledge, skills, abilities and personal qualities (inputs) required to achieve an effective level of performance in the job. The degree to which the job involves multiskilling, ie using a variety of skills, would also be established.
- *Responsibilities* — the level of responsibility the job holder has to exercise by reference to the scope and input of the job; the amount of discretion allowed to make decisions; the difficulty, scale, variety and complexity of the problems to be solved; the quantity and value of the resources controlled; and the type and importance of interpersonal relations.
- *Organizational factors* — the reporting relationships of the job holder, ie to whom he or she reports either directly (the line manager) or functionally (on matters concerning specialist areas, such as finance or personnel management); the people reporting directly or indirectly to the job holder; and the extent to which the job holder is involved in teamwork.
- *Motivating factors* — the particular features of the job that are likely to motivate or demotivate job holders if, in the latter case, nothing is done about them.
- *Developmental factors* — promotion and career prospects and the opportunity to acquire new skills or expertise.
- *Environmental factors* — working conditions, health and safety considerations, unsocial hours, mobility, and ergonomic factors relating to the design and use of equipment or work stations.

Job descriptions

Job descriptions are derived from the job analysis. They provide basic information about the job under the headings of the job title, reporting relationships, overall purpose and principal accountabilities and tasks or duties. Job descriptions are used for a number of different purposes such as to assist in organization design, for recruitment, as the basis of an employment contract, in job evaluation and in training. The basic data may therefore be supplemented by other information giving more details about the nature and scope of the job, the factors or criteria which indicate its level for job evaluation purposes, or the competences required as an aid to the preparation of training programmes and for use in assessment centres.

Methods of preparing job descriptions are described on pages 342–345.

Person specifications

Person specifications, also known as job or personnel specifications, set out the education, qualifications, training, experience, abilities and personal qualities job holders require to perform the job satisfactorily. Person specifications are used in recruitment and are dealt with in Chapter 17.

Training specifications

Training specifications define the knowledge and skills needed to achieve an acceptable level of performance. They are used as the basis for devising training and development programmes (see Chapter 20). Training specifications may be produced following a competence analysis.

Skills analysis

Skills analysis determines the skills required to achieve an acceptable standard of performance. It is mainly used for technical, craft, manual and office jobs.

Competence analysis

Competence analysis enables the behavioural dimensions affecting job performance to be defined as a means of providing guidance on:

- the qualities required for appointments and promotions;
- training and development needs and programmes;
- criteria for determining pay levels and progression.

It is mainly used for managerial, professional and scientific jobs.

Approach to job analysis

The essence of job analysis is the application of systematic methods to the collection of information about jobs. It leads to a job description, a person or training specification, or a factor analysis for job evaluation. Job analysis obtains information about the content of jobs (what employees do) and subjects this to analysis, using the following structural approach:

- *inputs* — what the job holder needs to know and be able to do.
- *process* — how the job holder applies knowledge and skills to do the work.

- *outputs* — the value added to the organization as a result of the job holder's efforts.

Job analysis is essentially about data collection and the basic steps are described below.

Data collection — basic steps

The basic steps required to collect information about jobs are as follows:

1. Obtain documents such as existing organization, procedure or training manuals which give information about the job.
2. Ask managers for fundamental information concerning the job, the overall purpose, the main activities carried out, the responsibilities involved and the relationships with others.
3. Ask the job holders similar questions about their jobs. It is sometimes helpful to get them to keep a diary or a detailed record of work activities over a week or two.
4. For certain jobs, especially those involving manual or clerical skills, observe job holders at work. Even with managers or professional staff it is helpful, if time permits, to spend time with them.

There are a number of job analysis techniques used for data collection; these are described below.

Job analysis techniques

The main methods of data collection for job analysis are the following:

- interviews
- observation
- self-description
- questionnaires
- check-lists and inventories
- diaries and logs
- critical incident technique
- repertory grid technique
- hierarchical task analysis.

These are described below. There are also a number of techniques used specifically for skills analysis; these are described on pages 336–39.

Interviews

To obtain the full flavour of a job, one must interview job holders and check the findings with their superiors. The aim of the interview should be to obtain all the relevant facts about the job, covering the areas listed above in the section on questionnaires.

To achieve this aim, job analysts follow these guidelines:

1. Work to a logical sequence of questions which help interviewees to order their thoughts about the job.
2. Pin people down on what they actually do. Answers to questions are often vague and information is given by means of untypical instances.
3. Ensure that job holders are not allowed to get away with vague or inflated descriptions of their work. If, for example, the interview is part of a job evaluation exercise, they would not be human if they did not present the job in the best possible light.
4. Sort out the wheat from the chaff: answers to questions may produce a lot of irrelevant data which must be sifted before preparing the job description.
5. Obtain a clear statement from job holders about their authority to make decisions and the amount of guidance they receive from their superiors. This is not easy. If asked what decisions they are authorized to make, most people look blank because they think about their job in terms of duties and tasks rather than abstract decisions.
6. Avoid asking leading questions which make the expected answer obvious.
7. Allow the job holder ample opportunity to talk by creating an atmosphere of trust.

The advantages of the interviewing method are that it is very flexible, can provide in-depth information and is easy to organize and prepare. But interviewing can be time-consuming and expensive and the results are not always easy to analyse. An example of an interview check-list for analysing an office job is given in Appendix H.

Observation

Observation means studying job holders at work, noting what they do, how they do it, and how much time it takes. It is appropriate for situations where a relatively small number of key jobs need to be analysed in depth, but it is time-consuming and difficult to apply in jobs which involve a high proportion of unobservable mental activities, or in highly skilled manual jobs where the actions are too speedy to observe accurately.

Self-description

Job holders can be asked to analyse their own jobs and prepare job descriptions. This saves the considerable time a job analyst can spend in interviewing or observing a job holder. But people do not always find this easy, perhaps because what they do is so much part of themselves that they find it difficult to be detached and dissect the information into its various elements. Some guidance is therefore required in most cases. If a number of job holders are involved, for example, in a job evaluation exercise, it is advisable to run special training sessions in which they practise analysing their own and other people's jobs. This method can be taken even further by getting the job holders together and, under the guidance of a job analyst, preparing their analyses and job descriptions on the spot. It is always helpful to produce a model job description to illustrate the format required.

Questionnaires

Questionnaires to be completed by job holders and approved by the job holder's supervisor are useful when a large number of jobs are to be covered. They can also save interviewing time by recording purely factual information and by helping the analyst to structure questions in advance in cover areas which need to be explored in greater depth.

Questionnaires should provide the following basic information:

- the job title of the job holder;
- the job title of the job holder's manager or supervisor;
- the job titles and numbers of staff reporting to the job holder (best recorded by means of an organization chart);
- a brief description (one or two sentences) of the overall role or purpose of the job;
- a list of the main tasks or duties that the job holder has to carry out; as appropriate, these should specify the resources controlled, the equipment used, the contacts made and the frequency with which the tasks are carried out.

These basic details can be supplemented by questions designed to elicit from the job holders some information about the level of their responsibilities and the demands made upon them by the job. Such questions are difficult to phrase and answer in a meaningful way. The replies may be too vague or misleading and usually have to be checked with the job holders' supervisors and in subsequent interviews. But they at least give job holders an opportunity to express their feelings about the job and they can provide useful leads for development in discussion. These questions can cover such aspects of the job as:

- the amount of supervision received and the degree of discretion allowed in making decisions.
- the typical problems to be solved and the amount of guidance available when solving the problems;
- the relative difficulty of the tasks to be performed;
- the qualifications and skills required to carry out the work.

The advantage of questionnaires is that they can produce information quickly and cheaply for a large number of jobs. But a substantial sample is needed and the construction of a questionnaire is a skilled job which should only be carried out on the basis of some preliminary fieldwork. It is highly advisable to pilot-test questionnaires before launching into a full-scale exercise. The accuracy of the results also depends on the willingness and ability of job holders to complete questionnaires. Many people find it difficult to express themselves in writing about their work, however well they know and do it.

Check-lists and inventories

A check-list for completion by job holders is similar to a questionnaire, but response requires fewer subjective judgements and tends to be of the YES or NO variety. Check-lists can cover as many as 100 activities; job holders tick those tasks that are included in their jobs.

Like questionnaires, check-lists need to be thoroughly prepared and a field trial is essential to ensure that the instructions for completion are adequate and that the responses make sense. Check-lists can be used only where a large number of job holders exist. If the sample is below 30, the results can be erratic.

Rating scales or inventories are an improvement on the relatively crude check-list. Like the check-list, they present job holders with a list of activities. But instead of simply asking them to mark those they carry out, scales are provided for them to give a rating, typically from one to seven, according to the amount of time spent and, sometimes, the importance of the job. These scales could look like those given in Table 6.1.

There are a number of general purpose inventories available, the most widely used of which is the Position Analysis Questionnaire developed by McCormick, Jeanneret and Mecham.[1] This was based on studies of over 3700 jobs, from which six major work factors were identified:

Table 16.1 Example of a job analysis rating scale

	Job analysis rating scale	
Activity description	Time spent — the activity occupies:	Importance of activity
Dealing with requests for information by telephone	1. Hardly any time (less than 10%)	1. Extremely unimportant
	2. A small proportion of the job (10%–24%)	2. Very unimportant
	3. Rather less than half the job (25%–44%)	3. Not very important
	4. About half the job (45%–54%)	4. Fairly important
	5. A fairly large proportion of the job (55%–74%)	5. Important
	6. A very large proportion of the job (75%–89%)	6. Very important
	7. Almost the whole of the job (90% or more)	7. Extremely important

1. the input of information;
2. mental processes; for example, decision making;
3. work input; for example, the use of machine controls;
4. relationships with people;
5. work environment;
6. other characteristics.

Scales were devised under each heading to measure specific requirements for almost 200 job elements. Each scale describes the activity and has 'benchmark' descriptions for each rating point, as in the example given in Table 16.2.

The Position Analysis Questionnaire has the advantage of being

Table 16.2 Position Analysis Questionnaire — example of benchmark
scale for an element (McCormick)

	Near visual discrimination (visual discrimination of objects within arm's reach)
7	Inspects precision watch parts for defect
6	Proofreads newspaper articles before publishing
5	Reads electric house meters
4	Makes entries on sales tickets
3	Observes position of knife when carving beef
2	Paints house walls
1	Sweeps street with push broom
0	Makes no near visual discrimination

generally applicable and comprehensive and having benchmarks. However, it is time-consuming to administer and requires some specialist knowledge.

Diaries and logs

This approach to job analysis has job holders analyse their own jobs by keeping diaries or logs of their activities. These can be used by the job analyst as the basic material for a job description. Job holders need guidance on how to prepare their diaries or logs. They can be asked to describe a typical day on an hour-by-hour basis, or they can record their activities in narrative form at the end of a period, usually a day.

Diaries and logs are best used for managerial jobs which are fairly complex and where the job holders have the analytical skills required, as well as the ability to express themselves on paper.

Critical-incident technique

The criticial-incident technique is a means of eliciting data about effective or less effective behaviour which is related to examples of actual events or 'critical incidents'. The critical-incident technique is used with individuals or groups as follows:

1. Explain what the technique is and what its aims are, ie to assess what constitutes good or poor performance by analysing events which have been observed to have a noticeably successful or unsuccessful

outcome, thus providing much more factual and 'real' information then by simply listing tasks and guessing performance requirements.

2. Identify the job to be analysed and then agree and list the key areas of responsibility — the principal accountabilities. To save time, the analyst can sometimes establish these prior to the meeting, but it is necessary to ensure that they are agreed provisionally by the individual or group — who can be told that the list may well be amended in the light of the analysis.

3. Taking each area in turn, ask for examples of critical incidents. If, for instance, one of the job responsibilities is dealing with customers, ask questions such as:

> I want you to tell me about a particular occasion at work which involved you — or that you observed — in dealing with a customer. Think about what the circumstances were, eg who took part, what did the customer request, what you or the other member of staff did, and what the outcome was.

4. Collect information on the critical incident under the following headings:

    (a) what the circumstances were;
    (b) what the individual did;
    (c) the outcome of what the individual did.

    The information should be recorded on a card or a flip chart.

5. Continue this process for each area of responsibility.

6. Refer to the cards or the flip chart and analyse each incident by obtaining ratings or the recorded behaviour on a scale such as 1 for least effective to 5 for most effective.

7. Discuss these ratings to obtain initial definitions of effective and ineffective performance for each of the key aspects of the job.

8. Refine these definitions as necessary following the meeting — it can be difficult to get an individual or group to produce finished definitions.

9. Produce the final job analysis, which will set out performance indicators or standards against each principal accountability, as illustrated in Appendix C.

Repertory grid

Like the critical-incident technique, the repertory grid can be used to identify the dimensions which distinguish good from poor standards of performance. The technique is based on Kelly's[2] personal construct theory. Personal constructs are the ways in which we view the world. They are personal because they are highly individual and they influence the way we behave or view other people's behaviour. The aspects of the system to which these 'constructs' or judgements are applied are called 'elements'.

To elicit constructs or judgements, we ask a group of people or an individual to concentrate on certain objects or elements, which are the tasks carried out by job holders, and develop constructs about those elements in terms of the qualities they have which indicate the essential requirements for effective performance.

The procedure to be followed by the analyst uses a triadic method of elicitation, as follows:

1. Identify the tasks or elements of the job to be subjected to repertory grid analysis. This is done by one of the other forms of job analyses, eg interviewing.
2. List the tasks on cards.
3. Draw three cards at random from the pack and ask the individual or members of the group to nominate which of these tasks is the odd one out in terms of the qualities and characteristics needed to perform it.
4. Probe to obtain more specific definitions of these qualities or characteristics in terms of expected behaviour. If, for example, a characteristic has been described as 'the ability to plan and organize', ask questions such as 'What sort of things indicate that someone is planning effectively?', or 'How can you tell if someone is not organizing his or her work particularly well?' This process is sometimes called 'laddering'.
5. Draw three more cards from the pack and repeat steps 3 and 4. It does not matter if the same cards are taken out — simply ask the individual or group to think of other ways in which one of the three cards may differ from the other two.
6. Repeat this process until all the cards have been analysed and there do not appear to be any more constructs to be identified.
7. List the constructs and ask the individuals to rate each task on every quality, using a six- or seven-point scale.
8. Collect and analyse the scores in order to assess the relative importance of the scores. A number of statistical ways to do this are decribed by Markham[3] and Smith and Robertson.[4]

Although a full statistical analysis of the outcome of a repertory grid exercise is helpful, the most important results which can be obtained are the descriptions of what constitutes good or poor performance in each element of a job. This is why the 'laddering' process is so important as a means of obtaining definitions in specific behavioural terms, ie what people do or don't do.

The advantage of this technique is that it helps people to articulate their views by reference to specific examples. The triadic approach makes it easier for them to identify specific constructs by defining and limiting the area of comparison. The approach provides a framework for discussion but it can be used flexibly. However, it does require a skilled analyst who can probe and draw out the descriptions of job characteristics.

Hierarchical task analysis

Hierarchical task analysis, as developed by Annet and Duncan,[5] breaks down jobs or areas of work into a hierarchical set of tasks, subtasks and plans. Tasks are defined in terms of objectives or end-products and the plan needed to achieve the objective is also analysed. The process starts with an analysis of the overall task. This is then subjected to further analysis in order to develop a hierarchy of subtasks, together with their outputs and produce definitions of the subplans needed to achieve them.

The method involves:

- using action verbs which describe, in clear and concrete terms, what has to be done;
- definining performance standards, ie the level of performance which has to be achieved in carrying out a task or operation satisfactorily;
- listing the conditions associated with task performance, which might include environmental factors such as working in areas of high noise.

This approach is mostly used for process or manufacturing jobs, but the principles of defining outputs and performance standards and analysing subtasks are relevant when analysing any type of job.

Choice of method

In the selection of a method of job analysis, the criteria for choice are the purpose for which it will be used, its effectiveness in obtaining the data required, the degree of expertise required to conduct the analysis and the resources and amount of time available for the analysis programme. The following is a summary of the advantages or disadvantages of each method:

- *Interviewing* — this is the basic method of analysis and, as such, is the one most commonly used. It requires skill on the part of the analyst and is time-consuming. Analysts need to be trained, and their effectiveness is increased by the use of a check-list, such as the one given in Appendix X which covers all aspects of job analysis.
- *Observation* is the most accurate technique for analysing job content (what people actually do). But it is so time-consuming that it is seldom used except when preparing training specifications for manual or clerical jobs.
- *Self-description* — this is the quickest and most economical form of job analysis. But it relies on the often limited ability of people to describe their own jobs. It is therefore necessary to provide them with guidance in the form of questionnaires and check-lists.
- *Questionnaires, check-lists, and inventories* — these can be a useful aid in helping individuals to describe their jobs, but it may be necessary to invest a lot of time in constructing and evaluating questionnaires, which, ideally, should be related to the particular job. If they are overgeneralized it will be too easy for job holders to provide vague or incoherent answers.
- *Diaries and logs* are most useful for managerial jobs but they make great demands on job holders and can be difficult to analyse.
- *The critical-incident technique* is a valuable method of ensuring that factual information, expressed in behavioural terms, is obtained about the job. It is most useful in competence analysis and when there is some ambiguity about what contributes to high-level performance. It can be used during interviews or in a group discussion where a helpful range of opinions will be elicited. It does, however, take time and the analyst must be skilled and experienced.
- *The repertory grid technique* also provides good insight into attitudes and opinions about job performance factors, but it is somewhat elaborate and requires considerable skill to administer.
- *Hierarchical task analysis* provides a helpful structure for job analysis in terms of outputs, plans (inputs) and relationships. It can be used when analysing the data obtained by interviews or other methods.

Skills analysis

Skills analysis is used as the basis for devising training programmes, as discussed in Chapter 20. It starts from a broad job analysis but goes into detail of not only what job holders have to do but also the particular abilities and skills they need to do it. The skills analysis techniques described below were mainly developed for use in manual or clerical jobs:

1. job breakdown
2. manual skills analysis
3. task analysis
4. faults analysis
5. job learning analysis.

Job breakdown

The job breakdown technique analyses a job into separate operations, processes, or tasks which can be broken down into manageable parts for instructional purposes.

A job breakdown analysis is recorded in a standard format of three columns:

1. *The stage column.* The different steps in the job are described — most semi-skilled jobs can easily be broken down into their constituent parts.
2. *The instruction column.* Against each step, a note is made of how the task should be done. This, in effect, describes what has to be learned by the trainee.
3. *The key points column.* Against each step, any special points such as quality standards or safety instructions are noted in order that they can be emphasized to a trainee learning the job.

Manual skills analysis

Manual skills analysis is a technique developed by W D Seymour from work study. It isolates for instructional purposes the skills and knowledge employed by experienced workers in performing tasks which require a high degree of manual dexterity. It is used to analyse short-cycle, repetitive operations such as assembly tasks and other similar factory work.

The hand, finger and other body movements of experienced operatives are observed and recorded in great detail as they carry out their work. The analysis concentrates on the tricky parts of the job which, while presenting no difficulty to the experienced operative, have to be analysed in depth before they can be taught to trainees. Not only are the hand movements recorded in great detail, but particulars are also noted of the cues (visual and other senses) which the operative absorbs when performing the tasks. Explanatory comments are added when necessary.

Task analysis

Task analysis is a systematic analysis of the behaviour required to carry out a task with a view to identifying areas of difficulty and the appropriate training techniques and learning aids necessary for successful instruction. It can be used for all types of jobs but is specifically relevant to clerical tasks.

The analytical approach used in task analyis is similar to those adopted in the job breakdown and manual skills analysis techniques. The results of the analysis are usually recorded in a standard format of four columns as follows:

1. *task* — a brief description of each element.
2. *level of importance* — the relative significance of each task to the successful performance of the whole job.
3. *Degree of difficulty* — the level of skill or knowledge required to perform each task.
4. *training method* — the instructional techniques, practice and experience required.

Faults analysis

Faults analysis is the process of analysing the typical faults which occur when performing a task, especially the more costly faults. It is carried out when the incidence of faults is high.

A study is made of the job and, by questioning workers and supervisors, the most commonly occurring faults are identified. A faults specification is then produced which provides trainees with information on what faults can be made, how they can be recognized, what causes them, what effect they have, who is responsible for them, what action the trainees should take when a particular fault occurs, and how a fault can be prevented from recurring.

Job learning analysis

Job learning analysis as described by Pearn and Kandola,[6] concentrates on the inputs and process rather than the content of the job. It analyses nine learning skills which contribute to satisfactory performance. A learning skill is one used to increase other skills or knowledge and represents broad catagories of job behaviour which need to be learnt. The learning skills are the following:

1. physical skills requiring practice and repetition to get right;

2. complex procedures or sequences of activity which are memorized or followed with the aid of written material such as manuals;
3. non-verbal information such as sight, sound, smell, taste and touch which is used to check, assess or discriminate, and which usually takes practice to get right;
4. memorizing facts or information;
5. ordering, prioritizing and planning, which refer to the degree to which a job holder has any responsibility for and flexibility in, determining the way a particular job activity is performed;
6. looking ahead and anticipating;
7. diagnosing, analysing and problem solving, with or without help;
8. interpreting or using written manuals and other sources of information such as diagrams or charts;
9. adapting to new ideas and systems.

In conducting a job learning analysis interview, the interviewer obtains information on the main aims and principal activities of the job, and then, using question cards for each of the nine learning skills, the interviewer analyses each activity in more depth, recording responses and obtaining as many examples as possible under each heading.

Competence analysis

Competence in its broadest sense consists of the knowledge, skills and qualities applied by individuals to the successful achievement of their job objectives. Competence analysis has evolved recently, mainly as a technique for use in management and career development. But the level of competence demanded for the effective performance of different jobs is a measure of the relative value of those jobs. The concept of competence can therefore be used as a form of job evaluation (see Chapter 25) and as a basis for the design of pay structures and performance-related pay systems (see Chapters 26 and 27).

Techniques of competence analysis

A competence analysis is often based on interviews, and/or questionnaires, although a 'workshop' approach can be adopted in which a number of people who are in the jobs being analysed, or have extensive knowledge of them, get together as a group to analyse the job[5].

During the interview or workshop, the questions concentrate on what people do, the situations they face and, importantly, what distinguishes performers at different levels of competence in terms of behaviours. This information can then be developed to assess what particular knowledge, skills and abilities are needed to behave appropriately at these levels and thereby deliver the required results.

The following check-list includes the main questions that should be asked in analysing competences.

1. What is the job holder expected to accomplish overall?
2. What are the actual objectives the job holder has to achieve?
3. What are the positive or negative indicators of behaviour which are conducive or non-conducive to achieving objectives. Consider these under the headings of:

    (a) personal drive;
    (b) impact;
    (c) ability to communicate;
    (d) team management;
    (e) interpersonal skills;
    (f) analytical power;
    (g) ability to innovate (creative thinking);
    (h) strategic thinking;
    (i) commercial judgement;
    (j) ability to adapt and cope with change and pressure.

4. Can you illustrate any of these with specific instances of effective or less effective behaviour?
5. What type of experience and how much of it is required to achieve a reasonable level of competence?
6. What type of education and training and level of qualifications are required to meet job objectives?

Although the straightforward interview or group discussion, using a check-list such as the one given above, is the normal method of defining competences, use can also be made of the critical-incident or repertory grid techniques, as described on pages 332–335.

Job descriptions — type and purpose

Job descriptions provide basic information on the overall purpose of the job and on the job holder's principal accountabilities. There will, however, be some variations according to the type of description, as described below.

Job descriptions for organizational, recruitment and contractual purposes

The basic job description can be used for each of the following purposes:

- to define the place of the job in the organization and to clarify for job holders and others the contribution the job makes to achieving organizational or departmental objectives;
- to provide the information required to produce person specifications for recruitment and to inform applicants about the job;
- to be the basis for the contract of employment.

Such job descriptions should not go into too much detail. What needs to be clarified is the contribution job holders are expected to make, expressed as the results to be achieved (principal accountabilities) and their positions in the organization (reporting relationships).

There are two factors to take into account when preparing this type of job description:

1. *Flexibility* — operational flexibility and multiskilling are becoming increasingly significant. It is therefore necessary to build flexibility into the job description. This is achieved by concentrating on results rather than spelling out what has to be done to achieve specified outputs. Emphasis can also be given, where appropriate, to the fact that the job holder may be required to carry out tasks or use skills which have not been specified in the job description to achieve the overall purpose of the job.
2. *Teamwork* — today's flatter organizations rely more on good teamwork and this requirement needs to be stressed.

Format
The format of a job description for organizational, recruitment or contractual purposes comprises simply:

- the job title;
- a definition of the overall purpose or objectives of the job;
- a list of principal accountabilities, key result areas, tasks or duties (what these are called does not matter too much, although the terms 'principal accountabilities' and 'key result areas' do emphasize the end results the job holder is expected to achieve).

Examples of organizational job descriptions are given in Appendices D and J.

Job descriptions for job evaluation purposes

For job evaluation purposes, the job description should contain the information included in an organizational description as well as an analysis of the job by reference to the job evaluation factors or criteria used to assess relative job values (see Chapter 25). In addition, it is often helpful to include a narrative describing the nature and scope of the job, as used in the Hay job evaluation system. This narrative gives general information on the environment in which the job operates. The nature of the job is described in broad terms to give evaluators an overall view of what sort of job it is. This puts flesh on the bones of a list of principal accountabilities. The scope of the job is defined wherever possible by quantifying the various aspects of the job, such as the resources controlled, the results to be achieved, budgets, the proportion of time spent on different aspects of the job, and the number of occasions over a certain period of time when decisions have to be made or actions taken.

A factor analysis attached to the job description describes the incidence in the job of each job evaluation factor such as knowledge and skills, responsibility, decisions, complexity and contacts. An example of a job description for job evaluation is given in Appendix E.

Job description for training purposes

For training purposes, the job description should be based on the format for an organizational job description, although the details on the nature and scope of the job and the factor analysis contained in job descriptions for job evaluations contain useful additional information. The training job description and specification include an analysis of the knowledge and skills required in the job. This means that a more detailed description of the tasks the job holder has to carry out is required. Further considerations on the preparation of training job descriptions and specifications are given in Chapter 20 (pages 431–432).

Writing a job description

Job descriptions should be based on a detailed job analysis and should be as brief and factual as possible. The headings under which the job description should be written and notes for guidance on completing each section are set out below.

Job title

The existing or proposed job title should indicate as clearly as possible the function in which the job is carried out and the level of the job within that function. The use of terms such as 'manager', 'assistant manager' or 'senior' to describe job levels should be reasonably consistent between functions with regard to gradings of the jobs. But this does not mean that all posts described, say, as 'manager', should be in the same grade. It is quite possible for someone correctly described as a manager in one function to have a less responsible job than a manager in another function.

Reporting to

The job title of the manager or supervisor to whom the job holder is directly responsible should be given under this heading. No attempt should be made to indicate here any functional relationships the job holder might have to other managers.

Reporting to job holder

The job titles of all the posts directly reporting to the job holder should be given under this heading. Again, no attempt should be made here to indicate any functional relationships that might exist between the job holder and other staff.

Overall responsibilities

This section should describe as concisely as possible the overall purpose of the job. The aim should be to convey in no more than two or three sentences a broad picture of the job which will clearly distinguish it from other jobs and establish the role of the job holders and the contribution they should make towards achieving the objectives of the company and their own function or unit.

No attempt should be made to describe the activities carried out under this heading, but the overall summary should lead naturally to the analysis of activities in the next section.

When preparing the job description, it is often best to defer writing down the definition of overall responsibilities until the activities have been analysed and described.

Principal accountabilities

The steps required to define principal accountabilities are the following:

1. Identify and produce an initial list of the main activities or tasks carried out by the job holder.
2. Analyse the initial list of tasks and group them together so that no more than about ten main activity areas remain. Most jobs can be analysed into seven or eight areas. If the number is extended much beyond that, the job description will become overcomplex and it will be difficult to be specific about accountabilities.
3. Define each activity area as a statement of accountability. An accountability statement expresses what the job holder is expected to achieve and will therefore be held responsible (accountable) for. The accountability should be expressed in one sentence which should:

    (a) Start with a verb in the active voice which provides a positive indication of what has to be done and eliminates unnecessary wording; for example: plans, prepares, produces, implements, processes, provides, schedules, completes, dispatches, maintains, liaises with, collaborates with. In managerial or supervisory positions, the active-voice verb may have to express actions such as directs, manages, supervises, ensures that.

    (b) Describe the object of the verb (what is done) as succinctly as possible; for example:

    -   tests new systems;
    -   posts cash to the nominal and sales ledgers;
    -   dispatches to the warehouse packed output;
    -   schedules production;
    -   ensures that management accounts are produced;
    -   prepares marketing plans.

    (c) State briefly why the activity is carried out (its purpose); for example:

    -   tests new systems to ensure they meet agreed systems specifications;
    -   posts cash to the nominal and sales ledgers in order to provide up-to-date and accurate financial information;
    -   dispatches the warehouse planned output so that all items are removed by carriers on the same day they are packed;

- schedules production in order to meet laid-down output and delivery targets;
- ensures that management accounts are produced which provide the required level of information to management and individual managers on financial performance against budget and on any variances;
- prepares marketing plans which support the achievement of the marketing strategies of the enterprise, are realistic, and provide clear guidance on the actions to be taken by the development, production, marketing and sales departments.

Examples of statements of accountability are given in Appendices C, D and E.

Nature and scope

The nature and scope section of a job description provides an opportunity to describe the job in more general terms, with examples of what is done and an indication of the relative significance of its different aspects. It is often easier to get job holders to write a narrative of their jobs, from which can be distilled the principal accountabilities. Nature and scope descriptions add 'flavour' to the job in order that job evaluators and trainers in particular, can obtain a better picture of what the job entails than from a mere list of principal accountabilities. There are no rules for writing nature and scope descriptions except that they should not be too long or repetitive.

An example of a nature and scope description is given in Appendix E.

Factor analysis

Factor analysis is the process of taking each of the job evaluation factors and assessing the level at which they are present in the job. When writing factor analyses, you should refer to the factor and level definitions in the job evaluation factor plan (see Chapter 25). The analysis should be backed up as far as possible with facts and examples. An example of a factor analysis is given in Appendix E.

References

1. McCormick, E J, Jeanneret, P R and Mecham, R C 'A study of job characteristics and job dimensions based on the Position Analysis Questionnaire (PAQ)', *Journal of Applied Psychology*, Vol. 56, pp. 347–68, 1972.

2. Kelly, G *The Psychology of Personal Constructs*. Norton, New York, 1955.
3. Markham, C *Practical Consulting*. Institute of Chartered Accountants, London, 1987.
4. Smith, M and Robertson, I *Systematic Staff Selection*. Macmillan, London, 1986.
5. Annet, J and Duncan, K *Task Analysis*. HMSO, London, 1971.
6. Pearn, M and Kandola, R *Job Analysis*. Institute of Personnel Management, London, 1986.

17

Recruitment and Selection

The recruitment and selection process

The overall aim of the recruitment and selection process should be to obtain at minimum cost the number and quality of employees required to satisfy the manpower needs of the company. This chapter discusses three stages of recruitment and selection:

1. *Definining requirements* — preparing job descriptions and specifications; deciding terms and conditions of employment.
2. *Attracting candidates* — reviewing and evaluating alternative sources of applicants, inside and outside the company; advertising; using agencies and consultants.
3. *Selecting candidates* — sifting applications, interviewing, testing, assessing candidates; offering employment, obtaining references; preparing contracts of employment.

The last section of the chapter covers induction and follow-up procedures for new employees.

The flow of work and main decisions required in a recruitment and selection procedure are shown in Figures 17.1 and 17.2.

Defining requirements

The number and categories of manpower required should be specified in the recruitment programme, which is derived from the human resource plan. In addition, there will be demands for replacements or for new jobs to be filled, and these demands should be checked to ensure that they are justified. It may be particularly necessary to check on the need for a replacement or the level or type of employee that is specified.

In a large organization it is useful to have a form for requisitioning staff,

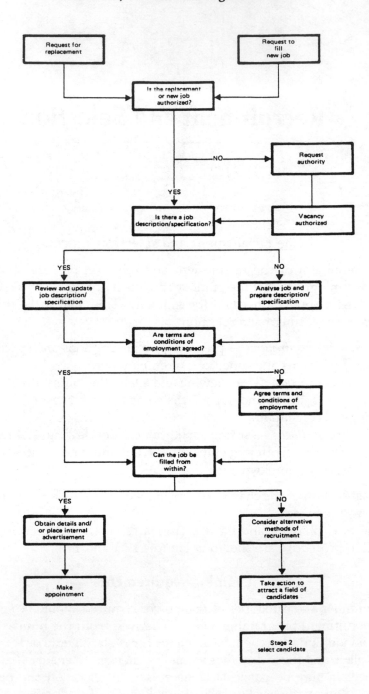

Figure 17.1 Recruitment flow chart — part 1: preliminary stages

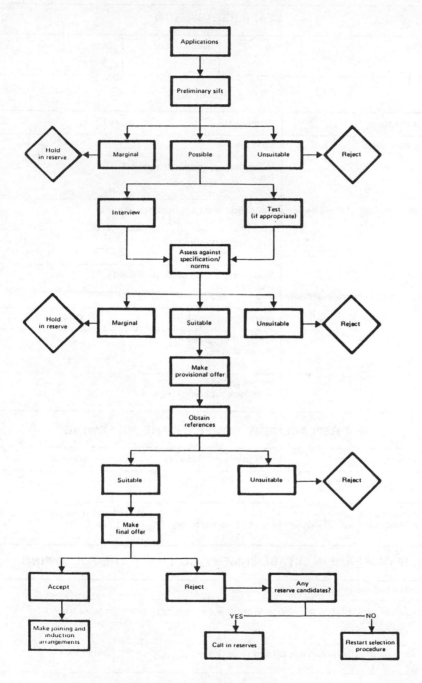

Figure 17.2 Recruitment flow chart — part 2: interviewing and selection stages

STAFF REQUISITION

To Personnel Department	From	Department	Date

REQUIREMENTS

Job title	Permanent ☐ Temporary ☐
Salary grade	Date needed
	If temporary, specify the period from to
Brief outline of main duties	Education and qualifications required
	Experience required
	Special skills, mental or personality requirements
	Age limits (if any)
	Who will supervise the employee?
	Whom will the employee supervise?

IF A REPLACEMENT, COMPLETE THE FOLLOWING

Employee replaced	Job title	Salary	Date terminated
Reason for termination			
Performance ☐ Above average ☐ Satisfactory ☐ Unsatisfactory		Would you re-engage? ☐ Yes ☐ No	

IF INCREASE IN ESTABLISHMENT, COMPLETE THE FOLLOWING

What has created the need for an increase?		
Explain why it is not possible to avoid this increase by organizational or other re-arrangements		
Increase in establishment approved	Signed	Date

Figure 17.3 Staff requisition form

as illustrated in Figure 17.3. However, even when a requisition form is completed, it may still be necessary to supplement the brief information contained in the form about the job, and it will almost certainly be necessary to check on the specification. If a requisition form is not available, then the job has to be analysed and a job description and job specification prepared. Existing descriptions and specifications should be checked to ensure that they are up to date. It is also necessary to establish or check on the terms and conditions of employment at this stage.

Person specifications

Person specifications, also known as recruitment, personnel or job specifications, define the qualifications, experience and personal qualities required by the job holder and any other necessary information on the special demands made by the job, such as physical conditions, unusual hours, or travel away from home. They should also set out or refer to terms and conditions of employment such as salary, fringe benefits, hours and holidays.

The information on qualifications, experience and qualities should be derived from an analysis of the knowledge and skills needed to carry out the job, as described in Chapter 16. These should therefore be specified: for example, the skills a machine operator requires to operate a machine or group of machines; the ability to read engineering drawings needed by a tool room fitter; the knowledge of word processing needed by a secretary; or the persuasive ability needed by a salesman. The list should be as exact as possible in order that at the interviewing stage the interviewer can ask direct questions about what the applicant knows or can do.

The biggest danger to be avoided at this stage is that of overstating the qualifications required. Perhaps it is natural to go for the best, but setting an unrealistically high level for candidates increases the problems of attracting applicants, and results in dissatisfaction among recruits when they find their talents are not being used. Understating requirements can, of course, be equally dangerous, but it happens much less frequently.

When the requirements have been agreed, they should be analysed under suitable headings. There are various ways of doing this; the most familiar being the seven-point plan developed by Rodger[1] and the five-fold grading system produced by Munro-Fraser.[2]

The seven-point plan (Rodger)
The seven-point plan covers:

1. *physical make-up* — health, physique, appearance, bearing and speech;

2. *attainments* — education, qualifications, experience;
3. *general intelligence* — fundamental intellectual capacity;
4. *special aptitudes* — mechanical, manual dexterity, facility in the use of words or figures;
5. *interests* — intellectual, practical constructional, physically active, social, artistic;
6. *disposition* — acceptability, influence over others, steadiness, dependability, self-reliance;
7. *circumstances* — domestic circumstances, occupations of family.

The five-fold grading system (Munro-Fraser)

The five-fold grading system covers:

1. *impact on others* — physical make-up, appearance, speech and manner;
2. *acquired qualifications* — education, vocational training, work experience;
3. *innate abilities* — natural quickness of comprehension and aptitude for learning;
4. *motivation* — the kinds of goals set by the individual, his or her consistency and determination in following them up, and success in achieving them;
5. *adjustment* — emotional stability, ability to stand up to stress and ability to get on with people

Choice of method

Of these systems the seven-point plan has the longer pedigree. The five-fold grading scheme is simpler, in some ways, and places more emphasis on the dynamic aspects of the applicant's career. Both provide a good framework for interviewing, although a simpler approach used by many interviewers is to start from the analysis of the knowledge and skills required and go on from there to define the minimum and the optimum education, qualifications, training and experience needed to succeed in the job. This leads on naturally to a specification of the personal and physical attributes required and to a definition of other requirements such as age limits, location of work, travel, and night or shift work. This information can be recorded on a person specification form, as shown in Figure 17.4. The more complex systems can be used in circumstances where the jobs themselves are fairly complicated and the numbers to be recruited or trained are large.

Attracting candidates

Attracting candidates is primarily a matter of identifying, evaluating and

Part 1: JOB DESCRIPTION	
Department	Section
Job title	Job grade
Reporting to (job title)	
Reporting to job holder (job titles)	
Overall purpose of job	
Main activities/tasks	
Special requirements (tools and equipment used, external contacts, etc)	
Other features of job: shift or night work, travel, working conditions, etc	
Location of job	

Figure 17.4(a) Person specification form (part 1)

Part 2: JOB REQUIREMENTS
Knowledge and skills
Education, qualifications, and special training
Experience
Personality requirements
Physical requirements
Other requirements Age Travel Hours Other

Figure 17.4(b) Person specification form (part 2)

using the most appropriate sources of applicants. However, in cases where difficulties in attracting or retaining candidates are being met or anticipated, it may be necessary to carry out a preliminary study of the factors that are likely to attract or repel candidates — the strengths and weakness of the organization as an employer.

Analysis of recruitment strengths and weaknesses

The analysis of strengths and weaknesses should cover such matters as the national or local reputation of the company, pay, fringe benefits and working conditions, the intrinsic interest of the job, security of employment, opportunities for education and training, career prospects, and the location of the office or plant. These need to be compared with competition in order that a list of what are, in effect, selling-points, can be drawn up as in a marketing exercise, in which the preferences of potential customers are compared with the features of the product in order that those aspects which are likely to provide the most appeal to the consumers can be emphasized. Candidates are, in a sense, selling themselves, but they are also buying what the company has to offer. If, in the latter sense, the labour market is a buyer's market, then the company which is selling itself to candidates must study their needs in relation to what it can provide.

The aim of the study might be to prepare a better image of the company for use in advertisements, brochures or interviews. Or it might have the more constructive aim of showing where the company needs to improve if it is to attract more or better candidates. The study could make use of an attitude survey to obtain the views of existing employees. One such survey mounted by the writer in an engineering company wishing to attract science graduates established that the main concern of the graduates was that they would be able to use and develop the knowledge they had gained at university. As a result, special brochures were written for each major discipline giving technical case histories of the sort of work graduates carried out. These avoided the purple passages used in some brochures (which the survey established were distinctly off-putting to most students) and proved to be a most useful recruitment aid. Steps were also taken to encourage research managers to make proper use of the graduates they recruited.

Sources of candidates

The main sources of candidates are the following:

- internal, by means of a search or 'trawl', as the Civil Service puts it more expressively, or by internal advertisements;

- external advertisements;
- employment agencies — private or government;
- education and training establishments;
- other external sources, such as unsolicited letters and casual callers, and recommendations from employees.

One source may suffice, or it may be necessary to tap a number of alternative sources. It depends upon the type of job to be filled, the relative difficulty of attracting candidates, the area in which the company operates and the history of success or failure in using different methods.

Clearly, if the job can be filled from inside, so much he better. Failing that, unsolicited enquiries and/or personal recommendations are to be preferred, if they are known to work and if the cost of maintaining an employment office to deal with enquiries is taken into account.

From a cost point of view, an approach to government employment agencies, schools, universities, or ex-servicemen's employment agencies may be preferred to advertising or to the use of private agencies or consultants. But the effectiveness of the alternative sources must be taken into account as well as the indirect costs of using them or of having to put up with a longer waiting period before recruits can be obtained. External advertising may have to be used as the only reliable method of attracting candidates or to supplement other sources, but it is essential to evaluate such advertising properly in terms of cost per reply from each insertion.

The first choice of method may depend on the type of job, and typical methods for different categories of jobs are shown below:

Job category	*Typical sources*
1. Juveniles	Schools, youth employment agencies
2. Clerical and secretarial staff	Private employment agencies
3. Manual workers	Government employment and training centres
4. Professional staff	Advertisements, including the professional institutions themselves, where they operate an employment service
5. Graduates	Direct from universities, polytechnics and business schools
6. Managerial staff	Advertisements, consultants

Advertising

Advertising is the most obvious method of attracting candidates. Nevertheless, the first question to ask is whether an advertisement is really justified. This means looking at the alternative sources mentioned above and confirming, preferably on the basis of experience, that they will not do. Consideration should be given as to whether it might be better to use an agency or a selection consultant. When making the choice, refer to the three criteria of cost, speed and the likelihood of providing good candidates. The objectives of an advertisement should be to:

- *Attract attention* — it must compete for the interest of potential candidates against other employees.
- *Create and maintain interest* — it has to communicate in an attractive and interesting way information about the job, the company, the terms and conditions of employment and the qualifications required.
- *Stimulate action* — the message needs to be conveyed in a manner which will not only focus people's eyes on the advertisement but also encourage them to read to the end, as well as prompt a sufficient number of replies from good candidates.

To achieve these aims, one must do six things:

1. Analyse the requirement.
2. Decide who does what.
3. Write the copy.
4. Design the advertisement.
5. Plan the media.
6. Evaluate the response.

Analyse the requirement

First it is necessary to establish how many jobs have to be filled and by when. Then turn to the job description and specification to obtain information on responsibilities, qualifications and experience required, age limits, and any other data needed to draft the advertisement.

The next step is to consider where suitable candidates are likely to come from; the companies, jobs or education establishments they are in; and the parts of the country where they can be found.

Finally, think about what is likely to attract them about the job or the company so the most can be made of these factors in the advertisement. Consider also what might put them off, for example, the location of the job, in order that objections can be anticipated. Analyse previous successes or failures to establish what does or does not work.

Decide who does what

When planning a campaign or recruiting key people, there is much to be said for using an advertising agency. An agency can provide expertise in producing eye-catching headlines and writing good copy. It can devise an attractive house style and prepare layouts which make the most of the text, the logo and any 'white space' round the advertisement. Moreover, it can advise on ways of achieving visual impact by the use of illustrations and special typographical features. Finally, an agency can advise on media, help in response analysis and take up the burden of preparing blocks and placing advertisements.

The following steps should be taken when choosing an advertising ageny:

1. Check its experience in handling recruitment advertising.
2. See examples of its work.
3. Check with clients on the level of service provided.
4. Meet the staff who will work on the advertisements.
5. Check the fee structure.
6. Discuss methods of working.

Write the copy

A recruitment advertisement should start with a compelling headline and then contain information on:

- the company;
- the job;
- the person required;
- the benefits provided;
- the location;
- the action to be taken.

The headline is all important. The simplest and most obvious approach is to set out the job title in bold type. To gain attention, it is advisable to quote the salary (if it is worth quoting) and to put 'plus car' if a company car is provided. Salaries and cars are major attractions and should be stated clearly. Applicants are rightly suspicious of clauses such as 'salary will be commensurate with age and experience'. This usually means either that the salary is so low that the company is afraid to reveal it, or that salary policies are so incoherent that the company has no idea what to offer until someone tells them what he or she wants.

The name of the company should be given. (Do not use box numbers — if you want to be anonymous, use a consultant.) Add any selling-points, such as growth or diversification, and any other areas of interest to potential candidates. The essential features of the job should be conveyed by giving a brief description of what the job holder will do and, as far as space permits, the scope and scale of activities. Create interest in the job but do not oversell it.

The qualifications and experience required should be stated as factually as possible and age limits (if any) should be given. There is no point in overstating requirements and seldom any point in specifying exactly how much experience is wanted. This will vary from candidate to candidate and the other details about the job and the salary should provide them with enough information about the sort of experience required. Be careful about including a string of personal qualities such as drive, determination, and initiative. These have no real meaning to candidates. Phrases such as 'proven track record' and 'successful experience' are equally meaningless. No one will admit to not having either of them.

The advertisement should end with information on how the candidate should apply. 'Brief but comprehensive details' is a good phrase. Candidates can be asked to write, but useful alternatives are to ask them to telephone or to come along for an imformal chat at a suitable venue.

Remember that the Sex Discrimination Act 1975 makes it unlawful to discriminate in an advertisement by favouring either sex, the only exceptions being a few jobs which can be done only by one sex. Advertisements must therefore avoid sexist job titles such as 'salesman' or 'stewardess'. They must refer to a neutral title such as 'sales representative', or amplify the description to cover both sexes by stating 'steward or stewardess'. It is accepted, however, that certain job titles are unisex and therefore non-discriminatory. These include director, manager, executive and officer. It is best to avoid any reference to the sex of the candidate by using neutral or unisex titles and referring only to the 'candidate' or the 'applicant'. Otherwise you must specify 'man or woman' or 'he or she'

The Race Relations Act 1976 has similar provisions, making unlawful an advertisement which discriminates against any particular race. As long as race is never mentioned or even implied in an advertisement, you should have no problem in keeping within the law.

Design the advertisement
The main types of advertisement are the following:

1. *Classified/run-on*, in which copy is run-on, with no white space in or around the advertisement and no paragraph spacing or indentation. They are cheap but suitable only for junior or routine jobs.

2. *Classified/semi-display*, in which the headings can be set in capitals, paragraphs can be indented and white space is allowed round the advertisement. They are fairly cheap and semi-display can be much more effective than run-on advertisements

3. *Full display*, which are bordered and in which any typeface and illustrations can be used. They can be expensive but obviously make the most impact for management, technical and professional jobs.

Professional advice in designing display advertisements is desirable. The aim should be simplicity. Logos, illustrations, pre-set headings and borders and different typefaces can all help to achieve impact, but avoid creating too cluttered an impression. Use of white space can be very effective.

Plan the media

An advertising agency can advise on the choice of media (press, radio, television) and its cost. *British Rates and Data* (BRAD) can be consulted to give the costs of advertising in particular media.

The quality papers are best for managerial, professional and technical jobs. The popular papers can be used to reach less qualified staff such as sales representatives and technicians. Local papers are obviously best for recruiting clerical, secretarial and manual workers. Professional and trade journals can reach your audience directly, but results can be erratic and it is often best to use them to supplement a national campaign.

Avoid Saturdays and be cautious about repeating advertisements in the same medium. Diminishing returns can set in rapidly.

Evaluate the response

Measure response to provide guidance on the relative cost-effectiveness of different media. Cost per reply is the best ratio.

Using agencies

Most private agencies deal with secretarial and clerical staff. They are usually quick and effective but quite expensive. London agencies charge a fee averaging 15 per cent of the first year's salary for finding someone. It can be cheaper to advertise, especially when the company is in a buyer's market. Shop around to find the agency which suits the company's needs at a reasonable cost.

Agencies should be briefed carefully on what is wanted. They produce unsuitable candidates from time to time but the risk is reduced if they are clear about your requirements.

Using selection consultants

Selection consultants generally advertise, interview and produce a short list. They provide expertise and reduce workload. The company can be anonymous if it wishes. Most selection consultants charge a fee based on a percentage of the basic salary for the job, ranging from 15 to 20 per cent. The following steps should be taken when choosing a selection consultant:

1. Check reputation with other users if there are any doubts.
2. Look at the advertisements of the various firms. An idea of the quality of a consultancy and the type and level of jobs with which it deals can thus be gained.
3. Check on special expertise. The large accountancy firms, for example, are obviously skilled in recruiting accountants.
4. Meet the consultant who will work on the assignment to assess his or her quality.
5. Compare fees, although the differences are likely to be small, and the other considerations are usually more important.

When using selection consultants, do the following:

1. Brief them clearly on their terms of reference.
2. Give every assistance to consultants in defining the job and the company's requirements. They will do much better if they know what type of person is most likely to fit well into the company.
3. Check carefully the proposed programme and the draft text of the advertisement.
4. Clarify the basis upon which fees and expenses will be charged.
5. Ensure that arrangements are made to deal directly with the consultant who will handle the assignment.

Using executive search consultants

Use an executive search consultant, or 'head hunter', for senior jobs where there are only a limited number of suitable people and a direct lead to them is wanted. They are not cheap. Head hunters charge a fee of 30–50 per cent of the first year's salary, but they can be quite cost-effective.

Head hunters first approach their own contacts in the industry or profession concerned; the more numerous the contacts, the better the head hunter. Some may be interested in the job themselves; others may provide leads to people who can be approached. If this fails, the consultant telephones likely people, even if there is no indication that they are interested. Those who receive unexpected calls from a head hunter are often flattered or interested enough to agree to see him. A fairly relaxed and informal meeting then takes place and the consultant forwards the names of suitable and interested candidates to his client.

There are some good and some not-so-good executive search consultants. Do not use one unless a reliable recommendation is obtained.

Selecting candidates

Sifting applications

When the vacancy or vacancies have been advertised and a fair number of replies received, the typical sequence of steps required to process and sift applications is as follows:

1. List the applications on a standard control sheet such as the one illustrated in Figure 17.5.

Ref		Vacancy					
Media							
No.	Media Ref	Name	Address	Grading	Acknow-ledge	Inter-view	Final letter
1							
2							
3							
4							
5							
6							
7							
8							
9							
10							

Figure 17.5 Recruitment control sheet

2. Send a standard acknowledgement letter to each applicant unless an instant decision can be made to interview or reject. If there is insufficient information in the initial letter, the applicant could be

asked to complete and return an application form. To save time, trouble, expense and irritation, it is best to make a decision on the initial letter rather than ask for a form.

3. Compare the applications with the key criteria in the job specification: qualifications, training, experience, age and location, and sort them initially into three categories:

   (a) possible
   (b) marginal
   (c) unsuitable

4. Scrutinize the possibles again to draw up a short list for interview. This scrutiny could be carried out by the personnel or employment specialist, and, preferably, the manager.

5. Invite the candidates to interview, using a standard letter where large numbers are involved. At this stage, candidates should be asked to complete an application form, if they have not already done so.

6. Review the remaining possibles and marginals and decide if any are to be held in reserve. Send reserves a standard 'holding' letter and send the others a standard rejection letter. The latter should thank candidates for the interest shown and inform them briefly, but not too brusquely, that they have not been successful. A typical reject letter might read as follows:

   Since writing to you on — we have given careful consideration to your application for the above position. I regret to inform you, however, that we have decided not to ask you to attend for an interview. We should like to thank you for the interest you have shown.

Application forms

Application forms are required as a means of setting out the information on a candidate in a standardized format. They provide a basis both for the interview and for the subsequent actions in offering an appointment and in setting up personnel records. An example of a form is given in Appendix L.

Interviewing arrangements

The interviewing arrangements will depend partly on the procedure being used, which may consist of individual interviews, an interviewing panel, a selection board or some form of group selection procedure. The main features of these alternative procedures are described later in this section but, in most cases, the arrangements for the interviews should conform broadly to the following pattern:

- The candidate who has applied in writing or by telephone should be told where and when to come and whom to ask for. The interview time should be arranged to fit in with the time it will take to get to the company. It may be necessary to adjust times for those who cannot get away during working hours. If the company is difficult to find, a map should be sent with details of public transport. The receptionist or security guard should be told who is coming. Candidates are impressed to find that they are expected.
- Applicants should have somewhere quiet and comfortable in which to wait for the interview, with reading material available and access to cloakroom facilities.
- The interviewers or interviewing panel should have been well briefed on the programme. Interviewing rooms should have been booked and arrangements made, as necessary, for welcoming candidates, for escorting them to interviews, for meals and for a conducted tour round the company.
- Comfortable private rooms should be provided for interviews with little, if any, distractions around them. Interviewers should preferably not sit behind their desks, as this creates a psychological barrier.
- During the interview or interviews, time should be allowed to tell candidates about the company and the job and to discuss with them conditions of employment. Negotiations about salaries and other benefits may take place after a provisional offer has been made, but it is as well to prepare the ground during the interviewing stage.
- Candidates should be told what the next step will be at the end of the interview. They may be asked at this stage if they have any objections to references being taken up.
- Follow-up studies should be carried out of the performance of successful candidates on the job compared with the prediction made at the selection stage. These studies should be used to validate the selection procedure and to check on the capabilities of interviewers.

Individual interviews

The individual interview is the most familiar method of selection. It involves face-to-face discussion and provides the best opportunity for the establishment of close contact — *rapport* — between the interviewer and the candidate. If only one interviewer is used, there is more scope for a biased or superficial decision, and this is one reason for using a second interviewer or an interviewing panel.

Interviewing panels

Two or three people gathered together to interview one candidate may be described as an interviewing panel. The most typical situation is that in which a personnel manager and line managers see the candidate at the same time. This has the advantage of enabling information to be shared and reducing overlaps. The interviewers can discuss their joint impressions of the candidate's behaviour at the interview and modify or enlarge any superficial judgements.

Selection boards

Selection boards are more formal and, usually, larger interviewing panels convened by an official body because there are a number of parties interested in the selection decision. Their only advantage is that they enable a number of different people to have a look at the applicants and compare notes on the spot. The disadvantages are that the questions tend to be unplanned and delivered at random, the prejudices of a dominating member of the board can overwhelm the judgements of the other members, and the candidates are unable to do justice to themselves because they are seldom allowed to expand. Selection boards tend to favour the confident and articulate candidate, but in doing so they may miss the underlying weaknesses of a superficially impressive individual. They can also underestimate the qualities of those who happen to be less effective in front of a formidable board, although they would be fully competent in the less formal or less artificial situations that would face them in the job.

Group selection

A group selection procedure involves gathering a number of candidates together (ideally, six to eight) in the presence of a group of interviewers/observers (ideally, two or three). The candidates are subjected to a series of exercises and tests, supplemented by individual or panel interviews.

The group exercises may be of the 'analogous' type in which the group is given a case study to discuss which includes features and problems similar to those they would meet if they joined the organization. Or the group may be asked to discuss a general social or economic problem. They may even be asked to agree among themselves what they are going to discuss.

Members of the group may be tested on leadership qualities by being asked to take turns in leading the group, or the groups may not have appointed leaders, in order that leadership qualities can emerge in discussion.

The observers rate or rank participants in respect of a set of factors such as:

- ability to think in a logical manner about the problem posed;
- realistic, practical approach to the problem;
- confidence in putting views to the group;
- willingness to follow and consider other people's opinion;
- tendency to emerge as a leader in the group;
- willingness to accept criticisms of his or her ideas.

Ranking on each of these characteristics is sometimes preferred to rating on a numerical scale because of the difficulty of ensuring that the raters maintain a uniform standard of judgement.

In addition to the group discussions, candidates may be tested on their ability to express themselves in writing by being given paper exercises. Their ability to express themselves and to present a case orally may be tested by asking them to deliver 'lecturettes' or to make a presentation of a proposal to the group based on the study of a brief.

Individual abilities and qualities can be discussed by administering a battery of intelligence, personality and aptitude tests.

Group selection procedures are time-consuming and expensive to run, but they appear to be a more comprehensive method of making selection decisions, ie they have 'face validity'. This is because they expose candidates to a number of more or less realistic situations and enable interviewers to see them in action with others as well as individually. A number of studies have been carried out on their *true* validity — that is, their value as a means of predicting future performance in the job, and one conducted for the Civil Service Commission showed that the selection procedure as a whole had a considerable degree of validity when judged in the light of follow-up information about the performance of successful candidates.

But Vernon sounded the following warning on group selection procedures:

They are likely to be somewhat superior to the conventional interview method of assessing people, because they provide a more prolonged and varied set of situations in which to observe and interpret. But they are just as dependent as the interview on the skill, experience and impartiality of the observer and they should be applied with all the more caution because they engender in the observers an undue measure of confidence in the accuracy of their judgements.[3]

The interview

The purpose of the interview is to obtain and assess information about a candidate which will enable a valid prediction to be made of his or her future performance on the job in comparison with the predictions made for any other candidates. Interviewing therefore involves processing and evaluating evidence about the capabilities of a candidate in relation to the job specification. Some of the evidence will be on the application form, but this must be supplemented by the more detailed or specific information about experience and personal characteristics that can be obtained in a face-to-face meeting. Further evidence may be obtained from selection tests or from references, but the interview remains the main source of information.

An interview has been described as a conversation with a purpose. It is a conversation because the candidates should be induced to talk freely with their interviewer about themselves and their careers. But the conversation has to be planned, directed and controlled to achieve the main purpose of the interview, which is to make an accurate prediction of the candidate's future performance in the job for which he or she is being considered.

Interviewers, however, have other aims. One is to provide the candidate with information about the job and the company. An interview is basically an exchange of information which will enable both parties to make a decision: to offer or not to offer a job; to accept or not to accept the offer. A further aim is to give the candidate a favourable impression of the company. This should encourage the good candidate to join and should leave the rejected candidates without any ill-feelings.

Good interviewers know what they are looking for and how to set about finding it. Finally, they have a method for recording their analyses of candidates against a set of assessment criteria.

Knowing what to look for
Knowing what to look for is a matter of knowing the job specification and the information needed to confirm whether or not the candidate meets the specification under each of its headings: qualifications, experience, knowledge, skills, physical and personality characteristics, and personal circumstances.

Knowing how to find it
Knowing how to find the information required is a matter first of planning the interview and then of conducting it in a way which will obtain all the data needed to make a balanced decision.

The interview should be planned round the candidate's application form to cover each of the headings on the job specification. It is therefore essential to read the application form thoroughly before the interview to decide on the line of questions and any areas where probing may be required. The aim is to establish exactly what applicants know and can do, or to fill any gaps in their employment record. A biographical approach is usually best, starting with applicants' education (especially younger candidates) and then moving progressively and naturally through work experience, job by job, discussing for each job: why they took it, what they did, what knowledge and skills they acquired, and why they left it. Clearly, the interview should concentrate on the most recent experience. There is no point in dwelling for long on the earlier experience of someone who has been in employment for a number of years.

The information required in an interview can seldom be obtained in fewer than 20 minutes, but it is usually unproductive to extend the information-gathering part of the interview beyond 30 or 40 minutes. Allowance has also to be made for the information-giving part of the interview and for the candidate's questions. For a managerial interview, a longer period may be necessary to discuss recent experience and ambitions more thoroughly. Time must also be allowed for information about the company and the job, and for the candidate to ask questions. The best approach is to start with a few welcoming remarks and explain how the interview is to be planned. Then carry out the biographical interview before telling the candidate about the job and discussing conditions of

Table 17.1 Dos and don'ts of interviewing

Do	Don't
☐ plan the interview	☐ start the interview unprepared
☐ establish an easy and informal relationship	☐ plunge too quickly into demanding questions
☐ encourage the candidate to talk	☐ ask leading questions
☐ cover the ground as planned	☐ jump to conclusions on inadequate evidence
☐ probe where necessary	
☐ analyse career and interests to reveal strengths, weaknesses, patterns of behaviour	☐ pay too much attention to isolated strengths or weaknesses
	☐ allow the candidate to gloss over important facts
☐ maintain control over the direction and time taken by the interview	☐ talk too much

employment, including pay and fringe benefits. There is no point in giving a lengthy dissertation about the company or the work to someone who is clearly unsuitable or uninterested. Allow time at the end for questions and round off the interview by telling the candidate what the next step will be. It is normally better not to announce the final decision during the interview. It may be advisable to obtain references and, in any case, time is required to reflect on the information received. Moreover, some candidates, especially senior staff and students, do not like to think that snap decisions are being made about them, even if they are favourable. These points are summarized in Table 17.1.

Assessment criteria

The criteria for assessing candidates and the method of recording assessments should either be standardized for regular recruitment exercises or, if a one-off recruitment is being carried out, drawn up in advance of the interviewing stage.

The criteria should obviously be those used in drawing up the job specification: for example, the seven points or the five factors in the two schemes referred to earlier in this chapter.

Admirable though these systems may be when they are used by a skilled personnel practitioner or a trained manager, they sometimes prove too complex for the typical line manager or selection board. It may therefore be necessary to devise a simplified set of criteria for their use which can be expressed in terms a layperson can understand with the minimum of training.

In any situation in which non-specialists are making selection decisions, it is best to use criteria which can be defined simply in familiar language and can easily be related to a job specification. The following criteria, which were mentioned earlier in this chapter when discussing job specifications, are used by managers in practice even if they do not necessarily analyse them under precisely similar headings:

- qualifications and training;
- experience;
- knowledge and skills — as acquired by experience, training and education or the natural abilities the individual possesses;
- overall impression — appearance, manner and speech, physique, health (physical characteristics);
- personality characteristics — leadership, drive, dependability, persistence, self-reliance, sociability.

Vacancy		Candidate					
			Rating				
Factor	*Comments*		A	B	C	D	E
Qualifications and training							
Experience							
Knowledge and skills							
Personality characteristics							
Overall impression							
Recommendation							
A = Very much above average; B = Above average; C = Average; D = Below average; E = Very much below average.							

Figure 17.6 Interview assessment form

An interview record form using these criteria is illustrated in Figure 17.6.

Whatever assessment criteria are used, it is essential to follow up interviews to find out if the assessments and predictions have been validated by performance on the job. This is the only way in which interviewers can ever find out how effective they are. It takes time and trouble, and valid criteria are not always easy to identify, but it is well worthwhile.

Psychometric tests

The purpose of a selection test is to provide an objective means of measuring individual abilities or characteristics. These involve the application of standard procedures to subjects which enable their responses to be quantified. The differences in the numerical scores represent differences in abilities or behaviour.

A good test has the following four characteristics:

1. It is a *sensitive measuring instrument* which discriminates well between subjects.
2. It has been *standardized* on a representative and sizeable sample of the population for which it is intended so that any individual's score can be interpreted in relation to that of others.

3. It is *reliable* in the sense that it always measures the same thing. A test aimed at measuring a particular characteristic, such as intelligence, should measure the same characteristic when applied to different people at the same or a different time, or to the same person at different times.
4. It is *valid* in the sense that it measures the characteristic which the test is intended to measure. Thus, an intelligence test should measure intelligence (however defined) and not simply verbal facility. A test meant to predict success in a job or in passing examinations should produce reasonably convincing (statistically significant) predictions.

The main types of psychometric tests used for selection are intelligence tests, aptitude and attainment tests, and personality tests.

Intelligence tests
Intelligence tests are the oldest and most frequently used psychological tests. The first test was produced by Binet and Simon in 1905, and shortly afterwards, Stern suggested that the test scores should be expressed in the form of intelligence quotients, or IQs. The IQ is the ratio of the mental age, as measured by a Binet-type test, to the actual (chronological) age. When the mental and chronological age correspond, the IQ is expressed as 100. It is assumed that intelligence is distributed normally throughout the population; that is, the frequency distribution of intelligence corresponds to the normal curve shown in Figure 17.7.

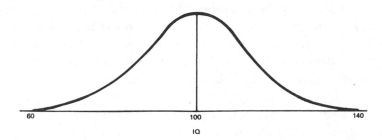

IQ

Figure 17.7 A normal curve

The most important characteristic of the normal curve is that it is symmetrical — there are an equal number of cases on either side of the mean, the central axis. Thus, the distribution of intelligence in the population as a whole consists of an equal number of people with IQs above and below 100.

The difficulty with intelligence tests is that they have to be based on a

371

theory of what constitutes intelligence and then have to derive a series of verbal and non-verbal instruments for measuring the different factors or constituents of intelligence. But intelligence is a highly complex concept. There is no agreed definition of it among psychologists and the variety of theories about intelligence and the consequent variations in the test instrument or battery available make the choice of an intelligence test a difficult one. For general selection purposes, a test which can be administered to a group of candidates is the best, especially if it has been properly validated, and it is possible to relate test scores to 'norms' in such a way as to indicate how the individual taking the test compares with the rest of the population, in general or in a specific area.

Aptitude and attainment tests

Aptitude tests are designed to predict the potential an individual has to perform a job or specific tasks within a job. They can cover such areas as clerical aptitude, numerical aptitude, mechanical aptitude and dexterity.

All aptitude tests should be properly validated. The usual procedure is to determine the qualities required for the job by means of a job analysis. A standard test or a test battery is then obtained from a test agency. Alternatively, a special test is devised by or for the company. The test is then given to employees already working on the job and the results compared with a criterion, usually supervisors' ratings. If the correlation between test and criterion is sufficiently high, the test is then given to applicants. To validate the test further, a follow-up study of the job performance of the applicants selected by the test is usually carried out. This is a lengthy procedure, but without it no real confidence can be attached to the results of any aptitude test. Many do-it-yourself tests are worse than useless because they have not been properly validated.

Attainment tests measure abilities or skills that have already been acquired by training or experience. A typing test is the most typical example. It is easy to find out how many words a minute a typist can type and compare that with the standard required for the job.

Personality tests

The term 'personality' is all-embracing in terms of the individual's behaviour and the way it is organized and co-ordinated when he or she interacts with the environment. There are many different theories of personality and, consequently, many different types of personality tests. These include self-report personality questionnaires and other questionnaires which measure interests, values or work behaviour.

Self-report personality questionnaires are the ones most commonly used. They adopt a 'trait' approach, defining a trait as a fairly independent but enduring characteristic of behaviour which all people display but to differing degrees. Trait theorists such as Cattell or Guilford identify examples of common behaviour, devise scales to measure these, and then obtain ratings on these behaviours by people who know each other well. These observations are analysed statistically, using the factor analysis technique to identify distinct traits and to indicate how associated groups of traits might be grouped loosely into personality 'types'. There are a number of questionnaires to choose from and reference should be made for further guidance on what is available to *Testing, Practical Guide* by Toplis, Pulewicz and Fletcher (Institute of Personnel Management, 1987), which covers the whole subject of tests very thoroughly.

'Interest' questionnaires are sometimes used to supplement personality tests. They assess the preferences of respondents for particular types of occupation and are therefore most applicable to vocational guidance but can be helpful when selecting apprentices and trainees.

'Value' questionnaires attempt to assess beliefs about what is desirable or 'good' or what is undesirable or 'bad'. The questionnaires measure the relative prominence of such values as conformity, independence, achievement, decisiveness, orderliness and goal-orientation.

Specific work behaviour questionnaires cover behaviours such as leadership (Fleischman's Leadership Opinion Questionnaire) or selling (The Poppleton-Allen Sales Aptitude Test).

Personality tests can provide interesting supplementary information about candidates which is free from the biased reactions that frequently occur in face-to-face interviews. But they have to be used with great care. The tests should have been developed by a reputable psychologist or test agency on the basis of extensive research and field testing and they must meet the specific needs of the user.

Choosing tests

It is essential to choose tests which meet the four criteria of sensitivity, standardization, reliability and validity. It is very difficult to achieve the standards required if a company tries to develop its own test batteries unless it employs a qualified psychologist or obtains professional advice from a member of the British Psychological Society. This organization, with the full support and understanding of the reputable test suppliers, exercises rigorous control over who can use what tests and the standard of training required and given. Particular care should be taken when selecting personality tests — there are a lot of charlatans about.

Do-it-yourself tests are always suspect unless they have been properly validated and realistic norms have been established. Generally speaking, it is best to avoid using them.

The use of tests in a selection procedure

Tests are most likely to be helpful when they are used as part of a selection procedure for occupations where a large number of recruits are required, and where it is not possible to rely entirely on examination results or information about previous experience as the basis for predicting future performance. In these circumstances it is economical to develop and administer the tests, and a sufficient number of cases can be built up for the essential validation exercise.

Intelligence tests are particularly helpful in situations where intelligence is a key factor, but there is no other reliable method of measuring it. It may, incidentally, be as important to use an intelligence test to keep out applicants who are too intelligent for the job as to use one to guarantee a minimal level of intelligence. A validation exercise with which the author was concerned on tests for van salesmen established that applicants above a certain level of intelligence should be rejected, unless they had promotion potential, because they could not settle down in the job.

Aptitude and attainment tests are most useful for jobs where specific and measurable skills are required, such as typing or computer programming. Personality tests are potentially of greatest value in jobs such as selling where 'personality' is important, and where it is not too difficult to obtain quantifiable criteria for validation purposes.

Tests should be administered only by staff who have been thoroughly trained in what the tests are measuring, how they should be used, and how they should be interpreted.

It is essential to evaluate all tests by comparing the results at the interview stage with later achievements. To be statistically significant, these evaluations should be carried out over a reasonable period of time and cover as large a number of candidates as possible.

In some situations a battery of tests may be associated, including various types of intelligence, aptitude and personality tests. These may be a standard battery supplied by a test agency, or a custom-built battery may be used. The biggest pitfall to avoid is adding extra tests just for the sake of it, without ensuring that they make a proper contribution to the success of the predictions for which the battery is being used.

Offers and references

After the interviewing and testing procedure has been completed, a provisional decision to make an offer by telephone or in writing can be made. This is normally 'subject to satisfactory references' and the candidate should, of course, be told that these will be taken up. If there is more than one eligible candidate for a job it may be advisable to hold one or two people in reserve. Applicants often withdraw, especially those whose only purpose in applying for the job was to carry out a 'test marketing' operation, or to obtain a lever with which to persuade their present employers to value them more highly.

References

The purpose of a reference is to obtain in confidence factual information about a prospective employee and opinions about his character and suitability for a job.

The factual information is straightforward and essential. It is simply necessary to confirm the nature of the previous job, the period of time in employment, the reason for leaving (if relevant), the salary or rate of pay and, possibly, the attendance record.

Opinions about character and suitability are less reliable and should be treated with caution. The reason is obvious. Previous or present employers who give references tend to avoid highly detrimental remarks either out of charity or because they think anything they say or write may be construed as slanderous or libellous (references are, in fact, privileged as long as they are given without malice and are factually correct).

Personal referees are, of course, entirely useless. All they prove is that the applicant has at least one or two friends.

Written references save time, especially if they are standardized. They may take the form of an invitation to write a letter confirming the employment record and commenting on the applicant's character in general. If brief details about the job are included (these may be an extract from the advertisement — they should certainly not be an over elaborate job description), previous employers can be asked to express their views about the suitability of the individual for the job. But this is asking a lot. Unless the job and companies are identical, how well can existing or ex-employers judge the suitability of someone they may not know particularly well for another job in a different environment?

More precise answers may be obtained if a standard form is provided for the employer to complete. The questions asked on this form should be limited to the following:

- What was the period of employment?
- What was the job title?

- What work was carried out?
- What was the rate of pay or salary?
- How many days' absence over the last 12 months?
- Would you re-employ (if not, why not)?

The last question is the key one, if it is answered honestly.

Telephone references may be used as an alternative or an addition to written references. The great advantage of a telephone conversation is that people are more likely to give an honest opinion orally than if they have to commit themselves in writing. It may also save time to use the telephone.

Employer references are necessary but they are unreliable. A satisfactory reference has to be treated at its face value — all one can be reasonably certain about is that the factual details are correct. A very glowing reference may arouse suspicion, and it is worth comparing it with a reference from another employer (two employment references are desirable in any case). Poor or grudging references must create some alarm if only because they are so infrequent. But allowance should be made for prejudice and a check should be made, by telephone if possible.

Confirming the offer

The final stage in the selection procedure is to confirm the offer of employment after satisfactory references have been obtained, and the applicant has passed the medical examination required for pension and life assurance purposes or because a certain standard of physical fitness is required for the work. The contract of employment should also be prepared at this stage.

Contracts of employment

The basic information that should be included in a written contract of employment varies according to the level of job, contracts of employment are dealt with in Chapter 37 (pages 802–804).

Induction

Induction is the process of receiving and welcoming employees when they first join a company and giving them the basic information they need to settle down quickly and happily and start work. Induction has three aims:

- to smooth the preliminary stages when everything is likely to be strange and unfamiliar to the starter;

- to establish quickly a favourable attitude to the company in the mind of the new employee so that he or she is more likely to stay;
- to obtain effective output from the new employee in the shortest possible time.

Company induction

The first stage in induction is when the employee arrives at the company. He or she should be welcomed by a responsible person (not simply a commissionaire or a junior wages clerk) who can provide basic information about the company and terms and conditions of employment. Some of the information will confirm what the employee has already been told, some will be new, but there is a limit to how much can be conveyed at this stage.

An employee handbook is useful for this purpose. It need not be too glossy, but it should convey clearly and simply what new staff need to know under the following headings:

- a brief description of the company — its history, products, organization and management;
- basic conditions of employment — hours of work, holidays, pension scheme, insurance;
- pay — pay scales, when paid and how, deductions, queries;
- sickness — notification of absence, certificates, pay;
- leave of absence;
- work rules;
- disciplinary procedure;
- grievance procedure;
- promotion procedure;
- union and joint consultation arrangements;
- education and training facilities;
- health and safety arrangements;
- medical and first-aid facilities;
- restaurant and canteen facilities;
- social and welfare arrangements;
- telephone calls and correspondence;
- travelling and subsistence expenses.

If the organization is not large enough to justify a printed handbook, the least that can be done is to prepare a typed summary of this information.

Company induction procedures, however, should not rely on the printed word. The member of the personnel department or other individual who is looking after new employees should run through the main points with each individual or, when larger numbers are being taken on, with groups of people. In this way, a more personal touch is provided and queries can be answered.

When the initial briefing has been completed, the new employee should be taken to his place of work and introduced to his manager or supervisor for the departmental induction programme. Alternatively, he or she may go straight to a training school and join the department later.

Departmental induction

The departmental induction programme should, wherever possible, start with the departmental manager, not the immediate supervisor. The manager may give only a general welcome and a brief description of the work of the department before handing new employee's over to their supervisors for the more detailed induction. But it is important for the manager to be involved at this stage so that he or she is not seen as a remote figure by the new employee. And at least this means that the starter will not be simply a name or a number to the manager.

The detailed induction is probably best carried out by the immediate supervisor, who should have five main aims:

- to put the new employee at ease;
- to interest the employee in the job and the company;
- to provide basic information about working arrangements;
- to indicate the standards of performance and behaviour expected from the employee;
- to tell the employee about training arrangements and how he or she can get on with the company.

Follow-up

It is essential to follow up newly engaged employees to ensure that they have settled in and to check on how well they are doing. If there are any problems it is much better to identify them at an early stage rather than allowing them to fester.

Following up is also important as a means of checking on the selection procedure. If by any chance a mistake has been made, it is useful to find out how it happened so that the selection procedure can be improved. Misfits can be attributed to a number of causes; for example: inadequate job description or specification, poor sourcing of candidates, weak advertising, poor interviewing techniques, inappropriate or invalidated tests, or prejudice on the part of the selector. If any of these are identified, steps can be taken to prevent their recurrence.

References

1. Rodger, A *The Seven-Point Plan*. National Institute of Industrial Psychology, London, 1952.
2. Munro Fraser, J *A Handbook of Employment Interviewing*. Macdonald and Evans, London, 1954.
3. Vernon, P E 'The Validation of Civil Service Board Selection Procedures', *Occupational Psychology*, Vol. 24, 1950 pp. 75–95.

18

Assessment Centres

Definition

An assessment centre is a programme (not a place!) which lasts from one to three days and uses a range of assessment techniques to determine whether or not candidates are suitable for a particular job or for promotion. It may also analyse their development needs.

Aims

In their original form, assessment centres were used exclusively for selection. Increasingly, however, they have concentrated more on diagnosing development needs.

The fundamental aim of an assessment centre is to give information about the participants' competences, to determine suitability for a job or promotion, and to provide guidance on what should be done by the organization or by the individual to develop these competences in line with the requirements of the organization.

Features

The aims and methods of assessment centres vary considerably according to the needs of the organization. There are, however, a number of typical features, which are as follows:

- The focus of the centre is on behaviour.
- Exercises are used to capture and simulate the key dimensions of the job. These include one-to-one role-plays and group exercises. It is assumed that performance in these simulations predicts behaviour on the job.

- Interviews and written exercises or tests may be used in addition to group exercises.
- Performance is measured in several dimensions in terms of the competences required to achieve the target level of performance in a particular job or at a particular level in the organization.
- Several candidates of participants are assessed together to allow interaction and to make the experience more open and participative.
- Several assessors or observers are used in order to increase the objectivity of assessments. Involving senior managers is desirable to ensure that they 'own' the process. Assessors must be carefully trained.
- Results are fed back to participants, with areas of strength and development needs identified.

Developing an assessment centre

The following steps are required to develop an assessment centre.

Define aims

It is necessary to be clear about the extent to which the centre is required to assess suitability for particular jobs, to identify potential for promotion to a higher level, or to diagnose development needs.

Define membership

Who will attend? How will they be selected? How many? The membership is clearly related to the aims of the centre, but in deciding what type or level of person should attend, should one refer to human resource planning data on future requirements. Candidates for assessment centres should be identified through the performance management system (see Chapter 19). The number attending a centre is typically six, certainly not fewer, and there is a limit to which this number can be increased before making the centre unwieldy and inoperable (eight is probably the maximum).

Define competences

Competences are the behavioural dimensions that affect job performance. The task of the job analyst, as described in Chapter 16, is to identify the behaviours that distinguish high performance. The results of this analysis are then classified to provide the list of criteria round which the assessment centre will be designed. These assessment dimensions should be defined in behavioural terms and should include only those which can be easily and economically observed in an assessment centre context.

There are lists of generic competences such as that compiled by Henley Management College, as reported by Dulewicz.[1] These are middle-management competences. The list is not in its final state, but at present it looks like this:

Intellectual:	Strategic perspective
	Analysis and judgement
	Planning and organizing
Interpersonal:	Managing staff
	Persuasiveness
	Assertiveness and decisiveness
	Interpersonal sensitivity
	Oral communication
Adaptability:	Adaptability and resilience
Results orientation:	Energy and initiative
	Achievement motivation
	Business sense

Many other lists have been compiled, as described by Woodruffe,[2] and there are many similarities between them. But it is best for organizations to do their own analyses and produce lists to which they can relate, as does W H Smith, whose list comprises:

- written communication
- oral communication
- leadership
- team membership
- planning and organizing skills
- decision making
- motivation
- personal strength
- analytical and reasoning skills.

The leadership dimension in the W H Smith list is defined as follows:

Positive indicators:

- takes account of the priorities and problems of others;
- helps to direct the group to the achievement of its goals;

- avoids 'making enemies';
- explains a situation clearly to others;
- is open in his or her dealings with other people;
- identifies the needs of the group and responds accordingly;
- works well as a member of a team.

Contra-indicators:

- excessive need to dominate other people;
- fails to take account of the needs and problems of other people;
- fails to disclose relevant information to others;
- is unhelpful and unsupportive;
- alienates others by his or her attitudes and actions.

Develop methods of assessment

It is usual to have a scoring system for rating against each dimension. The following are the W H Smith rating definitions:

- Rating is on an eight-point scale.
- Each pair of points on the scale corresponds to a classification of performance.
- The two points within each classification can be used by assessors to indicate whether performance is just within that classification or well within it.
- The classifications are *excellent, competent, fair* and *weak*.

Excellent (scale points 7 and 8)
This rating identifies a major strength shown by the candidate. It is a level of performance which is well above average, and which would be expected only from candidates of very high ability. No development action in respect of this factor would be proposed where a 7 or 8 rating is given.

Competent (scale points 5 and 6)
This rating identifies a good level of performance but not one which is a major strength. It is certainly a good enough standard of performance for the candidate's current job requirements, and development action would be undertaken only to prepare the candidate for a more demanding role.

Fair (scale points 3 and 4)
This rating identifies a level of performance which is adequate or just below adequate for the current job. Some development action should

probably be taken to improve current job performance, and a significant degree of development action would be required before moving into a more demanding role.

Weak (scale points 1 and 2)

This rating identifies a level of performance which represents a significant weakness. A significant degree of development action is probably required to bring performance up to an acceptable level in the current job. Ratings in this area would give serious concern in seeking to evaluate the potential of the candidate.

Decide on assessment instruments

The assessment instruments that can be used include the following.

Exercises

Some off-the-shelf material can be used as long as the tests or exercises are both valid and reliable as measures and predictors of behaviour in line with the required job dimensions or competences. Because of the emphasis on simulations, it is highly desirable to develop tailor-made material based on the tasks job holders actually perform in the organization. This material might include some or all of the following types of exercises:

- in-tray exercises in which participants have to deal with the problems or requests contained in a pile of specially devised letters, faxes or memoranda;
- role-plays, often on a one-to-one basis, in which participants may have to deal with a customer or handle a grievance or a group negotiating exercise;
- individual exercises in which participants are given a brief and are required to prepare a written report recommending action and/or to present their report orally;
- group problem-solving/decision-making exercises in which the group is presented with a situation or requirement and must prepare joint recommendations on the action to be taken.

There are no rules on how many exercises should be included, except that sufficient time should be allowed for each one to ensure that it can be completed by the average participant or group of participants, and to enable assessors to complete their ratings. Exercises typically take two to three hours or so, and their number should be limited to four or five to avoid exhausting participants *and* assessors. It is important, however, that the exercises should cover all the dimensions or factors, and each factor should be measured more than once. Woodruffe[2] gives good examples of exercises.

Interviews
Interviews can be used to supplement exercises and to assess specific dimensions, such as achievement motivation, by discussing the experiences of individuals — what they have done and how they have done it. Interviews should be planned, conducted and reported on specifically by reference to these dimensions.

Tests and inventories
Tests and inventories can provide useful information supplementary to observations and interviews, but again, they must be related to competences. Some assessment centre organizers prefer to rely on observations alone, although inventories such as the Myers-Briggs give helpful data for counselling sessions.

Self-assessment
Self-assessment questionnaires can be used where the assessment centre is primarily developmental. They can cover points such as the analysis of achievements or strengths in terms of knowledge, skills and development needs.

Prepare assessment forms and procedures

Examples of assessment forms are given below; they consist of:

- an observation sheet (Figure 18.1);
- an assessment report (Figure 18.2);
- an interview report (Figure 18.3);
- a rating summary sheet (Figure 18.4);
- assessment conference summary form (Figure 18.5);
- a feedback summary form (Figure 18.6).

The procedures to be developed are those concerning the administration of the centre (this needs to be carefully planned and an administrator will have to work full-time during the programme) and the method of assessment. The latter is carried out at an assessors' conference in which information on assessments is pooled and agreed, and decisions are made on actions and feedback.

Participant:	Assessor:
Activity:	

Time	Observation

Figure 18.1 Assessment centre observation sheet

Participant:	Assessor:
Activity:	

Competence dimension	Rating							
	Weak		Fair		Compt.		Exel.	
	1	2	3	4	5	6	7	8
	1	2	3	4	5	6	7	8
	1	2	3	4	5	6	7	8
	1	2	3	4	5	6	7	8
	1	2	3	4	5	6	7	8

Comments on strengths:

Comments on development needs:

Figure 18.2 Assessment centre activity assessment report

Participant:	Assessor:							
	Rating							
	Weak		Fair		Compt.		Exel.	
Adaptability	1	2	3	4	5	6	7	8
Leadership	1	2	3	4	5	6	7	8
Business sense	1	2	3	4	5	6	7	8
Commitment	1	2	3	4	5	6	7	8
Need to achieve	1	2	3	4	5	6	7	8
Comments on strengths:								
Comments on development needs:								

Figure 18.3 Assessment centre interview report

Participant:				Assessor:			

Competence dimension	Activities						
	In-tray	Individual project	Interview	Role-play	Group project	Group exercise	Dimension total
1. Self-organization			▒	▒	▒	▒	
2. Adaptability		▒		▒			
3. Problem solving/ decision making			▒	▒			
4. Leadership	▒	▒					
5. Interpersonal skills	▒	▒	▒				
6. Team skills	▒	▒	▒		▒		
7. Communication skills			▒				
8. Business sense				▒		▒	
9. Commitment	▒			▒	▒		
10. Need to achieve	▒			▒			
TOTAL SCORE	▒	▒	▒	▒	▒	▒	

Comments on strengths:

Comments on development needs:

Assessment centre rating summary sheet

Participant:										
Competence dimension	Comments	Consensus rating								
		Weak		Fair		Comp		Exel		
1. Self-organization		1	2	3	4	5	6	7	8	
2. Adaptability		1	2	3	4	5	6	7	8	
3. Problem solving/ decision making		1	2	3	4	5	6	7	8	
4. Leadership		1	2	3	4	5	6	7	8	
5. Interpersonal skills		1	2	3	4	5	6	7	8	
6. Team skills		1	2	3	4	5	6	7	8	
7. Communication skills		1	2	3	4	5	6	7	8	
8. Business sense		1	2	3	4	5	6	7	8	
9. Commitment		1	2	3	4	5	6	7	8	
10. Need to achieve		1	2	3	4	5	6	7	8	

Comments on strengths:

Comments on development needs:

Recommended action:

Assessment conference summary form

Name:
Strengths:
Development needs:
Outcome of discussion and action plan:
Signed   Date: Assessor: Participant:

Assessment centre feedback summary form

Construct programme

The following is an example of a two-and-a-half-day programme:

Day 1
1400–1430   Introduction
1430–1630   In-tray exercise
1700–1900   Group project
2100–2200   Project presentation

Day 2
0900–1100   Role-plays
1130–1230   Individual project
1400–1530   Individual project
1600–1900   Interviews
2030–2200   Group exercise

Day 3
0900–1030   Group exercise
1030–1300   Assessors' conference
1400–1600   Individual feedback

Select assessment staff

The centre will probably need a director who exercises overall control, acts as an assessor and chairs the assessors' conference; an organizer who briefs individuals and teams on the exercises, administers the tests and advises the assessment panel; an administrative assistant; and the assessors. Assessors should be line managers, preferably two levels above the participants. Their task is to rate behaviour from each exercise against the organization's *requirements* and reach consensus before drawing overall conclusions and recommendations in line with the objectives of the centre. Typically, a ratio of 1:2, assessors to candidates, is found most effective.

Train assessors

It is vital to train assessors thoroughly. Training often starts with their participation in a centre. They are then trained in observation and assessment techniques. It is essential that they know the behaviour dimensions that are being measured and how behaviour is revealed by each of the assessment instruments. It is unlikely that a training period of fewer than three days as well as experiencing a centre suffices to attain the minimum level of skill required. And more time may be desirable to reach a full level of competence. Training as assessors and taking part in assessment centres are good methods of developing senior managers in the important skill of analysing and understanding behaviour and taking appropriate action.

Feedback and follow-up

The results should be fed back to participants as soon as possible after the centre has finished. The aim should be to concentrate on development needs rather than emphasize weaknesses. If a candidate has not been assessed as eligible for promotion, this should be explained as gently as possible. Although candidates so assessed will naturally be disappointed, they should not feel that they are complete failures and should be encouraged, if appropriate, to believe that they still have opportunities for development at that level. They should also be counselled on what they need to do to develop themselves.

The career of those who have attended an assessment centre should be followed up and their performance should be related to the results of the centre. As necessary, improvements can then be made to the factor definitions, instruments and the training of assessors.

Introducing an assessment centre

The work described above takes time. It is often desirable to seek outside help from consultants on the design of the centre and the training of assessors. It is essential to pilot-test the centre with potential assessors before using it for real candidates.

Advantages and disadvantages

A well-conducted assessment centre can achieve a better forecast of future performance and progress than judgements made by line managers in the normal, unskilled way. Research quoted by Ungerson[3] indicated that face-validity is high — people are generally[3] impressed by the proceedings. So is reliability. Moses and Byham[4] quote a number of studies, including one by Huck, who estimated that the probability of selecting an above-average performer by choosing at random is 15 per cent, that appraisal data and interviews might raise this to 35 per cent, but that if this management information and assessment centre data are integrated, the probability could be raised to 76 per cent.

The problem with assessment centres is their cost. They are not worth doing if they are not done well, and this means that amateur efforts or the use of packaged systems without proper training are to be avoided. Assessment centres are time-consuming. Fairly senior managers have to be trained and to be away from their desks for several days. It may be difficult to get the right people unless top managers are convinced that this is essential.

But the use of assessment centres is growing — Mahcy[5] found in a 1989 survey that in the UK over a third of companies employing more than 1000 people had used an assessment centre in the past year, and the use of centres in the US is widespread. While it is unlikely that assessment centres would be cost-effective in smaller organizations, they have a lot to offer to any firm which is concerned about the development of its staff and is promoting people from within.

References

1. Dulewicz, V 'Assessment centres as the route to competence', *Personnel Management*, November 1989.
2. Woodruffe, C *Assessment Centres*. Institute of Personnel Management, London, 1990.
3. Ungerson, B 'Assessment centres: a review of research findings', *Personnel Review*, Summer 1974.
4. Moses, J L and Byham, W C *Applying the Assessment Centre Method*. Pergamon Press, Oxford, 1977.
5. Mahey, B 'The majority of large companies use occupational tests', *Guidance and Assessment Review*, June 1989.

Part V
Human Resource Development

The process of human resource development starts from the strategic plans of the enterprise which define where the business is going and, broadly, the resources required to get there. These strategies are translated by human resource planning into more specific definitions of how many and what sort of people will be needed in the future. Simultaneously, the business plan defines what levels of performance are required to achieve objectives.

Human resource development starts, therefore, with performance management, as discussed in Chapter 19. The prime aim of this process is to improve individual and therefore organizational performance — now and in the future. To achieve this aim, performance management systems assess how effectively people are working in their present jobs and what they need to do and know to perform even better. This information provides the basis for the three main areas of human resource development, which are discussed in the next three chapters:

1. training — the systematic development of the knowledge, skills and attitudes required to carry out a task or a job;
2. management development — improving the performance of managers and giving them opportunities for growth and development;
3. career management — ensuring that the organization has the people it needs to provide for growth and management succession, and that individual managers are given the guidance and help they require to realize their potential and develop their abilities.

19

Performance Management

Definition

Performance management is a means of getting better results from the organization, teams and individuals by understanding and managing performance within an agreed framework of planned goals, objectives and standards. Performance management therefore consists of a systematic approach to the management of people, using performance, goals, measurement, feedback and recognition as a means of motivating them to realize their maximum potential. It embraces all formal or informal methods adopted by an organization and its managers to increase commitment and individual and corporate effectiveness. It is a broader concept than performance appraisal or performance-related pay. These can indeed be important elements in a performance management system (PMS). But they are part of an integrated approach which consists of an interlocking series of processes, attitudes and behaviours which together produce a coherent strategy for adding value and improving results.

Perhaps the most important thing to remember about performance management is that it is a continuous process shared between managers and the people for whom they are responsible. It is concerned both with improving results and with the quality of working relationships. Good performance management means that people know what their priorities are, what they should be doing currently, what they should be aiming for and how well this contributes to both team and company performance. It grows from open, positive and constructive discussion between managers, individuals and teams to produce agreement on how to focus on doing the job better.

How performance management works

How performance management works is illustrated in Figure 19.1.

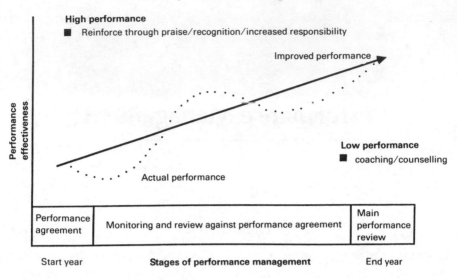

Figure 19.1 How performance management works

The process of performance management starts with a performance agreement which sets out objectives and development needs. During the ensuing period, usually a year, performance is continually monitored and assessed. High performance is reinforced with praise, recognition and the opportunity to take on more responsible work. Low performance is dealt with by coaching and counselling, which takes place at the time. It is not deferred until the formal review at the end of the year when it will have lost its immediacy and where the formality of the proceedings militates against a constructive discussion.

Both the individual and the manager prepare for the formal review. The former carries out a self-assessment of performance in achieving objectives and considers the points he or she would like to make about work and career prospects. The latter also considers the results obtained by the individual and decides how he or she wants to plan the meeting. The performance review meeting is, to a degree, a stocktaking exercise but its emphasis is on looking forward to next year and formulating a performance agreement rather than raking over past events.

It will be noted that performance-related pay (PRP) is not mentioned as part of this process. This is because performance management is essentially an objectives and development needs setting and review system. PRP, as described in Chapter 27, is an optional extra, which, in the right circumstances and for the right people, can reinforce the messages provided by the sequence of activities illustrated in Figure 19.1. Many organizations, however, have introduced performance management successfully without any element of PRP; others have found that PRP has not delivered the expected results when it has been grafted without sufficient thought to a performance management scheme.

The basis of performance management

A performance management system includes all the processes described above. It incorporates many of the features of results-orientated performance appraisal schemes which review performance against targets or standards. A performance management system, however, does not usually incorporate merit rating, which attaches numerical values or grades to judgements about the degree to which an individual possesses a characteristic such as initiative or judgement. The approach to performance management is based on the philosophy of management by objectives.

Management by objectives philosophy

Management by objectives (M by O), as an approach to performance appraisal, emphasizes the need to assess performance by reference to agreed outputs as defined by targets, tasks to be accomplished or standards of performance. It rejects the idea that managers should appraise the personality characteristics of their subordinates on the grounds that such judgements can not be substantiated, create tension between the appraiser and the appraised and imply, in McGregor's[1] words, that managers are 'playing god', a role for which they are singularly ill-equipped. He suggested that the emphasis should be shifted from appraisal to analysis. The philosophy of management by objectives was formulated originally by Drucker in the 1950s and then developed by McGregor is behavioural science terms.

Another problem with management by objectives, as introduced in the 1960s and '70s, was that it stressed the need to measure performance against quantifiable targets. This in itself is a fine principle but it was carried to excess. Frantic efforts were made to quantify the unquantifiable — most of the outputs of many service and support jobs can be assessed only in qualitative terms, as is usually the case with a number of key areas of responsibility in jobs, such as production and sales, which are largely concerned with measurable outputs.

The emphasis on quantification meant that broader but important qualitative objectives, such as developing staff, encouraging teamwork, and innovation, were neglected. Managers who were given profit, sales or output objectives tended to indulge in 'short-termism', ie going for quick results without thinking about the future. Managers also often felt they were unfairly treated when their performance was measured mechanistically and no account was taken of circumstances beyond their control.

Many of these manifestations of management by objectives were inconsistent with its basic philosophy as expressed by Drucker and McGregor. But their impact meant that 'M by O' fell into disrepute in the 1980s and performance management emerged like a phoenix from the ashes.

Performance management philosophy

Performance management philosophy emphasizes the agreement of objectives and development needs and the importance of self-assessment and self-development. It is positive and forward-looking and it regards development as a joint responsibility of the individual and the manager.

One shift of emphasis from management by objectives is the belief that in reviewing performance it is necessary not only to measure results but also to analyse the behaviour that contributed to those results. And this analysis refers to the behaviour of the individual *and* that of the manager in the latter's role of providing direction, guidance and support. Behavioural analysis in performance management, however, is not concerned with personality traits. Instead, it focuses on the evidence provided by the analysis of what individuals and their managers did or did not do as an explanation of the results achieved. This information is used positively to establish what needs to be done in the future. No time is wasted on recriminations about the past.

Another difference is that performance management provides more opportunities for individuals to discuss their work problems and aspirations with their managers in an atmosphere from which the daunting process of concentrating on quantifiable results has been removed.

Finally, an important feature of performance management is the importance attached to its being a continuous process — a natural aspect of management — rather than the potentially stressful annual event when people may be confronted with evidence that they have failed in some way to come up to standard, based on happenings long since forgotton or not dealt with at the time.

Developing a performance management system

When developing a performance management system, one must:

- define its purpose;
- determine the factors to be covered by the system in terms of what is to be assessed, eg the achievement of objectives, upholding core values, meeting development needs or potential;
- agree policies on 'transparency' (the degree to which employees are informed of the results of their appraisals) and on the link between performance reviews and rewards;
- decide on policies concerning performance-related pay and overall rating.

Purpose

The extent to which the system has to cater for some or all of the following requirements has to be made clear from the outset:

- Review of performance for training and development purposes — this is perhaps the most important reason for conducting reviews.
- Potential assessment for career development and management succession planning purposes — this tends to be given less prominence in current schemes and is often omitted completely because of the difficulties managers have in making realistic forecasts.
- Rating to determine eligibility for performance-related pay.

Factors to be covered by the system

The main factors that can be assessed in a performance management system are the following:

1. *The achievement of objectives* — performance management systems assess performance by reference to agreed objectives and include a performance agreement which spells out future objectives. Objectives may be expressed in terms of targets, standards of performance or tasks to be accomplished within a period of time and to an agreed specification.
2. *Observing core values* — performance management systems increasingly recognize that performance is not just achieving objectives. It is also behaving in a way which makes the core values of the organization a reality, not just a string of pious platitudes. A major multinational company, for example, assesses managers on the extent to which they observe core values under the headings of:

    (a) contribution in the job beyond normal expectations;

(b)   contribution to the work of others (this organization had problems with teamwork!);

(c)   contribution to change (the organization was trying to create a more flexible culture).

3.   *Personal qualities* — some performance appraisal schemes still ask managers to assess the personal qualities of staff under such headings as drive, judgement and initiative. Such approaches, however, mean that individuals are in danger of becoming passive objects, receiving judgements from on high. A joint review of how well individuals have achieved objectives will be rooted in the reality of their performance. It is concrete, not abstract, and it enables managers and individuals to take a positive look together at how performance can become even better in the future and how any problems in achieving objectives can be resolved. Individuals become active agents in improving their results and managers adopt their proper enabling role.

4.   *Potential* — performance management systems generally concentrate on the identification of development needs rather than attempting to rate potential. Unless managers have a very clear understanding of the competences required at higher levels of responsibility, such ratings are likely to be guesswork, and such understanding is rare. In any case, although it can be said that people generally have to perform well in the present to succeed in the future, good performance at one level does not guarantee success at the next or succeeding levels; hence the Peter Principle.

The measurement of potential is increasingly taking place at assessment centres (see Chapter 18) where the assessment criteria are related to well-researched and clearly defined core competences which are indicators of successful performance at higher levels in the organization. Such centres, incidentally, can and are used to identify development and training needs.

Policy on openness

There is no point in a performance management system in which the review process is not shared between the reviewer and the person being reviewed. The review's most important purpose is to be developmental — to assist in the improvement of performance. Unless employees are fully involved through self-assessment in the prereview stage and in the joint analysis of achievements and development needs during the actual review, they will not 'own' any of the performance improvement steps which should form part of the performance agreement or contract.

Policy on performance-related pay

The other major policy issue concerns the link between the performance review and performance-related pay. Some people object to any link because they say that a preoccupation with the existence and size of an award during the review will seriously contaminate the developmental purposes of the appraisal. These opponents of such a link are usually doubtful about the value of relating a reward to what they believe to be a largely subjective performance rating. Their views are also coloured by the fact that they have fundamental doubts about the motivational value of extrinsic rewards.

Those who support performance-related pay say, logically enough, that you must have a performance rating to determine the reward, and if that is not going to be produced at the performance review, where is it going to come from? Given a belief in PRP, this argument is unanswerable. One way to reconcile these opposed views is to conduct the assessment at a different time than the pay review. This enables those involved to concentrate on its developmental aspects. When the pay review is carried out, a 'read across' can take place between the assessment to provide the basis for the performance-related pay decision. It may be necessary to update the ratings in these circumstances, depending on the length of time between the reviews and the existence of any new factors.

Policy on overall rating

Performance assessment systems have traditionally included a section in the form for an overall rating; for example:

A   Outstanding performance in all respects.

B   Superior performance, significantly above normal job requirements.

C   Good, all-round performance which meets the normal requirements of the job.

D   Performance not fully up to requirements. Clear weaknesses requiring improvement have been identified.

E   Unacceptable; performance of many aspects of the job is well below an acceptable standard.

This rating is supposed to provide an overall assessment which sums up the job holder's performance. If there is a performance-related pay scheme, the rating may determine the amount of the merit payment. The problem with such ratings is that they force managers to make somewhat arbitrary and often indefensible judgements, and their use may prejudice the constructive discussion which lies at the heart of a performance management system. This is particularly true if the rating scale definitions include entirely negative words such as 'unacceptable'. If someone's performance is totally unacceptable, this fact should have been identified during the continuous process of monitoring results and actions taken at the time. This is not something that can wait for a number of months until the next formal review. To avoid this problem, you might well use a rating scale which provides positive reinforcement at every level, as in the following scale:

Very effective   Exceeds all objectives and requirements. Achievements are notable and outstanding and are far beyond the normal expectations of the job.

Effective   Achieves required objectives and standards of performance and meets the normal expectations of the job.

Developing   A contribution which is stronger in some aspects of the job than others; where most objectives are met but where performance improvements should still take place.

Basic   A contribution which on the whole meets the basic standards required, although a number of objectives are not met and there is clearly room for improvement in several definable areas.

This scale may remove the negative aspects of the conventional scale, and the fact that there are only four levels prevents raters from following a natural tendency to settle for the middle grade. But the problem remains that with this, as with all other rating scales, it is very difficult, if not impossible, to ensure that a consistent approach is adopted by raters. It is almost inevitable that some people are more generous than others — the 'swan effect', while others will be harder on their staff — the 'geese' effect. Ratings can, of course, be monitored and challenged if their distribution is significantly out of line and computer-based systems have been introduced for this purpose in some organizations. But many managers want to do the best for their staff, either because they genuinely believe that the staff are better or because they as managers are trying to curry favour. It can be very difficult in these circumstances to challenge them. The only solution may be to tackle the problem on a group basis by running workshops every year to reinforce the values of the scheme and the basis upon which ratings should be given. Ultimately, however, such judgements will always be subjective, and this is an argument which can be used against relating pay to performance assessed in this way.

Designing the performance management system

The performance management system operates as a continuous cycle, as illustrated in Figure 19.2, and this should be reflected in the operation of each of its main components, as described below:

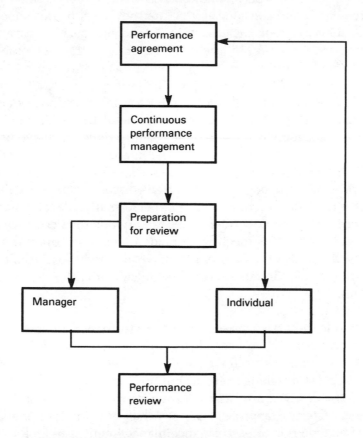

Figure 19.2 The performance management cycle

- *The performance agreement.* This sets out the key objectives for next year and the main development needs (areas where existing skills can be enhanced or performance improved). This agreement is concluded between the manager and the individual during the performance review meeting. It provides a point of reference when monitoring performance during the year. The emphasis in the performance agreement is on self-direction and self-control. Guidelines on agreeing objectives are given in Appendix M.

- *Continuous performance management.* Both the manager and the individual continually monitor performance in relation to the performance agreement and plan. As necessary, objectives are added or revised. New development needs may emerge and are also added to the plan.

- *Preparation for the review.* At the end of the assessment period immediately prior to the performance review, individuals assess their own performance and consider any points they wish to raise about their work, development or prospects. Managers also prepare for the review by referring to the agreement and the outcome of the continuous performance management process throughout the year.

- *The performance review meeting.* This is the meeting, usually annual, in which managers and individuals refer to their preparatory notes, the performance agreement and the outcome of the continuous performance management process. They jointly review achievements and progress, comments and ratings are made as required and a new performance agreement is concluded. Most importantly, these meetings provide the opportunity for a frank discussion between managers and the individuals about the latter's performance, development needs and prospects and how the former can provide the necessary support and guidance. The meeting should discuss not only the results achieved but also the factors that have affected those results. These factors may be, for various reasons, outside or within the individual's control.

There should be no surprises at the performance review meeting if performance issues have been dealt with as they should have been — during the continuous performance management process. In one sense the review is a stocktaking exercise, but this is no more than an analysis of where those involved are now, and where they have come from. This static and historical approach is not what performance management means. The true role of performance management is to look forward to what needs to be done to achieve the overall purpose of the job; to meet new challenges; to make even better use of the knowledge, skills and abilities of personnel; and to help them to develop their competences and improve their performance. This process also helps managers to improve their ability to lead, guide and develop their staff, as individuals or as a team.

It should be emphasized that although a system of this nature provides the basis for constructive discussions, the extent to which such discussions are successful depends very much on the skill and willingness of the manager to conduct the meeting properly and on the cooperation of staff. Performance assessment can be a nerve-racking occasion for both parties and, rather than conduct reviews badly, it is better not to hold them at all. A poorly run meeting can be an effective demotivating device. One of the more difficult skills managers need is counselling their staff and this skill is considered later in this chapter (pages 409–410).

The solution to the problem of performance assessment is, of course, not to give up but to ensure that all concerned are very thoroughly briefed and trained on the purpose of the system and the part they should play in it. It should be impressed on managers, for example, that their own performance will be assessed against agreed standards for operating the performance management system and developing their staff.

Performance management forms

A performance management system should not be allowed to get bogged down in paperwork or forms. There is no reason why the key points in a performance agreement, the preparatory notes and the conclusions reached at the end of the performance review meeting should not be recorded on the back of a proverbial envelope (or on blank sheets of paper), as long as everything has been covered and noted for future use and action.

In practice, it is helpful for all concerned to have a framework for recording agreements, notes, comments and action points. This framework can be provided by a set of forms such as those illustrated in Appendix N. These are not intended to be models of their kind — every organization needs to design its own performance management system to fit its culture and particular requirements. But they do illustrate what sort of headings can be included. This set of forms consists of:

- a manager's preparation form;
- an individual employee's preparation form;
- a performance review form which incorporates a performance agreement.

No rating scales are included.

In using forms of this kind it is essential to avoid too bureaucratic an approach. Although all concerned should be given guidance on how to complete them, they should be told that the important thing to do is to record the key points emerging from the various performance management processes. They should be concerned about the substance of what has been agreed, not how they express themselves in the form.

Introducing the performance management system

To make any impact at all, top management must put its whole weight behind the performance management system. The chief executive must demonstrate his or her total commitment to it and must make plain that all managers must be equally committed.

'Packaging' is important! Simple, straightforward, well-designed forms are best. At all costs, avoid forms which smack of officialdom and bureaucracy. People respond best to well-printed forms on good-quality paper. It is well worth issuing the description of the scheme and the notes for guidance in an elegantly designed and well-produced folder which in itself demonstrates the importance attached to performance management.

The performance management system should be introduced with a reminder of the purposes of the scheme and its benefits. The roles of reviewers and those being reviewed should be spelled out in a way which emphasizes their joint responsibility for the success of the system and explains how they should conduct the preparatory work, the meetings and the continuous process of appraisal. The information about the scheme should include:

- a statement of its objectives;
- guidance to managers on objective setting, how to conduct reviews and how to counsel and coach the individual members of their team;
- guidance to individuals on the part they play in completing the prereview form, agreeing objectives and development needs and preparing and implementing the performance and development plan;
- brief descriptions of how the documents are to be filled in and examples of well-completed forms;
- a statement emphasizing that the system should be regarded as a fundamental aspect of management throughout the organization.

Launching the system

The system should be launched by the chief executive, who should personally brief the management team. In smaller organizations this briefing should be extended to all employees. In larger concerns, the brief should be cascaded down the organization through a team briefing approach. A video can be used to good effect. Experience suggests that training in the concepts and practice of performance management should precede detailed briefing on the procedure to be used. This briefing and training process will be greatly enhanced if it is based on good material. This is why it is so important to make the procedures and documentation user-friendly and to present the material well.

Training

The effectiveness of performance management systems depends ultimately on the quality of the reviews carried out by managers and the attitudes of the staff to the system. An essential part of the implementation of a system is therefore a training programme for all managers. Ideally, this should take the form of a workshop, and both managers and their staff should be involved. The workshop should last at least one day (preferably two) and should include sessions concerned with:

- describing the system and the role of managers and their staff;
- analysing the skills required to set and review objectives, review and rate performance, identify development needs, prepare performance agreements and plans and provide guidance to individuals by means of counselling and coaching;
- practising the skills — this should comprise 75 per cent of the programme.

Use should be made of case-study material drawn from the organization, referring to typical performance problems; role-plays, and video. The aim would be to enable both managers and their staff to try out each other's roles in a safe environment where important lessons can be learned.

Counselling

Counselling is a vital part of performance management programmes if they are to achieve their prime purpose of helping people to improve and develop. But it is difficult to do well and many managers are reluctant to do it at all. In one unpublished study conducted by the writer, it was found that people were more dissatisfied after their counselling session than before. Even where a results-orientated approach is adopted, a clumsy interviewer can allow the discussion to degenerate into pointless arguments about where blame should be attached for something that has gone wrong.

There are three approaches to performance counselling:

1. *The tell and sell method*, in which the manager seeks first to let employees know how they are doing, then to gain their acceptance of the evaluation, and finally to get them to follow the plan outlined for improvement. The problem with this method is that considerable and unusual skill is required to get people to accept criticisms and to change in the required manner. There are occasions when people have to be told, but it may not always be possible to provide the motivation required for change, unless resort is made to crude threats or inducements.

2. *The tell and listen method*, in which the evaluation is communicated to the employee who is then allowed to respond to it. Instead of dominating the discussion, the interviewer sits back and becomes a non-directive counsellor during the second part of the interview. Employees are encouraged to think things out for themselves and to decide on what needs to be done, and the assumption is that they are more likely to change in these circumstances than if they had been told what to do. A further advantage of this approach is that the interviewer profits additionally from the interview by receiving feedback from the employee on how the job may be improved with regard to supervision, work methods and job assignments. But the method requires considerable skill on the part of the interviewer in listening, reflecting feelings and summarizing opinions.

3. *The problem-solving approach*, in which the interviewer abandons the role of judge and becomes a helper. The appraisal is not communicated to the employee. Instead a discussion takes place of the work problems of employees, who are encouraged to think through their own solutions to them, including the changes they have to make to their behaviour to achieve improvement. This approach motivates original thinking because it stimulates curiosity. It also provides the intrinsic motivation that can be derived from work itself and the process of tackling work problems. Job satisfaction can be improved by reorganizing or enlarging the job, by changing employees' perceptions of their role, and by increasing the manager's ability to provide guidance and help in the form it is needed. Again, this approach needs skill, but it is the most fruitful method and one which can clearly be linked to results-orientated review techniques.

The shift to performance management

It has become increasingly recognized in recent years that the performance management approach (whether or not it is called performance management) is likely to be the most effective one for use in any organization which attaches importance to development, especially self-development, and the need continually to get everyone concerned involved in seeking ways of improving performance. It appeals to organizations which believe in decentralization, recognize the need for flexibility and want to avoid mechanistic or bureaucratic systems. The philosophy of performance management, with its links to management by objectives and results-orientated appraisal, is also attractive to performance-orientated organizations which appreciate the extra dimension provided by the whole concept of performance management.

But there are other methods of performance appraisal which some organizations adopt because they meet their special needs. These are described below.

Other methods of performance appraisal

The main other types of performance appraisal are the following:

- overall assessment;
- guideline assessment;
- grading;
- merit rating.

Overall assessment

This approach simply asks managers to write down in narrative form their comments about the employee. They may be given a checklist of personality characteristics to consider, such as reliability, enthusiasm, appearance, and acceptability and, with a slight bow to the McGregor philosophy, they may be asked to comment on results achieved against targets.

This is the simplest approach and at least ensures that managers have to collect their thoughts and put them down on paper. But different people will consider different aspects of performance and there will be no consensus in the criteria selected for assessment. The value of the exercise also depends on the ability of managers to express themselves in writing. And managers tend to be evasive. As Rowe reported on the comments made in the six schemes she studied:

> A few suggested careful thought and a conscientious effort to say something meaningful but the vast majority were remarkable for their neutrality. Glib,

generalized, enigmatic statements abounded. Typical of such statements was 'a loyal, conscientious and hard-working employee'. Such a statement may well have been true but it is not very revealing.[2]

Guideline assessment

The guideline assessment approach is an attempt to obtain more specific judgements from assessors, who are asked to comment separately on a number of defined characteristics; for example, industry and application, loyalty and integrity, cooperation, accuracy and reliability, adaptability, knowledge of work and use of initiative. When assessing a characteristic such as industry and application, managers might be asked to 'Consider his application to work and the enthusiasm with which he approaches a task. Does he work quickly and stick to the job or is he slow and inclined to slack if not watched?'

In theory, this method should help managers to be more precise but, in practice, the guidelines are so vague that comments are uninformative, especially if they are about generalized characteristics such as industry and application.

Grading

Grading is a further development of the guideline approach which attempts to provide a framework of reference by defining a number of levels at which the characteristic is displayed and asking managers to select the definition which most closely describes the individual they are assessing. For example, in rating effective output the manager in a typical grading scheme is asked to choose between:

1. Outstanding — outstanding output of high-quality work;
2. Satisfactory — satisfactory level of output and effort;
3. Fair — completes less than the average amount of effective work;
4. Poor — low output and poor worker.

In themselves, definitions of this type are not particularly helpful — they are generalized and fail to establish actual standards against which judgements can be made. Assessments are therefore just as subject to variations and inconsistencies as in the other schemes.

Merit rating

Merit rating is similar to grading except that numerical values are attached to the judgements, so that each characteristic is rated on a scale of, say, 1 to 20. The ratings are then added up to produce a total score.

A variation of this approach is the graphic rating scale, in which the assessor ticks the place on a line running from very high to very low to indicate the employee's standing on each quality. In its most Machiavellian form, this method requires an *éminence grise* in the personnel department to attach values to ratings and adjust them when it is thought that managers are tending to over- or underassess their staff.

These merit rating schemes have rightly been discredited. Their only reason for survival is that they satisfy those people who are not happy unless they can quantify everything, even the patently unquantifiable judgements of personality characteristics. The other problem with this type of scheme, as with all the others, is that it does not ensure that assessors base their judgements on systematic and objective observations of the job behaviour of the people they are asked to describe.

References

1. McGregor, D 'An Uneasy Look at Performance Appraisal', *Harvard Business Review* Vol. 35, No. 3, May–June 1957, pp. 89–94.
2. Rowe, K H 'An Appraisal of Appraisals', *Journal of Management Studies* Vol. 1, No. 1, March 1964, pp. 1–25.

20

Training

The basis of training

Definitions

Training is the systematic modification of behaviour through learning which occurs as a result of education, instruction, development and planned experience. Learning has been defined by Bass and Vaughan[1] as 'a relatively permanent change in behaviour that occurs as a result of practice or experience'. The following is an extended definition of training, together with definitions of education and development, produced by the Manpower Services Commission.[2]

Training

A planned process to modify attitude, knowledge or skill behaviour through learning experience to achieve effective performance in an activity or range of activities. Its purpose, in the work situation, is to develop the abilities of the individual and to satisfy the current and future manpower needs of the organization.

Education

Activities which aim at developing the knowledge, skills, moral values and understanding required in all aspects of life rather than a knowledge and skill relating to only a limited field of activity. The purpose of education is to provide the conditions essential to young people and adults to develop an understanding of the traditions and ideas influencing the society in which they live and to enable them to make a contribution to it. It involves study of their own cultures and of the laws of nature, as well as the acquisition of linguistic and other skills which are basic to learning, personal development, creativity and communication.

Development

The growth or realization of a person's ability, through conscious or unconscious learning. Development programmes usually include elements of planned study and experience, and are frequently supported by a coaching or counselling facility.

Note that these definitions refer to *planned* experience. It is said that experience is the best teacher, but an essential feature of any effective training and development programme is that trainees are provided with the right sequence of experience and are helped to understand and learn from that experience.

Aims

The fundamental aim of training is to help the organization achieve its purpose by adding value to its key resource — the people it employs. Training means investing in people to enable them to perform better and to empower them to make the best use of their natural abilities. The particular objectives of training are to:

- develop the competences of employees and improve their performance;
- help people grow within the organization in order that, as far as possible, its future needs for human resources can be met from within.
- reduce the learning time for employees starting in new jobs on appointment, transfer or promotion, and ensure that they become fully competent as quickly and economically as possible.

Benefits

Effective training can:

- minimize learning costs;
- improve individual, team and corporate performance in terms of output, quality, speed and overall productivity;
- improve operational flexibility by extending the range of skills possessed by employees (multiskilling);

- attract high-quality staff by developing their competences and enhancing their skills, thus enabling them to obtain more job satisfaction, to gain higher rewards and to progress within the organization;
- increase the commitment of staff by encouraging them to identify with the mission and objectives of the organization;
- help to manage change by increasing understanding of the reasons for change and providing people with the knowledge and skills they need to adjust to new situations;
- help to develop a positive culture in the organization, one, for example, which is orientated towards performance improvement;
- provide higher levels of service to customers.

Understanding training

To understand how training should be developed and operated within an organization, we must appreciate:

1. *training philosophy* — the basis upon which training philosophies and policies should be developed;
2. *the process of training* — how systematic training programmes and interventions can be planned, implemented and evaluated;
3. *the process of learning* — how people learn (learning theory) and how that affects the design and operation of training programmes;
4. *identifying training needs* — establishing what type of training is required and ensuring that it is relevant to the requirements of individuals and the organization.
5. *planning training* — deciding how the longer- and shorter-term training needs of the organization and the teams and individuals working in it can be satisfied and selecting and using training techniques;
6. *conducting training* — running training programmes for different categories' of staff;
7. *responsibility for training* — determining who plans and executes training programmes;
8. *evaluating training* — establishing the extent to which training is achieving objectives by satisfying training needs.

The rest of this chapter deals with each of these aspects of training.

Training philosophy

The training philosophy of an organization expresses the degree of importance it attaches to training. Some firms adopt a *laissez-faire* approach, believing that employees will find out what to do for themselves or through, in the old phrase, 'sitting by Nellie'. If this sort of firm suffers a skill shortage, it is remedied by recruiting from firms who do invest in training. It is the existence of a large number of *laissez-faire* firms which explains why, in 1985, private-sector organizations devoted no more than 0.15% of their turnover to in-service training. In the same year, employees in West Germany received two and a half times as much off the job training as their UK counterparts.

Other companies pay lip service to training and indiscriminately allocate money to it in the good times. But in the bad times these firms are the first to cut their training budgets.

Organizations with a positive training philosophy understand that they live in a world of skills shortages, especially when demographic forces restrict the flow of qualified young people into the labour market. In hard commercial terms, these firms persuade themselves that training is an investment that will pay off. They understand that it may be difficult to calculate the return on that investment but they believe that the tangible and intangible benefits of training, as described earlier in this chapter, will more than justify the cost.

But it is not enough to believe in training as an act of faith. This belief must be supported by a positive and realistic philosophy of how training contributes to organizational success. This philosophy will cover the following headings, as discussed below:

- a strategic approach to training;
- integrated;
- relevant;
- problem-based;
- action-orientated;
- performance-related;
- continual.

A strategic approach to training

Training strategy takes a long-term view of what skills, knowledge and levels of competence employees of the company need. Training philosophy emphasizes that training and development should be an integral part of the management process. A performance management system (see Chapter 19) requires managers to review regularly, with their teams and the individuals reporting to them, performance in relation to agreed objectives, the factors that have affected performance and the development and training needs that emerge from this analysis. The satisfaction of these needs is a joint process between managers, teams and individuals by means of coaching, counselling and relevant training courses.

Relevant

While some organizations do not go in for training at all, others go in for 'training for training's sake'. The latter approach is as bad as, if not worse than, the former. Training must be relevant in that it satisfies identified and appropriate training needs.

Problem-based

Training should be problem-based in the sense that it should be planned to fill the gaps between what people can do and what they need to do, now and in the future. The problem may be a negative one in the form of a weakness that needs to be remedied. Or it may be positive because it refers to how the need to develop new skills or enhance knowledge to meet future requirements will be satisfied.

Action-orientated

Training philosophy should stress that training exists to make things happen, to get people into action. The objectives of any training event or programme should be defined in terms of 'deliverables' — this is what people will be able to do after training, and this is what they will achieve.

Performance-related training

A performance-related training philosophy involves relating training specifically to performance requirements — for example, those following the introduction of a new product or system. Murphy[3] has explained how it was done at Abbey National:

> Every time we designed or developed a new product we would involve a trainer in the development team. So, as the product was developed, the training was developed. Before the product was actually launched there was a training package designed for the branches so that each branch could start to train its staff in all aspects of the product before it was launched.
>
> We then extended this into the systems area, so that every time we developed a new computer system, a new investment system or a new mortgage system we involved the trainer in the systems development. The

benefits of this were twofold; one was that the trainers learned a lot more about the systems we were launching and, two, the systems designers learned a lot about how these systems had to be put over to the users, and more still about user-friendliness, etc. It pulled trainers into the fabric of the business and also pulled specialists into the fabric of the presentation of the new product, system or procedure.

W H Smith developed its performance-related training policy for managers following a systematic review of management training. Managers said they enjoyed attending courses and the level of nominations was rising. However, there was no proof that they were gaining any practical benefit from the courses or that W H Smith's investment of nearly £1m in 1985 was justified.

W H Smith was also aware that it was ignoring some important techniques which could make management training more effective in the workplace. As a result, it started to look for an approach to management training which would 'measurably improve job performance'. This meant making sure that managers understood and could implement the systems and procedures to ensure consistency throughout a geographically dispersed organization. It also meant leaving aside the universal theories of management in favour of much closer attention to the different detailed routines which apply in the various businesses within the W H Smith group.

In W H Smith's search for this new approach, it found many of the components it was seeking in such areas as skills training, student-centred learning and assessment centre methodology. In the latter case, the extensive use of assessment centres for all levels of management established that the analysis of behaviour during the programme was a valuable way of identifying development needs as well as establishing promotability.

W H Smith did not, however, find these components assembled together coherently and applied to management training. As a result, the company designed the approach it now calls 'performance-related training' (PRT). The purpose of PRT is to identify individual training needs and provide relevant and effective training to meet them.

An important part of the PRT process is the profiling of key skills. The newly appointed manager undertakes exercises in the key skills of the job to which he or she has been promoted. His or her performance is compared with the standard expected of an experienced manager in the same position. A below-standard performance indicates a training need which is met by the most suitable of a variety of different responses. These include residential courses, guided study, assignments or individual coaching. Following training, managers undertake a further exercise to confirm that their performance is now of the required standard.

W H Smith believes that performance-related training has enabled it to confirm the practical benefits of management training in measurable terms. It anchors management training firmly to the needs of the current job and ensures that managers have the competences and skills to carry out all the functions of the jobs for which they are being paid.

Continuing development

A philosophy of continuing development states that training is not just something that is provided for people by the organization at the start of their employment or at occasional points in their career. It should instead be regarded as a continuous process, with less emphasis on formal instruction and an increased requirement for trainees to be responsible for their own learning. Hence the development of such approaches as 'do-it-yourself training', action learning and computer-based training (these are all described in Appendix P).

The Institute of Personnel Management's 1987 code of practice on continuous development states:

If learning activity in an organization is to be fully beneficial both to the organization and its employees, the following conditions must be met:

- the organization must have some form of strategic business plan. It is desirable that the implications of the strategic plan, in terms of the skills and knowledge of the employees who will achieve it, should be spelled out;
- managers must be ready and willing (and able) to define and meet needs as they appear, all learning needs cannot be anticipated; organizations must foster a philosophy of continuous development;
- as far as practicable, learning and work must be integrated. This means that encouragement must be given to all employees to learn from the problems, challenges and successes inherent in their day-to-day activities;
- the impetus for continuous development must come from the chief executive and other members of the top management team (the board of directors, for example). The top management team must regularly and formally review the way the competence of its management and workforce is being developed. It is important too that one senior executive is charged with responsibility for ensuring that continuous development activity is being effectively undertaken;
- investment in continuous development must be regarded by the top

management team as being as important as investment in research, new product development or capital equipment. It is not a luxury which can be afforded only in the 'good times'. Indeed, the more severe the problems an organization faces the greater the need for learning on the part of its employees and the more pressing the need for investment in learning;

Money spent within the organization on research and development into human resource development itself is money well spent. An evaluation of current human resource development procedures can confirm the effectiveness of current practice or point the way towards necessary change. Such research is as valuable as technical research.

Training policies

Training policies are expressions of the training philosophy of the organization. They provide guidelines on the amount of training that should be given (eg everyone in managerial, professional, technical or supervisory positions should undergo at least five days' formal training every year); the proportion of turnover that should be allocated to training (eg 1 to 2 per cent, although the amount will vary according to the special needs of the business); the scope and aims of training schemes; and the responsibility for training. An example of a training policy statement is given in Appendix A.

The process of training

Systematic training

The concept of systematic training was originated by the Industrial Training Boards in the late 1960s. Systematic training is training which is specifically designed to meet defined needs. It is planned and provided by people who know how to train and the impact of training is carefully evaluated.

Systematic training is based on a simple four-stage model expressed as follows:

- define training needs;
- decide what sort of training is required to satisfy these needs;
- use experienced and trained trainers to plan and implement training;
- follow up and evaluate training to ensure that it is effective.

The model provides a good basis for planning training programmes, but it is oversimplified — training is a more complex process than this. Another drawback to the concept of systematic training is that insufficient emphasis is placed on the responsibilities of managers and individuals for training. And under the influence of the training boards, a 'training industry' developed in the 1970s which imposed or tried to impose overelaborate and bureaucratic routines on industry and commerce, an 'industry', which, understandably, was largely rejected. But the essential validity of the concept of systematic training was not destroyed by the fact that it was badly implemented. What needed to be done was to develop a more realistic approach, which is described below as 'planned training'.

Planned training

Planned training, as defined by Kenney and Reid[4] is 'a deliberate intervention aimed at achieving the learning necessary for improved job performance'. The process of planned training, as shown in Figure 20.1, consists of the following steps:

1. *Identify and define training needs* — this involves analysing corporate, team, occupational and individual needs to acquire new skills or knowledge or to improve existing competences (competence is defined as the ability and willingness to perform a task). The analysis covers problems to be solved as well as future demands. Decisions are made at this stage on the extent to which training is the best and most cost-effective way to solve the problem.
2. *Define the learning required* — it is necessary to specify as clearly as possible what skills and knowledge have to be learnt and what attitudes need to be developed.
3. *Define the objectives of training* — learning objectives are set which define not only what has to be learnt but also what trainees must be able to do after their training programme.
4. *Plan training programmes* — these must be developed to meet the needs and objectives by using the right combination of training techniques and locations.
5. *Decide who provides the training* — the extent to which training is provided from within or outside the organization will be decided. At the same time, the devision of responsibility between the training department, managers or supervisors and individuals has to be determined. (In practice, these decisions will be made concurrently with stage 4 when the training programmes are planned.)
6. *Implement the training* — ensure that the most appropriate methods are

used to enable trainees to acquire the skills, knowledge and attitudes they need.

7. *Evaluate training* — the effectiveness of training is monitored during programmes and, subsequently, the impact of training is assessed to determine the extent to which learning objectives have been achieved.

8. *Amend and extend training as necessary* — decide, on the basis of evaluation, the extent to which the planned training programme needs to be improved and how any residual learning requirements should be satisfied.

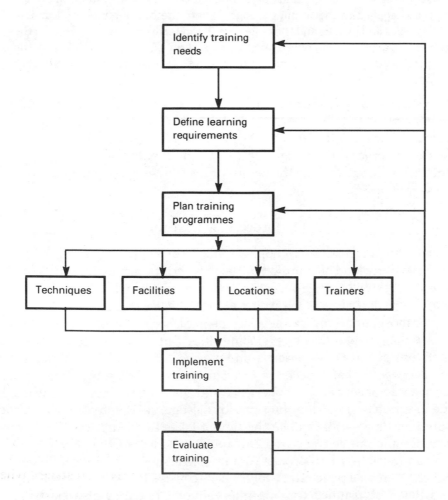

Figure 20.1 The process of planned training

The systems approach to planned training

The training process just described will work effectively only if it is fully integrated with the systems of relationships, structures, interdependence and work in the organization (cf the description of systems theory in Chapter 10). A systems approach to training has been defined by the Manpower Services Commission[2] as the process of:

Identifying inputs, outputs, components and sub-systems, and then seeking to identify the contribution that training can make to improving the operation by enhancing the contribution of the human components (people) as opposed to machinery and operational procedures. The systems approach is next applied to the training design, where the components are learning strategies and people, and the objectives are in terms of learning. Finally, the systems approach is applied to the interaction between training and the operation to produce a feedback which can be used to improve subsequent training.

A system approach requires those concerned with the preparation of training plans to take account of all the factors and variables that might affect learning. In other words, the programme of training for a job in one part of the organization might be affected by events elsewhere, within or outside the company, and the design of the course must take into account these interactions.

The process of learning

As Kenney and Reid[4] say: 'People cannot be brought into an organization to achieve any kind of common purpose without learning taking place. As a result they will change their behaviour in various ways.' The organization can be described as a learning environment.

The most important way in which people learn is through experience in undertaking new tasks or developing skills. But they need to be provided with the right sort of experience, and they need help and guidance to make the best use of that experience. A training course could be regarded as a formal way of condensing experience and ensuring that it is channelled in the direction of acquiring the right knowledge, skills and attitudes in the optimum time — this will be the time it takes to ensure that learning is retained and can be translated into appropriate action.

Learning is a natural process, but it is necessary to create conditions in which it can take place effectively. These consist, in the words of Kenney and Reid,[4] of 'planned training interventions' but they also exist when individuals are helped to make the best use of their own experience and to find out things for themselves. Training interventions and helping people to help themselves work best if they are conducted on the basis of an understanding of learning theory.

Basic learning theories

The four main learning theories are:

1. *Reinforcement,* which, in its positive sense, involves commending trainees when they have accomplished a task successfully, thus motivating them to extend their learning. Positive feedback and knowledge of results is an important way of ensuring that learning takes place. The concept of reinforcement has been strongly influenced by Skinner's[5] conditioning and social engineering theories and, although they are sometimes criticized as being simplistic, they continue to have a considerable effect on the design of training programmes.

2. *Cybernetic and information theories,* which, in essence, suggest that feedback can control people's performance in the same way that a thermostat controls a heating system. Trainees react to cues or stimuli which, if they are established by means of skills analysis, can be used as the basis for training programmes. If a task can be divided into a number of small parts, each with its own cue or stimulus, the learning of each part can be accelerated by ensuring that trainees concentrate on one easily assimilated piece of learning at a time.

3. *Cognitive theories* describe the way in which people learn to recognize and define problems and experiment to provide solutions. If, according to this theory, people can discover things for themselves they are more likely to retain the skill or knowledge and use it when required to. Cognitive theory is the basis for discovery or 'do-it-yourself' learning procedures and it provides the rationale for workshop, participative, and case study training, which help people to 'own' the solution as one they have worked out for themselves rather than something they have been forced to accept by an instructor.

4. *Experiential learning,* which was described by Kolb, Rubin and McIntyre[6] as a four-stage cycle:

   (a) the actual experience;
   (b) observations and reflections on that experience;
   (c) the formation of abstract concepts and generalizations which explain the experience and determine how it will be applied;
   (d) the testing of the implications of the concepts in new situations

and a return to the actual experience at the beginning of the cycle.

Every person has his or her own learning style and one of the most important arts that trainers have to develop is to adjust their approaches to the learning styles of the trainees. Trainers have also to help trainees to understand how best they can interpret and benefit from their experience.

Conditions required for effective learning

Learning theory suggests that there are ten main conditions required for learning to be effective:

1. *Individuals must be motivated to learn.* They should be aware that their present level of knowledge or skill, or their existing attitude or behaviour, needs to be improved if they are to perform their work to their own and to others' satisfaction. They must, therefore, have a clear picture of the behaviour they should adopt.

2. *Standards of performance should be set for learners.* Learners must have clearly defined targets and standards which they find acceptable and can use to judge their own progress.

3. *Learners should have guidance.* Learners need a sense of direction and feedback on how they are doing. Self-motivated individuals may provide much of this for themselves, but the trainer should still be available to encourage and help when necessary.

4. *Learners must gain satisfaction from learning.* Learners are capable of learning under the most difficult circumstances if the learning is satisfying to one or more of their needs. Conversely, the best training schemes can fail if they are not seen as useful by the trainee.

5. *Learning is an active, not a passive process.* Learners need to be actively involved with their trainer, their fellow trainees and the subject matter of the training programme.

6. *Appropriate techniques should be used.* Trainers have a large repertory of training tools and materials. But they must use these with discrimination in accordance with the needs of the job, the individual and the group.

7. *Learning methods should be varied.* The use of a variety of techniques, as long as they are equally appropriate, helps learning by maintaining the interest of the trainee.

8. *Time must be allowed to absorb the learning.* Learning requires time to assimilate, test and accept. This time should be provided in the training programme. Too many trainers try to cram too much into

their programmes and allow insufficient scope for practice and familiarization.

9. *The learner must receive reinforcement of correct behaviour.* Learners usually need to know quickly that they are doing well. In a prolonged training programme, intermediate steps are required in which learning can be reinforced.

10. *It must be recognized that there are different levels of learning and that these need different methods and take different times.* At the simplest level, learning requires direct physical responses, memorization and basic conditioning. At a higher level, learning involves adapting existing knowledge or skill to a new task or environment. At the next level, learning becomes a complex process when principles are identified in a range of practices or actions, when a series of isolated tasks have to be integrated or when the training deals with interpersonal skills. The most complex form of learning takes place when training is concerned with the values and attitudes of people and groups. This is not only the most complex area, but also the most difficult and dangerous.

The learning curve

When planning and implementing training programmes one must take account of the phenomenon known as the learning curve. This refers to the fact that it takes time for an inexperienced trainee to achieve a reasonable standard of skill in a task — this is usually called the 'experienced worker's standard' (EWS).

The standard learning curve is shown in Figure 20.2.

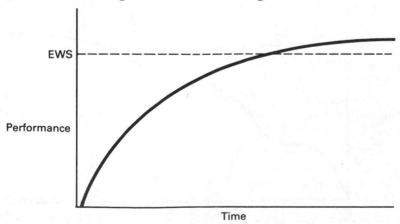

Figure 20.2 A standard learning curve

But rates of learning vary, depending upon the effectiveness of the training, the natural aptitude of the trainee, and the latter's interest in learning. Both the time taken to achieve the experienced worker's standard and the speed with which learning takes place at different times affect the shape of the curve, as shown in Figure 20.3.

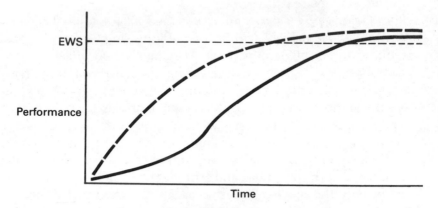

Figure 20.3 Different rates of learning

Learning is often stepped with one or more plateaux while further progress is halted. This may be because the trainees cannot continually increase their skills or speed of work and need a pause to consolidate what they have learnt. The existence of steps such as those shown in Figure 20.4 can be used when planning training to provide deliberate reinforcement periods when newly acquired skills are practised in order to achieve the expected standards. When one plans a training module which describes the

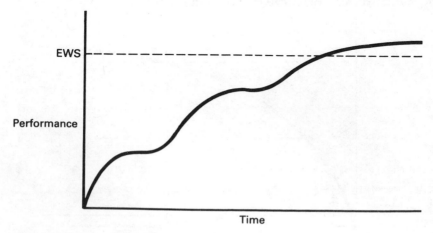

Figure 20.4 A stepped learning curve

training required to acquire a particular skill, it is often desirable to proceed step by step, taking one task at a time, reinforcing it and then progressively adding other parts, consolidating at each stage. This is called the progressive parts method of training.

Applying learning theory

Each of the ten conditions required for learning described above and the existence of the learning curve need to be applied in planning training and ensuring that it is effective. Particular attention should be given to motivation, providing satisfaction from learning, making training an active process, and reinforcement. Training is about changing behaviour and all these factors are important if change for the better is to take place. Hence the importance of what has been termed the behaviour modelling approach to training.

Identifying training needs

Training will not be effective unless it is based on an understanding of learning theory. But training must have a purpose and that purpose can be defined only if the training needs of the organization and the groups and individuals within it have been identified and analysed. Put like that, this seems a trite and obvious statement. Too much training in industry and commerce, however, has been training for training's sake. In effect, people have said: 'Training is a good thing; let there be training.' Perhaps the major contribution of the industrial training boards in the UK was to emphasize the importance of an analytical and systematic approach to training. And analysis starts at the beginning, with the study of training needs.

Training needs analysis — aims

Training needs analysis is partly concerned with defining the gap between what *is* happening and what *should* happen. This is what has to be filled by training (see Figure 20.5).

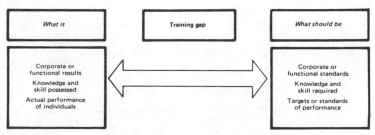

Figure 20.5 The training gap

But it is necessary to avoid falling into the trap of adopting the 'deficiency model' approach which implies that training is only about putting right things that have gone wrong. Training is much more positive than that. It is, or should be, more concerned with identifying and satisfying development needs — multiskilling, fitting people to take on extra responsibilities and increasing all-round competence.

Training needs analysis — areas

Training needs should be analysed, first, for the company as a whole — corporate needs; secondly, for departments, functions or occupations within the company — group needs; and thirdly, for individual employees — individual needs. These three areas are interconnected, as shown in Figure 20.6. The analysis of corporate needs will lead to the identification of training needs in different departments or occupations, while these in turn will indicate the training required for individual employees. The process also operates in reverse. As the needs of individual employees are analysed separately, common needs emerge which can be dealt with on a group basis. The sum of group and individual needs will define corporate needs, although there may be some superordinate training requirements which can be related only to the company as a whole — the whole training plan may be greater than the sum of its parts.

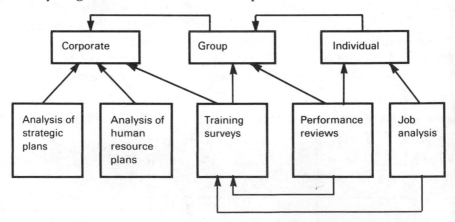

Figure 20.6 Training needs analysis — areas and methods

Methods of analysing training needs

The four methods of training needs analysis are:

1. analysis of human resource plans;

2. job analysis;
3. analysis of performance reviews;
4. training surveys.

Human resource plans

The training strategy of an organization should largely be determined by its human resource plans, which in turn are derived from its overall strategies. The plans should indicate in fairly general terms the types of skills that may be required in the future and the numbers of people with those skills who will be needed. These broad indicators have to be translated into more specific plans which cover, for example, the outputs from training programmes of people with particular skills or a combination of skills (multiskilling).

Job analysis

Job analysis for training purposes means examining in detail the content of jobs, the performance standards required in terms of quality and output and the knowledge and skills needed to perform the job competently and thus meet the performance standards.

The techniques of job and skills analysis were described fully in Chapter 16. For training purposes, it would be necessary to ensure that the information obtained from this analysis specifies:

- any problems faced by job holders in learning the basic skills and applying them successfully;
- any weaknesses in the performance of existing job holders arising from gaps in knowledge, lack of skill or poor motivation which need to be rectified by training;
- how training is carried out at present — and how effective it is.

The output of the job analysis should be a training specification, as described below.

Training specification

A training specification is a product of job analysis. It breaks down the broad duties contained in the job description into the detailed tasks that must be carried out. It then sets out the characteristics that the worker should have in order to perform these tasks successfully. These characteristics are:

431

- *Knowledge* — what the worker needs to know. It may be professional, technical or commercial knowledge. Or it may be about the commercial, economic, or market environment; the machines to be operated; the materials or equipment to be used or the procedures to be followed; or the customers, clients, colleagues and subordinates he or she is in contact with and the factors that affect their behaviour. Or it may refer to the problems that occur and how they should be dealt with.
- *Skills* — what the worker needs to be able to do if results are to be achieved and knowledge is to be used effectively. Skills are built gradually by repeated training or other experience. They may be manual, intellectual or mental, perceptual or social.
- *Attitudes* — the disposition to behave or to perform in a way which is in accordance with the requirements of the work.
- *Performance standards* — what the fully competent worker has to be able to do and achieve.

Performance reviews

A performance management system, as described in Chapter 19, should be a prime source of information about individual training and development needs. The performance management system is based on agreed objectives which are related to each of the key task areas in the employees' job. Both managers and individuals are required to review how well these objectives have been achieved and to analyse the factors that have affected performance. This analysis should reveal development or training needs which are agreed by both parties. An important part of this performance agreement is the preparation of joint plans for development. Managers are expected to agree how they will help to develop individuals and what training they will recommend. Individuals are required to prepare their own self-development plans, with the help of their managers. The latter can refer individuals to the personnel or training department for further help or guidance on their development plans.

The performance management approach to training concentrates on the preparation of performance improvement programmes which are related to jointly determined action plans. The emphasis is on continual development. Every contact between managers and individuals throughout the year is regarded as a learning opportunity.

Training surveys

Training surveys assemble all the information obtained from the other methods of analysis in order to provide a comprehensive basis for the development of a training strategy and its implementation. It may be necessary to supplement that information by interviewing managers to establish their views about training needs and by discussing with people undergoing training or who have just completed a training course their opinions about its effectiveness.

A training survey pays particular attention to the extent to which existing training arrangements are meeting training needs. Further information should be derived from training evaluations, as described below (pages 446–451). It may also be necessary to assess training programmes in terms of the quality of training provided, their output and the level of performance achieved by ex-trainees.

Planning training programmes

Every training programme needs to be designed individually, and the design will continually evolve as new training needs emerge, or when feedback indicates that changes are required. Before one considers special aspects of training programmes for managers, supervisors, craft and technical trainees and clerical staff, decisions are necessary in the following areas:

- the objectives of the programme;
- its content;
- its length;
- where it takes place;
- what techniques will be used;
- who will provide the training

Objectives

It is essential to consider carefully the objectives of the training programme. Objectives can be defined as 'criterion behaviour', ie the standards or changes of behaviour on the job to be achieved if training is to be regarded as sucessful. This should be a definition of what the trainee will be able to do when he or she goes back to work on completing the course; in other words, terminal behaviour. Transfer of training is what counts; behaviour on the job is what matters. Training objectives are best expressed as follows:

> On completing the training (or this part of the course) the trainee will be able to . . . (read a balance sheet, program a microcomputer, operate a word processor, work to a high degree of accuracy, etc).

Content

The content of the training programme should be determined entirely by the training needs analysis and an assessment of what needs to be done to achieve the agreed training objectives.

Length

The length of the training programme clearly depends on its content. But careful consideration should be given to how learning can be speeded up by the use of techniques such as computer-based training (see Appendix P). Thought should also be given to where more time needs to be allowed for 'discovery learning' to take place, or for the amount of involvement required to ensure that those undergoing training have the opportunity fully to understand and 'own' the new ideas or techniques to which they have been exposed.

Where should training take place?

There are three places where training can take place: in company, on the job, off the job; and external, off the job. Each has its uses, and its advantages and disadvantages.

In company, on-the-job

In-company, on-the-job training may consist of teaching or coaching by managers, supervisors or trainers at the desk or at the bench. It may also consist of individual or group assignments and projects. It is the only way to develop and practise managerial, supervisory, technical, selling, manual, and clerical skills. It has the advantage of actuality and immediacy. The trainee works, learns and develops expertise at the same time. Theory is put into practice immediately and its relevance is obvious. The disadvantages are that the effectiveness of the learning is strongly influenced by the quality of the guidance and coaching provided on the job. Many managers and supervisors are unskilled at training and disinclined to carry it out or to encourage it. Relying on fellow employees — 'sit by me' or 'sitting by Nellie' training — had equally obvious disadvantages. The instruction may be inadequate and the training may perpetuate bad habits. Above all, the trainee may be distracted by the environment and find it difficult to acquire the basic skills quickly. To overcome this problem, it is essential to train managers and supervisors how to train.

Training

In company, off the job

In-company, off-the-job training can take place on special courses or in training areas or centres which have been specially equipped and staffed for training. It is the best way to acquire advanced manual and clerical skills and to learn about company procedures and products. It helps to increase the identification of the trainee with the company as a whole, and the use of systematic training techniques, special equipment and trained trainers means that the basic skills and knowledge can be acquired quickly and often economically. The main disadvantage arises when trainees are transferred from the training course to a job to apply their knowledge and skills in practice. On a full-time manual skills course in a training centre, they will have been sheltered from the realities of the rough and tumble in most workshops, especially in batch production factories. At manager and supervisor level, the problem of transferring from the 'training situation' to 'real life' may be even more difficult.

External training

External training is useful for the development of managerial, supervisory, technical and social knowledge and skills, especially if the courses cover standard theory and practice which can easily be translated from the general to the particular. External training should be able to supply the quality of instruction which it might be uneconomic to provide from internal resources. It can be used to implant highly specialized knowledge or advanced skills and has the added advantage of broadening the horizons of those exposed to it. The main disadvantage is that of transferring learning into practice — even more acute with external courses. However effective the training, the knowledge and skills acquired may be quickly dissipated unless they are used immediately. It may also be difficult to select relevant courses from the bewildering variety available.

The art of designing training programmes is to select the right blend of on-the-job and off-the-job training. There are no rules for doing this. Each programme has to be considered individually. But the emphasis should always be towards putting learning into practice and, therefore, first consideration has to be given to what happens on the job. Off-the-job courses, whether internal or external, should be regarded as complementary and supplementary activities which may stimulate learning or provide knowledge and skills that cannot be obtained internally; but they are always subsidiary to what individuals do and learn in their normal place of work.

Training techniques

There is a wide variety of training techniques that can be used. These can be divided into:

1. *On-the-job techniques*, which are practised by the manager and the individual employee on a day-to-day basis or as part of a specially tailored training programme. These include demonstration, coaching, self-development programmes, do-it-yourself training, job rotation, planned experience and mentoring.
2. *Off-the-job techniques*, which are used in formal training courses away from the place of work. These include lectures, talks, discussions, the discovery method, case study, role-playing, simulation, group exercises, team building, distance learning, and workshops.
3. *On- or off-the-job techniques*, which include instruction, question and answer, action learning, assignments, projects, guided reading, computer-based training, instructional systems development, interactive video and video.

These techniques are described in Appendix P.

Who provides the training?

On-the-job training can be provided by managers, supervisors, colleagues or 'mentors' (fellow employees who are given a particular responsibility to guide, advise and generally look after trainees). As mentioned earlier, it is essential to train anyone involved in on-the-job training in techniques such as coaching, instructing and mentoring.

Off-the-job training may be provided by members of the training department, external education and training establishments, guest speakers or consultants. Line managers should be involved as much as possible to bring reality into the classroom, to ease the transference of learning to work (always a difficult problem) and to underline their prime responsibility for training. Anyone who provides off-the-job training must be carefully selected, briefed and monitored to ensure that they make the right contribution. Natural trainers are fairly rare and even professionals need all the guidance you can give them to ensure that they are providing relevant training.

Conducting training programmes

The only general rule for conducting training programmes is that the courses should continually be monitored to ensure that they are proceeding according to plan and within the agreed budget. This s the job of the head of training, who should be required to report on progress against plan at regular intervals.

There are, however, a number of considerations which affect the conduct of training for specific occupations, and those concerning managers and supervisors (these are considered jointly because the basic principles are similar), sales staff, craftsmen and office staff are discussed briefly below.

Management and supervisory training

As the old saying goes, managers learn to manage by managing under the guidance of a good manager. The emphasis should therefore always be towards on-the-job training, by planned experience, coaching or assignments. This can be supplemented — but never replaced — by off-the-job training to extend knowledge, fill in gaps, develop skills, or modify attitudes.

In his report on the experienced manager, Mant[7] said, on the basis of extensive research, that:

- the majority of managers do not benefit greatly from external management courses;
- managers benefit more from well-designed and well-conducted internal courses, variously termed 'in-company', 'in-plant', or 'in-house', which are linked to the job and involve problem-orientated project work;
- the organization, and not the individual, should be regarded as the main consumer of management training, the aim of which is to secure better results for the company.

Revans[8] has taken the same standpoint consistently over many years in developing his concept of 'action learning'. Action learning is based on the conviction that, valuable though specialist knowledge may be as a tool, the most effective resources available to those who want to improve performance are their own talents and experience. Action learning aims to help individuals and groups recognize and develop these natural resources and put them to good use. It is described in more detail in Appendix P.

Project training is a particularly valuable method of providing managers and supervisors with new experience and the opportunity to extend their knowledge over a wider range of problems and to exercise their analytical skills in solving them.

Training courses

Courses should be used judiciously. They can provide:

- concentrated knowledge;
- an opportunity to acquire new skills or to develop and practise existing skills;
- a framework for analysing past experience;
- the chance to reflect on ways in which better use can be made of future experience;
- a means of having new ideas accepted and changing attitudes through group activities not available on the job.

Internal courses

An important spin-off from internal courses, especially resident ones, is that the participants get to know more about their company and their colleagues. Their sense of identification with the organization is thereby increased.

The essential characteristics of an effective formal internal course are threefold. First, it should be problem-based. It must help participants to overcome the actual problems that have been identified as those most likely to prevent good performance. Secondly, it should be action-orientated. It must result in positive action which produces improvements in performance. The effectiveness of the course is primarily measured by the extent to which the desired action has resulted from it. Thirdly, senior managers should be involved in the course, thus demonstrating their support of the manager or supervisor and their recognition of his or her responsibilities and importance.

It goes without saying that the course should be highly participative, making the maximum use of discussion, case studies and group exercises. Throughout the programme, participants should be compelled to list the action points to which they will give attention when they return to their jobs. The course may aim to impart knowledge, but the emphasis should be on the skills required to make effective use of the knowledge the participants have or acquire on the course.

External courses

External general management courses should be used with caution. They can broaden the knowledge and skills of those attending and they can serve as a sort of accolade to demonstrate that someone has 'arrived' or is about to 'arrive'. But the problem of transferring learning back to work can be a formidable one.

Training

The purpose of an external general management course should be to develop the natural ability of managers and to build upon their experience by helping them to:

- think more clearly and critically about all aspects of their jobs;
- understand more about the management techniques that are available so that they can appreciate the ways in which these techniques overlap and are interdependent, and how they can be used to get results;
- obtain a broader understanding of business and organizational problems, thus overcoming any tendency towards insularity or a narrow departmental viewpoint.

Continuity

Whatever form of training is used, management and supervisory training should be seen as a continuous process. One of the greatest fallacies of the typical one-week internal management course, as described above, is that this is sufficient. This applies equally to longer external courses. The management and supervisory training programme should therefore be established as a continuing activity at all levels of management to avoid dissipation of the interest and enthusiasm that follows an isolated course, and to promote the progressive development of managerial and supervisory skills as new experiences are encountered and as conditions change.

Sales training

The aim of sales training should be to equip salespersons with the knowledge, skills, attitudes and habits required to meet or exceed their sales targets.

The first requirement is knowledge of the company and its products, customers, competitors and sales administration procedures.

Secondly, they have to acquire and develop skills: prospecting, making the approach, making presentations, handling objections, closing the sale, and handling complaints. Perhaps the most important skill to be developed, however, is analytical ability. Salespersons must be taught how to analyse their product into its technical characteristics and, most important, its selling points — those aspects of the product that are likely to appeal to particular customers. They must also be taught how to analyse their customers from the point of view of their buying habits and the features of the product that are most likely to appeal to them. In addition, they must be able to analyse themselves — their own strengths and weaknesses as salespersons in order that they can exploit their strengths and overcome their weaknesses.

Thirdly, training should aim to develop attitudes: of loyalty to the company and belief in its products, and of understanding and tolerance with regard to potential and existing customers. Salespersons have to believe in themselves; they must be given confidence and provided with the motivation to go out and sell — a task which requires courage, determination and persistence.

The fourth requirement is to develop sound work habits: organizing time, planning activities, following up leads, maintaining records and submitting reports.

Sales training, like any other form of training, should be based on an analysis of the job and the problems salespersons are likely to meet. The training programme should be continuous; there can never be a time in any salesperson's career when he or she would not benefit from training. Use should be made of classroom training to provide basic knowledge and an opportunity to practise skills. But most training should be carried out on the job by sales managers or supervisors who can demonstrate sales techniques and observe and comment on the efforts of the salesperson.

Classroom training should be highly participative and involve the trainees in practising every aspect of selling. The members of the course should be made to carry out detailed analyses of the selling-points of the company's products in comparison with those of competitors. They should also be asked to work out for themselves the sort of sales resistance they will meet and how they should handle objections. Above all, role-playing exercises should be used to give each trainee experience in every aspect of selling; closed-circuit television is invaluable as a training aid for this type of exercise. Sales training films are helpful, but they should not be relied upon too much. If one of the main aims of a classroom course is to increase the identification of the saleperson with the company and its products, then it is essential for the message to be given by company sales executives and sales training managers.

Field training should be complementary to classroom training. It should be carefully programmed in order that area or district sales managers know exactly what sort of training every salesperson under their control should be receiving at any time. Field sales managers and supervisors therefore need to be thoroughly trained themselves in coaching techniques and in running local sales meetings.

The field training programme should consist of an appropriate mix of live demonstrations with customers; of observations of the salesperson at work by the manager, followed immediately by 'kerbside' coaching sessions; and of more formal off-the-job counselling or training sessions. The latter may be restricted to the manager and an individual salesperson, or may consist of sales meetings which follow a programme of sales topics laid down by headquarters and supplemented by sessions dealing with local problems. It is essential for the field sales training programme to be monitored from headquarters by the sales training manager. Some field managers recognize the importance of training and are good at it. Others neglect it to pursue sales, or are not particularly effective trainers. These individuals need encouragement, stimulation and help.

Selling is a highly personal business and it is therefore important to recognize and meet individual training needs. A performance review system is required for this purpose which focuses attention on the results achieved and the areas where performance needs to be improved by training to obtain better results. The scheme should be linked to informal counselling and coaching sessions as well as more formal training activities.

Technical and skill or craft training

Technical and skill or craft training schemes can be divided into four main types:

Graduate — postgraduate training, usually lasting two years, leading to a professional qualification.

Student — a course of education and practical training leading to a degree or some other qualification as a technologist. In the UK the course may include 'block' release to college for periods of, say, four weeks. Or, more commonly, it is a 'thin sandwich' — periods of up to six months in college and at the works, or a 'thick sandwich' — one year's basic training, three or four years at university and one year's postgraduate training.

Technician — a course of education and training, which could last up to three or four years, leading to employment as a technician or draughtsperson and an appropriate technician's qualification.

Skill or craft — a course lasting up to three or four years, depending on the level of skill that has to be attained and often leading to a craft certificate or other record of achievement.

At one time such training schemes were always called apprenticeships and the indenture agreement laid down a fixed period of training. But it did not specify what training should take place or indicate what standards had been achieved.

The old apprenticeship agreement has generally been replaced by the training agreement. This stipulates the basic and general training, and the skill modules that have to be completed to satisfactory standards before the agreement can be discharged. A skill module is based on skills analysis and defines what training is required to achieve 'experienced worker's standard' in a particular skill or task. It sets out the exercises to be carried out and how attainments should be tested. The training agreement may also specify the part-time period of further education that has to be completed.

Phases of training
In the major craft industries — engineering, construction and shipbuilding — the practical training for all types of trainees or apprentices consists of the following three phases:

1. *Basic Training* — in which the trainee receives training in basic skills in a basic training workshop. This training should consist of a series of modules. Clearly, the standard modules should be chosen on the basis of an analysis of the knowledge and skills required, and additional modules should be specially developed if necessary. A basic course for an engineering craft apprentice may last a full year, by which time the apprentice should be fully equipped with all the basic skills.

   Each module should have defined objectives — criterion behaviour. There should also be predetermined methods of measuring terminal behaviour by tests or observations after the module has been completed. The training should be given by trained instructors in a space set aside for training.

2. *General training* — in which the trainees are given experience in a number of different shops, processes, or operations to consolidate training. If it is already decided that they are to become, say, tool room turners, they would be given an extended period of familiarization in the tool room. But they would also spend some time in related areas; for example, the jig and tool drawing office, the foundry, the machine shop and various fitting and assembly shops.

   Technician, student and graduate trainees in engineering would also spend a general period of training 'round the shops' but would then move into the engineering, design or development departments, depending on their speciality. A production specialist, for example, would spend time in the planning, jig and tool, production control, work study, rate fixing and quality control departments.

   During the period, graduate and student trainees should be given special projects which test their understanding of the design, development, engineering and manufacturing functions. Craft and technician trainees may return to the training school for advanced skill courses in machine operation, draughting or any other speciality.

The biggest danger to avoid in this period of general training is that trainees aimlessly wander from shop to shop and find themselves relegated to a tedious job out of harm's way because no one wants to know about them. The burr bench in a machine shop is a favourite dumping ground for unwanted trainees. To avoid this danger, it is essential to have a syllabus of training in every workshop which is based on an analysis of knowledge and skill requirements. There should be one trained supervisor responsible for training in each workshop and in a large department, such as a machine shop, there may be more than one full-time training supervisor. The training department should also monitor the progress of trainees carefully to ensure that they are following the syllabus and are acquiring the knowledge and skill they need. In a large organization there may be one or more full-time supervisors who spend all their time in the shops chasing shop supervisors and checking on the progress of trainees.

The trainees themselves should know what they are expected to learn at each stage in order that they can request a move if they feel they are wasting their time or are not covering the syllabus. They should also be required to keep logbooks to record what they have done. These should be seen regularly by their training officer as a check on their progress.

3. *Final training* — in which trainees settle down in the department of their choice, or the department for which they are best fitted. During this period trainees will probably be doing the same work as experienced craftsmen, technicians or technologists. The aim is to ensure that they are equipped to apply their learning in normal working conditions and at the pace and level of quality expected from a full experienced and competent individual.

Throughout these three stages the training department has to work closely with the educationists to ensure that, as far as possible, the theory is complementary to the practice.

The length of the period of training at each stage obviously depends on the level and complexity of the knowledge and skills that have to be acquired and on the type of apprenticeship. Traditional union agreements may lay down the length of training in some cases. The experience of any company conducting training along the lines described above, however, has shown that if the basic training is sufficiently comprehensive and the period of experience is adequately planned and monitored, the length of time to reach a fully experienced worker's standard may be considerably less than the traditional period.

Training for other skilled crafts should follow the same pattern of basic training: familiarization with the application of different aspects of the craft, and final consolidation of knowledge and skills. The basic training period, however, may not be so elaborate and may well be carried out in a local technical college which is better equipped to provide the skilled instruction required.

Integrating education and training

One of the main problems faced in running craft and technical training schemes is that of integrating education and training: that is, ensuring that the theoretical instruction provided by a university, polytechnic or technical college is of practical use. This particularly applies to graduate, student and technician.

It is, of course, impossible to ensure that all college instruction is directly relevant. And it would be undesirable to make the attempt. The aim of technical education should be to train the minds of apprentices and to equip them with understanding of general principles and concepts which they can put to use. But some parts of the course will deal with applications, and it is in these areas that integration is desirable.

Integration can be achieved by maintaining good liaison with the college, which should have industrial liaison officers for this purpose. It is also a good idea to keep in touch with lecturers and instructors and give them a chance to look at the work carried out by apprentices in the company.

Members of the training department should meet regularly to discuss progress in their studies and how they can make the best use of what they have learned. In some companies it may be helpful to have qualified engineers in the design, development, production engineering and manufacturing departments to act as tutors for groups of graduates, students or technicians. They can arrange individual or collective meetings regularly to discuss practical applications and to provide advice on the course of studies.

Training office staff

Office training is the most neglected form of training. Perhaps this is because both line and training managers often despise or at least underestimate the skill content of most office work. This feeling has been intensified because of the tendency of systems analysts to deskill office jobs.

But inefficiency in office work can be an important factor in reducing the efficiency of the organization as a whole. A company cannot afford to neglect training in office skills and departmental procedures.

Office training should be divided into three areas: basic training, further education, and continuation training. During the basic training stage, when the trainee is being taught how to carry out his or her first job, a foundation is being laid for the employee's career. During this period, young trainees should obtain background knowledge of the company and acquire the basic knowledge and skills they need.

Office trainees should be encouraged to follow a further course of studies leading to a professional or commercial qualification. The course of studies should be decided by agreement between the employee, the departmental manager and the training department.

The third area is continuation training. Training and development should be a continuous process. When trainees have completed their basic training programme and, preferably, have obtained a qualification, their abilities should be developed by providing broader experience within the company and by short technical courses. The aim at this stage should be to ensure that staff with potential are not allowed to stagnate within a department and that they are prepared for greater responsibility.

Responsibility for training

As has been made clear throughout this chapter, most learning occurs on the job through coaching, planned experience and self-development. The onus is on managers and individuals to ensure that it takes place. Senior management must create a learning organization in which managers recognize that training and development are a key part of their role and one on which their performance will be assessed.

The role of a specialized training department is to provide advice and guidance to managers on their training responsibilities. It will be necessary to monitor what is happening and stimulate action when necessary. The training department is also, of course, responsible for the following activities:

- developing training strategies which support the achievement of business strategies;
- analysing and identifying corporate and occupational training needs;
- developing proposals on how these needs should be satisfied;
- preparing plans and budgets for training activities;

- advising on external training courses for individuals or groups;
- organizing and conducting internal courses and training programmes;
- training managers, supervisors and mentors in their training responsibilities;
- providing help and guidance to individuals on their training and development programmes;
- monitoring the effectiveness of training throughout the organization.

Evaluation of training

It is at the planning stage that the basis upon which each category of training is to be evaluated should be determined. At the same time, it is necessary to consider how the information required to evaluate courses should be obtained and analysed.

The process of evaluating training has been defined by Hamblin[9] as: 'Any attempt to obtain information (feedback) on the effects of a training programme, and to assess the value of the training in the light of that information.' Evaluation leads to control which means deciding whether or not the training was worthwhile (preferably in cost-benefit terms) and what improvements are required to make it even more cost-effective.

Evaluation is an integral feature of training. In its crudest form, it is the comparison of objectives (criterion behaviour) with effects (terminal behaviour) to answer the question of how far training has achieved its purpose. The setting of objectives and the establishment of methods of measuring results are, or should be, an essential part of the planning stage of any training programme.

Evaluation is difficult because it is often hard to set measurable objectives and even harder to collect the information on the results or to decide on the level at which the evaluation should be made.

Evaluation levels

Hamblin[9] has suggested that there are five levels at which evaluation can take place:

1. *Reactions.* The reactions of trainees to the training experience itself: how useful or even how enjoyable they feel the training is, what they think of individual sessions and speakers, what they would like put in or taken out, and so on.
2. *Learning.* Evaluation at the learning level requires the measurement of what trainees have learned as a result of their training — the new knowledge and skills they have acquired or the changes in attitude

446

that have taken place. This is the terminal behaviour that occurs immediately after the training has finished.

3. *Job behaviour*. At this level, evaluation attempts to measure the extent to which trainees have applied their learning on the job. This constitutes an assessment of the amount of transfer of learning that has taken place from an off-the-job training course to the job itself. If the training is carried out on the job, there should be little difference between learning and job behaviour.

4. *Organization*. Evaluation at this level attempts to measure the effect of changes in the job behaviour of trainees on the functioning of the organization in which they are employed. The measurement might be in such terms as improvements in output, productivity, quality, morale (if that can be measured), contribution, or sales turnover. In effect, the question answered by this type of evaluation is not simply what behavioural changes have taken place, but what good have those changes done for the unit or department in which the employee works.

5. *Ultimate value*. This is a measure of how the organization as a whole has benefited from the training in terms of greater profitability, survival or growth. But it might also be defined in terms of the trainee's personal goals rather than those of the sponsoring organization. This could be a legitimate company goal for training if it is believed that what is good for the individual is good for the organization, or if the company feels that it has a social duty to educate and train its employees to the maximum of their capacity. Fundamentally, however, evaluation at this level is related to the criteria by which the organization judges its efficiency and its success or failure. The difficulty is assessing how far training has contributed to the ultimate results.

As Hamblin points out, the five levels are links in a chain: training leads to reactions, which lead to learning, which leads to changes in job behaviour, which lead to changes in the organization, which lead to changes in the achievement of ultimate goals. But the chain can be snapped at any link. Trainees can react favourably to a course — they can 'enjoy it' — but learn nothing. They can learn something, but cannot, or will not, or are not allowed to, apply it. They apply it, but it does no good within their own area. It does some good in their function, but does not further the objectives of the organization.

Evaluation can start at any level. Ideally, some people might say, it starts and finishes at levels four and five; organizational and ultimate value. This is all that really matters, they assert. But it may be difficult, if not impossible, to measure the effect of training in these respects. In any case, it may be desirable to work backwards to find out what went wrong at earlier levels if the ultimate benefits arising from training are inadequate.

Sources of information

The sources of information for training evaluation, as listed by Easterby-Smith,[10] are given below.

Observation

Trainers should be able to observe who is contributing and who is not. They gain fairly clear impressions of how much is being absorbed and how interested the trainees are in learning by noting reactions to the trainer and reactions between the trainees themselves.

Observations can be carried out more analytically by using the Bales interaction process analysis categories (Table 20.1) to classify statements made by trainees in group discussions.

Easterby-Smith[10] notes that one feature which has become increasingly common in management training is the feedback of interaction analysis to trainees as part of the process of encouraging them to try out new forms of behaviour. He gives as an example (Table 20.2) a check-list of types of interaction in a lecture which members of the audience are asked to complete.

Table 20.1 Bales interaction process analysis categories

Positive socio-emotional	1.	Shows solidarity
	2.	Shows tension release (jokes, laughs)
	3.	Agrees (understands, complies)
Gives task help	4.	Gives suggestion (direction)
	5.	Gives opinion (analysis, feelings)
	6.	Gives orientation (information, classification)
Requests task help	7.	Asks for orientation
	8.	Asks for opinion
	9.	Asks for suggestion
Negative socio-emotional	10.	Disagrees
	11.	Shows tension
	12.	Shows antagonism

Table 20.2 Observational check-list for delivery/interaction during a lecture

---

Try to recall specific examples from the lecture to illustrate some of the following:

1. A clear explanation of a point — how was this done; what use was made of examples/illustrations?

2. Summarizing something in the middle of the lecture before moving on to the next point.

3. Use of pauses and/or silence.

4. Bodily activity: one time when (s)he was very active; another time when (s)he was very still

5. Variations in tempo and themes.

6. Other approaches to maintaining interest and attention: jokes, stories, games, etc.

7. An attempt to gain involvement from the audience. How did (s)he do it?

Most training programmes generate written reports and comments and these can be collected and used for evaluation purposes by the trainer.

Individual judgements
The judgements of individuals who have attended the course, qualified observers, the managers of trainees and senior managers in general are an obvious and important source of material for observations. But these judgements are likely to be subjective and should not be relief upon entirely.

Data collection methods

The main data collection methods are the following.

Objective tests
Tests such as the Myers-Briggs or 16-PF personality tests can be used in the early diagnostic stages of a course to identify the personality traits of participants in order that the training and, later, the evaluation can be adjusted to the training needs of those attending the course. This type of test should not, however, be used to measure before-and-after personality traits. A good test should produce similar results when administered on separate occasions to the same people. The training course should not,

therefore, affect test performance; this only goes to show that training not only should not but also cannot change personalities (it can only modify attitudes and get people to reconsider and possibly change their values).

Attitude scales

Attitudes are enduring systems of beliefs about an object, feelings about the object, and tendencies to want to take action with respect to the object. An attitude scale takes a range of subjects covered in a training session or course, one of which could be delegation, and asks trainees to answer a series of *yes* or *no* questions about them; for example:

Can you delegate responsibility?   Yes   No

Attitude scales can be administered before and after the training session and used not only to evaluate how much learning has taken place but also to reinforce points that do not seem to have got across. Evaluation is worthwhile only if it leads to action which supplements, improves or reinforces learning or indicates where modifications are needed to training methods.

Rating scales

A rating scale can be used to evaluate reactions to:

1. The *inputs* to the course in the form of subject matter.
2. The *outputs* of the course in the form of what the trainee has learnt.
3. The *processes* of the course in the form of the effectiveness of the training.
4. The *impact* of the course in the form of what trainees are now going to do which they did not do before.
5. The *overall effectiveness* of the course — the extent to which trainees felt it had achieved its objectives.
6. The *administration* of the course.

A typical rating question could be:

The last session was:
Relevant to my work 1 2 3 4 5 6 7   Irrelevant to my work

Attainment tests

Attainment tests focus on the outcomes of training in the shape of increases in knowledge or skills. They can be administered before and after the course and often take the form of multiple-choice questions, as in Table 20.3.

Table 20.3 A multiple-choice question

Which of the following factors is likely to have the most effect on individuals' performance at work?

(a) the value of the rewards for improved performance (eg promotion, increased pay, higher status);

(b) the extent to which they feel that the reward will be related to the effort they put into the work;

(c) their ability to do the work;

(d) the extent to which they understand and accepts their responsibilities.

Questionnaires

End-of-course questionnaires typically ask questions such as:

- What specific changes would you suggest to improve this course?
- Were there any particular high or low points on this course and what do you think caused them?
- What was the most significant thing you learnt on this course and how did you learn it?
- What specific action(s) will you take following this course on return to work?

Questionnaires get data quickly and cheaply, but they can be subjective and partial.

Interviews

A two-way exchange of information about the impact of a course can be the most effective method of evaluation. An interview can be structured or open — the results of the former may be more consistent, while the latter may be more revealing. In any interview, whether or not it is structured, interviewers will get most out of it if they:

- know what they want to find out;
- ask the right questions;
- give feedback to the person being interviewed;
- phrase questions in such a way that they encourage the informant to open up, rather than simply answering 'yes' or 'no'.

Training strategy

The activities described in this chapter dealing with the formulation of training policies and the identification of training needs should be summarized in a training strategy. This should also take into account the other considerations described earlier relating to the design of training programmes and the responsibility for and organization of training.

Aims of training strategy

The training strategy constitutes a declaration of intent. In effect it says: 'We believe that training pays off and this is what we are going to do about it.' The strategy therefore provides the basis for training plans and programmes and provides a justification for the training budget.

Training philosophy statement

The basis of the training strategy should be a statement of the training philosophy of the organization, which could be expressed as follows: we believe that:

1. Training makes a major contribution to the successful attainment of the organization's objectives.
2. Training plans and programmes should be integrated with and support the achievement of business and human resource strategies.
3. Training should always be performance-related — designed to achieve specified improvements in corporate, functional and individual performance.
4. Everyone in the organization should be encouraged and given the opportunity to develop their skills and knowledge to the maximum of their capacity.
5. While the organization is prepared to invest in training and to provide appropriate training opportunities and facilities, the prime responsibility for development rests with the individual, who will be given the guidance and support of his or her manager and, as necessary, members of the personnel department.

Components of the training strategy

The training strategy should include statements of

● the training philosophy of the organization;

- the key strategic (longer-term) issues that training is required to address;
- the shorter-term training needs which are to be met;
- the priorities to be attached to meeting long- and short-term needs;
- the resources that will be made available for training;
- the allocation of responsibility for developing and implementing strategic training plans.

Strategy action points

The following are ten things to do when formulating training strategies:

1. Analyse business strategies to identify key issues to be addressed by training.
2. Analyse opportunities and threats facing the organization to establish how training could contribute to the achievement of business strategies by devloping opportunities or minimizing the impact of threats.
3. Assess the impact of change to determine how training can help with its management.
4. Analyse the culture of the organization to establish how training might help to achieve cultural change or to reinforce the existing culture.
5. Analyse organizational performance to identify failures or weaknesses that training might help to avoid in the future.
6. Assess human resource plans and analyse proposed organizational changes to determine the skills likely to be required in the future and the training requirements which follow from the need to develop new skills.
7. Assess the training implications of plans for increasing flexibility; for example, multiskilling.
8. Identify individual training and development needs through performance appraisal, assessment centres and analyses of the degree to which the competences required are possessed by individual job holders.
9. Ensure that managers and supervisors are fully aware of their training responsibilities and are equipped with the skills to fulfil them properly.
10. Seize every training opportunity as a chance to make a positive impact on corporate performance and the bottom line.

References

1. Bass, B M and Vaughan, J A *Training in Industry — the Management of Learning*. Tavistock, London, 1966.
2. Manpower Services Commission. *Glossary of Training Terms*. 3rd ed, HMSO, London, 1981.
3. Murphy, T quoted in Armstrong, *Personnel and the Bottom Line*. Institute of Personnel Management, London, 1989.
4. Kenney, J and Reid, M *Training Interventions*. 2nd ed, Institute of Personnel Management, London, 1988.
5. Skinner, B F *Science and Human Behaviour*. Macmillan, London, 1965.
6. Kolb, D A , Rubin, I M and McIntyre, J M *Organisational Psychology; a Book of Readings*. 2nd ed, Prentice-Hall, Englewood Cliffs, 1974.
7. Mant, A *The Experienced Manager*. British Institute of Management, London, 1970.
8. Revans, R W *Developing Effective Managers*. Longman, Harlow, 1971.
9. Hamblin, A C *Evaluation and Control of Training*. McGraw-Hill, Maidenhead, 1974.
10. Easterby-Smith, M *Evaluation of Management Education, Training and Development*. Gower, London, 1986.

21

Management Development

What is management development?

Management development aims to ensure that the organization has the effective managers it requires to meet its present and future needs. It is concerned with improving the performance of existing managers, giving them opportunities to growth and development, and ensuring, as far as possible, that management succession within the organization is provided for.

The objectives of management development are to increase the effectiveness of the organization by:

- improving the performance of managers by seeing that they are clearly informed of their responsibilities and by agreeing with them specific key objectives against which their performance will be regularly assessed;
- identifying managers with further potential and ensuring that they receive the required development, training and experience to equip them for more senior posts within their own locations and elsewhere in the organization;
- assisting chief executives and managers throughout the organization to provide adequate succession and to create a system whereby this is kept under regular review.

Role of the organization

The traditional view is that the organization need not concern itself with management development. The natural process of selection and the pressure of competition will ensure the survival of the fittest. Managers, in fact, are born not made. Cream rises to the top (but then so does scum).

The reaction to this was summed up in Humble's[1] phrase, 'programmitis

455

and crown princes'. Management development was seen in its infancy as a mechanical process using management inventories, multicoloured replacement charts, 'Cook's tours' for newly recruited graduates, detailed job rotation programmes, elaborate points schemes to appraise personal characteristics, and endless series of formal courses.

The true role of the organization in management development lies somewhere between these two extremes. On the one hand, it is not enough, in conditions of rapid growth (when they exist) and change, to leave everything to chance — to trial and error. On the other hand, elaborate management development programmes cannot successfully be imposed on the organization. As Drucker[2] says: 'Development is always self-development. Nothing could be more absurd than for the enterprise to assume responsibility for the development of a man. The responsibility rests with the individual, his abilities, his efforts.' But he goes on to say:

> Every manager in a business has the opportunity to encourage individual self-development or to stifle it, to direct it or to misdirect it. He should be specifically assigned the responsibility for helping all men working with him to focus, direct and apply their self-development efforts productively. And every company can provide systematic development challenges to its managers.

Executive ability is eventually something which individuals must develop for themselves on the job. But they will do this much better if they are given encouragement, guidance and opportunities by their company and managers. In McGregor's[3] phrase: managers are grown — they are neither born nor made. The role of the company is to provide conditions favourable to faster growth. And these conditions are very much part of the environment and organization climate of the company and the management style of the chief executive who has the ultimate responsibility for management development. As McGregor wrote:

> The job environment of the individual is the most important variable affecting his development. Unless that environment is conducive to his growth, none of the other things we do to him or for him will be effective. This is why the 'agricultural' approach to management development is preferable to the 'manufacturing' approach. The latter leads, among other things, to the unrealistic expectation that we can create and develop managers in the classroom.

Responsibility for management development

Management development is not a separate activity to be handed over to a specialist and forgotten or ignored. The success of a management development programme depends upon the degree to which all levels of management are committed to it. The development of subordinates must be recognized as a natural and essential part of any manager's job. But the lead must come from the top.

The basis of management development

Management development should be regarded as a range of related activities rather than an all-embracing programme. The use of the word 'programme' to describe the process smacks too much of a mechanistic approach.

This does not imply that some systematization is not necessary; first, because many managers have to operate in more or less routine situations and have to be developed accordingly; and secondly, because organizations will not continue to thrive if they simply react to events. There must be an understanding of the approaches that can be used to develop managers as well as means of assessing the existing managerial resources and how they meet the needs of the enterprise. And plans must be made for the development of those resources by selecting the best of the methods available. But this should not be seen as a 'programme' consisting of a comprehensive, highly integrated and rigidly applied range of management training and development techniques.

The management development activities required depend on the organization: its technology, its environment and its philosophy. A bureaucratic mechanistic type of organization, such as a large government department, a nationalized industry, a major insurance firm or a large process manufacturing company, will be inclined to adopt the programmed routine approach, complete with a wide range of courses, inventories, replacement charts, career plans and management-by-objectives-based review systems. An innovative and organic type of organization may rightly dispense with all these mechanisms. Its approach should be to provide its managers with the opportunities, challenge and guidance they require, seizing the chance to give people extra responsibilities, and ensuring that they receive the coaching and encouragement they need. There may be no replacement charts, inventories or formal appraisal schemes, but people know how they stand, where they can go and how to get there.

The learning organization

The organization itself, as managed from the top (or centre) and at all levels, can therefore create the conditions in which managers learn. The 'learning organization' has been described by Pedler *et al*[4] as 'an organization which facilitates the learning of all its members and continually transforms itself'. The characteristics of a learning organization, as defined by Mumford,[5] are that it:

- encourages managers to identify their own learning needs;
- provides a regular review of performance and learning for the individual;
- encourages managers to set challenging learning goals for themselves;
- provides feedback at the time on both performance and achieved learning;
- reviews the performance of managers in helping to develop others;
- assists managers to see learning opportunities on the job;
- seeks to provide new experiences from which managers can learn;
- provides or facilitates the use of training on the job;
- tolerates some mistakes, provided managers try to learn from them;
- encourages managers to review, conclude and plan learning activities;
- encourages managers to challenge the traditional ways of doing things.

Management development and learning

Management development is about learning: the learning required to do the present job better and the learning needed to tackle more responsible or demanding jobs successfully. Mumford,[5] in fact, defines management development as 'an attempt to improve managerial effectiveness through a learning process'. He emphasizes the importance of learning by informal means and believes, correctly, that 'a great deal of management development is not "planned and deliberate" — and, even more significantly, probably cannot be'.

It is possible to distinguish between learning and development along the lines of Pedler and Boydell,[6] who see learning as being concerned with an increase in knowledge or a higher degree of an existing skill, whereas development is a move towards a different state of being or functioning.

How managers learn

Management development processes must be based on an understanding of how managers learn. Honey and Mumford[7] have produced a research-based analysis of the managerial learning styles which constitute the learning cycle depicted in Figure 21.1.

Management learning involves all stages of the cycle and the different

Management Development

The learning cycle

Activists:

- try anything once;
- tend to revel in short-term crises; fire-fighting;
- tend to thrive on the challenge of new experiences;
- are relatively bored with implementation and longer-term consolidation;
- constantly involve themselves with other people.

Reflectors:

- like to stand back and review experiences from different perspectives;
- collect data and analyse them before coming to conclusions;
- like to consider all possible angles and implications before making a move;
- tend to be cautious;
- actually enjoy observing other people in action;
- often take a back seat at meetings.

Theorists:

- are keen on basic assumptions, principles, theories, models and systems of thinking;
- prize rationality and logic;
- tend to be detached and analytical;
- are unhappy with subjective or ambiguous experience;
- like to make things tidy and fit them into rational schemes.

Pragmatists:

- positively search out new ideas or techniques which might apply in their situation;
- take the first opportunity to experiment with applications;
- respond to problems and opportunities 'as a challenge';
- are keen to use ideas from management courses;
- like to get on with things with clear purpose.

Approaches to management development

It has often been said that managers learn to manage by managing — in other words, 'experience is the best teacher'. This is largely true, but some people learn much better than others. After all, a manager with ten years' experience may have had no more than one year's experience repeated ten times. Differences in the ability to learn arise because some managers are naturally more capable or more highly motivated than others, while some will have had the benefit of the guidance and help of their manager. The saying quoted above could be expanded to read: 'Managers learn to manage by managing under the guidance of a good manager.' The operative word in this statement is *good*. Some managers are better at developing people than others, and one of the aims of management development is to get all managers to recognize that developing their staff is an important part of their job. And for senior managers to say that people do not learn because they are not that way inclined, and to leave it at that is to neglect one of their key responsibilities — to improve organizational performance by doing whatever is practical to improve the effectiveness and potential of the managers.

To argue that managers learn best 'on the job' should not lead to the conclusion that managers are best left entirely to their own devices or that management development should be a haphazard process. The organization should try to evolve a philosophy of management development which ensures that consistent and deliberate interventions are made to improve managerial learning. Revans[8] wants to take management development back into the reality of management and out of the classroom, but even he believes that deliberate attempts to foster the learning process through 'action learning' (described in Appendix P, pages 922–923) are necessary.

It is possible to distinguish between formal and informal approaches to management development, as described below.

Formal approaches to management development

The formal approaches to management development include:

- *development on the job* through coaching, counselling, monitoring and feedback by managers on a continuous basis associated with the use of performance management systems to identify and satisfy development needs (see Chapter 19) and mentoring (see Appendix P);
- *development through work experience*, which includes job rotation, job enlargement, taking part in project teams or task groups, 'action learning', and secondment outside the organization;
- *formal training* by means of internal or external courses;
- *structured self-development* by following self-development programmes agreed with the manager or a management development adviser — may include guided reading or the deliberate extension of knowledge or acquisition of new skills on the job.

The formal approaches to management development are based on the identification of development needs through a performance management system or an assessment centre. The approach may be structured around a list of competences which have been defined as being appropriate for managers in the organization (see pages 464–66).

Informal approaches to management development

Informal approaches to management development make use of the learning experiences which managers meet during the course of their everyday work. Managers are learning every time they are confronted with an unusual problem, an unfamiliar task or a move to a different job. They then have to evolve new ways of dealing with the situation. They will learn if they analyse what they did to determine how and why it contributed to its success or failure. This retrospective or reflective learning will be effective if managers can apply it successfully in the future.

This is potentially the most powerful form of learning. The question is: can anything be done to help managers make the best use of their experience? This type of 'experiential' learning comes naturally to some managers. They seem to absorb, unconsciously and by some process of osmosis, the lessons from their experience, although in fact they have probably developed a capacity for almost instantaneous analysis, which they store in their mental data bank and which they can retrieve whenever necessary.

Ordinary mortals, however, either find it difficult to do this sort of analysis or do not recognize the need. This is where formal or at least semi-formal approaches can be used to encourage and help managers to learn more effectively. These approaches include:

- emphasizing self-assessment and the identification of development needs by getting managers to assess their own performance against agreed objectives and analyse the factors that contributed to effective or less effective performance — this can be provided through a performance management system;
- getting managers to produce their own development plans;
- encouraging managers to discuss their own problems and opportunities with their bosses or colleagues in order to establish for themselves what they need to learn or be able to do.

An integrated approach to management development

An integrated approach to management development will make judicious use of both the formal and informal methods as described above. There are five governing principles:

1. *The reality of management* — the approach to management development should avoid making simplistic assumptions on what managers need to know or do, based on the classical analysis of management as the processes of planning, organizing, directing and controlling. In reality, as described in Chapter 1, managerial work is relatively disorganized and fragmented, and this is why many practising managers reject the facile solutions suggested by some formal management training programmes. As Kanter[9] has said: 'Managerial work is undergoing such enormous and rapid change that many managers are reinventing their profession as they go.'

2. *Relevance* — it is too easy to assume that all managers need to know about such nostrums as quantitative analysis, strategic planning, balance sheet analysis, zero-based budgeting, etc. These can be useful but they may not be what managers really need. Management development processes must be related to the needs of particular managers in specific jobs and these processes may or may not include techniques such as those listed above. Those needs, however, may include not only what managers should know now but also what they should know and be able to do in the future, if they have the potential. Thus, management development may include 'broadening programmes' aimed at giving managers an understanding of the wider, strategic issues which will be relevant at higher levels in the organization.

3. *Self-development* — managers need to be encouraged to develop themselves and helped to do so. A performance management system will aim to provide this guidance.

4. *Experiential learning* — learning can be described as the modification of behaviour through experience. The principal method by which managers can be equipped is by providing them with the right variety of experience, in good time, in the course of their careers, and by helping them to learn from that experience. Action learning is a method of achieving this.

5. *Formal training* — courses can supplement but can never replace experience and they must be carefully timed and selected or designed to meet particular needs.

The use of competences in management development

Competences as a means of classifying areas for training or development became 'flavour of the month' in managerial development circles in the 1980s following the work of Boyatzis[10] and the Management Charter Initiative's proposals for a certificate-level qualification in management based on competences.

Definition of competence

The concept of competence for management development and training purposes has been defined in a number of ways; for example:

- 'A capacity that exists in a person that leads to behaviour that meets the job demands within the parameters of the organizational environment and that, in turn, brings about desired results.' (Boyatzis[10])
- 'The knowledge, skills and qualities of effective managers.' (Hornby and Thomas[11])
- 'The ability and willingness to perform a task.' (Burgoyne[12])
- 'Behavioural dimensions that affect job performance.' (Woodruffe[13])

Use of competences

Lists of competences such as analytical ability, persuasiveness and achievement motivation are used in the following ways:

- as criteria for judging a manager's performance in a conventional performance assessment system or an assessment centre;
- as a basis for identifying and classifying training needs;
- as a basis for identifying areas for self-development.

At Cadbury Schweppes, for example, as reported by Glaze,[14] a dictionary of competences has been developed to form a language for use in assessment centres, performance appraisal and management development.

The performance appraisal system measures two dimensions of a person's performance — results and behaviour. The aim was to strengthen the focus on future work priorities by requiring managers to explore sources of higher-quality performance rather than debate past failures. All managers were therefore asked to identify with subordinates those competences which would contribute to the achievement of objectives for the year ahead and to determine what action was necessary to address shortcomings. They were required to do this against the following dimensions:

- strategy
- drive
- relationships
- persuasion
- leadership
- followership (teamwork)
- analysis
- implementation
- personal factors.

Managers were then asked to express development needs, using the competence language, and the personnel department was required to provide professional and personalized advice on how these needs might be addressed. The thrust was to put pressure on and give information to the various parties who had the power to make things happen.

The success criteria adopted by Cadbury Schweppes for the competence project were:

- each manager should be able to define his or her job in competence terms and pursue improvements in personal competence by setting learning objectives at least annually;
- every newly appointed person should commence work with agreed development objectives;
- challenges, pressures and major change should be described in competence terms;
- the organization should be aware of and make optimum use of the strengths which it has available at any one time;
- people/job mismatches should be brought to the surface and addressed;
- more imagination should be introduced into the rotation of managers.

Defining competence

Methods of analysing competence were described in Chapter 16 (pages 339–340). Competences should be defined to meet the needs of the particular organization although most lists contain a number of common factors. The following are some examples of competence lists.

Competence lists

Boyatzis[10] has suggested the following clusters of competences:

- goal and action management;
- directing subordinates;
- human resources management;
- leadership.

As reported by Dulewicz,[15] Henley Management College has compiled the following list of middle-management competences:

Intellectual

- strategic perspective;
- analysis and judgement;
- planning and organization.

Interpersonal

- managing staff;
- persuasiveness;
- assertiveness and decisiveness;
- interpersonal sensitivity;
- oral communication.

Adaptability

- adaptability and resilience.

Results-orientation

- energy and initiative;
- achievement-motivation;
- business sense.

Burgoyne and Stuart[16] have developed the following three-level model of managerial skills:

1. *Data and facts* — command of basic facts and relevant professional understanding;
2. *Situation-specific skills and response tendencies* — continuing sensitivity to events, analytical skills, social skills (eg leadership), emotional resilience and inclination to respond purposefully;
3. *Meta-skills* (which enable the manager effectively to develop the other skills) — creativity, mental agility, balanced learning habits and self-awareness.

Reservations about competence analysis

A reservation some people have about the term 'competence' is that it carries the connotation of 'mere competency', which, as Burgoyne[12] says, implies 'a minimal, scraping through, satisfying level of ability'. To avoid this problem, it is best to use 'competency' in the 'total quality' sense as what managers should be able to do to achieve consistently high levels of performance.

Burgoyne, however, believes that breaking down this concept of total managerial competence into lists of managerial competences which purport to be relatively universal and easily measurable is not necessarily an appropriate thing to do, or a useful foundation to a complete prescription for the delivery of management development. He suggests that the following eight issues need to be considered before wholeheartedly pursuing the 'competency' approach:

1. *The divisibility of competence* — managing is not the sequential exercise of discrete competences. The separated list has, somehow, to be integrated. Earning separate competences does not necessarily mean that a manager can combine them effectively.
2. *Objective technical measurability* — no acceptable technical approach to the measurement of competence has emerged. The best that can be achieved is a process of 'informed and grounded judgement'.
3. *Universality* — 'All managerial jobs are different at a detailed level of resolution, and all managerial jobs are the same at a high level of abstraction.' Generic competences operate at that high level and are not particularly useful in guiding conduct in a specific situation.
4. *Moral and ethical issues* — 'competency' lists tend to emphasize the technical and leave out the moral and ethical issues; for example, the values of the organization.
5. *The nature of managing* — managing is a creative activity. The effective exercise of managerial 'competency' exhausts or renders obsolescent

the competences which achieve success and brings new ones into play.

6. *Many right ways to manage* — 'competency' lists should be flexible and adaptive enough to be compatible with this reality.
7. *Competent person* — being competent is different from having competences. Simply having competences begs the questions of how they are used, who is using them and how does the user develop.
8. *Collective competence* — high levels of individual member competences do not guarantee group or organizational competence and effectiveness.

Burgoyne's conclusion from this analysis is that, while 'competency' approaches have a valuable part to play in management development, it is inappropriate to consider them as universal, differentiated lists of managerial competences and therefore treat them mechanistically. They have to be used flexibly and with discretion, taking into account the eight issues listed above.

Management development strategies

Management development strategies define broadly how the organization intends to ensure that managers of the quality it needs are available now and in the future. Two examples of management development strategies are given below.

Management development at Cadbury Schweppes

The personnel function at Cadbury Schweppes defined the group's management development policy by reference to the sort of manager it wants:

As a fast-growth company, we need:

1. ability moving up, pushing our top people;
2. managers in the top two to three levels with an international perspective;
3. managers who are information-technology literate;
4. managers with capacities greater than their current job requires;
5. managers with commercial awareness but a human face;
6. a mix of managers who can:

    (a) integrate acquisitions;
    (b) manage and organize growth;
    (c) manage a maintenance environment;

7. a mix of managers with dominant skills for jobs requiring:

    (a) hands-on management;

(b) high-order integration skills;
(c) ideas-dominated leadership as the key for success.

The supporting recommendations to this policy were defined as being:

To undertake management development activities selectively and with clear focus. Priority should be given to activities with a big payback. We will develop our top people, who will pull the remaining up to new levels. To this end, we should:

- undertake a regular disciplined assessment of high-potential talent on an international basis;
- adopt a common language for management development, building upon the model of leadership excellence and competence dimensions;
- expand the general management training scheme on an international basis and have a small cadre from universities throughout the world who have planned careers;
- have selective, planned job rotation across streams, countries and functions;
- have a simple, flexible way for identifying and providing talent across streams;
- continue to adapt our organizational structure to fit the strengths and weaknesses of our people rather than try to change our people to fit the organizational structure.

The conclusion reached was that

People development must rank as a top priority. In a company like ours, with many executives and managers recruited from the outside, we must guard against paying lip service to this vital requirement for future growth.

Management development at General Electric

At General Electric the management development mission is expressed in the following points:

- To ensure that the best available talent is considered for each job and that each opening is considered for its developmental potential.
- To see that there is a reasonable yet selective flow of managers across the corporation.
- To ensure that the top organization structure is consonant with long-term company objectives and strategy, and enhances top executives' development.
- To provide a competitive compensation programme to attract, retain, and motivate key employees.

The basic management philosophy driving the General Electric system of executive development is described in the following 10 main points:

1. Ensuring development of managerial excellence in the company is the chief executive's most important responsibility.
2. Managers at all levels must be similarly responsible and must 'own' the development system(s).
3. Promotion from within, for motivational value, will be the rule, not the exception.
4. A key step in planning the development of managers is the manpower review process.
5. Managerial abilities are learned primarily by managing. Other activities are variable adjuncts.
6. Control of the selection process is essential in order to use openings developmentally.
7. The company can tolerate and needs a wide variety of managerial styles, traits, abilities, etc.
8. Several different managerial streams and development planning systems are needed to accommodate the company's size, diversity, and decentralization.
9. Occasionally it may be necessary to distort otherwise sound compensation practice and/or change organization structure to achieve developmental results.
10. Staff people must add value in these processes, but their roles are secondary to the managerial roles.

References

1. Humble, J 'Programmitis and crown princes', *The Manager*, December, 1963.
2. Drucker, P *The Practice of Management*. Heinemann, London, 1955.
3. McGregor, D *The Human Side of Enterprise*. McGraw-Hill, New York, 1960.
4. Pedler, M, Boydell, T and Burgoyne, J 'Towards the learning company', *Management Education and Development* Vol. 20, Part 1, 1989.
5. Mumford, A *Management Development: Strategies for Action*. Institute of Personnel Management, London, 1989.
6. Pedler, M and Boydell, T *Managing Yourself*. Fontana, 1985.
7. Honey, P and Mumford, A *Manual of Learning Styles*. Honey, London, 1986.
8. Revans, W *Action Learning*. Blond and Briggs, London, 1989.
9. Kanter, R M The new managerial work. *Harvard Business Review*. November 1989.
10. Boyatzis, R *The Competent Manager*. Wiley, New York, 1982.

11. Hornby, D and Thomas, R 'Towards a better standard of management', *Personnel Management*. January 1989.
12. Burgoyne, J *Competency Approaches to Management Development*. Centre for the Study of Management Learning, University of Lancaster, 1988.
13. Woodruffe, C *Assessment Centres*. Institute of Personnel Management, London, 1990.
14. Glaze, T 'Cadbury's dictionary of competence', *Personnel Management*, July 1989.
15. Dulewicz, V 'Assessment centres as the route to competence', *Personnel Management*, November 1989.
16. Burgoyne, J and Stuart, R Centre for the Study of Management Learning, University of Lancaster, 1987.

22

Career Management

Definition

Career management plans and shapes the progression of individuals within an organization in accordance with assessments of organizational needs and the performance, potential and preferences of individual members of the enterprise.

Overall aims

Career management has three overall aims:

1. to ensure that the organization's needs for management succession are satisfied;
2. to provide men and women of promise with a sequence of training and experience that will equip them for whatever level of responsibility they have the ability to reach;
3. to give individuals with potential the guidance and encouragement they need if they are to fulfil their potential and achieve a successful career with the organization in tune with their talents and aspirations.

Specific aims

The specific aims of career management policies and procedures are to:

- help employees identify the skills and qualities needed for both current and future jobs;
- align and integrate personal aspirations with organizational objectives;
- develop new career paths and plans that point outwards from the individuals in all directions, not just upwards;
- revitalize employees who are experiencing stagnation in their careers;

- provide employees with the opportunity to develop themselves and their careers;
- by the above means, provide mutual benefits for both the organization and individual employees.

The process of career management

The process of career management is illustrated in Figure 22.1. The key aspects of this process are discussed below.

Career dynamics

Career dynamics describes how career progression takes place — the ways in which people move through their careers and advance upwards, grade by grade, within the organization.

Career progression dynamics
Figure 22.2 illustrates the ways in which career progression proceeds through three main stages:

1. *expanding* at the start of a career, when new skills are being acquired, knowledge is growing rapidly and aspirations and inclinations are being clarified;
2. *establishing* the career path, when skills and knowledge gained in the expanding stage are being applied, tested, modified and consolidated with experience, and when aspirations are confirmed or amended;
3. *maturing* when individuals are well established on their career path and proceed along it according to their motivation, abilities and opportunities.

Through each of these stages people develop and progress at different rates. This means that at the maturing stage they either continue to grow, 'plateau-out' (although still doing useful work), or stagnate and decline.

The relevance of career dynamics
The study of career dynamics is a necessary prelude to the formulation of career management policies and the preparation of management succession plans. The study is carried out by analysing the progression of individuals within an organization — function by function — in relation to assessments of performance, as illustrated in Figure 22.3. This can be used to trace typical career progressions in relation to performance assessment and to compare actuals with the model that can be developed from the

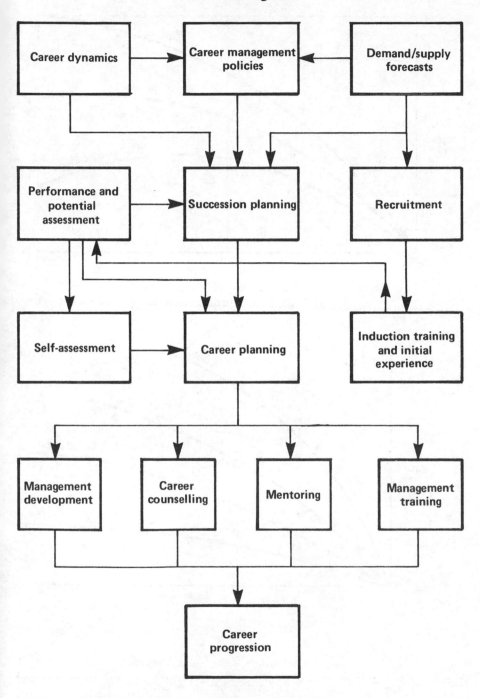

Figure 22.1 The process of career management

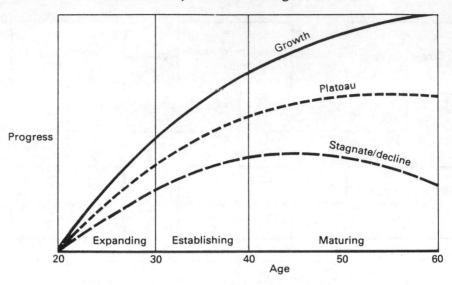

Figure 22.2 Career progression curves

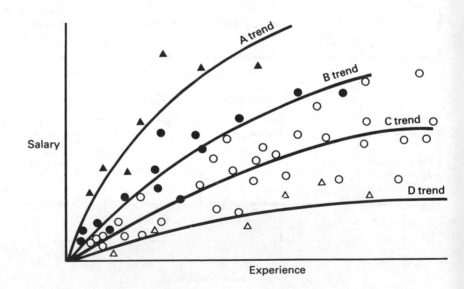

Figure 22.3 Progress analysis

empirically determined trend lines. An analysis of career dynamics can also point the way towards any actions required to alter career path trends for promising individuals by means of specific career management actions. Finally, the analysis reveals anomalies such as overpromotions (victims of the Peter Principle who have been promoted to the level of their own incompetence) or problems of managers who are stagnating or have gone over the hill.

Career management policies

Career management policies cover the following areas.

Make or buy decisions
The organization needs to decide on the extent to which it:

- makes or grows its own managers (a promotion from within policy);
- recruits or buys-in deliberately from outside (bringing 'fresh blood' into the organization) which means adopting a policy that accepts a reasonable amount of wastage and even takes steps in good time to encourage people, fairly gently, to develop their careers elsewhere if they are in danger of stagnating;
- will have to buy-in talent from outside because of future shortfalls in the availability of managers, as revealed by the demand and supply forecasts.

A make or buy policy may be expressed as follows: 'We plan to fill about 80 per cent of our management vacancies from within the organization. The remaining 20 per cent we expect to recruit from outside.'

Short or long-term policies
Policies for determining the time scale for investing in careers fall into one or other of the following categories:

- *Short-term performance.* Employers who adopt, consciously or unconsciously, this policy, concentrate on the 'here and now'. They recruit and train high performers who will be good at their present job and are rewarded accordingly. If they are really good, they will be promoted — there are plenty of opportunities — and the enterprise will get what it wants. Deliberately to train managers for a future that may never happen is considered a waste of time. Top managers in this type of organization may well say: 'If we can get good people to do good work, the future will take care of itself. They'll prove and mature their abilities in their present job and be ready and indeed eager to take on extra responsibilities when the occasion arises. The future can take care of itself. If there's no one around at the time, then we'll buy in someone from outside — no problem!'

- *Long-term plans.* Employers who believe in long-term career planning develop highly structured approaches to career management. They go in for elaborate reviews of performance and potential, assessment centres to identify talent or confirm that it is there, 'high-flyer' schemes, and planned job moves in line with a predetermined programme.

- *Long-term flexibility.* Employers who follow this policy appreciate that they must concentrate on getting good performance now, and that in doing so they will, to a considerable extent, be preparing people for advancement. To this extent, they adopt the same attitude as short-term employers. However, they also recognize that potential should be assessed and developed by training which is not job-specific and by deliberately broadening experience through job rotation or the redirection of career paths. This approach avoids the possible short-sightedness of the here-and-now policy and the rigidity and, often, lack of realism, inherent in the structured system. In conditions of rapid development and change, how far is it actually possible to plan careers over the long term? The answer must be, to a very limited extent, except in a static organization which has implicitly recognized that it provides a 'cradle-to-grave' career for people who, in general, are willing to wait for 'Buggins' turn'.

As a generalization, the short-term system is likely to be more common in smallish, rapidly growing, 'organic' businesses where form follows function and the organization is fluid and flexible. The longer-term system is more prevalent in larger, bureaucratic, 'mechanistic' types of organization, where accurate forecasts of future needs can be made, significant changes in skill requirements are not likely to take place and there is a steady flow, according to easily assessed performance, up the promotion ladder.

Specialists or generalists

Career management policies should cover the extent to which the organization is concerned about developing better and better specialists (broadly in line with the short-term approach) or whether it attaches equal, or even more, importance to developing the appropriate number of generalists who are capable of exercising effectively the managerial functions of planning, organizing, motivating and controlling. Obviously, all organizations have a mix of these two categories, but it may be a matter of policy to create a dual career structure with separate career ladders for pure specialists, who would be rewarded in accordance with their technical contribution and not in line with their place in a management grade hierarchy. There is no universal law that says a top-rate specialist who is not a manager and does not want to be one, must be paid less than someone who happens to have the skills and inclinations to take him or her along the management route.

Clearly, the policy depends on the type of organization, especially its technology and the extent to which it is a hierarchy of managers with a few specialists on the side (for example, an insurance company with a large branch network but with a select team of actuaries and investment managers at head office), or is a hi-tech, research-based operation where the technologist rules.

Dealing with the 'plateaued' manager

As Davies and Deighan[1] have suggested: 'Preoccupied with motivating and retaining our superstars, we have neglected the needs of the vast majority of managers who actually keep the business going. The problem is that, once they know they can rise no higher in the organization, they are likely to experience what has been called the "managerial menopause".'

These people fall into three categories, as defined by Davies and Deighan:

1. *Contented maturity* — people who have progressed well and feel that they have had a satisfying career in a good company. Although they have been overtaken by high-flyers, they are not too put out by this and are content to go on doing their job well, and they find satisfaction outside as well as inside work. In these cases, the policy should be to recognize the worth of this indispensable core, reward them appropriately, and strive to enlarge or enrich their jobs when this is possible. They make excellent mentors (mentoring systems are described later in this chapter).

    Many people are not as ambitious as some achievers think they are or ought to be. For those who are in a state of contented maturity, the organization should have a policy of registering how much it values their services and accepting that 'they have done jolly well and need not be driven any further'.
2. *Discontented maturity* — many people who have plateaued but, in spite of having progressed reasonably well, believe that they should go

further and are under pressure to do so because of their own ambitions (possibly unrealistic), the cult of success in the company or even the expectations of their spouse. Because of their frustrated expectations these people tend to be characterized by low morale, cynicism, staleness and depression. Revitalizing them is again a matter for job enrichment and enlargement as part of a programme for changing job structures, where possible. This approach should become a deliberate policy of the company, but it needs to be backed up by counselling which will help those affected adversely by plateauing to learn to live with it and, perhaps, positively enjoy the feeling that they no longer have to join in the 'rat race'. The policy on counselling should therefore incorporate help to plateaued managers as well as rising stars. Career management may primarily be concerned with development but it also has to take care of those people who are worth taking care of at each stage of their career.

3. *Thwarted rising stars* — people who have started well but are now burning themselves out and not living up to their own expectations or those of the organization. Counselling may help these individuals to become reconciled to their situation, but it will not necessarily work in this way. It may be necessary to have a policy which recognizes that thwarted rising stars need outplacement rather than job counselling; that is, help in restructuring their careers elsewhere.

Demand and supply forecasts

Demand and supply forecasts are provided by the use of human resource planning and modelling techniques (see Chapter 15). In larger organizations, modelling is a particularly fruitful method to use because it does allow for sensitivity analysis of the impact of different assumptions about the future (answering 'what if?' questions).

Expert systems, as described in Chapter 38, can also be used where this is an extensive database on flows, attribute requirements (person specifications), and performance and potential assessments. Such systems can establish relationships between the opportunities and the personal attributes they demand so that careers advisers can take a set of personal attributes and identify the most appropriate available opportunities. At the career planning stage, they can also identify people with the correct abilities and skills for particular jobs and provide information on the career management programmes required to ensure that attributes and jobs are matched and careers progress at an appropriate rate. Career management systems such as ExecuGROW (Control Data) have been specially developed for this purpose.

There is a limit, however, to sophistication. There are so many variables and unpredictable changes in both supply and demand factors that it may be possible to conduct only an annual check to see what the relationship is between the numbers of managers who will definitely retire over the next few years (no more than five) and the numbers at the next level who have the potential to succeed them. If this comparison reveals a serious unbalance, then steps can be taken to reduce or even eliminate the deficit or to consider other types of deployment for those who are unlikely to progress. This comparison is represented graphically in Figure 22.4, in which the two hypothetical examples illustrate a surplus and a deficit situation.

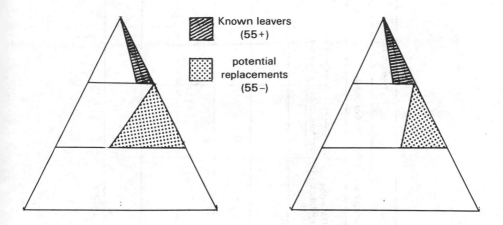

Figure 22.4 Demand and supply models

Succession planning

The aim of management succession planning is to ensure that, as far as possible, suitable managers are available to fill vacancies created by promotion, retirement, death, leaving, or transfer. It also aims to ensure that a cadre of managers is available to fill the new appointments that may be established in the future.

The information for management succession planning comes from organization reviews and demand-and-supply forecasts. The succession

MANAGEMENT SUCCESSION SCHEDULE

Department _____   Director/Manager _____

Present Managerial and Supervisory Staff

Name	Position	Age	Date due for replacement	Rating		If promotable, indicate what position and when
				Performance	Potential	

Possible successors

Names (1st and 2nd choice)	Positions	When ready

Figure 22.5 Management succession schedule

plans will be influenced by the career dynamics of the organization and also by the performance and potential assessments, which provide information on who is ready now and in the future to fill projected vacancies. This information needs to be recorded so that decisions can be made on promotions and replacements, and training or additional experience arranged for those with potential or who are earmarked for promotion.

The records need not be elaborate. In practice, complex inventories and detailed succession charts replete with colour codes and other symbols are a waste of time, except in the largest and most bureaucratic organizations. All the information required can be recorded on a simple management succession schedule such as the one illustrated in Figure 22.5.

A computerized personnel information system, as described in Chapter 38, can, with the help of competency modelling techniques, store inventories of the skills and experience of individual employees together with records of their performance and potential assessments. Lists of attributes for key jobs can also be stored, and this information can be linked to the other data mentioned above to provide guidance on who is available to fill present or future vacancies and on any career plans needed to ensure that potential is realized.

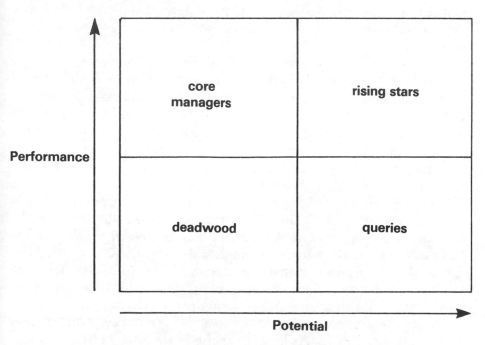

Figure 22.6 Categorization — performance and potential

Performance and potential assessment

The aim of performance and potential assessment is to identify training and development needs, provide guidance on possible directions in which an individual's career might go, and indicate who has potential for promotion. This information can be obtained from a performance management system, as described in Chapter 19. In addition to this type of assessment procedure, it may be interesting to categorize employees in one of the four squares set out in Figure 22.6.

The rising stars are the high-flyers with potential, who will benefit from career planning, wider experience and management training. The organization may wish to 'fast-track' them by rapid promotion or by offering more challenging opportunities. They should be listed and looked after. This may mean paying over the odds to demonstrate that the company values them and wants to keep them from straying further afield. It does not mean setting up a row of crown princes whose future is guaranteed and whose path to the top is made easy. They have to know that they have been given these opportunities only because they have performed well so far, and that the demands made on them in the future are going to be even greater. There is no easy way to the top and they must realize that they will have to work their passage, and that, while the company has its eye on them and is going to help their development, in the last analysis it will be up to them.

The core managers are the people on whom the organization depends to get things done. They are its backbone. They are sometimes called 'solid citizens', but this is a derogatory term. They are not necessarily going to rise much above their present level, but they are useful and dependable and they still need training in new techniques and skills. They also need the encouragement and motivation provided by varying their responsibilities, introducing new opportunities wherever this can be arranged, and assuring them that they are doing a worthwhile job.

The queries are those managers who for one reason or another do not seem to be making the grade. They may have the ability but not the motivation, or they may have the motivation but not the ability. In the latter case it is worth trying to establish and satisfy training needs. They are clearly worth saving, if that is at all possible. People with ability who lack motivation may present a bigger problem. It is a good thing to find out why they are not motivated and do something about it.

The deadwood are the people — one hopes few in number, if they exist at all — who ought to go. As long as all else in the shape of training and encouragement has failed, there is no point in keeping them — for their sake as well as that of the company. They could do better elsewhere if they can find a nice square hole into which they will fit.

Recruitment

Career management means taking into account the fact that the organization will inevitably need to recruit new managers, who will then have to prove themselves while gaining their initial experience and undergoing induction training. As soon as they have been with the company long enough to show what they can do and where they might go, their performance and potential can be assessed and they can be fed into the career management system.

Self-assessment

As mentioned in Chapter 21, the best form of development is self-development. Similarly, the most important contribution to individual career planning must come from managers themselves. They must be given the encouragement to assess what they want to do and become and the opportunity to discuss their aspirations and plans with their manager and a career counsellor or mentor.

Career planning

The process of career planning

Career planning is the key process in career management. It uses all the information provided by the organization's assessments of requirements, the assessments of performance and potential and the management succession plans, and translates it into the form of individual career development programmes and general arrangements for management development, career counselling, mentoring and management training.

Career progression — the competence band approach

It is possible to define career progression in terms of the competences required by individuals to carry out work at progressive levels of responsibility or contribution. These levels can be described as competence bands. Competences would be defined as the skills, knowledge and personal attributes needed to perform effectively at each discrete level in a job family or category. The number of levels would vary according to the range of competences required in a particular job family. For each band, the experience and training needed to achieve the competence level would be defined.

These definitions would provide a career map incorporating 'aiming points' for individuals, who would be made aware of the competence levels they must reach in order to achieve progress in their careers. This would help them to plan their own development, although support and guidance should be provided by their managers, personnel specialists and, if they exist, management development advisers or mentors (the use of mentors is discussed on pages 486–490). The provision of additional experience and training could be arranged as appropriate, but it would be important to clarify what individual employees need to do for themselves if they want to progress within the organization.

The advantage of this approach is that people are provided with aiming points and an understanding of what they need to do to reach them. One of the major causes of frustration and job dissatisfaction is the absence of this information.

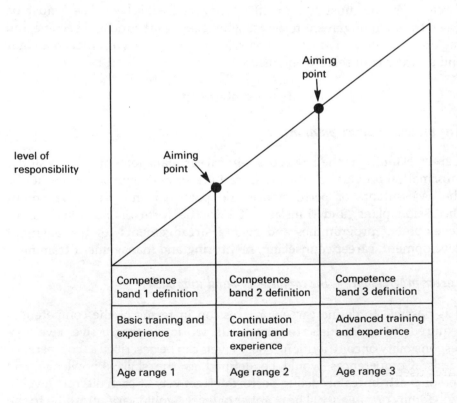

Figure 22.7 Competence band career progression system

A competence band career development approach can be linked to a pay curve salary structure, as described in Chapter 26, thus providing a fully integrated approach to career and reward management which recognizes the need to join these together. The operation of a competence band career progression system is illustrated in Figure 22.7.

Career planning is for core managers as well as high-flyers

The philosophy upon which career plans are based refers not only to advancing careers to meet organizational and individual requirements, but also to the need to maximize the potential of the human resources of the organization in terms of productivity and satisfaction under conditions of change, when 'development' does not necessarily mean promotion. As mentioned earlier in the chapter, an obsession with high-flyers and 'fast-tracking' may lead to a neglect of the majority of employees, who also need to be motivated, encouraged and given every opportunity to use their skills and abilities.

Career planning is for individuals as well as the organization

Career planning procedures are always based on what the organization needs. But they have to recognize that organizational needs will not be satisfied if individual needs are neglected. Career plans must therefore recognize that:

- members of the organization should receive recognition as *individuals* with unique needs, wants, and abilities;
- individuals are more motivated by an organization which responds to their aspirations;
- individuals *can* grow, change and seek new directions if they are given the right opportunities, encouragement and guidance.

Career planning techniques

Career planning uses all the information generated by the succession plans, performance, and potential assessments and self-assessments, to develop programmes and procedures which are designed to implement career management policies, achieve succession planning objectives and generally improve motivation, commitment and performance. The procedures used are those concerned with:

1. training and management development, as described in Chapters 20 and 21;

2.   career counselling and mentoring, as described below.

In addition, career planning procedures may cater for the rising stars by 'fast-tracking' them, that is, deliberately accelerating promotion and giving them opportunities to display and enlarge their talents. But these procedures should pay just as much, if not more, attention to those managers who are following the middle route of steady, albeit unspectacular, progression.

Career counselling

Performance management procedures, as described in Chapter 19, should provide for counselling sessions between individuals and their managers. These sessions should give the former the opportunity to discuss their aspirations and the latter the chance to comment on them — helpfully — and, at a later stage, to put forward specific career development proposals to be fed into the overall career management programme.

Career counselling is, however, a skilled job and the immediate boss is not always the best person to do it, although all managers should be trained in the techniques involved. Some large organizations have appointed specialists whose sole job is to provide a career counselling service to back up the efforts of line managers and to advise on what needs to be done for individuals or, more generally, by the organization as a whole. Mentoring systems, as described in the next section of this chapter, can also be used for this purpose.

The individuals concerned may need an increased level of self-awareness, better access to information about career opportunities and improved decision-making skills. Decision support systems have been developed, such as Career Builder (Hopson and Scally[2]), which explores the individual's values and skills, and RESOLVE (Wooler and Wisuda[3]), which is a programme for training in career decision making. These systems, however, are primarily of interest to young people starting their careers.

Mentoring

Definition

A mentor, according to the *Oxford English Dictionary*, is 'an experienced and trusted counsellor'. Mentoring is the process of using specially selected and trained individuals to provide guidance and advice which will help to develop the careers of the 'protégés' allocated to them.

Aims

The typical aims of the mentoring programme, as suggested by Clutter-buck,[4] are to:

- establish a cadre of broadly trained generalist managers at or just below middle-management level;
- speed up and improve the induction of specific types of recruits and reduce wastage during the early period of employment;
- help top management to assess the abilities of both individual young managers and the rising generation of managers as a whole;
- provide equal opportunities for disadvantaged groups of employees.

Some mentoring systems concentrate on the young high-flyers; some offer a company-wide service for all junior managers and professional or technical staff with some promise, even if they are not 'stars'; while others are concerned only with people entering the organization who need more help and guidance in learning their job and finding their feet than can be provided either by their immediate superior or by formal, induction training courses.

Mentoring is aimed at complementing learning on the job, which must always be the best way of acquiring the particular skills and knowledge the job holder needs. Mentoring also complements formal training by providing those who benefit from it with individual guidance from experienced managers who are 'wise in the ways of the organization'.

Mentoring, however, should have as its main purpose that of furthering the careers of individuals with a future in the organization. It is therefore a necessary part of a career management programme, although it is also an excellent training technique.

The role of the mentor

Mentors provide for the person or persons allocated to them (their 'protégés'):

- guidance on how to acquire the necessary knowledge and skills to do a new job;
- advice on dealing with any administrative, technical or 'people' problems individuals meet, especially in the early stages of their careers;
- information on 'the way things are done around here' — the corporate culture and its manifestations in the shape of core values and organizational behaviour (management style);

- coaching in specific skills, especially managerial skills such as leadership, communication, and time management;
- help in tackling projects — not by doing it for protégés but by pointing them in the right direction, that is — helping people to help themselves;
- a parental figure with whom protégés can discuss their aspirations and concerns and who will lend a sympathetic ear to their problems.

How mentors carry out their role

There are no standard mentoring procedures. Typically, however, a mentor is allocated one or more protégés and given a very general brief to carry out the functions described above.

This brief could be more specific for trainees who may be undergoing a fairly prolonged period of training in a number of departments. In these cases there may be a programme of training and a 'syllabus' defining what trainees have to learn. This could take the form of a 'do-it-yourself' training programme using 'discovery' techniques (both these approaches are described in Appendix K). The mentor's job is to meet the trainees regularly to review progress. Trainees report on what they have done and how they have coped with any problems they have met. They inform their mentor of what they have achieved in carrying out projects allocated to them. If they have been given questions to answer on functions they have been learning about, the mentor may test their understanding. Coaching in various management skills may form part of the programme.

With more experienced individuals for whom the mentor is more in a 'counselling' than a 'coaching' role, the arrangements may be more informal. Regular meetings could be held to discuss progress, aspirations and plans, but the mentor's function might often be no more than to act as a resource to whom people can go for help and advice when they need it.

Launching a mentoring system

The following steps are required to launch a mentoring system:

1. Define objectives.
2. Define the role and functions of mentors.
3. Obtain the support of management, starting at the top.
4. Appoint a senior manager to coordinate the mentoring programme.
5. Identify through performance and potential appraisals individuals who will be allocated to mentors as part of a career management

programme. Also list the trainees for whom mentors will be appointed.

6. Select mentors who have the following attributes:

    (a)   a reasonable degree of seniority;

    (b)   a sound and seasoned knowledge of the company and its political structure;

    (c)   the ability to encourage and motivate;

    (d)   the ability to create an open, candid atmosphere in order that their protégés confide in and trust them;

    (e)   good interpersonal skills for counselling and coaching;

    (f)   a good record for developing people;

    (g)   a wide range of skills and understanding to pass on;

    (h)   a good network of contacts and influence;

    (i)   above all, an interest in mentoring and a willingness to spend time in doing it well.

7. Train mentors in counselling, and coaching and teaching techniques and ensure that they fully understand their role and how they perform it.

8. Brief the managers of individuals who are to be allocated to mentors on what will happen and how they, the managers, as well as the individuals, will benefit. This is important. Without the support of middle management, mentoring systems fail.

9. Allocate protégés to mentors.

10. Follow-up to ensure that the system is working as planned — that mentors are carrying out their role properly, that protégés are benefiting and that their managers are supportive.

Maintaining a mentoring system

Mentoring systems can be launched on a wave of enthusiasm, but can rapidly sink with all hands unless strenuous efforts are made to keep them steaming away in the right direction — just keeping them afloat is not enough. Top management should be encouraged to take a continued interest in the programme, as they will if it is effective and they are told about how it is benefiting the organization. Mentors must be encouraged and, if interest is flagging, stimulated to greater activity. If they cannot or will not cope, they should be relieved of their responsibility. Mentors will come and go, and therefore it is always useful to have some trained people in reserve.

Benefits of a mentoring system

For the organization   The benefits of a mentoring system to the organization are that it will:

- enhance the efficiency and effectiveness of the training for those taking on new roles or being prepared for promotion;
- improve motivation and commitment and thus reduce the rate at which people that the organization needs in the future are lost;
- provide further information on promising individuals in order that career plans can be made for them which will satisfy the organizational requirements for management succession or a flow of well-equipped managers to meet future growth needs.

For individuals   The benefits of mentoring for individuals are that it will:

- enable them to acquire more quickly and comprehensively the skills and understanding they need;
- improve their self-confidence;
- help them to learn how to adjust to the corporate culture and the formal and informal processes that take place in the organization;
- provide them with a means to discuss their hopes and fears, and to realize the former and resolve the latter.

Career progression

A satisfying system of career progression is the overall aim and culminating point of a career management programme. There is a sequence of events and actions required to reach this point, starting with an understanding of the career dynamics and management requirements of the organization and, having defined career management policies, ensuring that each of the activities is coordinated as part of the overall programme.

The benefits of this approach are clear. The organization defines what it needs in the light of an understanding of its situation. Each activity can then be fitted into a systematically prepared action plan. It may never be possible to predict exactly what the organization will need, especially in times of change. Nor can a career management programme, such as the one described in this chapter, guarantee that the organization will get what it wants. But it is much more likely to do so if these methods are used.

An example of a career planning system is given below.

Career planning at W H Smith

Hank Bowen,[5] Divisional Director, Staff and Training for W H Smith, has said:

> Career planning is a prime function of general management at all levels, assisted and guided, but never replaced, by people like myself. The basis of career planning must be the efficient and correct measurement of performance and potential. . . .
>
> However, I must now face you with an unpalatable truth. It is a fact, which must be recognized, that in any organization, no matter how large or small, half the management team will have reached their ceiling half way through their career. . . . Management succession is a pyramid *not* a ladder. It is a balance between the aspirations, ambitions, hopes of the individual and the needs of the company for high potential, well motivated, highly trained and developed individuals, both for the present and the future. This does not mean that half the management team is on the scrap heap aged 40-plus. They have a very useful career and working life ahead of them. However, their chances of rising further in the hierarchy will be limited.

The career review procedure is designed to provide a framework within which both the individual and the company work together to make use of the individual's talents and aspirations and to assess the requirements for training and development. It is normally conducted for the top 250 managers every three years in addition to the annual performance review.

There are five sections to the review:

1. *Present facts:* i.e. educational, professional and technical qualifications, vocational and management training programmes attended, employment experience outside the company, employment within the company after a set period of years, and current job title.
2. *Personal qualities:* the individuals' perceptions of their own strengths and weaknesses.
3. *Individual future plans:* the individuals' plans and aspirations for the future.
4. *The assessment of managerial skills:* by a director or senior manager.
5. *Future intentions:* long-term possibilities of career development. These are not firm plans or intentions but a summary of possibilities that enable individuals to be trained and developed. This part is completed under divisional director guidance and remains confidential information.

The review process involves assessors (senior managers plus directors) in:

1. agreeing or otherwise the individual's personal assessment;

2. discussing the individual's ambitions and proposed development;
3. grading the individual on performance in the present job;
4. grading the individual's readiness to be promoted to the next level;
5. commenting on the individual's aspirations;
6. proposing any career development steps, which might include further experience in the same job or a job at the same level as well as or instead of training;
7. identifying training needs for longer-term development;
8. indicating mid- and long-term potential and possible job moves over the next five years together with an estimate of when the manager will be able to take up his or her next job (this section is completed by directors).

Finally, career reviews for managers in the top three grades are seen by their executive director, while the chairman and the managing director see the reviews of all the top-level managers.

References

1. Davies, J and Deighan, Y 'The Managerial Menopause', *Personnel Management*, March 1986.
2. Hopson, B and Scally, M *Career Building: A Computer Programme for Managing Your Own Career*, Lifeskills Associates/UHA, Leeds, 1984.
3. Wooler, S and Wisuda, A 'An educational approach in designing computer-based career guidance systems', *British Journal of Educational Technology* 16(2), 1985.
4. Clutterbuck, D *Everyone Needs a Mentor*, Institute of Personnel Management, London, 1985.
5. Bowen, H, as reported in Armstrong, M *Personnel and the Bottom Line*. Institute of Personnel Management, London, 1989.

Part VI
Reward Management

Reward management means designing, implementing and maintaining pay systems which are geared to the improvement of organizational performance. This aspect of personnel management used to be called salary administration, but this is now regarded as a limited description of one aspect of the whole subject of payment which is concerned only with administering the pay system and exercising control over the implementation of pay policies. The alternative phrase 'compensation management' is used in the US and is gaining recognition in the UK. It is generally used to represent a more up-to-date approach to creating and managing pay systems, but the use of the word 'compensation' seems to imply that work is an unpleasant necessity which people have to be compensated for doing rather than spending their time more rewardingly elsewhere.[1] 'Reward management' is the term used in this book because it describes a more positive approach to paying people for what they have done and can do for the enterprise and for themselves by contributing effectively to the achievement of organizational objectives.

In this part, the basis of reward management is examined first. Consideration is given to reward management strategies and policies, the factors affecting pay levels, and the importance of communicating to employees information about the benefits they receive. A vital consideration throughout this part of the handbook is how to get value for money out of the reward management system by ensuring that it fits the organization's strategies, underpins organizational values, aids recruitment *and retention, increases motivation and commitment and generally adds value by providing leverage for the improvement of performance and productivity.*

It is, however, noted that financial rewards are not the only way to achieve motivation and commitment. Emphasis is placed on the role of intrinsic motivation and the part played by various forms of non-financial reward in enhancing it.

Chapters 24 and 25 examine the two principal criteria which govern pay systems and levels: first, the need to be competitive and therefore the importance of establishing market rates to track the organization's relative position in the marketplace, and, secondly, the need to be internally equitable and the process of achieving this, as far as possible, by means of job evaluation.

Chapter 26 reviews the various kinds of pay systems and structures for salaried staff (or for all employees when terms and conditions have been harmonized). Chapter 27 considers all aspects of performance-related pay and Chapter 28 examines wage payment systems, noting, however, that these are increasingly being integrated with salary systems.

23

The Basis of Reward Management

Definition

Reward management is the process of developing and implementing strategies, policies and systems which help the organization to achieve its objectives by obtaining and keeping the people it needs and by increasing their motivation and commitment. It therefore means rewarding people in accordance with their value to the organization as measured by their actual and potential contribution. It also means recognizing that people have their own needs and goals and that the organization must be constantly aware that it must match its rewards and incentives to these people.

Thus, reward management is concerned with both financial and non-financial rewards and although this part of the book is about various forms of remuneration, that does not mean that the significance of the non-financial elements is underestimated. Beer[1] put this point well:

> Organizations must reward employees because in return they are looking for certain kinds of behaviour: they need competent individuals who agree to work with a high level of performance and loyalty. Individual employees, in exchange for their commitment, expect certain intrinsic rewards in the forms of promotions, salary, fringe benefits, perquisites, bonuses or, stock options. Individuals also seek intrinsic rewards such as feelings of competence, achievement, responsibility, significance, influence, personal growth, and meaningful contribution. Employees will judge the adequacy of their exchange with the organization by assessing both sets of rewards.

The reward management system — strategy and processes

The reward management system is illustrated in Figure 23.1 as a set of relationships between the various reward management processes and

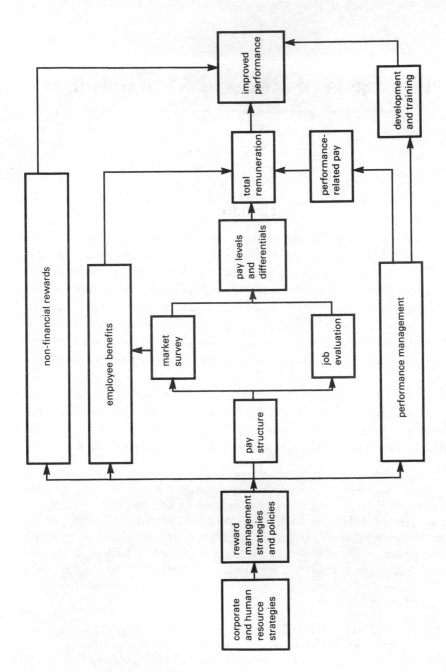

Figure 23.1 Reward management — strategy and processes

corporate strategy. This shows that reward management strategies and policies are driven by corporate and human resource management strategies. These provide guidance on the processes required in four main areas: (a) non-financial rewards; (b) employee benefits; (c) pay structure; and (d) performance management. All of these contribute as follows to the ultimate aim of improved performance:

- Non-financial rewards satisfy individual needs for variety, challenge, responsibility, influence in decision making, recognition, and opportunity.
- Employee benefits satisfy employees' needs for personal security and provide remuneration in forms other than pay, which meet other needs and which are also frequently tax efficient.
- Pay structures, by combining the results of market surveys (which also contribute to decisions on benefit levels) and job evaluation, define levels of pay and differentials and pay progression limits.
- Performance management, on the basis of continuing as well as formal reviews of performance against targets and standards, leads to the design of the performance-related pay (PRP) systems and development and training programmes.
- Employee benefits and basic and performance-related pay combine to form total remuneration.

Reward management strategies

Definition

Reward management strategies define the intentions of the organization on the remuneration policies and systems required to ensure that it continues to obtain, motivate and retain the committed and competent people it needs to accomplish its mission.

Purpose and aim

Reward management strategies address critical, longer-term issues concerning how employees should be rewarded. As declarations of intent, they provide the basis for deciding how the reward system can help to achieve the objectives of the organization and how the system should be designed and managed.

For a business, the aim of reward management strategies should be to help it to achieve sustainable competitive advantage. In a non profit-making organization, the aim should be to enable it to reach higher levels of service and performance. These aims are achieved by developing and reinforcing high levels of performance to meet the requirements of the organization.

The basis of reward strategies

Reward management strategies must:

- be congruent with and support corporate values and beliefs;
- emanate from business strategy and goals;
- be linked to organization performance;
- drive and support desired behaviour at all levels;
- fit desired management style;
- provide the competitive edge needed to attract and retain the high level of skills the organization needs.

The contribution of reward strategies

Reward strategies can make a significant contribution to the achievement of corporate and functional objectives by:

- developing a positive culture — in Kanter's[2] words, 'a culture of pride and a climate of success';
- underpinning the organization's values, especially those concerned with excellence, performance, teamwork and quality;
- conveying a message to prospective high-calibre employees that the organization will satisfy their reward expectations;
- ensuring that the right mix and levels of reward are provided in line with the culture of the organization, the needs of the business, the needs of employees and the economic, competitive, and market environment in which the business operates;
- linking reward policies, systems and procedures to the key business and human resource strategies for innovation, growth, development and the pursuit of excellence;
- developing a strong orientation toward the achievement of sustained high levels of performance throughout the organization by recognizing successful performance and increases in levels of competence, thus contributing to the processes of empowering, enabling, and energizing all employees;
- indicating to existing employees what types of behaviour will be rewarded and how this will take place, thus increasing motivation and commitment and improving performance.

The components of reward management strategy

Reward management strategy covers the following areas:

- *reward policies* — the roles of different elements of the reward system: how the system should fit the culture of the organization and can help to reinforce or reshape it; the types and levels of rewards to be offered; the design of the system; how the system relates to the external environment; and how the tension between the aims of a reasonable degree of internal equity and external competitiveness can be managed (see below);
- *pay levels and relativities* — the analysis of market rates and the use of job evaluation to develop pay structures (see Chapters 24 and 25);
- *reward structures* — the development and design of pay structures (see Chapter 26);
- *paying for performance* — the design and management of systems of performance-related pay, relating to individual, group, or corporate achievements (see Chapter 27);
- *employee benefits and total remuneration* — the development of the employee benefit package and the use of a total remuneration approach to reward management (see Chapter 29).

Integrating reward management strategies

Reward management strategies should flow directly from these human resource strategies, which in turn are derived from the overall strategies of the organization. The following are ten ways in which reward management strategies can help to implement human resource and business strategies:

1. stimulate and direct effort towards the achievement of corporate goals for added value and competitive gain;
2. convey clear messages on corporate values relating to innovation, endeavour, performance, teamwork and quality;
3. underpin these values by linking rewards to accomplishment and contribution;
4. establish and clarify priorities for people in terms of their principal accountabilities;
5. attract high-quality people who fit the culture of the organization and grow and contribute to its success;
6. encourage enterprise and strategic thinking;

7. ensure that high-quality staff prosper and stay with the organization;
8. deliver messages to poor performers that they must improve or go;
9. avoid demotivating the people the company wishes to retain;
10. motivate the majority of reliable 'core' performers as well as the minority of high-flyers.

The basis of reward management policies

Policies on how rewards should be managed need to be formulated as guidelines on the implementation of reward management strategies.

Reward policies cover areas such as: levels of reward; paying for performance; the reconciliation of the tension between the need to achieve external competitiveness as well as a reasonable degree of internal equity; the extent to which decisions on pay can be delegated to line managers; the type of salary structure which is most appropriate; and the degree to which a flexible approach can realistically be adopted toward total remuneration — allowing some element of choice for employees on the level and mix of employee benefits and cash.

The starting-point must be the philosophy of the organization toward rewards. The policies can then be developed in the light of this philosophy and an understanding of the factors affecting (a) reward policies; and (b) actual and potential satisfaction with the reward system.

Reward philosophies

As stated in the Top Pay Unit's 1990 publilcation, *Putting Pay Philosophies into Practice*,[3]

> Behind every pay system is a pay philosophy — a set of aims and assumptions which underpins the reward structure and determines its form. A pay philosophy can reflect an existing company culture, or it can be used as an agent for change. . . . Having a well-considered pay philosophy is the first step towards creating a salary structure which will assist in the recruitment and retention of high-quality executives and specialists.

The pay philosophy should be articulated because it governs the company's approach to how it rewards its employees, the objectives it wants the pay system to achieve and the way in which it wants to manage the system.

Reward philosophies have been influenced strongly by changes in the environment in which companies operate. The enterprise culture, as a product of the 1980s, may not seem so relevant in the less aggressive

1990s, although it has created the strong pressures for flexibility, performance-related pay and responsiveness to the market which still prevail. However, pay philosophies increasingly recognize that financial rewards are not the only way to increase motivation and commitment. Many people responsible for human resource management know that attention has to be paid to adopting an integrated approach to reward and performance management which makes use of intrinsic as well as extrinsic motivators.

Developing reward policies

Within the framework of the organization's pay philosophy, reward policies should be developed on the basis of an understanding of:

1. the factors affecting employee performance and motivation;
2. the factors affecting reward levels;
3. the influence of corporate culture and organization;
4. the factors influencing employee satisfaction with the reward system.

The factors that affect performance and motivation

The ingredients of high performance
High performance requires that employees be:

- energized to perform because they are well motivated and highly committed;
- empowered to perform because they have the ability, skills and know-how needed to achieve the levels of competence required;
- enabled to perform through the guidance and support provided to them, the quality of leadership and the autonomy they are given to decide, act and exercise control over their work.

Motivation
The role of money as a motivator was discussed fully in Chapter 7, which concluded that although money in itself has no intrinsic meaning, it can acquire significant motivating power because it may symbolize so many intangible goals. Pay is undoubtedly an important factor in attracting and retaining people. But financial rewards act as incentives only if people's expectations that they can earn them are high, the reward is worth the effort and there is a clear link between effort and reward. Performance improvements result from a multiplicity of factors of which money is only one.

Factors influencing reward levels

The factors influencing reward levels are the following:

- individual worth;
- external relativities;
- internal relativities;
- union pressures.

Individual worth

The value of the contributions made by individuals to achieving organizational goals should determine their rewards. This process must not be constrained by the artificial barriers built into rigid salary structures.

External relativities

A salary or wage rate is a price indicating, like any other price, the value of the service to the buyer and seller: the employer and the employed. Those who emphasize the importance of market forces assert that a job is worth what the market says it is worth. There is much to be said for this point of view. If insufficient attention is given to market rates, a company may be unable to attract and retain good-quality staff. External equity is a fundamental aim of any reward system: most people look first at the salary level stated in advertisements when seeking a job. Within a company, staff study advertised salaries to find out if they are being paid fairly in relation to the market, and this provides data which help them to decide whether to stay or to look around for another job.

The external value of a job — the market rate — is primarily determined by the laws of supply or demand. If people in a particular occupation are in short supply, they are in a seller's market and can force up prices (ie pay levels). The opposite applies in a buyer's market where there is a surplus of labour. But the labour market is generally not a perfect market. Employers and unions can exert monopolistic pressures to counteract free-market focus. People are not always guided by purely economic factors. They may seek or accept substitutes for their present jobs for what may be largely subjective reasons, rather than on the grounds of an analysis of relative economic values. And one of the factors they consider is the quality of life the organizations provide — job satisfaction, the work environment and, importantly, the opportunity to use their skills and develop their careers.

Those who assert the supremacy of market forces say that because reward systems are caused by the market, the systems themselves cannot be deemed unfair or inappropriate because they are at the mercy of the market — they are incapable of causing anything. In reality, because it can be difficult to link pay directly to performance, all the market does is to allow us to assume that people occupying equal positions tend to be paid equally, and that people with similar experience and education tend to be worth about the same. As Kanter[2] put it: 'The process is circular . . . . we know what people are worth because that's what they cost in the job market, but we also know that what people cost in the market is just what they're worth.'

Be that as it may, no enterprise can afford to ignore the 'going rate' or, as it should properly be described, the going range, if it wants to attract and retain good-quality staff. Although internal salary structures are not directly and instantaneously responsive to market forces at all points, the general structure must move up or down and differentials must expand or contract in response to the changing pressures of the market. The points of pressure are most likely to be at the intake points in a structure, for example, among newly qualified accountants, computer specialists or experienced brand managers.

Internal relativities

The value of a job within an organization is relative. There is no such thing as absolute value. The value of anything is always comparative.

Within an organization, pay levels are affected by real or perceived differences between the value of jobs and the individual contributions made by job holders. Differentials have to be maintained, although these may be distorted by the influence of accepted market differentials. It could be argued, however, that differentials established in a market from which a company recruits are correct simply because they are there, and internal differentials have to take account of what the market dictates.

Trade union pressures

To achieve their aims, as described earlier in this chapter, trade unions exert pressure on pay levels. This impact on the reward system, will, of course, depend on their bargaining power. It is interesting to note that where staff associations have been fostered by management to keep unions out, they have often been able to enforce higher awards because the company has been over-anxious to preserve the staff association's independence against all comers from the real trade union movement.

In the new climate, unions are becoming much more involved in the whole process of productivity, quality and performance improvement. In many cases a more flexible approach is being encouraged by a new generation of more sophisticated negotiators who appreciate that this will benefit their members by increasing their prosperity and their security in a thriving organization.

Corporate culture

The reward system should fit the corporate culture, but it can also be used as a lever for change. Some cultures, for example, in voluntary organizations, do not support incentive payment schemes because they are too individualistic. The culture in aggressively entrepreneurial businesses may, however, result in a reward system with a strong emphasis on individual incentives. The reward system can help to shape culture by underpinning values such as high performance. It can be used to deliver messages on what the company believes is important by relating rewards to specific aspects of performance.

Organization

A tightly organized company may prefer a bureaucratic pay system which controls everything at the centre. A more loosely organized company, especially one which is growing and changing rapidly, will not want to overformalize its procedures. It needs flexibility to respond quickly to change. An autocratic style of management will result in control from the top, no participation in formulating policies and as little disclosure of information by the company as possible.

A flattened or de-layered organizational structure requires better teamwork among managers, and therefore group rather than individual bonus or incentive schemes might be more appropriate. A highly decentralized organization might allow a fair degree of leeway to enable local management to develop its own approaches to the reward system (for example, type of structure or bonus scheme), as long as certain broadly defined corporate policies are followed.

The factors that affect satisfaction with the reward system

The degree to which employees are satisfied with the reward system is related to the following factors:

1. *Fairness* — the extent to which they think the system is fair in that rewards are commensurate with ability, contribution, and effort. This is what Jaques[4] describes as the 'felt-fair' principle. He believes that

there is an unrecognized system of norms for fair payment and that individuals are 'unconsciously aware of their own potential capacity for work, as well as the equitable pay level for that work'. To be fair, pay must be felt to match the level of work and the capacity of the individual to do it.

2. *Expectations and value* — satisfaction is highest when rewards meet expectations as to their value and the value of the reward is commensurate with the effort and skill needed to obtain it.

3. *Internal comparisons* — employees are more likely to be satisfied if they feel they are being paid correctly in relation to what other employees who are doing similar jobs at a similar level of competence are receiving. Dissatisfaction may be caused by perceived inequities because people have insufficient information on how salary policy affects them and are therefore not in a position to compare their worth with others; hence the importance of a fair and open job evaluation system and a convincing demonstration that pay is fairly related to performance. Given the problem of achieving effective communication and the innate suspicion with which many employees view their company's pay policies, this can be very difficult. It is hardly surprising in these circumstances that many performance-related pay schemes are more successful at demotivating than motivating people.

4. *External comparisons* — satisfaction and commitment to stay with the organization are most probable if people feel that present *and* future rewards are likely to be higher within the organization than elsewhere. This is often a matter of perception, which may be misguided (based on the 'grass is greener on the other side of the fence' principle). It is therefore sometimes difficult for organizations to reduce feelings of dissatisfaction in this area, especially if promotion prospects are limited.

5. *Self-evaluation* — if rewards are in line with what people feel they are worth then satisfaction will result. The problem is that, as Beer[1] points out, individuals tend to overrate their own performance: 'It has been found that many employees rate their performance in the eightieth percentile. Given the fact that an organization cannot pay everyone at the eightieth percentile it is not surprising that many employees feel they are being underpaid'.

6. *The total reward package* — overall satisfaction depends on the result of a mix of rewards rather than any single reward. Beer suggests: 'The evidence seems to be clear that intrinsic rewards and extrinsic rewards are both important, and that they are not directly substitutable for each other. Employees who are paid well for repetitive, boring work

will be dissatisfied with the lack of intrinsic rewards, just as employees paid poorly for interesting, challenging work may be dissatisfied with extrinsic rewards.'

Overall implications for reward policy

This analysis of the factors affecting reward management suggests that the following considerations should be taken into account when formulating reward policies:

1. An appropriate mix of rewards is required which is flexible enough to satisfy, as far as possible, the needs of both the organization and its employees.
2. The reward system should be geared to the attainment of goals but should also recognize the importance of ensuring that there is a clear relationship between effort/ability and reward.
3. Attention has to be given to determining the right levels of financial rewards in relation to the needs of the organization to attract, retain and motivate (or avoid demotivating) staff, the ability of the organization to provide the rewards, and the needs and expectations of employees.
4. In deciding on reward levels, one must consider external comparisons (market rates) and the achievement of a reasonable degree of internal equity.
5. The type of pay structure and how employees should be rewarded in relation to their performance have to be considered in the light of the culture of the organization and employee expectations. This also affects the degree of freedom managers are allowed with which to manage reward.
6. The degree to which employees are involved in developing reward policies and practices needs to be determined.
7. Employees should be informed about the system and the way it affects them. Also, their expectations should be managed within the bounds of what is realistic in their particular circumstances.

Reward policy areas

The main areas in which policies need to be formulated are:

- the relationship of rewards to business performance;
- flexibility;
- the level of rewards;
- market rates;

- equity;
- performance-related rewards;
- pay structures;
- delegation and control;
- balancing financial and non-financial motivators;
- the reward mix and the total;
- communicating the benefits.

The relationship of rewards to business performance

A policy needs to be formulated on how pay levels should respond to fluctuations in business performance. Raising basic salaries during times of business buoyancy can create problems. The resulting higher salaries could be a serious cost burden in future years if there is a downturn in the business. Furthermore, it implies that the ability to pay is sufficient justification for higher salaries and this may conflict with other remuneration policies which lay down that individual rates of pay should be related only to performance, competence and responsibility. Business success is best shared with employees either through a profit-sharing scheme (see Chapter 27) or by one-off bonus payments which do not have a cost commitment in future years.

Flexibility

Reward policies should allow for flexibility in operating the reward system in response to business fluctuations, the rapidly changing pressures to which the organization and its employees are likely to be subjected, the demand for different types of skills and variations in market rates for different categories of staff.

Flexibility can be achieved by:

- increasing the proportion of variable performance-related pay in the total package;
- avoiding the use of rigid, hierarchical pay structures by such means as the use of pay curves, where progression is dependent on competence and performance (see Chapter 26);
- not having a mechanistic system of relating rewards to performance;
- relating pay awards entirely to merit and increases in market rates, thus avoiding a separate and explicit link with increases in the cost of living, and giving scope to reward the good performers more and the poor performers less;

- allowing greater choice in the range of benefits employees receive;
- recognizing that the organization must respond quickly to the problems created by skill shortages and market rate pressures, and flexing the pay arrangements accordingly.

Levels of reward

The policy on reward levels should determine whether or not the company needs to be a high payer. This is sometimes called its pay posture, the policy on where rates of pay and fringe benefit packages should lie in relation to what comparable companies pay for similar jobs. This policy is linked to the one on market rates.

Fast-moving, profitable companies want top people and, if they want to stay in front, pay top rates, or at least in the upper quartile of the range of pay for similar jobs in comparable companies. They go to great efforts to ensure that they maintain that position. Small concerns, such as advertising agencies working on high margins which depend entirely on the talent of their staff, pay exceptionally good salaries and provide some magnificent benefits. So much so, that the companies outside this particular 'magic circle' cannot possibly compete.

Other organizations may seek to pay closer to the median — to keep pace with market rates. The author has rarely come across companies which admit that it is their policy to pay below the median. Obviously, however, that is where half of them are, possibly because they are unaware of the fact, and not through any deliberate actions on their part.

Performance-related rewards

The extent to which performance governs rewards and how the two are linked together depends absolutely on the core values of the organization. Thrusting, thriving and growing companies have to be entrepreneurial. And they must encourage what Pinchot[5] describes as an *intrapreneurial* spirit. He defines this as taking hands-on responsibility for creating innovation of any kind within an organization. The intrapreneur may not be the creator or inventor but is always the dreamer who figures out how to turn an idea into a profitable reality.

Intrapreneurship within an enterprise should flourish if people believe that the game is worth the candle, ie that potential rewards justify the effort or the risk that have to be put into achieving them. They must *expect* that the value of their contribution to the organization will be rewarded appropriately.

Market rate policy

How far should market rate pressures be allowed to affect or possibly distort a salary structure? They cannot be ignored completely, but there is an element of choice. It might be decided that the salaries for certain jobs have to keep pace with the market. These would be distinguished as special market rates in the salary structure ('red circled') or put into a separate market group. The salaries of other jobs would primarily be fixed by internal comparisons, possibly using as upper and lower limits the chief executive's salary and the salary levels required to maintain a reasonable differential between first-line supervision and the clerical staff or operatives they control. Alternatively, salary levels for all key jobs may be assessed by reference to market rates, which would also indicate differentials between functions and between levels in the hierarchy. The main factor in assessing the influence that external salary levels should be allowed to exercise internally is the degree to which there is open market competition for staff. The less the need to go to the market, the less the need to react to short-term pressures.

In formulating market rate policy, one should remember that the company is probably operating in several different labour markets. There are the local market for more junior employees; the national market for managerial, professional and highly technical staff; and, possibly, the international market. The increasing importance and relevance of international influences as more and more companies base themselves in the UK, and overseas firms look for talent in the UK, may strongly influence reward policies. Labour markets are becoming increasingly fragmented — between different sections of industry or commerce, for different occupations and in different areas.

Market rate policies have therefore to be flexible and continuously under review in order that they can be quickly and easily adjusted to the needs of the organization and changes in the labour markets.

Equity

Equity is a perceived sense that pay policies are just and fair because pay matches individual contribution, capacity and the level of work carried out; pay differentials are related to finite differences in the degree of responsibility; and equal pay is received for equal work. Absolute equity is an unattainable ideal, but the policy should be to achieve as high a degree of equity as possible by adopting a systematic and analytical approach to establishing the value of jobs. It is, however, often difficult to reconcile the two aims of being equitable *and* competitive. It may be hard to avoid paying higher than internal rates for comparable jobs in order to attract the right people. Market forces sometimes have to be allowed to prevail.

This does not imply that elaborate job evaluation schemes are essential. It is possible to be both systematic and analytical, without calling on the aid of an overcomplicated job evaluation scheme. In this context, 'systematic' means a methodical collection of facts about market rates and contents of the jobs, and 'analytical' means the resolution of the data into elements to increase the ease and accuracy with which comparisons can be made between different jobs. The choice of method is wide and the alternatives are discussed in Chapter 25.

Pay structures

The main policy questions to be answered about pay structures are the following:

- Is a formal structure required?
- If a formal structure is necessary, what sort of structure should it have?

Some companies work without a formal structure quite successfully. They decide on a starting rate for a job on some *ad hoc* basis and adjust it as and when required. They can operate flexibly and react quickly to events, and this may be desirable in a fluid situation. The obvious danger is that salaries will be dealt with inconsistently and inequitably, unless there is rigid central control, which is not always possible of desirable. By its very name, a salary structure implies a certain amount of rigidity. But this need not be so. A structure can and should be no more than an understood framework within which consistent salary policies can be applied. It is possible to design and operate salary structures which enable a sufficient degree of flexibility to be achieved but allow for an adequate amount of control in order to avoid inequities and excessive costs. The pay curve system, as described in Chapter 26, is a means of achieving this.

Control

The extent to which control can be exercised is partly determined by the choice of salary progression system and salary structure, but it is also a matter of the amount of freedom that is allowed to managers to fix and change the salaries of their staff. This, like so many other aspects of reward management, depends largely on the management style of the company (ie the degree to which decisions are centralized and autocratic or are decentralized and independent). Some central control over the implementation of salary policies and salary costs is necessary, but the aim should be to delegate as much authority as possible to managers. The reward management procedures of the company must, therefore, be designed to achieve a delicate balance between the extremes of rigidity or anarchy.

Balancing financial and non-financial rewards

Reward policy has to strike a balance between the mix of intrinsic (entirely non-financial) and extrinsic (mainly financial) rewards. Neither should be neglected, bearing in mind that financial rewards are important as a means of attracting and retaining staff and achieving short-term motivation, while non-financial rewards are more likely to achieve longer-term motivation and commitment.

Total remuneration

There is usually some choice in deciding the best mix of the various elements of remuneration: basic salary, bonus, profit sharing, pensions, life insurance, cars and other fringe benefits. The mix may vary at different levels. For junior staff, the best approach may be to concentrate on straight salary with some scope for progression according to merit, together with the usual pension and life insurance provisions, and either subsidized canteens or luncheon vouchers as the only additional benefit. At senior-management level where individuals will appreciate, and, indeed, where the market dictates a wider range of benefits, the mix could become much more complicated.

At this level (or below), it could be decided, as a matter of policy, that the aim should be to concentrate on paying a competitive salary at a rate high enough to allow individuals to purchase for themselves the benefits they need. This could be held to be preferable to imposing fringe benefits on individuals who may not want them, or providing fringe benefits on an inequitable basis to a favoured few who happen to become eligible for them. On the other hand, the tax advantage to the company or the individual may make the provision of a benefit such as a car or a generous pension scheme preferable to an addition to basic salary. In areas of very high pay, tax planning still has a very important part to play.

Communication

If money is a motivator, it is right and proper that people be told what is available to them in order that they can be motivated by it. If equity is the first consideration, the fairness of the system has to be seen to be believed. But how can the system motivate if left to its own devices? — if people are unsure why the system was developed, suspect that it is unfair, or are unsure about how their pay is linked to performance, or what their future rewards are going to be as they take on greater responsibility? And how can the company get any mileage out of its logical, equitable, competitive, and even creative reward system; its high level of rewards; or its generous employee benefits package if it does not tell its employees all about them?

Payment systems can sometimes demotivate even more effectively than they motivate, as Herzberg[6] established by his classic study, *The Motivation to Work*. This is because they often seem to be unfair. Pay is perceived as being either inequitable or not commensurate with performance. Jaques'[5] felt-fair principle states that people feel their pay ought to be fair in relation to their personal contribution, to what other people are being paid within the organization, and to what is being paid by other organizations for similar jobs. If management wants to motivate its employees, these expectations must be satisfied. It is worth remembering that the most respected theory of motivation — the expectancy theory — states that it is what people *expect* to get, if it is worth having, which motivates them most effectively, not what they already have.

Therefore it is important to motivate people by telling them that what they have is worth having — if that is the case — and even more important to tell them what they can expect. This starts with the recruitment process and ends with the way in which retirement or, indeed, severance is handled. If they have been rewarded for doing well, that has to be communicated to them. If they are going to get higher rewards for doing even better in the future, that must also be communicated, but more forcibly.

The following is what you should communicate to staff in general and to individual employees:

Staff in general

1. *The company salary policy*: This sets out the principles followed in setting pay and benefit levels.
2. *The pay and benefits structure*: This defines the salary brackets for each grade and the benefits available, including details of the pension scheme.

3. *Methods of grading and regrading jobs*: Where job evaluation exists, details will be given of the job evaluation scheme, including how evaluations are carried out and the right to appeal against gradings.
4. *Salary progression*: The method by which salaries are progressed within grades or within a salary curve system.
5. *Incentive/bonus schemes*: Details of any incentive, bonus, profit sharing, or share purchase schemes, including how bonuses or profit shares are calculated and distributed and the procedures for purchasing shares.
6. *Reward systems and organizational change*: How remuneration policy is affected by mergers/takeovers, change in corporate direction and, indeed, the bad news of liquidation and closure.

Individual employees

1. *Job grade*: What their grade is and how it has been determined.
2. *Salary progression*: The limit to which their salary can go in their present grade and the rate at which it can progress through the grade, depending on performance.
3. *Potential*: Their potential for higher salaries following promotion, subject to meeting defined performance criteria and the availability of suitable positions. In other words, this information, plus that contained under the heading of salary progression, should create expectations of what staff can get and define the action or behaviour they have to do to get there.
4. *Performance appraisal*: How performance and potential are assessed, including details of the criteria used, the method of assessment and the right of the employee to know what his or her assessment is and why it has taken that form.
5. *Salary levels* The reasons for the level of reward employees are getting or the salary increase at the last review and what they must do to get more.
6. *Benefit statement*: The value of the benefits the individual employee receives in order that he or she appreciates the level of his or her total remuneration.

Managing reward to improve results

The following are ten approaches which can be adopted to make sure that, in practice, reward management strategies, policies and systems fulfil their promise of improving organizational effectiveness and performance:

1. Relate pay systems to organizational needs and culture.

2. Relate pay to contribution.
3. Establish performance criteria.
4. Assess performance against the criteria.
5. Evaluate jobs systematically to achieve a reasonable degree of equity.
6. Monitor market rates to maintain competitiveness.
7. Segment the pay structure into market groups as required.
8. Ensure that the pay system promotes rather than discourages flexibility.
9. Communicate the message about the system and how and why it benefits employees.
10. Remember the other forms of intrinsic and extrinsic motivation.

References

1. Beer, M 'Reward systems', from Michael Beer, Bert Spector, Paul R Laurence, and D Quinn Mills *Managing Human Assets*. Free Press, New York, 1984.
2. Kanter, R *When Giants Learn to Dance*. Simon & Schuster, London, 1989.
3. Top Pay Unit *Putting Pay Philosophies into Practice*. Incomes Data Services, London, 1990.
4. Jaques, E *Equitable Payment*. Heinemann, London, 1961.
5. Pinchot, G *Intrapreneuring*. Harper & Row, New York, 1985.
6. Herzberg, F *et al*, *The Motivation to Work*. Wiley, New York, 1959.

24

Establishing Market Rates

Purpose

Competitive salary levels and pay structures can be developed and maintained only if the external market is regularly and systematically checked. This can be done by using a range of sources, from large-scale, formal salary and benefits surveys to job advertisements, companies' annual reports, informal confidential contacts and other forms of market intelligence.

Job evaluation schemes can be used to determine internal relativities, but, in themselves, they cannot put a price to the job. To a large extent, pay levels are subject to market forces which have to be taken into account in negotiations and in fixing the rates for particular jobs. Some specialized jobs may not be subject to the same external pressures as others, but it is still necessary to know what effect market rates are likely to have on the pay structure as a whole before deciding on internal pay differentials which properly reflect levels of skill and responsibility. It has also to be accepted that market pressures and negotiations affect differentials within the firm. An employer may be unwilling to submit to individual pressure because of the danger that it will distort the structure. But it may sometimes be necessary to recognize the compelling force of market or union demands in one area and adjust rates accordingly. Wherever possible such adjustments should be regarded as special measures and an attempt should be made to contain their influence on other scales by isolating them as exceptions ('red-circling').

The purpose of both published and privately conducted surveys is to provide accurate and representative data on the current range of salaries or wage rates paid for the jobs or levels of responsibility in question. These need to be looked at in relation to company size, industry type, ownership, location, and other factors such as particular market pressures which affect what the market is prepared to pay.

Despite great improvements in sampling and analysis, salary surveys and other forms of pay analysis can sometimes be misleading and should perhaps never be taken entirely at face value. The concept of the market rate, even in the local labour market, is an inexact one. It is noticeable that for identical jobs there is always a range of rates paid by different employers. This is particularly so in managerial jobs and other occupations where duties can vary considerably between companies, even if the job title is the same. It is therefore possible to use pay surveys only to provide a broad indication of market rates. Judgement has to be used in interpreting the results of special enquiries or the data from published surveys. There is usually plenty of scope for selecting evidence which supports whatever case is being advanced.

Information on the rates paid by other firms can come from the following sources:

- company surveys;
- club surveys;
- local surveys conducted by employers, unions or other bodies;
- general published surveys;
- analyses of job advertisements.

Company surveys

Company surveys are conducted when specific information is required of the pay and benefits provided by comparable companies for similar jobs. The steps required to conduct a company survey are to:

1. Draw up a list of suitable companies which are compatible with regard to industry, size and the sort of jobs they are likely to have.
2. Approach each company. It is clearly best to maintain a list of friendly contacts who, from experience, are known to give reliable information. These may develop into a 'club' which can operate at various levels of formality in exchanging information on a regular or an as-required basis. If such contacts or a club are not readily available it may be necessary to approach a company out of the blue and ask for information. This has obviously to be provided on a reciprocal basis and it may sometimes be possible to offer the *quid pro quo* of an anonymous summary of the results. In such contacts, the messages that have to be got across are that:

    (a) A responsible individual is conducting the survey.

(b) The survey will be carried out competently and in confidence.

(c) The reciprocal information provided will be relevant and useful.

(d) The company being approached will not be put to too much trouble.

3. Prepare job data and, if necessary, survey forms. It may be possible to obtain the information required over the telephone, but it is necessary to have information about the jobs ready to ensure that like is being compared with like. If a postal survey is being conducted, it is even more necessary to provide basic data about the duties and responsibilities of the jobs to assist in making valid comparisons. A pro forma may be prepared by the surveying company for completion by the participating company to save time and trouble and to help in the subsequent analysis. The form should provide spaces for the information required on pay scales, actual salaries paid, overtime earnings and, for wage earners, details of basic rates, regular total earnings, variations in earnings, the make-up of total earnings (base rates, bonuses, overtime, shift payments, etc) and hours worked.

4. Where it is difficult to make valid comparisons by telephone or post by reference to outline job descriptions, it may be possible to carry out on-the-spot enquiries, if other companies are willing to participate. Much more can be got out of a face-to-face discussion which will clarify any differences in responsibilities that may affect comparisons. The best results are obtained if the parties agree to benchmark jobs being analysed and compared, using a common method of job evaluation which compares agreed factors as in a points or factor comparison scheme.

5. Analyse the information obtained from the survey, ensuring that as far as possible like jobs are being compared and that the details provided on pay distinguish between basic rates and piecework, overtime, and shiftwork earnings. It is also important to establish that the earnings are regular and not distorted by special circumstances. If, when comparing earnings, they are brought down to an hourly rate to eliminate the effect of overtime, it is worth remembering that a simple division of the total earnings by the hours will not remove the impact of overtime if the effect of overtime premiums is not discounted.

6. Present the analysis in a form which can be easily assimilated and reveals the range of rates of pay or earnings for the jobs covered by the survey. The presentation may show the range of pay or earnings from highest and lowest, the median rate and the upper and lower

quartile. The median is the middle item in the distribution of salaries or wage rates — 50% of the jobs are paid more than the median and 50 per cent of the jobs paid less. The upper quartile is the rate above which 25 per cent of the jobs are paid more; the lower quartile is the rate below which 25 per cent of the jobs are paid less.

Club surveys

Salary clubs have been around a long time and employers seem to place a high value on them. It was as long ago as 1974 that the Government Pay Board wrote:

> Our studies showed most employers used quite a number of surveys — indeed it was exceptional for an employer to rely on one or two. However, where employers belong to a 'pay club' we found that the information obtained from the 'club' was regarded as more relevant than that contained in the general surveys partly because the other club members were considered to be the main competitors for that type of staff.

Clubs may be administered either by management consultants or by companies themselves. Clubs tend to operate in single industries, although some cover a range of industries — a survey of 'blue chip' companies, for instance. Many cover all managerial and professional grades, although there are those which cover only one employee category — graduates, for example, within one industry. When a single employee category is chosen, this is normally because there is strong competition for people with skills which are in demand.

The major advantage of running a salary club is that participants in the survey know who the other participants are and that their data are relevant. When members of the same club are in the same industrial sector, they may be thought of as competitors for the same type of staff in the same salary market. This is particularly true for managers and specialists whose skills are easily transferable from one company to another in a similar line of business. At managerial level, members of the same club typically employ a rather homogeneous group of staff in terms of the experience required, the demands of the job and their qualifications. Some clubs exchange salary information only on managerial and specialist grades, eg from first line to senior management, while others cover technical and professional grades, clerical, or, indeed, only manual employees.

The establishment of a salary club may start from a more informal exchange of salary information between two or more companies who employ similar types of staff. A club may be the result of individual initiatives by one or two compensation specialists within companies. In some industries, the computer industry, for example, there is a more regular exchange of salary information than in others. Some consultants specialize in club survey work in certain industrial groups. If the target group is sufficiently finely defined, as, for example, in the international banking sector and the pharmaceutical industry, then not only is a homogeneous group of employees being surveyed, but also a very high proportion of the potential number of participants probably takes part.

General published surveys

The number of surveys continues to grow, but the quality of the data they provide varies enormously. Both the Top Pay Unit of Incomes Data Services and the Pay and Benefits Bulletin published by Industrial Relations Services publish regular reviews of these surveys and analyses of the trend data they contain. The Top Pay Unit also publishes a *Directory of Salary Surveys* every two years which is essentially a consumer's guide to the salary survey market. It gives full information on the jobs covered, sample data cost and availability as well as comments on the quality and reliability of the data.

General surveys such as those produced by Remuneration Economics, Monks/Charterhouse, Inbucon, Reward and the Executive Compensation Service (now part of the Wyatt Company) are based on data collected from as large a number of participating organizations as they can attract — typically from mailshots to a large number of employers. They cover base salary and total earnings levels paid on a given date and a certain number of data on benefits entitlements. The most usual company analyses are by industrial sector, and size in terms of annual sales turnover and/or numbers of employers. Most surveys include some indication of regional variations and can be expected to add to this, given the interest in regional pay differences for jobs; here local market influences are more important than national trends. Clerical and shop-floor jobs that are recruited by using local sources need local pay analyses to give an acceptable picture of the market — especially among smaller organizations. National data are always needed, however, for jobs which are recruited on a national basis. It is important to remember that where, for instance, there appear to be regional differences in management pay, this will almost always turn out, on deeper analysis, to be related to the size of the job and the nature and age of the industry rather than the location. Traditional engineering companies tend to pay less than their high-tech counterparts and they tend to be located in different parts of the country. They also often do not demand the same academic background and level of skills from the managers they employ. Nor, sadly, are some of them in a position to afford higher pay — for better qualified managers able to improve profitability through innovation and improved financial management.

Most surveys also provide data on annual salary movement.

Advertisements

Advertisements are often used to give information on salary or wage levels. But they should be treated with caution. The rates quoted may be inflated to attract candidates and the information about the job may be too imprecise to permit useful comparisons to be made.

Analysing and presenting the results

As survey returns come in, they should be checked carefully to ensure that acceptable matching or pricing has been given for each job. Any doubtful figures should be referred back to participants and discussed with them. Where comparisons turn out not to be close enough to be acceptable, the data should be rejected — preferably with the agreement of the participant concerned.

Salary club surveys can generally be processed very quickly and participants typically expect a report within a month of sending in their returns. Strict deadlines usually have to be set and enforced to ensure that this is possible. Whoever is responsible for the survey should ensure that the analysis of results can begin as soon as the first few returns have come in and been checked.

The methods used in the analysis and presentation of survey results depend on the number of returns received and the degree of sophistication in salary policy of both the survey producer and the participants. It can therefore vary from simple histograms (bar charts), either set out on graph paper or drawn by computer, showing the salary scales or actual ranges paid by participants and coded company by company, to complex statistical analyses producing computer printouts which present the data in relation to a number of different variables. In selecting which forms of analysis yield the most meaningful results and present the data in a way which helps the salary policy decision-making process, it helps to concentrate on what the data are actually based on and who will use the findings. The use of multiple regression analysis, correlations and standard deviations looks very sophisticated and is therefore sometimes seductive. For data based on large samples, such techniques have their value and can be used to good effect. But the application of sophisticated statistical techniques to rather tentative data collected in a small-scale salary survey has all the subtlety of a sledgehammer crushing a nut. What matters most is to present a limited amount of directly relevant market data in a way which shows that the actual operating salary range for any given job is where the extremes of practice lie as well as the midpoint — backed by a brief commentary on the underlying influences affecting the distribution.

A statistical summary of research data might look like that shown in Table 24.1.

Table 24.1 Summary of salary data: production managers

Job title	Salary range (£)			Actual salary (£)		
	Lower quartile	*Median*	*Upper quartile*	*Lower quartile*	*Median*	*Upper quartile*
Production manager	16,100– 18,800	18,000– 20,000	19,500– 22,300	*17,800*	19,100	20,200

Salary data can also be represented graphically in various ways. Figure 24.1 illustrates the relationships between salary ranges and actual salaries for a number of companies and the relative position of the originating company. This approach has considerable visual impact and is also particularly useful for internal salary policy deecision making.

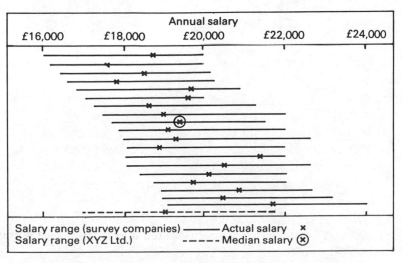

Figure 24.1 Salary survey data presented graphically

Using survey data

The translation of salary market data into an acceptable company salary structure is a process based on judgement and compromise. The aim is to extract a derived market rate based on effective estimates of the reliability of the data, and to strike a reasonable balance between the competing merits of the different sources used. However 'scientific' the approach, this is essentially an intuitive process. Once all the data available have been collected and presented in the most accessible manner possible (ie job by job for all the areas the structure is to cover), a proposed scale midpoint has to be established for each level, based on the place in the market the company wishes to occupy, ie its 'market posture'. The establishment of this midpoint will be based not only on assessment of current and updated salary data, but also on indications of movement in earnings and the cost of living which are likely to affect the life of the whole structure. For organizations needing to stay ahead of the market, this point will often be around the upper quartile; for others, closer alignment with the median is adequate.

25

Job Evaluation

Job evaluation is a system of comparing different jobs to provide a basis for a grading and pay structure. An analysis of market rates will provide the information needed to ensure that a reward management system is competitive, but it is still necessary to maintain a pay structure into which jobs can be slotted according to their relative value. This will be strongly influenced by market forces, but attention has also to be paid to internal relativities in order to achieve, as far as possible, both appropriate differentials to reward different levels of contribution and equity in the form of equal pay for work of equal value.

A pay structure consists of a hierarchy and decisions have to be made on how and where jobs should be fitted into that hierarchy. The aim of this chapter is to assist in making those decisions by:

- Defining job evaluation.
- Setting out the aims of evaluation.
- In the light of these descriptions, considering the pros and cons of job evaluation.
- Developing a strategy for selecting a method of evaluation and introducing it.
- Reviewing in detail the implications of the equal pay for work of equal value legislation in the UK. Job evaluation schemes can be used to ensure that inequalities are not allowed to happen or to continue, but they can also be used to defend differentials as being based on a proper comparative analysis of job values. In cases where equal value claims are heard by industrial tribunals, the tribunal can appoint independent experts to carry out job evaluations. The pressure for evaluation is therefore increasing where equal value claims are possible. These, however, are more likely to happen at junior levels — supervisors, clerical staff and manual workers.

523

- Outlining the developments taking place in job evaluation following the introduction of new technology, organizational changes and the trend towards the harmonization of the terms and conditions of employment for white- and blue-collar staff.

What is job evaluation?

Job evaluation is a method of establishing the relative positions of jobs in a job hierarchy. Job evaluation schemes do not directly determine rates of pay, with the exception of the obsolete factor comparison method. The rate for the job or the salary bracket for a job grade are influenced by a number of factors outside the scope of most schemes. These include market rate pressures, trade union negotiations and traditional patterns of pay differentials between jobs.

Job evaluation schemes set out to measure the relative value of the job, not of the job holder. Ideally, the performance of the individual should not enter into job evaluation, although in practice it may be difficult to dissociate individuals from their jobs where they have been in a position to influence what they do. This applies particularly to senior or specialist jobs where the position has been built round the personal skills and abilities of the job holders.

Job evaluation is concerned with relationships, not absolutes. It cannot measure in definitive terms the inherent value of a job to the organization. It is essentially a comparative process: comparisons with other jobs, comparisons against defined standards, or comparisons of the degree to which a common criterion or factor is present in different jobs.

Job evaluation schemes

The main types of job evaluation schemes are:

1. *non-analytical schemes:* ranking, paired comparison (a refined process of ranking), and job classification;
2. *analytical points rating schemes:* where the jobs are analysed and compared by reference to different factors.

In addition, competence or skill-based pay structures involve a form of job evaluation.

Ranking

Ranking is the simplest form of job evaluation. It is a non-analytical approach which aims to judge each job as a whole and determine its relative place in a hierarchy by comparing one job with another and arranging them in order of importance.

Method of comparison

Jobs may be compared by reference to a single criterion or factor such as responsibility, which might be defined as the particular obligations that have to be assumed by any person who carries out the job; or evaluators may be asked to define several facets of the job, for example:

1. decisions: difficulty, judgement required, extent to which the tasks are prescribed (amount of discretion allowed);
2. complexity: range of tasks to be carried out or skills to be used;
3. knowledge and skills: what the job holder is required to know and be able to do.

A list of factors to be considered may be helpful because it steers thinking towards definable aspects of the content of the job rather than dealing with overgeneralized concepts such as responsibility. But there are dangers. Ranking may be distorted because evaluators attach different weights to the factors, emphasizing some and not others. But they will do this anyway. Without a defined list, they will, consciously or unconsciously, evaluate by reference to their own choice of factors and weight them according to their own whim or prejudice.

Ranking procedure

The ranking procedure is to:

1. Analyse and describe the jobs, bringing out in the description those aspects which are to be used for comparison purposes.
2. Identify key or benchmark jobs; the most and least important jobs, a job midway between the two extremes, and others at the higher or lower intermediate points.
3. Rank the other jobs round the jobs until all jobs are placed in their rank order of importance.
4. Divide the ranked jobs into grades. In effect, this means that the grades are now defined by the jobs that have been placed in them. In future, new jobs can be graded or existing jobs regraded by reference to the established gradings on a job-to-job basis.

Grading jobs in a ranking exercise

There are no fixed rules for determining grade boundaries or the number of grades required. At this stage, job evaluation becomes even less objective than it has been before. The aim is to produce grades which are administratively feasible and which conform to broad levels of responsibility in the organization. Their purpose is to collect jobs of comparable responsibility into broad bands before pricing the structure by attaching salary brackets to the bands.

Some guidance on the division of jobs into grades may be provided by a natural promotion ladder: junior clerk to clerk, to section leader, to group leader and so on. The danger of this approach is that the existing hierarchy may simply be reproduced, which could defeat the purpose of the scheme.

Pay structures do not necessarily have to have rigidly defined job grades (see Chapter 26). But grades have their advantages. Grouping jobs together into a grade means that they are considered to be roughly equal and can be priced within the same salary range. This helps to overcome the fundamental problem of ranking, that of placing closely related jobs one above the other on the basis of subjective judgements which cannot be validated.

The process of job grading means that a dividing line has to be placed between adjacent jobs in the rank order. This division can be invidious if, as is often the case, the difference between the importance of the two jobs on either side of the boundary is not significant. This problem is shared by all forms of job evaluation although, in theory at least, points schemes enable divisions to be made where there are natural breaks between bunches of points. This problem can be alleviated by the use of overlap between salary ranges, ie where the maximum salary of a lower range extends beyond the minimum point of the next range above.

Advantages of ranking

Ranking produces a hierarchy without having to analyse the job content or parts of a particular job individually. This means that the evaluation can be done very quickly and, if the final order is acceptable, the structure can be implemented easily, without excessive cost in terms of cost or resources.

Those who favour ranking claim that the process of assessing the overall importance of the job as a whole to the organization is, in practice, what people do even when they go through the analytical motions of assessing the different facets of a job in a points-rating scheme.

Ranking schemes can be used as a check on the results obtained by other more sophisticated schemes to ensure that the hierarchies produced are 'felt-fair'.

Disadvantages of ranking

The disadvantages of ranking are the following:

1. There is no rationale to defend the final rank order if it is challenged. Ranking one job higher or lower than another becomes a matter of opinion, although, to a degree, even the more sophisticated methods of job evaluation do no more than channel opinions into specified areas. The opinion is confined to one aspect of the job and guidance is given in how to exercise it, but ultimately, it is still an opinion. However, ranking systems cannot, for this reason, be used convincingly to deal with equal value problems.
2. Judgements become multidimensional when a number of jobs have to be placed in order of importance. Inconsistencies can occur because different individuals give more weight to one factor than to others because they do not know what complex of factors is operating or what the balance is between them.
3. While it may be easy to establish the extremes in a rank order, it may be difficult to discriminate between the middling jobs. Consensus on the correct rank order may therefore be hard to obtain.
4. Ranking does not provide a clear basis for grading or regrading jobs and a graded salary structure is, after all, often the main reason for having a job evaluation scheme.

To overcome these formidable disadvantages, one can try paired comparisons, job classification or points schemes.

Paired comparisons

Paired or forced comparisons are a refinement of job ranking. This approach introduces an element of scoring to give an indication of the degree of importance between two jobs. As with job ranking, the method is more appropriate for smaller organizations or where jobs within a similar job family are being assessed.

Specially designed score charts are necessary and the use of a computer to correlate the results reduces the time an evaluation takes. The method is easily understood and is quick. As with job ranking, the approach is hard to defend rationally, even though decisions represent the consensus when an evaluation was done.

How the method is used

As with job ranking, the job evaluation panel analyses each job as a whole. The panel then goes on to compare it with all other jobs in turn (this may not be necessary with basic job ranking). If a job is considered more demanding, it scores two points; if it is as demanding, it scores one point; and if it is less demanding, it scores nothing. By totalling up the scores a rank order is produced, as illustrated below:

Job	A	B	C	D	E	Total score	Rank order
A	—	0	2	0	2	4	2
B	2	—	2	2	2	8	1
C	0	0	—	2	0	2	5
D	2	0	0	—	1	3	3
E	0	0	2	1	—	3	3

Number of calculations

One problem with paired comparisons is that as the number of jobs increases, the number of paired comparisons rises rapidly so that evaluating 50 jobs involves 1225 comparisons. With the use of a computer, however, this need not be a great drawback.

Advantages

This method combines the advantages of ranking, notably speed and simplicity, with a more efficient way of checking the consistency of the ranking. The number of individual assessments, which may be inconsistent because of bias, is reduced.

The advantages can be summarized as:

- The method is quick and easy to understand.
- Jobs are assessed as a whole, so that more general questions such as creativity or financial responsibilities can be considered without attempting to quantify each particular job factor.

Disadvantages

Paired comparisons may help to eliminate some of the subjectivity and inconsistencies of whole job ranking, but this method still fails to answer why a job is necessarily more important or more demanding. While analysing jobs as a whole does give an important 'feel' for the job, paired comparisons assume that everyone reaches the same conclusions about each job — if this consensus does not exist, then it becomes hard to justify where the job should be placed.

The disadvantages can be summarized as:

- It is difficult to justify why jobs are considered more important.
- The number of calculations is impractical for a large number of jobs unless computer facilities are available.
- The evaluation relies on the team's ability to come to a consensus on where a job should be ranked.

The paired comparison method can be applied to all types of jobs. It is well suited to manual jobs where there is already an established feeling about how important jobs are in comparison with one another, ie where an organization does not have to justify why certain jobs are more demanding or are considered more important.

Job classification

Job classification is based on an initial definition of the number and characteristics of the grades into which the jobs are placed. The grade definitions attempt to take into account discernible differences in skill and responsibility and may refer to specific criteria, such as level of decisions, knowledge, equipment used and education or training required to do the work. Jobs are allotted to grades by comparing the whole job description with the grade definition.

A job classification scheme for clerical jobs may be based on the Institute of Administrative Management's grading scheme. Alternatively, a job classification scheme can be built up within a company following a ranking or points evaluation exercise. The number of grades can be determined along the lines suggested above when grading procedures in ranking schemes were discussed. The ranking or points system indicates the grades into which the benchmark jobs are placed and the descriptions of these jobs provide guidance when writing grade definitions. The benchmark jobs can then be used as reference points to illustrate the necessarily generalized grade descriptions.

Advantages of job classification

The advantages of job classification are that, first, it is simple to operate and, second, standards of judgement are provided in the form of grade definitions. It is often a good system to use in an organization that wants to introduce job evaluation quickly without elaborate and costly studies and wants an easy method of slotting new or changed jobs into an established structure.

Disadvantages of job classification

The disadvantage of job classification is that it cannot cope with complex jobs which will not fit neatly into one grade. It is less suitable for senior positions where grade definitions have to become so generalized that they provide little help in evaluating borderline cases. It also tends to be inflexible in that it is not sensitive to changes in the nature and content of jobs.

The problem with job classification is that even with clerical jobs, where it seems to have more relevance, it is still better in practice to evaluate by comparing jobs with jobs rather than by comparing jobs with job descriptions. Once the initial grades into which the benchmark jobs have been slotted are established, the system is usually expendable. In addition, like ranking or paired comparisons, job classification cannot readily be used in equal pay for work of equal value cases.

Points rating

Points rating schemes are based on an analysis of separately defined characteristics or factors which are assumed to be common to all the jobs. It is further assumed that differences in the extent to which the characteristics are found in the jobs will measure differences between the jobs. Points schemes are sometimes loosely called factor comparison schemes, although, strictly speaking, this term should be used for an outdated approach which apportions agreed rates of pay between factors in accordance with the extent to which the factor is present in the job.

The factors selected in points schemes are those considered to be most relevant in assessing the comparative value of jobs. Typical factors include skill (of various kinds), responsibility, decisions, complexity and contacts with other people.

Each factor is given a range of points so that a maximum number of points is available. The relative importance or 'weighting' of a factor is determined by the maximum number of points allotted to it. In each factor, the total range of points is divided into degrees according to the level at which the factor is present in the job. The characteristics of each degree in terms of, say, level of complexity, are defined as yardsticks for comparison purposes.

Points rating procedure

Jobs are evaluated by studying job descriptions containing analyses of the degree to which the factor is present in the job and comparing them with the factor level definitions. The jobs are graded for each factor and the points for each grading are added to produce a total score. This score can then be related to the scores of other jobs to indicate the rank order. For example, an evaluation of two jobs by using a typical scheme could produce the results shown in Table 25.1.

Table 25.1 Points rating evaluation

Factor	Job A		Job B	
	Level	*Points*	*Level*	*Points*
Resources	4	20	5	25
Decisions	4	60	4	60
Complexity	5	25	3	15
Knowledge and skills	3	15	3	15
		120		115

Grading jobs in a points rating exercise

To develop a grade structure, one plots the points scored against salaries. Any clustering of scores helps to establish the divisions between job grades, and when the salary ranges have been fixed with the help of information on market rates, the dimensions of each grade can be re-evaluated and slotted into the structure according to their points rating.

Advantages of points schemes

The advantages of points schemes are as follows:

1. Evaluators are forced to consider a range of factors which, as long as they are present in all the jobs and affect them in different ways, avoid

the oversimplified judgements made when using non-analytical schemes.
2. Points schemes provide evaluators with defined yardsticks which should help them to achieve some degree of objectivity and consistency in making their judgements.
3. They at least appear to be objective even if they are not, and this quality makes people feel that they are fair.
4. They provide a rationale which, however specious, helps in the design of graded salary structures.
5. Under the Equal Pay legislation, they are the preferred method of evaluation in equal value cases. The assumption is that an analytical approach produces more accurate results. Whether or not that assumption is correct, the fact that Industrial Tribunals favour analytical schemes following the Appeal Court's decision in *Bromley* v *Quick* (which stated that they should be the basis for equal value decisions) is a powerful argument for their use.

Disadvantages of points schemes

Points schemes have three disadvantages:

1. They are complex to develop, install and maintain.
2. They give a spurious impression of scientific accuracy, though it is still necessary to use judgement in selecting factors, deciding on weightings, defining levels within factors, and interpreting information about the jobs in relation to the often rather generalized definitions of factors and factor levels.
3. They assume that it is possible to quantify different aspects of jobs on the same scale of values and then add them together. But skills cannot be added together in this way.

Competence and skill analysis

Evaluation based on competence or skill requirements in a job is, in effect, a single factor approach. The competence or skill requirements of a job are analysed by using one of the techniques discussed in Chapter 16. Hay Management Consultants is developing this method, which is relatively new. This company's system is described by Murlis and Fitt,[1] who define competence as 'an underlying characteristic of an individual which can be shown to have a causal link with high performance in a defined role'. Competence scale definitions are used in the Hay System to develop a skill matrix which defines factors and factor levels, as in the example shown in Table 25.2. A further example of a Hay competence scale definition for a sales manager is given in Table 25.3.

Table 25.2 Example of skill matrix factor and definitions for an engineering job family (Hay Management Consultants)

Factors:

- knowledge
- application of knowledge
- integration
- autonomy
- people management
- management of relationships
- creativity
- project management

Factor definition:

Integration: 'Your ability to integrate directly technologies, skills or knowledge.'

Factor levels:

1. Capable of working within own speciality.
2. Capable of coordinating some elements within a speciality.
3. Capable of integrating a group of specialities within a discipline, or a number of relevant disciplines on a product, component, process, or system.
4. Capable of the integration of all specialities within a discipline, or the integration of all relevant disciplines on a major project, component process, or system.

Murlis and Fitt point out that in a competence or skills-based evaluation scheme the factor definitions refer to skill and capability but are also, in effect, descriptions of job content. This is because an individual's competences must always be related to organizational requirements. There is clearly no purpose in rewarding people for the possession of knowledge or skills which are not operationally relevant.

Advantages of competence and skills analysis

1. Levels, grades or bands are related to one readily definable factor.
2. Competence requirements are clearly key inputs to be assessed when determining the level of jobs.

Table 25.3 Example of a competence scale definition within a sales management job family (Hay Management Consultants)

Organizational sensitivity and awareness

Factor definition: An accurate understanding of others at the organizational level — their feelings, their reasons for their actions and interactions, their intentions. It also involves understanding how organizations function and how people function in organizations

Behavioural indicators:

1. Response to explicit customer requests only.
2. Recognizes formal customer hierarchy.
3. Recognizes organizational constraints, understands informal interactions in customer's organization.
4. Understands key decision makers and the power and politics of the organization.

3. Competence definitions are much more specific about knowledge and skill requirements than the factor definitions in most conventional evaluation schemes.
4. The factor levels can provide a career map or series of aiming points for individuals which will define what they need to know and be able to do if they are to progress within the organization. This aspect was explored more thoroughly in Chapter 22 (pages 471–92).
5. This approach is particularly appropriate for professional, scientific, technical, and highly skilled jobs where, to a large degree, what people do is determined by the level and range of skills they possess rather than their position in an organizational hierarchy. These are people who develop their knowledge and skills progressively as they gain experience and go through various training modules. The content of the work may not always appear to differ significantly between individuals. It is what they bring to the work in terms of the ability to deploy a high level or a variety of skills which counts rather than some arbitrary and often indefinable distinction between, say, what a senior and a principal scientist or engineer do.
6. It is particularly relevant in flatter organizations where there is increased emphasis on flexibility and teamwork. It is also appropriate in high-technology, research or development organizations where, again, flexibility and teamwork are important. A skills-based approach may be best on the shopfloor or in development units where

Table 25.4 Characteristics, advantages and disadvantages of different job evaluation schemes

Scheme	Characteristics	Advantages	Disadvantages
1. Ranking	Whole job comparisons made to place them in order of importance.	Easy to apply and understand.	No defined standards of judgement: difference between jobs are not measured.
2. Paired comparisons	Panel members individually compare each job in turn with all the others being evaluated. Points are awarded according to whether the job is more, or less, or equally demanding than or as each of the jobs with which it is being compared. These points are added to determine the rank order, usually with the help of a computer. The scores are analysed and discussed in order to achieve consensus among the members of the panel.	Ranking is likely to be more valid on the principle that it is always easier to compare a job with one other job than with the whole range of disparate jobs.	As with ranking, the system neither explains why one job is more important than another nor assesses differences between them.
3. Job classification	Job grades are defined and jobs are slotted into the grades by comparing the whole job description with the grade definition.	Simple to operate, and standards of judgement are provided in the shape of the grade definitions.	Difficult to fit complex jobs into a grade without using elaborate grade definitions.
4. Points rating	Separate factors are scored to produce an overall points score for the job.	The analytical process of considering separately defined factors gives the impression that the evaluation is objective. Consistency in judgement is helped by having defined factor levels. Regarded as the best system in equal value.	Complex to install and maintain. Objectivity is more apparent than real: subjective judgement is still required to rate jobs of different factors.
5. Competence/skills grading	Jobs placed in grades or bands in accordance with level of competence or skill.	Based on key input factor. Direct link to pay structures and PRP systems.	Non-analytical; may be difficult to differentiate clearly between competence or skill levels.

multiskilling is a requirement and there are autonomous work groups.

7. It facilitates the development of pay curves, as described in Chapter 26, and 'technical ladder' or skill-level types of pay progression, as described in Chapters 27 and 28.

Disadvantages

1. The system is non-analytical in the strict job evaluation use of that term. It may therefore be difficult to use in dealing with an equal value claim.
2. It may be hard to differentiate clearly between competence or skill levels.
3. It is difficult to apply in a hierarchical and bureaucratic type of organization.

Characteristics of job evaluation schemes

The characteristics and advantages and disadvantages of each type of evaluation scheme are summarized in Table 25.4.

Pros and cons of job evaluation

Each of the schemes described in Table 25.2 has its advantages and disadvantages, but before choosing them it will be useful to consider in general the points for and against formal job evaluation schemes.

Pros

The point usually made in favour of the more formal types of job evaluation systems, especially analytical schemes, is that they are 'objective'. This adjective means, according to the *Oxford English Dictionary*, 'treating a subject as to the actual facts, not coloured by the feelings or opinions of the writer'. This claim cannot be substantiated. The only factual basis for job evaluation is the job description, but this can never convey the full flavour of a job, however carefully written. And no existing system of job evaluation can eliminate the colouring provided by the feeling or opinions of the evaluators.

It is also claimed that job evaluation provides the basis for a logical pay structure. This is a true statement, as far as it goes, but there is no proof that the more elaborate forms of job evaluation produce more logical salary structures.

Perhaps the most convincing claim that can be made for formula job evaluation schemes is that they are demonstrably more fair than entirely subjective managerial judgements, as long as the schemes are fully disclosed to staff who participate in them. This is where the more elaborate approaches come into their own. Points, guide charts, paired comparisons and multiple regression analysis with the help of a computer all give the impression that schemes are accurate, scientific and, above all, objective. They are felt to be fair, whether they are or not, and that is what counts when gaining acceptance of the results they produce.

Cons

The main point made against the more elaborate job evaluation schemes is that they can be costly to install and maintain. The installation costs include management consultants' fees, if they are used, which can be considerable, plus the time spent by management and staff in working with the consultants or designing a company scheme. When job evaluation is used to develop a new pay structure or to revise an old one, inevitable costs arise when staff are slotted into new grades. If any jobs are downgraded, it is most unusual for the people concerned to suffer any reduction in salary. Instead, they are 'red-circled' by being given personal-to-job-holder gradings which mean that they retain their present salary and expectations of fixed increments if they are on a scale. When jobs are upgraded, however, it is customary to increase salaries at least to the minimum of the new grade. If the costs are really exceptional, it may be possible to phase increases over a period of time, but this is only deferring the expense. New or revised structures therefore increase the pay of some staff (and the number could be considerable) without balancing this increase by decreases elsewhere. The cost may be a 3 per cent increase in the pay bill or more, if considerable changes are made to the pay structure.

Maintenance can also be expensive, especially if job evaluations are carried out by committees, although computerized job evaluation schemes can save time and administrative costs, more than recovering the initial investment in software (see pages 548–549).

Moreover, job evaluation is not the universal panacea that some companies think it to be. Handling its introduction can be a very delicate matter, especially if trade unions are involved. Evaluations can upset long-standing differentials and gradings and thus create more problems than they solve.

The disadvantages mentioned above mainly arise from the operation of job evaluation schemes, but there are more serious limitations to the process of job evaluation itself.

1. No scheme has been proved to be valid in that it measures what it sets out to measure, or reliable in that it produces consistent results. An act of faith is required to believe in job evaluation.
2. 'Whole-job' comparison schemes look wrong because they seem to oversimplify, but analytical systems are also suspect — apples and pears cannot be added together. The quantification of subjective judgements does not make them any more objective.
3. Job evaluation relies on human judgement. Its methodology may be logical and it may provide guidelines on the exercise of judgement, but these are subject to different interpretations and varying standards among assessors, and their preconceived notions ensure that subjectivity creeps in. This tendency to make *a priori* judgements about how jobs should be ranked or graded means that the deliberations of evaluators often take the form of a series of self-fulfilling prophesies.
4. Averaging a group of subjective judgements, as in consensus schemes, does not make them any more objective.
5. All evaluation schemes deteriorate as the organization changes and as evaluators become more skilled at manipulating the system. Grade drift — unjustified upgradings as a result of the manipulation — occurs and the pay structure is no longer equitable.

To sum up, job evaluation attempts to impose objectivity on a process of subjective judgement. It can never fully succeed in the task. In the last analysis, all job evaluation schemes boil down to organized rationalization.

Job evaluation strategy

Is job evaluation necessary?

The pros for job evaluation as given above appear to be self-evident, but the cons are formidable and reading them prompts the question, 'Is job evaluation really necessary?' The answer is, of course, yes. You cannot avoid evaluating jobs. That is what you do every time you decide on what one job should be paid in relation to another. The question needs to be re-stated as, 'Is a formal system of job evaluation necessary?'

Informal or formal?

A completely informal approach means relying on judgement without the benefit of any form of job analysis or a systematic analysis of market rates.

Except in the smallest organizations, it is unlikely to work.

A semi-formal system can work for some companies. This involves job analysis, so that even if internal comparisons are fairly crude, they are at least based on fact rather than opinion. Additionally, market rate information is collected regularly and, where the market-place is competitive, these rates will have a dominant influence on the structure. They will largely determine differentials between jobs in different market groups or jobs within a hierarchy where there are well-established market rates at different levels. For example, this will apply in marketing organizations where there are clearly defined rates for different grades of product or brand managers.

A semi-formal approach linked to market rate intelligence often works well in loosely structured, dynamic, market-orientated, or fairly small companies, and it can form the basis for a 'spot-rate' pay structure, as described in Chapter 26. But in larger organizations which are less subject to change and in which equity is a more important consideration, a more formal method is desirable to establish fair and sensible differentials and to achieve consistency in grading jobs. When you decide on what approach is required, the following questions need to be answered:

1. Who should be covered?
2. How many schemes?
3. Should the scheme(s) be specially designed for the company?
4. Should one of the standard schemes offered by consultants (the 'proprietary brands') be used? If so, which one?

Who should be covered?

Ideally, every job should be evaluated in order that comparisons can be made, ideally throughout the organization, or at least between staff in comparable occupations at different levels. Some companies, however, exclude directors and possibly senior managers on the grounds that their salary levels are largely determined on a personal basis. Senior jobs are often built round the skills of particular individuals and they can change, sometimes quite radically, when one manager leaves or is promoted and is replaced by another. Where this happens, job evaluation would clearly mean evaluating the individual, not the job.

How many schemes?

The tendency has been to have different systems for, say, managers, clerical staff and manual workers because of the difficulty of designing a scheme which is equally applicable at all levels of responsibility or for completely different types of work. Job evaluation is based on explicit or implicit factors or criteria which are believed to define the relative value of jobs. The factors typically used in executive jobs are unlikely to be appropriate for manual workers. But the attempt to introduce common factors too often results in a scheme which does not discriminate effectively at different levels. And even if a 'whole job ranking' system is used (as described on pages 524–527), comparisons at all levels may still be difficult because the criteria that are implicitly used in such schemes are seldom universally applicable.

Attempts are, however, being made, although it is not easy, to extend a single scheme to all or at least a wider range of employees. There are two reasons for this. First, the equal value legislation in the UK has made it necessary to compare levels of responsibility across the previously rigidly separated boundaries of clerical and manual staff. The second reason is the drive to harmonize conditions of employment for white- and blue-collar employees. Such extensions are probably most effective when different occupational categories need to be evaluated which are at roughly equivalent levels in the organization structure, although the type of work and conditions of employment are dissimilar. In other words, schemes can be extended horizontally without too much difficulty. The problems arise when vertical integration is attempted. This is why many organizations still have one scheme for managerial staff and another for clerical and manual workers. A compromise found in some large organizations is to use the same approach from top to bottom but to vary the factors in a tailor-made, points-rating scheme to meet the evaluation needs at different levels.

Tailor-made scheme?

The main advantage of a scheme specially designed for the company is clearly that it can take into account any unique features of the organization, such as the need to cover different categories of staff. Special factors can be introduced at different levels and appropriate weightings can be applied. Tailor-made schemes can also be designed to fit the salary administration systems of the firm. They are not necessarily less expensive to introduce than a job evaluation package because account has to be taken of the opportunity costs in the shape of the considerable amount of executive time that has to be spent in designing, developing and introducing a special company scheme. This time can be reduced by getting a firm of management consultants to design a tailor-made scheme.

What type of scheme?

When developing a tailor-made scheme, you have the choice between using a 'whole job' ranking, paired comparison, or job classification system, or introducing a more complex points scheme. The natural way to evaluate jobs is to compare one whole job with another — people do this almost instinctively. However carefully factors are analysed and however carefully they are told to compare jobs factor by factor, evaluators bring to the table their preconceived ideas of the overall relativities between jobs. These intuitions inevitably colour their judgements. The tendency is to manipulate points scores to produce a result which coincides with the views that people have already formed, ie the process of organized rationalization mentioned above. In the light of this phenomenon, there is much to be said for a ranking or classification approach which is realistic enough to recognize that nothing will stop people from behaving in this way.

Points schemes may be used in complex situations where it is felt that only a highly analytical approach provides an acceptable basis for evaluation, and they can provide a useful basis for designing a salary structure. Their elaborate nature may make them difficult to understand and their objectivity may be suspect. But their use may be justified if it is considered that staff are going to be favourably impressed both by the sheer quantity of time and trouble involved in introducing a scheme, and by the apparent fairness or the process of analysis.

Points schemes have been steadily increasing in popularity, partly because they are thought to be the best way of dealing with equal value problems, but also because of their 'face validity'. People *feel* that they are scientific and therefore they must be all right. They may, of course, work as well as any other approach, given thorough job analysis, the effective training of evaluators and the joint determination of management, staff and trade unions to see the exercise through. But no one should be starry-eyed enough to believe that, given these inputs, a points scheme will in itself produce more accurate results than other methods.

Competence and skills-based schemes are appropriate in relatively fluid organizations, especially those in the high-tech, scientific or research and development fields. They are particularly relevant for professional, scientific, technical and highly skilled workers and where career development tends to be progressive rather than a series of steps.

Introducing job evaluation

Having decided on the approach to be adopted, the steps required to introduce a scheme are to:

- inform staff and agree on how they should be involved;
- clarify trade union attitudes, where appropriate;
- select benchmark jobs;
- plan the job evaluation programme.

Informing and involving staff

Staff must obviously be informed about the exercise. It affects them deeply and their help is required in analysing jobs. The objectives and potential benefits should be discussed and it should be made absolutely clear that it is the jobs which are to be evaluated and not the people carrying out the jobs. The way in which staff are consulted will depend on the company's normal policies for consultation and negotiation.

There is much to be said for involving staff in the job evaluation programme. They can assist in selecting, analysing and evaluating benchmark jobs. It is becoming increasingly common to set up job evaluation committees to establish and maintain the scheme and to hear appeals.

Trade union attitudes

If the company is unionized, the form in which consultation and participation takes place will be strongly influenced by union attitudes. Staff unions may insist on being involved in the job evaluation programme, although they might not be prepared to commit themselves in advance to accept its findings. The guidelines on job evaluation issued by one major union are:

1. A preliminary meeting should be held between management and union to establish the need for job evaluation and the method to be used.
2. A job evaluation committee should be set up to define the scheme's terms of reference and the extent and method of communication between management and union.
3. A decision should be made as to which union members should take an active part in the scheme.
4. An appeals procedure should be set up.
5. Revision of the scheme should be carried out at regular intervals in

order to identify changes both in individual jobs and in company objectives.

One union has stated very firmly that no job evaluation scheme should be allowed to undermine the traditional role of collective bargaining in determining pay. The function of job evaluation, according to this union, is to deal with the job structure. The pay structure is a matter for negotiation.

Another union produced the following list of reservations about job evaluation:

1. Error-prone management judgements will replace negotiations and weaken the joint determination of wage rates and structures.
2. The wage system arrived at can be rigid, whereas wage systems should be dynamic and part of a continuous process.
3. Job evaluation can emphasize 'the rate for the job' and overlook the importance of 'the rate for the ability to do the job'.
4. At the time of introduction there is the possibility that the new pay structure will involve no more than a rearrangement of the old structure and not include any increase or benefit for employees as a whole.

These guidelines and attitudes are typical. They should be taken into account in any organization where staff are represented by unions or by staff associations with negotiating rights.

Select benchmark jobs

In any exercise where there are more than 30 or 40 jobs to be evaluated, it is necessary to identify and select a sample of benchmark jobs which can be used for comparisons inside and outside the organization. The benchmark jobs should be selected to achieve a representative sample of each of the main levels of jobs in each of the principal occupations.

The size of the sample depends on the number of different jobs to be covered. It is unlikely to be less than about 5 per cent of the total number of employees in the organization, and it would be difficult to produce a balanced sample unless at least 25 per cent of the distinct jobs at each level of the organization were included. The higher the proportion the better, bearing in mind the time required to analyse jobs (seldom less than one man-day for each job).

Draw up job evaluation programmee

The steps to be taken in drawing up and implementing a job evaluation are

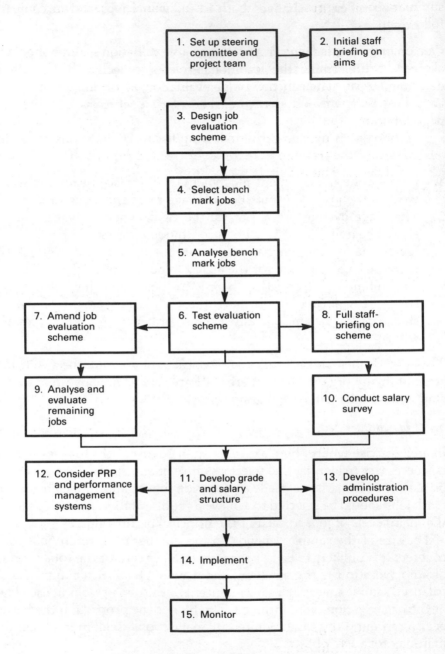

Figure 25.1 Job evaluation programme

summarized in Figure 25.1. The particular points to be covered are the following:

1. *Staffing:* who is responsible for analysis, evaluation, pay comparisons and the design of the salary structure.
2. *Briefing:* of management, staff and unions on the objectives of the exercise and how they are to be achieved.
3. *Procedures:* the terms of reference, membership and methods of working of any job evaluation committee.
4. *Training:* the training to be given to full and part-time analysts and evaluators. This is a vital part of the programme. If training is carried out thoroughly, many of the limitations of job evaluation referred to earlier can be minimized.
5. *Pay comparisons:* methods of conducting market rate surveys and the timetable for completing them.
6. *Job evaluation:* methods and procedures, including appeals, and the timetable for completing the programme.
7. *Job analysis:* the methods to be used in job analysis, the jobs to be covered and the timetable for completing the programme.
8. *Design the structure:* the methods to be used and the timetable for completing the design.
9. *Communication and negotiation:* the approach to communicating the results of the exercise to staff and for negotiating the structure with unions. It is highly desirable to produce a booklet explaining the scheme.
10. *Maintenance:* the procedures for maintaining the scheme, including regradings and appeals.

When the programme has been drawn up, the detailed work of job analysis, pay comparisons and design of the structure can be carried out.

Staffing the job evaluation exercise

Responsibility for the overall coordination of the introduction of job evaluation should be in the hands of a senior executive who can then report on progress to the board and advise it on ensuing salary policy developments.

Where there is a developed personnel function, the personnel manager will take control. In larger organizations with a salary administration department, the executive in charge of this function will normally take responsibility for the introduction and maintenance of the scheme. Provided adequate training is given at the outset, job analysis is an excellent way for new personnel or other company trainees to familiarize themselves with the company and the work done in its different departments. Many larger organizations expect their personnel trainees to spend a year or more working on job analysis as an essential addition to their background experience. Analysts must be taught the basic skills of interviewing and the elements of a concise descriptive style for writing job descriptions.

The use of analysts either to write job descriptions or check on those written by job holders and their supervisors often greatly improves the quality of job descriptions submitted for evaluation.

Staffing the job evaluation committee is a fairly delicate exercise. A balance has to be struck between the different divisions or departments in the organization and the different levels of staff covered by the scheme. Again, the process of job evaluation is an excellent training ground because it exposes committee members to a detailed analysis of the kinds of work done elsewhere in the organization and to an extended period of discussion and negotiation with other staff of different levels. Where trade unions are involved, it is usual for them to nominate an agreed number of representatives, balanced by management nominees and a mutually acceptable chairman, often the personnel manager.

Briefing for job evaluation

Effective briefing of all staff involved at the introduction stage of a job evaluation scheme is usually crucial to its success. This can be done at a meeting or series of meetings at which the executive responsible for the introduction of the scheme outlines its aims and emphasizes the long-term benefits for both company and staff of a properly evaluated basis for the new salary structure. A simple question-and-answer sheet given out at the meeting and covering the common, if basic, questions employees normally ask will also help remove any misgivings that may arise. Some of the most common questions are the following:

- What is job evaluation?
- Why does this company need job evaluation?
- How will it work?
- How does it affect promotion policy?
- How will the system be kept up to date?
- Does job evaluation mean that everyone whose job is in the same grade gets the same rate of pay?
- How does the publication of job grades and salary bands affect confidentiality?

- How does the system cater for additions to or alterations in jobs?
- What happens if individuals disagree with their grading?
- How quickly will appeals on grading be dealt with?
- How will the company go about grading new jobs created as the result of change or expansion?

Answers should be tailored to proposed company practice.

Briefing the job evaluation committee

Much of the success of a job evaluation committee depends on how it is briefed and the way in which an *esprit de corps* is developed. The first meeting should discuss the collective responsibilities of the committee, answer members' questions and perhaps try a few 'practice runs' before formal gradings get under way.

Briefing is usually the chairman's responsibility or that of the personnel manager if he or she is not chairman. The main points that need to be covered at the first meeting are:

- restatement of the purpose of job evaluation;
- detailed briefing on every aspect of the company's own scheme;
- reminders that the committee has the right to go back to the individual or supervisor for further details and clarification as often as necessary and the right not to evaluate any job until it is completely satisfied that the job description is adequate.

Committee proceedings are usually confidential, but minutes summarizing the reasons for grading each job should be kept.

How much time is involved?

However much the company may want to get the scheme fully implemented, it is unwise to rush job evaluation. Even the keenest evaluation committee can grade only a limited number of jobs in a day: eight is probably a realistic average maximum. After this, the quality of evaluation tends to drop, and more time has to be spent later in checking and assessing the validity of grading. The final review of all the grades allocated to check that no inconsistencies have occurred should be done meticulously and with enough time allowed for re-evaluation if necessary. Extra time devoted at this stage will help reduce appeals to the inevitable few. Careful preparation for the communication of job grades and of the handbooks or other documents describing the scheme and its operation will also assist acceptance.

Appeals procedure

Even the most committed and highly trained job evaluation committees make mistakes. Add to this, 'political' considerations, as shown by managers who expect the people they supervise to be more highly graded as a reflection of departmental status and individuals who feel the importance of their job has been undervalued, and the need for an appeals procedure is inevitable. Unions will want to negotiate the basis for appeals when the introduction of job evaluation is agreed. A fairly typical appeal sequence covering unionized and non-unionized staff would be the following:

1. Appeal goes to supervisor.
2. Supervisor and employee appeal to grading committee.
3. If the decision is not acceptable:

    (a) unionized staff involve branch officials;
    (b) non-unionized staff go through their own grievance procedure to higher authority.

4. Ultimately the appeal goes to a top management committee for final decision.

Use of computers

A job evaluation exercise can generate a lot of paper and take considerable time. The use of knowledge-based software systems, usually referred to as export systems, can organize the analytical processes in a way which makes the best use of the database, assists in making consistent judgements and records decisions to be added to the database. An expert system will do this by:

- defining the evaluation rules relating to the weighting of factors; the points, levels, or degrees attached to each factor; and the assessment standards which guide evaluators to the correct rating of jobs — these may take the form of benchmark jobs and/or level definitions;
- programming the computer to ask appropriate questions concerning each factor in a job to enable it to apply the evaluation rules;
- applying the rules consistently and determining the factor score for the job;
- grading the job;
- sorting the job into position in the rank order;
- storing the job information entered in the form of a factor analysis into

the computer's memory in order that it can be called to the screen or printed at any time.

An example of a computerized job evaluation system is given in Chapter 38 (pages 841–842).

Equal value

Under the equal value amendment to the UK Equal Pay Act, *any* woman can claim equal pay with *any* man if she believes her work is equally demanding under such factors as 'effort, skill and decision-making'. Equal value claims can be made whether or not job evaluation schemes exist, and they can cut across traditional boundaries, so that blue-collar workers can compare their jobs with those of white-collar workers and vice versa. Vulnerability to claims is highest where traditional, sex-based job segregation exists.

Claims are heard by industrial tribunals, who may ask 'independent experts' appointed by ACAS (the Advisory Conciliation and Arbitration Service) to assess equality of value between claimant and comparator. The experts carry out their evaluation by applying sets of factors to the job analysis such as:

- responsibility, effort, skills, 'know-how';
- physical demands, environment, planning and decision making, skill and knowledge;
- skills and experience, working conditions, effort.

The independent experts start with the job description to identify any areas where the content of the job is the cause of conflict. They attempt to get agreement on the facts and ask the employer to justify the differential. A precise point rating for each factor is usually considered neither necessary nor appropriate, but a general statement comparing the demands of each job under each factor heading is essential.

The existence of a company job evaluation scheme which assigns values to the jobs under review can be used to prove that no discrimination is taking place only if the scheme itself is non-discriminatory. Job evaluation schemes can be discriminatory in the choice of factors and in the weightings attached to the factors as well as in the grading process — reflecting underlying discrimination. The Equal Opportunity Commission has stated that job evaluation should not give a spurious objectivity to the *status quo*: 'A commitment to a fair job evaluation may require that some traditional assumptions are changed regarding the value attributed to work predominantly carried out by women.' It also advises that extremely high or low weightings should not be given to factors which are exclusively found in jobs performed predominantly by one sex.

Once factors are selected and weightings applied so that sex bias is avoided, the administration of the scheme should be in line with good personnel practice. Hay Management Consultants has published a useful code of practice, the main points of which are summarized below:

- Formation of steering and review panels should have regard to the distribution of men and women across the organization.
- Where it may not always be easy to persuade women to be involved, appropriate education should be provided in order to bring home the importance of active participation.
- Individuals involved should be thoroughly trained in the techniques and approaches they are required to assess and monitor and should be briefed to avoid sex bias (both direct and unintentional).
- Allocation of jobs across more than one evaluation panel should avoid adherence to any traditional occupational grading or historical difference in the sex of job holders.
- An appointed chairperson should monitor panel operation and encourage active involvement of all panel members in the process.
- Evaluators should possess the qualities of open-mindedness and fair judgement and, in addition to being thoroughly trained in the job evaluation method, they should be specifically briefed on guarding against sex bias in their interpretation of job descriptions and subsequent evaluation.
- Evaluation of jobs should be the result of panel consensus based purely on job content without reference to job holders or historical position in the pecking order.
- Evaluations should be updated to reflect changes in jobs and results should be regularly audited to ensure that sex bias does not creep in.
- Where a series of benchmark jobs is fully evaluated and other jobs are subsequently positioned within that framework, the benchmark sample should be equally representative of typically female- and typically male-dominated jobs and where possible include jobs populated by both.
- Evaluation and appeals panels should comprise a cross-section of individuals representative of the range of job groups/occupations to be evaluated and reflect the distribution of men and women.
- Detailed descriptions of all jobs should be prepared, using a uniform format.
- Where job analysts are involved in the preparation of job descriptions,

both men and women should be selected with reference to their distribution across the range of jobs.

- All individuals involved in the preparation of job descriptions should, in addition to receiving appropriate training in the approach to collection and presentation of information, be briefed to avoid sex bias in discussion, interpretation and choice of words used to describe jobs.
- Job descriptions should be agreed as representative of the job by job holders, line management and, where appropriate, the job analyst and union/staff association representative.
- Job titles appearing on job descriptions should avoid any indication of the sex of the job holder (eg not 'manageress').
- The name and gender of the job holder should be avoided on copies of descriptions put forward for panel evaluation.

References

1. Murlis, H and Fitt, D 'Job evaluation in a changing world', *Personnel Management*, May 1991.

Pay Structures

Definition

A pay structure consists of an organization's pay levels or scales for single jobs or groups of jobs. In a graded pay structure, these are defined by the minimum and maximum rates of pay in each grade for the jobs placed in the grade. Within each grade there will be scope for progression according to merit or service or a combination of the two (salary progression systems are described in Chapter 27). However, a system of individual job rates without any defined grades but, possibly, with scope to earn more by merit or by means of a payment-by-results scheme, could equally well be described as a pay structure.

In one organization there may be a wage structure for manual or hourly paid workers and a separate salary structure for white-collar staff, who are paid monthly or, less frequently, by the week. Harmonization of terms and conditions for all employees in the shape of single-status companies is, however, becoming more common. Traditional status symbols are, rightly, going, and the only distinction made between employees is their rate of pay, which is governed by the value of their contribution and by the market rate for their job. Unified grading systems occur in high-tech firms and where overseas companies, particularly Japanese firms, are setting up factories in the UK.

This chapter starts by considering the criteria for any pay structure — wage, salary or unified, and the considerations affecting the number of structures. It continues to deal with the main types of salary structures:

1. graded;
2. individual job range;
3. pay curves;
4. job family system;

5. spot rates;
6. pay spine;
7. rate for age.

Wage payment systems are dealt with in Chapter 28.

Criteria for pay structures

The criteria that should be used when selecting or modifying a pay structure are that it should:

- be appropriate to the needs of the organization, in terms of its culture, its size, the degree to which it is subject to change, the need for flexibility and the type and level of employees to be covered;
- be flexible in response to internal and external pressures, especially those related to market rates and skill shortages;
- provide scope for rewarding high-flyers while still providing appropriate rewards for the bulk of employees on whom the organization depends;
- ensure that rewards are given in line with performance and achievement;
- provide a basis for career planning which will motivate ambitious employees;
- facilitate consistency in the treatment of varying levels of responsibility and performance.

How many structures?

The advantage of having one structure to cover all grades of employees is that a consistent approach to gradings, differentials and control can be adopted from top to bottom. The problems of borderline cases between two structures are avoided and the overall structure is easy to explain and understand.

It may not, however, be feasible to have one structure covering all staff which satisfies all the criteria listed above. It may be necessary to separate senior managers from the rest because their terms and conditions of employment are different or because more scope is needed to recognize variations in responsibility and performance than would be possible in a conventional graded structure used for other staff. At this level, each job might have its own salary bracket or 'spot rate'. At the other end of the scale, it might be necessary to separate junior staff, either because they are paid a rate for age or because they are in jobs where the opportunity to improve performance is limited and they should therefore be paid a flat rate or placed within a fairly small salary bracket.

Separate structures for different occupations may be necessary because the salaries of some categories of employees are negotiated with trade unions, or because there are special market rate pressures which make it difficult to fit them into the general salary structure. Some salary systems have a number of different structures for 'market' groups such as computer staff, brand managers or accountants. The salaries for these groups are fixed primarily by reference to market rates and the salaries in one group are not compared specifically with those in other groups. However, a consistent approach to the salary structure may be used across the company with regard to differentials within groups and the width of salary brackets.

Graded salary structures

A graded salary structure, as illustrated in Figure 26.1, consists of a sequence of salary ranges or grades, each of which has a defined minimum and maximum. It is assumed that all the jobs allocated into a range are broadly of equal value, although the actual salaries earned by the individuals in a range depend on their performance or length of service.

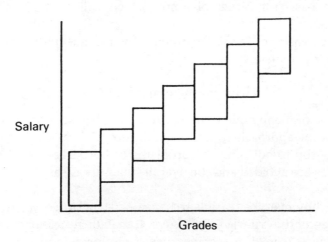

Figure 26.1 A graded salary structure

Main features

The main features of a graded salary structure are the following:

1. All jobs are allocated into a salary grade within the structure on the

basis of an assessment of their internal and external value to the organization.

2. Each salary grade consists of a salary range or band. No individual holding a job in the grade can go beyond the maximum of the salary range unless he or she is promoted.

3. The jobs allocated to a salary grade are assumed to be broadly of the same level. In other words, they normally have the same minimum and maximum rates, which correspond with the grade boundaries.

4. The range may be defined in terms of the percentage increase between the lowest and highest points in the range, for example:

minimum £	midpoint £	maximum £	range %
20,000	23,000	26,000	30
20,000	24,000	28,000	40
20,000	25,000	30,000	50

Alternatively, the range may be defined as a percentage of the midpoint, for example:

minimum %	midpoint %	maximum %	range %
90 (£22,500)	100 (£25,000)	110 (£27,500)	(22)
85 (£21,250)	100 (£25,000)	115 (£28,750)	(35)
80 (£20,000)	100 (£25,000)	120 (£30,000)	(50)

5. The midpoint of the range is the salary level which represents the value to the organization of any job in that grade in which the performance of the job holder is fully acceptable. It may be regarded as the 'target salary' for the grade, which would be the average salary of the staff in the grade, assuming a steady movement of people through the range.

   The midpoint is aligned to the market rates for the jobs in the grade. The salary policy, or 'posture', of the organization determines whether the midpoint is equated to the median market rate or whether it is related to another point, for example, the upper quartile market rate or 10 per cent above the median market rate.

6. The rate of salary progression through a range is determined by performance (variable increments) or by time (fixed increments).

Fixed incremental scales are rapidly disappearing in the private sector after their introduction in the 1970s to combat the impact of incomes policies. They still exist in the public sector, mainly in the form of 'pay spines', as described below, although a certain amount of flexibility has been introduced through accelerated increments or 'range points', which are used to reward high performance in the Civil Service and other agencies and local authorities.

All staff in a performance-related system may eventually progress to the top of the range but at varying rates depending on performance, as illustrated in Figure 26.2. Alternatively, there may be a range of 'target' salaries for staff according to their level of performance, as illustrated in Figure 26.3. Salary progression systems are considered in more detail in Chapter 27.

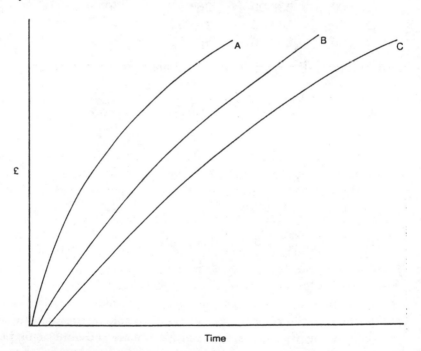

Figure 26.2 Progression to the top of a range at rates varying according to performance

7.   The number of salary ranges required depends on:

(a)   the upper and lower salary levels of the jobs to be covered by the structure, which give the overall range of salaries within which the individual salary ranges have to be fitted;

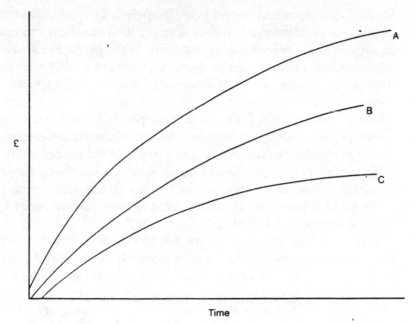

Figure 26.3 Progression to varying target salaries according
to performance

(b)   the number of distinct levels of responsibility in the hierarchy
which need to be catered for by separate grades;
(c)   the size of the differentials between each range (see below).

While the grade structure should take account of the main promotion ladders, it should pay more attention to the distinct levels of
responsibility in the organization as established by job evaluation. It
is necessary to ensure that specialist jobs outside the promotion
ladder are accommodated at appropriate levels, sometimes through
separate technical or professional 'dual ladder' scales.

It is also necessary to distinguish between jobs in different functions
which, although broadly at the same level as other jobs, exhibit
special features which require them to be graded slightly above or
below them. The grade structure must allow for some flexibility in
grading and this is achieved by adjusting differentials and range
widths (and, consequently, overlaps) to meet the needs of the
company.

A structure to cover jobs whose midpoint salaries range from
£10,000 to £30,000 would require seven grades if differentials were
20 per cent. Research has shown that the average number of grades

for managerial, executive and professional staff in the 1970s used to be ten, but as differentials widen at upper limits to allow more scope to attract top people or to reward high performers, and as organizations embark on the necessary process of de-layering, the number of grades is diminishing — sometimes to no more than three.

8.   There is a differential between the midpoints of each salary range which provides adequate scope for rewarding increased responsibility on promotion to the next higher grade but does not create too wide a gap between adjacent grades or reduce the amount of flexibility available for grading jobs. This differential should normally be 15–25 per cent, but 20 per cent of the midpoint of the lower grade is a typical differential.

   If differentials between ranges are too close — less than 10 per cent — many jobs would become borderline cases and frequent reassessments would be required. There would be endless arguments about gradings which could not be resolved by job evaluation, which is too blunt an instrument for making marginal decisions. Staff would be upgraded without adequate increases in responsibility, and this tendency towards 'grade drift' erodes the salary structure. It was, however, a ploy used under the incomes policies of the 1970s to engineer promotion increases on regrading.

   If differentials for junior staff and middle management are too wide — more than 25 per cent — injustices may be done when jobs are considered to be on the borderline between ranges and it would not be easy to allow for the finer gradations that exist between salaried jobs in most organizations, except at the highest levels.

   Experience has shown that in most companies a differential of from 15 to 20 per cent between salary ranges is appropriate for the bulk of staff. This is large enough to provide an adequate increase for promotion between grades. It also avoids an excessive number of grades and reduces the endless arguments about marginal cases. These arguments inevitably result in grade drift when pressure is applied for upgrading rather than a specific market response and in such cases, this can be difficult to resist because of the small variation in responsibility between grades.

   There is a good case for wider differentials at higher levels when increases in responsibility are more significant. A structure can start with 15 per cent differentials for junior staff and then have 20 and 40 per cent or more for middle and senior managers, respectively.

9.   The salary ranges are sufficiently wide to allow recognition of the

fact that people in jobs graded at the same level can perform differently, and should be rewarded in accordance with their performance. To allow room for progression, the ranges at junior clerical level need to be no wider than 15–20 per cent of the minima for the grade. At senior levels, however, where there is more scope for improvements and variations in performance, the ranges could be 35–60 per cent, although the most typical width is about 50 per cent, or plus or minus 20 per cent of the midpoint of the range.

10. There is an overlap between salary grades which acknowledges that an experienced person doing a good job can be of more value to the company than a newcomer to a job in the grade above. Overlap, as measured by the proportion of a grade which is covered by the next lower grade, is usually 25–50 per cent. A large overlap of 40–50 per cent is typical in companies with a wide variety of jobs, where a reasonable degree of flexibility is required in grading them. It results in a larger number of grades than is required for a typical promotion ladder within a department, and implies that in some circumstances a grade can be jumped following promotion.

General increases in salary levels following reviews of market movement, pay negotiations or changes in market rates or the cost of living (usually expressed in percentage terms) are dealt with by proportionate increases to the midpoints of each salary range. Assuming that the policy is to maintain range widths, this would result in proportionate increases to the maxima and minima of each grade.

Jobs can be regraded within the structure when it is decided that their value has altered because of a change in responsibilities or the level of competencies required, or a pronounced movement in market rates. In the latter case, it is necessary to note that this is a special market rate or premium for the job imposed by external circumstances and does not imply that jobs previously placed by job evaluation at the same level should also be regraded. Increasingly, in the fragmenting UK salary market, market premiums of various kinds have to be paid. At their peril, however, do organizations allow jobs to be regraded to match the market — so destroying the integrity of internal relativities and embarking on the reward management 'sin' of grade drift.

Designing the salary structure

The simplest way to design a salary structure is to take the following steps:

Step 1: Establish by market rate surveys and studies of existing structures and differentials the salary levels of the most senior and most junior jobs to be covered by the structure.

Step 2: Draw up a salary grade structure between the upper and lower limits, as established in step 1, according to policies for differentials, the width of salary grades and the size of overlap between grades.

Step 3: Conduct a job evaluation exercise.

Step 4: Obtain market rate data, bearing in mind that there is likely to be a range of market rates rather than a precise figure.

Step 5: Slot the jobs into the grade structure in accordance with the results of both the job evaluations and the market rate surveys. It is here that judgement is required. While some decisions on grades will be obvious, others will be more difficult. If in doubt, re-evaluate the borderline cases to help make the final marginal decision. One advantage of an overlapping structure is that such decisions are less critical.

More detailed guidance on designing salary structures is provided by Armstrong and Murlis.[1]

Alignment with market data

A critical factor to be considered when designing or modifying pay structures is how they should be aligned to market rates. The most appropriate reference point is the midpoint of the salary range. This is the salary level which represents the value to the organization of any job in that grade in which the performance of the job holder is fully acceptable. Recruitment salaries, although normally at the bottom of the range, may have to go as far as this level to obtain a fully qualified and experienced individual. The midpoint salary should therefore not be below the average of the market rates for the jobs in the grade.

The salary policy, or 'market posture' (sometimes called 'salary posture'), of the company determines the relationship between market rates and the midpoint of salary ranges. If, for example, the policy is to pay at the 'upper quartile' (ie the salary level above which the top 25 per cent of the jobs in the survey are paid), the salary curve or salary policy line joining the midpoint of the salary ranges would correspond broadly to the upper quartile of the range of market rates for the jobs in each grade. An 'upper quartile' posture, although it may be desirable in a company wanting to attract and retain above-average quality staff (eg one in a start-up position) could be expensive and inherently inflationary. It is, however, a perfectly viable place to be in a business start-up dependent on high-flyers, or where leading edge, ie upper quartile, people have to be recruited and kept.

If the company is prepared to accept that it should do no more than keep pace with the market by paying average market rates, the policy line might be set to correspond with the median market rates (ie the middle item in the distribution of all the comparable jobs for which survey data are available). Fifty per cent of the jobs will be paid more than the median and 50 per cent of the jobs will be paid less. An intermediate position between the median and upper quartile might be established by a policy of paying, say, 10 per cent above the median rate. This is illustrated in Figure 26.4.

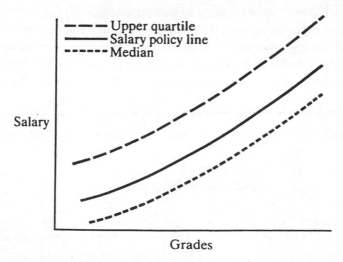

Figure 26.4 Relationship of salary structure to market rates

Advantages of graded structures

The advantages of this type of structure are that:

1. The relative levels of jobs in different functions can be readily assessed and recognized.
2. Consistent methods of grading jobs and establishing differentials between them can be maintained.
3. A well-defined and comprehensible framework exists within which salary and career progression can be planned and controlled.
4. Better control can be exercised over salaries for new starters, merit increments and promotion increases.

Disadvantages of graded structures

The main disadvantage of graded structures is that they are inflexible. Many organizations believe that this is more of a virtue than a defect because graded structures facilitate order, consistency and control. Others find that fixed grades make it more difficult to accommodate the many changes to which reward structures are subject because of internal or external (market rate) pressures. They also argue that the sort of people they employ cannot be confined within rigid range boundaries — their progression may depend on an increase in competence over a time continuum rather than a series of predetermined steps. Flexible organizations and flexible people need flexible pay structures.

Graded structures bring people to top of the range barriers where they stick if there are no opportunities for promotion to the next grade. This problem can be alleviated by granting lump sum bonuses to the highly rated staff in this category on an annual or sometimes less frequent basis (sometimes called continuing good performance bonuses). But these barriers may be largely artificial for those whose market rate is steadily increasing and who are making a real added value contribution to the company.

Individual job range

Where the content of jobs is widely different, or where flexibility in response to rapid organizational changes or market rate pressures is vital, an individual job range system may be preferable to a graded structure. In these circumstances, differences should not be blurred by the procrustean process of forcing a number of dissimilar jobs within the rigid confines of a salary grade.

Individual job range systems, as illustrated in Figure 26.5, simply define a salary bracket for each job. The midpoint of the range is related to market rates and the limits are expressed as plus or minus a percentage of the midpoint salary, typically, at senior levels, plus or minus 20 per cent.

The advantages of the individual job ranges are that they are more flexible and avoid the inevitable problems which occur when positions are evaluated just below grade boundaries. But they are more difficult to control and require more administrative time and effort.

Individual job ranges are probably best for senior jobs or for rapidly growing companies where a conventional grade structure would be too stultifying. They are often associated with points-based job evaluation schemes which provide a basis for assessing relativities between jobs and fixing benefits. They are obviously easier to manage in the context of a well-designed, computer-based salary management system.

It may be necessary to superimpose a benefit grade structure on top of a job range system. Each benefit grade defines the benefits that can be obtained, such as a company car or an improved pension scheme. Jobs can be slotted into benefit grades by means of job evaluation or by a more subjective assessment of what benefits are required to provide increased rewards for greater responsibility or to compete with market rates. A benefit grade structure is shown in Table 26.1.

Table 26.1 Benefit grade structures

Management grade	Salary range (midpoint) £	Company car £	Petrol	Pension scheme	Medical insurance
A	35,000– 50,000	19,000	Yes	Senior fund; $\frac{2}{3}$ of final salary after 20 years' service	Yes
B	25,000– 35,000	15,000	Yes	Senior fund; $\frac{2}{3}$ of final salary after 30 years' service	Yes
C	19,500– 25,000	9500	No	Normal fund; $\frac{2}{3}$ of final salary after 40 years' service	Yes

A benefit grade structure superimposed on an individual job range structure is illustrated in Figure 26.5.

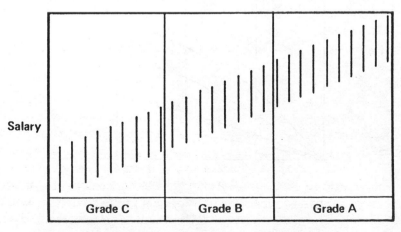

Figure 26.5 Individual job ranges and benefit grades

Pay curves

The types of salary structure just described work well when market rates and/or the process of job analysis and evaluation can clearly discriminate between different levels of responsibility in terms of the work people are doing, rather than their capacity to do the work. They may not, however, be as appropriate in companies or departments where the work is predominantly carried out by young professional staff, engineers, scientists or technologists. It may be more difficult to grade jobs, especially in research and development departments, and staff in these categories often have more opportunities to compare their prospects with those employed elsewhere.

In these circumstances, the critical factors determining salary levels and progression are, first, the extent to which individuals can contribute whatever they are expected to do in terms of meeting objectives and performance standards and, secondly, the market rates for those individuals.

The ability to deliver desirable results can be described as the level of competence individuals have attained. Market rates will govern what individuals should be paid now and in the future as their competence and hence their marketability increase.

A competence progression curve, as illustrated in Figure 26.6, relates salaries for people in a particular family of jobs, such as scientists or

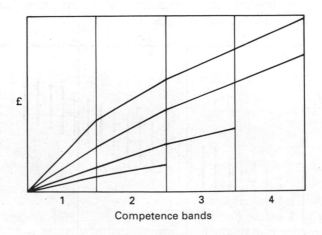

Figure 26.6 A pay curve system

computer staff, to levels of competence defined as points to be attained (as in this example) or as bands, on the assumption that competence develops progressively rather than between a number of fixed points. The rate of pay for each level or band of competency is determined by reference to market rate data, which may have to be collected specially from comparable firms when comparisons between competence levels and payments can be made.

In a competence progression curve, the assumption is made that salaries will not increase beyond certain points unless individuals have attained the right level of competence. The pay curve system may, however, be refined by allowing for different rates of progression up the salary scale according to performance. Competence-based pay curves are developed by using the analytical and job evaluation techniques described in Chapters 16 (pages 334–340) and 25 (pages 532–534) respectively.

Job family system

The advantages of operating one pay structure for all jobs in terms of achieving consistency and facilitating control seem to be obvious. But it becomes progressively more difficult to do this in situations when market rate pressures impinge so strongly on particular categories of employees that the existing grade structure can no longer accommodate them. An overrigid structure can make it difficult to reward individuals according to their levels of competence and contribution.

A job family system recognizes that there are different market rates for different categories of staff in the organization. It also recognizes that rates of progression may have to vary according to individuals and the jobs they are in.

Job families or market groups might, for example, be created to cover research and development engineers, marketing and sales staff, IT specialists, production managers and engineers, personnel professionals, lawyers, accountants and other categories of administrative or support staff. Separate job families could be linked within the same discipline to distinguish, for example, between those with professional and those with managerial competences. This might involve accepting the principle that top professionals or specialists in a field could progress to a higher salary band than managers in the same area, thus recognizing that although professionals and managers use different skills, they can, in their own way, make equally important contributions which could be reflected in their relative market rates.

This type of structure is strongly orientated towards market rates and individual competences. Strict considerations of equity may not be so prominent and unless great care is taken to justify differences in terms of competences and market rates, it could be difficult to ensure that the principle of equal pay for work of equal value is maintained.

Spot rate structures

In its simplest form, a spot rate or individual job rate system allocates a specific rate for a job. There are no salary brackets. There may, however, be what might be termed 'salary zones' which define the benefits that employees receive and may also indicate the basis upon which salaries are fixed and progressed within the zone. Rates are fixed by reference to market rates or by negotiation with trade unions — spot rate structures remain almost universal for manual workers. Job evaluation can be used to establish the hierarchy, but this may not be the case if rates are negotiated in relation to traditional craft demarcations or if there are considerable market pressures.

Modifications to the spot rate system

The basic system can be modified in one or more of the following ways:

1. Performance-related bonuses can be earned on top of the basic rate.
2. Additional payments can be made to the spot rate for special skills or responsibilities. This is common in structures for manual workers.
3. Scope may be allowed for some discretion to pay people below the spot rate if they are not fully qualified to do the job. The assumption is that if the spot rate is the market rate then the company has to pay to attract and retain someone who is fully capable of meeting the standards expected by the company. If those standards are higher than those of its competitors, then the company spot rate would be higher than the external market rate; for example, it would be located at the upper quartile of the distribution of market rates. People appointed or promoted to a job for which they are not yet suitably qualified could be paid up to, say, 10 per cent less than the spot rate and progressed towards that rate as quickly or as slowly as their progress warrants. This salary would remain below the rate if they did not progress, in which case their continued retention by the company would be under question.

Pay spines

Pay spines are mainly used in the public sector, or in agencies and organizations which have adopted a public sector approach to reward management.

They consist of a series of incremental points extending from the lowest to the highest paid jobs covered by the system. Pay scales or ranges for the various grades are then superimposed on the pay spine, as illustrated in Figure 26.7 (this represents only part of a typical pay spine).

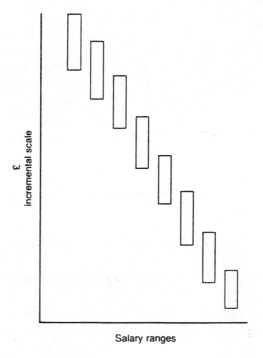

Figure 26.7 A pay spine system

Pay spines are essentially incremental scales, but if performance-related or flexible pay is introduced, individuals can be given accelerated increments. The Civil Service adds range points on top of the normal scale which enable staff who achieve very high or consistently high performance ratings to advance above the scale maximum for their grade.

Rate for age

A rate for age system is usually an incremental scale in which a specific rate of pay or a defined pay bracket is linked to each age for staff in certain jobs. Rates for age scales are reserved for young employees under training or for junior office or laboratory staff carrying out routine work. The assumption behind rate for age scales is that the staff are on a learning curve which means that their value to the company is directly linked to increased experience and maturity.

The simplest structure consists of one rate for each age as shown in Figure 26.8.

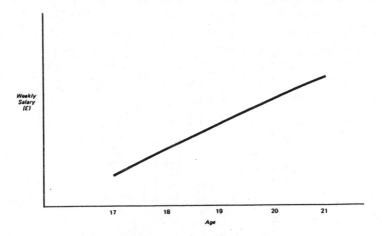

Figure 26.8 Rate for age structure

A more complex structure to accommodate three different job grades is shown in Figure 26.9.

It may be thought desirable to allow some scope for merit at each age and Figure 26.10 shows how merit can be catered for in a rate for age scale.

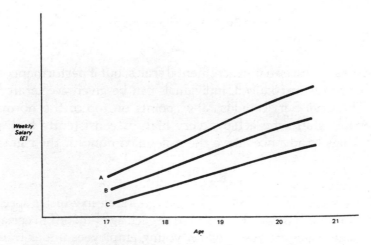

Figure 26.9 Rate for age structure for three job grades

Rate for age scales of the basic type illustrated in Figure 26.8 are inflexible but they may have to be used because they are a tradition in the local labour market and with a highly mobile form of labour it is essential to keep pace with market rates. Their great advantage is that they are easy to administer — invidious decisions about the relative merit of people under training do not have to be made and the scales achieve complete equity. They may be worth retaining for these reasons, but there is a lot to be said for relating pay to age *and* performance as in Figure 26.10 rather than to the arbitrary criterion of age.

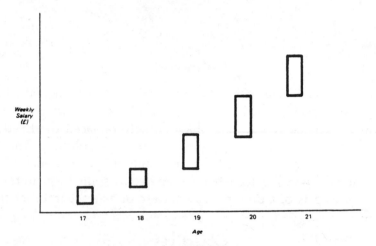

Figure 26.10 Rate for age structure with merit bands

References

1. Armstrong, M and Murlis, H *Reward Management*, Kogan Page, London, 1991.

27

Performance-related Pay

Definition

Performance-related pay (PRP) links financial rewards to individual, group or corporate performance, or any combination of these three Performance-related pay systems have largely replaced the fixed incremental systems that were a legacy of the incomes policies of the 1970s They are most commonly applied to managerial, professional, technical and clerical staff, but they have been extended by some firms to the shop floor, either as part of a uniform pay system or as a separate scheme.

Objectives

The objectives of PRP are to:

- motivate all employees, not just the high-flyers;
- increase the commitment of employees to the organization by encouraging them to identify with its mission and values;
- reinforce existing cultures and values where these foster high levels of performance, innovation and teamwork;
- help to change cultures where they need to become more performance- and results-orientated, or where the adoption of other new and key values should be rewarded;
- discriminate consistently and equitably on the distribution of rewards to employees according to their contribution;
- deliver a positive message about the performance expectations of the company — one of the main merits of PRP is that it focuses attention on key performance issues;
- direct attention and endeavour where the organization wants them by specifying performance goals and standards;

- emphasize individual performance or teamwork as appropriate — personal schemes focus on individual contribution and group schemes foster cooperation — although, as many UK employers have learned, it is wise to ensure that individual schemes also reward good team performance as a 'core' value;
- improve the recruitment and retention of high-quality staff — many employees expect PRP to be part of a well-managed working environment;
- flex pay costs in line with company performance.

Factors to be taken into account in achieving the objectives

The gap between the simple idea of paying for performance and successful implementation of performance-related pay systems is wide. PRP is not a panacea which will cure all your problems by instantly motivating staff to achieve significantly higher levels of performance. Introducing performance-related pay is an act of faith based on the assumption that people perform more effectively if offered financial incentives to do so. Most people act implicitly on that assumption, but no convincing research evidence has yet been produced to prove that it is true — principally because we know that a multiplicity of factors is involved in most performance improvements, and most of these factors are interdependent. What recent research has taught us is that badly designed and poorly implemented PRP schemes probably demotivate staff more effectively than well-designed and implemented schemes motivate them. And inadequate schemes will be produced if:

- They do not match the culture and value systems of the organization.
- Managers and those who implement systems are not committed to making them work and properly prepared and trained to do so.
- Performance rewards are not closely linked to the business, do not support overall strategy and are not flexible enough to respond to changes in strategic direction.
- The key performance indicators and critical success factors are not clearly identified.
- The system is unfair in that rewards are arbitrary and not linked clearly to competences and achievements through an effective performance management system, which should be in place *before* PRP is introduced.
- Performance targets are too mechanistic — qualitative targets and standards can be just as important to success as quantitative ones.
- Provision is not made for monitoring, evaluating and reviewing the

system to ensure that it can develop and respond to changing needs. Systems 'set in stone' are dangerous — they fail to reflect the need for organizations to learn from and build on experience gained from year to year.

These are difficult criteria to satisfy, and even if they are met, account has to be taken of the arguments that can be advanced against PRP when contemplating its introduction. These may be voiced by managers fearful of the new responsibilities PRP brings as well as by trade unions and individual employees who doubt management's ability to conduct the performance review process openly and fairly.

Arguments against PRP

The criticisms most frequently levelled at PRP are as follows:

- It is difficult to measure individual performance objectively, and subjectivity may lead to unfair assessments.
- It can encourage people to focus narrowly on the tasks which will earn them Brownie points fast, to do them as quickly as possible, to be less concerned about quality and longer-term issues and to take fewer risks.
- Study after study has shown that intrinsic interest in a task — the sense that something is worth doing — typically declines when someone is given only external reasons for doing it.
- Getting people to chase money can produce nothing except people chasing money — waving 20-pound notes in front of employees can lead them to think of themselves as doing work *only* for the reward.
- Financial rewards may work for some people because their expectations that they will receive them are high. But these people tend to be well motivated anyway, and less confident employees may not respond to incentives which they do not expect to receive.
- If there is undue influence and emphasis on individual performance, essential teamwork and cooperation may suffer.
- It can lead to pay rising faster than performance if the control systems are not strong enough — experience shows that there is a strong tendency for performance-related pay to drift upwards.

Counter-arguments

The counter-arguments to these criticisms are the following:

- An analytical and systematic approach to developing PRP, as described below, should minimize the risk of producing an inadequate scheme.

- While it has not been proved that PRP guarantees better motivation, neither has it been disproved. The concept that people react positively to financial incentives has considerable face validity — as long as you do not simplistically imply that money is *all* they work for.
- Controls can successfully be built into a scheme to minimize the danger of pay drift — cost iterations on computerized payroll systems greatly assist the achievement of this.
- PRP may be necessary simply because of market pressures and employee expectations that it will be part of competitive practice.
- While it may be argued that PRP has a limited effect as a motivator, in some circumstances it can still play an important role in focusing effort, defining the performance expectations of the company and increasing commitment — many organizations have found that the joint discussions of managers and employees in this area have significant value in themselves.
- It is not suggested that PRP is the only, even the best, long-term motivator — attention should also be given to the development of non-financial approaches to motivation, as described in Chapter 14. The total approach to performance management, as advocated in Chapter 19, involves using the right mix of non-financial and financial motivators.

Rules for successful PRP

Mike Langley, past Vice-President of the Institute of Personnel Management's National Committee for Pay and Employment Conditions and first Chairman of the IPM Compensation Forum, has defined the following five golden rules for successful PRP schemes:

1. Individuals need to be clear about the targets and standards of performance required, whatever they may be.
2. They should be able to track performance against those targets and standards throughout the period over which performance is being assessed.
3. They must be in a position to influence their performance by changing their behaviour or decisions.
4. They should be clear about the rewards they will receive for achieving the required end results.
5. The rewards should be meaningful enough to make the efforts required worthwhile — and the communication of the rewards should be positively handled.

Considerations to be taken into account when introducing PRP

These requirements for success are very demanding. PRP in any form — be it performance-related salary increases, bonuses or incentives — is not an easy option. Before embarking on the introduction of PRP, one must take the following factors into account:

- *Matching the culture.* PRP schemes cannot be taken off the shelf. There is no magic scale of performance measures and simple set of rules waiting for adoption on a universal basis. Successful PRP schemes need to match the culture and core values of the organization. It is only by understanding and working with the culture that it is possible to develop systems which underpin a bias to action.
- *Linking PRP to the business strategy.* If PRP is to be an effective strategic tool, it must be linked to business strategy. The focus needs to be on issues which emerge from the business planning process, such as profitability, research initiatives, product development, market penetration and shareholder value.
- *Balancing quantitative and qualitative measures.* While most PRP schemes rely on quantitative measures of performance, there is a strong case for introducing qualitative factors, which may be related to the degree to which individuals behave in line with corporate values in such areas as innovation, teamwork, customer service and delivery.
- *The need for flexibility.* Many PRP schemes at top management level tend to pay out only if a profit or other quantified target has been completely achieved. But in some circumstances there is a case for flexibility in making 'milestone' payments which convey the right messages for the future.
- *The need to promote teamwork.* Bad PRP schemes can produce a lot of raving individualists. The importance of teamwork should be recognized in structuring the scheme and defining critical success factors and performance indicators. Individuals should be informed that achieving their targets at the expense of others is not competent performance.
- *The need to avoid short-term thinking.* Poor PRP schemes can focus attention on short-term results at the expense of other, more important, longer-term objectives. This must be avoided by setting long-term as well as short-term goals and by discussing short-term objectives in their overall context.
- *Involvement in the design process.* Designing PRP schemes should be and usually is an iterative process — trying and testing ideas on measures and structure with those who will eventually be involved in a scheme. It is also a valuable learning process which can throw up fundamental

strategic and business issues. Those due to benefit from the scheme should have an input into agreeing critical success factors and performance indicators for both themselves and the organization.

- *Getting the message across.* All types of PRP are very powerful forms of communication. To get the right messages across for any scheme, one must make key decisions on the following:

  (a) How can the scheme achieve the best possible launch?
  (b) Is it better to give no pay-out rather than a low pay-out?
  (c) What is the best psychological moment for pay-out?
  (d) What communications should be used to gain maximum motivational impact from payments?
  (e) How should communications be handled when the scheme requires change?

Introducing PRP

The sequence of activities in introducing PRP is illustrated in Figure 27.1. The following questions need to be answered at each stage:

1. Why and how do we want to do it?

    (a) Why does the organization want to introduce PRP?
    (b) What does it want to get out of it?
    (c) How much money and effort should be put into designing and operating the scheme?
    (d) To whom should the scheme apply?

2. Are we ready?

    (a) Will it fit and support the culture and value systems of the organization?
    (b) Is the concept of PRP supported at all levels in the organization?
    (c) What is the attitude of the trade unions or staff associations to PRP?
    (d) Is there an effective performance system in operation to provide the basis for PRP?
    (e) Can we administrate a PRP scheme fairly and efficiently?

3. Should we go ahead? Decide on the basis of the results of the stages 1 and 2 analyses whether or not to go ahead with PRP.

4. If we decide against PRP, what else can we do? If the decision is not to go ahead with PRP, consider other forms of motivation and recognition the organization could provide, for example:

    (a) improved training;

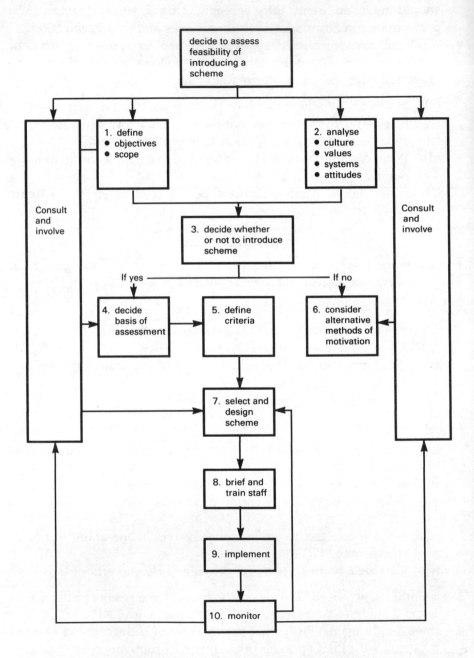

Figure 27.1 Introducing performance-related pay

(b) better succession planning;

(c) sympathetic career development counselling;

(d) non-cash individual or team awards to mark special and identifiable achievements.

Types of schemes

The types of scheme available are the following:

1. individual merit payment schemes:

    (a) salary range schemes;

    (b) pay spine;

    (c) variable increment;

    (d) competence-related;

2. individual bonus payments;

3. group bonuses;

4. profit sharing;

5. executive bonus schemes;

6. salesforce incentives.

These are discussed below.

Individual merit payment schemes

Salary range schemes

Basic features

These schemes are commonly found in the private sector. Their basic feature is that salary progresses within a salary range according to performance. The differential between the minimum and maximum of the range is specified, and the midpoint represents the rate for a fully competent person in the job (the relationship of this rate to the market rate is determined by the market posture of the company). Typical salary ranges are 90–110 per cent, 85–115 per cent, and 80–120 per cent. An individual merit scheme will provide for progression through the range to be covered by performance ratings, as illustrated in Figure 27.2. There will be different rates of progression over time and limits (merit bars) beyond which employees with certain ratings cannot progress.

Dealing with those reaching the top of their scale

Some organizations when faced with the problem of good employees reaching the top of their scale without any immediate prospects of promotion — one of the implications of the flatter organization structures

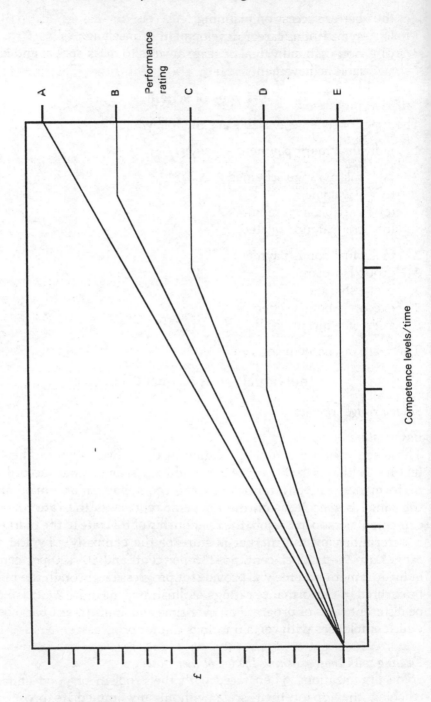

Figure 27.2 Individual merit pay progression within a grade

of today — are prepared to ignore scale ceilings and pay above the range for truly exceptional performance. Others deal with this situation by paying lump sum bonuses, a measure which avoids distorting the salary structure. It is, however, dangerous to adopt this practice in response to market rate pressures. These should be dealt with by separately identified market premiums.

Rating scales

Merit payments are usually determined by an overall rating, for example:

A = Exceptional performance
B = Very effective performance
C = Well-balanced performance
D = Not entirely effective
E = Ineffective

Further examples of rating scales for use in determining performance-related pay were given in Chapter 19. The rating classifications need to be defined with great care, and managers should be given explicit guidance on the approach they use in making this assessment. The whole purpose of performance-related pay can be undermined if such ratings are inconsistent, biased or unduly subjective. One of the strongest arguments against PRP is that it is very difficult to avoid these problems unless continuous effort is directed to monitoring ratings to ensure that they are distributed fairly and are based on well-balanced assessments.

Ranking systems

One method of dealing with biased ratings is to adopt a ranking system. The approach used by Marks and Spencer, The Alliance and Leicester Building Society and others is to rank staff in order of merit and then distribute gradings through the rank order, for example, by giving the top 10 per cent an A rating, the next 15 per cent a B rating, the next 60 per cent a C rating and the remaining 15 per cent a D rating. This is, in effect, a forced distribution, which eliminates a skewed allocation of ratings but still depends on the accuracy of the rankings. The rank order may be produced by scoring various merit factors for each member of a group of staff and adding them to produce a total score. Even this somewhat mechanistic approach cannot eliminate inequitable ratings if the basic assessment is unfair.

Relationship between ratings and the size of merit increases

The ratings determine the size of the merit increase expressed as a percentage of base salary. For example, guidelines could be issued as follows:

Exceptional performance = 10% plus
Excellent performance = 7% to 10%
Well-balanced performance = 5% to 7%

These increases could be in addition to an across-the-board cost-of-living award. But many companies are now combining merit and cost-of-living increases in one payment which, although it makes allowance for underlying inflation, is geared entirely to merit. This provides for greater flexibility — there is more scope to discriminate between different levels and give really significant increases to outstanding staff — 20 per cent or more. It also enables companies effectively to reduce the real salary of poor performers by giving them an increase which is less than inflation.

Size of increases
The size of increases is affected by the following factors:

- The organization's ability or willingness to pay.
- The rate of inflation.
- Increases in market rates which may be broadly in line with inflation, although some increases will be greater or less, depending on supply and demand factors.
- What is regarded as a worthwhile increase for different levels of performance. There are no absolute standards for what is 'worthwhile', but it is pointless to give an increase of less than 3 per cent, and that should be reserved for the below-average performers. Anyone who is doing reasonably well deserves an increase of at least 5 per cent on top of inflation, and really high levels of performance deserve rewards of 10 per cent or more.

Guidance on the market rates of progression can be obtained by studying market surveys which provide data on the increase in pay of matched samples of individuals over a period of time. If such a survey indicates that the average total increase has been, say, 12.4 per cent, this is a good starting point for a decision on the average increase (merit plus inflation) that the company should consider awarding.

Flexibility and control
In some schemes there is a fair amount of flexibility with regard to the size of merit payments and the rates at which individuals can move through a salary bracket. There may be an overall budget of x per cent of payroll, but

managers may be allowed to exercise discretion on how they distribute their own budget. This inevitably means that distributions and rates of progression vary between departments.

But it can be argued convincingly that if you are going to hold managers totally accountable for achieving their objectives by making the best use of their human resources, then, within a financial budget, you ought to allow them to stand or fall on their ability to distribute rewards fairly and to motivate their staff in ways which they believe will work. This approach assumes that you have competent and well-trained managers, and that it is still necessary to provide advice to those managers who need it on the distribution of payments. Heads of remuneration in companies which adopt this policy of delegation support it because it is in accordance with the belief in today's flatter, decentralized, flexible and responsive organizations that more authority should be devolved to line managers. But they know that they may still have to engage in a lot of 'hand holding' while managers learn how to exercise their newly granted authority.

Some companies, however, do not feel that they can trust their managers to act responsibly and they adopt a more rigidly controlled, even mechanistic, approach (although it may be asked, parenthetically, how anyone can ever *be* responsible if never trusted?). And low-trust organizations can be unpleasant and demotivating to work in.

Rate of progression

The size of the merit payment obviously determines the rate of progression through a salary range, which will vary according to ratings. For example, in an 80–120 per cent range, say, £16,000 to £24,000, an 'A' rating may result in an increase of 10 per cent of the bottom of the scale. Someone who consistently received an 'A' would therefore progress through the range in five years. A 'C' rating might result in a 5 per cent increase, which would mean that it would take ten years to move through the range.

Performance matrices

Some organizations are quite happy to allow a fair degree of flexibility in the system so that merit increases and the rate at which people progress is a matter for individual judgement. Others, the majority, prefer to be explicit about the size of increases on the grounds that consistency and, therefore, equity in the distribution of merit payments occur only if managers are given explicit rules to follow rather than broad guidelines.

A frequently used method of controlling the distribution of rewards and the rate of progression is to have a performance matrix, such as the one

performance assessment \ position in salary band	90–94%	95–99%	100%	101–105%	105–110%
	% increase	% increase	% increase	% increase	% increase
A Far exceeds requirements in all areas	15	15	15	12	12
B Consistently exceeds requirements in most areas	12	12	12	10	10
C Meets requirements	10	10	10	8	0
D Does not meet requirements in a number of areas	8	8	5	0	0
E Fails to meet requirements	0	0	0	0	0

Figure 27.3 Performance matrix

illustrated in Figure 27.3, which indicates the total increase, including an allowance for inflation or increases in market rates (in this example, this is assumed to be 5 per cent). The matrix provides for increases to be related to both performance and the position of the individual in the salary range. Such systems also spell out the limits (merit bars) within a salary range beyond which salaries for people rated at lower levels cannot progress.

The performance matrix is constructed with reference to the remuneration policies of the organization, especially those concerned with the size of increases and the consolidation of merit and general increases. A performance matrix has to be reconstructed at the time of the salary review to allow for market rates, inflation, and the firm's ability to pay. Many organizations flex the merit payment 'pool' according to company performance by setting an overall percentage limit to the payroll increase and then deciding how that pool should be divided. The division may be determined by an analysis of the distribution of performance ratings. A computerized system is very helpful, and, in large organizations, it is essential in conducting this analysis.

Pay spine scheme

This is a typical approach in the public sector. The 'box' rating given in the assessment determines whether or not an individual should get additional increments on the pay spine or whether or not an increment should be withheld. The use of merit bars and range points means that relatively few staff can progress further and then only to a limited extent. These schemes may provide for a modicum of flexibility but are not powerful motivators.

Variable increment schemes

Although fixed incremental scales, in which people progress through a salary grade for 'being there' rather than in relation to their competence, are now much less common in the private sector, they do still exist in the more bureaucratic or trade-union-dominated organizations (trade unions can still fight against merit pay because they believe it is fundamentally unfair). Some companies have, however, wanted to provide a measure of performance-related pay on the grounds that it is more inequitable *not* to reward people according to their contribution than to pay everyone the same irrespective of their performance. To cater for this need, these firms have provided for extra increments to be paid, or for increments to be withheld, according to performance, much as in pay spine schemes.

Competence-related schemes

This is a relatively new approach to PRP and, although competence-related schemes are not strictly merit schemes, they are most conveniently listed under this heading. They are also referred to as skill-based or knowledge-based schemes, although these terms are sometimes reserved for skilled craft and other manual workers (see also Chapter 28 which describes the operation of these schemes in wage payment systems).

The analysis of competences is playing an increasing part in management development, as discussed in Chapter 21, and it is logical to extend its application to reward. Linking pay to levels of competence embraces the fundamental belief that rewards should be related to the demonstrated ability to apply knowledge, skills and ability to deliver results.

Basis
A competency scheme typically divides the range of competency requirements for a category of employee, such as scientists, into a series of competence bands. Bands are defined in terms of competences and any formal education or training required. Each competence band has a broad pay range and progression within the band depends on performance assessed by reference to the competence requirements. A competence and

performance-related scheme contains explicit guidelines in the shape of pay curves, as illustrated in Figure 27.4.

These schemes recognize that the rate of pay of individuals is determined by three factors:

1. their level of competence — ie their ability to apply knowledge and skills to reach a satisfactory level of performance;
2. the level of performance they achieve in whatever competence band they are in;
3. the market rate for the levels of competence and performance they have achieved.

Main features of competence schemes
The main features of a competence and performance-based scheme are as follows:

- The horizontal axis on the chart shown in Figure 27.4 represents the level of competence individuals achieve. In this example, four competence bands have been established, although the competence development line along this axis represents a continuum of progression rather than four finite steps. No times would be set for moving through these bands — this would depend on the level of performance. It could be assumed, however, that continuing satisfactory performance would take individuals through the bands at a certain rate, thus indicating the length of time, on average, it might take to reach each competence band.
- The curves represent different levels of performance. In this example, there are five rates, C being regarded as the normal level. Six- or four-level scales could be used. The curves govern pay progression, although this could be limited if an individual cannot advance to a higher competence band. Pay within each competence band would vary according to performance.
- The vertical axis represents the rate of pay appropriate for different levels of competence and performance. These would be linked to market rates.
- The rate of increase in pay according to performance would have to be determined. Clearly, increases have to be meaningful. The example indicates a reduction in the rate of pay progression at higher levels, but it might well be considered that percentage increases should continue at the same rate.
- There would be scope to give a lump sum bonus equivalent to the

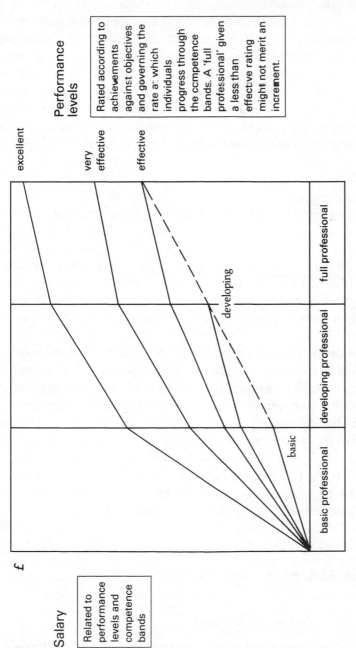

Figure 27.4 Competence and performance-related pay curve

The rate at which individuals move through the bands depends on achievement — thus, an effective individual would move through over a standard period while higher-rated individuals would move faster. Individuals given a 'basic' or 'developing' rating can move only so far through the competence bands unless they receive a higher rating.

normal pay increment for high-level performers who have reached the limits of their salary bands.

- Although the system would be designed to relate pay to competence and performance, it would also provide the basis for career planning and development. Individuals could be made aware of career 'aiming points' expressed in terms of what they must be able to do and, as appropriate, the qualifications, training and experience they need to reach a defined level of competence. This provides additional motivation and, when the company supports the development programme, a means of increasing commitment and retaining valued staff.

Design of competence schemes

The design of a competence or skill-based scheme requires an analysis of the different levels of knowledge, skills and abilities within 'job families'. These can result in fairly generalized descriptions of competence levels. But some companies have prepared much more detailed analyses of skills which they have defined as modules. Employees are assessed on the degree to which they have acquired the skills or knowledge, and, as long as there is an operational requirement for these qualities, their pay is adjusted accordingly.

A competence or skill-based scheme may be linked to training programmes designed to increase or widen skills. In some cases, payment is made for reaching a skill level even if that skill is not being used at present by the employee, although it must be one which is required within the job family to which the employee belongs. Grades may be defined for job families in terms of these skill modules, and points schemes may be applied which allocate points for the acquisition of skills in order to determine gradings. This analytical approach, however, is more common in wage payment systems or when terms and conditions of employment are harmonized. It is described in more detail in Chapter 28.

Advantages of individual merit payment schemes

These advantages are that these schemes:

- directly link performance and salary progression;
- provide individualized progression rates;
- recognize increasing competence gained through experience.

Disadvantages

These are as follows:

- The schemes are dependent on the quality of appraisal, which can be arbitrary, subjective or inconsistent, especially when the appraisers have been inadequately trained.
- Unless they are very carefully conceived and managed, they can demotivate a lot of people who, although they may not be delivering spectacular results (and therefore not receiving spectacular rewards) are still important.
- Merit payments, as distinct from bonuses, create extra payroll costs when benefits such as pensions are related to base pay.
- A merit payment is, in effect, a permanent increase in salary, yet the quality of performance in future years may not justify this payment.
- Because it results in increases in base salary, merit pay can result in an upward drift in payroll costs without a commensurate improvement in performance.
- Merit pay is effective as a motivator only if rewards are clearly related to performance and are of a significant value, but it is difficult for conventional schemes to discriminate properly, and the size of the award may have to be controlled to offset the cost factors mentioned above.

Design of individual merit payment schemes

The points to be considered are the following:

- the amount of money available for distribution expressed as a percentage of the payroll (the merit payment pool);
- how the merit payment pool will or can be flexed in relation to company performance;
- the range of payments to be made, expressed as a percentage either of base salary or the lowest part of the salary range;
- the distribution of rewards in such a way that the scheme contributes to the motivation of the core of competent performers upon whom the organization largely depends, as well as of the high-flyers;
- the amount of freedom to be given to managers within their budgets to determine merit increases;
- what happens to highly rated staff who have 'topped out', ie have reached the top of their scale and for whom there are no immediate prospects of promotion (consideration may have to be given to bonus

payments in these circumstances);
- how the quality of assessments and ratings will be monitored and controlled;
- how budgets for merit increases and payroll costs will be controlled;
- how staff are going to be convinced that the scheme is fair, equitable and reasonably rewarding, not only for the superachievers but also for the more modest but essential contributors to success.

Individual bonus schemes

Definition

Individual performance bonuses are payments made in addition to base salary which are related to the achievement of specified targets, the completion of a project or a stage of a project to a specified standard, the receipt of an appropriate performance rating, or a combination of any of these. An individual bonus for those at the top of their salary scale could be the normal merit payment according to performance, converted into a lump sum.

Bonuses can, however, be more explicitly linked to performance if they are related to the degree to which targets have been achieved. For example, three levels of bonus may be paid according to whether individuals:

- only just achieved the target — the threshold bonus;
- completely achieved the target — the full bonus;
- significantly exceeded the target — the exceptional bonus.

Individual bonuses were at one time paid only to senior managers, senior sales representatives and others whose performance could be targeted with precision, using such criteria as profitability or sales. Their use is now spreading generally to more junior levels and jobs where targets are more difficult to quantify. This is because organizations are trying to contain consolidated payroll costs and benefit from the reality that bonuses can, if well implemented, give very strong performance messages. One reason for the effectiveness of bonuses as part of a reward system is the simple fact that people often spend bonus money differently from a 'drip feed' pay increase. They remember and appreciate the extra luxury or weekend in Paris on which they spent the award.

Advantages

These are as follows:

- The reward is immediately payable for work well done.
- The bonus can be linked to specific achievements and future targets, and this constitutes both a reward and an incentive.
- The payment is not perpetuated as part of base salary irrespective of future performance.
- Lump sum payments appeal to some people.
- Additional rewards can be given to people at the top of their salary scale without damaging the integrity of the salary structure.
- The arrangements can be flexible.
- The system can be designed for easy administration.

Disadvantages

These are as follows:

- It is more difficult to apply to people whose jobs have less tangible outputs.
- An individualistic rather than a team approach may be encouraged.
- People may be diverted away from the innovative and developmental aspects of their work because they are concentrating on the task in hand.
- It could be difficult to establish a fair and consistent relationship between the results achieved and the level of the reward, which could be seen as arbitrary and inequitable.
- It might be hard to discriminate fairly between those on long-term projects, who could wait for some time before they are rewarded, and those with shorter-term and more visible objectives, who could be rewarded more rapidly.

Design of individual bonus schemes

The points to be considered are the following:

- the constituents of the bonus in terms of the mix of the payments related to target achievement, ratings or company results;
- the method of defining targets and standards of performance for tasks to be completed;
- the basis upon which performance ratings could be translated into

bonus payments (including the range of payments that can be made);
- how agreement should be reached with individuals on their targets or tasks;
- how performance should be measured and by whom;
- the amount of money to be made available for bonuses, and how and when bonuses should be paid;
- how to make the scheme differentiate rewards in relation to performance in a fair, consistent and relevant way, having regard to the disadvantages listed above.

Group bonus schemes

Definition

Group or team bonus schemes related the reward to the satisfactory completion of a project or stage of a project, or the achievement of a group target.

Advantages

Group bonuses are increasingly being used by organizations that want to underpin and reward collective effort. They are particularly helpful in areas such as research and development and information technology where work is project-based. They can:

- promote the value and successful operation of teamwork;
- facilitate the setting of group targets where results depend on joint effort;
- be less invidious than individual payments, especially when these are affected by the work of other people in the team which is outside the employee's control.

Disadvantages

Group bonuses:

- are feasible only where it is possible to identify teams who are working together to achieve defined tasks;
- can dilute individual motivation because the relationship between individual effort and reward may be remote;
- can cause ill-directed peer-group pressure which punishes weaker performers.

Design of group bonus schemes

The points to be covered are the following:

- the identification and definition of the groups to be included in the scheme;
- methods of defining targets;
- how agreement should be reached with groups on their targets;
- how the performance of groups should be measured;
- the formula for deciding on bonus payments (including minima and maxima) and the extent to which a discretionary element is required;
- the amount of money available for group bonus payments and how and when bonuses should be paid;
- the procedure for monitoring the scheme.

Profit sharing

Definition

Profit sharing is a plan under which an employer pays to eligible employees, as an addition to their normal remuneration, special sums in the form of cash or stock related to the profits of the business. The amount shared is either determined by an established formula, which may be published, or left entirely at the discretion of management. Profit-sharing schemes are generally extended to all employees of the company except directors.

Objectives of profit sharing

Most companies which operate profit-sharing schemes have one or more of the following objectives in mind:

- to encourage employees to identify themselves more closely with the company by developing a common concern for its progress;
- to stimulate a greater interest among employees in the affairs of the company as a whole;
- to encourage better cooperation between management and employees;
- to recognize that employees of the company have a moral right to share in the profits they have helped to produce;
- to demonstrate in practical terms the goodwill of the company towards its employees.

It is generally recognized that schemes which share profits according to some universal formula among all or most employees do not provide any real incentive because they fail to satisfy the three basic requirements of an incentive scheme, namely:

- that the reward should bear a direct relation to the effort;
- that the payment should follow immediately or soon after the effort;
- that the method of calculation should be simple and easily understood.

Types of schemes

The main types of profit-sharing schemes are the following:

1. *Cash* — a proportion of profits is paid in cash direct to employees. This is the traditional and still the most popular approach.
2. *Stock* — a proportion of profits is paid in stock. This is much less popular, especially since the advent of the approved deferred share trust scheme with its considerable tax advantages.
3. *Approved deferred share trust (ADST)* — the company allocates profit to a trust fund which acquires shares in the company on behalf of employees.
4. *Mixed schemes* — an ADST scheme is sometimes offered in addition to a cash scheme, or the latter is made available to staff before they are eligible for ADST shares or as an alternative to ADST shares.

In addition, the UK government introduced in 1987 its profit-related pay scheme, which provides income tax relief for approved schemes.

A survey of profit sharing in 356 firms published by the Glasgow University Centre for Research into Industrial Democracy and Participation revealed that in the two-thirds of the survey firms which operated profit sharing, the most popular scheme, especially among the smaller firms, was the simple cash-based option. The ADST type scheme is, however, gaining in popularity. Profit sharing was much more common among US-based companies (64 per cent) than their European counterparts (29 per cent), and the schemes were more prevalent in London and the South than in the Midlands and the North.

Cash schemes

The main characteristics of typical cash schemes can be analysed under the following headings, which are discussed below:

- eligibility;

- formula for calculating profit shares;
- method of distributing profit shares;
- amount distributed;
- timing of distribution.

Eligibility

In most schemes all employees except directors are eligible. The normal practice is to require one year's service to be completed before a share in profits can be received. Profit shares are then usually paid in relation to the pay earned or the time served between the date on which one year's service was completed and the date on which the profit shares are paid.

Formula for calculating profit shares

There are three basic approaches to calculating profit shares. The first is to use a predetermined formula for distributing a fixed percentage of profits. This formula may be distributed to staff to show that the company is committed to using it. The advantages of this approach are that it clarifies the relationship between company profits and the amount distributed, and demonstrates the good faith of management. The disadvantages are that it lacks flexibility, and that the amount paid out may fluctuate widely in response to temporary changes in profitability.

The second approach is for the board to determine profit shares entirely at its own discretion without the use of any predetermined or published formula. The decision is based on a number of considerations, including the profitability of the company, the proportion of profits that it is felt should reasonably be distributed to employees, estimates of the expectations of employees about the amount of cash they are going to receive, and the general climate of industrial relations in the company. This is the more common approach, and its advantages are that it allows the board some flexibility in deciding the amount to be distributed and does not commit it to expenditure over which it has no control. Random fluctuations can be smoothed out, and the profit-sharing element of remuneration can be adjusted easily in relation to other movements in pay within the company. The disadvantage is that a secret formula or the absence of a formula appears to contradict one of the basic reasons for profit sharing: the development among employees of a firmer commitment to the company because they can identify themselves more clearly with its successes and appreciate the reasons for its set-backs. The scheme is no longer a completely realistic profit-sharing device if employees feel that they are insufficiently rewarded for improved performance or insulated from reverses. These arguments against flexibility are powerful ones, but, on balance, a flexible approach is to be preferred because it does not commit the company to distributing unrealistically high sums when profits are shared out.

The third approach is a combination of the first and second methods. A formula exists in the sense that a company profit threshold is set below which no profits will be distributed. A maximum limit is set on the proportion of profits that will be distributed, for example, 5 per cent and/ or that percentage of salary that will be distributed as a profit share, for example, 10 per cent.

Methods of distributing profit shares
The main ways of distributing profit shares in cash schemes are to:

- Distribute profits as a percentage of basic pay with no increments for service. This is a fairly common arrangement, and those who adopt it do so because they feel that profit shares should be related to the individual contribution of the employee, which is best measured by pay. Service increments are rejected because the level of pay received by individuals should already take into account the experience they have gained in the company.
- Distribute profits as a percentage of earnings, with payments related to length of service. This approach is also frequently used, and its advocates argue that it ensures that loyalty to the company is suitably encouraged and rewarded. They assert that to rely on pay as the sole arbiter of profit shares would be unjust because many valuable employees have, through no fault of their own, limited opportunities to move out of their present occupation or grade.
- Distribute profits in proportion to pay and some measure of individual performance. This approach is rare below board level because of the difficulty of measuring the relationship between profits and performance and because it is considered that individual effort should be rewarded directly by merit increments or promotion.
- Distribute profits as a fixed sum irrespective of earnings or service. This completely egalitarian approach is rare.

The choice of approach is usually between distributing profit shares either in relation to pay or in relation to pay and service. The arguments for and against each approach are finely balanced, but there is a good case for providing some uplift for long-service staff in any situation where a company relies on its experienced staff to contribute their specialized skills and knowledge to its success and cannot ensure that its normal policies for paying merit increments to or promoting staff adequately reward their loyalty to the organization.

Amount distributed

A survey conducted by Incomes Data Services in 1986 revealed that rather more than half of the companies surveyed leave the amount to be distributed to 'directors discretion'. Others provide limits within which the directors decide. A maximum of 5 per cent of profits is typical, but this may be paid only if it is triggered by profits reaching a defined level. At British Home Stores, for example, there is a maximum of 5 per cent of profit, providing profits exceed £23 million.

Other surveys into the amounts distributed in UK profit-sharing schemes have indicated that the proportion of pay shared out can vary from as little as 2 to 20 per cent or more. The Glasgow University survey showed that in 60 per cent of the firms surveyed which had profit-sharing schemes, the share amounted to less than 6 per cent of pay. Ideally, however, the share should be somewhere between 5 and 10 per cent of pay in order to be meaningful without building up too much reliance on the amount to be distributed.

Timing of distribution

Most schemes distribute profits annually, although a few share out profits

Table 27.1 Attitudes to profit sharing — Industrial Participation Association

	Agree strongly	Agree	Don't know	Disagree	Disagree strongly
	%	%	%	%	%
1. Profit sharing created a better attitude in the firm.	10	55	16	18	1
2. It is popular because people like to have the bonus.	24	69	4	3	—
3. It strengthens people's loyalty to the firm.	6	41	12	34	2
4. It makes people try to work more effectively so as to help the firm to be more successful.	6	45	15	31	3
5. It is good for the company and its employees.	14	72	11	3	—

twice a year. Distribution is usually arranged to fall in good time for either the summer holidays or Christmas.

Employees' attitudes

The Industrial Participation Association (IPA) recently questioned 2700 employees in 12 companies about their attitudes to profit sharing. The results of the survey are summarized in Table 27.1.

The IPA believes that the survey 'suggests that profit sharing does significantly improve employee attitudes and employee views of their company'. They reach this view essentially by adding together the percentages recorded under *Agree Strongly* and *Agree*.

However, the Incomes Data Services 1986 study of profit sharing commented: 'Another interpretation would be to add up all the responses except those under *Agree Strongly*, the one clear positive statement. This would suggest that most employees do not have a particularly positive attitude.'

Of course, employees like the cash, but their gratitude to the company is probably short-lived. Company profits are remote figures to people in the offices and on the shop-floor. They express some interest in their size, because it affects the hand-out, but the idea of working harder to generate more profit for someone else does not necessarily appeal to them.

Benefits of profit sharing

Profit sharing and profitability
A survey carried out by Wallace Bell and Hanson[1] in 1985–6 sought to establish a correlation between profit sharing and profitability. They surveyed 113 profit-sharing companies and 301 non-profit-sharing companies and compared their performance on the basis of nine economic ratios over a period of eight years. Taking the composite results of all 414 companies, the average performance of the profit sharers over the eight years was better than that of the non-profit sharers on every one of the nine economic ratios used. And on an average of averages, the average ratios of the profit sharers were 27 per cent higher than those of the non-profit sharers. Of course, as Wallace Bell and Hanson say, the profit-sharing companies were not better just because they had profit sharing. It was because they were good companies that they introduced profit sharing.

The particular features of how these companies achieved success were that managers:

- had clear and defined objectives and the ability to harness the resources needed to achieve them;
- recognized that their most important resource is people;
- saw employees not in terms of 'them and us', as adversaries, but as part of a team that should be working together for the success of the enterprise and sharing in its success;
- were able to generate a reciprocal attitude among the employees and thus overcome the 'them and us' feelings that are found equally, and sometimes more strongly, among employees;
- were able to generate a commitment to success.

Profit sharing and industrial relations

The Glasgow University survey referred to earlier expressed the more pessimistic view that the influence of profit sharing on industrial relations is marginal. The researchers concluded that profit sharing was used by employers as an effort-reward operation and not as an attempt to involve employees more closely in the decision-making apparatus. Yet, the evidence that profit sharing does increase effort hardly exists at all, and that is simply because, as was mentioned earlier, the link between effort and reward is so tenuous. What, therefore, is the point of having a profit-sharing scheme if it is not used to increase productivity by means of involving employees and mounting a communications campaign pointing out how *they* benefit from increased output and profitability?

Conclusions

It is worth noticing that a number of companies have introduced profit sharing primarily because they feel that it is their duty to share their prosperity with their employees. If this view is held, then any uncertainty about the benefits arising from profit sharing is not an argument against its introduction. It is, of course, possible to take the opposite view; that profits are the wages of capital and that a company is not under any moral obligation to share profits with its employees, although it has the duty of treating them fairly and providing them with the rewards, benefits, and conditions of employment that are appropriate to the contribution they make.

For anyone contemplating the introduction of profit sharing or wondering whether to continue an existing scheme, the fundamental question is, 'Do you consider that in addition to all the benefits already provided by the company to its employees, it has a moral obligation to share its prosperity with them?' If the answer to this question is in the affirmative, a profit-sharing scheme is what you want. If the answer is in the negative, alternative means of rewarding employees and increasing their identification with the company should be sought, as described elsewhere in this book.

Executive bonus schemes

There are innumerable formulae for executive bonus schemes, and each company must adopt one which suits its own circumstances. The simplest formula is for a percentage out of net profits before tax to be paid *pro rata* to the executive's basic salary. In some schemes, dividend payments and provisions for reserves are deducted from net profits before the distribution of bonuses, and there is usually an upper limit to the amount of bonus that can be paid. These schemes are crude but do provide a direct incentive as long as results are directly influenced by the actions of the executives in the scheme. Such schemes can get out of hand unless an upper limit is strictly applied, and their emphasis on profits may make some executives seek short-term gains at the expense of the long-term development of the company.

Other schemes are based on a formula which measures company performance. Bonuses are paid when a target figure is attained and increased further as the target figure is exceeded. The increase of bonus may be on a straight-line basis, ie directly proportionate to the improvement in results. Alternatively, it may be geared either by decreasing the rate of bonus the more the target is exceeded, which is generally regarded as poor practice, or by increasing the rate, which could be an expensive device. A straight-line progression is to be preferred.

The formula in some schemes is directly applied to the executive's salary. In other schemes, a percentage of profits on an increasing scale is released into a bonus pool which is distributed in proportion to salary.

Incentive schemes for sales staff

Where it is felt that sales staff need to be motivated by an incentive commission scheme, the majority of companies find that the best approach is a basic commission on sales volume or, in more sophisticated firms, on the contribution to fixed costs and profits of the sales of each product group or product. The standard commission is typically set at about one-third of salary to provide a noticeable incentive without adversely affecting feelings of security.

A successful sales commission plan should satisfy all the criteria listed above for bonus schemes. But it is particularly necessary to ensure that:

- The reward is fair in relation to the efforts of the sales representative. This means that attention has to be paid to setting and agreeing realistic and equitable targets, making allowances for special circumstances outside the control of the sales representative which might affect sales, and splitting commission fairly when more than one person has contributed to the sale.
- The scheme directs sales effort in accordance with management's policy on the product mix and does not encourage the representative to concentrate on what is easiest to sell.
- The scheme does not encourage high-pressure selling, which results in an unacceptable level of returns, cancellations and complaints.
- The scheme does not encourage representatives to neglect their indirect selling activities, such as servicing customers.

These criteria are not always easy to satisfy, and a cautious approach is therefore needed before introducing an incentive scheme. A straight salary may be more appropriate where there is a wide range of products, a highly technical product, a high proportion of non-selling activities such as merchandizing to be carried out, or when flexibility is required in allocating salesmen to customers, territories or products.

Choice of performance-related pay scheme

The matrix illustrated in Figure 27.5 is designed to help in the choice of scheme or mix of schemes by summarizing the impact of different approaches in terms of motivation, commitment, retention and time-scale.

	individual motivation	team motivation	commitment/ retention
immediate	individual bonus	group bonus	—
short-term	merit pay	—	—
medium-term	deferred pay	gain-sharing	profit-sharing
long-term	—	—	share option phantom option

Figure 27.5 PRP choice matrix

It is advisable, however, to reinforce the impact of the selected scheme or schemes by taking additional steps to increase long-term motivation by the use of non-financial incentives and rewards such as:

- recognition of achievement;
- additional responsibility;
- greater autonomy;
- involvement;
- enhancement of skills and knowledge;
- career development.

Reference

1. Wallace Bell, D and Hanson, C *Profit Sharing and Profitability*. Kogan Page, London, 1987.

28

Wage Payment Systems

Increasingly, firms are harmonizing the terms and conditions of all members of staff — managers, team leaders, professional and technical staff, production workers and any other employees who work in distribution, maintenance or other ancillary functions. This is particularly the case with high-technology firms which have a preponderance of knowledge workers and other highly skilled employees, and with firms starting up on a greenfield site. Full harmonization involves paying everyone on the same basis, usually a monthly salary. There is one unified pay structure and all employees are entitled to the same benefits. Separate dining facilities for managers, privileged parking spaces or other barriers to an egalitarian atmosphere, such as clocking on for shop-floor workers, do not exist. Some companies, however, have gone only partly along the route to harmonization, and the majority retain a separate wage payment system for their manual, distribution and other non-office workers.

This chapter concentrates on wage payment systems as applied only to non-salaried staff, although some applications, such as skill-based schemes, are operated in all-salaried systems, and performance-rated pay may be used for wage earners.

The basis of the wage payment system

Wage payment systems consist of the pay structure and the methods used to motivate and reward workers for their efforts, to settle pay levels and to consult on pay systems.

Objectives of management

The objectives of management in developing and maintaining wage payment systems are to achieve the purposes of the organization by attracting, retaining and motivating workers in order that maximum productivity and quality are obtained at minimum cost. The assumption behind most payment systems is that pay is the key motivating factor. This is not necessarily completely valid. But it is certainly reasonable to assume that pay is a major factor in obtaining and retaining workers and can be an important cause of dissatisfaction, even if it is not by any means the only motivator.

Management's job is, therefore, to assess what level and type of inducements it is able to offer in return for the contributions it requires from its workforce.

The effort bargain

The worker's objective is to strike a bargain with management about the relation between what he or she regards as a reasonable contribution, and what the employer is prepared to offer to elicit that contribution. This is termed the 'effort bargain' and is, in effect, an agreement between managers and unions which lays down the amount of work to be done for the agreed wage, not just the hours to be worked. Explicitly or implicitly, all employers are in a bargaining situation with regard to payment systems. A system will not be effective or workable until it is recognized as fair and equitable by both sides.

Pay settlements

The level of pay settlements depends on the relative bargaining strengths of the two parties, but it is, of course, influenced by the 'going rate' (the levels of settlements reached by other employers) as well as the company's ability or willingness to pay and the state of the labour market (shortages or surpluses of skills). Agreement also has to be reached with the trade union on the introduction of new types of payment schemes or the amendment of existing ones. There will, for example, be tight rules in an agreement on a payment-by-results system on the circumstances in which piece or time rates can be altered by management.

Consultation on pay systems

Even when a company is not unionized, it still makes sense for its managers to consult employees on the design and operation of the payment system even if pay levels are determined unilaterally by management. The scheme will work only if employees feel it is fair, and this belief is more likely to be engendered if they are involved in decisions about it.

Features of wage payment systems

A pay system for wage earners consists of the rates paid to employees in a factory or other establishment. The structure will incorporate pay differentials between jobs which reflect real or assumed differences in skill and responsibility but are influenced by pressures from the local labour market, by custom and practice and by the settlements reached between management and trade unions.

The pay system may incorporate a number of 'spot rates', that is, fixed base rates for each job which do not vary according to merit or degree of skill. Alternatively, there may be a formal structure in which there are defined job grades into which jobs are slotted according to their levels of skill or responsibility. There may be a fixed rate for each job in the grade, or there may be a pay bracket to allow for individual skill or merit payments to be made above the minimum time rate.

The pay levels within the structure are determined in various ways. They may be imposed by national, local or plant negotiations, or they may be fixed by management by reference to the national minimum rates, the local going rates, as established by pay surveys and, possibly, job evaluation.

Differentials may also be determined in a number of ways: by tradition, by reference to market rate relativities, by national or plant negotiations or by job evaluation. Frequently, however, there is no formal structure, or the structure is limited to a crude division of jobs into skilled, semi-skilled or unskilled categories. In these cases, differentials within or between categories may be haphazard, dictated by custom and practice or by the way in which a payment-by-results scheme rewards particular classes of employees.

Unplanned structures may easily result in a mass of overlapping and confused grades without any acceptable pattern of rational differentials between jobs. Such structures offer endless scope for argument and conflict over grading and upgrading issues.

The case for a planned and rational pay structure is overwhelming, although achieving order from chaos is usually a formidable task. Differentials which have been built into the system over a number of years are hard to change. This is where a job evaluation programme which involves the full participation of both management and unions can be so valuable (job evaluation schemes are dealt with in Chapter 25).

The ideal structure should have the minimum number of grades required to accommodate the clearly differentiated levels of skill and responsibility that exist in the organization. The more straightforward the production process, the less reason to have numerous grades. Current practice is to aim for five to seven grades covering all factory personnel. It is important to have adequate pay differentials between each grade in order that a significantly increased reward results from an upgrading, and to avoid the arguments about regradings which result if the increases between grades are too small.

The structure will have to take account of any payment-by-results schemes in operation. Pay rates may, therefore, be divided into a basic time rate for the job which is paid according to the hours worked, and a piece-work rate which varies according to the amount earned under the piece-work system. Traditionally, the ratio of basic rate to incentive has been 2:1, but the current trend is nearer 4:1 to minimize fluctuations in earnings and to control wage drift (increases in piece-work earnings which have not resulted from specific pay increases achieved by negotiated settlements or granted by an employer). There might also be a guaranteed, or 'fall-back', rate for piece-workers which could be equivalent to the consolidated rate for time-workers carrying out a similar job. Additionally, the pay structure incorporates overtime and shift premium rates and allowances for dangerous or dirty work or for special responsibility.

The structure may be determined by a skills- or knowledge-based pay system, as described on pages 615–619. It also has to take account of the need for flexibility and multiskilling.

Methods of payment

The six principal methods of payment which can be used selectively in wages systems are the following:

1. Time rate;
2. Incentive schemes (payment by results systems):

    (a) straight piece-work — individual scheme;
    (b) differential piece-work — individual scheme;
    (c) measured daywork — individual scheme;
    (d) group incentive schemes;

3. Gainsharing (company-wide bonus schemes);
4. Skills-based schemes;
5. Flexibility-based schemes;
6. Performance-related pay.

Time rate

Time rate, also known as day rate, daywork, flat rate, or hourly rate, is the system under which operators are simply paid a predetermined rate per week, day or hour for the actual time they have worked. The basic rate for the job is fixed by negotiation, by reference to local rates, or by job evaluation, and varies only with time, never with output or performance.

In some circumstances, what are termed high day rates are paid which are higher than the agreed minimum rates. The high day rate may include a consolidated bonus element and is probably higher than the local going rate in order to attract and retain labour. High day rates have been a feature in some parts of the UK motor industry where above minimum earnings are expected because of a history of payment by results, and where there is a high proportion of machine control of output. They are most appropriate in assembly lines where workers can be trained to produce work of a specified standard and to maintain a fixed working pace determined by work study.

Time rates are most commonly used where it is thought that it is impossible or undesirable to apply a payment-by-results system, for example, in maintenance work. But they may also be adopted as an alternative to an unsatisfactory piece-work system. From the point of view of operators, the advantages of time rates are that earnings are predictable and steady, and they do not have to engage in endless arguments with supervisors and rate-fixers about piece rate or time allowances.

The obvious accusation made against time rates is that they do not provide the motivation of a direct incentive relating the reward to the effort. The logical point is that people want money and will work harder to get more of it. The argument is a powerful one, and explains the high proportion of workers on payment-by-results schemes — for example, one half of manual workers in the UK engineering industry. But it ignores all the problems associated with piece-work, which are discussed below, and pays insufficient attention to the other motivating factors intrinsic to the job or provided by management. It is true, however, that time rate systems, especially high day rates, make greater demands on management and supervision.

Incentive schemes

Incentive or payment-by-result schemes relate the pay or part of the pay received by employees to the number of items they produce or process, or to the time they take to do a certain amount of work. They usually provide for pay to fluctuate with performance in the short term, but they can, as in measured daywork, provide for a long-term relationship.

Arguments for and against incentive schemes

For

The main argument put forward by those in favour of any payment-by-results system is, of course, that people work to make money — the more money they make the happier they are, and they will work harder if, and only if, they are paid more money. Higher output becomes what both management and workers want and everyone is happy. Underlying this argument is the assumption that piecework operators have the power to control the amount of effort they put into the job, and that they adjust their effort solely or mainly in relation to the monetary return they get from it.

Against

Arguments against the 'economic man' philosophy of piecework and its practical effects have been gaining ground over a number of years, especially since a number of research projects into what actually happens on the shop-floor have exposed the inadequacies of the system — for example, those carried out by Lupton.[1]

The argument against the 'economic man' rationale for payment-by-results schemes is that it is a naive view of motivation. People at work have much more complicated goals than the simple pursuit of money and are not so many donkeys to react as required to the carrot or the stick. One of the earlier formulations of this argument came from McGregor,[2] who wrote:

> The practical logic of incentives is that people want money, and that they will work harder to get more of it. Incentive plans do not, however, take account of several other well-demonstrated characteristics of behaviour in the organizational setting: (1) that most people also want the approval of their fellow workers and that if necessary they will forego increased pay to obtain this approval; (2) that no managerial assurances can persuade workers that incentive rates will remain inviolate regardless of how much they produce; (3) that the ingenuity of the average worker is sufficient to outwit any system of controls devised by management.

The more specific arguments against payment by results systems are that they:

- are not effective in themselves — they do not increase effort or output;

- cause more trouble than they are worth in the shape of conflict between management and workers, arguments about rates, jealousies between those on piece-work and those on lower time rates, damage to pay structures where carefully calculated relativities are upset because one group of workers is fortunate enough to benefit from a loose rate, and frustrations to workers who suffer from unstable and unpredictable earnings;
- are a major cause of wage drift — the inflation of earnings outside the normal pattern of negotiated pay settlements.

Conclusion

The argument that people work harder only if they can earn more money may appear to be simplistic. But Goldthorpe[3] in his research on what motivated car workers found that they preferred their repetitive, boring jobs which paid higher wages to the much more interesting jobs for lower pay available to them nearby. Of course, people work for other things besides money, but money can be an effective motivator because it provides the means for satisfying so many needs. Incentive schemes do work if they satisfy the criteria for success set out below.

Criteria for success

The criteria for the success of an incentive scheme are that:

1. It should be appropriate to the type of work carried out and the workers employed.
2. The reward should be clearly and closely linked to the effort of the individual or group.
3. Individuals or groups should be able to calculate the reward they get at each of the levels of output they are capable of achieving.
4. Individuals or groups should have a reasonable amount of control over their efforts and therefore their rewards.
5. The scheme should operate by means of a defined and easily understood formula.
6. The scheme should be properly installed and maintained.
7. Provision should be made for controlling the amounts paid to ensure they are proportionate to effort.
8. Provision should be made for amending rates in defined circumstances.

Types of incentive (individual) schemes

Straight piece-work

The most common type of incentive scheme which is purely individual in character is what is called straight piecework. This means payment of a uniform price per unit of production, and it is most appropriate where production is repetitive in character and can easily be divided into similar units.

Straight piecework rates can be expressed in one of two main forms, 'money piecework' or 'time piece-work'. In the case of money piecework, the employee is paid a flat money price for each piece or operation completed. In the case of time piecework, instead of a price being paid for operation, a time is allowed (this is often called a time-allowed system). Workers are paid at their basic piecework rate for the time allowed, but if they complete the job in less time they gain the advantage of the time saved, as they are still paid for the original time allowed. Thus, an operator who completes a job timed at 60 hours in 40 would receive a bonus of 50 per cent of the piecework rate, ie $[(60-40)/40] \times 100$.

Piece rates may be determined by work study, using the technique known as effort rating to determine standard times for jobs. In situations where work is not repetitive, especially in the engineering industry, times may be determined on a much less analytical basis by rate-fixers using their judgement. This often involves prolonged haggles with operators.

Differential piecework

Straight piecework systems result in a constant wage cost per unit of output, and management objections to this feature led to the development of differential systems where the wage cost per unit is adjusted in relation to output. The most familiar applications of this approach have been the premium bonus systems such as the Halsey/Weir or Rowan schemes. Both these systems are based on a standard time allowance, not a money piece rate, and the bonus depends on the time saved. Unlike straight piecework, the wages cost per unit of production falls as output increases, but the hourly rate of workers' earnings still increases, although not in proportion to the increased output. For obvious reasons, these systems are viewed with suspicion by unions and workers, and many variations to the basic approach have been developed, some of which involve sharing the increments of higher productivity between employers and workers.

Measured daywork

In measured daywork, the pay of employees is fixed on the understanding that they will maintain a specified level of performance, but the pay does not fluctuate in the short term with their performance. The arrangement relies on work measurement to define the required level of performance and to monitor the actual level. Fundamental to measured daywork is the concept of an incentive level of performance, and this distinguishes it clearly from time rate systems. Measured daywork guarantees the incentive payment in advance, thereby putting the employee under an obligation to perform at the effort level required. Payment by results, on the other hand, allows employees discretion as to their effort level but relates their pay directly to the output they have achieved. Between these two systems are a variety of alternatives that seek to marry the different characteristics of payment by results and measured daywork, including banded incentives, stepped schemes, and special forms of high day rate.

Measured daywork seeks to produce an effort-reward bargain in which enhanced and stable earnings are exchanged for an incentive level of performance. The criteria for success in operating it are the following:

- total commitment of management, employees and their unions, which can be achieved only by careful planning, joint consultation, training, and a staged introduction of the system;
- an effective work measurement system, and efficient production planning and control and inventory control procedures;
- the establishment of a logical pay structure with appropriate differentials from the beginning of the scheme's operation — the structure should be developed by the use of job evaluation and in consultation with employees;
- the maintenance of good control systems to ensure that corrective action is taken quickly if there is any shortfall on targets.

The disadvantage of measured daywork is that the set performance can become an easily attainable norm and is difficult to change without renegotiation.

Group incentive schemes

Group or team incentive schemes provide for the payment of a bonus either equally or proportionately to individuals within a group or team. The bonus is related to the output achieved over an agreed standard or to the time saved on a job — the difference between allowed time and actual time.

Group bonus schemes are in some respects individual incentive schemes writ large — they have the same basic advantages and disadvantages as any payment-by-results system. The particular advantages of a group scheme are that it encourages team spirit, breaks down demarcation lines, and enables the group to discipline itself in achieving targets. In addition, job satisfaction may be achieved through relating the group more closely to the complete operation. Group bonuses may be particularly useful where groups of workers are carrying out interdependent tasks and when individual bonus schemes might be invidious because workers have only limited scope to control the level of their own output and are expected to support others, to the detriment of their personal bonus.

The potential disadvantages of group bonus schemes are that management is less in control of production — the group can decide what earnings are to be achieved and can restrict output. Furthermore, the bonus can eventually cease to be an incentive. Some opponents of group schemes object to the elimination of personal incentive, but this objection would be valid only if it were always possible to operate a satisfactory individual incentive scheme.

Group schemes may be most appropriate where people have to work together and teamwork has to be encouraged. They are probably most effective if they are based on a system of measured or controlled daywork where targets and standards are agreed by the group, which is provided with the control information it needs to monitor its own performance.

Designing an incentive scheme

The following factors should be taken into account when designing an incentive scheme:

1. How performance will be measured.
2. The employees who will take part in the scheme and who will therefore have part of their pay directly linked to their own performance or that of their group.
3. The employees who will not take part in the scheme (supervisors, maintenance workers, inspectors, etc) and how they will be compensated. In the case of immediate supervisors, there should at least be a reasonable differential, say, 10 to 20 per cent, between their pay and the average pay for a standard week, including bonus, earned by the people they supervise.
4. Whether or not the scheme will be an individual one or one linked to group performance or related to plant performance.
5. Whether the bonus payments will be related to basic pay and therefore higher for those on higher basic rates, as in individual schemes, or whether bonus payments will be equal for all members

of the group, as in group incentive schemes.

6. The proportion of pay which can be earned as bonus. This may have to be fixed as a percentage for standard performance, say, 33.33 per cent, and, as an upper limit, say, 50 per cent.

7. The full basic rate — this could be the basic rate, but some schemes allow a minimum bonus payment of, say, 10 per cent.

8. The relationship between output/effort and reward, ie the extent to which, if at all, there is a differential built into the scheme which shares the results of higher productivity between the company and the workers.

9. The basis upon which employees not earning bonuses will be paid when, for example, they are on waiting time, attending meetings on company business, working on a new job which has not yet been rated, or on holiday or sick. Shop-average bonus is a fairly typical method of payment, although individual average bonuses are also paid.

10. The timings of bonus payments (the period of work for which bonuses are paid) and the lapse of time before payments are made.

11. The arrangements, if any, to alleviate the problems of large fluctuations in bonus payments.

12. The methods to be used to maintain the scheme and to inform employees of their earnings.

Maintaining the incentive scheme

Incentive schemes degenerate. The consultants and work study engineers who install them say such schemes should not degenerate, but they do. In an ideal world they would not. Managers and supervisors would exercise control as the consultants advise. But the latter do not always live in the real world, where there are numerous opportunities for workers to gain more from an incentive scheme than they have earned. Individual and group incentive schemes are prone to this type of degeneration, a process which is called wage or earnings drift.

Causes of degeneration

The main causes of degeneration are:

1. *Special allowances.* All schemes have allowances for the payment of shop-average earnings or some other figure which includes a premium over the base rate in certain circumstances. The most

common are for unmeasured work or waiting time. Clearly, the higher the proportion of this time when pay is unrelated to effort, the more the scheme degenerates. Allowances are, in theory, controllable by management, but supervisors closer to the shop-floor have been known to make their lives easier by granting allowances too easily. And this can be done on an hour-to-hour basis and in small increments which can all too readily be missed by more senior managers.

Allowances can also be manipulated by, for example, workers booking in waiting time rather than time on a difficult job which earns a less than average bonus.

2. *Erosion of standards.* The type of work or the work mix can change almost imperceptibly over a period of time. It may not be possible to point to a change in method significant enough to justify a retiming of the job under the rules of the scheme.

The original ratings, although not slack, may not have been particularly tight — workers themselves and their representatives will have seen to that. As time goes on, workers learn how to take short cuts (sometimes risky ones) which increase or maintain earnings for less effort.

3. *Cross-booking.* Workers sometimes cross-book from difficult tasks to easier ones from a bonus-earning point of view. Work measurement is not an exact science, whatever work study engineers may say, and some ratings are easier than others. The ability of work people to get to know ways round the scheme should never be underestimated. An important US study by Roy[4] showed that productivity could be held back even when a payment-by-results scheme was in operation. He observed that in a time-allowed scheme where bonus is directly linked to the amount of time saved in doing the task from the original time allowed, some timings were inevitably tighter than others. If there is a reasonably generous fall-back rate (the basic rate paid, whatever the effort or results), as there frequently is, employees may work more slowly and thus save their effort on the difficult jobs, but still earn a reasonable standard rate, while working hard and fast on the easier jobs to achieve the bonus earning they want. Research studies have frequently shown that workers set their own level of bonus earnings and adjust their effort accordingly. Sometimes, they can be under pressure from their fellow workers not to work too hard and thus 'bust' the rate, or at least inspire management to indulge in a rate-cutting exercise.

To prevent management from becoming aware that some jobs are easier than others, workers sometimes do not record all their time on these jobs, thus keeping earnings down. Workers then allocate their time to other jobs to raise them into the bonus-earning range, or simply take it easy. They operate, as it were, on borrowed time.

Remedies

To avoid degeneration, one must:

1. Introduce a bonus scheme only where the following conditions apply:
    (a) short-cycle, repetitive work;
    (b) changes in work mix, tasks or methods are infrequent;
    (c) shop-floor hold-ups are rare and not prolonged;
    (d) management and supervision are capable of controlling the scheme, not only technically, but also from the point of view of being able to prevent manipulation and skiving;
    (e) productivity is so low that the stimulus of a bonus scheme, even when it might create problems later, is still worth while.

2. Take care, in introducing the scheme, to use the best work study engineers available in order that accurate and even standards are obtained.

3. Ensure that the rules of the scheme as agreed with a trade union allow for retimings because of changes in the task (including, importantly, work mix), changes in method or errors in the original bonus calculation.

4. Institute recording systems or rules for booking time on non-bonus-earning activities which minimize the risk of allowance manipulation or cross-booking.

5. Train managers, supervisors and industrial engineers in how to manage and control the scheme. Impress on them that they will be held accountable for productivity and for ensuring that the scheme does not degenerate.

6. Continuously monitor bonus performance and crack down on any drift. Ensure that new jobs are timed properly, and that the implications of any changes in work mix or methods are understood and reflected in altered standards.

7. Keep on emphasizing to managers and supervisors their responsibility for controlling the scheme and take them to task if they do not.

Gainsharing

Gainsharing schemes provide for all workers in the company or factory a bonus which is related to an overall measure of performance. They are sometimes called share-of-production plans or factory-wide incentive schemes. The overall measure may be output or, more frequently, added value, which is usually defined as:

- *income* from sales of the product or service (output); less
- *expenditure* on materials and other purchased services (input); leaves
- *added value*, which is either distributed as wages, salaries, pensions, interests on loans, taxes, and dividends, or retained in reserves or for investment and depreciation.

Gainsharing schemes using the added value concept can operate, as in the original Rucker plan, by establishing over a period the proportion of added value which is represented by payroll costs (typically 40 to 50 per cent) and then calculating the amount distributed as follows:

Added value is:	£800,000
40 per cent of added value is:	£320,000
Actual payroll is:	£280,000
Distributed to employees:	£40,000

A variant of this example is to agree that the employee savings, that is, £40,000, should be divided on an agreed basis, say, 50 per cent for employees and 50 per cent for the company, the latter proportion being needed by the company to provide, among other things, for a return on new investment.

An added value scheme operating in Perkin Elmer is based on the proportion of value added that had in practice been distributed to employees in the form of pay — the employees' share. Over a period of five years this was remarkably constant at 47.9 per cent. Value added is then calculated quarterly, and if the employee share is greater than the pay already distributed, 75 per cent of that surplus is distributed in the form of a bonus. The remaining 25 per cent is transferred to a reserve account which accumulates throughout the year and provides a buffer against quarters in which the employee share of value added may be found to be less than the money that has already been paid. Any surplus remaining in the reserve account at the end of the year is then finally distributed as a terminal bonus. Bonuses have averaged about 20 per cent. Any deficit is absorbed by the company, so that a new reserve account is always started with the new financial year.

An important feature of the Perkin Elmer plan, which is an essential feature of gainsharing schemes, is the extensive involvement of employees in analysing performance and, jointly with management, agreeing on ways to improve productivity and thus increase their share. John Leare[5] of Perkin Elmer has said that the single most important benefit of operating the plan has been

> The identification of a common purpose for both management and employee. Morale is high and there is much wider trust and co-operation. The annual pay negotiations have lost their edge since total remuneration is already agreed and any increases in basic rates of pay, which are already automatically linked to the Retail Price Index, merely lead to a corresponding reduction in bonus levels.

The main argument against any type of factory-wide incentive scheme is that it does not provide a direct incentive because the link between individual effort and the eventual reward is tenuous. A gainsharing scheme can, however, be effective if it provides reasonably high bonuses, 10 per cent or more, and includes arrangements for participation in jointly analysing the factors that have contributed to the size of the added value and what can be done to improve the share allocated to employees. Such schemes can minimize the problems of degeneration and constant bickering between employees and management which plague most conventional payment-by-results systems.

Skills-based schemes

Skills-based schemes, also called knowledge-based schemes, link pay to the acquisition of additional skills or knowledge. Employees are rewarded through direct payments for the ability to perform an operationally related range of tasks or skills rather than for the actual work performed at any given time. Skills-based schemes determine the vertical rate of progression through grades as higher levels of skill are reached. Flexibility-based schemes, as described below, reward the horizontal acquisition of additional skills at broadly the same level as those already possessed by the employee and are linked to dual and multiskilling programmes. The distinction between these two approaches, however, is blurred — reaching a higher level of skill could be a difference of degree, but it could equally well be a difference of kind.

Both skills-based and flexibility-based schemes require the company to offer training for employees to enable them to acquire new skills. This training is usually provided on a modular basis, ie training packages are developed which concentrate on a particular skill or group of skills (sometimes referred to as 'skill blocks'). Skills-based schemes are founded on the same principles as the competence-based schemes for staff described in Chapter 27.

Reasons for the development of skills-based schemes

The main reason for the development of skills-based schemes is the pressure to increase the ability of employees to meet the greater level of skill required for the new technology and working practices introduced by companies in recent years. As Holder[6] commented: 'Ten to fifteen years ago, it was common for direct labour to account for 35 to 40 per cent of total produce costs. With such high figures, managers sought to maintain control over this cost by using incentive schemes.' These schemes were essentially geared to volume, with large batches of components and material piled up around workstations. Now, with more efficient work practices and investment in capital equipment, direct labour typically accounts for 6 to 12 per cent of product cost. The emphasis has shifted to material costs and from direct to indirect labour. Quality, customer service and the operation of just-in-time systems mean that performance is largely determined by the quantity of materials carried by a company as well as by efficient resource utilization. As Holder says: 'In this climate, traditional incentive schemes have little place. The objective is to make what you need, when you need it, to the right specification and as efficiently as possible. There is no point giving people a bonus purely on the basis of the number of widgets they can knock out in an hour.'

Competitive advantage is achieved by having a skilled, flexible and committed labour force, and skills-based schemes have been developed to respond to this need. Such schemes do not exist simply to allow individual employees to pick up additional skills. Their purpose is rather to build and maintain a comprehensive mix of key skills over the whole workforce in order to enhance flexibility, productivity and quality.

Developing a skills-based scheme

A skills-based scheme can be developed as follows:

1. *Identify jobs to be covered by the scheme.* These may be entirely hourly paid jobs but, as the distinction between skilled production or process workers and technicians or other knowledge workers diminishes with the development of new technology, so the skills-based scheme may be extended to include salaried staff. This is a step towards harmonization and could result in a single competence/skills-based system extending to all employees.

2. *Define job families.* This means analysing the individual jobs and grouping them into families where the operational or support tasks and basic skill requirements are similar, although a range of skills at different levels may be used within the family. For example, a job family of assemblers might be identified, consisting of four or five previously distinct jobs. However, although the fundamental skills required may be similar, the family could range from, at one extreme, fairly straightforward 'bolting on' work, to, at the other extreme, highly intricate assemblies for a number of products. A job family for machine operators could have a range of skills starting with basic machining tasks using, say, a simple drilling machine and leading to the operation of computer-controlled machines requiring a wide range of high-level skills.

3. *Analyse skills within job families.* Each skill used in a job family is identified and described.

4. *Define skill bands.* By reference to skill analysis, the different skill bands are defined — there should be a distinct step in skill levels between each band. The bands may contain a number of associated skills, each of which has its own training module. Alternatively, the band may be described in terms of the general level of skills used in accomplishing certain tasks, but this general level would be defined in a way which indicates exactly what the employee has to do as a basis for the training programme. Typically, there are three or four bands in an extended job family.

5. *Devise skill training modules.* Training modules are devised for each major skill or group of skills in the bands which set out what should be learnt and how that learning should be achieved.

6. *Design training and job rotation programmes.* The 'cross-training' programmes for each module to develop multiskilling and enhance skills are designed to take place on- or off-the-job. If training is on-the-job, managers and team leaders should be briefed on their training duties. Off-the-job training should be geared to the development of specified skills and should incorporate tests wherever possible. Job rotation is planned to enlarge experience and develop new skills.

7. *Decide on methods of testing and assessment.* If appropriate tests are available, they should be used to determine whether or not an employee has reached a defined skill level (there are no half measures). Alternatively, the manager, team leader or training officer makes an assessment of the extent to which the employee has achieved the level of skill required and can apply it to meet operational standards of output, accuracy and quality. This assess-

ment should be carried out as objectively as possible, using checklists which define explicitly the performance standards required for each skill. Some firms use the NCVQ (the National Council for Vocational Qualifications) to develop and validate skill blocks. Outside assessments can add extra validity to the scheme.

8. *Establish base rates for job families.* The base rates for job families may have to be established by negotiation with a trade union. The aim is to establish competitive rates which will attract and retain good-quality employees. To this end, market surveys should be carried out.

9. *Define range of payments for skill.* The extra payment for achieving the skill level required in a higher band is defined by reference to market rates for skills. These rates are also influenced by custom and practice, and, if the company is unionized, have to be negotiated. A four-banded system, for example, may operate as follows:

Band 1	100 per cent
Band 2	105 per cent
Band 3	115 per cent
Band 4	125 per cent

10. *Establish procedures for progressing through the bands.* These procedures would set out the testing and training arrangements and indicate that extra skill payments would be made only if they could be used operationally.

There are many variations on this pattern. For example, progression may be based on the accumulation of points related to skill acquisition. At the Oilwell Cable Division of the TRW Electronic Components Group, as reported by Ziskin,[7] the 'knowledge-based pay' system provides for employees to progress at the rate of ten points a pay level through nine levels of skill to achieve a maximum level of 90 points. Varying numbers of points are attributed to different skills, according to how difficult the skill is to learn or how critical the skill is to the production process. To progress to a new skill and pay level, employees are required to demonstrate through a practical examination that they have reached the skill level.

Advantages

The advantages claimed for skills-based schemes are that they:

● develop individual skills through the extended take-up of training;

- provide for greater workforce flexibility;
- reduce staffing levels;
- improve teamwork as a result of job rotation and cross-training;
- increase productivity.

Disadvantages

Potentially, however, skills-based schemes have the following disadvantages:

- They incur increased payroll costs — these schemes aim to be self-financing, but it has not yet been proved that they are.
- They are complex to install and administer.
- They incur increased training costs.
- The concept of paying employees for the ability to perform an operationally related area of tasks or skills, rather than for the actual work performed at a given time, may be difficult for management to accept. Even if it is agreed, as in the Pirelli General scheme, that the number of skill modules an individual can attain is limited by the plant's ability 'to effectively utilize these modules for its operational requirements', there is still plenty of scope for argument as to whether a skill level has been attained and, if so, whether or not this is usable operationally by the individual concerned.

These disadvantages appear to outweigh the advantages, but skills-based schemes are a valid option for companies where the diversity of skills is high, where flexibility and teamwork are a key requirement, and where there has been a shift from direct to indirect labour and from labour to material costs.

Flexibility-based pay schemes

Flexibility-based pay schemes also link reward to the acquisition of skills, but do not necessarily link progression to skill bands or grades as in skills-based schemes. Flexibility pay is usually provided for in multiskilling agreements. For example, BP Chemicals' skill development programme provides for cumulative annual supplements (worth £344 per capita in 1989). These are paid on the basis of allowing anyone to use their skills in areas currently restricted by demarcation. At Lyons Tetley's Eaglescliffe site, an immediate payment of 5 per cent of the basic rate was made for the removal of restrictive practices and enhanced flexibility with, again, further payments linked to multiskilling at a later date.

As reported in the IRS *Pay and Benefits Bulletin*,[8] the following are examples of pay agreements which incorporate multiskilling arrangements and grade payments:

Birds Eye Walls — Craft (1987)

Multi-site agreement that craft workers are 'willing to apply both electrical and mechanical skills to the limit of their capability'. All certified craft workers agreed to initial assessment and counselling programme. On completion, moved to new multiskilled stage 1 rate (worth 4.6 per cent). Those willing to receive multi-skill training could then move to a higher pay band — once formally validated as having successfully completed training lasting 9–18 months. This rate of pay is 14.9 per cent more than original certified craft rate.

Inca Alloys (1987)

'Skill flexibility scheme.' Agreement grouped jobs into four main skill areas; within each area employees required to acquire additional skills to increase their competency across the whole of their group as well as to ensure a basic knowledge of mechanical and engineering skills through a modular training programme. Staged pay rises (in addition to general pay deal) were linked to progress of training: 4 per cent on completion of 25 per cent of all modules; 2.5 per cent on completion of 50 per cent; 2.5 per cent on completion of 75 per cent; and a final rise of 6 per cent on completion of all modules by all participants: 15 per cent in all as payments were not compounded.

Performance-related pay

Performance-related pay (PRP) schemes on the shop-floor relate a proportion of pay to indicators of performance such as quality, flexibility, contribution to teamwork, and ability to hit targets. They are, in fact, based on exactly the same principles as the merit payment schemes for salaried staff described in Chapter 27 — namely, a system of assessment which leads to merit increases and progresses pay through a range.

Shop-floor PRP schemes have been in existence for a long time but their number has increased over the last decade because of the general pressure to introduce such schemes and because of the belief that they are more appropriate in high-technology, multiskilled environments where piece-work systems are likely to be ineffective.

Aims

Companies which install PRP schemes on the shop-floor generally aim to increase the commitment and capability of their employees. As Kinnie and

Lowe[9] comment on the basis of their research, the firms they contacted wanted 'to get "better value" from both manual and non-manual employees but not necessarily in a way that resulted in an immediate reduction in cost or improvement in profits. The aim, more broadly, was to bring about a longer-term improvement in the motivation and performance of the work force as a whole, rather than simply paying a chosen few more.'

It was established by Kinnie and Lowe that PRP in these firms often formed part of an overall approach aimed at focusing attention on the individual employees in the organization. 'It could be used as a key component in a wide-ranging attempt to change the management style or even the whole culture of an organization.'

Benefits

The firms contacted by Kinnie and Lowe asserted that they had gained the following benefits from PRP:

- Improvement in the quality of relationships between team leaders and the members of their teams — this arose because of the need to clarify performance requirements and discuss results against agreed expectations.
- Employees gained increased awareness of critical factors affecting performance such as quality, cost and delivery.
- Employees gained more information about their company and what it was trying to achieve.
- Employees were more prepared to put forward ideas for improving work methods.
- The commitment and capability of employees were improved.

Problems

But PRP on the shop-floor suffers from the same problems as in the office, namely, subjectivity, lack of commitment or ability to review performance among supervisors, and the difficulty of translating assessments fairly and consistently into pay awards. In addition, shop-floor PRP schemes often arouse the hostility of trade unions, who object to what they believe to be a potentially unfair dependence on the judgement of supervisors on pay awards for their subordinates. These problems have to be considered carefully before introducing PRP on the shop-floor, and it should always be remembered that performance-related pay is only one of the factors affecting performance.

Selecting a payment system

As Bowey and Thorpe[10] have commented, 'Many managers still believe that as long as an incentive scheme is designed, maintained and "operated" correctly, higher performances will follow automatically.' But managers usually admit that decay is inevitable and seem prepared to accept this uncomfortable fact.

Both these assumptions can be challenged. A payment-by-results scheme will work only if it is appropriate and if full consultation has taken place during its introduction. Degeneration can be controlled but, again, this is only possible where the scheme fits the circumstances, although control action, as described in the later section of this chapter dealing with degeneration, may still be required.

Initial steps

The initial steps required to select a payment system are the following:

1. Define objectives and assumptions.
2. Analyse the existing situation.
3. Evaluate alternative systems.

Define objectives and assumptions

Everyone starts by wanting a system which will help with the recruitment of good-quality employees and reduce labour turnover. Managements also want the system to provide direct incentives to increase output, although some may recognize the limits to which this can be done in their environment and attach importance to one or more of the following objectives:

- obtaining consistency in performance;
- containing labour costs;
- reducing pay disputes;
- improving product quality;
- improving delivery times;
- improving equipment utilization;
- obtaining a lower level of rejects;
- reducing the level of work in progress;
- gaining control over the pay structure in order to reduce wage drift and problems of differentials;
- improving methods, planning, work loading and labour flexibility.

The analysis of objectives should define priorities and assess how far they are being achieved by the present payment system. But it is also necessary to examine and, if necessary, challenge the assumptions that management holds about payment systems. Rightly or wrongly it may be assumed that 'the workers in this plant are only interested in money', or that 'the existing system is the best one we've got, so why change it?', or 'all we need to do is to tighten up the loose rates' (rather than find out why the rates are loose in the first place), or 'that's the way the workers want it', and so on.

Analyse the existing situation

The existing situation should be analysed by obtaining answers to the following questions:

1. What is the system of work — batch, mass production, flow-line process?
2. How long is the average work cycle?
3. To what extent is the work high- or low-tech; skilled, semi-skilled, or unskilled; repetitive or varied?
4. Is the flow or cycle steady or intermittent and is the work method constant or varied?
5. To what extent do changes in methods occur?
6. How often does the type of work carried out change because of new products or design modifications?
7. Is work carried out mainly on an individual basis, or do workers operate together in teams?
8. What proportion of workers are able to participate individually or in groups in a direct incentive scheme?
9. What is the incidence of wasting time?
10. To what extent is the pace of work tightly controlled by, for example, the production line?
11. How tightly are workers supervised?
12. What is the general climate of employee relations — cooperative, hostile, neutral?
13. What level of productivity/work rate is being achieved now?
14. What is the scope for increasing existing work rates?
15. If productivity can and should be increased, is an incentive scheme the best or the only way to do it?
16. Have the alternatives of improved work organization, methods or supervision been considered?

17. Will managers and supervisors be capable of controlling an incentive scheme?
18. Has the firm the resources required in the shape of industrial engineers to install and maintain the scheme? If not, can they be obtained?
19. What is the union's attitude to incentive schemes?
20. How likely are employees to respond positively to a payment-by-results system?

Evaluate alternatives

The main alternatives should be evaluated in general against the criteria given in Chapter 27 (page 599) and the particular points relating to each system as given below.

Time rates
Time rates may be appropriate where:

* individual or team effort does not determine output;
* achieving a fair and consistent relationship between performance, skill levels and reward is difficult;
* it is not easy to establish accurate standards by means of work measurement;
* there are many modifications or design changes;
* product changes are numerous;
* job stoppages are numerous;
* there is a tradition of unsatisfactory shop-floor relations;
* it is believed that the time and cost involved in operating an incentive scheme are likely to outweigh any of its (dubious) benefits;
* the company is confident that other means of achieving motivation and commitment are likely to be more successful. These may include non-financial incentives, job design, teamwork and the quality of management and supervision.

Individual piece-work
This may be appropriate when individual effort clearly determines output and:

* the job cycle is short;
* the number of modifications is small;
* the work requires purely manual skills and/or only single-purpose hand tools or simple machine tools are used;

- product changes and modifications are limited;
- job stoppages are small;
- a high proportion of tasks is specified;
- effective work measurement techniques are in use;
- good-quality work study and rate fixing staff are available; reasonably stable industrial relations are maintained on the shop-floor.

Measured daywork

Measured daywork may be appropriate where individual effort largely determines output, and:

- conditions are inappropriate for individual piecework;
- operations are of the process type or are assembly line;
- the job cycle is long;
- accurate work measurement of operations is possible, so that acceptable standards can be agreed;
- high-quality work study staff are available;
- high-quality management negotiators are available;
- the unions are responsive to the advantages of measured day work, and there is a reasonable chance of reaching agreement on the system and the standards adopted.

Group piecework

Group piecework systems may be suitable if collective effort clearly determines output, and the other features necessary for individual piecework systems are present.

Gainsharing

Factory-wide incentive schemes are appropriate when:

- the company believes that jointly created wealth should be shared with employees;
- a conventional piecework system would be difficult to manage;
- there is scope for participation in considering methods of improving productivity — and willingness on all sides to get involved;
- added value or some other measure of overall performance can be easily calculated and the relationship between individual performance and eventual results can be clearly established.

Skills-based schemes

Skills-based schemes may be appropriate when:

- skill diversity is high;

- flexibility and teamwork are important;
- productivity is mainly dependent on capital costs;
- labour costs as a percentage of material costs are low;
- cross-training is important;
- job rotation can readily be arranged;
- managers and supervisors support the idea of paying for skill.

Flexibility pay

Flexibility pay is arranged in addition to other forms of payment and does not therefore constitute an alternative scheme. It is clearly desirable where multiskilling is important.

Performance-related pay

A performance-related pay system is worth considering when:

- the company wants to focus the attention of employees on such critical success factors as quality, costs and delivery, as well as output;
- it is believed that supervisors can become fully committed to the system and can learn the new skill of performance appraisal;
- a consistent and fair relationship between performance and reward can be achieved;
- the company has PRP for salaried staff and wants to move towards harmonization;
- employees and trade unions are likely to support the scheme.

Prerequisites for success when introducing a scheme

Following its research into payment systems and productivity, the Pay and Rewards Research Centre, Strathclyde University, concluded that the three essential prerequisites for introducing a successful scheme were the following:

1. The top of the organization is committed to a programme of change.
2. A team of managers is developed who know what is required of them and have the enthusiasm to make it work.
3. The rest of the workforce is convinced that the project is worthy of their support, is shown how to make it work, and is assisted in its operations.

The importance of participation

Bowey and Thorpe[10] emphasized the importance of the last of these requirements — a participative approach. There is no point in introducing a scheme which aims to increase productivity without involving employees in discussing how to obtain improvements and how they will benefit financially from them. It is equally necessary to discuss at each development stage the design of the scheme and how it will operate. Work measurement techniques should be demonstrated; many companies train selected employee representatives in work measurement in order that they can agree timings and, importantly, retimings. It is essential at this stage to prepare employees for the fact that rates will have to be altered as a result of changes in work, work mix, and methods. Any agreement should spell out and indicate how retiming will be made in consultation with representatives and employees. Management has to be completely open about the scheme while making it clear that it will not allow the scheme to deteriorate. The latter point is vital, as will be seen from the following analysis of why payment-by-results schemes degenerate.

Monitoring the wage payment system

The steps that should be taken to avoid degeneration have already been discussed in this chapter. To ensure that the operation of the system is properly monitored, managers require the following information regularly.

Any payment system can erode or decay, however carefully its installation was managed. It is essential to review the system in operation regularly to ensure that it continues to achieve its objectives. The review should consider labour unit costs and performance as well as measuring earnings in different sections and jobs in order to spot anomalies. It may be particularly important to analyse overtime earnings, as these are often responsible for creating semi-permanent distortions in the earnings structure when overtime is not controlled properly. Attention might also be directed towards shift premiums and other special allowances for dirty or dangerous work or unsocial hours, to ensure that they are reasonable and in tune with market rates. Finally, a review should consider the equal pay situation to ensure that the arrangements conform with equal pay legislation — in the UK, that separate male and female rates should not exist, and that women should be paid the same as men if they are employed on the same or broadly similar work as men, or on work of equal value.

A review of the payment system could include an analysis of present arrangements, as described earlier in this chapter. The other matters that could be looked at specifically include:

● labour cost per unit of output;

- output figures and performance levels;
- the proportion of bonus to total pay;
- levels of earnings in different departments and jobs;
- percentage of time paid on average bonus when normal bonus work was available;
- percentage overtime worked;
- percentage shift premium in total pay;
- average earnings compared with the salary levels of first-line supervisors.

The aim of the review should be to ensure that management is prepared to take corrective action in good time when the payment system is not operating effectively.

References

1. Lupton, T *On the Shop Floor*. Pergamon, Oxford, 1963.
2. McGregor, D *The Human Side of Enterprise*. McGraw-Hill, New York, 1960.
3. Goldthorpe, J *The Affluent Worker: Industrial Attitudes and Behaviour*. Cambridge University Press, Cambridge, 1968.
4. Roy, D 'Quota Restrictions and Goldbricking in a Machine Shop', *American Journal of Sociology*, Vol. 67, No. 2, 1952.
5. Leare, J 'The Value-added Approach to Sharing Company Wealth', *Personnel Management*, October 1987.
6. Holder, R 'A rewarding strategy that pays dividends', *Works Management*, May 1990.
7. Ziskin, T 'Knowledge-based pay — a strategic analysis', Report Vol. 24, No. 1 New York State School of Industrial and Labor Relations, Ithaca, NY, 1986.
8. *Pay and Benefits Bulletin*, No. 243, IRS, November 1989.
9. Kinnie, N and Lowe, D 'Performance related pay on the shop floor', *Personnel Management*, September 1990.
10. Bowey, A and Thorpe, R *Payment Systems and Productivity*. Macmillan, London, 1986.

29

Employee Benefits

Definition

Tangible employee benefits are elements of remuneration given in addition to the various forms of cash pay, that is, basic salary and incentive or bonus payments. They provide a quantifiable value for individual employees, which may be deferred or contingent, such as a pension scheme, insurance cover or sick-pay, or may provide an immediate benefit such as a company car. Tangible employee benefits also include elements which are not strictly remuneration, such as annual holidays.

Intangible benefits provided by organizations can, in practice, provide an equally and, in some cases, more important means of increasing the commitment of employees to the organization than the tangible benefits. Most of these intangible benefits are strongly related to the need for personal recognition and the desire to go on learning and developing as a career goes through different stages. People generally prefer to work for an employer who is caring as well as challenging and successful.

The items 'fringe benefits' and 'perks' (perquisites) are sometimes used derogatorily, but they should be reserved for those employee benefits which do not fundamentally cater for personal security and personal needs.

Purposes

The main purposes of employee benefits are as follows:

- to motivate employees and increase their commitment to the organization;
- to provide for the actual or perceived personal needs of employees, including those concerning security, financial assistance and the provision of assets in addition to pay, such as company cars and petrol;

- to demonstrate that the company cares for the needs of its employees;
- to provide a tax-efficient method of remuneration which reduces tax liabilities compared with those related to equivalent cash payments.

Types of benefits

Benefits can be divided into the following six categories:

1. *Pension schemes.* These are generally regarded as the most important employee benefit. They are sometimes referred to as deferred pay because they are financed by contributions which build up rights to a guaranteed income for employees or their dependants on retirement or death.
2. *Personal security.* These are benefits which enhance the individual's personal security with regard to illness, health, accident or redundancy.
3. *Personal needs.* Entitlements which recognize the interface between work and domestic needs or responsibilities, eg holidays and other forms of leave, child care, retirement counselling, financial counselling, health and recreational facilities.
4. *Financial assistance.* Loans, house purchase assistance, relocation assistance, discounts, and fees to professional bodies.
5. *Company cars and petrol.*
6. *Other benefits.* These are improvements in the standard of living of employees such as subsidized meals, clothing allowances, refund of telephone costs and credit card facilities.

Pension schemes

Pension schemes are designed to provide employees with security by currently building up rights which will give a guaranteed income to employees or their dependants on retirement or death. Pensions are financed by contributions from the company and in most, but not all, cases the employee.

Pensions are generally regarded as the most important employee benefit after basic pay, although many employees, especially younger ones, express little interest in their pension arrangements until, in many cases, it is too late.

The need to ensure that the pension arrangements are the best the company can afford arises for three reasons:

1. A company has a moral obligation to do the best it can to provide a

reasonable degree of security for its employees, especially its long-service employees.

2. A good pension scheme demonstrates that the company has the long-term interests of its employees at heart.

3. A good scheme will help to attract and retain high-quality staff, especially older staff employed at senior levels who are likely to be most interested in pension rights.

The most significant change in recent times was perhaps the requirement that from April 1988 membership of a company pension scheme can no longer be compulsory. Employees can opt out of the company scheme and are then free to choose whether or not to make their own personal pension arrangements or rely solely on the State pension scheme. The employer is less able to adopt a paternalistic approach in deciding what is 'best' for employees, and new attitudes may range from 'this is the company pension scheme, take it or leave it' to a concerted effort to provide good benefits and to sell the advantages of the company scheme over the personal pension or 'State pension only' routes.

State earnings related pension scheme (SERPS)

The Social Security Pensions Act 1975 changed the whole face of UK pensions practice and introduced the new State Earnings Related Pension Scheme (SERPS) on top of the State Basic Pension. SERPS started on 6 April 1978 and originally provided a pension of 1.25 per cent of a person's average annual 'revalued band earnings' for each year completed after April 1978, up to a maximum of 25 per cent by 1998.

Revalued band earnings are earnings between a lower and upper earnings limit, which are increased in line with earnings inflation for the period up to retirement. The lower earnings limit is approximately equal to a quarter of the national average earnings, and the upper earnings limit is about one-and-three-quarters times national average earnings.

Subsequently, the Government considered that the cost of SERPS would be too high in the next century, and has introduced changes in the Social Security Act 1986 which became effective from 6 April 1988. The changes should not affect the SERPS pension of anyone reaching state pension age before the end of this century. The SERPS pension for anyone retiring after that will be gradually reduced to an ultimate level of 20 per cent, rather than 25 per cent, of average revalued band earnings. Furthermore, this average will be based on all earnings rather than the best 20 years as originally provided.

Contracting out

The 1975 Act empowered good occupational pension schemes to contract out of SERPS. This meant that the occupational pension scheme undertook to provide benefits at least equal to a guaranteed minimum pension (GMP) in place of the SERPS pension, in return for a reduction in employer and employee National Insurance contributions. A person's GMP is calculated like the SERPS pension.

Until April 1988, only final salary schemes which guarantee a minimum level of earnings-related pension could contract out of SERPS. The Social Security Act 1986, however, allowed schemes to contract out of SERPS from April 1988 without having to guarantee any level of minimum benefits. Such schemes are Contracted Out Money Purchase schemes, or COMP schemes, and provide benefits equal to whatever the contributions accumulated for a member will buy at the time of retirement.

Main features of pension schemes

Pension schemes are usually complex affairs, and their provision can vary considerably. Professional advice from pensions specialists is always required when reviewing pension arrangements to assess what the company needs, what it can afford, and all the legal and tax considerations surrounding pension schemes. The following is a list of the main features that have to be dealt with when reviewing pension schemes.

Pension formulae.　　There are four main types of formulae for determining pensions on retirement:

1. Final salary (salary service), in which the pension is calculated as a fraction of the salary at retirement or as an average over the closing years or months of service. If the arrangement is to pay one-sixtieth of final salary for every year's service, the formula would be described as $n/60$ths. In this case, people on retirement with 40 years' service would obtain 40/60ths of their final salary as a pension, the maximum allowed in the UK under the Inland Revenue code of approval for pension schemes.
2. Average salary (salary graded), in which fixed amounts of pension are given for each year spent in a salary bracket.
3. Flat rate, in which a flat-rate payment is made which is quoted as a given rate for each year of service.
4. Money purchase, in which contributions are fixed and accumulate in a 'pool' for each employee.

A final salary scheme is clearly preferable for the employee because the pension will be based on earnings just before retirement, which should keep pace with increases in the cost of living. But in inflationary times, which are always with us, a final salary scheme can be very costly.

Contributions.   Schemes can be either contributory — requiring contributions from both the employer and the employee   or non-contributory, in which case only the employer makes the contribution. The contributions of employees tend to average about 5 to 6 per cent of basic salary.

The arguments advanced in favour of a contributory scheme are that sharing the cost means that more money is available to buy better benefits, and that employees appreciate benefits more when they have had to pay for them. The arguments in favour of non-contributory schemes are that they are an attraction to employees, are more flexible in response to change, and cost less to run.

Entry age.   The entry age can be fixed at 25 or, preferably, 21. There is usually a qualifying period of six months to a year.

Retirement age.   The retirement age has commonly been fixed at one level for men (often 65) and another for women (often 60). Some organizations retire more senior executives at an earlier age. But since a legal decision in the European Court, it has been necessary for employers to equalize retirement ages for men and women. A typical approach, adopted by W H Smith, is to equalize at the higher retiring age for men of 65 but provide for either men or women to retire from 60 years onwards without loss of pension rights as long as they have had a minimum period of pensionable service (two years).

Post-retirement pensions increases.   Pension schemes can be more or less inflation-proofed by the process of escalation — allowing for increases in pensions in response to change in the cost of living. This is a highly desirable but potentially expensive feature.

Lump sum on retirement.   Pension schemes can offer the right of communication of pension on retirement, which allows the exchange of part of the pension for a tax-free lump sum. This provides a useful aid to those wanting to buy a retirement home, or it can be used for special purchases or investment.

Widows' benefits.   Pension schemes support a widow whose husband has died in service either by providing a lump sum, a reduced widows' pension, or a combination of the two. If wisely invested, a lump sum can often provide a better income than a pension. During his working life, a man should know that there will be adequate provision for his dependants.

Arrangements for paying a widow's pension after the husband's death in retirement vary widely. The best method is to provide a pension of up to two-thirds of the husband's pension.

Early and late retirement.   Early retirement pensions are usually calculated at a reduced rate, and schemes may define the reduction that will apply for each year between the year of early retirement and the normal retiring age. If an employee retires early through ill-health, he or she should at least be entitled to the pension earned up to retirement age. A more favourable arrangement is to pay an improved pension which would take account of potential service up to normal retirement age.

There may be situations in which the company wants employees to stay on after normal retiring age, but their continued service should be reviewed regularly from the point of view of their health. Pension schemes should always provide for a 'late retirement increment' under which employees who continue to work after their normal retirement date can receive an enhanced pension without any further contributions from them or their employers.

'Top hat' arrangement.   A 'top hat' arrangement is one in which a pension scheme for directors or senior staff is topped up by means of an additional non-contributory scheme. A 'top hat' scheme is offered when a company wishes to provide a greater benefit to individuals over and above that supplied under its main fund. Such benefits could usually be provided by augmentation within the fund but there are sometimes internal company reasons for requiring a separate policy.

Additional voluntary contributions.   A good scheme includes provisions for additional voluntary contributions (AVCs) which enable employees to top up their pension to the Inland Revenue limits, although the amount they can contribute is restricted at present to 15 per cent of their pay. This is a very tax-effective form of saving for the future. AVCs can now be made outside the company's schemes through an insurance company.

Funding.   All schemes have to be funded so that the money is available to pay the promised benefits. The usual arrangement is to build up funds by contributions which are invested in securities or in an insurance policy or both. The basic choice is between running a private, self-administered fund through trustees or operating a scheme through an insurance company. Private schemes require considerable investment expertise and administrative effort to organize, although some large companies feel they can run a better and less costly scheme if they go it alone with specialist actuarial advice. The majority of schemes are designed and administered for their clients by insurance companies who have the actuarial, investment and administrative skills required.

Choice of scheme

Pension schemes are complicated affairs and are subject to a number of legal and fiscal considerations. The choice of what goes into the scheme in the shape of alternative types and levels of benefits depends largely on what the company can afford to pay. It may be necessary to trade off one benefit against another by, for example, reducing the pensions formula from $n/60$ths to $n/80$ths in order to introduce a 50 per cent widows' pension. If there is any choice within a budget, employees should be consulted about their preferences.

The cost of pension schemes can be considerable; therefore, it is worth taking care in setting them up and maintaining them. They should be reviewed regularly with the help of expert advice to ensure that they are properly funded and that a reasonable mix of benefits is being provided for the money subscribed by the company and its employees.

Personal pension plans

The rules for personal pension plans are different from occupational (company) schemes. They are arranged on the money purchase principle, and the main difference is that the contributions are restricted according to age and scale, but the amount of the pension that can be bought has no limit. Each contract is an individual one, but employers can contribute and can obtain some advantage by organizing a group arrangement for their company. Alternatively, an individual, who must not be a member of an occupational scheme for the same employment, may effect a personal pension scheme without reference to the employer. Personal pensions are thus 'portable'.

Personal security benefits

Extra statutory sick pay

This supplements the statutory provision by continuing payment beyond the statutory period. Typically, it is service related and provides for a given period at full pay and then a further period at half pay until the scheme's provisions are exhausted.

Permanent health insurance

Also called long-term disability cover, this form of insurance provides for continued income once the provisions of the company sick-pay scheme are exhausted. It is used to provide security of income for those struck down by chronic or permanent illness or disability. It is normally payable until retirement or death and the income typically ranges from one-half to two-thirds of salary at the time illness occurs.

Medical treatment insurance

There are two basic forms of medical treatment insurance:

1. Schemes which cover the costs of private hospital treatment at rates which vary with the location and status of the hospital selected by the employee (eg BUPA, PPP, WPA).
2. Schemes which pay out cash to those being treated under the National Health Service (eg Hospital Savings Association).

The former scheme is the more common and can be offered in one of the following two ways:

1. on a group discount basis, so that employees can obtain cover more cheaply for themselves and their families;
2. at no cost to the employee — this free cover may relate only to the employee or may be extended to his or her family.

Health screening

Health screening may cover basic provisions for X-rays and cervical smears but can be extended to regular full health check-ups. The latter are more often provided for executives.

Personal accident and travel insurance

Personal accident insurance is usually limited to selected employees or to staff who travel or are stationed abroad. Travel insurance can provide extra protection for accidents not causing death which may not be fully covered by the company's pension scheme.

Redundancy

Additional redundancy protection can be provided by increasing the statutory minimum payments to, say, twice the statutory payment for those with more than ten years' service. Redundant employees can be offered counselling or outplacement (ie help in getting another job) services.

Personal needs

Holidays

Annual leave entitlements are a major benefit. Few UK companies give less than four weeks to employees and basic holiday entitlements can be as much as five weeks. Six weeks is usually the maximum, either to senior executives or very long-serving staff. Holiday entitlements often increase on a rising scale in accordance with length of service.

Compassionate leave

Compassionate leave can be provided for as part of the employee benefits policy. It is usually allowed for a limited period on full pay and then the leave becomes unpaid.

Maternity and paternity leave

Employees can provide for longer maternity leave than that given by statute. They may also provide for extra maternity pay on top of the statutory amount. More organizations are now providing paternity leave as an entitlement, recognizing that the amount of leave taken will be relatively small but that the benefit will be great.

Other forms of leave

Policies need to be determined for leave to do with reserve training in the armed forces, jury service and other civic duties.

Sabbaticals

These are rare in the UK but can be a useful retention factor for long-serving professional employees. Leave can vary from a few weeks to a year and is often linked to programmes of research to enhance the knowledge of employees and therefore their contribution to the company.

Child care

In order to attract or retain employees with young dependent children, companies such as the Midland Bank are providing workplace nurseries or crèches.

Retirement counselling

To ease what for some people is a drastic change in circumstances when they retire, counselling can be provided which helps people to understand their financial position, advises them how to cope with being retired and suggests ways of spending their time. Companies such as W H Smith provide counselling by means of residential weekends which are held about a year before people retire and to which spouses are also invited.

Financial counselling

Financial counselling may be made available on investments and tax matters. This benefit is usually restricted to senior executives.

Health and recreational facilities

Although larger companies still retain their traditional recreational clubs and sports fields for employees, there is an increasing tendency for smaller firms to provide or subsidize health programmes by, for example, making facilities available at a reduced cost in a local health and fitness centre.

Financial assistance

Loans

The most common loan facility, especially in London and the Home Counties, is the season ticket loan. This is usually interest free and is repaid in instalments over the year. Loan schemes may also provide for modest sums to be lent interest free or for more substantial sums to be lent at a favourable interest rate. Smaller sums may be lent in cases of hardship, but larger ones are usually for a specific purpose, such as buying a car. The loans are repaid in instalments by deductions from salary. The facility for larger loans is more common in financial institutions.

House purchase (mortgage) assistance

House purchase assistance can be provided by subsidizing interest payments on mortgages up to a defined amount, so that the employee has to pay no more than about 5 per cent. This benefit is mainly confined to the finance sector and is usually provided to all employees, subject to age and service qualifications. Bridging loans are sometimes provided for employees who move at the company's request and have to purchase a new house before they have sold their old one.

Relocation assistance

Companies have to provide some form of relocation assistance when employees are moved at the company's request. The relocation package may reimburse legal and agent's fees, removal costs, and buying new carpets and curtains, as well as compensate for the personal upheaval involved. In order to attract new employees from other parts of the country, companies may have to offer a relocation package providing at least for the payment of removal expenses and usually extending to all or most of the benefits included in the relocated employee's package.

Company discounts

Retail companies usually allow employees to buy goods from their shops at discounted rates which can be as high as 25 per cent off the retail price. The value of the goods they are allowed to purchase in a year may be limited.

Fees to professional bodies

Fees for recognized professional bodies, such as the Institute of Chartered Accountants or the Institute of Personnel Management, may be refunded.

Company cars and petrol

The company car is regarded by many employees and employers as the most significant benefit after pensions, holidays, and sick-pay. Even though the tax advantage is being progressively reduced, employees appreciate this highly visible benefit. Recent research has shown that employees would like a company car even if taxation entirely removed the financial benefit, mainly because they may well have a much better car than they would buy on their account, but also because they are provided with relatively worry-free motoring.

Worth of a company car

The cash value to an employee of a company car can be as much as £5000 to £7000 a year (or more) depending on the model.

Conditions for use

Employees, their spouses, and sometimes their children are generally allowed to use the company car for private motoring. This can sometimes be restricted to the UK. It is usual to reimburse all running costs except petrol and oil. This includes road fund licence, insurance, maintenance and repairs. Employees are sometimes required to make a contribution to the costs of running a car, but this is likely to be significantly less than the financial benefit to them.

Methods of provision

Cars may be bought outright by the company. Alternatively, they may be obtained under:

1. a contract hire arrangement, in which the employer pays a fixed monthly sum to the contract hire company which is related to the value of the car and estimated usage. The contract hire company pays all repair charges and service bills.
2. a lease, in which the leasing company provides the car for rental but takes no responsibility for upkeep or maintenance.

The decision on which method to adopt depends upon an analysis of the tax and cash-flow considerations applicable to the company.

Allocation of cars

Cars can be allocated simply on a need-to-use basis ie only those who have to use a car on business get one provided by the firm. This includes people such as sales representatives, but the principle may be extended generously to managers above a certain level. Because of the significance attached to a company car as a benefit, firms often allocate them to all staff above a certain level.

One of the most vexed questions faced by those formulating benefit policies is whether or not there should be a hierarchy of company cars to match the job hierarchy and, if so, what is the starting point, and what sort of cars should be allocated to each grade? These decisions are critical because of the size of the benefit but also because of the emotion that can be aroused over the allocation of such a *visible* benefit which is often regarded as a powerful prestige symbol.

A hierarchical allocation of cars is best accomplished if there is a graded salary structure based on systematic job evaluation and if the rules on who gets what type of car (or the value of the car that can be obtained) are clear and unequivocal. Even when such rules are clearly defined, eg under a contract hire system where employees in a certain grade can obtain a car for a hire cost within a stipulated bracket, there is plenty of scope for argument at the margin, especially concerning extras.

Replacement of cars

The other key decision to be made about company cars is on when they are to be replaced. The optimum period financially is between two and three years, but some companies lay down a four-year replacement period.

Car allowances

Rather than provide a company car, some firms give car allowances which contribute to running costs, such as repairs and maintenance, and/or a mileage allowance when the car is used on company business.

Petrol

Free petrol to be purchased by a company credit card and used for both business and private purposes is a much appreciated perk. The alternative is a car allowance for employees using their cars on business (currently 35p per mile) or a refund of the costs of petrol if a company car is used on business and a credit card arrangement does not exist.

Other benefits

There is a wide range of other benefits which can improve the employee's standard of living. These include:

- subsidized meals;
- luncheon vouchers;
- refund of telephone costs;
- credit card facilities;
- clothing allowances.

Benefits policies

Policies on employee benefits need to be formulated in the following areas:

- *Range of benefits provided* — some benefits such as pensions and holidays are mandatory; others, such as permanent health insurance, are optional extras.
- *Scale of benefits provided* — the size of each benefit, taking into account its cost to the company and its perceived value to employees. Note that the perceived value of some benefits such as company cars, or pension schemes (in the case of older employees), can be greater than their actual cash value.
- *Proportion of benefits to total remuneration.* In cash terms, a mandatory benefit such as a pension scheme can cost the company from 5 to 10 per cent of an employee's total remuneration. A decision has to be made on the proportion of total remuneration to be allocated to other benefits which incur expenditure of cash by the company. This policy decision is, of course, related to decisions on the range and scale of benefits provided, and it can be affected by decisions on allowing choice of benefits and on the distribution of benefits. Many companies are moving towards a 'clean cash' policy which maximizes the number and scale of fringe benefits.
- *Allowing choice.* A policy is required on the extent to which the company should allow its employees to choose the benefits they want.
- *Allocation of benefits.* The policy on the allocation of benefits determines the extent to which it is decided that a single status company should be created. If the policy is to have a hierarchy of benefits, then the allocation of these at different levels has to be determined.

Factors which affect benefits policy

Tax-efficiency

A tax-efficient benefit is one for which the tax payable on the cost of providing the benefit is less than the tax that would be payable by the employee on the equivalent cash sum. In the past, tax-efficiency was one of the main reasons for the proliferation of benefits, but it has become progressively less important as governments have tightened up the fiscal rules relating to employee benefits. Pension schemes, however, are still highly tax-efficient, as are company cars, although in the latter case this is being steadily eroded by government legislation.

Choice and cafeteria systems

Benefits are most effective in the process of attracting and retaining employees when they satisfy individual needs. But individual needs vary so much that no benefits package or single item within the package can satisfy all employees equally. Younger employees may be more interested in housing assistance than a company pension plan. Some employees have ethical or political objections to medical insurance schemes. Not everyone wants a company car. Many people, especially those to whom tax-efficiency is less important, may prefer cash to an automatic benefit which is not precisely what they want.

One way of dealing with this situation is to introduce a cafeteria system. This allows employees to exercise choice over a range of benefit options within the constraint of total remuneration. Employees, particularly executives with a wider range of benefits, can alter the balance between the range of benefits by cutting back the level of benefits that have less value to them and using the surplus this generates for redistribution to other benefits. For example, an allowance of £500 a month for the contract hire of a car could be reduced to £300 a month, freeing £200 to be allocated to other benefits or, possibly, to be paid as additional salary.

A cafeteria system can enable companies to:

- discover which benefits are popular and which are not, leading to more effective concentration of resources on those benefits welcomed by employees;
- develop mechanisms to manage benefit costs more effectively;
- inform employees about the real costs of benefits;
- make use of a single strategic concept to meet diverse employee needs.

A typical way of managing flexibility in a cafeteria system is to establish a core package of benefits topped up by a percentage of gross pay available for additional components. But a cafeteria system can be an elaborate affair because of the need to produce comparative valuations of different parts of the package and construct methods of transferring the cash released by foregoing the whole or part of a benefit to another benefit or aspect of remuneration.

Some companies are moving away from a complex benefit package to a 'clean cash' system which provides basic core benefits, such as pensions, sick-pay and holidays but translates all other items into cash. This may conflict with a policy of maximizing tax efficiency, especially in the case of company cars, but it does give freedom of choice and also reduces administrative costs.

Harmonization

In the new flatter organizations, where flexibility and multiskilling are important and new technology is eliminating the old distinction between white- and blue-collar workers, harmonization of benefit packages is increasingly taking place. The objectives are to increase unity of purpose and improve teamwork by abolishing invidious distinctions between benefits, and to reward different levels of responsibility and contribution by pay alone. Single-status companies are becoming much more common.

Full harmonization means that there are no distinctions at any level in the hierarchy between the benefits provided, which may vary only with length of service. Partial harmonization may provide the same basic benefits in some areas, such as pensions, holidays, sick-pay, and redundancy for white- and blue-collar staff, but have a hierarchy of benefits above this base according to job grades. These benefits could include company cars, topped-up pension schemes or medical treatment insurance.

Market considerations

Whatever degree of choice or harmonization is decided upon, the precise arrangements will be affected by market considerations. It may be possible to attract and retain some key staff only by, for example, offering a company car in line with what other organizations are doing for similar jobs. To attract a senior executive, it may be necessary to offer him or her a special pension arrangement. As in all aspects of pay, market considerations and the need to offer competitive packages may have to override the principle of equity.

Trade unions

Trade unions are increasingly concerned with the whole remuneration package and therefore may be involved or ask to be involved in negotiating the provision and level of benefits. Many companies, however, resist negotiating such items as pensions although they are prepared to consult unions or staff associations on benefit arrangements.

Total remuneration

The total remuneration concept is based on the belief that all aspects of pay and employee benefits should be treated as a whole, the different parts of which can be adjusted according to the needs of the company and the individual. This means that, in setting levels of remuneration, account is taken of the value to employees and the cost to the company of each of the benefits to which job holders are entitled as well as their basic salary and bonus payments. Remuneration is thereby treated as a total package in order that employees can be told about the complete value of what they are getting, valid comparisons can be made with other companies, and an appropriate balance can be achieved between the different components of remuneration.

The concept applies to all levels of staff, but it is of more importance at higher levels because of the tax advantages that may be achieved by providing certain benefits as an alternative to basic salary. However, as tax authorities tighten up on their regulations, the scope for tax planning to reduce the incidence of income tax on higher earnings is becoming increasingly restricted.

Total remuneration and the company

The approach to total remuneration should be to decide on the mix of basic pay, bonuses and other employee benefits that should be provided at different levels by reference to company policies on differentials and external comparisons. Ideally, the value of each element should be assessed in terms of the benefit received by individuals — gross and net of tax — at different salary levels and the cost to the company, also gross and net of tax. By comparing remuneration on both a gross and net basis, the scope for using fringe benefits to reduce the effect of progressive taxation can be identified. It is unlikely that benefits other than basic salary, especially pensions, will take up an increasing proportion of total remuneration as responsibility increases.

Total remuneration and the individual

Everyone starts off by wanting a good basic salary to provide for the necessities of life and satisfy the basic needs in Maslow's hierarchy of human needs — to survive and to achieve security. Thereafter other needs become more important, and these are the ones that can best be satisfied by the intrinsic motivators present in the work itself. At the same time, people begin to seek alternative means of providing for their needs and, particularly at higher levels, may not find the package offered by the company fully acceptable. Hence the importance of choice, as mentioned earlier. What the company must not do is force benefits on people who may not appreciate them. If money is to motivate, it should satisfy real rather than assumed needs.

30

Salary Administration

Salary administration procedures

Salary administration procedures are concerned with the implementation and control of salary policies and with the control of salary costs against budgets. Control is an essential element of salary administration, and this section will therefore begin with a general discussion of the desirable features of a control system. It will then deal more specifically with the following procedures:

- salary budgets;
- cost-of-living or general reviews of salary levels;
- individual salary reviews;
- fixing salary levels on joining the company or on promotion;
- salary control.

Desirable features of control

To achieve effective salary control, the salary administration procedures should have the following features:

1. defined ranges with minima and maxima to which all jobs are allocated on the basis of their value, with all employees paid within the ranges for the jobs performed;
2. defined methods of progress within the range based on specific criteria;
3. a detailed salary budget based on the number of staff required to carry out the forecast volume of work; forecast salary levels taking into account the effects of general and incremental increases; forecasts of promotions and promotional increases and numbers joining and leaving the organization; and forecasts of the likely effect on salary

costs of changes in the numbers employed and of differences between the salary levels of those joining or leaving;

4. clear statements of the degree of authority at each management level to award or to confirm increments with arrangements for authorizing proposed salary changes and checking their consistency with policy;

5. clear salary review guidelines defining the limit to which the payroll costs of each department can increase as a result of merit awards, together with other instructions on, for example, the maximum awards that can be given and the distribution of awards according to performance and between the population in each salary grade;

6. procedures for auditing increases and salary levels to ensure that they are in accordance with salary policies, and for monitoring actual salary costs against budgeted costs.

Salary budget

A salary budget is a statement in quantitative and usually financial terms of the planned allocation and use of resources to meet the operational needs of the company. All budgets are based on a planned level of activity or volume of output which determines the resources required. In the case of the salary budget, the forecast levels of activity indicate the numbers of different categories of staff that are needed for the budget period. The annual salary budget is a product of the numbers of staff to be employed and the rates at which they will be paid.

The salary budget has to take account of the financial resources available to the company. This will affect the ability to pay general or individual merit increases, or the numbers employed, or both. Salary budgets in large organizations are prepared by departmental managers in accordance with instructions issued by the accounts department. They are often based on current salary levels and are inflated at a later stage when decisions are made about how much money can be allocated for individual and general salary increases. An example of a budget form is shown in Figure 30.1.

Historical control over salary costs is achieved by comparing budgeted costs with actual costs, analysing any variances, and deciding on corrective action, which could take the form of a reduction in manning levels or in the budget for merit increases if salary costs are over the budget. A cost comparison form is illustrated in Figure 30.2.

But backward-looking controls are not enough. It is also necessary to ensure that the salary policies and guidelines laid down by management

				Salary budget for year ending					
Department:				**Proposed by:**				**Approved by:**	
Actual — previous year...........				Forecast — forthcoming year.........					
No.	Salary cost	Overtime cost	Total cost	Category of staff	No.	Salary cost	Overtime cost	Total cost	Increase or decrease in total cost
				Managers					
				Supervisors					
				Clerical staff					
				Temporary staff					
				Total					
Reasons for forecast increase/decrease over previous year:									

Figure 30.1 Salary budget form

Department				COST COMPARISON STATEMENT	Quarter ending:				
This quarter				Category of staff	Year to date		Forecast for year		
Number		Payroll cost			Payroll cost		I Payroll cost		
Actual	Variance	Actual	Variance		Actual	Variance	Actual	Variance	
				Managers					
				Supervisors					
				Clerical staff					
				Temporary staff					
				Total					
Reasons for variance and proposed actions:									

Figure 30.2 Salary cost comparison form

are implemented, and the procedures required for this purpose are described below.

General and market rate salary reviews

General salary reviews take place when it is necessary to increase all or

649

most salaries in response to increases in the cost of living or in market rates, or as a result of settlements affecting either staff or hourly paid employees.

General reviews tend to be an annual event, although external market pressures may mean that they have to take place at different times of the year to individual merit reviews. Changes in market rates generally, or, which is more likely, in particular market groups, may require adjustments to pay as and when necessary, rather than in accordance with a fixed timetable. If market pressures are acute for an important category of employee, then it does not make sense to delay a review until it is too late and key staff have been lost. In competitive situations, a flexible approach to salary administration is essential.

Companies without staff unions who operate a secret salary policy often try to differentiate between a general and merit increase. Their staff receive their annual award and do not know how much is general or how much is particular to them. Companies pursue secrecy in salary policies because it enables them to exercise complete control, that is, until the staff lose patience and move into the ever-welcoming arms of the trade unions. Companies are frightened of divulging their salary structure or review policies to staff because they feel that this may open the door to recognition claims and pay negotiations. The other reason for not publishing salary scales, which is not admitted to so freely, is that the structure is so illogical that it would be impossible to explain or to justify it to the staff.

It is difficult to reconcile this point of view, especially with regard to merit increments, with the equally prevalent view that money is the great motivator. How can money motivate effectively if everyone is kept in the dark about the relationship between effort and reward?

The best approach is to distinguish between general and individual increases, even if they are paid at the same time. The general increase is paid to everyone, although some companies reserve the right to withhold general increases or to give smaller increments to staff whose performance is below average or who are overpaid. At the same time, the salary brackets are adjusted, usually at both ends, by the same amount. It is equally important to keep individuals informed of how they stand in the salary structure and the rewards they are getting or can obtain.

Individual salary reviews

The purpose of an individual salary review is to decide on the merit increments that should be given to staff. The usual practice is to have one annual review for all staff, with the possibility of a half-yearly review for younger staff with high potential who need encouragement more than once a year. Some companies phase increases throughout the year on birthdays or on the anniversary of staff joining the company. This, they say, enables more individual attention to be paid to staff and removes the emotional atmosphere that surrounds the annual review. But phased reviews are more difficult to administer and control except where a fixed increment system is in use, and most organizations prefer one or two fixed dates for a review. Individual salary reviews require the preparation of budgets and guidelines for management in accordance with the principles of salary control, as set out at the beginning of this chapter.

Salary review guidelines

Salary review guidelines are necessary to inform managers of what they can pay and how they should distribute it among their staff. The aim should be to give managers the maximum amount of authority to determine merit increments within a budget as long as this freedom does not result in unacceptable inconsistencies in the awards given to staff. It has to be faced that any merit review system which relates rewards to performance and not to a time-scale will result in inconsistencies. Even if rigid guidelines are laid down on the amount and distribution of awards, the ultimate decision on who gets what will depend on the largely subjective judgement of someone. It is best, however, for this judgement to be exercised by people in direct charge of staff rather than by remote control.

The various types of guidelines available are:

1. *Overall cost guidelines*, in which a budget of, say, 4 per cent of payroll is imposed for merit reviews. This is the essential guideline, and managers may be left to distribute the pool as they please, or they may be subject to various degrees of control on the grounds that they might otherwise make eccentric awards such as giving everyone exactly the same small amount, or giving a limited number of people excessively high increases.

2. *Guidelines on maximum and minimum increases*, in which managers are told that they cannot give an increase of more than, say, 10 per cent or less than, say, 3 per cent, on the grounds that too high an increase could produce inequities and too low an increase is meaningless — 3 or 4 per cent is generally regarded as the minimum worthwhile increase. These limiting guidelines are not too restrictive and can easily be added to the basic budget figure to produce a reasonable balance

between excessive control and excessive freedom.

3. *Guidelines on the relationship between performance and reward*, in which it is laid down that awards should be related to an overall assessment of performance on a scale such as this:

Assessment	Increment (%)
A — outstanding	9–10
B — very satisfactory	7–8
C — satisfactory	4–6
D — barely satisfactory	3*
E — unsatisfactory	0

    The problem with this approach is that the assessments are entirely subjective. There will be no common standards of judgement between departments and the distribution of awards will be as inconsistent as ever. All that such guidelines can do is to provide some indication to managers about how they might distribute the pool of money made available to them among their staff.

4. *Guidelines on the distribution of increments*, in which, in an attempt to overcome the varying standards of judgement leading to an 'all my geese are swans' approach to rewarding staff, managers are required to conform to a forced distribution of merit increases. For example, they are not allowed to give an increase of 9 per cent to more than 10 per cent of their staff. The distribution scale may be related to the guidelines on increments like this:

Assessment	Increment %	Distribution %
A — outstanding	9–10	10
B — very satisfactory	7–8	20
C — satisfactory	4–6	40
D — barely satisfactory	3	20
E — unsatisfactory	0	10

In this example a normal distribution is followed, but this may be rejected, quite rightly, by managers as an entirely arbitrary device. They will assert that their departments are exceptional and will refuse to accept any contention that the abilities of their staff conform to the normal distribution of the population as a whole. They will assert, and they might even be right, that they have trained and developed a body of exceptional men and women, and that they have taken great care

---

* but only if there is hope of improvement and the individual needs encouragement.

both to avoid selecting duds and to remove any who have slipped through the net. Distributions can, of course, be altered to conform to this viewpoint by increasing the proportion of higher increments, thus conceding that the normal distribution of abilities does not apply. But this is still an entirely arbitrary process.

5. *Guidelines on rates of progression,* in which managers are helped to plan salary progression by being given an indication of the number of years it should take staff at different levels of performance to reach the top of the grade and, in a zones salary range, the limits within the range which can be reached according to their performance. For example:

Assessment	Limit in grade	Years to limit from grade minimum
A	Grade maximum	7–8
B	Qualified zone maximum	7–8
C	Midpoint	8–9
D	Learning zone maximum	5 or more
E	Not normally retained	—

Again, such guidelines may be helpful in salary planning, but it would be wrong to apply them too rigidly.

There is a danger of going too far with guidelines and imposing so much rigidity on the system that it collapses under the strain. There is a limit to the extent to which it is appropriate or possible to direct increments in any situation where decisions are not all made centrally. Constraints in the form of budgets and upper and lower limits can and should be applied, but the other guidelines on amounts and distribution should never be used as mandatory controls. They can be helpful in showing managers how the system can work but as examples only.

The best form of guideline, other than the essential budget limits, is the briefing and training that should be given to managers who are recommending increments. Thereafter, guidance should be based on an analysis of recommendations from the centre in order that managers who adopt a seemingly eccentric approach can be asked to justify it. If they cannot, they must be persuaded to think again and do better next time.

Procedures for grading jobs

The procedures for grading or regrading jobs should lay down that new jobs or jobs where the responsibilities have changed can be graded or regraded only when a job evaluation has taken place. This should require the preparation of job descriptions which can be matched with other jobs and grade definitions, or which can be used as a basis for an analytical job evaluation.

Managers who wish to regrade a job or increase a salary because of market rate pressures or because a member of staff is 'holding a pistol at their heads' by threatening to leave for a higher salary should be required to produce evidence to support their case. The evidence should be positive. It is not enough to refer to one or two carefully selected advertisements. And it is always dangerous to succumb to blackmail, however valuable the individual appears to be. Panic measures should be avoided by keeping a careful watch on market rate trends and taking any necessary action in good time.

Fixing salaries on appointment or promotion

Control over starting salaries should be exercised by providing guidelines on the policies to be followed and by defining who has the authority to approve salaries. The guidelines should state that the normal practice is to start inexperienced staff at the bottom of the range, but salaries up to, say, 15 per cent above the minimum can be offered if this would not cause embarrassment by appointing an outsider at a higher salary than existing staff. Appointments at a salary above this level would only be made with the approval of a higher authority.

Promotions should be dealt with as they arise rather than being left to the annual review. The increase should be meaningful, say, 10 per cent or more, and the starting-point in the new salary grade should provide adequate scope to reward performance in the new job. Ideally, therefore, the starting-point should not be higher than 15 per cent or so above the minimum rate for the grade.

Salary control procedures

Salary control procedures are concerned with:

- salary review budgets;
- generating and using control information;
- monitoring gradings within the salary structure by the use of compa-ratios (comparative ratios);
- understanding and using the principle of salary attrition.

Salary review budgets

The best way to plan and control the individual or merit review is to determine the increase to the payroll that can be allocated for merit payments. The review budget can then be expressed as, say, 5 per cent of payroll costs, and this is the limit given to each manager for increasing the payroll. The following factors influence the size of the budget:

- The salary policies of the company on the rates at which staff of different levels of ability should progress through their salary ranges.
- The extent to which the actual salaries in each grade differ from the target salary, which is usually the midpoint in the grade and, ideally, should correspond to the average salaries of the job holders in the grade. The information used for this purpose is the compa-ratio, as described below.
- The potential effect of what is termed salary attrition on average salaries over the year. Attrition is the reduction in salary costs which can take place over a period of time as a result of staff joining the company at a lower salary than those who leave. This process is also discussed below.
- The amount the company thinks it can afford to pay on the basis of forecasts or revenue, profits and payroll costs and an analysis of the effects of salary attrition on costs.
- The effect of government regulations on pay increases.

Control information

In a small or even medium-sized organization, control over the implementation of individual salary reviews is easily achieved by checking through recommendations and ensuring that they appear to be reasonable and that the total increase to the payroll does not exceed the budget.

In a larger organization it may be advisable to exercise control by means of a salary review form for each department, such as the one illustrated in Figure 30.3.

Overall control can be maintained quite simply by requiring each department to produce a summary of the individual recommendations which shows the percentage increase to the payroll and the distribution of merit awards of different amounts. A more elaborate approach, suitable only for organizations which want to exercise close central control, is to use a summary sheet showing details of average salaries and increments in each grade, as illustrated in Figure 30.4.

FUNCTION/DEPARTMENT			PROPOSED BY					DATE		APPROVED BY			DATE	
		Date		Job grade	Last increase			Present salary	Assess-ment (2)	Proposed increase		Approved increase		Comments
Name	Job title	of birth	of joining	started present job		Amount	Date	Reason (1)			Amount	New salary	Amount	New salary	
(1)	(2)	(3)	(4)	(5)	(6)	(7)	(8)	(9)	(10)	(11)	(12)	(13)	(14)	(15)	(16)
									Total	Totals					
Total number															

NOTES

1. Reasons for last increase:
   M = merit
   P = promotion

2. Assessment
   A – Outstanding   C – Satisfactory
   B – Very satisfactory D – Barely satisfactory
                 E – Unsatisfactory

Figure 30.3 Individual salary review form

656

DEPARTMENT   PROPOSED BY   DATE   APPROVED BY   DATE

Grade	Present			Proposed											
	No. in grade	Salary bill £	Average salary £	Distribution of merit increments (number)			Number not receiving increment			Distribution in grade (number)			Salary bill £	Average salary £	% Increase
				A	B	C	Assessed D/E	On maximum	On midpoint	Premium zone	Qualified zone	Learning zone			
	(1)	(2)	(3)	(4)	(5)	(6)	(7)	(8)	(9)	(10)	(11)	(12)	(13)	(14)	(15)
1															
2															
3															
4															
5															
6															
7															
8															
9															
10															
11															
12															
13															
14															
15															
16															
17															
18															
Total															

Approved total

Figure 30.4 Salary review summary sheet

Compa-ratios

A compa-ratio (short for comparative ratio) is a measure of the extent to which the average salaries in a grade deviate from the target salary. It is used to compare actual averages with the target salary to indicate the extent to which salary levels are high or low, and thus suggest where action may have to be taken to limit increases or to adopt a more generous policy. The formula for calculating a compa-ratio is:

$$\frac{\text{Average of all salaries in the grade}}{\text{Midpoint of the salary range}} \times 100$$

A compa-ratio of 100 indicates that the average salary is aligned to the midpoint of the salary grade and that no corrective steps need to be taken. An average salary of £9600 compared with a midpoint of £12,000 would produce a compa-ratio of 80 and would indicate the need to investigate why average salaries were low and possibly no longer competitive. This could have arisen because of an influx of new staff or those promoted into a salary grade.

A compa-ratio of 120 arising if average salaries were £14,400 in a grade where the midpoint was £12,000 would suggest either there were a lot of long-service staff in the grade (which could be a cause of congratulation or alarm) or that staff were being overpaid, and that increases needed to be modified. Compa-ratio analysis can therefore reveal a situation where earnings drift has taken place — the natural but not necessarily appropriate tendency for salaries to drift towards the upper range or top of a salary range irrespective of the merits of the individuals concerned.

Information on compa-ratios and changes in the average salaries can be recorded on a form, such as the one illustrated in Figure 30.5, and used for

		Number in grade		Average salary		Compa-ratio	
Grade	Salary range	Last year	This year	Last year	This year	Last year	This year

Figure 30.5 Compa-ratio summary form

manual comparisons and to provide guidance on the likely effects of salary attrition.

Salary attrition

Attrition to the costs of awarding merit increments takes place when the average salary of leavers in a company exceeds the average salary of joiners. This is the normal situation and it means that an increase in the salary bill of, say, 3 per cent at the beginning of a year could be steadily eroded during the year as a result of the inflows and outflows of staff.

In practice, the difference between the salaries of leavers and joiners is not likely to correspond exactly with the cost of the merit increase. But if there are movements in and out of a company or a salary grade, and if the salaries of leavers are higher than those of joiners, which is highly probable, then there must be some attrition.

The importance of attrition for salary control purposes is that it is possible to assume that it will finance the cost of merit increases wholly or in part during the year. Alternatively, it can be assumed that merit increases in a fixed incremental system, where people are likely to be moving steadily into, out of, and through grades, are not inflationary.

Some companies have developed attrition models which they use to determine in advance the cost of merit awards. Other companies adopt the less sophisticated approach of calculating attrition as the residual figure which remains after general and merit increases, expressed as a percentage of payroll, have been subtracted from the percentage increase in average salaries.

Computerized salary administration

The scope for computerizing salary administration systems is considerable and should be exploited. This is covered in Chapter 38.

Salary problems

No system of reward management can ensure that a company is not faced with salary problems. Reward management takes place in dynamic conditions, and unpredictable changes are inevitable. Salary levels and grading ultimately affect employees, collectively and as individuals. Salary policies and reviews arouse strong feelings which must be dealt with.

Most of the likely problems have been considered in earlier chapters, but, at the risk of some repetition, it would be useful to review the main issues in this chapter to highlight the pressure points that occur in salary systems. The problems discussed below are:

- absorbing market rate pressures;
- widening differentials;
- performance pay;
- staff reaching the top of their salary league;
- deteriorating job evaluation schemes.

Absorbing market rate pressures

Market rate forces — the 'hidden hand' in remuneration policies, to paraphrase Adam Smith — produce the perennial problem of reconciling the need to keep pace with what other companies pay with the need to preserve equitable internal relativities. The problem arises when general and individual salary reviews have not enabled the company's salary levels to keep pace with increases in market rates. It is exacerbated if the company is expanding and is compelled to obtain key staff who are in short supply.

The problem occurs in its most acute form when the grading given to specialist jobs, such as computer programmers, within the company does not place them on a salary range which is competitive with market rates. If this is genuinely the case, there are five possible courses of action that can be taken:

1. Create a separate 'market group' structure for these jobs. This isolates the problem to a degree, but invidious comparisons can still be made within the company, and a proliferation of salary structures can cause administrative difficulties.
2. Create a special salary range for the jobs, which need not correspond with any existing job grade salary range. Again, this does not prevent comparisons, and intermediate salary ranges of this kind can destroy the integrity of the structure if indulged in to excess. But this method provides a measure of isolation without the administrative complexities of a completely separate structure.
3. Pay a market rate premium to job holders who retain the original grading given to their jobs. This is a variation of the second choice, which in certain circumstances may be easier to justify and administer. It is also easier to remove a premium than to abolish a grade.
4. Place the jobs in question in a higher grade but identify them as special cases (known in the trade as 'red-circling'). This can be quite an effective way of dealing with isolated cases, but one of the earlier three

choices provides a more easily controllable method of dealing with a large number of similar jobs.

5. Recruit staff at a higher point in the salary range. This is the easiest solution, but it can be used only as a short-term expedient because it restricts salary progression and may be difficult to justify to staff in other jobs in the grade.

None of these choices present the ideal solution because no such solution exists. The circumstances will indicate whether a short- or a long-term method is best and the degree to which isolation on a permanent basis is necessary.

Widening differentials

Differentials are widening between and within companies in the following areas:

1. Between high- and low-paying organizations — the variations in prosperity between differing sectors of industry and commerce and between different regions are major contributors to this problem.
2. Between companies paying bonuses or incentives and those paying straight salaries — this arises not just because of the bonus element but also because the bonus-paying companies tend to have higher base salaries, a reflection of their policy of demanding results but expecting to have to pay over the odds to get the extra performance they require.
3. Between top and middle management within companies — this is partly incentive led; bonuses are given more readily to top management, and the amounts tend to be considerably higher as a proportion of the base salary. But the widening of differentials has also taken place because of a deliberate policy of redressing the situation of the 1970s when differentials were squeezed and 'head room' was lacking. This increase in differentials as a response to the more onerous demands made on top management is usually desirable, but it has sometimes meant that middle managers have felt neglected, and they are still important.
4. Between executives recruited by search and those with a one-company career — key people in short supply are increasingly being recruited by executive search consultants or head-hunters. The best executives will already be paid in the upper quartile of the salary range before they are offered a 20 per cent or higher increase to move companies.

To a degree, the widening of differentials is a fact of life that everyone working in an enterprise culture has to accept. When it happens between companies or sectors, the problem is one of market pressure and can be dealt with only by one of the methods suggested earlier. Within companies the aim should be to ensure that differentials are justified, that they truly reflect differences in contribution, and that they properly reward achievement.

Performance pay problems

The emphasis in the 1980s on performance-related pay was an appropriate response to the ever increasing pressure for results. However, bonus schemes and merit awards can be divisive if they are awarded only to top people and the favoured few whose results can be measured. The supporting staff who do the hard work should be remembered too, but companies often neglect them. It can, of course, be difficult to develop performance-related pay schemes for office staff, a problem which is very evident in the Civil Service. But there are means of varying progression according to merit, as described in Chapter 28.

Performance-related pay can also cause problems because merit assessments are too often based on subjective and biased judgements. This can be avoided only by the intensive training of assessors and by carefully monitoring the appraisal scheme.

Staff reaching the top of their salary range

Staff who reach the top of their salary range may feel demotivated if there are no prospects of promotion. The blow will be softened if they are fully aware of the policy of the company on limiting progression to the top of the salary range and can be told that the company's policy of relating the salary range midpoint to market rates means that they are well paid compared with what they could earn elsewhere. Feelings of disappointment can be further reduced, if not eliminated, by assuring staff that every attempt will be made to maintain the purchasing power of their salaries and that jobs will be regraded if there is a sufficient increase in responsibilities.

It is possible to deal with this problem by introducing on top of the normal salary range a premium zone which is reserved for outstanding staff whose promotion is blocked. This may provide for a 10 per cent or more uplift in salary. The use of premium zones must be controlled very carefully.

However, the problem returns when staff get to the top of their premium zone. They may have been told clearly that they are now paid well above the going rate but, especially if they have been used to regular increments, they may still feel aggrieved if they come to a grinding halt. One solution to the problem is to pay non-consolidated bonuses for exceptional work. But these must not be handed out too liberally or they will lose any incentive effect they might have had. People at the top of their scale should already be well paid. If they want more they must earn it.

Starting salaries

The problem of starting new staff at higher rates than existing employees should, in theory, be minimized if internal salary levels are regularly reviewed in comparison with market rates. In practice, especially when a government imposes pay restrictions, salaries within a company often lag behind those outside, and anomalies are almost inevitable. If normal salary structure review and control procedures fail to control this problem, the anomalies should be noted and special steps taken to overcome them at the time of the next salary review by giving higher increases to those left behind, or by restricting the increases of the higher paid staff, unless their performance justifies the retention of their differential.

Deteriorating job evaluation schemes

Job evaluation schemes can deteriorate for a number of reasons. The scheme may not have been controlled properly, so that grade drift occurs through unjustifiable upgradings as a result of pressures from managers or staff. Or the scheme may have lost credibility because it no longer gives acceptable solutions. Or the administration of the scheme may have become so bureaucratic that the time taken to produce answers is unduly prolonged.

The facile answer to these problems is to say that effective administration should prevent grade drift, remove doubts and speed up results. But the evaluation scheme itself may be at fault because it is no longer appropriate (if it ever was), or because it is difficult to administer. Job evaluation systems are inherently prone to these defects because they are subjective and rely on large acts of faith backed up by time-consuming analysis. Simple schemes, even if they are rather crude, are often more effective in the long run.

It is tempting to scrap the existing scheme when it goes wrong and replace it with a new and much more elaborate system. This temptation should be resisted unless the situation is desperate. New schemes are expensive to introduce, and they can cause more trouble than they are worth because of the expectations they create among staff, which are often disappointed. It is preferable to make a determined effort to tighten controls and speed up administration, making only minor modifications to the scheme itself. These changes should be in the direction of simplication.

Part VII
Employee Relations

Employee relations consists of all those aspects of personnel management where employees are dealt with collectively. The primary aims of employee relations policies and procedures are to improve cooperation, to minimize unnecessary conflict, to enable employees to play an appropriate part in decision making, and to keep them informed on matters that concern them.

Wherever there are trade unions, industrial relations are a major preoccupation of personnel management. Industrial relations policies and procedures need to be developed and operated in the light of an understanding of the processes at work in collective bargaining, where the 'web of rules' is developed by formal and informal negotiations and by discussions between management and the trade unions. Chapter 31 therefore starts with an analysis of industrial relations as a system of rules developed by formal and informal processes of collective bargaining. It goes on to discuss the framework of industrial relations and the roles of the various parties involved, before considering the established industrial relations system, including the structure of collective bargaining, recognition and procedural agreements, and the formal and informal elements within the system. Next, a number of important trends in industrial relations are reviewed. These include single-employer and decentralized bargaining, single-union and 'new style' agreements, single-table bargaining, dispute resolution, flexibility and the HRM approach to employee relations.

The remaining chapters in this part then examine the important subjects of participation, consultation and communications and the means available to develop procedures and techniques which create a climate of employee relations conducive to cooperation and trust.

31

Industrial Relations

The essence of industrial relations

Industrial relations is concerned with the formal and informal relationships which exist between employers and trade unions and their members. It involves:

- The development, negotiation and application of formal systems, rules and procedures for collective bargaining, handling disputes and regulating employment. These serve to determine the reward for effort and other conditions of employment, to protect the interests of both employees and their employers, and to regulate the ways in which employers treat their employees and how the latter are expected to behave at work.
- Informal as well as formal processes which take the form of continuous interactions between managers and supervisors on the one hand and shop stewards and individuals on the other. These may happen within the framework of formal agreements but are often governed by custom and practice and the climate of relationships that has been built up over the years.
- A number of parties, each of different roles. These consist of the State, management, the trade unions, individual managers and supervisors, personnel managers, shop stewards and employees.
- The bargaining structures, recognition and procedural agreements and practices which have evolved to enable the formal system to operate.

This chapter deals with the complex and ever-changing subject of industrial relations under the following seven main headings:

1. *fundamental concepts of industrial relations* — the system of rules, types of

regulations and rules, the basis of collective bargaining, industrial relations and the individual and the principle of voluntarism;

2. *industrial relations institutions* — the parts played by the government, the trade unions, and the employers' associations;
3. *industrial relations roles* — the roles of the principal players in the system as defined above;
4. *the established industrial relations system* — the Donovan analysis, the structure of collective bargaining, the form and content of recognition and procedural agreements, and formal and informal elements in the system;
5. *trends in industrial relations* — single employer and decentralized bargaining, single-union and 'new style' agreements, single-table bargaining, dispute resolution, the closed shop, new technology, individualism, flexibility and the HRM (human resource management) approach to employee relations;
6. *negotiations* — concluding agreements with trade unions or employee representatives;
7. *industrial relations strategy.*

Fundamental concepts of industrial relations

Industrial relations as a system of rules

Industrial relations can be regarded as a system or web of rules regulating employment. In the words of Thomason,[1] systems theory 'concentrates on those relationships which establish, contain and apply the rules by which people behave at work'.

The systems theory of industrial relations, as propounded by Dunlop,[2] states that the role of the system is to produce the regulations and procedural rules which govern how much is distributed in the bargaining process and how the parties involved, or the 'actors' in the industrial relations scene, relate to one another. The output of the system takes the form of:

> The regulations and policies of the management hierarchy; the laws of any worker hierarchy; the regulations, degrees, decisions, awards or orders of governmental agencies; the rules and decisions of specialized agencies created by the management and worker hierarchies; collective bargaining arrangements and the customs and traditions of the workplace and work community.

The system is expressed in many more or less formal or informal guises:

in legislation and statutory orders, in trade union regulations, in collective agreements and arbitration awards, in social conventions, in managerial decisions, and in accepted 'custom and practice'. They may be defined and coherent, or ill-defined and incoherent. Within a plant the rules may mainly be concerned with doing no more than defining the *status quo* which both parties recognize as the norm from which deviations may be made only by agreement. In this sense, therefore, an industrial relations system is a normative system where a norm can be seen as a rule, a standard, or a pattern for action which is generally accepted or agreed as the basis upon which the parties concerned should operate.

Systems theory, however, does not sufficiently take into account the impact of the State (see pages 671–672). Nor does it adequately explain the role of the individual in industrial relations (see page 681).

Types of regulations and rules

Job regulation aims to provide a framework of minimum rights and rules. Internal regulation is concerned with procedures for dealing with grievances, redundancies, or disciplinary problems and rules concerning the operation of the pay system and the rights of shop stewards. External regulation is carried out by means of employment legislation, the rules of trade unions and employers' associations, and the regulative content of national or local agreements.

The rules can be of two kinds:

1. *procedural*, which deal with such matters as the methods to be used and the rules to be followed in the settlement of disputes, to regulate the behaviour of the parties to the agreement;
2. *Substantive*, which refer to working hours or to other job terms and conditions in the area of employment covered by the agreement. These rules regulate the behaviour of employers and employees as parties to individual contracts of employment.

Procedural rules are intended to regulate conflict between the parties to collective bargaining, and when their importance is emphasized, a premium is being placed on industrial peace, and less regard is being paid to the terms on which it may be obtained. Substantive rules settle the rights and obligations attached to jobs. It is interesting to note that in the UK the parties to collective agreements have tended to concentrate more on procedural rather than on substantive rules. In the US, where there is greater emphasis on fixed-term agreements, the tendency has been to rely more on substantive rules.

Collective bargaining

The industrial relations system is regulated by the process of collective bargaining, defined by Flanders[3] as a 'social process that continually turns disagreements into agreements in an orderly fashion'. Collective bargaining aims to establish by negotiation and discussion agreed rules and decisions in matters of mutual concern to employers and unions as well as methods of regulating the conditions governing employment.

It therefore provides a framework within which the views of management and unions about disputed matters that lead to industrial disorder can be considered with the aim of eliminating the causes of the disorder. Collective bargaining can also be regarded as a joint regulating process, dealing with the regulation of management in its relationships with work people as well as the regulation of conditions of employment. It has a political as well as an economic basis — both sides are interested in the distribution of power between them as well as the distribution of income.

Collective bargaining takes two basic forms, as identified by Chamberlain and Kuhn.[4]

1. *conjunctive bargaining*, which 'arises from the absolute requirement that some agreement — *any* agreement — may be reached so that the operations on which both are dependent may continue', and results in which a 'working relationship in which each party agrees, explicitly or implicitly, to provide certain requisite services, to recognize certain seats of authority, and to accept certain responsibilities in respect of each other';
2. *cooperative bargaining*, in which it is recognized that each party is dependent on the other and can achieve its objectives more effectively if it wins the support of the other.

A similar distinction was made by Walton and McKersie,[5] who referred to *distributive bargaining* as the 'complex system of activities instrumental to the attainment of one party's goals when they are in basic conflict with those of the other party', and to *integrative bargaining* — 'the system of activities which are not in fundamental conflict with those of the other party and which therefore can be integrated to some degree. Such objectives are said to define an area of common concern, a purpose.'

Both forms of collective bargaining emphasize that in industrial relations the parties cannot withdraw, or not for long; they are dependent upon each other for performance of their specialist functions and for their survival (except in the isolated cases where workers' cooperatives independently keep a firm going after its financial collapse). Conjunctive or distributive bargaining is a recognition of this mutual interdependence, but it is limited and negative. Cooperative or integrative bargaining is based on both the mutual interdependence of management and employees *and* their recognition that they can achieve more for themselves by adopting this approach.

Voluntarism and its decline

The essence of the systems theory of industrial relations is that the rules are jointly agreed by the representatives of the parties to employment relations, an arrangement which, it is believed, makes for readier acceptance than if they were imposed by a third party such as the State. This concept of voluntarism was defined by Kahn-Freund[6] as 'the policy of the law to allow the two sides by agreement and practice to develop their own norms and their own sanctions and [to abstain] from legal compulsion in their collective relationship'. It was, in essence, voluntarism which came under attack by government legislation from 1974 onwards, including the principle of 'immunities' for industrial action and the closed shop. The role of the government is discussed in the next section of this chapter.

Industrial relations institutions

The rule-making and regulating processes of industrial relations take place within the framework of national institutions which operate according to certain stated or unstated principles. These comprise the government, the trade unions and the employers' associations, all of which impinge at corporate or plant level.

The government

According to its political persuasion, the government creates a legal framework which regulates the conduct of trade unions and confers rights on employees and duties on employers. It also, in the UK, has established institutions such as the Advisory, Conciliation and Arbitration Service (ACAS) and a network of industrial tribunals to hear unfair dismissal, equal pay and equal opportunity cases and other matters raised where employers are alleged to have failed to comply with the provisions of employment legislation. The Employment Arbitration Tribunal (EAT) has been set up to hear appeals from industrial tribunal decisions. Above this level, appeals are heard by the Court of Appeal and, ultimately, the House of Lords.

Interventionism

Since 1979, the UK government has become more interventionist in dealing with the system as a whole, while not intervening at all in disputes (no more beer and sandwiches at Number 10). According to Mackie,[7]

> The central strategic objective behind government legislative policies since 1979 has been a simple one: to shift the balance of power from trade unions to employers. The philosophy behind this aim was the belief that the trade unions had abused their privileged position, exercising industrial pressure regardless of the country's social or economic interests. . . . Underpinning the desire to set union conduct within a more constructive framework, lies a government drive to ensure business competitiveness and 'free market' conditions.

The legal framework — trade union legislation

The legal framework for this process of intervention in the system was provided by the Employment Acts 1980 and 1982, the Trade Union Act 1984, the Wages Act 1986 and the Employment Act 1988.

The main provisions in these Acts were as follows:

- Trade unions can be sued for unlawful industrial action where called by a 'responsible person'.
- Ballots are required for any union-supported action before it can be made official.
- Industrial action to enforce union membership is unlawful.
- Secondary and sympathetic action is unlawful unless the employer has contract with primary employer.
- Secondary picketing is unlawful.
- Union members have the right to prevent industrial action without a ballot, not to be 'unjustifiably disciplined' for not supporting industrial action, and to pursue grievances against their union.
- Individuals have the right to claim unreasonable expulsion or exclusion from union membership, and the right not to be dismissed or victimized for non-union membership.

Perhaps the two most significant aspects of this legislation are, first, the opportunity it gives to employers to sue trade unions for unlawful industrial action. This has resulted in the courts imposing fines and sequestering union assets. Secondly, closed-shop agreements are faced with complete elimination by the outlawing of industrial action aimed at ensuring the organization of trade unionism in the workplace and by regulations protecting employees from dismissal because they will not join a trade union.

The trade unions

Objectives

The objectives of trade unions can broadly be defined as being:

- to redress the bargaining advantage of the individual worker *vis-à-vis* the individual employer by substituting joint or collective action for individual action;
- to secure improved terms and conditions of employment for their members and the maximum degree of security to enjoy those terms and conditions;
- to obtain improved status for workers in their work;
- to increase the extent to which unions can exercise democratic control over decisions that affect their interests by power sharing at the national, corporate, and plant level.

Exertion of union power

Union power is exerted primarily at two levels — at the industry-wide level, to establish joint regulation on basic wages and hours with an employers' association or equivalent; and at the plant level, where the shop stewards' organizations exercise joint control over some aspects of the organization of work and localized terms and conditions of employment. Unions are party to national, local, and plant procedure agreements which govern their actions to a greater or lesser extent, depending on their power and on local circumstances.

The role of unions

Unions could be said to be in the business of managing discontent; Clive Jenkins once described the professional union bargainer as sitting on 'a pinnacle of institutionalized indignation'. But it does not follow that unions introduce conflict — Jenkins also suggested that 'a union official is vocationally a gladiator because the work of the union is basically defensive'. It can be said that the role of a union is simply to provide a highly organized and continuous form of expression for sectional interests which would exist anyway. Such conflicts of interest are inherent in working relationships, and unions can contribute to their solution by bringing issues out into the open and jointly defining with employers procedures for dealing with them.

Types of unions

The structure of the UK trade union movement is highly complex, with its overlapping and interlinking forms of organization cutting across occupations, skills, and industrial boundaries. The various types of unions in the UK, include *craft unions*, the oldest kind, which require entry by apprenticeship and try to maintain standards by the joint control of apprenticeships and by resisting 'dilution' of the craft by those who have not become full members of the union; *general unions*, the largest kind, which take in recruits without being concerned about their level of skill, occupation or industry; *industrial unions*, which confine recruitment and representation to one industry; *sectoral unions*, which cater for one sector of employment only, such as the civil service; *manual unions*, which recruit what are normally termed manual workers; and *white-collar unions*, a growing field, which include workers who are removed by one or more degrees from direct production or direct service, such as clerks, supervisors, technicians, scientists, and managers. These types of unions can be combined or overlap; for example, there are white-collar sections in general unions, or unions catering for one sector such as banking which are exclusively for white-collar workers.

Most of the unions are federated on a fairly loose basis to the Trade Union Congress, which exerts political influence and tries with varying degrees of success to coordinate and regulate the trade union movement — a difficult task because of the jealously guarded independence of individual members.

Individual unions are run by full-time central and district officials, with local committees of members. Their organization extends into the place of work through shop stewards whose role is discussed on pages 680–681.

Trends in union membership and power

Trade union membership has declined steeply. Total losses between 1979 and 1987 were almost 2.9 million or 21.7 per cent. Trade union density, ie actual trade union membership, as opposed to potential membership, declined from 54.2 per cent in 1979 to 42.0 per cent in 1987. The reasons for this decline are not primarily disenchantment with the unions. There are a number of other and more important factors which have affected membership levels; these were listed by Bain and Price[8] as follows:

1. The composition of potential union membership, which includes the impact of the growing numbers of women and white-collar workers in the labour force, accompanying the shift in the economy towards the service industries.
2. The economy, in particular the impact of inflation and unemployment.

3. Employer policies and government action.
4. Personal and job-related characteristics such as age, gender and the incidence of part-time employment.
5. Industrial structure, which includes decentralization and the decline in the number of workplaces employing large numbers of people. There has consequently been a weakening in the links between the large corporations and the unions, and a reduction in their opportunities to recruit members.
6. The influence of union leaders on the recruitment and retention of members. It is interesting to note that union officials are increasingly being assessed on their success in recruiting members as much as on their negotiating skills.

Too much significance, however, should not be attached to the decline in trade union membership, whatever the reason. Where trade unions are well established at workplace level, their influence has continued to be important.

Responses by the trade union movement

The trade union movement has responded to these factors and the growth in new technology in two ways, as described by Towers:[9]

1. *New realism*, as propounded by the electricians (EEPTU) and, to a lesser extent, the engineers (AEU). They have argued that the primary purpose of trade unions is to improve the pay and conditions of their members, and they accept the need to adjust union strategies and tactics to changes in technology, company organization and the economic circumstances which affect company performance. The new realists represent some of the 'core' groups of craftsmen and have been associated with 'new style' agreements (see pages 691–692) which involve the joint identification with management of the causes of industrial conflict and the best methods of dealing with these causes. The new realism movement has been dismissed by Macintyre[10] as no more than new pragmatism, and the TUC and many of its affiliated unions will have nothing to do with it, perhaps because it seems to them to fit in too well with what management wants. Hence the rise of the new traditionalists.
2. *New traditionalism*. The new traditionalists are led by the big general unions, the TGWU and the GMB. They represent the non-core groups (semi-skilled workers and what the GMB calls 'the servant class'). The aim of the new traditionalists is to extend membership into the sector, adopt a wider, community-based approach and represent

their members on matters of national interest as well as on their terms and conditions of employment.

Employers' associations

Employers' associations have traditionally existed to advise and assist their members on commercial and/or industrial relations matters. They may handle national negotiations on behalf of their members, but the tendency towards single-employer bargaining (see pages 687–689) is reducing their importance in this area. The main natural employer's organization is the Confederation of British Industry (CBI) which does not get directly involved in negotiations although it does conduct research and express views on industrial relations issues on behalf of its members.

Industrial relations roles

Management

The unitary view

Management typically sees its function as that of directing and controlling the workforce to achieve economic and growth objectives. To this end, it believes that it is the rule-making authority. Management tends to view the enterprise as a *unitary* system with one source of authority — itself — and one focus of loyalty — the company. It extols the virtue of teamwork, where everyone strives jointly to a common objective, each pulls his weight to the best of his ability, and each accepts his or her place and function gladly, following the leadership of the appointed manager or supervisor. These are admirable sentiments, but they sometimes lead to what McClelland[11] has referred to as an 'orgy of avuncular pontification' on the part of the leaders of industry. This unitary view, which is essentially autocratic and authoritarian, is sometimes expressed in agreements as 'management's right to manage'.

The pluralist view

In contrast, the *pluralist* view, as advanced by Fox,[12] is that an industrial organization is a plural society, containing many related but separate interests and objectives which must be maintained on some kind of equilibrium. In place of a corporate unity reflected in a single focus of authority and loyalty, management has to accept the existence of rival sources of leadership and attachment. Management has to face the fact that in Drucker's[13] phrase, a business enterprise has a triple personality: it is at once an economic, a political and a social institution. In the first, it produces and distributes incomes. In the second, it embodies a system of government in which managers collectively exercise authority over the managed, but are also themselves involved in an intricate pattern of political relationships. Its third personality is revealed in the plant community which evolves from below out of face-to-face relations based on shared interests, sentiments, beliefs and values among various groups of employees.

The role of management is to exercise authority as well as to build up teamwork, and it is concerned with the development of rules for this purpose. But management has increasingly to accept that it no longer has absolute authority. To a very great extent, management and unions are mutually dependent. For each, the achievement of its own function is dependent upon a working relationship with the other.

The trusteeship theory

The *trusteeship theory* regards the manager as the trustee of the many interests in the undertaking: shareholders or political masters, customers or clients *and* employees. This concept suggests that management 'has the *duty* to manage' rather than the right to manage.

The interdependence of management and trade unions

There are three factors which are important in the relationship between management and trade unions if the pluralist/trusteeship views are held. The first is stability — a firmly established basis for interaction between management and employees. This is why many managers deplore closed shops in theory as an infringement of liberty, but in practice accept that there is less likelihood of trouble if all employees in a job category or unit are members of one union. For the same reason, one union covering all members of the plant may be preferred as a way of reducing the fragmentation of bargaining and of avoiding inter-union rivalries and demarcation — 'who does what' — disputes, even though a monolithic union may be more powerful. The second factor is trust — a belief that when the bargaining is over and the agreement is reached, both parties will keep their word. The third factor is understanding of each other's point of view. This does not mean that the parties must always be at one about the fundamental issues that affect them. But they must know how each side sees these issues if a collective agreement is eventually to be negotiated, or if a relatively stable working relationship is to be maintained.

Lack of involvement by management

At the highest level, management has often been too remote from the unions and their members. Winkler's[14] interesting piece of research on this subject, published under the apt title of *The Ghost at the Bargaining Table*, revealed that: 'Most directors have no significant contact with any manual or clerical staff other than their secretaries. . . . Non-contact was also just as much the norm for production directors and for those normally responsible for personnel matters.' According to Winkler, their withdrawal is a coping device which enables low-level compromises with unions to take place on a pragmatic basis which does not threaten any fundamental principles.

Sir Michael Edwardes, when he was chairman of British Leyland, took a different view from the directors interviewed by Winkler. In *Back from the Brink*, Edwardes emphasized his conviction that leadership in industrial relations had to come from the top and had to include direct contact with workers. His objective in tackling the sad state of industrial relations in BL was, as he put it,

> not to destroy or weaken the unions. On the contrary, it was to rebalance the whole order of things so that, together with management, national union officials would be able to play a proper role without finding their authority eroded by strong stewards, weak management, and a lack of understanding of what management was trying to achieve. This mixture has led to chaos in the past.[15]

The HRM approach

The 'HRM' (human resource management) approach to employee relations originated in the US where the emphasis has increasingly been focused on commitment and mutuality. This was advocated by people such as Walton,[16] whose article in the *Harvard Business Review*, entitled, significantly, 'From control to commitment', has exerted a great deal of influence. The essential features of the HRM approach are as follows:

- a belief that employees should be managed as efficiently and tightly as any other resource in order to maximize added value, ie the difference between the value of sales (outputs) and the cost of resources (inputs such as employment costs);
- a drive towards achieving competitive advantage by gaining commitment through intensive training and indoctrination programmes — this is coupled with a belief in the benefits of 'mutuality', as described in Chapter 8;
- the organization of complementary forms of communication, such as

team briefing, alongside traditional collective bargaining — ie approaching employees directly as individuals or in groups rather than through their representatives;

- the use of employee involvement techniques such as quality circles or improvement groups;
- continuous pressure on quality — total quality management;
- increased flexibility in working arrangements to provide for the more cost-effective use of human resources;
- emphasis on teamwork;
- a strategy of training employees in the particular package of skills appropriate to their own technologies rather than buying in or training skilled craftsmen — this enhances the employee's dependence on the employer by isolating them occupationally and also limits trade union control.

The HRM approach has been taken up by a number of firms in the UK, perhaps because it appears to be in accord with the trusteeship theory of management (although they would not put it that way) while at the same time seeming to support the unitary view of management (although they might not be prepared to admit this).

Managers and supervisors/team leaders

Managers and supervisors, or teamleaders (as they are increasingly being called), have a crucial role in industrial relations, a role that is not always recognized. It is they who are in constant contact with shop stewards and individual union members. If there is disagreement or conflict, they are in the front line. The informal processes of interaction, which are the essence of industrial relations at office and shop-floor level, are their responsibility. To carry out this role effectively, they need support and training in handling interpersonal relationships.

Personnel managers

The personnel manager's role in industrial relations is to give the support managers and teamleaders need and to provide advice and guidance to management on industrial relations strategies, politics and tactics. Personnel managers are involved in negotiations and the implementation and administration of dispute, grievance and disciplinary procedures. But they are not there to usurp the role of line managers, who should be primarily responsible for the management of industrial relations.

It is a difficult role to carry out well. Batstone[17] came to this rather damning conclusion about the part played by personnel managers in industrial relations: 'While personnel managers have succeeded in formalizing and centralizing industrial relations procedures and decision-making, they have done little about the content of these procedures and decisions. Indeed, they may have exacerbated the conflict.' Moreover, Marsh's[18] 1982 study found that personnel directors spent much of their time performing non-personnel functions, and that boards discussed employee relations problems rather than policies. And the situation has not, in the writer's experience, changed significantly since then.

Shop stewards

The role of shop stewards is to represent their members to management in all matters that affect them. They negotiate and resolve disputes, but they may also deal with a host of day-to-day issues affecting the interests of their members.

Shop stewards can help management and supervision by squashing unreasonable complaints, or by dealing with issues as they arise on the shop-floor, thus preventing escalations into major disputes. Commenting on his study of industrial relations in a UK car factory, Clack[19] wrote that 'the convenors and shop steward organization at the factory did not appear as a driving force behind labour unrest, but could more validly be regarded as "shock absorbers" of the industrial relations machinery'.

The popular stereotype of the difficult, aggressive, and often surly shop steward as a common feature of the UK industrial scene has been largely dispelled by research such as that carried out by Marsh, Evans, and Garcia[20] on workshop industrial relations in over 400 UK engineering establishments. This revealed that the overwhelming proportion of the managers in the survey thought that shop stewards were helpful (80 per cent) — 9 per cent thought they were obstructive, and the remaining 11 per cent had no firm views on the subject. There are, of course, difficult shop stewards, just as there are difficult managers and supervisors. And shop stewards are militant when they feel they have to be; as Phillip Higgs,[21] convenor of a Midlands engineering factory said: 'It is our job to do more damage to the enemy than he does to us. If you can get a limited objective with very few casualties, you are all the more ready to move on to the next step. With each such advance we secure a little more control, a little more of managerial function is taken from management.'

A satisfactory climate of relationships with unions and shop stewards cannot be achieved either by exaggerating militancy or by underestimating it. The approach management should use is to take steps to understand why it exists and to develop strategies, rules and procedures which will enable conflict to be managed by cooperative as well as conjunctive processes of collective bargaining. These approaches are discussed in the next section.

Individual employees

Much of industrial relations is based on the reasonable assumption that individual employees are mainly influenced by their trade unions, group pressures from their co-workers, and actions by management designed to increase their motivation and commitment. Systems theory also makes the assumption that employees are conformist and rule-orientated. But orientation and reactance theory, as described in Chapters 6 and 7 respectively, suggest that individuals are more autonomous than is generally supposed.

The established industrial relations system

The industrial relations system, as it existed in 1968, was thoroughly analysed by the Royal Commission on Trade Unions and Employers' Associations (the Donovan Commission). The extent to which this analysis still holds good as a description of the industrial relations system today is assessed below. This section then examines the main features of the established system, namely, collective bargaining, recognition and procedural agreements, and the significance of the informal elements present in the system.

The Donovan analysis

The key findings of the Donovan Commission were that at plant level, bargaining is highly fragmented and ill-organized, based on informality and custom and practice. The Commission's prescription was for a continuation of voluntarism, reinforced by organized collective bargaining arrangements locally, thus relieving trade unions and employers' associations of the 'policing role', which they so often failed to carry out. This solution involved the creation of new, orderly and systematic frameworks for collective bargaining at plant level by means of formal negotiation and procedural agreements.

Since Donovan, comprehensive policies, structures and procedures to deal with pay and conditions, shop steward facilities, discipline, health and safety, etc have been developed at plant level to a substantial extent. As Wooldridge[22] comments: 'Today these policies, structures and procedures, are indeed an enduring record of the report's impact.' But he also posed the question, 'Are they really all too often the backcloth of industrial relations rather than the vehicle for finding solutions to industrial relations problems?' The survey carried out by Marsh[18] in 1982 showed management to be generally more alive to relations with their workers than ever before, with much of the Donovan machinery in place. However, the use of this machinery was patchy and the preference for informality remained.

The collective bargaining system

The pay of 60 to 70 per cent of the UK workforce is determined, either directly or indirectly, through collective bargaining. As stated by the IRS,[23] 'It is perhaps the fundamental basis of industrial relations in Britain. The structure of collective bargaining in Britain is characterized not only by its extent but also its diversity and complexity.'

There are generally only two main levels of bargaining:

1. *multi-employer or national bargaining*, including wages councils, national joint industrial councils and regional negotiations;
2. *single-employer or company bargaining*, which can be further subdivided into corporate negotiations covering more than one, but not necessarily all, establishments of a company, and plant or workplace negotiations, restricted to employees at one site.

However, the actual pay received by an employee may be the result of negotiations conducted at a number of different levels.

A survey conducted by the CBI[24] showed that, in 1986, 87 per cent of employees in plants with collective bargaining had their basic rates of pay negotiated at establishment or company level. But the survey also showed that multi-employer bargaining still forms an important part of the framework of industrial relations in the UK.

The two-tier system frequently operates by fixing national rates, which are supplemented by domestic negotiations, as in the Chemical Industries Association, which described the system in 1989[25] as 'a highly flexible and efficient concept'.

National pay bargaining in the private sector does not result in all workers in the industry concerned being paid the same. Few industry agreements set *actual* rates of pay, and in many industries natural rates are regarded as no more than minimum earning levels with wide variations existing between and within local labour markets to meet particular circumstances. In fact, domestic rates are normally well in excess of the national minimum, which is regarded as no more than a benchmark. Hours of work and holiday entitlements, however, are still heavily influenced by multi-employer or industrial bargaining.

There are many strong arguments in favour of multi-employer or centralized bargaining, but there is a tendency to move towards single-employer or decentralized systems, as described in the next section of this chapter (pages 687–689).

Union recognition agreements

Union recognition has been one of the biggest industrial relations problems that can face a company, whether it is a case of recognizing any union in a non-unionized company, or of recognizing additional unions in a company which is already partly unionized. It is not so much of an issue today, partly because of the stronger line being taken by managements (prompted by more stringent economic conditions) and partly as a result of some weakening in the resolve of unions to pick off new employers (they tend to be more interested in widening their membership with existing employers). Another important factor has been the actions of the government: first, in repealing schedule 11 of the 1975 Employment Protection Act, which allowed trade unions to claim recognition from an employer by means of ACAS conciliation, investigation and recommendation; and, secondly, in the 1982 Employment Act, which removed the legal right of employers to require other employers (those tendering for contracts) to recognize, consult, or negotiate with trade unions, or to employ union labour only.

Managements in recent years have increasingly been derecognizing unions. A survey by the National Institute for Economic and Social Research has indicated that 13 per cent of companies which recognized unions in 1984 had by 1990 partially or completely derecognized them. Other movements to change the system at workplace level, have included single-union deals and single-table bargaining. These are discussed on pages 690–693.

Procedural agreements

Since the Donovan Commission report in 1968, the use of written procedures has expanded significantly, and, according to the investigation by Millward and Stevens,[26] the proportion of surveyed establishments possessing some form of industrial relations procedure increased from 85 to 94 per cent between 1980 and 1984.

Advantages and disadvantages

The advantages of written procedures, as listed by Brewster,[27] are as follows:

- The mere act of writing joint procedures encourages discussion of their purpose and scope.
- An agreed text reduces the possibility of misunderstanding and ambiguities of meaning.
- Written documents can be readily transmitted to, and retained by, those to whom the procedures relate.
- Managers and trade union representatives leave and go elsewhere, taking with them their recollections of oral agreements.

But, as Brewster points out, written procedures have their drawbacks, including:

- a reduction in the autonomy of both parties;
- the introduction of a 'legalistic' element into industrial relations, which can prejudice a relationship between management and unions which relies upon mutual trust, flexibility and a preparedness to compromise;
- the possibility that the removal of oral arrangements or 'custom and practice' can reduce the scope for trying out different arrangements without commitment on either side.

Content of procedural agreements

The scope and content of a procedural agreement do and should vary considerably according to the needs and wants of the parties involved. But the following are typical areas or details that might be incorporated in an agreement:

1. a preamble defining the objectives of the agreement;
2. a statement that the union is recognized as a representative body with negotiating rights;
3. a statement of general principles, which includes a commitment to use the procedure (a no-strike clause) and may additionally include a status quo clause which restricts the ability of management to introduce changes outside negotiated or customary practice;
4. a statement of the facilities granted to unions, including the rights of shop stewards and the right to hold meetings;
5. provision for joint negotiating committees (in some agreements);

6. the negotiating or disputes procedure;
7. provision for terminating the agreement.

A more detailed description of the possible contents of each part of a procedural agreement is contained in Appendix Q.

Developments in procedural agreements

The main developments in procedural agreements are the 'new style' agreements usually associated with single-union deals. These are described in the next section of this chapter (pages 691–692).

Informal approaches to industrial relations

Purcell[28] has referred to the 'self-perpetuating web of distrust' in UK industrial relations, and Wooldridge[22] has commented that, in order to break out of this situation, 'maybe we will always have to seek joint solutions in spite of the systems and procedures rather than within them. Perhaps we shall always have to live with such an imperfect formula so that we can create the real fabric of industrial relations — which is woven through relationships, not through procedures.'

This is confirmed by my own experience in industrial relations, including 3 years as a 'shop-floor' personnel officer in the engineering industry, 5 years as a personnel manager in the same industry, and 12 years as a director of personnel in a publishing firm. All of these establishments were heavily unionized.

On the shop-floor I quickly came to realize that the key to successful industrial relations was the day-to-day contact between management and shop stewards. This virtually ignored the existence of written procedures and joint consultation arrangements. Issues were settled because people knew, understood and, on the whole, trusted one another. Even with the leader of the then communist-dominated and militant electricians' union (Dai Thomas, known to his friends as Tommy the Commy), I found that it was possible to get on terms with him which enabled us to defuse problems without involving higher management or full-time officials.

In the publishing industry my experience of dealing with a highly organized and often militant SOGAT closed shop confirmed that peace and, indeed, goodwill, were best maintained by the continuous informal contacts made between the warehouse management and the members of the Chapel Committee, especially the Father and, latterly, the Mother of the Chapel. We found that day-to-day issues and even pay negotiations were best settled at Chapel level, largely on an informal or semi-formal basis, although negotiations were concluded with a formal agreement. Trouble occurred only when higher management and full-time union officials appeared on the scene to confront one another in a formal setting. Our strategy was therefore to leave everything to be sorted out at Chapel level within policy guidelines only — and it worked.

Industrial relations trends

The overall trend

The industrial relations system in the UK is in a state of constant change. More companies are derecognizing their unions. Monolithic bargaining structures are breaking up by moving from multi-employer to single-employer negotiations and by decentralizing bargaining to profit centres or units within groups. Local bargaining arrangements are being simplified to meet the particular needs of the business. Procedure agreements are still being set up formally, but the informal processes of industrial relations are receiving more attention.

Single-union and new-style agreements have incorporated different approaches to dispute resolution aimed at eliminating strikes by using pendulum arbitration. These agreements have also encouraged the harmonization of terms and conditions of employment and stressed the need for flexibility.

Other trends which are significantly affecting industrial relations in the workplace are the decline, if not the demise, of the closed-shop or membership agreement and the impact of new technology.

It is true that collective bargaining and consultative machinery continue as the major means through which employers and employees deal with one another. Many employers welcome trade unions in the face of the possible alternatives and will continue to do so. For whatever reasons, relationships in many companies have generally improved. 'Macho-management' tactics emerged in some areas in the 1980s, for example, in the newspaper industry, but they remain the exception rather than the rule.

There has, however, been a move in some quarters, although not a very pronounced one, from collectivism to individualism, and there has been considerable emphasis on achieving greater flexibility. The 'HRM approach', which aims to enhance commitment and mutuality with or without the cooperation of trade unions, is gaining ground.

These trends in industrial relations are discussed in more detail in this section under the following headings:

1. the shift from multi-employer to single-employer bargaining;
2. the pressure for decentralized bargaining;
3. single-union agreements;
4. new-style agreements;
5. single-table bargaining;
6. harmonization;
7. dispute resolution;
8. the decline and fall of the closed shop;
9. the impact of new technology;
10. individualism;
11. flexibility;
12. the HRM approach.

The shift from multi-employer to single-employer bargaining

The Workplace Industrial Relations Survey of 1984, as reported by Millward and Stevens,[26] identified a shift to single-employer bargaining away from national or industry-wide negotiations. The CBI survey[24] of trends during the period 1979–86 found that there was a 'market domination' in the influence of multi-employer, industry wide agreements which was matched by a pronounced growth in single-employer bargaining at company or establishment level. A study by Brown[29] in 1989 revealed that multi-employer bargaining is now the principal means of fixing pay for only one in five private sector employers and that 'Many surviving national agreements now provide no more than fall-back minimum rates which have little or no influence upon those whose earnings are already higher.'

Reasons for change
The reasons for this trend were summed up by the Chairman of Thames Water who said: 'If you believe, as we do, that our employees are the most important asset of the business, then it is difficult to justify delegating the responsibility for their pay and conditions of employment to an outside body.' This desire of companies to control their own destiny was prompted by the drive during the 1980s to restructure payment systems to secure greater flexibility and relate pay more closely to performance. As the IRS[23] commented: 'This more strategic approach to pay was clearly difficult to reconcile within the framework of national agreements and reinforced the tendency for companies to pursue idiosyncratic pay policies.'

Arguments for and against multi-employer bargaining

As might be expected, strong views have been expressed by the trade union movement in favour of multi-employer bargaining, and in 1986 the TUC argued that:

● National pay bargaining was viewed by both employers and trade unions as valuable because it established a minimum rate for the job, a floor below which no employer could fall, a basis for planning and, in many cases, a framework within which local negotiations could take place.
● Greater regional variations in pay would not reduce unemployment.
● National pay rates are simple to administer, enhance labour mobility and contribute to stability in industrial relations.
● National rates represent the rate for the job, which is the foundation of an equitable payment system.

The Institute of Personnel Management, in its comments to the Department of Employment on the question of the inflationary effect of multi-employer bargaining, said that 'the alleged deficiencies of national bargaining did not stand much scrutiny'. The Institute was unconvinced that national bargaining results in higher wages than is the case under regional or local arrangements: 'It is not the small employers who pull out of the national bargaining arrangements for their industry but the large employers who find the nationally set rates too low to meet their recruitment and retention needs and too inflexible for the needs of modern human resource planning.' The CBI, however, has stuck to its view that the lessons of the 1980s were that pay should be more closely related to performance, which requires the decentralization of bargaining.

The arguments for multi-employer bargaining can be summarized as follows:

● It provides a 'safety net', for union members, guaranteeing minimum terms and conditions.
● It prevents pay leap-frogging and more vulnerable companies from being 'picked off' by unions.
● It provides a basis for company negotiations.
● It is cost-effective, saving a lot of time and trouble at employer level.

The arguments against multi-employer bargaining are that it:

● creates inflexible arrangements which do not take account of differing local circumstances;
● does not allow for pay arrangements to be fine-tuned to reflect factors

such as company profitability, competitiveness and the supply and demand for workers in a locality;

- takes control over a large element in costs out of the hands of individual employers;
- inhibits the development of coherent and appropriate pay systems in individual companies in which pay can be related to performance.

Whether the advantages outweigh the disadvantages or vice versa, very much depends on the views the parties take of their own best interests and the particular circumstances of the industry bargaining system (eg the extent to which variations from the going rate are allowed). But in the larger organizations at least, the gains perceived from autonomy make single-employer bargaining the more attractive option.

The pressure for decentralized bargaining

The shift towards single-employer bargaining has been accompanied by pressure in larger organizations to decentralize pay negotiations to the level of the business unit, profit centre or plant. An IRS survey in 1989[30] gave examples of ten major companies, including Cadbury Schweppes, Pilkington, STC and Legal and General which have taken this step.

As noted by the IRS survey, the principal impetus for pay decentralization was provided by the reform of organizational and business structures, most notably the devolution of corporate responsibilities into separate budget, profit and product centres. Linked to this was a growing desire on the part of employers to secure greater flexibility and relate pay more closely to performance. Research conducted by Purcell[28] and the IRS survey indicates that the main gains from decentralization can be:

- enhanced roles for unit managers, giving them fuller authority to run their own parts of the business, including pay negotiaions;
- more scope to tailor employee pay packages to meet specific business needs;
- better links between pay movements and productivity;
- closer contact with shop stewards and employees;
- easier introduction of technical and organizational change.

The drawbacks, which many organizations believe to be overwhelming, are the duplication of effort in pay negotiations and the danger of leap-frogging pay claims.

Whether or not to decentralize depends very much on the culture of the company (how much authority it is prepared to devolve to unit managers) and its structure. If the firm is already divided into separately accountable profit centres, the decentralization of bargaining may be highly desirable. But it may still be necessary to provide coordination and guidance from the centre. The lessons drawn by Jackson and Leopold[31] from their analysis of the initial experience of the Coats Viyella decentralization programme included:

- the need for careful planning;
- the need to win the support of the senior line managers who have to implement the change;
- the need to train such managers properly in their new roles and responsibilities;
- the need to keep employees informed of developments;
- the need to reassure the union of its role in representing employees.

Single-union agreements

Single-union agreements are built round a single union representing all staff, flexible working practices, well-understood pay systems and an open communications system between management and employees, accompanied by more involvement of the latter in company affairs at the local level. They may also include provisions for pendulum arbitration and for making strikes unnecessary.

The reasons for the move towards single-union agreement were explained by Brewster[27] as follows:

> As managerial pressure for flexibility and adaptability has increased, so managers are developing policies built around the concept of single bargaining units. Managers are insisting that they will only meet with the unions as a single body; they are refusing to deal with each union in turn and asking the unions to resolve any differences among themselves before any subject is brought to management. Such a strategy risks uniting the unions against management, but diminished union power has reduced any threat here. The corresponding benefits for management are substantial.

Single-union deals, from management's point of view, eliminate the fragmentation, inter-union disputes and leap-frogging that exist in a multi-union situation. It makes life simpler to deal with one body rather than a number of disparate unions and union officials. This is why firms which decide in start-up situations that they *do* want to recognize a union (because they feel it promotes more settled relationships or because of a local tradition of trade unionism) may opt for a single-union 'new style' agreement, as described below.

The TUC in 1988 expressed its concern about single-union agreements because they can cause particular difficulties between unions when they:

- exclude other unions who may have some membership in the unit covered by the agreement, or exclude unions which previously held recognition or bargaining rights;
- exclude other unions who, while having no members in the unit concerned, have recognition agreements in other UK units operated by the same employer;
- represent an intrusion by one union into areas considered to be the province of another union, or the exclusion by a union or unions representing particular occupations;
- are agreed by one union, where another has been previously campaigning for membership, perhaps over a long period;
- lead unions to compete with each other for employers' approval, which encourages dilution of trade union standards and procedures.

The following guidelines were also proposed by the TUC in 1988 to deal with single-union deals:

- A union should notify the TUC when it intends making a single-union agreement.
- The TUC should then issue guidelines about whether any other unions on the site had a significant membership, and whether any unions were recognized by the same employer for similar groups elsewhere.
- Unions should not sign any clause which removed the right of the union to take industrial action — this recommendation does not affect arbitration clauses, which can be triggered unilaterally or by mutual agreement.
- Unions should have regard for the general terms and conditions which have already been agreed with the company concerned and take all possible steps to avoid undermining them.

New style agreements

The so-called new style agreements were developed first by the EETPU and a number of Japanese firms. They are based on the principle that the mutually accepted rights of parties will be expressed in the recognition agreement. The remaining differences of interest, especially pay, should be resolved by in-company negotiations, but there is an 'inexhaustible disputes procedure' which provides for a compulsory final stage of pendulum arbitration (see below) which aims to produce a binding solution to the dispute.

The other main features of a new-style agreement are: 1. single-union bargaining, 2. single status, 3. commitment to involvement and disclosure of information, 4. flexibility as an accepted method of working, 5. attempts to make strikes unnecessary and 6. a joint statement expressing a community of interest and mutuality between the employer and union members.

Single-table bargaining

Single-table bargaining brings together unions representing both manual and non-manual workers as a single bargaining unit.

Research conducted by Marginson and Sisson[32] into the experience of 13 large companies with a single bargaining table established three main reasons for making this move:

1. A concern that existing multi-unit bargaining arrangements not only are inefficient in terms of time and management resources but are also a potential source of conflict.
2. The desire to achieve major changes in working practices, with or without new technology, which can be achieved only through single-table bargaining.
3. A belief in the necessity of introducing harmonized or single-status conditions.

This research also highlighted a number of critical issues which need to be resolved if single-table bargaining is to be introduced successfully. These comprise:

* the commitment of management to the concept;
* the need to maintain levels of negotiation which are specific to particular groups below the single bargaining table;
* the need to allay the fears of managers that they will not be able to react flexibly to changes in the demand for particular groups of workers;
* the willingness of management to discuss a wider range of issues with union representatives — this is because single-table bargaining adds to existing arrangements a top tier in which matters affecting all employees, such as training, development, working time and fringe benefits can be discussed;
* the need to persuade representatives from the various unions to

forget their previous rivalries, sink their differences and work together;
- the need to allay the fears of trade unions that they may lose representation rights and members, and of shop stewards that they will lose the ability to represent members effectively.

These are formidable requirements to satisfy, and however desirable single-table bargaining may be, it will never be easy to introduce or to operate.

Harmonization

Harmonization is the process of introducing the same conditions of employment for all employees. It is distinguished by Roberts[33] from single status and staff status as follows:

1. *Single status* is the removal of differences in basic conditions of employment to give all employees equal status. Some organizations take this further by putting all employees into the same pay and grading structure.
2. *Staff status* is a process whereby manual and craft employees gradually receive staff terms and conditions of employment, usually upon reaching some qualifying standard, for example, length of service.
3. *Harmonization* means the reduction of differences in the pay structure and other employment conditions between categories of employee, usually manual and staff employees. The essence of harmonization is the adoption of a common approach and criteria to pay and conditions for all employees. It differs from staff status in that, in the process of harmonization, some staff employees may have to accept some of the conditions of employment of manual workers.

According to Duncan,[34] the pressure towards harmonization has arisen for the following reasons:

- *New technology.* Status differentials can obstruct efficient labour utilization and concessions on harmonization are invariably given in exchange for an agreement on flexibility. Moreover, technology, by deskilling many white-collar jobs and enhancing the skills of former blue-collar workers, has made differential treatment harder to defend.
- *Legislation.* Equal pay, the banning of sex and racial discrimination, and employment protection legislation have extended rights to manual workers previously the preserve of staff. The concept of equal value has been a major challenge to differentiation between staff and manual workers.

- *Improving productivity* by the more flexible use of labour.
- *Simplifying personnel administration* and thereby reducing costs.
- *Changing employee attitudes*, thus improving commitment, motivation and morale.

In Roberts' view, questions of morality are probably of least importance.

ACAS[35] has suggested that organizations, before pursuing a programme of harmonization, should seek answers to the following questions:

- What differences in the treatment of groups of employees are a rational result of differences in the work or the job requirements?
- Is it possible to estimate the direct costs of removing these differences?
- What differences in status are explicitly recognized as part of the 'reward package' for different groups in the labour force? What would be the possible repercussive effects of harmonization?
- How do the existing differences affect industrial relations in the organization?

Dispute resolution

Government policy in the 1980s was to leave the parties in a dispute very much to their own devices. Courts of inquiry have disappeared, the right of unilateral access provided by the 1975 Employment Protection Act was removed in 1985, and, according to Sir Pat Lowry,[36] formerly head of ACAS and President of the Institute of Personnel Management, there is some evidence to show that the government also sought to use its influence to bring to an end any arrangements, where they existed, for unilateral access to arbitration as a means of settling disputes.

Independently of the government, the two major developments that took place in dispute resolution during the 1980s were the so called no-strike agreements and pendulum arbitration, both of which often feature in the 'new-style' agreements described in pages 691–692.

No-strike agreements
A lot of heat but not much light was generated in no-strike agreements during the row between the electricians (EEPTU) and the rest of the trade union movement in 1988. In fact, only an agreement which specifies conventional or pendulum arbitration as a compulsory final stage justifies that label. The Toshiba agreement (exceptionally) makes such a provision. The Nissan agreement (typically) does not.

Sir Pat Lowry[36] said that 'no collective agreement can ever guarantee there will never be a strike'. Procedure agreements can usually do no more than discourage strikes (sometimes very positively) in the following ways:

- peace clauses which defer industrial action until the procedure has been fully utilized;
- term agreements, such as a 12 months' pay settlement, which in effect prohibit strikes over pay for 12 months;
- a clause in the procedure agreement which at the final stage requires a clear decision, as provided by pendulum negotiation, as distinct from permitting an inconclusive failure to agree.

Pendulum arbitration

Pendulum arbitration gives the arbitrator terms of reference which confine him or her to awarding the union's final claim in direct negotiation or the employer's final offer. In other words, the arbitrator is denied the middle ground. Pendulum arbitration is also known as final-offer arbitration, or straight-choice arbitration. This describes the process more accurately than 'pendulum', which implies a swing back and forth between two alternatives rather than a choice of one or the other.

The advantage claimed for pendulum arbitration is that the two negotiating parties, faced with the prospect of this kind of arbitration, will realize that an extravagant claim or an unreasonably low offer is likely to be penalized by the arbitrator. As Lowry[36] says, 'They will thus abandon extreme positions and together so narrow the gap that they can eventually reach agreement without the need to resort to arbitration at all.' Support for pendulum arbitrations is also based on the false assumption that arbitrators always 'split the difference'. However, the fact that this assumption is false may not influence the effectiveness of the approach. It is the strength of the assumption that counts, not its validity.

Review bodies

Review bodies in the public sector, such as the one recently set up for nursing and hospital staff, cover the pay arrangements of some 950,000 people. They rely to a considerable extent on pay comparability arguments, as do the Civil Service negotiating bodies (the Treasury and the Civil Service unions), for whom the Office of Manpower Economics provides information on pay movements and levels in the private sector.

Conciliation

The conciliation service provided by ACAS dealt with over 14,000 collective disputes in the 1980s, and successful conciliations, according to Lowry, regularly amounted to some 80 per cent of the cases handled. This success is attributable to the unique nature of the conciliation process, the ability of the counciliator to rebuild bridges, and a belief that the last-minute search for compromise is better than confrontation.

Flexibility

Flexibility arrangements, as a means of achieving the most efficient use of human resources, take the following forms:

- contract-based — new forms of employment contracts;
- time-based — shift working and flexible hours;
- practice-based — job-related flexibilities concerned with multiskilling and the removal of demarcation boundaries;
- work organization-based — the use of contract workers and part-timers.

Contract-based flexibility

Contract-based flexibility refers to employee contracts which specify flexibility as a key aspect of terms and conditions. Job descriptions are written in terms which emphasize the overall purpose of the job and its principal accountabilities. These are broadly related to the achievement of corporate or departmental objectives. The job description does not specify in detail the duties to be carried out by the job holder and may contain a catch-all phrase such as 'accountable for the performance of such other duties as are required to achieve the overall purpose of the job'. Contract-based flexibility is also achieved by employing contract workers who are required to work on any task or in any area appropriate to their range of skills.

Time-based flexibility

Time-based flexibility can be achieved by the use of flexible hours. The most familiar method is flexitime in which employees can vary their daily hours of work on either side of the core-time when they have to be present, providing that the longer-term required hours are completed. Time flexibility can be achieved in companies with marked seasonal fluctuations in labour requirements, such as photoprocessing, by negotiating annual hours agreements. These specify the annual hours to be worked and paid for but within that total, they incorporate provisions for longer hours at peak periods and shorter hours during troughs.

Multiskilling

Multiskilling involves:

1. providing people with a range of skills and knowledge which will equip

them to undertake a variety of different tasks;

2. moving people who have the necessary skills to undertake different tasks, possibly in different areas of the office or plant, in accordance with the needs of the business.

The need for multiskilling has arisen because of the trends towards flatter, more flexible and more responsive organizations. Just-in-time systems, for example, which involve manufacturing units delivering to the next unit precisely what that unit requires to carry out the next stage of manufacture and just in time for that work to start, require a highly flexible approach to the deployment of labour.

The trend towards creating autonomous work groups, as described in Chapter 13, means that more flexibility is required within such groups because work is shared between their members, who have to be able to undertake any task.

Demarcation

The major battles for ending demarcation (limiting the allocation of work to individuals in a particular craft trade union) were fought in the 1970s and '80s when demarcation agreements were concluded as quid pro quos in package deals. Any remaining restrictions are likely to be eliminated in the 1990s. Single-union agreements usually provide for the elimination of demarcation barriers and multiskilling.

Organizational approaches to flexibility

There is an increasing trend for companies to reorganize work into a core group which performs specific tasks essential to the firm; a secondary, flexible labour group which includes part-timers, job shares and short-time contract workers; and a peripheral group consisting of self-employed workers and agency temporary staff. The core group may consist of members of craft unions with whom a flexibility agreement may have been concluded. The secondary and peripheral groups are treated as an entirely flexible labour force.

HRM

The HRM approach, as described on pages 678–679, is being increasingly adopted by firms who see this, if they take a 'hard' HRM line, as a means of bypassing the unions and appealing directly to the workforce. Those who take a softer HRM line are more interested in generally increasing 'mutuality' and see this as complementary to maintaining good relationships with trade unions.

Negotiations

Negotiations take place when two parties meet, one or both aiming to win as much as they can from the other while giving away as little as possible. Negotiating can be a war game. It is a battle in the sense that the bargainers are pitting their wits against each other while also bringing in the heavy artillery in the shape of sanctions or threatened sanctions. As with other battles, the negotiation process can produce a pyrrhic victory in which both sides, including the apparent winner, retire to mourn their losses and lick their wounds. It is a game in the sense that both sides are trying to win, but there are various conventions or rules which the parties tacitly adopt or recognize, although they may break them in the heat of the battle.

Negotiations can normally be broken down into four stages:

1. Preparing for negotiation: setting objectives, defining strategy and assembling data.
2. Opening.
3. Bargaining.
4. Closing.

Before analysing these stages in detail it may be helpful to consider the process of bargaining and list the typical conventions that operate when bargaining takes place.

The process of bargaining

The process of bargaining consists of three distinct, though related, functions. First, bargainers state their bargaining position to their opposite numbers. Second, they probe weaknesses in the bargaining position of their opposite numbers and try to convince them that they must move, by stages if this is inevitable, from their present position to a position closer to what the bargainer wants. Third, they adjust or confirm their original estimate of their own bargaining position in the light of information gleaned and reactions from their opposite numbers, in order that, if the time comes to put an estimate of bargaining position to the test, the ground chosen will be as favourable as possible.

The essence of the bargaining process was well put by Peters[37] in *Strategies and Tactics in Labour Negotiations*:

> In skilful hands the bargaining position performs a double function. It conceals and it reveals. The bargaining position is used to indicate — to unfold gradually, step by step — the maximum expectation of the

negotiator, while at the same time concealing, for as long as necessary, his minimum expectation. By indirect means, such as the manner and timing of the changes in your bargaining position, you, as a negotiator, try to convince the other side that your maximum expectation is really your minimum breaking-off point. . . . Since you have taken an appropriate bargaining position at the start of negotiations, each change in your position should give ever clearer indications of your maximum expectation. Also, each change should be designed to encourage or pressure the other side to reciprocate with as much information as you give them, if not more.

Bargaining conventions

There are certain conventions in collective bargaining which most experienced and responsible negotiators understand and accept, although they are never stated and, indeed, may be broken in the heat of the moment, or by a tyro in the bargaining game. These conventions help to create an atmosphere of trust and understanding which is essential to the maintenance of the type of stable bargaining relationship that benefits both sides. Some of the most generally accepted conventions are listed below:

1. Whatever happens during the bargaining, both parties are using the bargaining process in the hope of coming to a settlement.
2. Attacks, hard words, threats, and (controlled) losses of temper are perfectly legitimate tactics to underline determination to get one's way and to shake the opponent's confidence and self-possession. But these are treated by both sides as legitimate tactics and should not be allowed to shake the basic belief in each other's integrity or desire to settle without taking drastic action.
3. Off-the-record discussions are mutually beneficial as a means of probing attitudes and intentions and smoothing the way to a settlement. But they should not be referred to specifically in formal bargaining sessions unless both sides agree in advance.
4. Each side should normally be prepared to move from its original position.
5. It is normal, although not inevitable, for the negotiation to proceed by alternate offers and counter-offers from each side which lead steadily towards a settlement.
6. Concessions, once made, cannot be withdrawn.
7. Firm offers must not be withdrawn, although it is legitimate to make and withdraw conditional offers.
8. Third parties should not be brought in until both parties are agreed that no further progress would be made without them.

9. The final agreement should mean exactly what it says. There should be no trickery, and the terms agreed should be implemented without amendment.
10. If possible, the final settlement should be framed in such a way as to reduce the extent to which the opponent obviously loses face or credibility.

Preparing for negotiation

Negotiations take place in an atmosphere of uncertainty. You do not know how strong your employees' bargaining team is and what it really wants. The members of that team do not know how much you are prepared to concede or the strength of your convictions.

In a typical wage negotiation the union or representative body making the claim will define three things:

- the target it would like to achieve;
- the minimum it will accept;
- the opening claim which will be most likely to help them achieve the target.

You as the employer will define three related things:

- the target settlement you would like to achieve;
- the maximum you would be prepared to concede;
- the opening offer you will make which will provide you with sufficient room to manoeuvre in reaching your target.

The difference between their claim and your offer is the negotiating range. If your maximum exceeds their minimum, this will indicate the settlement range. This is demonstrated in Figure 31.1. In this example the chance of settlement without too much trouble is fairly high. It is when your maximum is less than their minimum, as in Figure 31.2, that the trouble starts. Over a period of time a negotiation where a settlement range exists proceeds in the way demonstrated in Figure 31.3.

Objectives
Your objectives should be defined in the form of your target settlement and your initial and maximum offers. These will be conditioned by:

- the relative strengths of your case and that of the union;
- the relative power of the company *vis-à-vis* the union;
- the size of the union's claim and whether it is realistic;

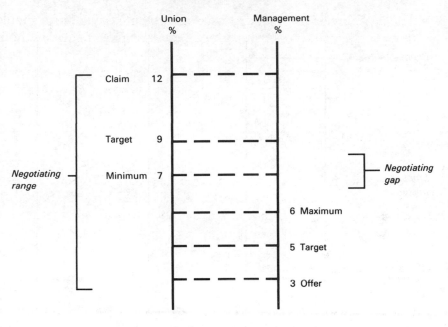

Figure 31.1 Negotiating range with a settlement zone

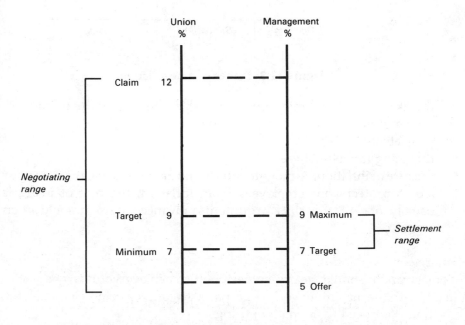

Figure 31.2 Negotiating range without a settlement zone

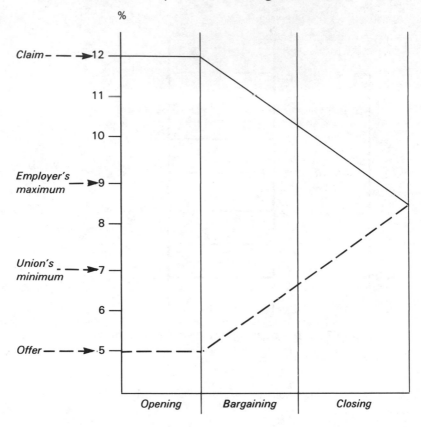

Figure 31.3 Stages of a negotiation

- the likely target and minimum acceptable offer set by the union;
- the amount of room for negotiation you want to allow;
- your ability to pay;
- the going rate elsewhere;
- the rate of inflation. Although you should never concede that it is your job to protect your employees from inflation, the cost of living is usually one of the chief arguments advanced by a union for an increase.

Strategy

Your strategy should clearly be designed to achieve your target settlement, with the maximum you are prepared to concede being your fall-back position. You need to decide two things:

1. The stages you would ideally like to follow in moving from your

opening to your closing offer. This is dependent on the amount of room for negotiation you have allowed.

2. The negotiating package you want to use in reply to whatever package the union has put forward. Your aim should be to provide scope for trading concessions during the course of negotiations. There is also much to be said for having in reserve various conditions which you can ask the unions to accept in return for any concessions you may be prepared to make. You might, for example, ask for an extended period before the next settlement in return for an increase in your offer.

Preparation steps

It is essential to prepare carefully for negotiations so that you do not, in Aneurin Bevan's phrase, 'go naked to the conference table'. The following steps should be taken:

1. List the arguments to be used in supporting your own case.
2. List the likely arguments or counter-arguments that your opponent is likely to use.
3. List your own counter-arguments to the arguments of your opponent.
4. Obtain the data you need to support your case.
5. Select the negotiating team. This should never have fewer than two members, and for major negotiations should have three or more: one to take the lead and do most of the talking, one to take notes and feed the negotiator with any supporting information required, and the others to observe opposite numbers and play a specific part in negotiations in accordance with their brief.
6. Brief the members of the negotiating team on their roles and the negotiating strategy and tactics that are to be adopted. If appropriate, prepared statements or arguments should be issued at this stage to be used as required by the strategic plan.
7. Rehearse the members of the team in their roles. They can be asked to repeat their points to other members and deal with responses from them; or someone can act as devil's advocate and force the leader or other members of the team to handle awkward points or negotiating ploys.

At this stage it may be possible to meet the opponents informally to sound out their position, while they sound out yours. The 'early warning' system can be used to condition the opponents to modify their likely initial demands by convincing them of the strength of your own position or your determination to resist.

Opening

Your tactics when opening the negotiation should be as follows:

1. Open realistically and move moderately.
2. Challenge your opponents' position as it stands; do not destroy their ability to move.
3. Explore attitudes, ask questions, observe behaviour and, above all, listen in order to assess your opponents' strengths and weaknesses, their tactics and the extent to which they may be bluffing.
4. Make no concessions of any kind at this stage.
5. Be non-committal about proposals and explanations (do not talk too much).

Bargaining

After the opening moves, you begin the main bargaining phase, during which you narrow the gap between the initial positions and try to persuade your opponents that your case is sufficiently strong to force them to close at a less advantageous point than they had planned. Employ the following tactics:

1. Always make conditional proposals: 'If you will do this, then I will consider doing that.' The words to remember are: 'if . . . then. . .'.
2. Never make one-sided concessions: always trade off against a concession from the other party: 'If I concede x, then I expect you to concede y.'
3. Negotiate on the whole package: do not allow your opponent to pick you off item by item, and keep the issues open to extract the maximum benefit from your potential trade-offs.

Closing

When and how you close is a matter of judgement, and depends on your assessment of the strength of your opponents' case and their determination to see it through. There are various closing techniques:

1. Making a concession from the package, preferably a minor one which is traded off against an agreement to settle. The concession can be offered more positively than in the bargaining stage: 'If you will agree to settle at x, then I will concede y.'
2. Doing a deal: splitting the difference, or bringing in something new,

such as extending the settlement time-scale, agreeing to back payments, phasing increases, or making a joint declaration of intent to do something in the future (eg introducing a productivity plan).
3.   Summarizing what has happened to date, emphasizing the concessions that have been made and the extent to which you have moved, and stating that you have reached your final position.
4.   Applying pressure through a threat of the dire consequences which will follow if your offer is not accepted.
5.   Giving your opponent a choice between two courses of action.

Do not make a final offer unless you mean it. If it is not really your final offer and your opponent calls your bluff, you will have to make further concessions and your credibility will be undermined. He will, of course, attempt to force you into revealing the extent to which you have reached your final position. Do not allow him to hurry you. If you want to avoid committing yourself and thus devaluing the word 'final', state as positively as you can that this is as far as you are prepared to go.

Industrial relations strategy

Overall aim

The overall aim of the industrial relations strategies of a company should be to ensure that corporate objectives can be achieved by gaining the maximum amount of commitment from employees and by minimizing the amount of industrial unrest.

Why have a strategy?

An industrial relations strategy is necessary to provide a sense of direction and a framework within which industrial relations can be managed and good relationships with trade unions and employees developed and maintained. It ensures that industrial relations are handled consistently and in accordance with the philosophy of the company about how it wants to relate with trade unions and its employees.

Content

The strategy should be based on principles developed in accordance with the employee relations philosophy and corporate culture of the organization. The following areas may be included:

• recognition;

- the form and content of procedural agreements;
- bargaining structure;
- harmonization;
- flexibility;
- employee participation.

The questions which should be answered in formulating the employee relations philosophy of the company and strategies in each of these areas are set out below.

Employee relations philosophy

1. To what extent is it believed that management has the *right* to manage or the *duty* to manage?
2. Does management believe that employees should or should not join a trade union, or does it care either way?
3. On balance, is it thought that the company gains or loses by recognizing trade unions?
4. To what extent does management accept the implied assumption of the HRM (human resource management) approach, which regards employees as just another factor in the input–output equation, to be managed as efficiently and tightly as any other resource?
5. If the HRM assumption is accepted, how is it proposed to cope with the fact that this particular resource is unique — it thinks and reacts?
6. Does management believe that harmony will best be achieved by negotiating and implementing formal procedure agreements with unions? Or
7. Does it think that such harmony is promoted more effectively by the informal relations maintained at all levels between management, unions and their members? Or
8. Would management prefer to deal direct with groups of employees or individuals through such means as briefing groups, quality circles or other channels of direct communication, thus bypassing the established union representative system, if one exists?
9. Is it believed that all employees should have the same status, ie basically similar terms and conditions of employment.
10. To what extent is it believed that the responsibility for conducting industrial relations should be devolved to line management at unit level?
11. How far is the company prepared to allow employees to become involved in its affairs?

12. How far is the company prepared to go in divulging information to its employees?

Recognition

13. In what circumstances, if at all, would the company be prepared to recognize a union for all employees, or for particular categories of employees if they are currently unrepresented?
14. What is the attitude of the company to recognition of a union in a greenfield site?
15. Has the company any preferences for any union if it feels it should recognize one?
16. Would the company prefer a single-union recognition agreement and, if so, how does it propose to achieve it?
17. If a union is to be recognized, is the company prepared to give it full negotiating rights or only representational rights?
18. If the company is not in favour of trade unions, what steps is it proposing to take to keep them at bay? The steps can include setting up its own staff association (which often fails to prosper), paying above the odds, or setting up extensive HRM-type procedures such as team briefing and closer involvement in company affairs through employee councils, quality circles, etc.
19. Would the company like to derecognize its union or one of its unions? If so, how should this be achieved and what are the potential problems?

Procedural agreements

20. To what extent is it believed that procedures should be formalized?
21. What should be included in a procedure agreement, eg disputes, grievances, discipline, redundancy?
22. Are there any features of the so-called new-style agreements which management would like to adopt, eg flexibility, single status, pendulum arbitration?

Bargaining structures

23. If the company's rates of pay and other terms and conditions of employment are fixed by a national multi-employer agreement, does it want to continue to be a party to that agreement?

24. If not, what are the advantages and disadvantages of negotiating directly with a union or unions as a single employer?
25. If the advantages outweigh the disadvantages, what steps should be taken to disengage the company from national negotiations while ensuring that a satisfactory negotiating procedure can be maintained?
26. To what extent does the company want to decentralize negotiations to its individual units?
27. If the company wants to decentralize bargaining:

    (a) What aspects of pay and terms and conditions should be decentralized?
    (b) How much authority should be given to local management?
    (c) To what extent will the centre coordinate negotiations?
    (d) How will leap-frogging be divided?
    (e) What training will be given to local management to develop negotiating skills?

Harmonization

28. Does the company want to achieve:

    (a) total harmonization?
    (b) partial harmonization? (if so, in which areas?).

29. What are the benefits and the costs of harmonization?
30. How is harmonization to be achieved to whatever degree is believed to be appropriate?

Flexibility

31. To what extent is increased flexibility in the use of labour desirable?
32. How is any desired increase in flexibility to be achieved? eg:

    (a) multiskilling and the removal of demarcation barriers;
    (b) single status;
    (c) introducing variable working patterns such as flexitime;
    (d) the reorganization of work.

Employee participation

33. How far is it possible to gain employee commitment to corporate goals for quality, productivity and competitiveness by increasing the

degree to which employees participate in the company's affairs?

34. Will planned changes be more acceptable if employees are made aware of the circumstances confronting the company, the reason behind the need for change, and the alternative courses of action that can be considered?

35. To what extent should we — can we — involve employees in discussing future plans and contributing their own views on courses of action?

36. What information can we — should we — give to employees on matters of concern to them?

37. How can we gain access to the ideas and enthusiasms of individuals and groups of employees, eg by the use of quality circles or improvement groups?

38. What information should we give to employees about what is going on and what we are planning to do, and how should we convey this information (eg team briefing)?

39. Do we need to introduce other forms of participation or joint consultation, taking into account the implications of the EC Social Charter?

40. How can we convey through briefings, training programmes and workshops the mission and values of the company to employees in order that they accept and are committed to them?

References

1. Thomason, G T *A Textbook of Industrial Management*. Institute of Personnel Management, London, 1984.
2. Dunlop, J T *Industrial Relations Systems*. Holt, New York, 1958.
3. Flanders, A *Management and Unions: The Theory and Reform of Industrial Relations*. Faber and Faber, London, 1970.
4. Chamberlain, N W and Kuhn, J *Collective Bargaining*. McGraw-Hill, New York, 1965.
5. Walton, R E and McKersie, R B *A Behavioural Theory of Labour Negotiations*. McGraw-Hill, New York, 1965.
6. Kahn-Freund, O *Labour and the Law*. Stevens, London, 1972.
7. Mackie, K J 'Changes in the law since 1979: an overview'. In Towers, B (ed.), *A Handbook of Industrial Relations Practice*. Kogan Page, London, 1989.
8. Bain, G S and Price, R I 'Union growth, dimensions, determinants and destiny'. In Bain, G S (ed.), *Industrial Relations in Britain*. Blackwell, Oxford, 1983.
9. Towers, B 'British industrial relations and the trade unions: change and its

consequences'. In Towers, B (ed.), *A Handbook of Industrial Relations Practice.* Kogan Page, London, 1989.

10. Macintyre, D 'Eclipse of the new realism', *Personnel Management*, November 1984.
11. McClelland, G *British Journal of Industrial Relations*, p. 278, June 1963.
12. Fox, A 'Industrial sociology and industrial relations', *Royal Commission on Trade Unions and Employers' Associations Research Paper No. 3.* Her Majesty's Stationery Office, London, 1966.
13. Drucker, P *The New Society.* Heinemann, London, 1951.
14. Winkler, J T 'The ghost at the bargaining table: directors and industrial relations', *British Journal of Industrial Relations*, Vol. XII, No. 2, July 1974.
15. Edwardes, M *Back from the Brink.* Collins, London, 1983.
16. Walton, R 'From control to commitment', *Harvard Business Review.* March–April 1985.
17. Batstone, E 'What have personnel managers done for industrial relations?' *Personnel Management*, June 1980.
18. Marsh, A *Employee Relations Policy and Decision Making.* Gower, Aldershot, 1981.
19. Clack, G *Industrial Relations in a British Car Factory.* Cambridge University Press, Cambridge, 1967.
20. Marsh, A, Evans, E, and Garcia, P *Workplace Industrial Relations in Engineering.* Kogan Page, London, 1971.
21. Higgs, P 'The convenor', *Work 2*, Penguin, Harmondsworth, 1969.
22. Wooldridge, E 'The Donovan analysis: does it still stand?' *Personnel Management*, June 1989.
23. IRS *Employment Trends*, No. 440, May 1989.
24. *The Structure and Processes of Pay Determination in the Private Sector 1974–1986.* CBI, London, 1988.
25. IRS *Employment Trends*, No. 443, July 1989.
26. Millward, N and Stevens, M *British Workplace Industrial Relations 1980–1984.* Gower, Aldershot, 1986.
27. Brewster, C 'Managing industrial relations'. In Towers, B (ed.), *A Handbook of Industrial Relations Practice.* Kogan Page, London, 1989.
28. Purcell, J 'How to manage decentralized bargaining', *Personnel Management*, May, 1989.
29. Brown, W *Trends in Public Service Pay.* Public Finance Corporation, London, 1989.
30. IRS *Employment Trends*, No. 454, December 1989.
31. Jackson, M and Leopold, J 'Casting off from national negotiations', *Personnel Management*, April 1990.
32. Marginson, P and Sisson, K 'Single table talk', *Personnel Management*, May 1990.
33. Roberts, C (ed.) *Harmonization: Whys and Wherefores.* Institute of Personnel Management, May, 1990.
34. Duncan, C 'Pay and payment systems'. In Towers, B (ed.) *A Handbook of Industrial Relations Practice.* Kogan Page, London, 1989.

35. ACAS *Developments in Harmonization: Discussion Paper No. 1*. London, 1982.
36. Lowry, P 'The unsung heroes of dispute resolution', *Personnel Management*, August 1990.
37. Peters, J *Strategies and Tactics in Labour Negotiations*. Duckworth, New York, 1968.

32

Participation and Joint Consultation

What is participation?

Participation takes place when management and employees are jointly involved in making decisions on matters of mutual interest where the aim is to produce solutions to the problems which will benefit all concerned. Participation does not mean that the parties subordinate their own interests entirely. But it does mean that they aim to achieve objectives which are not in fundamental conflict with those of the other party, and which can therefore be integrated to some degree. Participation does not require total and bland agreement all the time, and bargaining about issues is not excluded. It is akin to integrative or cooperative bargaining in which the parties find common or complementary interests and solve problems confronting both of them.

Participation should be distinguished from negotiation which, although it involves joint decision making, does this by a process of distributive or conjunctive bargaining where the sole aim is to resolve pure conflicts of interests.

Participation is more than joint consultation, which is the process by which management seeks the views, feelings and ideas of employees through their representatives, prior to negotiating or making a decision. Although joint consultation may involve the discussion of mutual problems and is a necessary aspect of participation, it leaves to management the ultimate responsibility for making decisions. Participation is also more than communications, which is the process of keeping people informed about intentions, opinions, results, or decisions on matters that interest them, although effective two-way communications are necessary to successful participation and joint consultation.

The purpose of participation

The purpose of participation should be to advance the well-being of all concerned — owners and managers as well as workpeople. It should be a means of enabling the enterprise to achieve its objectives, as long as it is understood that those objectives include acting in a socially responsible way to employees as well as the maximization of profits.

The objective of participation is not, therefore, simply to provide people with job satisfaction because they feel that they are involved. This is an important and legitimate aim, but it is not the only one. Participation should do more than help people to feel good. It should provide them with the means of identifying their own interests with those of the enterprise in which they work in order that both can flourish. Participation should therefore provide employees with the opportunity to contribute to the success of the organization by involving them in decision making by means of joint consultation, productivity committees, suggestion schemes and, the latest development, quality circles.

Participation and industrial democracy

Are participation and industrial democracy the same thing? To some, industrial democracy is an alternative way of describing more or less traditional forms of joint consultation. To others, it comprises the joint regulation or control by unions and management of decisions and actions which affect the present and future conduct of the business. This implies trade union participation in decision making at all levels in the enterprise, including the highest level, the board. This view, as held by trade unionists, rejects conventional joint consultative arrangements or paternalistically based profit-sharing schemes as a charade of participation which gives workpeople none of the substance of control that has been firmly based with the leading shareholders. The demand for two-tiered board structures and for union representation on the board arises from this latter viewpoint.

The debate on industrial democracy has often been concerned with means rather than with ends. It is the *form* and extent of participation that has caused most argument, not the objective. There has been a fair measure of agreement on both sides of industry with the following definition of the two basic purposes of industrial democracy prepared by the Industrial Participation Association (UK) for its evidence to the Committee of Inquiry on Industrial Democracy:

(a)   That it is both reasonable and just that the employees of a company

713

should have the means to influence the major decisions that may determine the conditions of their own working lives, and thereby the lives of their families — decisions that are commonly taken at a level where at present it is not usual for employees to be directly involved or represented.

(b)   That an essential purpose of industrial democracy must be to improve the efficiency and productivity of the enterprise, by enabling employees at all levels to make a more effective contribution — increased productivity being the context in which employees' interests, as well as the interests of other parties, can best be advanced.[1]

Forms of participation

Participation can vary according to the level at which it takes place, the degree to which decision making is shared, and the mechanisms of a greater or lesser degree of formality which are used.

Levels of participation

Participation takes various forms at different levels in an enterprise. These levels were classified by the Industrial Society[2] as:

- job level;
- management level;
- policy-making level;
- ownership level.

Participation at the job level involves the supervisor and his immediate group, and the processes include the communication of information about the work, the delegation of authority, and the interchange of ideas about how the work should be done. These processes are essentially informal.

Participation at management level can involve sharing information and decision making about issues which affect the way in which work is planned, coordinated and controlled, and the conditions under which the work is carried out. There are limitations. Management as a whole, and individual managers, must retain authority to do what their function requires. Participation does not imply anarchy. But it does require some degree of willingness on the part of management to share its decision-making powers. At this level, participation becomes more formalized, through consultative committees, briefing groups or other joint bodies involving management and trade unionists.

At the policy-making level, where the direction in which the business is going is determined, total participation implies sharing the power to make the key decisions on investments, disinvestments, new ventures, expansions, and retractions which affect the future well-being of both the company and its employees. Ultimately, it means that such decisions are made fairly by directors who represent the interests of the owners, the management, and the workpeople. The proposal to have a supervisory board upon which worker representatives have the power to veto major investment decisions, mergers or take-overs, and closures or major redeployment is not full participation, but it is in accordance with the reality of the divided loyalties that worker representatives would have if they had to share the responsibility for unpopular decisions by becoming full board members in the accepted sense.

At the ownership level, participation may imply a share in the equity, which is not meaningful unless the workers have sufficient control through voting rights to determine the composition of the board. Workers' cooperatives are also participative in the sense that the workers, including managers and supervisors, *are* the management and must therefore be involved in joint decision making at board level.

The degree to which decision making is shared

At the one end of the scale, management can make decisions unilaterally; at the other end, much more rarely, workers decide unilaterally. Between these extremes there is a range of intermediate points which can be expressed (Figure 32.1) as a scale.

The point on this scale at which participation should or can take place at any level in an organization depends on the attitudes, willingness and enthusiasm of both management and employers. Management may be reluctant to give up too much of its authority except under pressure from the unions, or from legislation aimed at developing industrial democracy (the political term for participation). Unions may prefer not to be over-involved in decision making in order that they can shoot from the sidelines when they want to.

Mechanisms for participation

At the job level, participation should be as informal as possible. Groups may be called together on an *ad hoc* basis to consider a particular problem, but formal committees should be avoided in small departments (say, fewer than 250 people) or at section level. Team briefing (see Chapter 33) can be used to provide for informal two-way communications.

At the next higher level, more formality may be appropriate in larger organizations. There is scope for the use of joint consultative committees

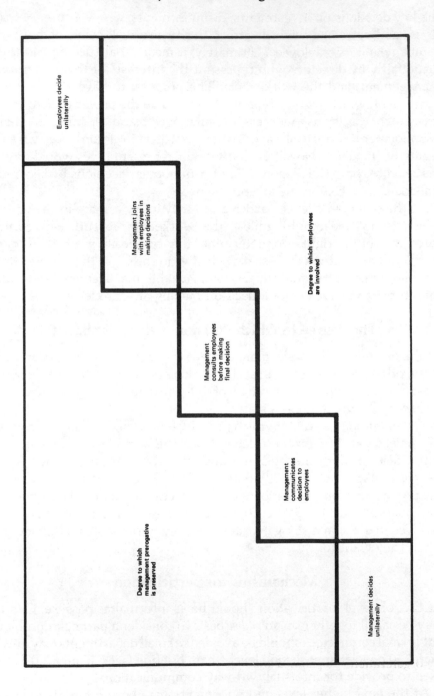

Figure 32.1 Scale of participation

or joint negotiating committees with carefully defined terms of reference on the matters they can discuss.

At the policy-forming level, participation becomes more difficult to organize. This is when management is most reluctant to abandon its prerogatives unless forced to by legislation. Unions, as already mentioned, do not like to be put in a position where they may have to endorse unpopular decisions. Works Councils may be given the chance to discuss policy issues, but if the final decision on any matter which is clearly not negotiable is made at board level, the works council may be seen as an ineffectual body.

Arguments for and against participation

The arguments for and against participation are not evenly balanced; they cannot be. They represent totally different points of view or, to put it more plainly, prejudice. And there is prejudice on both sides. Essentially, the favourable arguments are optimistic about human nature while the unfavourable ones are pessimistic. It would be a pity if the pessimistic view prevailed in this as in other spheres. But a favourable view on participation should not be allowed to develop into idealism.

In favour	*Against*
• It satisfies the individual's basic need for involvement in affairs that affect him or her.	• The board must exercise direction and control, and management must manage — managers cannot be effective unless they are allowed to exercise their authority with the minimum of interference.
• It makes better use of the skills and capacities available in the enterprise.	
• It gives people the opportunity to influence events which will have a direct or indirect effect on their present and future prosperity and security.	• Direction and management are specialized skills which are not shared by all employees. The extent to which workers' representatives at board level and elsewhere can make a real contribution is limited.
• It recognizes the reality of life today, in which traditional authoritarian patterns of behaviour are being steadily eroded.	• Power-sharing implies information-sharing — the necessarily confidential nature of much top management decision making would be seriously impaired if workpeople were involved.
• It is better to develop a participative system within an organization in a planned and orderly way rather than have it forced upon the company by the government or the unions.	

- The unions do not want it because it might impair their negotiating power or put them in an indivious position if they have to support unpopular management decisions.
- Employees do not want increased participation, either because they are apathetic or because they do not see any advantage to themselves in it.
- Participation may drive key decisions under cover if directors or managers form cabals or starve workers' representatives of the information they need to make a proper contribution.

A touch of realism along the lines suggested by the pessimists is required to make participation work.

Requirements for successful participation

Irrespective of the level at which participation takes place or the degree to which it is formalized, there are ten basic requirements for success:

1. The objectives of participation must be defined, discussed and agreed by all concerned.
2. The objectives must be related to tangible and significant aspects of the job, the process of management or the formulation of policies that affect the interests of employees. They must not relate to peripheral matters such as welfare or social amenities, ie, in Herzberg's phrase, they should not be concerned with the 'hygiene' factors alone.
3. Management must believe in and must be seen to believe in participation. Actions speak better than words and management must demonstrate that it will put into effect the joint decisions made during discussions.
4. The unions must believe in participation as a genuine means of advancing the interests of their members and not simply as a way of getting more power. They should show by their actions that they are prepared to support unpopular decisions to which they have been a party.
5. Joint consultation machinery should be in line with any existing

systems of negotiation and representation. It should not be sup-ported by management as a possible way of reducing the powers of the union. If this naive approach is taken, it will fail — it always does. Joint consultation should be regarded as a process of integrative bargaining complementary to the distributive bargaining that takes place in joint negotiating committees. A separate consultative system may not be necessary in a well-organized, 100 per cent union establishment.

6. If management does introduce joint consultation as a means of keeping unions out, it should be prepared to widen the terms of reference as much as possible to cover issues which might normally be the subject of negotiation with unions. This approach can backfire if the staff representatives acquire a taste for negotiation and turn to the unions if they find they are not getting what they want. It is an approach which should be used with extreme caution. It has been known to work with white-collar unions, but it can be difficult to resist strong union demands for recognition. It would be a pity in these circumstances to lose face by abandoning a management-sponsored system.

7. Joint consultative committees should always relate to a defined working unit, should never meet unless there is something specific to discuss, and should always conclude their meetings with agreed points which are implemented quickly.

8. Employee and management representatives should be properly briefed and trained and have all the information they require.

9. Managers and supervisors should be kept in the picture.

10. Consultation should take place *before* decisions are made.

Joint consultation

Joint consultation is the most obvious method of participation. It is essentially a means for management and employees to get together to discuss and, where appropriate, determine matters affecting their joint or respective interests.

In its simplest form, joint consultation is the informal exchange of views between individual employees and their managers; it takes place all the time in a well-run enterprise. But where the number of employees, or a complex organization, makes access difficult from employees to manage-ment, or from management to employees, then informal methods need to be systematized.

Objectives of joint consultation

The objectives of joint consultation should be to provide a means of jointly examining and discussing problems of concern to both management and employees. It involves seeking mutually acceptable solutions through a genuine exchange of views and information. Joint consultation allows management to inform employees of proposed changes which affect them and employees to express their views about the proposed changes. It also provides a means for employees to contribute their own views and knowledge on such matters as productivity and safety.

Topics for joint consultation

Joint consultation does not mean power-sharing — involving employees in policy decisions on such matters as investments, marketing and product development plans and mergers. These would be the subject of joint decision making only if full participation at board level were to take place.

The terms of reference to joint consultative committees often exclude the discussion of basic terms and conditions of employment such as wage rates and premium payments, hours of work and holidays. These are either regarded as part of management's prerogative in a non-unionized plant or are dealt with through the normal negotiation machinery. This leaves matters such as methods of work, job evaluation, works rules and safety as usual — and important — topics for joint consultation.

Joint consultation and negotiation

There are dangers in having two separate systems of employee representation. If the firm is strongly unionized, the unions will dominate the consultative committee, which is wasteful and often leads to the consultative committee system dealing with trivialities and falling into disrepute. It may be useful to have a place where people can argue about the quality of the sausages in the canteen, but if that is all they ever talk about (and sometimes this appears to be the case), then it would be better to abandon formal joint consultation altogether and rely on other channels. A reverse situation can sometimes occur when companies set up joint consultation as an alternative to a union negotiating committee. What may happen is that the joint consultative committee members persuade or force management to negotiate with them, with the result that there are two competing negotiating bodies, which is a recipe for disaster.

The argument in favour of keeping negotiating issues outside the terms of reference of joint consultation committees is that it gives the latter more opportunity to deal calmly with non-controversial matters. Negotiating committees may get into so many conflict situations that they are no longer capable of looking dispassionately at even the least controversial issues. There is some truth in this argument, but the ideal approach in a strongly unionized plant is to have one system of representation, and for all concerned to do everything in their power to develop a cooperative climate for consultation as well as negotiation.

When a company is involved in negotiations there is no easy answer to the problem of reconciling the machinery required for that purpose with the system most appropriate to joint consultation. It is no good, however, clinging to an effete joint consultative arrangement if all the real decisions are made with union representatives through the negotiating machinery. Separate joint consultation arrangements should be maintained only if they do provide proper representation for non-unionists and a genuine opportunity for employee representatives to discuss real issues which might be neglected in the hurly-burly of negotiations.

An interesting approach to solving this problem was developed at Glacier Metal by Brown[3] with the help of Jaques.[4] In *The Changing Culture of a Factory* the latter describes the process of working through problems in the developing representative system, while in *Exploration in Management* Brown describes how the representative, legislative, and appeals system functioned. The representative system was the basic machinery through which employees could express their views, but a legislative system was established above, and not in parallel with the representative system, which 'comprises councils . . . in which the executive and representative systems meet and by means of which every member can participate in formulating policy and in assessing the results of the implementation of that policy'.[3]

Constitution of consultative committee

Before deciding on detailed terms of reference, one must determine the aims and scope of joint consultation, paying particular attention to the question of the extent to which committees can become involved in policy or negotiating issues. It is also necessary to consider who should be covered by the committee system. A choice has to be made. It could cover only non-managerial or supervisory employees, or supervisors and even managers could be catered for separately. Finally, decisions have to be made on the committee structure, which in a large organization often consists of separate councils for each major department or group of departments and an overall works council. It is sometimes best to start in a modest way with one or two pilot schemes in large departments before setting up too elaborate a system. Some large companies, however, have restricted the system to one works council on the grounds that departmental matters are best dealt with informally by local management.

The following points should be covered in the constitution of a consultative committee:

1.   the objectives of the committee.
2.   its terms of reference — the matters which it can and cannot discuss.
3.   its composition:

    (a)   employee representatives (number, constituencies);
    (b)   management representatives;
    (c)   co-option provisions;
    (d)   officers;

4.   the period of office of members and arrangements for their retirement;
5.   election procedure:

    (a)   who organizes;
    (b)   when held;
    (c)   qualifications of candidates and voters;
    (d)   nominations;
    (e)   voting arrangements;

6.   committee meetings:

    (a)   frequency;
    (b)   where held;
    (c)   procedures for placing items on the agenda;
    (d)   arrangements for minutes;

7.   facilities for committee members:

    (a)   liaising with constituents;
    (b)   payment while attending meetings.

Quality circles

It can be argued that one of the greatest failings which result from the 'top-down' type of management prevailing in the UK and many other Western countries is that it ignores the knowledge that exists at the lowest level in the organization. Many investigators who have been trying to establish the secret of the success of Japan's industry have decided that a major ingredient is the degree to which collective or group management is practised.

One of the techniques of group involvement used successfully in Japan (although the idea originated in the US in the 1950s) is quality circles. Quality circles grew out of Japan's great need in the early 1960s to lose its postwar reputation as a clever producer of shoddy copies of Western products and to raise the quality of its goods. The approach owes a lot to the strong attachment to working in cohesive groups which exists in Japan. The first circle was registered in 1963 within the Nippon Telegraph and Telephone Public Corporation, and now there are hundreds of thousands of circles operating in Japan. Virtually all big companies use them.

Definition

Quality circles are small groups of volunteers who are engaged in related work and who meet regularly to discuss and propose ways of improving working methods or arrangements under a trained leader.

Aims

The aims of quality circles are to:

- give those doing the job more scope to use their experience and know-how;
- provide opportunities to tap the knowledge of employees, who may know more about work problems which are hidden from more remote managers and supervisors;
- improve productivity and quality;
- improve employee relations;
- win commitment to the organization.

Essential features

The essential features of quality circles are that they:

- consist of volunteers;
- have a trained leader, usually but not always a superior;
- hold regular meetings which are strictly limited in duration — often one hour;

- have five to ten members;
- usually select which problems to tackle but may be steered away from problems which are clearly beyond their scope or are already being dealt with;
- use systematic and analytical techniques in which they have been trained to solve problems;
- may use brainstorming to identify possible solutions (brainstorming involves the group listing as many solutions as they can think of — some good, some not so good — and then refining them and ranking them in merit order);
- present their results to management;
- implement accepted proposals.

Prerequisites for success

Management support
The first prerequisite is that top management believes in the value of quality circles and is committed to their success. Middle management and supervision must also be involved in their introduction. They are the people who are most likely to have reservations about quality circles because they can see them as a threat to their authority and reputation — for example, when a problem is overcome by a circle rather than by the supervisor. Without management support, quality circles die, as they often do.

Trade unions
Trade unions should also be informed of the plan to introduce quality circles. Some unions are hostile because they feel that quality circles can reduce their influence and power, and that management is deliberately introducing them for this purpose.

Facilitator
The introduction and maintenance of a quality circle needs a 'facilitator' who trains, encourages and guides quality circle members; ensures that they are given the resources they need; and sets up presentation sessions. The facilitator is often a line manager rather than a personnel officer or a trainer. This vital role also involves encouraging the circles and ensuring that top management backing continues by keeping them informed of the benefits provided by quality circles — publicity on their achievements is important. The facilitator can also deal with any problems quality circles meet in getting information or in dealing with management.

Training

Training is an important part of the quality circles. Team leaders need an initial two- to three-day training course in the analytical techniques they will use and in team building and presentation skills. They also need refresher training from time to time. Team leaders, with the help of facilitators, also train the members of their team. This training effort is a valuable spin-off from a quality circle programme. Instruction in leadership, problem solving and analytical skills is a useful way of developing existing or potential supervisors. Membership of a quality circle is also a means of developing skills as well as getting more involved.

Typical projects

The University of Manchester Institute of Science and Technology's (UMIST) 1983 research into quality circles in the UK[5] classified the proportions of projects in different areas as follows:

- quality improvement 18%
- cost reduction 15%
- production processes 14%
- productivity improvement 12%
- waste prevention 10%
- plant improvements 9%
- communications 6%
- service processes 5%
- safety 4%
- other 7%

Maintenance of a quality circle programme

The facilitator, as mentioned earlier, has the key task of keeping the programme going — encouraging the quality circles and ensuring that management is told about their achievements. The UMIST survey established that the major obstacles to quality circle programmes, as established by the reasons for failure, were:

- suspicion 19%
- slow management response to proposals 14%
- lack of support 14%
- overambitious projects 13%

It is up to top management and the facilitator, but especially the latter, to overcome these problems.

Benefits

The UMIST research listed the following benefits in the order of importance given by management:

- increased involvement of employees 25%
- improvement of communications 21%
- improvement of quality and productivity 17%
- reduction in barriers between management and shop-floor 17%
- reduction in operating costs 10%
- encouraging employees to establish an identity 9%
- encouraging labour to become more flexible 1%

Suggestion schemes

Suggestion schemes can provide a valuable means for employees to participate in improving the efficiency of the company. Properly organized, they can help to reduce the feelings of frustration endemic in all concerns where people think they have good ideas but cannot get them considered because there are no recognized channels of communication. Normally, only those ideas outside the usual scope of employees' duties are considered, and this should be made clear, as well as the categories of those eligible for the scheme — senior managers are often excluded.

The basis of a successful suggestion scheme should be an established procedure for submitting and evaluating ideas, with tangible recognition for those which have merit and an effective system for explaining to employees without discouraging them that their ideas cannot be accepted.

The most common arrangement is to use suggestion boxes with, possibly, a special form for entering a suggestion. Alternatively, or additionally, employees can be given the name of an individual or a committee to whom suggestions should be submitted. Managers and supervisors must be stimulated to encourage their staff to submit suggestions, and publicity in the shape of posters, leaflets and articles in the company magazine should be used to promote the scheme. The publicity should give prominence to the successful suggestions and how they are being implemented.

One person should be made responsible for administering the scheme. He or she should have the authority to reject facetious suggestions, but should be given clear guidance on the routing of suggestions by subject matter to departments or individuals for their comments. The administrator deals with all communications and, if necessary, may go back to the individual who submitted the suggestion to get more details of, for example, the savings in cost or improvements in output that should result from the idea.

It is desirable to have a suggestion committee consisting of management and employee representatives to review suggestions in the light of the comments of any specialist functions or executives who have evaluated them. This committee should be given the final power to accept or reject suggestions but could, if necessary, call for additional information or opinion before making its decision. The committee could also decide on the size of any award within established guidelines, such as a proportion of savings during the first year; usually not less than 10 per cent and not more than 33⅓ per cent. There should be a standard procedure for recording the decisions of the committee and informing those who made suggestions of the outcome — with reasons for rejection if appropriate.

Planning for participation

The form of participation appropriate for a company depends upon the attitudes and relative strengths of management and unions, its past experience of negotiation and consultation, and the current climate of employee relations. The form may also be affected by government legislation; but, whatever method is adopted, it is essential to take into account the requirements for successful participation listed earlier in this chapter and to plan its introduction or development in the following stages:

1. Analyse and evaluate the existing systems of consultation, communication and other formal and informal means of participation.
2. Identify the influences within and without the company which affect the climate of industrial relations and suggest the most appropriate form in which participation should take place.
3. Develop a plan for improving or extending participation in whatever form is appropriate to the company.
4. Discuss the plan in depth with all concerned — management, supervisors, workpeople and unions. The introduction of improved participation should itself be a participative process.
5. Brief and train those concerned with participation in their duties and how they should be carried out.
6. Introduce new schemes on a pilot-scheme basis — do not expect immediate results and be prepared to modify them in the light of experience.
7. Keep the whole system under continuous review as it develops to ensure that it is operating effectively.

References

1. *Industrial Democracy — The Way Forward*. Industrial Participation Association, London, 1976.
2. *Practical Policies for Participation*. The Industrial Society, London, 1974.
3. Brown, W *Exploration in Management*. Heinemann, London, 1960.
4. Jaques, E *The Changing Culture of a Factory*. Tavistock, London, 1951.
5. Dale, B G and Ball, T S *A Study of Quality Circles in UK Manufacturing Organizations*. Department of Management Sciences, University of Manchester Institute of Science and Technology, 1984.

33

Communications

The nature of communications

Communications are concerned with the creation, transmission, interpretation and use of information. The communication can be on a person-to-person basis, as when a boss tells someone what to do and when a subordinate reports to a superior, or it can be on a departmental/corporate basis when general instructions or pieces of information are passed down the line, and reactions, reports and comments float, more or less effectively, up again.

Communications start with the communicator wanting to say something; he or she then decides how it is to be said and transmitted. the communication reaches recipients who form an impression of what they have heard and interpret it against their own background of attitudes and experiences (Figure 33.1).

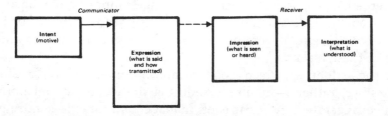

Figure 33.1 The process of communication

The basic problem in communications is that the meaning which is actually received by one person may not be what the other intended to send. The communicator and the receiver are two people living in different worlds; any number of things can happen to distort the messages that pass between them. People's needs and experiences tend to colour what they see and hear. Messages they do not want to hear are repressed. Others are magnified, created out of thin air or distorted.

The importance of communications

Organizations function by means of the collective action of people, yet each individual is capable of taking independent action which may not be in line with policy or instructions, or may not be reported properly to other people who ought to know about it. Good communications are required to achieve coordinated results.

Organizations are subject to the influence of continuous change which affects the work employees do, their well-being and their security. Change can be managed only by ensuring that the reasons for and implications of change are communicated to those affected in terms they can understand and accept.

Individuals are motivated by the extrinsic reward system and the intrinsic rewards that come from the work itself. But the degree to which they are motivated depends upon the amount of responsibility and scope for achievement provided by their job, and upon their expectations that the rewards they will get will be the ones they want and will follow from the efforts they make. Feelings about work and the associated rewards depend very much on the effectiveness of communications from their boss and within the company.

Above all, good two-way communications are required in order that management can keep employees informed of the policies and plans that affect them and employees can react promptly with their views about management's proposals and actions. Change cannot be managed properly without an understanding of the feelings of those affected by it, and an efficient system of communications is needed to understand and influence these feelings.

But the extent to which good communications create satisfactory relationships, rather than simply reducing unsatisfactory relationships, can be exaggerated. A feature of management practices during this century is the way in which different management theories become fashionable or influential for a while and then decline in favour. Among these has been the 'good communications' theory of management. This approach to dealing with management problems is based upon the following assumptions:

1. The needs and aims of both employees and management are, in the long run, the same in any organization. Managers' and employees'

ideas and objectives can all be fitted together to form a single conceptual framework.
2. Any differences in opinion between management and employees are due to misunderstandings that have arisen because communications are not good enough.
3. The solution to industrial strife is to improve communications.

This theory is attractive and has some validity. Its weakness is that the assumptions are too sweeping, particularly the assumption that the ultimate objectives of management and workers are necessarily identical. Experiences in countries, such as Yugoslavia, which have had long experience of industrial democracy, suggest that workers' representatives who are appointed to the board of a company concern themselves mainly with pay and conditions and are not greatly interested in other aspects of the company's business. The good communications theory, like paternalism, seems to imply that the company can develop loyalty by keeping people informed and treating them well. But people working in organizations have other and, to them, more important loyalties elsewhere; and why not?

The existence of different loyalties and points of view in an organization, however, does not mean that communication is unimportant. If anything, the need for a good communications system becomes even greater when differences and conflict exist. But it can only alleviate those differences and pave the way to better cooperation. It cannot solve them.

Communication problems

Communication problems fall into four main categories:

1. People are not aware of the need to communicate.
2. People do not know what to communicate.
3. People do not know how to communicate.
4. Proper facilities for communicating are not available.

These problems are equally important, although inadequacy in any one area can lead to communication failures, and they are not easy to correct. To overcome them, one must formulate a strategy for communications which will form the basis for developing communications systems, and to maintain a continuous programme of education and training in communication techniques. The strategy, systems and training programmes should, however, be founded on an understanding of the barriers to communication.

Barriers to communications

So many barriers exist to good communications that the constant cry in all organizations that communications are bad is hardly to be wondered at — it is amazing that any undisturbed messages get through. Some of the main barriers are summarized below.

Hearing what we expect to hear
What we hear or understand when someone speaks to us is largely based on our own experience and background. Instead of hearing what people tell us, we hear what our minds tell us they have said. We all tend to have preconceived ideas of what people mean: when we hear something new we tend to identify with something similar that we have experienced in the past. People like predictability and 'one of the most time-consuming passions of the human mind is to rationalize sentiments and to disguise them as logic' (Roethlisberger and Dickson).[1]

When people receive a communication which is consistent with their own beliefs, they accept it as valid, seek additional information and remember accurately what they heard.

Ignoring information that conflicts with what we already know
We tend to ignore or reject communications that conflict with our own beliefs. If they are not rejected, some way is found of twisting and shaping their meaning to fit our preconceptions. Communications often fail when they run counter to other information that the receiver already possesses, whether that information is true or false.

The technical term for what happens when people receive irreconcilable information is *cognitive dissonance*, a theory, developed by Festinger, which asserts that individuals experience discomfort when they hold logically inconsistent 'cognitions' (individual views or images of events which shape people's social behaviour) about an object or an event, and that they are thus motivated to reduce the discomfort or dissonance by changes to their views or attitudes. Cognitions are selectively organized to reflect an individual's own environment, experience, wants and goals, and physiological structure. This provides the frame of reference against which the properties of a particular object or piece of information are judged. People resist change or the communication asking them to change because the new ideas are outside their frame of reference.

Where communication is inconsistent with existing beliefs, receivers reject its validity, avoid further exposure to it, easily forget it and, in memory, distort what they hear.

Perceptions about the communicator

Not only do receivers evaluate what they hear in terms of their own background, but they also take the sender into account. Experience or prejudice may ascribe non-existent motives to the communicator. Some people see every collective action as a conspiracy. Others look behind the message to read into it all sorts of motives different from those apparent on the surface. It is extremely difficult for us to separate what we hear from our feelings about the person who says it.

Influence of reference group

The group with which we identify — the reference group — influences our attitudes and feelings. 'Management' and 'the union' as well as our family, our ethnic background, our political party and our reglious beliefs (if any) constitute a reference group and colour our reactions to information. What each group 'hears' depends on its own interests. Shared experiences and common frames of reference have much more influence than exhortations from management in which people with whom employees feel they have nothing in common hand on messages containing information which conflicts with what they already believe.

Words mean different things to different people

This is the problem of semantics. As Strauss and Sayles put it: 'Essentially language is a method of using symbols to represent facts and feelings. Strictly speaking we can't convey *meaning*, all we can do is convey *words*. And yet the same words may suggest quite different meanings for different people. The meanings are in the people not the words.'[2]

Words may have symbolic meanings for some people, with the result that they convey a quite different impression from the one intended. 'Profits', to management, are a prerequisite for survival and growth: to employees, they represent ill-gotten gains from keeping down pay or overpricing. 'Closed shop', to a trade unionist, means an appropriate device for maintaining stability and strength and ensuring that employees contribute to the organization: to managers, 'closed shop' may suggest a fundamentally illiberal device restricting the freedom of both management and workers.

In short, do not assume that something which has a certain meaning to you will convey the same meaning to someone else.

Jargon

All professions and trades develop their own special language, or 'jargon'. It is a convenient way of communicating technical terms among those who know the jargon, but it is an effective and irritating barrier between those who know and those who do not.

Non-verbal communication
In trying to understand what people are saying to us, we use many cues besides language — what have come to be called 'body language'. Looking at the eyes, the shape of the mouth, the muscles of the face, and even bodily posture, may tell us more about what other people really think than the words they use. In a sense, this is an aid to communication if the real meaning of what we are saying is conveyed by the expression on our face rather than by the actual message. But it can become a barrier if people misinterpret our 'body language'.

Emotional context
Our emotions colour our ability to convey or to receive the true message. When we are insecure or worried, what we hear and see seems more threatening than when we are secure and at peace with the world. When we are angry or depressed, we tend to reject out of hand what might otherwise seem like reasonable requests or good ideas. During arguments, many things can be said which are not understood or are badly distorted.

Noise
'Noise', in the sense of outside factors interfering with the reception of the message, is an obvious barrier. It may be literal noise which prevents words from being heard, or figurative noise in the shape of distracting or confused information which distorts the message. The awkward forms in which messages are communicated — unclear syntax, long unwieldy sentences with polysyllabic words — all help to produce noise.

Size
The sheer size and complexity of modern organizations is one of the main barriers to communication. Messages have to penetrate layer upon layer of management or move between different functions, units, or locations. They thus become distorted or never arrive. Reliance is placed more on the written than the spoken word to get the message through, and this seriously restricts the effectiveness of the communication.

With size goes formality, and with formality go restrictions to the freedom with which communication can take place. E F Schumacher has suggested that 'small is beautiful', and this certainly applies to communications. His theme was applied more to the encouragement of creativity

734

than to the development of good communications, but it is equally relevant to both. On the question of creativity, he wrote:

> In any organization, large or small, there must be a certain clarity and orderliness: if things fall into disorder nothing can be accomplished. Yet, orderliness as such is static and lifeless; so there must be plenty of elbow-room and scope for breaking through the established order, to do the thing never done before, never anticipated by the guardians of orderliness, the new, unpredicted and unpredictable outcome of a man's creative idea.[3]

Organizations, he wrote, have to strive continuously for the 'orderliness of *order* and the disorderliness of creative freedom'. He did not say, but well might have, that a free flow of communication is essential to bridge the gap.

Overcoming barriers to communication

The overall implication of this formidable collection of barriers is that no one should assume that every message sent will be received in the form intended. But communications can be improved, even if perfect understanding between people is impossible.

Adjusting to the world of the receiver

When you communicate, the tendency is to adjust to yourself. You have the need to say something and to say it in a particular way. But to get the message across, you have to adjust to the receivers. This means thinking ahead and trying to work out how they will perceive the message — understanding their needs and potential reactions. It also means using feedback and reinforcement techniques, as discussed later.

Effective communicators try to predict the impact of what they are going to write or say on receivers' feelings and attitudes. They try to tailor the message to fit the receivers' vocabulary, interests, and values, and are aware of the possible ways their information can be misinterpreted because of the symbolic meanings attached to phrases, the influence of the reference group and the tendency for people to reject what they do not want to hear.

Overcoming barriers requires *empathy* — the ability to put oneself in someone else's shoes and understand how he or she is likely to hear and interpret the message.

Using feedback

Feedback is the process of obtaining information on performance in order to take corrective action where this is necessary. In communications, feedback means ensuring that communicators get a message back from the receiver which tells them how much has been understood. This is why face-to-face communication is so much more effective than the written word, as long as the communication is truly 'two-way'; in other words, the receivers are given adequate opportunity to respond and react.

Using reinforcement
The message may have to be presented in a number of different ways to get it across. Good speakers know that if they can get more than three important ideas across in a 30-minute talk, they are lucky, and that they must repeat each idea at least three times in different ways to ensure that the message has been received and understood. In giving complicated directions, it is wise to repeat them several times, perhaps in different ways, to guarantee successful transmission.

Using direct, simple language
This seems so obvious as hardly to be worth stating. But many people seem unable to express themselves clearly and without the use of jargon or an excessive number of adjectives, adverbs and sub-clauses.

Reinforcing words with actions
Communications are only effective if they are credible. If management says a thing, then it must do it. Next time, it is more likely to be believed. The motto should be 'suit the action to the words'.

Using face-to-face communication
Face-to-face communication is more effective than the written word for the reasons already mentioned. First, the sender is able to experience direct feedback from the receiver on what the latter is or is not hearing. The way in which the message is presented can then be adjusted by being expressed in different terms or reinforced. If necessary, the message itself can be changed in the light of immediate reactions. Secondly, most people express themselves more clearly and directly when they use the spoken rather than the written word. Thirdly, a spoken message can be delivered in a much more human and understanding way — this helps to get over prejudices against the speaker. It also means that criticisms can be expressed in a more constructive manner. A written reproof seems much more harsh and condemnatory than one delivered orally.

Using different channels of communication
Some communications have to be in writing to get the message across promptly and without any danger of variations in the way in which it is delivered. But, wherever possible, written communications should be supplemented by the spoken word. Conversely, an oral briefing should be reinforced by a written confirmation.

Reducing problems of size
Communication problems arising from size can be reduced structurally by cutting down the number of levels of management, reducing spans of control, ensuring that activities are grouped on the basis of ease of intercommunication, and decentralizing authority into smaller, self-contained although accountable units. An appropriate degree of informality in relationships within the structure can be encouraged, and organization development programmes can be used to increase trust and understanding. Techniques such as briefing groups, as described later in this chapter, can be used to disseminate oral communications more effectively throughout the organization.

Making communications work

Overcoming barriers to communication can be a slow and, for long periods, an unrewarding task. Communications can only be effective in an atmosphere of trust and cooperation. A sudden conversion to the 'good communications' philosophy, resulting in a massive communication campaign, will not convert a bad situation into a good one overnight. Trust and understanding have to be built up over a long period during which management demonstrates that it really believes in explaining and listening to people about the things that concern them.

To achieve good results, communication should be seen as a strategic matter to be planned, developed and controlled on the basis of a full understanding of the requirements, problems and needs of everyone in the organization.

Communications strategy

The starting point for the formulation of a communications strategy should be an analysis of the different types of communication with which the strategy should be concerned. Communication studies embrace all human activities in an organization, and the analysis must narrow the field down to well-defined areas in which action can be taken. The main areas and the objectives to be attained in them are set out in Table 33.1.

Table 33.1 Communication areas and objectives

	Communication Area	Objectives
I. MANAGERIAL	1. The communication downwards and sideways of corporate or functional objectives, policies, plans and budgets to those who have to implement them.	To ensure that managers and supervisors receive clear, accurate and prompt information on what they are expected to achieve to further the company's objectives.
	2. The communication downwards of direct instructions from a manager to a subordinate on what the latter has to do.	To ensure that the instructions are clear and precise and provide the necessary motivation to get people into action.
	3. The communication upwards and sideways of proposals, suggestions and comments on corporate or functional objectives, policies and budgets from those who have to implement them.	To ensure that managers and supervisors have adequate scope to influence corporate and functional decisions on matters about which they have specific expertise and knowledge.
	4. The communication upwards and sideways of management information on performance and results.	To enable management to monitor and control performance in order that, as necessary, opportunities can be exploited or swift corrective action taken.
II. INTERNAL RELATIONS	5. The communication downwards of information on company plans, policies or performance.	To ensure that (i) employees are kept informed of matters that affect them, especially changes to working conditions, and factors influencing their prosperity and security; (ii) employees are encouraged to identify themselves more completely with the company.
	6. The communication upwards of the comments and reactions of employees to what is proposed will happen or what is actually happening in matters that affect them.	To ensure that employees are given an opportunity to voice their suggestions and fears and that the company is in a position to amend its plans in the light of these comments.
III. EXTERNAL RELATIONS	7. The receipt and analysis of information from outside which affects the company's interests.	To ensure that the compoany is fully aware of all the information on legislation and on marketing, commercial, financial and technological matters that affect its interests.
	8. The presentation of information about the company and its products to the government, customers and the public at large.	To exert influence in the interests of the company, to present a good image of the company, and to persuade customers to buy its products or services.

Communications

Employee relations are mainly affected by managerial and internal communications, although external communications are an additional channel of information. The strategy for managerial communications is concerned with planning and control procedures, management information systems and techniques of delegating and giving instructions. These matters are outside the scope of this book, except in so far as the procedures and skills can be developed by training programmes.

The strategy for internal communications, which is the main concern of this chapter, should be based on analyses of:

- what management wants to say;
- what employees want to hear;
- the problems being met in conveying or receiving information.

These analyses can be used to indicate the systems of communication that need to be developed and the education and training programmes required to make them work. They should also provide guidance on how communications should be managed and timed. Bad management and poor timing are frequently the fundamental causes of ineffective communication.

What management wants to say

What management wants to say depends upon an assessment of what employees need to know, which, in turn, is affected by what they want to hear.

Management should aim to achieve three things: first, to get employees to understand and accept what management proposes to do in areas that affect them; secondly, to get employees to act in the way management wants; and, thirdly, to get employees to identify themselves more closely with the company and its achievements and to help them appreciate more clearly the contribution they make to those achievements.

Communications from management should therefore be about plans, intentions and proposals (with the opportunity for feedback from employees) as well as about achievements and results. Exhortations should be kept to a minimum if used at all. No one listens to them. It is better to concentrate on specific requirements rather than resorting to general appeals for abstract things such as improved quality or productivity. The requirements should be phrased in a way which emphasizes how all concerned will actually work together and the mutual benefits that should result.

What employees want to hear

Clearly, employees want to hear about and to comment upon the matters that affect their interests. These will include changes in working methods and conditions, changes in the arrangements for overtime and shift working, company plans which may affect pay or security, and changes in terms and conditions of employment. It is management's job to understand what employees want to hear and plan its communications strategy accordingly. Understanding can be obtained by making formal enquiries, by means of attitude surveys, by asking employee representatives, by informally listening to what employees say, and by analysing grievances to see if improved communications could modify them.

Analysing communication problems

Specific examples of employee relations problems where communication failures have been the cause or a contributory factor should be analysed to determine exactly what went wrong and what needs to be done to put it right. The problems may be any of those listed earlier in this chapter, including lack of appropriate channels of communication, lack of appreciation of the need to communicate, and lack of skill in overcoming the many formidable barriers to communication. Problems with channels of communication can be dealt with by introducing new or improved communications systems. Lack of skill is a matter for education and training.

Communication systems

Communication systems can be divided into those using the written word such as magazines, newsletters, bulletins and notice-boards, and those using oral methods such as meetings, briefing groups and public address systems. The aim should be to make judicious use of a number of channels to make sure that the message gets across.

Magazines

Glossy magazines or house journals are an obvious way to keep employees informed about the company and are often used for public relations purposes as well. They can extol and explain the achievements of the company and may thus help to increase identification and even loyalty. If employees are encouraged to contribute (although this is difficult), the magazine can become more human. The biggest danger of this sort of magazine is that it becomes a public-relations-type exercise which is seen by employees as having little relevance to their everyday affairs.

Newsletters

Newsletters aim to appear more frequently and to angle their contents more to the immediate concerns of employees than the glossier form of house magazine. To be effective, they should include articles specifically aimed at explaining what management is planning to do and how this affects the company. They can also include more chatty 'human interest' material about the doings of employees to capture the attention of readers. Correspondence columns can provide an avenue for the expression of employees' views and replies from management, but no attempt should be made to censor letters (except those that are purely abusive) or to pull punches in reply. Anonymous letters should be published if the writer gives his name to the editor.

The key factor in the success of a newsletter or any form of house magazine is the editor, who should be someone who knows the company and its employees and can be trusted by everyone to be frank and fair. Professional expertise is obviously desirable, but it is not the first consideration, as long as the editor can write reasonably well and has access to expert help in putting the paper together. It is often a good idea to have an editorial board consisting of management and employee representatives to advise and assist the editor.

Companies often publish a newsletter in addition to a house magazine, treating the latter mainly as a public relations exercise and relying on the newsletter as the prime means of communicating with employees.

Bulletins

Bulletins can be used to give immediate information to employees which cannot wait for the next issue of a newsletter; or they can be a substitute for a formal publication if the company does not feel that the expense is justified. Bulletins are useful only if they are distributed quickly and are seen by all interested employees. They can simply be posted on notice-boards or, more effectively, given to individual employees and used as a starting point for a briefing session if they contain information of sufficient interest to merit a face-to-face discussion.

Notice-boards

Notice-boards are an obvious but frequently misused medium for

741

communications. The biggest danger is allowing boards to be cluttered up with uninteresting or out-of-date material. It is essential to control what goes on to the boards and to appoint responsible people to service them by removing out-of-date or unauthorized notices.

A more impressive show can be made of notices and other material if an information centre is set up in the canteen or some other suitable place where the information can be displayed in a more attractive and compelling manner than on a typical notice-board.

Consultative committees

Joint consultative committees, as discussed in Chapter 32, exist to provide a channel for two-way communication. Sometimes, however, they are not particularly effective, either because their thunder has been stolen by union negotiation committees, or because their proceedings are over-formalized and restricted. It is essential to disseminate the information revealed at committees around the offices and works, but it is impossible to rely on committee members to do this. Minutes can be posted on notice-boards, but they are seldom read, usually because they contain too much redundant material.

Videos

Specially made videos can be a cost-effective method of getting across personal messages (eg from the chief executives) or information about how the company is doing.

Team briefing

The concept of team briefing (previously called briefing groups), as developed by the Industrial Society, is a device to overcome the restricted nature of joint consultative committees by involving everyone in an organization, level by level, in face-to-face meetings to present, receive and discuss information. Team briefing aims to overcome the gaps and inadequacies of casual briefings by injecting some order into the system.

Team briefing should operate as follows:

1. *Organization:*

    (a) cover all levels in an organization;
    (b) fewest possible steps between the top and bottom;
    (c) between 4 and 18 in each group;

(d)   run by the immediate leader of each group at each level (who must be properly trained and briefed).

2.   *Subjects:*

(a)   policies — explanations of new or changed policies;
(b)   plans — as they affect the organization as a whole and the immediate group;
(c)   progress — how the organization and the group is getting on; what the latter needs to do to improve;
(d)   people — new appointments, points about personnel matters (pay, security, procedures).

3.   *Timing and duration:*

(a)   a minimum of once a month for those in charge of others and once every two months for every individual in the organization — but meet only if there is something to say;
(b)   duration not longer than 20–30 minutes.

The merit of team briefing is that it enables face-to-face communications to be planned and, to a reasonable degree, formalized. It is easy, however, for it to start on a wave of enthusiasm and then to wither away because of lack of sufficient drive and enthusiasm from the top downward, inadequately trained and motivated managers and supervisors, reluctance of management to allow subjects of real importance to be discussed throughout the system, and insufficient feedback upwards through each level.

A team briefing system must be led and controlled effectively from the top, but it does require a senior manager with specific responsibility to advise on the subject matter and the preparation of briefs (it is important to have well-prepared material to ensure that briefing is carried out consistently and thoroughly at each level), to train managers and supervisors, and to monitor the system by checking on the effectiveness and frequency of meetings.

Education and training in communications

Communication is ultimately one person passing on a message to another and listening to the reply. Formal channels of communication have to be provided for, but their effectiveness depends on the attitudes, skills, and enthusiasm of those responsible for using the system.

Education and training programmes are required to develop the attitude that communication is an important part of management and thus to ensure that a prime consideration when making any decision is how, where, and to whom it should be communicated. Communicators need to be made aware of the barriers to communication and the skills of perception and analysis they need to overcome them. Finally, training should be given in specific communication skills — speaking, writing, running meetings and, most important, listening. The training in many of these skills can be conducted by means of more or less traditional courses, but the maximum use should be made of group exercises and role-playing, in order that people can practise and develop their skills. Sensitivity, or 'T-Group', training (see Appendix P) is one method of increasing the individual's understanding of the impact he or she makes on other people, and the way in which they hear what he or she has to say. Such training, as its name implies, should make people more sensitive to the effect they have on others as well as providing them with new tools to analyse the interactions that take place when people work together.

Twelve rules for internal communications

To sum up, the following are the 12 golden rules of internal communications:

1. There is no such thing as absolute certainty in business decisions, and it is important everyone in a business realizes this.
2. If a board cannot or will not spell out its business strategy, employees are entitled to assume it does not have one.
3. Assume that in an information vacuum people will believe the worst.
4. Never take it for granted that people know what you are talking about.
5. Always take it for granted that people doing a job know more about it than you do.
6. Telling people something once is not much better than not telling them at all.
7. Never assume that people will tell you anything that reflects unfavourably upon themselves.
8. Remember that employees read newspapers, magazines and books; listen to the radio; and watch TV.
9. Do not be afraid to admit you were wrong; it gives people confidence that you know what you are doing.
10. Asking for help, taking advice, consulting and listening to others are signs of great strength.
11. Communicating good news is easy, but even this is not often done by management; bad news is often left to rumours and the grapevine.

12. Changing attitudes to change behaviour takes years — changing behaviour changes attitudes in weeks.

References

1. Roethlisberger, F and Dickson, W *Management and the Worker*. Harvard University Press, Cambridge, MA, 1939.
2. Strauss, G and Sayles, L R *Personnel: The Human Problems of Management*. Prentice-Hall, Englewood Cliffs, NJ, 1972.
3. Schumacher, E F *Small is Beautiful*. Blond and Briggs, London, 1973.

Part VIII
Health, Safety and Welfare

This part deals with the services provided by the personnel function in order to help the organization meet its legal and social responsibilities to provide a healthy and safe place of work and look after the welfare of its employees.

The importance of these aspects of personnel management should never be underestimated, although, sadly, they frequently are. Too often, the responsibility for health and safety and for welfare is relegated to poorly appreciated and under-resourced individuals and sections.

Welfare in particular, a much despised area of personnel management in the recent past, has become more significant as organizations learn to appreciate that they have a social responsibility to their members.

34

Health and Safety

Health and safety policies and programmes are concerned with protecting employees — and any other people affected by what the company produces or does — against the hazards arising from their employment or their links with the company.

Occupational health programmes deal with the reactions of workpeople to their working environment and with the prevention of ill-health arising from working conditions and circumstances. They consist of two main elements — occupational medicine, which is a specialized branch of preventive medicine concerned with the diagnosis and assessment of health hazards and stresses at work; and occupational hygiene, which is the province of the chemist and the engineer engaged in the measurement and physical control of environmental hazards.

Safety programmes deal with the prevention of accidents and with minimizing the resulting loss and damage to persons and to property. They relate more to systems of work than to the working environment, but both health and safety programmes are concerned with protection against hazards, and their aims and methods are closely interlinked.

This chapter therefore treats health and safety as two aspects of the same problem, although the particular considerations affecting occupational hygiene or accident prevention are treated separately, as are special areas of the subject such as fire precautions.

Health and safety programmes need to be considered against the background of the factors that affect health and safety at work, and the chapter begins with an analysis of these factors and a discussion of the basic principles that influence policies and procedures. This is followed by a description of the elements of the overall health and safety programme, and the chapter then deals with each of these elements, namely:

- the identification and analysis of health and safety hazards and problems;
- health and safety policies;
- the organization of health and safety;
- occupational health programmes and procedures;
- accident-prevention programmes and procedures;
- the prevention of fire and explosions;
- education and training in health and safety precautions;
- the measurement and control of health and safety performance.

Factors affecting health and safety

The work and writings of a number of distinguished practitioners and researchers in health and safety have resulted in a range of basic principles, concepts and approaches which need to be understood by anyone concerned with the development and implementation of health and safety programmes.

The first and most influential of the practitioners was Heinrich,[1] who developed his axioms of industrial safety to underline his thesis that the conventional approach to prevention, by concentrating on injuries that had happened rather than on accidental occurrences that might be predicted, looked at only a fraction of the total problem and looked at it backwards. From this analysis a considerable body of literature has developed advocating the techniques of 'damage control' and 'total loss control'. The basic message of these approaches, which were mainly North American in origin, is that the employer who wants to prevent injuries in the future, to reduce loss and damage, and to increase efficiency must look systematically at the total pattern of accidental happenings — whether or not they caused injury or damage. He must then plan a comprehensive system of prevention rather than rely on the *ad hoc* patching-up of deficiencies which injury-causing accidents have brought to light.

Principles of health and safety management

An analysis of the contributions of various schools of thought on health and safety matters suggests that there are five basic principles which should determine the approach to be used in health and safety management.

1. Industrial disease and accidents result from a multiplicity of factors, but these have to be traced to their root causes, which are usually faults in the management system arising from poor leadership from

the top; inadequate supervision; insufficient attention to the design of health and safety into the system; an unsystematic approach to the identification, analysis and elimination of hazards; and poor education and training facilities.

2. The most important function of health and safety programmes is to identify potential hazards, provide effective safety facilities and equipment, and take prompt remedial action. This is only possible if they are:

    (a) comprehensive and effective systems for reporting all accidents causing damage or injury;
    (b) adequate accident records and statistics;
    (c) systematic procedures for carrying out safety checks, inspections and investigations;
    (d) methods of ensuring that safety equipment is maintained and used;
    (e) proper means for persuading managers, supervisors and work-people to pay more attention to health and safety matters.

3. The health and safety policies of the organization should be determined by top management, who must be continuously involved in monitoring health and safety peformance and in ensuring that corrective action is taken when necessary.
4. Managers and supervisors must be made fully accountable for health and safety performance in the working areas they control.
5. All employees should be given thorough training in safe methods of work and should receive continuing education and guidance on eliminating health and safety hazards and on the prevention of accidents.

These principles are underpinned by health and safety legislation, as summarized in Chapter 36 (page 800).

Health and safety programmes

The essential elements of a health and safety programme are the following:

*   analysis — of health and safety performance, problems and potential hazards;
*   development — of policies, organization, procedures and training systems;
*   implementation — of the programme by means of training schemes, inspections, investigations and audits;

- evaluation — of control information and reports and of the effectiveness of the organization and training systems. This evaluation should provide feedback to be used for improving performance.

The constituents of the health and safety programme are shown in Figure 34.1.

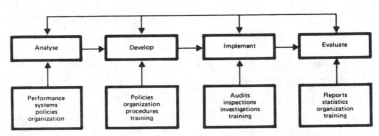

Figure 34.1 Health and safety programme

Health and safety programmes are the responsibility of top management, but they should enlist the support of middle management, supervisors and workpeople in conducting the initial analysis and in developing and implementing the programme. Assistance and guidance can be provided internally by specialist health and safety advisers, and externally by the government inspectorate (in the UK the Health and Safety Executive); bodies concerned with health and safety such as, in the UK, the Royal Society for the Prevention of Accidents; or employers' associations, some of whom have strong safety departments. But advisory services do not detract from the ultimate responsibility of management for health and safety performance.

Analysis of health and safety performance

Health and safety programmes must be based on an analysis of the facts on the organization of health and safety as it exists, and on the procedures used and results obtained.

The facts should be analysed under the following headings:

- policies — the extent to which health and safety policies are defined and implemented;
- the organization — the role and effectiveness of management, supervision and workpeople, health and safety staff and safety committees;
- systems and procedures — for carrying out inspections and investigations; reporting and recording accidents; ensuring at the design or

development stage that equipment, facilities, plant, processes or substances are not dangerous; providing safety equipment; educating and training employees;

- performance — the health and safety record of the company as shown by statistics, reports, special investigations and sample checks.

Such an analysis involves discussions with managers, supervisors, work-people, shop stewards, factory inspectors and insurers, as well as a review of standard procedures and an examination of safety records.

Health and safety policies

Written health and safety policies are required to demonstrate that top management is concerned about the protection of its employees from hazards at work and to indicate how this protection will be provided. There are, therefore, first, a declaration of intent; secondly, a definition of the means by which that intent is to be realized; and, thirdly, a statement of the guidelines that should be followed by management and workpeople in implementing the policy. The policies should provide a base for organization, action and control, as shown in Figure 34.2.

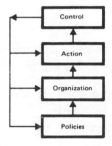

Figure 34.2 The role of health and safety policies

The policy statement should consist of three parts:

1. The general policy statement.
2. The description of the organization for health and safety.
3. Details of the arrangements for implementing the policy.

The general policy statement

The general policy statement should be a declaration of the intention of the employer to safeguard the health and safety of the employees. It should emphasize four fundamental points: first, that the safety of employees and the public is of paramount importance; second, that safety takes precedence over expediency; third, that every effort will be made to involve all managers, supervisors and employees in the development and implementation of health and safety procedures; and, fourth, that health and safety legislation will be complied with in the spirit as well as the letter of the law. (See Appendix A.)

Organization

This section of the policy statement should describe the health and safety organization of the company through which high performance standards are set and achieved by people employed at all levels in the organization.

The statement should underline the ultimate responsibility of top management for the health and safety performance of the company. It should then indicate how key management personnel are to be held accountable for performance in their areas. The role of safety committees and safety representatives should be defined, and the duties of specialists such as the safety adviser and the medical officer should be summarized.

Health and safety arrangements

The description of health and safety arrangements should indicate how the general policy statement is to be put into effect. It should cover:

- procedures for reporting accidents, illness and safety and health hazards; fire precautions; first aid;
- arrangements for monitoring the atmosphere and maintaining high standards of hygiene with regard to potentially harmful substances;
- arrangements for instructing workpeople in safe working methods and for training employees in health and safety matters;
- good housekeeping requirements covering storage facilities, adequate space for machinery and plant, the provision of gangways, and welfare arrangements;
- special rules for work done at a height, in confined spaces, on certain electrical equipment or on unguarded machinery;
- the maintenance of equipment and the provision of proper inspection and testing arrangements;
- general rules on safe working habits;
- special rules for internal transport drivers;
- arrangements for checking new machinery and materials;
- safety inspections;

- the provision of personal protective equipment, and rules as to its use;
- suggestions on safety matters.

Health and safety organization

Health and safety concerns everyone in an establishment, although the main responsibility lies with management and supervision for formulating and implementing safety policies and procedures.

The role of management

The role of management is to develop health and safety policies and procedures with the help of its medical and safety advisers. Management must then ensure that the procedures are implemented by making supervisors accountable for health and safety performance in their areas and by providing them with the help, guidance and training they need to carry out their responsibilities. Management must also set up information and control systems so that the health and safety performance can be monitored and corrective action initiated when required.

It is essential to have a director with specific responsibility for health and safety matters. His job is to advise the board on policies, to ensure that the agreed policies are implemented, and to report back to the board on health and safety performance. He should also be responsible for the overall management of the health and safety organization.

The role of supervision

Supervisors can exert the greatest influence on health and safety. They are in immediate control of employees and work processes, and it is up to them to keep a constant watch to reveal potentially unsafe practices or conditions. But they need all the support and encouragement they can get from higher management to fulfil these responsibilities. If the emphasis from above is purely on output and cost reduction, supervisors can hardly be blamed if they neglect safety precautions. Exhortations on safety from management or safety advisers are useless unless it can be demonstrated that health and safety considerations will be given priority if there is any conflict between them and the output and cost budgets.

Supervisors need training and guidance on their safety functions. This can be provided by the safety and training departments, if any, but the existence of well-defined safety rules and procedures should also help.

The role of the medical adviser

Medical advisers have two functions: preventive and clinical. The preventive function is the more important, and this covers advising on health precautions, conducting inspections and enquiries, establishing health standards, and conducting medical examinations. Their clinical function is to deal with industrial accidents and diseases and to advise on the steps necessary to recover from injury or illness. It is not their job to usurp the role of the family doctor, but their special knowledge of the factory should enable them to give more relevant advice on matters concerning health at work.

Only large companies can afford full-time medical officers, but any company with more than 100 employees should be able to call on the part-time advice of a local doctor who is interested and able to help.

The role of the safety adviser

The main functions of the safety adviser should be to:

- advise on health and safety policies and standards, rules and procedures;
- advise on the health and safety aspects of the design and use of plant and equipment;
- advise on the use of safety equipment and protective clothing;
- plan and carry out safety audits and inspections;
- conduct investigations into accidents;
- maintain safety records and statistics;
- liaise continually with management, supervision and safety representatives;
- liaise with the health and safety inspectorate.

The role of the safety committee

Safety committees should be concerned with reviewing unsafe practices and conditions and making suggestions on methods of improving health and safety performance. Like all such committees, they are most effective when they can be involved in real issues and can see their recommendations put into effect. That is why they should take part in formulating health and safety policies, procedures and rules; carrying out safety audits and inspections; investigating accidents; and analysing accident reports and statistics.

Occupational health programmes

Occupational health programmes are concerned with the identification and control of health hazards arising from toxic substances, radiation, noise, fatigue and the stresses imposed upon body and mind at work.

Basic approach

In each of these areas the same basic approach is necessary. The first stage is to identify the substances, conditions or processes which are actually or potentially dangerous. The second stage is to evaluate how the hazard arises by studying the nature of the substance or condition and the circumstances in which the danger occurs. This means establishing the point at which a substance or an environmental condition is in danger of becoming harmful in terms of the intensity of exposure and the duration of exposure. It also means that the effect of working methods and processes on the human body and mind has to be examined. Industrial hygiene research into these matters should be carried out by specialist medical advisers working closely with process engineers and chemists. In particularly hazardous environments, research and advice may be required from members of the growing profession of occupational hygienists.

The final stage is to develop methods for minimizing the risk by exercising control over the use of dangerous substances or over the environment in which the hazard occurs. Control of occupational health and hygiene problems can be achieved by:

- eliminating the hazard at the source by means of design and process engineering, which may, for example, ensure that harmful concentrations of toxic substances are not allowed to contaminate the worker;
- isolating hazardous operations or substances in order that workers do not come into contact with them;
- changing the process or substances used, to promote better protection or to remove the risk;
- providing protective equipment, but only if changes to the design, process, or specification cannot completely remove the hazard;
- training workers to avoid risk by eliminating dangerous practices or by using the protective equipment provided;
- maintaining plant and equipment to minimize the possibility of harmful emissions;
- good housekeeping to keep premises and machinery clean and free from toxic substances;

- regular inspections to ensure that potential health risks are identified in good time (Procedures for conducting safety inspections which also cover occupational health hazards are discussed below.);
- pre-employment medical examinations and regular checks on those exposed to risk;
- ensuring that ergonomic considerations (ie those concerning the design and use of equipment, machines, processes and workstations) are taken into account in design specifications, establishing work routines, personnel specifications and training.

Toxic substances

Many toxic substances are present in working environments in the form of dusts (eg lead oxide), liquids (eg carbon disulphide) and gases (eg chlorine) and can be absorbed into the body through the lungs, mouth or skin. The increasing use in industry of potentially harmful chemical substances is producing new and more subtle hazards against which constant vigilance is necessary.

The work of environmental hygienists in the control of toxic substances must be firmly based on medical intelligence. But chemists, engineers, and doctors should be part of one team working on the scientific assessment of the risks and the precise quantification of preventive standards in the form of agreed maximum levels of exposure expressed in threshold limit values (in the UK these are published by the Health and Safety Executive for a wide variety of substances used in industry).

It is the job of line managers in a factory to ensure that they get information and advice from their own specialists or those who can be made available from government agencies. This should enable the company to identify and list hazards from toxic substances and decide on the control actions required. These could be any combination of the control steps listed above, but, in addition, specific instructions and training should be made available for each operator exposed to risk on what should be done to avoid contamination and disease.

Environmental controls need to cover dust, fumes, gases, smoke and vapour in addition to the materials used in manufacturing processes. These create health risks, but they also result in pollution of the atmosphere, and control over pollution is a legal requirement as well as a social responsibility.

Radiation

Radiation hazards are so well known as to have generated an ultra-cautious attitude to the use of radioactive substances, resulting in the imposition of elaborate controls. This is an area where expert advice is essential for any employer who is not familiar with the subject in order that protection can be provided by monitors, remote control systems, special clothing, and rigid control over the doses of radiation any person is allowed to receive.

Noise

Noise is an aspect of occupational health which is probably more neglected than any other. Yet excessive noise can cause fatigue, speech interference, loss of hearing and emotional stress. Any of these could be instrumental in producing lasting physical damage or in increasing the likelihood of an accident.

A noise control programme should be based on a survey of the factory to identify the areas of noise and determine the abatement methods that can be used. The main problem is that noise reduction is something which should be catered for at the design stage — once the plant has been installed, it becomes an expensive business to attack noise.

Fatigue

Fatigue is the inevitable result of continued exertion — either mental or muscular. The factors that increase fatigue are badly designed machines, high temperature or humidity, excessive noise, inadequate lighting or glare, the nature of the floor upon which workers have to stand, and the absence of training in how to perform tasks with the least amount of exertion.

Fatigue induces carelessness and is therefore a potential cause of accidents. It can be attacked by paying attention to all the factors listed above when designing plant and fitting out factories or offices, carrying out work study exercises and designing training programmes.

Physical and mental stress

Physical and mental stress can result from fatigue or from the strains and pressures built into the system of work. This problem also needs to be tackled at the design stage in order that the machine (or office procedure) can be designed to fit the person rather than the person made to fit the machine. This is the science of ergonomics, and some large companies, such as Pilkingtons, employ full-time ergonomists, who join teams in the design stages of factory programmes and advise on the physical and mental factors that should be heeded when developing office systems and procedures. It is a highly technical and important discipline, but it is sad that so little attention is paid to it in training design or system engineers.

Musculo-skeletal conditions such as tenosynovitis need to be minimized by ergonomic design, selection screening, and training. Strain from the use of VDUs has also to be eliminated as far as possible.

The avoidance of strain from lifting heavy objects or from bad posture is also a matter of designing a safe work system. But this is an area where intensive training and constant propaganda are required to reduce risks.

Medical checks

The importance of preventive medicine in industry can hardly be overemphasized. It is the role of the medical adviser in cooperation with occupational hygienists, engineers, chemists and ergonomists to identify health risks and establish general threshold limits for exposure to the risks and individual standards of health and physique for employees.

The aim should be to develop health standards for each occupation and use these as a selection and placement criteria when carrying out pre-employment medical examinations, which are a must in any situation where there are health risks.

A continuing programme of preventive medicine is required which should include checks on the extent to which employees are being exposed to health hazards, inspections to review and revise exposure threshold limits and health standards, and regular examinations for anyone at risk. It is essential to produce a detailed programme for this purpose, and medical advisers should be required to keep top management informed of their programme and the results of their work.

Accident prevention

The prevention of accidents is achieved by:

- identifying the causes of accidents and the conditions under which they are most likely to occur;
- taking account of safety factors at the design stage — building safety into the system;
- designing safety equipment and protective devices and providing protective clothing;
- carrying out regular inspections and checks and taking action to eliminate risks;

- investigating all accidents resulting in damage to establish the cause and to initiate corrective action;
- developing an effective health and safety organization;
- maintaining good records and statistics in order to identify problem areas and unsatisfactory trends;
- conducting a continuous programme of education and training on safe working habits and methods of avoiding accidents.

Identifying the causes of accidents

The process of identifying causes is mainly one of conducting inspections, checks and investigations, as described below. Some consideration should be given, however, to the general factors that induce accidents, as these will indicate the approach that should be used at the design and inspection stages.

Fundamentally, it is the system of work to which human beings are exposed that is the cause of accidents. Carelessness, fatigue, lack of knowledge, inexperience, inadequate training, or poor supervision may, in different degrees, be the immediate causes, but all these factors are related to the basic system of work.

The causes of accidents can therefore be divided into two main areas:

1. those related to the system at work, which is the basic reason for most accidents;
2. those related to immediate individual factors, which in most cases arise from the system of work, but which might not have happened if there had been no human failure at or near the time when the accident occurred.

System of work factors
The main factors in the system of work which induce accidents are the following:

- unsafely designed machinery, plant and processes;
- congested layouts;
- unguarded or inadequately guarded machinery;
- defective plant, materials or working conditions; rough, sharp or obstructive objects; slippery or greasy conditions; decayed, corroded, frayed or cracked containers, wires, conveyor belts or piping; badly maintained machinery;
- poor housekeeping — congestion; blocked gangways or exits; inadequate disposal arrangements for swarf or other waste products; lack of

storage facilities; unclean working conditions;
- overloading of machines, transport vehicles or conveyor belts;
- inadequate lighting, glare;
- inadequate ventilation or systems for removing toxic fumes from the working environment;
- lack of protective clothing or devices.

It should be noted that although these factors are all connected with the system of work, they all result from a human failure at some time.

Immediate factors
The immediate, direct and personal factors causing accidents are the following:

- using unsafe equipment;
- using equipment unsafely — deliberately or through fatigue;
- unsafe loading and placing of materials or parts on machines or transport systems;
- operating without sufficient clearance;
- operating at an unsafe speed;
- making safety devices inoperative to reduce interference and speed up work;
- distractions from other people, noise or events taking place in the workshop;
- failure to use protective clothing or devices.

Any of these factors may result from personal failures such as carelessness, recklessness, laziness, impatience, lack of consideration, or inadequate knowledge, training, skill or supervision.

Building safety into the system

The hazards to employees who operate and maintain machines arise from the belts and pulleys, gears, projecting parts, shaft ends, clutches and other moving parts used to stamp, press, cut or shape materials. Transmission and transportation arrangements and the layout of plant and processes are also hazardous areas.

The prevention of accidents should be a major factor when designing plant or work processes. It is much more effective and economical to build safety into the system at the design stage rather than try to add makeshift safety devices later. It is equally important to specify the procedures and methods to be used in operating machines safely.

Designers should obtain feedback on accidents that may have been caused by a design fault, in order that accidents can be eliminated by modification to existing and future designs.

Safety inspections

The purpose of safety inspections is to locate and define the faults in the system and the operational errors that allow accidents to occur. It is essential to develop a systematic and thorough programme of inspections and spot checks which will cover all parts of the factory at regular intervals. The five steps required are described below:

1. *The first step* is to define the general points that should be covered in any area in which an inspection takes place. These should be included in a check-list.
2. *The second step* is to divide the plant into areas (which may or may not follow existing departmental boundaries) and list the specific points to which attention should be given.
3. *The third step* is to determine methods of inspection. These can take four forms.

   (a) Check-lists are prepared of the points to be covered, and a programme is planned to deal with them at regular intervals or over a series of inspections covering particular areas or safety points. This may be described as the audit approach, and the aim is to carry out a comprehensive review of all aspects of health and safety. Figure 34.3 is an example of the layout of a form that can be used for this purpose.

Audit area		Audited by		Date	
Points to be checked	Symptoms	Causes	Action recommended	Responsibility for action	Date for completion

Figure 34.3 Safety audit form

   (b) Spot checks can be made in each area on a random sample basis or to cover special problems, such as the inadequate use of protective clothing. In their simplest form these may simply enumerate the

763

unsafe acts or conditions observed by the inspector or inspection team and thus identify areas where more detailed investigations are required. A numerical count of this nature can also be done on a comprehensive basis prior to a thorough inspection. An example of the layout of a sample inspection form is shown in Figure 34.4.

Area	Check carried out by			Date
	Number of observations			
Unsafe act or condition	Department A	Department B	Department C	Department D

Figure 34.4 Safety sample inspection form

(c)   Supervisors can be required to make daily checks of safety points in the areas under their control. They should list the problem conditions and indicate the action to be taken either by the supervisor himself, management, or the safety adviser. An example of a supervisor's check-list is shown in Figure 34.5.

Department	Supervisor	Date
Item	Condition	Immediate action taken	Future action proposed

Figure 34.5 Supervisor's daily check-list

(d)   Regular inspections, as required by legislation or by insurance companies, of boilers, pressure vessels, pipelines, dangerous processes, lifts, hoists, etc.

The best approach is to use all four methods. The comprehensive audit can be a continuous, Forth Bridge-type operation, but spot checks should be used to supplement the audit and keep supervisors and workpeople alert. The supervisor's check-list is also required to formalize the inspection procedures, and this should be regarded as one of his or her key responsibilities. Statutory or insurance company inspections are obligatory, of course.

4. *The fourth step* is to define the responsibility for planning, conducting, and acting on safety inspections. A safety adviser or the manager responsible for health and safety can prepare the check-lists and programmes, although this should be done in consultation with managers, supervisors and workpeople. The inspections themselves should involve everyone concerned with safety; they should not be left to the safety adviser. This means that managers, supervisors and safety representatives should physically check conditions in their working areas. They may do this individually, but it is best done by a joint team working under the aegis of a health and safety committee. The safety adviser will still, of course, carry out his or her own investigations, but the prime responsibility for completing the preplanned programme and taking action should rest with line management and the people working in the factory.

5. *The fifth step* should be to set up systems of reporting on the results of inspections and on the action taken or proposed. It is essential that top management should take a direct interest in the inspection programme and that control procedures should be installed to ensure that audits, spot checks and inspections take place. The safety adviser can help top managers to exercise control, but the ultimate responsibiity is theirs.

Accident reports and investigations

A standard system for reporting accidents should be used to classify all accidents under appropriate headings, indicate the likely cause of the accident, and suggest any remedial action that should be taken. It is necessary to have a standard classification system for accidents under headings such as those listed below:

1. *Type of accident:*

    (a) falls of persons;
    (b) falls of material;
    (c) flying material;
    (d) handling (manual);

(e)   handling (mechanical);
(f)   stepping on or striking against stationary objects;
(g)   hand tools;
(h)   railways and vehicles;
(i)   escapes of gas, fumes, etc;
(j)   escapes of steam, hot water, liquids, etc;
(k)   machinery in motion;
(l)   electricity;
(m) welding, brazing, burning, etc;
(n)   fires;
(o)   explosions.

2.   *Location of the injury:*

(a)   head and neck;
(b)   eyes;
(c)   back;
(d)   upper limb;
(e)   lower limb;
(f)   hand;
(g)   fingers;
(h)   foot and toes;
(i)   body system.

3.   *Severity of the injury:*

(a)   fatal injury;
(b)   permanent injury, total disablement;
(c)   permanent injury, partial disablement;
(d)   temporary injury, total incapacity for work;
(e)   temporary injury, capable of carrying out alternative work;
(f)   temporary injury, able to continue work.

An example of a simple report form is shown in Figure 34.6.

Accident-reporting systems can work only if supervisors and medical or first-aid staff are trained in how to prepare reports. It is also necessary to keep on emphasizing the importance of the reports as a means of identifying causes and preventing the recurrence of accidents in order to ensure that they are completed accurately, comprehensively and in good time.

A report is useless unless it can contribute to increased understanding of health and safety problems and to the formulation of action programmes. In the case of minor and isolated incidents, it may not be

Department		
Name of injured	Date of injury	
	Date/time of return to work	
Where and how did the accident occur?		
Nature of injury		
Name(s) of witnesses		
Classification of accident		
Type of accident	Location of accident	Severity of injury
Measures taken and proposed to avoid repetition		
Signed _____ Date _____		

Figure 34.6 Accident report form

necessary to follow up every report, although statistical trends should be kept under review to reveal areas where accidents are increasing and thus show the need for a special investigation.

More serious incidents must, of course, be investigated by the safety adviser or manager responsible for safety. Line management and supervisors should also be involved in the investigation of accidents in their areas, and safety representatives should be included in major investigations. The aim of the investigation should be to decide what needs to be done to avoid future incidents. It should not simply be a matter of apportioning blame. The results of the investigation, however, may well be used as evidence in later inquiries or court actions and it is essential to document all the circumstances, record the observations of eyewitnesses, take photographs and ensure that defective machines or parts are isolated.

Prevention of fire and explosions

The prevention of fire and explosions is achieved by adopting the same basic procedures as those used in preventing accidents. The steps required are to appraise the risks and to develop the basic precautionary measures.

Appraising the risks

The appraisal should be carried out in conjunction with the local fire brigade, the Health and Safety Inspectorate, insurers, architects and process engineers.

Developing precautionary measures

After the initial survey of the premises and plant, it is necessary to list the precautions required to minimize risk. These precautions can be classified under these headings:

- preventive maintenance programme;
- regular inspections to identify potential risks;
- safety rules;
- detection and warning devices;
- procedures and devices for dealing with fires and explosions, evacuating the premises and calling in outside help.

In each of these areas, expert advice from specialists in the prevention of fires and explosions should be obtained.

Education and training

Health and safety conditions at work do not simply happen. They have to be planned and managed, and an essential part of this process is the education and training of managers, supervisors and workpeople.

Educational programmes

The aim of educational programmes should be to ensure that all staff are fully aware of the hazards they meet at work and the potential consequences of hasty or thoughtless actions. They should be designed to create and maintain interest, using all the formal and informal means of communication available — safety bulletins, posters and notices, films and slides, and talks and discussions.

Educational programmes should be continuous — they should not rely on intermittent spurts of activity, although they can include campaigns to deal with specific problems such as strains from lifting heavy objects. The message should be delivered straight to the people who need to hear and learn from it. This is why generalized campaigns are less effective than those aimed at people in their own workshop by the supervisors with whom they are in contact every day.

This can be done informally, but it is better to have an organized programme which supervisors can be trained to administer. Such a programme is the 'Safety Contact Scheme' developed by the Distillers Company, the essential elements of which are as follows:

- Supervisors are required to contact each employee in their sections at least once in every four-week period to discuss with them a safety topic which has been selected for them by management.
- The supervisors are trained in how to run the contact sessions and given carefully prepared notes for guidance on the subject matter which summarize the main points to be made and provide illustrations which help to get the message across.
- After each contact the supervisor records it on a record card, which is inspected regularly by a manager to ensure that the programme is being followed.

Health and safety training

Health and safety training programmes should be derived from an analysis of training needs. This should refer to the hazards generally present in the company as well as the specific hazards associated with individual jobs.

Managers, supervisors, safety advisers and safety representatives should be trained in such techniques as conducting inspections and investigations, collecting and analysing statistical data and communicating with people on health and safety matters.

Employees should be provided with general induction training as well as training in the hazards present in specific occupations.

Induction training

Induction training should aim to give new employees a general understanding of what they must do to avoid risks and how the safety policies and facilities of the company will help them to avoid occupational illnesses and accidents. The points that should be covered include:

- the health and safety policies of the company, with particular reference to the duties of employees to work safely;
- the organization of the safety function;
- the arrangements for safety training;

- the main hazards that employees are likely to face and what they should do about them;
- the methods of working, including posture to be adopted, to minimize risks to health or safety;
- the unsafe practices to avoid;
- the use of protective clothing and safety equipment;
- the safety rules and procedures of the company;
- the procedure for reporting accidents;
- evacuation procedures in case of fire or explosion;
- first-aid facilities.

Job training

Job safety training should be based on an analysis of the special hazards presented by a job. The job should then be broken down into its constituent parts, and the safety points to which the operator must pay attention should be defined for each part.

Measurement and control of health and safety performance

Effective measurement and control is primarily a matter for action by management and supervision with the help of health and safety advisers. The procedure for carrying out surveys and inspections and for investigating accidents referred to earlier in this chapter provides the best means of monitoring performance and identifying where preventive or corrective action needs to be taken.

These measures, however, should be supplemented by safety statistics — not as an end to themselves (which they too often are) but as a basis for comparisons, inside and outside the company, and as a means of identifying undesirable trends which may not be revealed so clearly by the normal inspection procedures.

Statistical measures

The most commonly used measure in the UK is the 'incidence rate', which is the number of reportable injuries (involving absence for over three days) per 1000 manual workers employed; thus:

$$\text{Incidence rate} = \frac{\text{Number of reportable injuries in period}}{\text{Average number of manual employees in period}} \times 1000$$

Other measures include the 'frequency rate', which is the number of disabling injuries per 1,000,000 man-hours, and the 'severity rate', which is the days lost through accidents per 1,000,000 hours worked.

The problem with these indices is that they deal only with reportable accidents, and in smaller companies the number of such accidents may be so small that the statistics do not provide a reliable indication of trends. It may be better in these circumstances to measure the incidence of all accidental injuries, or even of all accidents causing damage.

Measuring the cost

These statistics also ignore the cost of accidents, and those who advocate the 'total loss control' approach emphasize the need to look at accidents from the point of view of their cost to the company as a whole as well as their effect on the individuals who sustain them. This approach, they assert, provides a much greater incentive for commercially minded managements to take action.

The costs of accidents, other than the cost of insurance and special medical and safety facilities, can be allocated under the following headings:

1. wages paid to injured workers who are off work;
2. wages paid to workers who are not personally involved in the accident but lose time as a result of it;
3. damage to machines, equipment, materials and buildings;
4. loss of production because of damage or because workers are less effective when they return to work after an accident;
5. salaries paid to managers, supervisors and other staff dealing with the accident and investigating its cause;
6. other costs, including public library claims, additional overtime, and the cost of renting equipment.

If these costs can be analysed (which could prove difficult), it is possible to work out a 'cost severity rate', which is the total cost of accidents per 1,000,000 man-hours worked, thus:

$$\text{Cost severity rate} = \frac{\text{Total cost of accidents over a period}}{\text{Total man-hours of production and maintenance during the period}} \times 1,000,000$$

Conclusions

Inspection, investigations, reports, and statistics are all necessary to the improvement of health and safety performance. But they depend for their effectiveness entirely upon the will-power of the managers and supervisors concerned, who in turn depend upon the leadership exercised by top management. That is why the Robens Committee report on Safety and Health at Work emphasized that:

> Promotion of safety and health at work is an essential function of good management. We are not talking about legal responsibilities. The job of a director or senior manager is to manage. The boardroom has the influence, power and resources to take initiatives and to set the pattern.[2]

References

1. Heinrich, H W *Industrial Accident Prevention.* McGraw-Hill, New York, 1959.
2. *Safety and Health at Work: Report of the Committee 1970–72* Cmnd 5034, Her Majesty's Stationery Office, London, 1972.

35

Employee Welfare

Why welfare?

Welfare includes such activities as private advice on any type of personal problem; assistance with problems of health or sickness; special responsibilities for young people and elderly and retired staff; and the provision of sports and social facilities. The first question to be answered is why any organization should be concerned with these matters.

The case against welfare

The arguments against are obvious. Welfare implies 'do-gooding'; the personnel management fraternity has spent many years trying to shake off its association with what it, and others, like to think of as at best peripheral and at worst redundant welfare activities. Welfare is provided for by the state services — why should industrial, commercial or public sector organizations duplicate what is already there? The private affairs of employees and their out-of-work interests should not be the concern of their employers. It is selfish to maintain large playing fields and erect huge sports pavilions if they are going to be used by a minute proportion of staff for a very limited period of time — the space and facilities could be better used by the community. The argument that the provision of welfare services increases the loyalty and motivation of employees has long been exploded. If welfare services are used at all, they are taken for granted. Gratitude is not a prime motivating factor.

The case for welfare

The case against welfare is formidable; the last point is particularly telling and there is some truth in each of the others — although there are limitations to their validity. State welfare services are, in theory, available to all, but the ability of social workers to give individual advice, especially on problems arising from work, is limited in terms both of time and knowledge. It is all too easy for people to fall into the cracks existing in the edifice of the welfare state.

The case for welfare has to rely mainly on the abstract grounds of the social responsibility of organizations for those who work in them. This is not paternalism in the Victorian sense — turkeys at Christmas — nor in the Japanese sense, where the worker's whole life centres on the employer. Rather, it is simply the realization that in exchange for offering their services, employees are entitled to rather more than their pay, statutory fringe benefits and healthy and safe systems of work. They are also entitled to consideration as human beings, especially when it is remembered that many of their personal problems arise in the context of work and are best dealt with there. People's worries arise from work — about security, pay, health, and relationships with others. But they also bring their personal problems to work; and many of these cannot be solved without reference to the situation there — they may require time off to deal with aged parents or sick wives, or advice on how to solve their problems and so minimize interference with their work.

The argument for welfare services at work was well put by Martin:

> Staff spend at least half their waking time at work or in getting to it or leaving it. They know they contribute *to* the organization when they are reasonably free from worry, and they feel, perhaps inarticulately, that when they are in trouble they are due to get something *back* from the organization. People are entitled to be treated as full human beings with personal needs, hopes and anxieties; they are employed as *people*; they bring themselves to work, not just their hands, and they cannot readily leave their troubles at home.[1]

The social argument for welfare is the most compelling one, but there is also an economic argument. Increases in morale or loyalty may not result in commensurate or, indeed, in any increases in productivity, but undue anxiety can result in reduced effectiveness. Even if welfare services cannot increase individual productivity, they can help to minimize decreases. Herzberg's two-factor model, in effect, placed welfare among the hygiene factors, but he did not underestimate the importance of 'hygiene' as a means of eliminating or at least reducing causes of anxiety or dissatisfaction.

A further practical argument in favour of welfare is that a reputation for showing concern helps to improve the local image of the firm as a good employer and thus assists in recruitment. Welfare may not directly increase productivity, but it may add to general feelings of satisfaction with the firm and cut down labour turnover.

A case for welfare therefore exists, and the real question is not 'Why welfare?' but 'What sort of welfare?' This question needs to be answered in general terms before discussing the type of welfare services that can be provided and how they should be organized.

What sort of welfare?

Welfare services fall into two categories:

1. Individual or personal services in connection with sickness, bereavement, domestic problems, employment problems, and elderly and retired employees.
2. Group services, which consist of sports and social activities, clubs for retired staff and benevolent organizations.

Principles of personal casework

Individual services require personal casework, and the most important principle to adopt is that this work should aim to help individuals to help themselves. The employer, manager, or welfare officer should not try to stand between individuals and their problems by taking them out of their hands. Emergency action may sometimes have to be taken on behalf of individuals, but, if so, it should be taken in such a way that they can later cope with their own difficulties. Welfare action must start on the basis that disengagement will take place at the earliest possible moment when individuals can, figuratively, stand on their own two feet. This does not mean that follow-up action is unnecessary, but it is only to check that things are going according to plan, not to provide additional help unless something is seriously wrong.

Personal services should be provided when a welfare need is established, and a welfare need exists where it is clear that help is required, that it cannot be given more effectively from another source, and that the individual is likely to benefit from the services that can be offered.

In an organizational setting, an essential element in personnel casework services is confidentiality. There is no point in offering help or advice to people if they think that their personal problems are going to be revealed to others, possibly to the detriment of their future careers. This is the argument for having specialized welfare officers in organizations large enough to be able to afford them. They can be detached in a way that line managers and even personnel managers cannot be.

Principles for providing group services

Group services, such as sports or social clubs, should not be laid on because they are 'good for morale'. There is no evidence that they are. They are costly and should be provided only if there is a real need and demand for them, arising from a very strong community spirit in a company or lack of local facilities. In the latter case, the facilities should be shared in an agreed and controlled way with the local community.

Individual welfare services

Sickness

These services aim to provide help and advice to employees absent from work for long periods because of illness. The practical reason for providing them is that they should help to speed the return of the employee to work, although it is not part of the welfare function to check up on possible malingerers. The social reason is to provide employees with support and counsel where a welfare need exists. In this context, a welfare need exists where employees cannot help themselves without support and where such aid is not forthcoming from the state medical or welfare services or the employees' own families.

Welfare needs can be established by keeping in touch with an absent employee. This should be done by rushing round as soon as anyone has been absent for more than, say, ten days or has exhausted sickness benefit from work. It is generally better to write to sick absentees, expressing general concern and good wishes for a speedy recovery and reminding them that the firm can provide help if they wish, or simply asking them if they would like someone to visit them — with a stamped, addressed envelope for their reply. Such letters should preferably be sent by the employee's line manager.

There will be some cases where the employee is reluctant to request help or a visit, and the company may have to decide whether a visit should be made to establish if help is required. This will be a matter of judgement based on the known facts about employees and their circumstances.

Visits can be made by the line manager, a personnel officer, or a specialized full- or part-time welfare officer. Alternatively, arrangements can be made for a colleague to pay the visit. The aims of the visit should be, first, to show employees that their company and colleagues are concerned about their welfare; second, to alleviate any loneliness they may feel; and, third, to provide practical advice or help. The latter may consist of putting them in touch with suitable organizations or ensuring that such organizations are informed and take action. Or more immediate help may be provided to deal with pressing domestic problems.

Bereavement

Bereavement is a time when many people need all the help and advice they can get. The state welfare services may not be able to assist and families are often non-existent or unhelpful. Established welfare organizations in industry, commerce or the public sector attach a lot of importance to this service. The advice may often be no more than putting the bereaved employee or the widow or widower of an employee in touch with the right organizations, but it is often extended to help with funeral arrangements and dealing with will and probate matters.

Domestic problems

Domestic problems seem the least likely area for welfare services. Why should the company intervene, even when asked, in purely private matters? If, for example, employees get into debt, that is surely their own affair. What business is it of the company?

These are fair questions. But employers who have any real interest in the welfare of their staff cannot ignore appeals for help. The assistance should not consist of bailing people out of debt whenever they get into trouble, or acting as an amateur marriage guidance or family casework officer. But, in accordance with the basic principle of personal casework already mentioned, employees can be counselled on how to help themselves or where to go for expert advice. A counselling service at work, whether operated by full-time welfare officers or by others on a part-time basis, can do an immense amount of good simply by providing an opportunity for employees to talk through their problems with a disinterested person. There is a limit to how much can or should be done in the way of allowing employees to pour out their troubles but, used with discretion, it is a valuable service.

Employment problems

Employment problems should normally be solved by discussion between the individual and his or her boss, or through the company's grievance procedure. There may be times, however, when employees have problems over interpersonal relations, or feelings of inadequacy, about which they want to talk to a third party. Such counselling talks, as a means of relieving feelings and helping people to work through their problems for themselves, can do a lot of good, but extreme caution must be displayed by any company officials who are involved. They must not cut across line management authority, but, at the same time, they must preserve the confidentiality of the discussion. It is a delicate business, and where it affects superior/subordinate relationships, it is one in which the giving of advice can be dangerous. The most that can be done is to provide a counselling service which gives employees an opportunity to talk about their problems and allows the counsellor to suggest actions the employee can take to put things right. Counsellors must not comment on the actions of anyone else who is involved. They can comment only on what the employee who seeks their help is doing or might do.

Elderly and retired employees

Welfare for elderly employees is primarily a matter of preparing them for retirement and dealing with any problems they have in coping with their work. Preparation for retirement is a valuable service that many firms offer. This may be limited to advising on the classes and facilities local authorities provide for people prior to retirement, or when they have retired, or it may be extended to sponsoring special classes held during working hours. Some companies have made special provision for elderly employees by setting aside jobs or work areas for them. This has its dangers. Treating employees as special cases ahead of their time may make them over-aware of their condition or too dependent on the services provided for them. There is everything to be said for treating elderly employees as normal workers, even though the health and safety services may take particular care to ensure that the age of the worker does not increase the danger of accident or industrial disease.

Retired employees, particularly those with long service, deserve the continuing interest of their former employer. The interest need not be oppressive, but continuing sick visiting can be carried out, and social occasions can be provided for them.

Group welfare services

Group welfare services mainly consist of sports and social clubs, although some companies still support various benevolent societies which provide additional help and finance in times of need.

A massive investment in sports facilities is usually of doubtful value unless there is nothing else in the neighbourhood and, in accordance with the principles mentioned earlier, the company is prepared to share its facilities with the local community. In a large company in a large town, it is very difficult to develop feelings of loyalty towards the company teams or to encourage people to use the sports club. Why should they support an obscure side when their loyalties have always been directed to the local club? Why should they travel miles when they have perfectly adequate facilities near at hand? In the writer's experience, such clubs are usually supported by small cliques who have little or no influence over the feelings of other employees, who leave the enthusiasts to get on with whatever they are doing.

The same argument applies to social clubs, especially those forced on employees by paternalistic companies. It is different when they arise spontaneously from the needs of employees. If they want to club together, then the company should say good luck to them and provide them with a reasonable amount of support. The subsidy, however, should not be complete. The clubs should generate their own funds as well as their own enthusiasm. Facilities can be provided within the firm's premises if they are needed and readily available. An investment in special facilities should be made only if there is a real likelihood of their being used regularly by a large proportion of employees. This is an area where prior consultation, before setting up the facility, and self-government, when it has been established, are essential.

Provision of welfare

It seems obvious that the personnel department should provide welfare services. Inevitably, personnel staff will be dealing with cases and providing advice because they are in constant contact with employees and may be seen to be disinterested. It is to be hoped that they will also have some expertise in counselling.

Increasingly, however, it is being recognized that employee welfare is the responsibility of line management and supervision. If the latter take on their proper role as team leaders rather than their traditional autocratic and directive role, they should be close enough to each member of their team to be aware of any personal problems affecting their work. They should be trained in identifying symptoms and at least be able to refer them for counselling if it is clear that the employee needs more help than the team leader can provide.

Welfare can be provided for either internally by means of a counselling service or externally through an agency which runs employee assistance programmes (EAPs).

Internal counselling services

Internal welfare services can be provided by permanent, full-time volunteers, as at British Telecom, which has a highly organized welfare services department dating back to its origins in the Post Office. The department employs more than 70 officers, one for each of the company's business units. Officers are recruited within the organization from all disciplines in the belief that existing employees will best understand the welfare issues most relevant to BT. No specific qualifications are required, but applicants are carefully assessed for suitability and relevant experience and, if successful, they receive up to six months' training in counselling and welfare issues on-site and at BT's own training centre. The posts are permanent, rather than secondments, and officers who have left have moved more often into other welfare-related jobs than back into their former discipline.

The welfare officer's duties include providing help and advice to BT employees coping with bereavement, disablement, psychiatric illness and housing problems, among others, and offering support to managers. They are expected to have a sound knowledge of relevant state services and benefits.

British Airways has developed the following approach relying on volunteer and seconded counsellors. The first line of contact for an employee with a problem is a 'helper' with approximately one week's training, who will identify the problem and refer the employee to a 'counsellor'. Counsellors are employees on six-month secondment from their departments who are given training in a range of counselling skills. There is a facility for cross-departmental referral, so that a helper in the engineering department can refer an employee to a counsellor in flight operations in order that employees do not have to discuss problems with close colleagues. Counsellors receive support from British Airways health services, which can take on any health-related problems such as alcoholism or drug abuse.

Employee assistance programmes

Employee assistance programmes (EAPs) originated in the US in the 1960s where they are now commonplace. The idea was slow to catch on, but is now subscribed to by more than 100 organizations, including Whitbread,

General Electric, Du Pont and the Commission for the New Towns.

There are a number of external agencies which provide EAP services. They offer, on a contractual basis, a 24-hour phone service giving employees and their families access to counselling on a range of problems including stress, alcohol and drug abuse, marital breakdown and financial and legal problems. Most services identify the problem and arrange for a relevant specialist to phone back, although face-to-face counselling may also be offered, either at local offices or at surgeries on company premises. In addition, employers may refer employees direct to the service. Where long-term treatment relating to alcohol and drug problems or psychological problems is needed, employees are referred to state services.

Confidentiality is guaranteed by all EAPs to users, although employers are usually provided with a periodic statistical report on take-up of the service, which may be broken down by sex, seniority, department or type of problem. Advocates of the programmes argue that the anonymity they offer makes them particularly suitable for use in this country since it helps overcome the traditional British reluctance to discuss personal matters. Larger EAP providers offer clients the option of reports on average statistics based on work for comparable companies. Additional services include workplace seminars on problems identified as particularly prevalent, training of managers and personnel staff and related literature. The service may be charged for at a per capita rate or according to take-up, which can be as much as 25 per cent of the workforce.

Reference

1. Martin, A O *Welfare at Work*. Batsford, London, 1967.

Part IX
Employment and Personnel Administration

This handbook emphasizes the importance of strategic consid-erations in formulating personnel policies and planning personnel programmes to achieve defined objectives. The fact remains, however, that much of personnel management is about dealing with the problems that will always arise when people work together and have to be managed, and the various services and facilities needed to ensure that both employees and the organization feel that their needs are being satisfied.

Employment policies and practices have to be developed within the legal framework, as described in Chapter 36. They include the areas of personnel administration described in Chapter 37, which are terms and conditions of employment; procedures for handling grievances, discipline, redundancies and promotions; and policies and practices concerning attendance, age and employment; ethnic monitoring; smoking; substance abuse; and AIDS.

Finally, the function of the Personnel Department is to keep personnel records and, increasingly, to develop and maintain a computerized personnel information system. This operates from a database that provides the means for achieving efficiency in personnel administration as well as the opportunity to make decisions which are founded on a deeper understanding of what is happening now and what may occur in the future.

36

The Legal Framework

Personnel management policies, procedures and practices have to operate within the legal framework provided by employment legislation and the associated case law. The aim of this chapter is to provide a broad survey of the main features of the law relating to employment as of mid-1991. The aspects considered are the following:

- contracts of employment;
- termination of employment;
- unfair dismissal;
- redundancy;
- maternity rights;
- equal pay;
- sex discrimination;
- race relations;
- health and safety.

Contracts of employment

A contract is an agreement between two or more parties which the law will enforce. Contracts may contain (1) express terms (defined in writing or orally — a contract does not have to be written down); (2) implied terms (those that can be implied into the contract of employment by nature of the relationship, by the conduct of the parties or by custom and practice); and (3) terms implied by statute (the duty of the parties to conform to statutory law). Contracts may consist of one or more of the following documents: the letter of appointment, a written statement of express terms or other documents such as employee handbooks or works rules which are expressly referred to in the letter of appointment or written statement.

The legislation on contracts deals with written particulars and changes in terms of employment.

Written particulars

Written particulars of the terms of employment must, under the Employment Protection (Consolidation) Act 1978, as amended by Schedule 2, Employment Act 1982, be given to all employees not later than 13 weeks after they start work. Employees working fewer than 16 hours a week are excluded, but those working from 8 to 15 hours a week inclusive are entitled to a written statement within 13 weeks of completing 5 years' service.

The written statement must contain or refer to particulars of the following terms:

1. name of the employer and the employee;
2. starting date;
3. commencement of continuous service;
4. the scale or rate of remuneration, or the method of calculating remuneration;
5. the intervals at which remuneration is paid (eg weekly, monthly);
6. hours of work and normal working hours;
7. entitlement to holidays, including public holidays;
8. entitlement to holiday pay, including entitlement to accrued holiday pay on terminating employment;
9. provision of sick-pay, if any;
10. pensions and pension schemes;
11. the length of notice which the employee is obliged to give and is entitled to receive to terminate his contract of employment;
12. the title of the job which the employee is employed to do;
13. the disciplinary rules which apply to the employee (or reference can be made to a document specifying these rules which is reasonably accessible to the employee) — these rules will specify:

    (a) the person to whom the employee can apply if he or she is dissatisfied with any disciplinary action;
    (b) the disciplinary procedure which will be followed, eg the various warning stages before disciplinary action is taken and the right of appeal;
    (c) a person to whom the employee can apply for the redress of any grievance relating to his or her employment and the manner in

which any such applications should be made (ie grievance procedure).

Changes in terms of employment

If there is any change in the terms of employment as specified in the statement, the change must be announced not more than one month after the change by individual notification to each employee; or by telling employees where details of changes can be seen on a notice-board or in some reasonably accessible place; or by entering the change in a specified document, provided that employees are told that this would be done in their original statement or in a subsequent change.

Termination of employment

The Employment Protection (Consolidation) Act 1978 (EPCA) states that the written particulars must specify 'the length of notice which the employee is obliged to give and entitled to receive to determine his contract of employment'. The notice required to be given by the employer to terminate the contract of employment of a person who has been continuously employed for one month or more must be not less than:

- one week's notice if the period of continuous employment is less than two years;
- one week's notice for each year of continuous employment if the period of continuous employment is two years or more but less than 12 years;
- twelve weeks' notice if the period of continuous employment is 12 years or more.

It can be given orally or in writing.

These provisions do not apply to part-timers who work for less than 16 hours a week, unless they have been employed for five years or more and work eight hours or more a week.

Unfair dismissal

The legal provisions concerning unfair dismissal are contained in the Employment Protection (Consolidation) Act 1978, as amended by the Employment Act 1980 and the Employment Act 1982. Under the legislation, an employee who has been employed for two years or more has the right not to be unfairly dismissed. Complaints by an employee that he or she has been unfairly dismissed are heard by industrial tribunals.

Definition of dismissal

Legally, dismissal takes place when:

- the employer terminates the employee's contract with or without notice – a contract can be terminated as a result of a demotion or transfer as well as a sacking;
- the employee himself terminates the contract (he resigns) with or without notice by reason of his employer's behaviour in the sense that his employer's conduct was such that the employee could not be expected to carry on his job — this is termed 'constructive dismissal';
- the employee is employed under a fixed-term contract of one year or more which is not renewed by the employer when it expires;
- an employee resigns while under notice following dismissal;
- an employee is not re-engaged after a strike, when others who were on strike have been selectively engaged;
- en employee is unreasonably refused work after pregnancy.

Basic approach

The legislation lays down that industrial tribunals should obtain answers to two fundamental questions when dealing with unfair dismissal cases:

1. Was there sufficient reason for the dismissal, ie was it fair or unfair?
2. Did the employer act reasonably in the circumstances?

Fair reasons for dismissal

Dismissals may be held by an industrial tribunal to be fair if the principal reason was one of the following:

- incapability, which covers the employee's skill, aptitude, health and physical or mental qualities;
- misconduct;
- failure to have qualifications relevant to the job;
- a legal factor that prevents the employee from continuing work, ie he or his employer would contravene some other law if he stays in his job;
- redundancy — where this has taken place in accordance with a customary or agreed redundancy procedure;
- the employee broke or repudiated his contract by going on strike — as long as he was not singled out for this treatment, ie all striking

employees were treated alike and no selective re-engagement took place;
- some other substantial reason of a kind which would justify the dismissal of an employee holding the position which the employee held.

Dismissals may be unfair if:

- the employer has failed to show that the principal reason was one of the admissible reasons as stated above, or if the dismissal was not reasonable in the circumstances (see below);
- a constructive dismissal has taken place, ie a situation in which the employer's conduct is such that the employee would be entitled to regard the contract of employment as having been repudiated by the employer;
- they are in breach of a customary or agreed redundancy procedure, and there are no valid reasons for departing from that procedure.

The Employment Act 1980 removed the onus of proof on employers to show that they had acted reasonably in treating the reason for dismissal as sufficient. The industrial tribunal is required, in considering the circumstances, to take into account the size and administrative resources of the employer's undertaking.

Reasonable in the circumstances

Even if the employer can show to a tribunal that there was good reason to dismiss the employee (ie if it clearly fell into one of the categories listed above, and the degree of incapability or misconduct was sufficient to justify dismissal), the tribunal still has to decide whether or not the employer acted in a reasonable way at the time of dismissal. The principles defining 'reasonable' behaviour on the part of an employer are as follows:

- Employees should be informed of the nature of the complaint against them.
- The employee should be given the chance to explain.
- The employee should be given the opportunity to improve, except in particularly gross cases of incapability or misconduct.
- The employee should be warned of the consequences in the shape of dismissal if specified improvements do not take place.
- The employer's decision to dismiss should be based on sufficient evidence.

- The employer should take any mitigating circumstances into account.
- The offence or misbehaviour should merit the penalty of dismissal rather than some lesser penalty.

Remedies

Industrial tribunals which find that a dismissal was unfair can make an order for reinstatement or re-engagement and state the terms on which this should take place. The tribunal can consider the possibility of compensation for unfair dismissal, but only after the possibility of reinstatement or re-engagement has been examined (see paragraph 86).

Compensation

The three kinds of compensation (as of mid-1991) which an employer might be required by a tribunal to pay are as follows:

- a basic award related to the employee's service, maximum 30×158 (£4740);
- a compensatory award to reflect the employee's loss (£8000);
- an additional award for failure to comply with a reinstatement or re-engagement order, maximum 26×158 (£4108).

The total maximum award is £16,848.

However, if failure to reinstate or re-engage followed an unfair dismissal on grounds of trade union membership or non-membership, or contravention of the Race Relations Act or the Sex Discrimination Act, the upper limit for the additional award is £8216, making a total liability for the employer of £20,956.

Redundancy

An employer who recognizes an independent trade union must consult a representative of that union about proposed redundancies. This consultation must take place before any dismissals are carried out and applies equally:

- to a non-member of the union if that union covers the group or category of employees to which the individual belongs;
- to voluntary redundancies.

This consultation should begin at the earliest opportunity, but, if 10 or more employees are to be made redundant over a relatively short period, consultation must begin not later than the following specified minimum times:

- at least 30 days if 10 or more employees may be dismissed as redundant at one establishment over a period of 30 days or less;
- at least 90 days if 100 or more employees may be dismissed as redundant at one establishment over a period of 90 days or less.

The minimum times for consultation with the unions may run concurrently with the individual periods of notice for the employees concerned.
   The employer must tell the union:

- the reasons for the proposals;
- the numbers and descriptions of employees it is proposed to dismiss as redundant;
- the total number of employees of any description employed by the employer at the establishment in question;
- the proposed method of carrying out the dismissals, taking account of any agreed procedure, including the period over which the dismissals are to take effect.

It is up to the representatives to reply to the employer. If they do, the latter must consider any points they make, reply to them and give reasons for rejecting any of them. If the representatives do not reply, the employer need take no further action.
   There may be special circumstances where it is not reasonably practicable for an employer to meet fully the requirements for minimum consultation periods, disclosure of information, or the manner of dealing with the union's representatives. In such circumstances, employers must do all they can reasonably be expected to do to meet the requirements.

Maternity rights

General provisions

Employees who are absent from work as a result of pregnancy or confinement have the following rights if they fulfil the qualifying conditions:

- statutory maternity pay;
- return to work;
- not to be unfairly dismissed because of pregnancy.

Statutory maternity pay (SMP)

Qualification
An employee qualifies for SMP if:

- she has been continuously employed for a period of at least 26 weeks ending with the 15th week before the expected week of confinement;
- she is pregnant at, or has been confined, before reaching the 11th week before the expected week of confinement;
- her normal weekly earnings are not less than the lower earnings limit in force under the Social Security Act 1975.

Notification
The employee must give 21 days' notice of her impending absence which is due to pregnancy or confinement or, if that is not reasonably practicable, such notice as is reasonably practicable. She must also provide a maternity certificate certifying that she is pregnant and stating the expected week of confinement if required by the employer.

SMP is not payable if the employee's contract has terminated before the qualifying week — the week immediately preceding the 14th week before the expected week of confinement, except when:

- the employer has dismissed the employee to avoid SMP liability and she has been continuously employed for at least eight weeks;
- the employee has been dismissed for a pregnancy-related reason (eg incapable of continuing work because of pregnancy), provided that she has been continuously employed for at least eight weeks and has had at least 26 weeks' service by the qualifying week.

Payment

SMP is payable for a maximum period of 18 weeks (the maternity pay period). SMP starts from the 11th week before the expected date of confinement unless the employee has been confined before then. It cannot start later than the sixth week before the expected week of confinement. The maternity pay period ends not later than the end of the 11th week following the expected week of confinement. SMP cannot be paid in addition to Statutory Sick-Pay.

Right to return to work

Basic rights
The right of an employee to return to work after her confinement is

subject to her fulfilling the conditions set out below. The right is to return to work with her original employer, or a successor, at any time before the end of the period of 29 weeks, beginning with the week in which the date of confinement falls, in the job in which she was employed under the original contract of employment, and on terms and conditions not less favourable than those which would have been applicable to her if she had not been absent.

If her previous job is not available because of redundancy, she is entitled to be offered a suitable and equivalent alternative job where there is a suitable available vacancy. If it is not reasonably practicable for a reason other than redundancy for an employee to be given her old job back, she may be offered suitable alternative work — this could arise if it had been possible to recruit only a permanent replacement.

A woman loses her reinstatement rights if her employer has fewer than six employees and it is not reasonably practicable to give her old job back to her or offer suitable alternative work.

Subject to the provisions set out above, if the same job is not offered, ie one in which the nature of the work is in accordance with her contract — the employee is entitled to claim unfair dismissal.

Conditions for entitlement

An employee is entitled to return to work within 29 weeks after having had her baby if she satisfies the following requirements:

1. She continues to be employed up to the 11th week before the expected week of confinement.
2. She has been continuously employed for at least two years at the beginning of the 11th week.
3. She supplies a medical certificate as to the expected week of confinement if so required by the employer.
4. She informs her employer:

    (a) that she will be absent from work because of her expected confinement;
    (b) that she intends to return to work;
    (c) of the expected week of confinement, at least 21 days before taking maternity leave or as soon thereafter as is reasonably practicable.

5. Within 29 weeks from the date of her confinement, she notifies her employer at least 21 days in advance of the date on which she intends to return.

6.   When requested by her employer in writing not earlier than 49 days after the expected week or date of confinement, she provides written confirmation of her intention to return to work within 14 days of receiving the request or as soon thereafter as is reasonably practicable.

Postponement of return to work
An employee may postpone her return by a further four weeks if she supplies a medical certificate for absence. If an employee cannot return because of an interruption of work arising from a strike or other cause, she can delay her return beyond the statutory period of 29 weeks by up to 28 days after the end of the interruption. The employer may delay the date of return by up to four weeks after the date notified by the employee.

Dismissal rights

A woman with two years' continuous service who works 16 hours or more a week (five years' service for those working more than eight but fewer than 16 hours a week) has the right:

- not to be dismissed because of pregnancy;
- to be given other suitable work if she cannot do her own work and there is a suitable vacancy.

A pregnant employee can be dismissed only if any of the following conditions apply:

- The dismissal is fair in accordance with unfair dismissal legislation and is not because of or connected with her pregnancy.
- She is incapable of doing her work properly because of her pregnancy and no suitable alternative work is available.
- Continuing at work would contravene an enactment relating to pregnant women and no suitable alternative work is available.

Equal pay

The Equal Pay Act 1970, as amended by the Equal Pay (Amendment) Regulations 1983, requires equal treatment in respect of pay for men and women in the same employment when women are employed on:

- like work with men;
- work rated as equivalent with that of men;
- work of equal value to that of men.

The equality clause

An equality clause specifies that women and men will be paid the same when the work is like, equivalent, or of equal value. If an equality clause does not exist in the contract of employment, it is assumed to have one. An employee who alleges that his or her employer is in breach of the actual or assumed equality clause must show both:

- that there is or was a comparator of the opposite sex in the same employment (either on like work, on work rated as equivalent or on work of equal value);
- that the contract of the comparator contains a clause which is more favourable to him or her than the equivalent clause of the complainant's contract or, alternatively, that the comparator's contract contains a beneficial clause which is not present in the complainant's contract.

If the complainant shows the above breach, the employer has a defence only if it can be shown that there is a genuine material difference not based on sex between the two cases.

Like work

A woman is regarded as being on like work with a man if her work and his are of the same or of a broadly similar nature, and the differences between the things that she does and the things that he does are not of practical importance in relation to the terms and conditions of employment. When making comparisons between men's and women's work, account should be taken of the frequency or otherwise with which any such differences occur in practice as well as the nature and extent of the differences.

Equal value

A woman is to be regarded as employed on work of equal value with a man if her work is, in terms of the demands made on her (for instance, under such headings as effort, skill and decisions), of equal value to that of a man in the same employment. A claim can be made under the equal value provision only if it cannot be made under the like work or work of equivalent value measures. In a tribunal hearing the man with whom the woman wants to compare herself must be identified and, if the tribunal decides that there are reasonable grounds for determining the work is of equal value, a report must be commissioned from an independent expert as to the relative worth of the jobs before determining the question.

Sex discrimination

The Sex Discrimination Acts 1975 and 1986 aim to make certain kinds of sex discrimination and discrimination on the grounds of marriage unlawful.

Definition of discrimination

Discrimination on the grounds of sex takes place when, in similar circumstances, a man or woman is:

- treated less favourably than persons of the opposite sex (direct discrimination); and/or
- unjustifiably required to comply with a rule which, though applying equally to men and women, has unequal effects on them (indirect discrimination).

Discrimination on grounds of marital status is unlawful, where the discrimination is against a married person, eg a 'marriage bar' would be unlawful. Discrimination also occurs when a person is victimized for either bringing proceedings or giving evidence or information with regard to the Sex Discrimination or Equal Pay Acts.

Discrimination in employment

It is unlawful for an employer to discriminate on the grounds of sex or marital status in relation to:

- who is offered employment;
- the terms under which employment is offered and the benefits and facilities offered;
- the provision of opportunities for promotion, transfer or training and other benefits;
- dismissal or other detrimental acts (eg placing employees on short-time).

Discrimination is permitted if the sex of a person is a genuine occupational qualification. The Act gives the following circumstances in which discrimination for this reason would be allowable:

- where authentic male or female characteristics are required, eg modelling or acting;
- in order to preserve decency or privacy, eg lavatory attendants;
- where the person has to sleep on the premises and it is not possible to

provide separate sleeping and sanitary facilities for men and women;
- where the nature of the establishment requires the job to be done by a man or woman, eg a hospital or a prison;
- where personal, welfare or educational services can be provided only by a man or a woman;
- where the job needs to be held by a man because of health, safety or welfare legislation restricting the employment of women;
- where the work is carried out by a married couple.

Discrimination and retirement

Since 7 November 1987, or earlier by order, it has been unlawful for an employer to:
- set different compulsory retirement ages for men and women;
- discriminate on grounds of sex in promotion, transfer and training in relation to retirement;
- demote or dismiss a woman for reasons connected with retirement when a comparable male employee would not have been so treated.

Discrimination in training

Employers may discriminate in favour of women or men by providing special training for them in situations where very few members of the same sex are employed.

Advertising

When advertising, it is unlawful to use a 'sexist' job description such as postman, salesgirl or stewardess unless the advertisement states that the job is open to both men and women.

Race relations

The Race Relations Act 1976 prohibits discrimination on racial grounds and between racial groups, but it excludes discrimination based on religion, politics or culture. The Act applies to actual discriminatory practices or direct discrimination and to circumstances in which an employer operates potentially discriminatory practices which would result in indirect discrimination if an individual were to complain of them. However, only the Commission for Racial Equality can bring proceedings on these grounds.

Direct discrimination

A person discriminates against a person if, on racial grounds, he treats that person less favourably than he treats other persons.

Indirect discrimination

Indirect discrimination consists of treatment which is apparently fair but in operation and effect is discriminatory. It arises when an employer applies a requirement or condition to a person which he or she applies equally to persons not in the same racial group as that other, but:

- a considerably smaller proportion of people of the same racial group as the person involved can comply with it than people not in that group; and
- the employer cannot show that the condition or requirement is justifiable on non-racial grounds; and
- it is to the detriment of the person concerned because he or she cannot comply with it.

Discrimination by way of victimization

People discriminate by way of victimization if they treat someone less favourably than they would treat other persons in the same circumstances, because the person concerned has or is suspected of having:

- brought proceedings against the discriminator under the Race Relations Act; or
- given evidence or information in relation to such proceedings; or
- made allegations that the discriminator has committed an offence under the Act, as long as the allegations are not false or have not been made in bad faith.

Discrimination in recruitment

It is unlawful to discriminate on grounds of race against a candidate:

- in the arrangements made for the purposes of determining who should be offered employment (eg racially biased advertisements); or
- in the terms on which employment is offered; or
- by refusing or deliberately omitting to offer employment.

Discrimination against existing employees

It is unlawful to discriminate on grounds of race against employees:

- in the terms of employment given to them;
- in the way in which they are afforded opportunities for promotion, transfer, training or access to any other benefits, facilities or services;
- by dismissing them or subjecting them to any other detriment.

Exceptions

Positive discrimination is allowed if it takes the form of either:

- giving employees of a particular racial group access to facilities for training;
- encouraging members of a particular racial group to apply for work in the establishment.

But such positive discrimination is lawful only if during the previous 12 months the proportion of persons doing the particular work in the particular establishment was small in comparison with the proportion of the group among either:

- all those employed at the establishment; or
- the population of the area from which the employer normally recruits for that establishment.

Note, however, that positive discrimination in favour of one racial group when deciding whom to appoint is not permitted. Advertising for a particular racial group is unlawful if this racial group possesses a genuine qualification for the job.

Enforcement

Individual complaints are dealt with by industrial tribunals. The burden of proof lies with the complainant. Employers are not liable for the discriminatory acts of their employees as long as they can prove that they have taken all the reasonable steps available to them as employers to prevent their employees from committing an offence under the Act.

A tribunal may order one or more of the following remedies where it is fair and equitable to do so:

- a declaration of the parties' rights;
- an order for the discriminator to pay compensation;

- a recommendation to take action to obviate or reduce the adverse effects of the discriminatory acts.

Health and Safety at Work etc Act (HASWA)

The main provisions of this Act are the following:

- The creation of a framework best able to unify, streamline and systematize the legal requirements for health and safety at work, both now and for the future.
- A statutory declaration of principles relating to the basic and overriding responsibilities of employers, employees and others engaged in work activities. For example, the basic duties of an employer are spelt out: to install a safe working system; to provide safe premises, a safe working environment, and safe equipment; to employ trained and competent personnel; and to give adequate instruction and supervision necessary for the job. For the employee's part, it is his or her duty to observe the legal health and safety provisions and to act with due care for himself or herself and others.
- A national authority for health and safety at work is provided for with a comprehensive range of executive powers and functions.
- The maximum use will be made of 'approved' standards and codes of practice, which are seen to be the most flexible and practical means of promoting progressively better (rather than minimum) conditions.
- Employers are required to set out written statements of their health and safety policy backed by the organization and arrangements which they have in force to further the intention of the policy. Employers are also obliged to consult with their employees on measures for promoting health and safety: this implies discussing the contents of the policy with them before it is published. Annual reports of companies registered under the Companies Act are required to include prescribed information about accidents and occupational diseases suffered by the company's employees and about preventive measures taken by the company.

Control of Substances Hazardous to Health (COSHH) Regulations

The COSHH regulations require employers to:

- assess the risks to health caused by workplace exposures to hazardous substances, taking into account the particular circumstances of the workplace, and decide what precautions are necessary (in all but the simplest cases, the assessment should be recorded). Where circumstances change, the assessment should be reviewed.

- prevent such exposures or, where this is not reasonably practicable, implement control measures.
- ensure that control measures are used and that equipment is properly maintained and procedures observed.
- where necessary, monitor atmospheric contaminants and keep records of the measurements obtained. Where records refer to individual exposures, they should be kept for 30 years, or in any other case for five years.
- in certain cases, carry out and record health surveillance.
- inform, instruct and train employees about risks and the precautions to be taken.

The data protection act

This Act requires that personal data stored in computers should be:

- held only for specified purposes;
- not disclosed in a manner incompatible with those purposes;
- adequate, relevant and not excessive in relation to these purposes;
- accurate, up to date and not held for longer than is necessary for those purposes;
- available for inspection at reasonable intervals by individuals concerned who are entitled to be informed of what personal data is held relating to them;
- maintained securely.

37

Employment Practices and Procedures

Employment practices and procedures need to be defined in the following areas:

- terms and conditions of employment;
- contracts of employment;
- grievances;
- discipline;
- redundancy;
- transfers;
- promotions;
- attendance management;
- age and employment;
- sexual harassment;
- ethnic monitoring;
- smoking;
- substance abuse at work;
- AIDS.

For further information on employment practices, refer to Warren's[1] *Personnel Administration Manual*.

Terms and conditions of employment

Terms and conditions of employment which apply generally or to groups of employees need to be defined in the areas included in the contract of employment as described below.

Contracts of employment

Individual contracts of employment must satisfy the provisions of contracts of employment legislation (see Chapter 36). They will include a statement of the capacity in which the person is employed and the name or job title of the individual to whom he or she is responsible. They will also include details of pay, allowances, hours, holidays, leave and pension arrangements and refer employees to relevant company policies, procedures and works rules.

The basic information that should be included in a written contract of employment varies according to the level of job, but the following checklist sets out the typical headings:

1. job title;
2. duties, including a phrase such as 'The employee will perform such duties and will be responsible to such person, as the Company may from time to time direct';
3. date when continuous employment starts and basis for calculating service;
4. rate of pay, allowances, overtime and shift rates, method of payment;
5. hours of work including lunch break and overtime and shift arrangements;
6. holiday arrangements:

   (a) days paid holiday per year;
   (b) calculation of holiday pay;
   (c) qualifying period;
   (d) accrual of holidays and holiday pay;
   (e) details of holiday year;
   (f) dates when holidays can be taken;
   (g) maximum holiday that can be taken at any one time;
   (h) carry-over of holiday entitlement;
   (i) public holidays;

7. sickness:

   (a) pay for time lost;
   (b) duration of sickness payments;
   (c) deductions of national insurance benefits;
   (d) termination due to continued illness;
   (e) notification of illness (medical certificate);

8. length of notice due to and from employee;
9. grievance procedure (or reference to it);
10. disciplinary procedure (or reference to it);

11. works rules (or reference to them);
12. arrangements for terminating employment;
13. arrangements for union membership (if applicable);
14. special terms relating to rights to patents and designs, confidential information and restraints on trade after termination of employment;
15. employer's right to vary terms of the contract subject to proper notification being given.

Grievances

It is often said that the best way to settle grievances is to get the facts and then settle on an equitable solution. This is easier said than done. The problem is frequently hedged round with matters of opinion, and it is essential to attempt to penetrate the façade — the ostensible problem or grievance — and reach the real feelings. In any case, facts are always subject to interpretation and feelings are, by definition, subjective. It is not possible to reach behind the façade or achieve the cooperation of the individual in solving the problem if an autocratic or directive approach is adopted —ie *telling* someone what is wrong and how to improve. More cooperation and more information will be obtained if the following non-directive approach is used:

1. *Listen with intelligence and sympathy.* People in difficulty cannot fail to benefit if they are allowed to discuss their problems with a sympathetic listener: attentive silence is often the interviewer's best contribution.
2. *Define the problem.* Ideally, interviewees define the problems for themselves with the aid of sympathetic listening and brief, well-directed questions. It is essential to get the problem clearly stated and accepted as a problem by interviewees as well as interviewers. A considerable amount of listening and questioning may be necessary before the point becomes clear since strong emotions and clarity of expression seldom go together. When you think you understand the interviewee's viewpoint, it is often helpful to ask a summarizing question — 'Is that what you mean?' — without stating any moral judgement at this stage.
3. *Stay alert and flexible.* Plan the interview in advance to decide broadly how you will tackle it, but be prepared to change direction in the light of new information.
4. *Observe behaviour.* While listening to the words being spoken, take note

of gestures, manner, tone and inflexion, pauses and other ways of responding.

5. *Conclude the interview.* Try to get the interviewees to summarize their problem and suggest a possible solution. If this response is not forthcoming, help them either by a summarizing question or a crystallizing statement, such as 'Am I right in thinking that your problem boils down to this?'

The aim should be to get to the root of the matter and, if there is no justification for being aggrieved, let individuals work it out for themselves with prompting from the interviewer as necessary. If there is something in the complaint, time and trouble should be taken to identify causes rather than just dwelling on symptoms.

Individuals should be given the right to appeal if they feel that their complaint has not been adequately dealt with. A grievance procedure should allow people to take their case through higher levels of authority to the chief executive of the organization if they want. An example of a grievance procedure is given in Appendix R.

Discipline

In the UK the way in which disciplinary problems are handled is very much influenced by the statute law on unfair dismissal as interpreted by case law and backed up by the code of disciplinary practice and procedures in employment. Although only applicable in the UK, the regulations are based on principles of natural justice which are, or should be, universal.

When handling disciplinary problems, you should be aware of what these accepted principles of natural justice are and, building on this foundation, understand:

- the basic provisions of the law, such as the law of unfair dismissal, as summarized in Chapter 36;
- the general approach that should be used to deal with disciplinary matters as set out in the code of practice;
- the particular approaches to be used in dealing with specific branches of discipline or with cases of unsuitability, especially incapability, misconduct, absenteeism and lateness.

Natural justice

There are three basic principles which should govern the way in which you handle potential discipline problems:

1. Individuals should know the standards of performance they are expected to achieve and the rules to which they are expected to conform.
2. They should be given a clear indication of where they are failing or the rules are being broken.
3. Except in cases of gross misconduct, they should be given an opportunity to improve before disciplinary action is taken.

Four further principles governing how disciplinary cases should be dealt with have been defined in case law:

1. Individuals should know the nature of the accusation against them.
2. They should be given the opportunity to state their case.
3. The disciplinary tribunal should act in good faith.
4. Employees should be allowed to appeal.

Approach to handling disciplinary cases

The approach should be clearly governed by the principles of natural justice and the legal considerations set out above. There should be a disciplinary procedure which is understood and applied by all managers and supervisors.

A disciplinary procedure should provide for a three-stage approach before action is taken:

1. Informal oral warnings.
2. Formal oral warnings, which, in serious cases, may also be made in writing. These warnings should set out the nature of the offence and the likely consequences of further offences.
3. Final written warnings which should contain a statement that any recurrence would lead to suspension, dismissal or some other penalty.

The procedure should provide for employees to be accompanied by a colleague or shop steward at any hearing. There should also be an appeal system and a list of offences which constitute gross misconduct and may therefore lead to instant dismissal. An example of a disciplinary procedure is given in Appendix S.

Managers and supervisors should be told what authority they have to take disciplinary action. It is advisable to have all final warnings and actions approved by a higher authority. In cases of gross misconduct, supervisors and junior managers should be given the right to suspend, if higher authority is not immediately available, but not to dismiss. The importance of obtaining and recording the facts should be emphasized. Managers should always have a colleague with them when issuing a formal warning and should make a note to file of what was said on the spot.

Incapability

Incompetence can be shown to exist by comparing actual against expected performance. But where measurement is difficult, as in managerial jobs, it can still be shown if a responsible employer has come to the conclusion over a reasonable period of time that a manager is incompetent. Employees should normally be given a reasonable period to improve. But, if there is clear evidence of inherent and irredeemable incapability such that an opportunity to improve is most unlikely to have any effect, the employer can fairly and lawfully dismiss the employee without going through the whole procedure, although the complaint should have been brought to the attention of the employee over a period of time.

It is often not possible to judge performance against clearly defined standards. A gradual decline in overall competence is particularly difficult to judge and, if someone has been allowed to get away with it in the past, it becomes progressively more difficult to do anything. That is why it is better for everyone's sake to take action at the time, if only to give a warning, rather than to let things slide. A soft approach now can lead to real problems in the future. .

Those problems which are hardest to solve arise when 'the face doesn't fit' or attitudes to work are incompatible. Who is to blame if the boss cannot get on with his or her subordinates, or vice versa? How is it possible to substantiate accusations that someone is uncooperative or upsets colleagues? What is the point of warning people that things must improve or else, when the problem is one of an inherent personality characteristic which individuals may not accept as being a defect and, even if they did, could not do much about changing? In any case, people who are vaguely accused of being uncooperative frequently respond with remarks such as 'everyone is out of step but me'.

Criticisms of behaviour are difficult to make and even more difficult to back up. The only way to do it is to produce evidence of the effects of such behaviour or performance — of employees or of other people — and make them recognize the fault and work out for themselves how to overcome it. And it is no good making blunt accusations. The best approach is to spot unsatisfactory behaviour when it starts and discuss it informally, using the non-directive interviewing techniques mentioned earlier.

Redundancy

Redundancy, or what is now sometimes called 'downsizing', is the saddest and often the most difficult problem concerning people personnel managers ever have to deal with. There are five things which can be done to make it less painful:

1. Plan ahead to avoid redundancy.
2. Use other methods of reducing numbers or man-hours to avoid or minimize the effects of redundancy.
3. Call for voluntary redundancy.
4. Develop and apply a proper redundancy procedure.
5. Provide help in finding new jobs, ie 'outplacement', as it is now called.

Plan ahead

Planning ahead means anticipating future reductions in manpower needs and allowing natural wastage to take effect. A forecast is needed of the amount by which the labour force has to be reduced and the likely losses through labour turnover. Recruitment can then be frozen at the right moment to allow the surplus to be absorbed by wastage.

The problem is that forecasts are often difficult to make, and in periods of high unemployment, natural wastage rates are likely to be reduced. It is possible therefore to overestimate the extent to which they will take up the slack. It is best to be pessimistic about the time it will take to absorb future losses and apply the freeze earlier rather than later.

Ideally, steps should be taken to transfer people to other, safer jobs and retrain them where possible.

Use other methods

The other methods which can be used to avoid or at least minimize redundancy include, in order of severity:

● calling in outside work;
● withdrawing all subcontracted labour;
● reducing or preferably eliminating overtime;
● developing work-sharing: two people doing one job on alternate days or splitting the day between them;
● dismissing part-timers;
● temporary lay-offs.

Voluntary redundancy

Asking for volunteers — with a suitable pay-off — is one way of relieving the number of compulsory redundancies. The amount needed to persuade people to go is a matter of judgement. It clearly has to be more than the statutory minimum, although one inducement for employees to leave early may be the belief that they will get another job more easily than if they hang on until the last moment. Help can be provided to place them elsewhere.

One of the disadvantages of voluntary redundancy is that the wrong people might go, ie good workers who are best able to find other work. It is sometimes necessary to go into reverse and offer them a special loyalty bonus if they agree to stay on.

Outplacement

Outplacement is the process of helping redundant employees to find other work or start new careers. It may involve counselling, which can be provided by firms who specialize in this area.

Redundancy procedure

If you are forced to resort to redundancy, the problems will be reduced if there is an established procedure to follow. This procedure should have three aims:

- to treat employees as fairly as possible;
- to reduce suffering as much as possible;
- to protect management's ability to run the business effectively.

These aims are not always compatible. Management will want to retain its key workers. Trade unions, on the other hand, will want to adopt the principle of last in, first out, irrespective of the value of each employee to the company.

The following points should be included in any redundancy procedure:

1. Early warnings and consultation with unions and staff: in the UK, firms are required by law to inform the union and the Department of Employment if 10 or more employees are to be made redundant, giving at least 30 days' notice.
2. Means to be adopted to avoid or reduce redundancies, eg cutting back overtime and the use of temporary staff, short-time working, or transfers to other jobs with an appropriate trial period (4 weeks required in law).
3. The basis of selection for redundancy. The starting-point may be the

principle of last in, first out, but the right has to be reserved to deviate from this principle where selection on the basis of service would prejudice operational efficiency.

4. The basis of compensating for redundancy, ie payments made by the company which are additional to the statutory minimum.
5. The help of the company will give to redundant employees to find other work.

An example of a redundancy procedure is given in Appendix T.

Transfer procedures

Redeployment in response to changing or seasonal demands for labour is a necessary feature in any large enterprise. The clumsy handling of transfers by management, however, can do as much long-lasting harm to the climate of employee relations as ill-considered managerial actions in any other sphere of personnel practice.

Management may be compelled to move people in the interests of production. But in making the move, managers should be aware of the fears of those affected in order that they can be alleviated as much as possible.

The basic fear will be of change itself — a fear of the unknown and of the disruption of a well-established situation: work, environment, colleagues and workmates, and travelling arrangements. There will be immediate fears that the new work will make additional and unpalatable demands for extra skill or effort. There will be concern about loss of earnings because new jobs have to be tackled or because of different pay scales or bonus systems. Loss of overtime opportunities or the danger of shift or night work may also arouse concern.

Transfer policies should establish the circumstances when employees can be transferred and the arrangements for pay, resettlement and retraining. If the transfer is at the company's request and to suit the convenience of the company, it is normal to pay the employee's present rate or the rate for the new job, whichever is higher. This policy is easiest to apply in temporary transfers. It may have to be modified in the case of long-term or permanent transfers to eliminate the possibility of a multitiered pay structure emerging in the new location, which must cause serious dissatisfaction among those already employed there.

When transfers are made to avoid redundancy in the present location, the rate for the job in the new department should be paid. Employees affected in this way would, of course, be given the choice between being made redundant or accepting a lower-paid job.

The policies should also provide guidelines on how requests from employees for transfer should be treated. The normal approach should be to give a sympathetic hearing to such requests from long-serving employees, especially if the transfer is wanted for health or family reasons. But the transferred employees would have to accept the rate for the job in their new department.

The procedures for handling transfers may have to include joint consultation or discussions with workers' representatives on any major transfer programme. If regular transfers take place because of seasonal changes, it is best to establish a standard procedure for making transfers which would include payment arrangements. Individual transfers would be managed by departmental supervisors, but they should be made aware of company policies and procedures and the need to treat the human problems involved with care and consideration.

Promotion procedures

The aims of the promotion procedures of a company should be, first, to enable management to obtain the best talent available within the company to fill more senior posts and, second, to provide employees with the opportunity to advance their careers within the company, in accordance with the opportunities available and their own abilities.

In any organization where there are frequent promotional moves and where promotion arrangements cause problems, it is advisable to have a promotion policy and procedure which is known to both management and staff. The basic points that should be included in such a procedure are the following:

- Promotion vacancies should be notified to the personnel department.
- Specified vacancies should be advertised internally unless there is a recognized successor or, because of unusual requirements, there is no suitable candidate within the company.
- Departmental managers should not be allowed to refuse promotions within a reasonable time unless the individual has been in the department for less than, say, one year, or the department has recently suffered heavy losses through promotions or transfers.
- Promotion opportunities should be open to all, irrespective of race, creed, sex or marital status.

An example of a promotion procedure is given in Appendix U.

Attendance management

Attendance management is the process of minimizing lateness and absenteeism. The traditional method was to require hourly paid wage earners to clock on, and to deduct pay for lateness or unauthorized absence. There is now an increasing tendency to harmonize conditions of employment by granting full staff terms and conditions to manual workers, which includes payment when absent from work. Some 'single-status' organizations require all employees to clock on; others, such as Nissan, have abolished clocking on altogether. Whether or not harmonization has taken place or clocking on is in operation, it is still necessary to control lateness and absenteeism.

Timekeeping

The approach used by firms such as Nissan and Continental Can to control timekeeping is to rely on self-generated discipline within the group, giving the supervisor the responsibility for maintaining good timekeeping. The supervisor maintains the records (which might be computerized, as described in Chapter 38) and takes whatever action is required if the trust bestowed on employees is abused. In serious cases this could mean pay deductions and, ultimately, more stringent disciplinary action. But it is the responsibility of the supervisor to exercise leadership and develop the team spirit which will minimize such actions.

A policy on timekeeping may be negotiated with the union along the lines of the agreement made between Continental Can and its unions, as described by Wickens.[2] This included the following statement:

> The company trusts its employees to act responsibly and to be at work on time. . . . In the event of this trust being abused and the Company being dissatisfied with an employee's timekeeping record, he will be liable to be stopped pay and may be required to comply with a more rigorous form of timekeeping. He will also be liable to disciplinary action. . . . The company and the union recognize that it is in the interests of all parties to minimize lateness and will work together in whatever way necessary to this end.

Absenteeism

The control of absenteeism is also best carried out, as at Nissan and Continental Can, on the basis that employees are to be trusted. Those companies provide sickness benefit for all workers and rely upon the commitment and motivation of their employees (which they work hard at achieving) to minimize abuse. But they reserve the right to review sickness benefit if the level of sickness absence is unacceptable. At Nissan, sickness absenteeism has been remarkably low — 3 per cent compared with national averages for manual workers of from 7 to 8 per cent.

Age and employment

Recruitment, employment and training practices should take into account the following key facts about age and age discrimination as listed by the Institute of Personnel Management:[3]

- Age is a poor predictor of job performance.
- It is misleading to equate physical and mental ability with age.
- More of the population than ever before are living active, healthy lives as they get older.
- There is an increasing number of older workers in the labour market.
- Age is rarely a genuine employment requirement.
- Society's attitudes may encourage compliance with outmoded personnel practices regarding recruitment, promotion, training, redundancy and retirement.
- Reduced self-confidence, self-esteem, and motivation, together with loss or reduction of financial independence for individuals and their dependants, are some of the harmful effects of age discrimination.

Ethnic monitoring

The Commission on Racial Equality's (CRE) guide on ethnic monitoring recommends that analyses of the workforce should be conducted in sufficient detail to show whether there is under-representation in more skilled jobs and grades, as well as whether there are general concentrations of ethnic minority employees in certain jobs, levels or departments in the organization. The Institute of Personnel Management Equal Opportunities Code suggests that the most important processes to monitor are recruitment and selection since these are easily influenced by prejudice or indirect discrimination. But the proportion of ethnic minorities at different levels in the organization should also be checked regularly.

The CRE has suggested that ethnic monitoring should collect employment information under the following ethnic classifications:

- white
- black-Caribbean
- black-African
- black-other
- Indian
- Pakistani

- Bangladeshi
- Chinese
- other (those describing themselves in this category should be invited to provide further information).

The results of ethnic monitoring should be used to establish whether:

- in comparison with the workforce as a whole, or in comparison with the local labour market, ethnic minority workers are significantly under- or over-represented in any area;
- representative numbers of ethnic minorities apply for and are accepted for jobs;
- higher or lower proportions of employees from ethnic minorities leave the organization;
- there are any disparities in the proportion of members of ethnic minorities.

If necessary, positive affirmative action, as recommended by the CRE, can be taken along the following lines:

- job advertisements designed to reach members of under-represented groups;
- the use of employment agencies and careers offices in areas where these groups are concentrated;
- recruitment and training for school-leavers designed to reach members of these groups;
- encouragement to employees from these groups to apply for promotion or transfer opportunities;
- training for promotion or skill training for employees of these groups who lack particular expertise but show potential.

Sexual Harassment

Sadly, sexual harassment has always been a feature of life at work. Perhaps it is not so blatant today as it has been in the past, but it is still there, in more or less subtle forms, and it is just as unpleasant.

Persons subject to harassment can take legal action but, of course, it must be the policy of the company to make it clear that it will not be tolerated.

Problems of dealing with harassment

The first problem always met in stamping out sexual harassment is that it can be difficult to make a clear-cut case. An accusation of harassment can be hard to prove unless there are witnesses. And those who indulge in this practice usually take care to carry it out on a one-to-one basis. In this situation, it may be a case of one person's word against another's. The harasser, almost inevitably a man, resorts to two defences: one, that it did not take place ('it was all in her mind'); and two, that if anything did take place, it was provoked by the behaviour of the female. In these situations, whoever deals with the case has to exercise judgement and attempt, difficult though it may be, to remove any prejudice in favour of the word of the man, the woman, the boss or the subordinate.

The second problem is that victims of sexual harassment are often unwilling to take action and in practice seldom do so. This is because of the factors mentioned above about the difficulty of proving their case. But they may also feel that they will not get a fair hearing and are worried about the effect making such accusations will have on how they are treated by their boss or their colleagues in future — whether or not they will have made their case.

The third and possibly the most deep-rooted and difficult problem of all, is that sexual harassment can be part of the culture of the organization — a way of life, a 'norm', practised at all levels.

Solutions

There are no easy solutions to these problems. It may be very hard to eradicate sexual harassment completely. But an effort must be made to deal with it and the following approaches should be considered:

1. Issue a clear statement by the chief executive that sexual harassment will not be tolerated. The absolute requirement to treat all people equally, irrespective of sex, role, creed, sexual orientation or disability, should be one of the fundamental values of the organization. This should be reinforced by the explicit condemnation of harassment as a direct and unacceptable contravention of that value.
2. Back up the value statement with a policy directive on sexual harassment which spells out in more detail how the company deplores it, why it is not acceptable and what people who believe they are being subjected to harassment can do about it.
3. Reinforce the value and policy statements by behaviour at senior level which demonstrates that they are not simply words but that these exhortations have meaning.
4. Ensure that the company's policy on harassment is stated clearly in

induction courses and is conveyed to everyone in the form of a strong reminder on promotion.

5. Create a special procedure for hearing complaints about sexual harassment. It is probably best to have a panel on which, of course, both sexes are represented.

6. Ensure that hearings are conducted fairly, both parties being given an equal opportunity to put their case.

7. Where sexual harassment has taken place, crack down on it. It should be stated in the policy that it is regarded as gross industrial misconduct and, if it is proved, makes the individual liable to instant dismissal. Less severe penalties may be reserved for minor cases but there should always be a warning that repetition will result in dismissal.

8. Ensure that where action has been taken, people hear about it. There is no need to publish the case on notice boards or in the company newsletter, and the name of the victim must never be mentioned. There is, however, no harm in letting the word get around that the company means business when it says it will not tolerate this type of behaviour.

Smoking

Smoking policies at work are designed to provide employees with a healthy and efficient workplace and to avoid conflict. A smoking policy should be developed in consultation with staff and may involve the use of an opinion survey. Most smokers agree to the right of non-smokers to work in air free from tobacco smoke. Smoking policies can involve a total ban on all smoking except, usually, in a smoking-permitted area away from the workplace. Sometimes, by agreement, there is a partial ban with separate working areas for those who wish to smoke. Kitchens and lifts are always non-smoking areas and rest rooms generally are.

It is sometimes appropriate to introduce smoking bans in stages, starting by restricting smoking in meeting rooms, corridors and canteens before extending the restriction to other communal and work areas.

Substance abuse

Substance abuse is the use of alcohol, drugs or other substances which cause difficulties at work such as absenteeism, low performance standards and interpersonal problems such as unpredictable reactions to criticism, paranoia, irritability, avoiding colleagues, borrowing money or physical or verbal abuse of colleagues. A policy on how to deal with incidents of substance abuse is necessary because:

- most employers have some employees with a drink problem and possibly a drug problem;
- substance abuse may be a result of work pressures, for which employers must take some responsibility;
- employers are required to maintain a safe and healthy work environment.

The Institute of Personnel Management has produced guidelines for a substance-abuse policy which suggest that the following issues are the ones most likely to be covered:

- an assurance that employees identified as having abuse problems will be offered advice and other necessary assistance;
- any reasonable absence from work necessary to receive treatment will be granted under the organization's sickness scheme provided that there is full cooperation from the employee;
- an opportunity to discuss the matter once it has become evident or suspected that work performance is being affected by substance-related problems;
- the right to be accompanied at any discussion by a friend or employee representative;
- the right to full confidentiality;
- the provision of agencies to whom an employee can be referred for help or a commitment to provide the same expertise where employers operate their own treatment or counselling services;
- the safeguarding of all employment rights during any reasonable period of treatment, including the right, if proven capable, of returning to the same job or to suitable alternative employment;
- the links between substance-abuse policy and the disciplinary procedure;
- the policy to deal with subsequent recurrences (recurrences will be given due consideration and evaluated on their merits);
- the procedure for monitoring, evaluating and reviewing the policy;
- the designation of responsibilities for ensuring that the policy is carried out, and the selection of the person primarily responsible for its implementation;
- a commitment to an employee education programme, and a training programme for designated staff to provide them with the skills and knowledge necessary to carry out their duties under the policy.

AIDS

There are no logical reasons why AIDS should be treated differently from any other diseases which employees may be carrying, many of which are contagious and some of which are fatal. However, AIDS is a new, frightening and threatening disease which has received enormous publicity, not all of which has been accurate. Because of this fact it is necessary to develop a company policy, which might include the following points:

1. The risks of infection through workplace contact are negligible.
2. Where the occupation does involve blood contact as in laboratories, hospitals, and doctors' surgeries, the special precautions advised by the Health and Safety Commission will be implemented.
3. Employees who know that they are infected with HIV will not be obliged to disclose the fact to the company, but if they do, the fact will remain completely confidential.
4. There will be no discrimination against anyone with, or at risk of acquiring, AIDS.
5. Employees infected by HIV or suffering from AIDS will be treated no differently from anyone else suffering from a serious illness.

References

1. Warren, C *Personnel Administration Manual*. Kogan Page, London, 1990.
2. Wickens, P *The Road to Nissan*. Macmillan, London, 1987.
3. Institute of Personnel Management *Age and Employment*. London, 1991.

38

Computerized Personnel Information Systems

Background

The rapid expansion of information technology in recent years, especially in the use of microcomputers or PCs (personal computers) and the development of new facilities for using databases more flexibly and for networking, have combined to produce what Colin Richards-Carpenter of the Institute of Manpower Studies (IMS) has described as 'the astonishing growth in computer applications within the personnel field.'[1] This growth has produced increasingly sophisticated packages covering almost every aspect of human resource management.

Against this background, this chapter deals with:

1. The overall role of the computerized personnel information system (CPIS);
2. CPIS applications in such areas as personnel records, human resource planning, salary modelling and expert systems;
3. selecting the system;
4. developing the system;
5. operating the system.

The role of the computerized personnel information system (CPIS)

The role of a CPIS is to:

- improve administrative efficiency by speeding up the provision of data, by reducing the resources required to carry out routine administration, and by freeing resources for the higher-value activities which are fundamental to the success of business management;

- provide decision support — information which gives a factual basis for decisions concerning the planning, acquisition, development, utilization and remuneration of human resources.

Strategic decision making

Peter Wickens,[2] Director of Personnel and Information Systems at Nissan, has identified from his experience the following ways in which computerized information can assist strategic decision making:

- the organizational structure and how it might be modified to meet future needs;
- determination of performance and personality characteristics of the people who will be successful in the organization;
- analysis of future recruitment requirements based on the planned development of the company, labour turnover, promotions, etc;
- assessment of the 'health' of the organization measured by attitude surveys, turnover statistics, exit interviews, etc;
- determination of future training and development needs and the establishment of a continuous development programme to ensure that the company has people equipped to perform the tasks necessary for the development of the company;
- monitoring of performance and reward systems to ensure that the profiles between departments are maintained within previously established guidelines;
- health and safety management so as to determine problem areas and facilitate subsequent action;
- attendance management.

Fulfilling the role

A CPIS fulfils its role by:

1. *Data capture* — maintaining a database of personnel records and other information.
2. *Administrative actions* — using the database to:
    (a) produce listings of employees by age, length of service, job category, job grade, rate of pay, etc;
    (b) generate reports analysing distribution in such areas as relationships between age or service and job grade or pay;
    (c) initiate and print internal memoranda and documents such as notification of pay increases or contracts of employment;

(d) produce external letters such as offers of employment;

(e) use electronic mailing facilities to transmit data and correspondence between terminals.

3. *Decision support* — using the database to answer 'what if?' and other *ad hoc* enquiries, to carry out modelling and trend analysis and to produce projections.

Applications

The main applications for which a CPIS can be used are described below under the following headings:

- personnel records;
- integrated systems;
- human resource planning;
- recruitment;
- reward management;
- organization planning and development;
- performance management;
- human resource management;
- absence control;
- equal opportunity monitoring;
- competency modelling;
- expert systems.

Personnel records

The database

The personnel record system is essentially the electronic file, but it also provides the database for the whole CPIS.

A database is a collection of integrated data stored so that it can be accessed by authorized users with simple, user-friendly dialogs, ie information retrieval devices. The physical database is the form in which data are actually held in the storage media. From this can be developed one or more logical databases which comprise the database as viewed by the user. The structure of the data in a logical database need not be the same as in the physical database. The two main types of database are:

1. *The relational database.* This comprises a collection of relations between different items of data which can be manipulated and reconfigured by the database management system. This provides a high degree of flexibility in the use of the system.

2. *The hierarchical or network database.* This is a database which allows records to be related to one another in a predetermined network. In this system, the data structure is defined at the outset, and after that the links between records are automatically forged. The advantages claimed for this type of database are that it is easier for the user to operate the system, no duplicate information needs to be kept, mass updates are immediately reflected throughout the database, and it is quicker to operate than a relational one, particularly as the database expands. But a hierarchical database could be less flexible than a relational one.

Types of records

The main types of personnel records, as described below, are the following:

- personal details;
- job details;
- employment contracts;
- salary details;
- performance appraisal;
- contacts and addresses;
- employee transactional data.

```
┌11:19──────────────────PERSONAL DETAILS───────────────22/03/88┐
│Surname    P...................  Initials   ...  Reference No     .........│
│Forenames  ...............       ................................. Title    ....│
│Known as   ...............       Prev Sname .................... Sex       . │
│Birthdate  / /      Age __   Mar Status ..  Children   0. Mobility . │
│Eth Orig   ../...    Nationality .../...     Union        ..........│
│Join Date  / /       Int Tel No  .............  Car Reg     ..........│
│Address                                       Post Code   ..........│
│           ...............................    Telephone   .............│
│           ...............................    Free Field1 ...............│
│           ...............................    Free Field2 ...............│
├──────────────────────────────────────────────────────────────┤
│Newman       CE  :  073 │
│Njie         A   :  255 │
│O'Brien      JR  :  204 │
│O'Neill      PM  :  228 │
│Parrott      JA  :  229 │
│Pataki       L   :  249 │
│Patel        M   :  221 │
│Peluso       L   :  226 │
└──────────────────────────────────────────────────────────────┘
```

Figure 38.1 A personal details screen — Percom PMS system

```
┌─00:07────────────────────────JOB DETAILS────────────────────────01/01/80─┐
│Job No  PD.... Job Family Code DIR...    Job Title   Production Director......│
│Dept    PROD.. Production                Div MFG     Manufacturing           │
│Company SI     Sunrise Industries Plc    CstC AB123. Automation Budget 123   │
│Grade   DIR... Date 10/06/83 ITB         JobT D..... Director                │
│Rep to  MD.... Managing Director_____  Loc  WAR    Warrington              │
│        036____ Powell_____           Int Tel No 157......... FTE 1.0000 │
│Free Field1    ...................       Free Field3 ..........              │
│Free Field2    ...................       Free Field4 .......... Vac No ......│
│                                                                            │
├────────────────────────────────────────────────────────────────────────────┤
│Surname  Peters              Initials FG   Reference No          090        │
│Assignment Date      06/04/1986                                             │
│                                                                            │
│                                                                            │
│                                                                            │
│                                                                            │
└────────────────────────────────────────────────────────────────────────────┘
```

Figure 38.2 A job details screen — Percom PMS system

Personal details

Personal details contain all the information which is personal to the employee such as sex, a 'known as name', marital status, etc. An example of a personal details screen, as provided by Percom's PMS system, which uses a hierarchical database, is shown in Figure 38.1.

The Percom system provides a standard screen for these personal details and also a 'window', which enables additional information to be displayed. In this example, the top half comprises the standard screen which includes a range of personal information, including ethnic origin and union membership, and two free fields to record other personal duties such as first aider, fire officer, shop steward, or registered disabled. The lower half of the screen caters for data which can usefully be stored in this basic record such as job, salary and grade details.

Job details

This screen (Figure 38.2) gives details of the job the employee holds rather than the employee, ie the establishment record. Each job is identified by a code number and can be classified into larger generic groups. In this example the production manager is in the job type 'manager' and the family 'technical manager'. Other information includes reporting relationships, location and a vacancy number so that the user can flag it for establishment report purposes. The window shows the name of the job holder and the comments screen (Figure 38.3) can be used as a note pad to record any other items of information about the employee that cannot be held elsewhere.

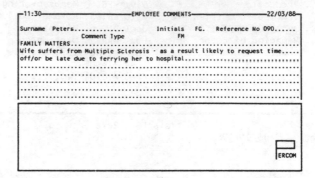

Figure 38.3 Employee comments screen — Percom PMS system

Employment contract

An example of the information that can be shown on an employment screen is shown in Figure 38.4.

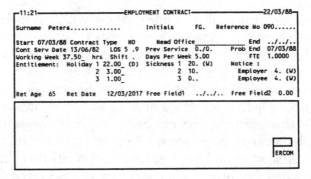

Figure 38.4 Employment contract screen — Percom PMS system

Salary details

A salary detail screen is illustrated in Figure 38.5. The standard screen gives details of salary review dates, job grade, basic salary, earnings, and, in the free fields, bonuses or other payments. There is scope to record the total cost of employment, including National Insurance contributions and allowances. The window shows the employee's salary history.

Performance appraisal

The performance appraisal screen shown in Figure 38.6 holds information

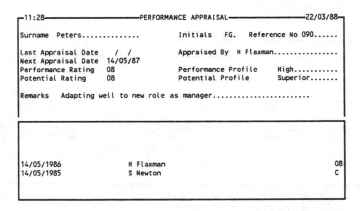

```
┌─11:21─────────────────────SALARY DETAILS──────────────────22/03/88─┐
│                                                                    │
│  Surname   Peters..............      Initials FG.   Reference No 090......  │
│                                                                    │
│  Review Date              / /        Reason   AR.  Next Review   01/01/88  │
│  NI No      XT237837C...             Personal Grade   ...... (.)    │
│  Job Grade DIR___                    Grade Point      0            │
│  Basic Salary/Wage      26375.0000   Period A Currency ST.  Payroll Code S │
│  Earnings 1             21500.00     Earnings 2              23000.00  │
│  Free Field 1               0.0000   Free Field 3       ...............  │
│  Free Field 2               0.00     Free Field 4       ...............  │
│                                                                    │
├────────────────────────────────────────────────────────────────────┤
│  01/01/1987      AR      26375.0000     JG DIR        PG            │
│  01/10/1986      AR      25000.0000     JG DIR        PG            │
│  30/06/1985      AR      20000.0000     JG MGT2       PG            │
│  30/06/1984      AR      19750.0000     JG           PG            │
│  13/08/1983      PRO     17500.0000     JG           PG            │
│  15/06/1983      AR      15000.0000     JG           PG            │
│  13/06/1982      AR      13500.0000     JG           PG            │
│                                                                    │
└────────────────────────────────────────────────────────────────────┘
```

Figure 38.5 Salary details screen — Percom PMS system

relating to both performance and potential (accessible to the employee under the UK Data Protection Act). The appraisal history can be shown in the window.

```
┌─11:28─────────────────────PERFORMANCE APPRAISAL──────────────22/03/88─┐
│                                                                      │
│  Surname  Peters..............      Initials   FG.   Reference No 090......  │
│                                                                      │
│  Last Appraisal Date     / /        Appraised By  H Flaxman...............  │
│  Next Appraisal Date  14/05/87                                       │
│  Performance Rating   08            Performance Profile   High...........  │
│  Potential Rating     08            Potential Profile     Superior.......  │
│                                                                      │
│  Remarks   Adapting well to new role as manager......................  │
│                                                                      │
├──────────────────────────────────────────────────────────────────────┤
│                                                                      │
│                                                                      │
│  14/05/1986            H Flaxman                              08     │
│  14/05/1985            S Newton                                C     │
│                                                                      │
└──────────────────────────────────────────────────────────────────────┘
```

Figure 38.6 Performance appraisal screen — Percom PMS system

Contacts and addresses
If the personnel department wants to keep additional addresses relating to employees such as those for the previous employer, an emergency contact, next of kin, spouse's workplace, and bank, these can be held in a contacts and addresses file, as shown in Figure 38.7.

Employee transactional data
A computerized record system can also be used to hold all these special items of information that companies need about their employees such as qualifications, special skills, training, absence, medical records and discipline. In the Percom system, what is termed a flexiscreen is used for this

```
┌─11:29─────────────────CONTACTS / ADDRESSES───────────22/03/88─┐

  Surname Peters..............    Initials FG.    Reference No 090......

  Address Type BNK. Address   Midland Bank.................
                              44 Hatton Road.................
                              Warrington....................
                              Lancs.........................
                 Post Code WE3 5RD...
  Telephone     0295-38599... / .............
  Contact Name  Mr H Arnold............. Relationship   Bank Manager...
  Free Field1   30·20·40...........   Free Field2 01VH842.............


                                                            ┌──┐
                                                            └──┘
                                                         ERCOM
```

Figure 38.7 Contacts and addresses file — Percom PMS system

purpose, as illustrated in Figure 38.8, where the screen displays the somewhat unhappy medical record of Mr Peters. Additional data can be expanded on a supplementary screen, as shown in Figure 38.9, which contains detailed records of qualifications which can be linked to a skills inventory (see below).

```
┌─11:31─────────────────EMPLOYEE TRANSACTIONAL DATA──────────22/03/88─┐
│                                                                      │
│ Surname  Peters..............       Initials FG.   Reference No 090......
│                                                                      │
│ Trans Group    AA                   Group Name  Absence_____    │
│ Trans Type     SI....               Type Name   Sickness_____   │
│                                                                      │
│                                                                      │
│ Start    End      Code        Reason        NoWkDays  SSP Days  SM Au│
│ ------------------------------------------------------------------   │
│ ./../.. 03/03/88 06.... Broken Hand.........  12.00    9.00   M. KL  │
│                                                                      │
├──────────────────────────────────────────────────────────────────── │
│ 17/02/1988 03/03/88 06   Broken Hand       12.00    9.00    M  KL    │
│ 02/01/1985 03/01/85 02   Upset Stomach      1.00    0.00    S        │
│ 24/10/1984 30/10/84 01   Influenza          5.00    2.00    S  KL    │
│ 21/08/1984 23/08/84 04   Stiff Back         3.00    0.00    S  KL    │
│ 17/07/1984 22/07/84 01   Heavy Cold         4.00    1.00    S  KN    │
│ 10/05/1984 18/05/84 02   Back Pain          7.00    4.00    S  KN    │
│ 21/03/1984 25/03/84 02   Gastroenteritis    5.00    2.00    M  KN    │
│                                                                      │
└──────────────────────────────────────────────────────────────────── ┘
```

Figure 38.8 Employee transactional screen — Percom PMS system

Integrated systems

A database approach to using the computer in personnel management means making the most of any personal data stored in the mainframe computer or in any other mini- or microcomputers in the organization. The database can be the starting-point for the various applications

Computerized Personnel Information Systems

```
┌11:32─────────────EMPLOYEE SUPPLEMENTARY DATA───────────22/03/88┐
│                                                                │
│ Surname  Peters..............      Initials FG.   Reference No 090......
│                                                                │
│ Supplement Type EDQ                Description  Education Qualifications
│ ...............................................................
│ Level   HND.......        .......... CSE    .. O Level 7..      0.00
│ School  12/09/66  End Dt  16/06/72   A Level 3. S Level ...      0.00
│ Univ    04/10/72  End Dt  06/05/75   OND     .. HND    ...      0.00
│ Degree  BSc Engineering..............RSA     .. C&Guild ...      0.00
│ Univ/Co Lincoln College-Oxford.......Other   ..       ...       0.00
│                                                                │
│                                                                │
│                                                                │
│                                                         ┌──┐   │
│                                                         └──┤   │
│                                                      ERCOM     │
└────────────────────────────────────────────────────────────────┘
```

Figure 38.9 Employee supplementary data screen — Percom PMS system

described below, but it can also be used to integrate three main areas of administration: people, payroll and pensions. An integrated database system such as the one developed by Peterborough Software allows payroll, pension and statutory sick-pay applications to use the data stored on the computerized personnel information system. The advantages of swifter and cheaper administration arising from linking these areas is obvious.

Human resource planning

Human resource flows

A CPIS can be used to model the effects on groups of people within the organization of change over time in the numbers and structure of each group and movements into, through and out of each group. A model such as MICROPROSPECT, developed by the Institute of Manpower Studies, looks as the organization, using a manpower system consisting of grades and flows. The user has considerable freedom in defining the number and type of flows required whether into, through, or out of each level of the system, ie:

- flows in — recruitment, transfers in;
- flows out — transfers out, retirement, resignation (uncontrolled losses), early retirement (controlled losses).

The user can control the way in which the flow is operated by specifying recruitment as numbers to be 'pushed in', percentages to be 'pulled out' to meet a target, or proportions by age or length of service bands.

827

Wastage monitoring and control

Computer models can monitor and help in the control of wastage. They can therefore provide a critical input to other areas of human resource decision making such as policies on recruitment, promotion, redeployment, training and career planning.

The Institute of Manpower Studies' WASP model offers the following modules which can be specified by using either age or length of service bands:

1. *cohort* — wastage or survival rates for the same group of people over a specified period of time;
2. *census* — a cross-sectional analysis of current wastage patterns for a particular group of people;
3. *plot* — a display of up to four sets of data, eg wastage rates and services;
4. *projections* — the age or length of service distribution for a group of people projected into the future under specified influences of policies;
5. *compare* — a statistical comparison of two wastage patterns for two groups of people or the same group of people over time.

Scheduling human resources

The CPIS can be used to provide an integral system for gearing human resources to business needs. The process of scheduling human resources to meet output in processing targets is becoming increasingly complex with the availability of more flexible ways of deploying people. They include multiskilling (employees who are capable of carrying out different tasks and are not subject to trade-union-imposed constraints in doing so), the use of contract workers, the use of outworkers (people working at home or in another centre, a process which is facilitated by computer networking and electronic mailing), twilight shifts, more part-timers, job sharing, etc.

Human resource planning is an interactive process which is always using output from one part of the process to influence another part of the process. Thus, assessments of the demand and supply of people, scheduling policies and possibilities, and the scope for flexing workloads and the use of people all influence the human resource supply policies adopted by the organization.

A CPIS provides the best basis for modelling this whole interrelated and iterative process, which is illustrated in Figure 38.10.

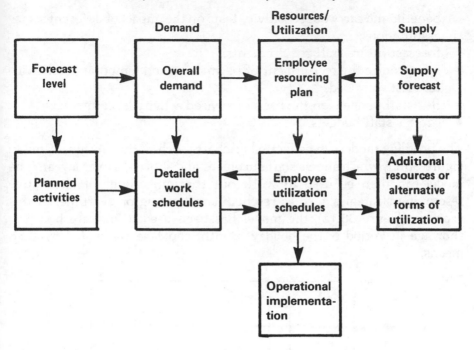

Figure 38.10 The CPIS human resource planning process

Profiling

Profiling is a particular aspect of employee scheduling concerned with the matching of staff to workloads and ensuring that the right number of people are available to meet fluctuations in activity levels over time. Profiling techniques are used where there are measurable volumes of work that can be costed and forecast with reasonable accuracy. Profiling can be linked with staff budgeting control in the sense that the use of staff resources is both constrained and influenced by the cash budget and performance and staff established targets.

Profiling models such as the one developed by the Department of Health and Social Security in association with the Institute of Manpower Studies can be used to:

- monitor and analyse staff usage;
- disentangle the interactive effects between staff in-post targets and other staffing constraints;
- test the effects of moving some activities to different times of the year and analyse their predicted impact on the staffing profile;
- monitor movements in expenditure on pay and other employee

829

benefits and carry out sensitivity tests on the impact of different salary assumptions;
- forecast future staff requirements;
- synchronize the recruitment of permanent and temporary staff with forecast workloads;
- flex staff budgets on the basis of revised activity level forecasts;
- control staff budgets.

The profiling model can generate bar charts such as the one illustrated in Figure 38.11, which shows staff surpluses and shortfalls over a year. The model can then be used to work out the implications of alternative resourcing strategies such as rescheduling training or overtime. In this example (Figure 38.12), the model has been used to indicate how the shortage in Period 6, the holiday month, could be eliminated by such means.

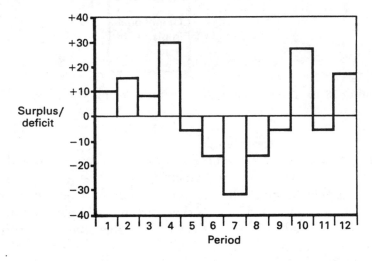

Figure 38.11 Staff usage profile before adjustment

Recruitment

A CPIS recruitment system can carry out four basic administrative tasks:

1. Storage of applicant's details.
2. Retrieval and amendment of those details.
3. Letter writing (linking the system to word-processing facilities) — acknowledgements, invitations to interview, offers and rejections.
4. Management reports, analysis of response by media and monitoring recruitment costs.

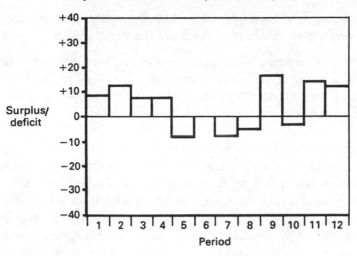

Figure 38.12 Staff usage profile after adjustment

Automated recruitment control packages, such as the one developed by Hall Associates, not only automate recruitment correspondence (coupling the CPIS with word processors) but also enable users to determine instantly who has applied for which post, track progress in recruiting for a specific post and match and process internal candidates from the organization's own human resources bank.

The Percom personnel recruitment system maintains three sets of records:

1. Applicant records with personnel details.
2. Vacancy records with job and recruitment details.
3. Applicant processing, which enables information extracted from the database to be put directly into the text of the letter for reproduction on a word processor. The *ad hoc* enquiry facility enables users to match applicants with vacancies in order that shortlists can be made; to list applicants by source, vacancy, and ethnic origin; to diarize follow-up actions; to calculate recruitment costs; and to carry out statistical analyses of the number of applications, interviews, offers, rejections, and the cost-effectiveness of the recruitment source, medium or internal recruiter.

The Nissan recruitment management system

The recruitment management system (RMS) at Nissan, as described by

Wickens, helps in handling some 30,000 applications a year, which generate around 40,000 letters. It allows the company to:

- hold vacancy details, including the skills and qualifications required;
- store the range of selection techniques to be used for each position;
- record the media used, including timing, cost, response, etc;
- input applicants' details and match the stated skills against those specified;
- record all test and interview results;
- most importantly, record the progress of applicants and generate all written communications, including offer and reject letters;
- obtain progress reports on unfilled vacancies with an inbuilt system for prioritizing action; write 'We have not forgotten you' letters to candidates whose application is not being actively progressed;
- monitor the time it takes to fill a position and thus guide in determining the lead times necessary to recruit people for expansions;
- calculate statistics, such as cost per applicant and cost per hire, allowing evaluation of alternative recruitment programmes — which media to use or even whether retraining might be more cost-effective;
- correlate subsequent performance as assessed on the appraisal system with test results achieved at the selection stage. The organization is then able to refine selection techniques in order to achieve an even higher success rate. It is also possible to assess the correlation between selection and wastage.

Reward management

A CPIS can be used for salary modelling and to carry out a number of salary administration activities. It can also be used in job evaluation as described on pages 548–549.

Salary modelling

Salary models provide the answers to 'what if?' questions such as, 'How much would it cost if we gave x per cent to this part of the company, y per cent to another part of the company, and implemented the following special package across these job functions?' A typical model such as PERSIS, developed by IBM, starts from a database that defines the concrete elements of the cost of salaries, such as the number of staff, average pay level for each group of employees, starting and leaving rates, overtime rates and so on. The model takes the personnel database, with its movements of job level, promotions, starters, leavers, etc, and uses parameters such as the expected level of promotions and range increases contained in the salaries policy files to calculate the cost of the salary review in a particular year, taking into account factors such as attrition (the erosion of the cost of salary increments over a period of time as a result of the average salary of leavers exceeding the average salary of joiners).

Salary administration

A CPIS can:

- Analyse and report on average salaries or salary distributions by job, grade, age or length of service — this could be expressed initially in the form of a scattergram, as illustrated in Figure 38.13. Regression lines showing trends can then be plotted on a vertical axis, as shown in Figure 38.14, which divides the salary progression curves into deciles.

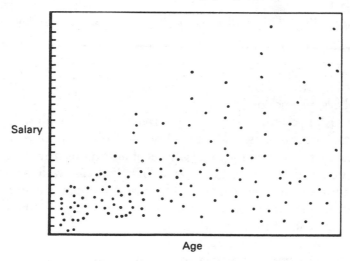

Figure 38.13 Scattergram of distribution of salaries by age

- Calculate compa-ratios to show how average salaries in a range differ from the target salary of the midpoint of the range — a compa-ratio is calculated as follows:

$$\frac{\text{average of all salaries in grade}}{\text{midpoint of range}} \times 100$$

- Calculate the effects of attrition.
- Estimate the costs of salary reviews.

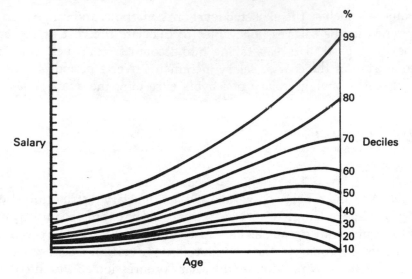

Figure 38.14 Distribution of salaries — regression (trend) lines

- Provide the basis for preparing and monitoring salary bands.
- Forecast future salary costs on the basis of given assumptions about numbers, promotions and pay levels.
- Administer pay reviews, producing review forms, analysing proposals against the budgets and agreed values of distributions of merit increases, calculating the implications of alternative review guidelines, and generating instructions to adjust pay as well as letters to individuals informing them of their rises. If there are any formulae governing the relationship between merit assessments and merit increases, the CPIS can work them out.

Organization planning and development

The CPIS database can be used in more advanced applications to assist in:

- experimenting with and amending the organization structure in the face of changing market or technology demands;
- designing or redesigning new or existing jobs within the structure against which specific goals and performance standards can be developed;
- establishing selection profiles incorporating the standards against which potential job holders can be assessed in order that the right people can be appointed to or promoted into jobs.

Performance management

A CPIS can help to operate a performance appraisal and management system, generating appraisal forms, analysing and reporting on the result of performance reviews showing the distribution of people with different degrees of potential or performing at different levels, and highlighting individuals with particular skills or special promise. This system can be linked to others to provide an integrated basis for creating and implementing human resource management policies (see competence modelling and expert systems below).

Human resource development

Training administration (computer-managed learning)

A CPIS can be used for training administration by:

- analysing the training recommendations contained in performance appraisal reports to identify collective and individual training needs;
- identifying suitable training courses to meet training needs;
- making arrangements for off-the-job courses (booking facilities, inviting speakers);
- informing managers and staff about the arrangements for courses;
- handling correspondence about training courses;
- storing data on standard or individually tailored induction, continuation or development training programmes, including syllabi, routings, responsibilities for giving training, test procedures and progress reporting;
- generating instructions and notes for guidance for all concerned with providing or undergoing on-the-job training programmes;
- storing progress reports and monitoring achievements against training objectives;
- producing reports summarizing current and projected training activities and calculating the output of training programmes — this can be linked to human resource planning models including those designed to determine the input of apprentices or trainees required for training schemes;
- recording and monitoring training expenditure against budget.

Computer-based training

Computer-based training (CBT) is a form of individualized learning and, as such, is a manifestation of educational technology. It uses the power of the computer to assist in the constant need to train and retrain workers in new processes and procedures. It also plays an important part in 'distance learning' in the fields of occupational training and higher education for institutions such as the Open University.

CBT starts with the process of instructional systems design (ISD). Each individual lesson is planned on the basis of careful job analysis, sequencing and testing. The experience gained in the 1960s in the development of teaching machines, feedback classrooms and programmed instruction has had a powerful influence on CBT.

CBT enables instructors to build into their sessions the adaptablity that a truly interactive process of learning should provide. Using a computer, the author can devise an interactive sequence in which the responses the students make will determine their route through the training unit or programme — a route which will be unique to them.

CBT uses hardware such as that illustrated in Figure 38.15.

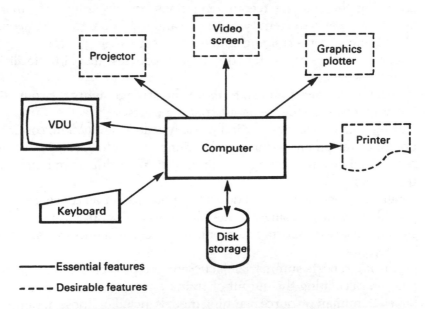

Figure 38.15 Computer-based training hardware
(Source: *The Personnel Training Databook*. Kogan Page)

Most CBT systems get trainees to study text on a visual display unit (VDU). They respond to problems which appear on the screen by typing an answer on a keyboard. More advanced systems use interactive video, as described in Appendix K on training techniques.

Skills inventory

Many organizations need to store detailed information about the skills and experience of the individuals they employ. A separate skills inventory can be linked to a personnel database in order that any individual changes in experience or additional training can be fed through automatically to it. This provides a basis for assessing the strengths and weaknesses of the organization in terms of available skills, and leads to the design of special training programmes to fill any gaps.

Career management

A CPIS can help in the implementation of career management policies and procedures which embrace both career planning and management development. The system does this by analysing the progression of individuals and comparing the results of that analysis, first, with assessments of organizational requirements as generated by the human resource planning models and, secondly, with the outputs of the performance management system.

The system developed by Royal Insurance:

- assesses the 'supply' side of career development as shown by salary progression (see Figures 38.13 and 38.14) and extrapolates, on the basis of the last four years' average increases, the progression of each individual for a period of five years ahead;

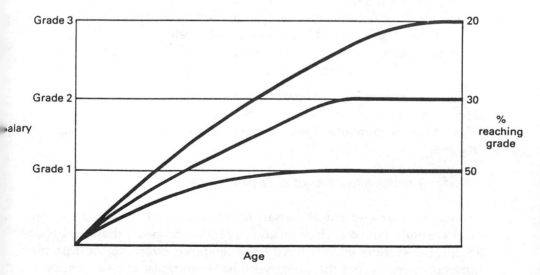

Figure 38.16 Career progression analysis

- identifies from their assessment those whose progression is such that they could move into the next level and also those who are 'plateauing out' or appear to be slipping;
- shows the number of vacancies likely to arise;
- lists possible candidates against those vacancies.

The output of this and similar systems can be used to plan for management succession and to devise collective or individual management development training programmes.

Career progression curves can be produced by using computer techniques to show the percentage of those recruited or in-post at a certain age who are likely to finish their careers in a particular grade. A simplified product of this type of analysis is given in Figure 38.16, which shows that 50 per cent of those engaged at a certain age who remain with the organization are likely to get no further than Grade 3 when they retire, while 30 per cent will achieve Grade 2 and 20 per cent Grade 1.

Absence control

Absence control can be carried out with the help of computerized time recording and attendance systems which:

- record clocking-on or -out time and the hours actually worked;
- enable employees to record the time spent on particular jobs;
- get employees to explain the reason for late arrival, early departure, or any other absence;
- can be linked to the payroll system for pay and bonus calculation purposes and to a flexible working hours system;
- provide supervisors with a statement on the first day back to work, showing the length and reasons for absence.

Advanced systems link information obtained from clocking-on or -out direct to a screen in supervisors' offices in order that they can have instant information on how many people are at work and on the incidence of lateness.

Attendance management system at Nissan

Attendance management at Nissan is the responsibility of supervision. Staff are not required to clock on and pay is not stopped if they are late or absent. Supervisors initially recorded attendance, overtime, shift premiums, etc manually, but this paperwork has been replaced by a computerized system with the following features: Each supervisor has access to data on the people in his section and is daily presented with a 'register' on which *exceptions* are input. Thus, the system's assumption is that everyone has attended work and has done no overtime unless it is advised otherwise. Shift patterns are already in the system. At the end of a month the supervisor must confirm the input for the whole month by using a special screen.

In addition to this, the system allows:

- messages to be passed between the supervisor and the personnel or finance departments;
- holiday recording, including the determination of amount of holiday left;
- appraisal due reminders (these can be switched off only by personnel);
- patterns of absenteeism to be analysed;
- more effective control over labour cost reporting in that, as a system integrated with finance, it allows immediate reports of labour dispositions — whether people are in training, lent to other sections, etc.

Equal opportunity monitoring

The CPIS can store records of the racial composition of the labour force. This information can be analysed to produce data on the distribution of ethnic minorities by occupation, job grade, age, service and location. The sort of information the analysis could provide is the overall proportion of ethnic minority employees compared with the proportion in each job grade. Similar statistics can be produced for men and women. The analysis can be extended to cover career progression, splitting the results of the overall analysis into comparisons of the rate at which women and men of different ethnic groups progress.

Competence modelling

Competence modelling brings together organization planning and perfor-mance management data to establish the skills or competences required to do particular jobs. This assists in appointment, promotion and training decisions. Competence analysis looks both at what tasks have to be carried out and at the skills required. Profiles can then be developed by the computer and matched to assessments of current job holders or job applicants.

Expert systems

Expert systems are computer programs which contain knowledge about particular fields of human activity and experience, which, through linkages and rules built into the system design, can help solve human resource management problems. Unlike a database system which stores, sorts, manipulates, and presents bits of information — ic data — expert systems store, sort, manipulate and present managers with ready-to-use knowledge of management practice, written in a language that management understands, as opposed to computerese.

Expert systems are developed through a process of knowledge engineering which starts from a knowledge base containing facts and a body of expertise ('heuristics', or rules of thumb) about the use of those facts. These 'rules' enable decisions to be made on the basis of factual information presented to the computer. Thus, a fact may be information on labour turnover during the last three years, and the rule of thumb may be the method by which turnover could be predicted over the next three years. These facts and rules are processed by what is termed the 'inference engine', which solves problems or makes predictions, and the results of this process are presented to the user in the 'user interface'.

An expert system can produce a list of suitable candidates for promotion by using information from the database. If more information was required, it would ask the user to answer questions. It would also respond to users' questions about why particular candidates had been identified, by giving details of qualifications, performance appraisal results and so on.

Example of a personnel expert system

The expert system developed in British Shipbuilders began by defining about 70 'job dimensions', which are discrete activities from which a combination can be selected to provide a specification for any possible job. Each dimension can operate at from four to six levels of responsibility. The next stage was to define all the attributes that people needed to perform each of the dimensions at the different levels — 50 attributes were identified, each scaled at from five to six levels.

The software engineering that followed these analyses linked attributes with dimensions in such a way as to identify the optimum attribute level for each dimension level. Because of the numbers of possible combinations, this could be done only with the help of a computer. A user-friendly package was then developed for analysing any job, and models were produced to maintain, monitor and control vacancy procedures to help in performance appraisal, to evaluate jobs, to advise on training needs, to administer psychological tests, and to produce organization charts.

Example of a job evaluation expert system

The Link Group Consultants Ltd uses 'Jeeves', a computerized system which is tailor-made to assist in the whole process of evaluating jobs.

Jeeves is an expert system shell which can be tailored to any analytical job evaluation scheme. An expert system shell is a form of computer program into which can be entered a body of expertise in the form of 'rules' which enable decisions to be made on the basis of factual information presented to the computer.

Jeeves assumes that each scheme has:

- weighted factors;
- a demand scale or a matrix for each factor, eg points, levels, degrees;
- assessment standards for each factor which guide evaluators to the correct rating of jobs; these may take the form of benchmark jobs and/ or level definitions.

It also requires that there be adequate information available on benchmark jobs in the form of job descriptions and factor information.

The rationale behind the Jeeves system is that in every analytical job evaluation scheme there must be clear and discernible reasons why jobs have been placed in the various degree or demand levels of each factor. Indeed, if there were no apparent reasons or 'rules', the job evaluation system could not function in a consistent manner. At the same time the system recognizes that the 'rules' may be both detailed and complex.

In essence, Jeeves has been so constructed that:

1. the evaluation 'rules' can be defined both qualitatively and/or quantitatively;
2. the rules can be enshrined in the expert system shell;
3. the computer can be programmed to ask sufficient questions about each factor to enable it to apply the evaluation rules;
4. when the job information has been entered, the computer can apply the rules and determine the factor score.

Once the system has been set up, Jeeves will therefore consistently apply the rules each time and produce an evaluated score for a factor.

By also entering factor weights and grade line positions in the system, Jeeves can go on to:

- score the job;

- grade the job;
- sort it into position in the rank order;
- store the job information entered in the form of a Factor Analysis.

Sample screens for Jeeves are given in Figure 38.17.

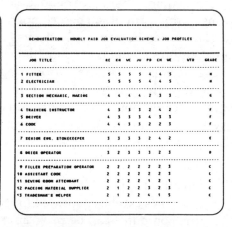

Figure 38.17 Sample 'Jeeves' screens

Selecting the system

When you select the computer system, the considerations that should be taken into account are:

- what is to be computerized?
- bureau or in-house?

- mainframe, mini or PC?
- package or in-house development?
- the extent to which it has to be user-friendly.

What to computerize?

A CPIS can be used simply to provide administrative support, or its use can be extended to provide decision support in a number of areas. If it is to be no more than an electronic filing system, this will obviously simplify the whole development programme, but it would be a pity to neglect all the other applications that could be derived from the database. Requirements for decision support should therefore be considered from an early stage. Another factor to be taken into account is the need for the system to be flexible in order that it can expand and link with other systems.

Bureau or in-house?

Bureaux operate and maintain computers externally and charge out on a time-sharing basis. They are worth considering when large quantities of batch processing are involved which cannot be dealt with on company hardware, or where powerful computer facilities are needed but not in any great quantity. Bureaux are often used by small or medium-sized companies for their payroll or for pensions administration.

Bureaux are, however, not so appropriate when the company wants an integrated administrative system and/or a decision support facility. Members of the personnel department must obviously have immediate access to data and the ability to obtain answers to enquiries and to use the computer in association with word processors as a memorandum, letter-writing and report production facility. The full development of a CPIS is possible only if it is operated in-house.

Mainframe, mini, or PC?

Mainframes and minis are more robust than PCs, they hold more information, they process data faster and there is more software available (although this situation as far as micros are concerned is changing rapidly as software packages proliferate). Mainframes and minis therefore offer greater scope for the wider applications of database management.

PCs are, of course, less expensive and the personnel department can have sole use of them for its own purposes. They are at their best in applications involving calculations rather than heavy information. But they have plenty of potential as integrated administration systems, provided that:

- the personnel department concerned is small enough to be happy with a single-user application;
- certain limits are placed in the number of data to be stored (these limits are not very severe but could become relevant in a company employing thousands rather than hundreds of people);
- certain compromises concerning the robustness of the system are acceptable to the users;
- the software has been written in a highly efficient way.

Package or in-house development?

A package is a software system which is already fully written. It is sufficiently flexible to be applicable in different organizations, although the software houses are increasingly marketing packages which are relevant for particular businesses. Packages are being developed in increasing numbers by a number of specialist firms.

The likelihood of finding an appropriate software package, even if the choice is somewhat bewildering, is enhanced by the fact that suppliers are dealing with data requirements that are common to many if not all organizations. Everyone wants to store such things as personal details, employment history and pay, benefits and job grade information.

In-house development seems to offer a more flexible approach at less cost, but these advantages may be illusory. As mentioned above, there is plenty of choice for packages which are increasingly flexible in use. And the cost of buying software, although seemingly high, may well be only one-tenth of the true cost of developing a system in-house.

User-friendly?

Whatever type of hardware or software is adopted, the system must be user-friendly. That is, members of the personnel department without specialized computer skills or elaborate training must be able to input data, access the information they require, and use the system for administrative purposes or as decision support without difficulty.

Implementing the system

The ten steps required to implement a CPIS are:

1. *Determine objectives* — are they to save administrative costs, speed up

processing, provide advanced decision support, or a combination of any of these?

2. *Carry out a feasibility study* to consider applications and their likely costs and benefits. This study could be carried out in-house or with the help of outside consultants or software houses who provide a consultancy service. The feasibility study will broadly analyse and define user requirements and ensure that all concerned are aware of what is being planned, how they will benefit from it and the contribution they will be expected to make to the development and application of the system. The information the system will be required to store and process and the uses to which the information will be put should be specified. Account should be taken of the provisions of the Data Protection Act (see page 801).

3. *Prepare a requirements specification* which will set out in detail what the system is expected to do and how the company would like to use it. This specification can be used to brief hardware and software suppliers before selecting the system.

4. *Select the system* in the form of the hardware and the software required. This may involve decisions on the extent to which existing hardware or systems (eg payroll systems) will be used. The need and scope for networking, that is, linking users by means of terminals, and the employment of word processors will also need to be considered. At this stage caution has to be exercised not to limit the value of the CPIS by relying too much on the use of existing facilities. There are apparent attractions, not least cost savings, in using the mainframe or the payroll system, but these could restrict the development of a fully integrated system which can be used flexibly by the personnel department.

5. *Plan the implementation programme* to ensure that the objectives will be achieved within a given time-scale and in line with the cost budget.

6. *Involve users* to ensure that everyone who will benefit from the system (line managers as well as members of the personnel department) can contribute their ideas and thus feel that it is *their* system rather than one imposed upon them.

7. *Control the project* against the implementation programme to ensure that it delivers what is required, on time and within the budget.

8. *Provide training* to all users to ensure that they can operate and get the most out of the system.

9. *Monitor performance* to ensure that the system lives up to expectations.

10. *Continually develop* the basic system to extend its use in administration and decision support.

References

1. Richards-Carpenter, C 'Achieving Practical Solutions — Current Concerns', *Computers in Personnel*. Institute of Personnel Management and Institute of Manpower Studies, 1987.
2. Wickens, P 'The importance of computerized information in strategic personnel decision making', *Computers in Personnel*. Institute of Personnel Management and Institute of Manpower Studies conference, London, 1990.

39

Personnel Records

The need

Personnel record and information systems are required for three main purposes:

1. To store for reference the personal details of individual employees.
2. To provide a basis for decision making in every area of personnel work, especially:

   (a) manpower forecasting and planning;
   (b) recruitment and selection;
   (c) employment, including promotion, transfers, disciplinary procedures, termination, and redundancy;
   (d) education and training;
   (e) pay administration;
   (f) health and safety.

3. To provide data for returns to government departments and agencies.

Personnel records and information procedures can be based on an entirely manual system but, increasingly, they are being computerized to a greater or lesser degree. The use of personal computers is accelerating this process. There are, however, certain basic principles and practices which apply to any system and these are considered in the first three sections of the chapter: requirements of a good record system, identifying information requirements and designing the system. The next section deals with basic forms and returns which may exist only as a manual system or may be linked to a computer. The use of computers was discussed in Chapter 38.

Requirements of a good record system

Personnel records, like any other records, must be simple, easy to maintain, comprehensive and relevant to the needs of the undertaking.

Simplicity and ease of maintenance are vital; records can be expensive to set up and maintain. A universal hatred of form filling and paperwork generally will be enhanced to the total detriment of accuracy and utility if forms and records are complex, difficult to complete, or hard to understand. This means designing forms such that entries can be made in logical and convenient sequence, left to right across the paper and from top to bottom. As far as possible, the method of completing the form should be self-explanatory — elaborate notes for guidance should be avoided. Plenty of space should be provided for each item; if different units of information are 'boxed' in, the form will be easier to complete and to read. Particularly vital pieces of information should be given prominence and may be placed in a more heavily defined box. Space should be provided for alterations and additions. One side of one sheet of paper is the ideal size although, clearly, some records, such as application forms, may have to be longer.

It is also important to ensure that records are not unduly duplicated, and this may mean taking care when assessing the degree to which records should be centralized or decentralized (discussed below).

Accuracy partly depends upon ensuring that clear definitions are made of the information that has to be entered on the form. If there is any ambiguity about, for example, a job title, the resulting entry may produce misleading information later for manpower planning or training surveys. It is important to place accurate information on the record. It is equally important to remove redundant information from the card or dossier. Many employee dossiers are full of useless documents which take up unnecessary space and increase the difficulty of getting at essential information. A regular review of records is required to clear out useless data.

A comprehensive system of records covers all the information required about individual employees or needed for personnel decision making. But the information must be relevant. Every piece of information must be challenged with the questions, 'What purpose will this serve?', 'To what use will it be put?' The first point to clarify when setting up a record system is the objective of each item in terms of the decisions it will help to make, its contribution to the assembly of essential statistical information, or its importance as a reference point in dealing with matters affecting individual employees.

Personnel Records

It is necessary to avoid gaps in information essential to decision making. It is equally necessary to avoid gathering useless data or maintaining elaborate statistics to which no one ever refers. Too often, a 'one-off' request for information leads to the setting up of a permanent record or data collection system, although the information may never be requested again. Regular reviews should be made of all records and returns to ensure that they are serving a useful purpose and that they are generally cost-effective. In some circumstances, it may be cheaper to maintain manual records than to computerize. It may be less time-consuming and costly to carry out a special exercise than to maintain a permanent record, just in case.

Identifying information requirements

The starting point should be an analysis of the decisions that the company makes or may need to make about individuals, groups of employees, or the workforce as a whole. This should be followed up by an analysis of the information required by government departments and agencies and by employers' associations.

Personnel decisions requiring statistical data

The main decisions for which statistical information or individual data may be required include:

- forecasting the future supply of manpower by analysing, for each category of staff, labour turnover, age distribution, absenteeism and promotions;
- forecasting the future demand for manpower by ratio-trend analysis (calculating current ratios of manpower to activity levels and forecasting future ratios by reference to projected activity levels) and other statistical means;
- the introduction of productivity improvement or cost reduction campaigns based upon analyses of present manpower productivity levels and costs (eg manpower cost per unit of output, or the ratio of manpower costs to sales turnover or profit);
- planning recruitment campaigns on the basis of analyses of the results of previous campaigns, especially sources of recruits, media costs and success rates, and the relative pulling power of different inducements and recruitment methods;

- introducing new or improved interviewing and testing techniques on the basis of comparisons between interview and test assessments and subsequent performance;
- identifying people with particular skills or potential for new appointments or promotion;
- improving disciplinary procedures or amending work rules by analysing disciplinary cases;
- introducing new or improved timekeeping methods or considering the introduction of flexitime by reference to timekeeping records;
- planning redundancies — consulting unions, transferring or retraining employees, selecting employees for redundancy, or helping to place redundant employees;
- planning training programmes — subjects to be covered, types and numbers of courses — by reference to analyses of future changes in manpower (numbers and skills), performance review records and job and training specifications;
- taking steps to improve job satisfaction and morale by reference to statistics on labour turnover, absenteeism, sickness, accidents, discipline cases and grievances;
- changing pay systems on the basis of statistics of wage drift, fluctuations in earnings, the proportion of employees on average earnings rather than payment by results, cost per unit of output, fluctuations in earnings, and the number and consequences of arguments over job rates;
- reviewing pay structures and levels of pay by reference to statistics of earnings in the company, rates of pay elsewhere, and the distribution of rates in each pay grade (eg compa-ratios for salary structure analysis, as described in Chapter 30);
- controlling merit reviews by analysing the distribution of merit awards in relation to budgets and guidelines and by assessing the implications of salary attrition (see Chapter 30);
- taking steps to improve employee relations by analysing the causes of disputes;
- determining the information that should be communicated to unions and employees about the company or to assist in negotiations and joint consultation;
- improving health, safety and fire precautions by analysing reports on industrial disease, accidents and dangerous occurrences; monitoring returns on exposure to health hazards in relation to predetermined threshold limits; and studying reports on health, safety and fire inspection, spot checks and audits.

Personnel returns

The personnel returns required may include (in the UK):

- manpower and earnings statistics to the Department of Employment or employers' associations;
- training statistics to industrial training boards;
- health and safety statistics to the Health and Safety Executive.

Individual data

Individual information should include:

- the application form, giving personal particulars;
- interview and test record;
- job history after joining the firm, including details of transfers, promotions and changes in occupation;
- current pay details and changes in salary or pay;
- education and training record with details of courses attended and results obtained;
- details of performance assessments and reports from appraisal or counselling sessions;
- absence, lateness, accident, medical and disciplinary records with details of formal warnings and suspensions;
- holiday entitlement;
- pensions data;
- termination record, with details of exit interview and suitability for re-engagement.

Collective data

Collective information may include:

- numbers, grades and occupations of employees;
- absenteeism, labour turnover and lateness statistics;
- accident rates;
- age and length of service distributions;
- total wage and salary bill;
- wage rates and salary levels;
- employee costs;
- overtime statistics;
- records of grievances and disputes;
- training records.

Designing the system

The type and complexity of the personnel records and information system must obviously depend upon the company and its needs. Small companies may need only a basic card index system for individual employees and a simple set of forms for recording information on numbers employed, labour turnover and absenteeism. But a larger company will almost certainly need a more complex system because more information has to be handled, many more decisions have to be made, and the data change more often. Card indexes are not enough, because supplementary records may be needed to give more detailed information about individual employees.

The key decisions to be made when designing the system concern:

- the design of the basic records, forms and input material;
- the use of computers;
- the extent to which records should be centralized or decentralized;
- the procedures and programme for collecting, recording, updating and disseminating information.

The design of basic records and forms

The basic records and forms must be designed in accordance with the principles of simplicity, clarity, cost-effectiveness, and relevance discussed earlier. Examples of typical forms and statistical returns are given at the end of this chapter and can be found elsewhere in this book.

Centralization and decentralization of records

In a small company, or one in which operations are concentrated on one site, the issue of centralization and decentralization may not be an important one. However, even in the latter case, there may be problems of duplication if departments insist on keeping records of their own employees in addition to those maintained centrally.

The advantages of centralization are that there is less expenditure on space and equipment, company statistical analyses can more easily be prepared and duplication is avoided. The disadvantages are that local departments or units may not have ready access to the information they need, while there may be delays in obtaining the data required by central records.

The advantages of decentralization are that departments have the information they need on the spot, and delays in transmitting data are reduced. The disadvantages are additional costs because of space requirements and duplicated efforts and possible loss in effectiveness at the centre because of difficulties in analysing the total situation in the company.

In a divisionalized company, where these problems are likely to be most pressing, the answer is usually a compromise. Divisions maintain all their own personnel records, but a standardized set of returns is devised for transmission to the central personnel information office to be processed by the computer or manually in order that the group statistical analyses and returns can be prepared. In this situation, the aim should be to keep the central returns to a minimum, possibly covering only basic data on manpower numbers and trends, and earnings.

Procedures

The procedures to be used in collecting, analysing, disseminating, and updating information should be laid down at the design stage in order that everyone knows what to do and when to do it. Decisions should be made at this stage as to whether data should be *event triggered* or *time triggered*.

Event-triggered data are recorded when prespecified events occur, giving information about the occurrence or non-occurrence of a particular event, eg an accident, or someone's leaving, which is important for control purposes. *Time-triggered* recordings are generated at prespecified intervals of time, eg earnings surveys.

The procedures for disseminating information should list who initiates the report, to whom it goes, and, where appropriate, what action should be taken. Updating procedures may include reviews of the relevance and accuracy of data as well as systems to ensure that changes in data are recorded quickly and accurately.

Examples of forms and statistical returns

The following are examples of basic forms and statistical returns:

Type of Form	Figure No.
Basic personnel record card	39.1
Quarterly return — employment, labour turnover, and earnings	39.2
Monthly analysis of leavers	39.3
Monthly/annual summary of absence	39.4

Name		Date joined
Date of birth	Marital status	No. of children
Address		Home telephone no.
Qualifications		
Languages		

Previous employment		
Company	Position	Dates

Present employment		
Department	Position	Dates
Date left	Reason for leaving	

Front

Salary — Performance — Potential Record			
Date	Salary	Performance rating	Potential rating

Training received	
Date	Course

Reverse

Figure 39.1 Basic personnel record card

QUARTERLY RETURN — EMPLOYMENT, LABOUR TURNOVER, AND EARNINGS										*Quarter ending*
	Number on payroll			Labour turnover annual rate %			Average weekly earnings			
	This quarter	Increase(+) or decrease(-) since:		This quarter	Increase(+) or decrease(-) since:		This quarter	Increase(+) or decrease(-) since:		
Occupation		Last quarter	Same quarter last year		Last quarter	Same quarter last year		Last quarter	Same quarter last year	
Total										

Figure 39.2 Quarterly return — employment, labour turnover and earnings

MONTHLY ANALYSIS OF LEAVERS

Month of _____ 19 ___   Department _____   Occupation(s) _____

| Length of service | Sex | Discharge | | Personal better-ment | Reasons for Leaving | | | | | | Domestic reasons | Retire-ment | Death | Unknown | Total |
| | | Unsuit-able | Redun-dancy | | Pay | Dissatisfaction with: | | | | | | | | | |
		Discipline				Work	Working conditions	Hours	Manage-ment	Other factors					
Less than 1 month	M														
	F														
1–3 months	M														
	F														
4–12 months	M														
	F														
1–5 years	M														
	F														
Over 6 years	M														
	F														
Total	M														
	F														

Labour turnover rate expressed as an annual rate%*

	This month	Last month	Same month last year
Male			
Female			
Total			

* Monthly labour turnover rate expressed as an annual rate% =

$$\text{Monthly labour turnover rate} = \left(\frac{\text{Number of leavers during month}}{\text{Average number employed during month}} \right) \times 100 \times 12$$

Figure 39.3 Monthly analysis of leavers

MONTHLY/ANNUAL SUMMARY OF ABSENCE

Year		Department/company			Occupation(s)			
Month		Hours of absence					Total planned hours (including overtime)	% lost of planned hours (including overtime)
		Sickness or accident		Other absence		Total absence (including lateness)		
		Certified	Uncertified	Authorized	Unauthorized (inc. lateness)			
January								
February								
March								
April								
May								
June								
July								
August								
September								
October								
November								
December								
Total for year								

Figure 39.4 Monthly/annual summary of absence

Part X
Conclusions

The introduction to this book and its first two chapters reviewed the development of personnel and human resource management and the main influences on the role and activities of the personnel function.

The further 9 parts described current thinking and practice in each area of the subject. This concluding chapter summarizes the key issues facing personnel management and considers the main trends in the development of personnel management in the 1990s.

40

Personnel Management — Key Issues and Trends

Key issues

The key issues affecting personnel management in the 1990s can be grouped under the following 12 headings:

1. resourcing;
2. change;
3. organizational;
4. performance;
5. quality;
6. reward;
7. employee relations;
8. Europe and globe markets;
9. competition;
10. social and environmental factors;
11. employee expectations;
12. the changing role of the personnel function.

Resourcing

- *Skills provision* — obtaining and developing people with both higher levels and wider ranges of skills (multiskilling).
- *Demographics* — shortfalls in the numbers of educated young people entering the labour market.
- *Knowledge workers* — learning how to employ and make the best use of people carrying out high-level professional and technical work in

organizations dominated by new technology, especially information technology.

- *Career management* — providing development opportunities to meet both people's aspirations and the needs of the organization, bearing in mind that people may want to build a 'portfolio' of careers while organizations cannot, indeed may not want to, guarantee a long-term future.
- *Plateaued managers* — motivating managers whose careers are no longer progressing.
- *Creating a learning organization* — one which creates opportunities for continuous learning and development.
- *Training provision* — ensuring that training resources are available and that training is delivered which will help people to acquire the competences they need.

Change

- *Continuous renewal* — helping the process of self-renewal when business is difficult, and the survival of firms is hazardous within an environment which is increasingly unpredictable, competitive and fraught with danger.
- *New paradigms* — changing mind-sets or ways of looking at things in order to cope with new demands and pressures.
- *Change management* — recognizing that change cannot often be achieved successfully by means of an organization-wide change programme and that it may have to be introduced incrementally, although within a strategic framework.
- *Transformational leadership* — providing the support required by leaders who are transforming the culture, structure and processes of the organization.

Organizational

- *Flexibility* — providing for greater operational flexibility within a strategic framework which maintains a strong sense of direction.
- *De-layering* — eliminating unnecessary layers of management and supervision.
- *Decentralization* — devolving operational decisions to decentralized business units or federated activities while ensuring that the centre still gives strategic guidance, coordinates effort and provides financial and senior management resources.

- *Teamwork* — developing teamwork at all levels in the organization from a 'collegiate' top management team at the centre to autonomous work groups on the shop-floor.
- *Collectivism versus individualism* — reconciling the tension between collectivism, as represented by a collegiate or teamwork approach and the need to encourage individuals to be innovative and entrepreneurial and to operate independently.

Performance

- *Motivation* — using the right mix of financial and non-financial rewards to motivate not only the high-flyers but also the core workers on whom the organization ultimately depends.
- *Performance management* — creating a performance-orientated culture through leadership, motivation, reward management, training and the use of a developmental performance management system.
- *Productivity* — increasing the efficiency with which human resources are utilized, with particular emphasis on developing flexibility in the type of people employed (increasing the proportion of peripheral workers round the core) as well as flexible working arrangements.

Quality

- *Total quality management* — the generation throughout the organization of total commitment to quality.
- *Customer service* — getting the message across that 'every contact with a customer is an opportunity to add value and quality'.

Reward

- *Strategic and cultural fit* — ensuring that reward management systems fit corporate strategies and culture, and underpin core values.
- *Flexible rewards* — developing flexible reward systems with features such as:

    (a) a high proportion of variable element;
    (b) maximum choice of benefit;
    (c) pay related to skill and competence levels;
    (d) fast response to market rate indicators;
    (e) pay curves rather than rigid structures.

- *Pay progression* — relating pay progression to performance and market-ability (not cost of living).

- *Paying for performance* — creating and maintaining cost-effective, performance-related pay schemes which

    (a) are based on corporate as well as individual success criteria;
    (b) relate both to quantitative and qualitative factors;
    (c) deliver clear messages about performance expectations.

- *Equity versus competitiveness* — maintaining a balance between the often competing goals of internal equity and external competitiveness.
- *Value for money* — making sure that money spent on remuneration pays dividends in terms of motivation and commitment.

Employee relations

- *Identification* — developing shared values and a sense of common purpose throughout the organization and thus increasing the identification of its members with the organization's mission and strategies.
- *Harmonization* — moving towards single-status organizations.
- *HRM approaches* — considering the introduction of HRM approaches of communication and involvement which aim to increase 'mutuality' and are aimed directly at work teams and individuals, thus bypassing union channels.
- *Union recognition* — deciding whether to recognize or derecognize trade unions.
- *Bargaining structures:*

    (a) decentralizing bargaining without losing control;
    (b) getting agreement to single-table bargaining.

- *Union agreements* — achieving agreement as required on:

    (a) flexibility (multiskilling);
    (b) 'no strike' clauses and pendulum arbitration.

Europe and globe markets

- *Getting ready for Europe,* especially in the following areas:

    (a) involvement and participation;
    (b) mobility of labour and increased competition for scarce skills;
    (c) development of expertise among management in dealing with European business matters;
    (d) the impact of competition in the internal market on labour costs.

- *Operating in the global market* — working within a global business environment and developing human resource plans in multinational organizations.

Competition

- *The search for competitive advantage* — competition is fiercer both at home and abroad. Competitive advantage can be achieved by innovation and making the best use of the distinctive competences of the organization. The personnel function has to play its part in developing a positive culture and ensuring that the right people are available and that they are well motivated.
- *Added value* — competitiveness depends on achieving the highest levels possible of added value per employee. This means ensuring that there is a proper return on any investments in people, especially in relation to resourcing, training and remuneration costs.

Social and environmental pressures

- *Social pressures* — organizations have to respond to social pressures which require them to act responsibly towards all their stakeholders, who include employees, customers, suppliers and the public at large, as well as their owners or political masters. As Barry Curnow,[1] President of the Institute of Personnel Management, wrote: 'All enterprises must adopt public affairs and community investment policies and frequently the personnel director is the natural custodian of the "conscience" of the board of directors in such matters.'
- *Environmental pressures* — meaning that the link between any irresponsible behaviour by an organization and its business performance and reputation is much more obvious. As Curnow points out: 'In recruitment of young people a company's fundamental beliefs and philosophies come under close scrutiny by a generation quick to detect humbug and conscious of their own scarcity, potential and worth.'

Changing employee and employer expectations

- *Employee expectations* — according to Curnow, employees traditionally expected security of job employment; recognition for loyalty, service and good behaviour (long-service and good-conduct medals); and paternalistic employee benefits. Increasingly, however, they want cash now rather than deferred rewards that come in the shape of promotions, status and long-term service benefits which they may well not be around to enjoy under the present climate of company and labour market insecurity and job change.

- *Employer expectations* — employers, for their part, have wanted good behaviour, loyalty, continuity (cradle-to-grave careers), team spirit and employees who would fit in with the corporate culture. However, employers now need immediate performance and no longer want to link rewards to time. They can no longer offer job security because of technological and market changes and are not so concerned with providing lifelong careers. In fact, they expect to supply their human resource needs much more from short-term contract or temporary staff.

The changing role of personnel management

- *Strategic capability* — the ability of the head of the function to be fully involved in the development of corporate strategy.
- *Strategic integration* — integrating human resource and business strategies through understanding of both the needs of the business and the key people issues.
- *Intervention* — the capacity to intervene as necessary in any issue affecting people.
- *Enabling* — the role of the function in enabling and empowering people within the organization to reach higher levels of performance in achieving organizational goals.
- *Contribution to the bottom line* — ensuring that all the activities of the personnel function are directed towards achieving improved bottom-line performance for the good of the organization and of all its stakeholders, including owners, employees, customers, suppliers and the public at large.
- *Social responsibility* — exerting influence to ensure that there is no conflict between achieving business or corporate objectives and fulfilling social as well as legal responsibilities.
- *The impact of HRM philosophies* — deciding on how far an HRM approach as described in the introduction to this book is valid.
- *The responsibility for human resource management* — determining the extent to which human resource management is the responsibility of line managers and, if it is believed that it *is* their responsibility (as it should be), working out what the role of the personnel function is in these circumstances.

The future of personnel management

The following three factors will govern future trends in personnel management:

- The future of the economy.
- The future of organizations.
- The future of work.

The future of the economy

The trend has been towards the high-tech and service industries which broadly have favoured the South against the North. Manufacturing industry will thrive, as it does now in part, but only if it accepts and implements technological and organizational change, and adapts its human resource management policies to current thinking, rather than living in the past.

Market economies, of course, do not always run smoothly, as many people found out on 19 October 1987 — Black Monday. Prosperous countries which have relied on one product, for example, oil, have got into difficulties in the past and might do so again in the future, and this could happen here, although the UK economy is, fortunately, not unduly dependent on North Sea oil.

The future of organizations and the future of work, which are considered below, are obviously affected to a considerable degree by government economic policy and trends in both world and home markets. The future of organizations, work and, therefore, personnel management, is just as unpredictable as the economic future. But it does not seem unreasonable to suppose that, give or take a few hiccoughs, present trends will continue.

The future of organizations

In 1988, Drucker,[2] as trenchant as ever after all these years, wrote:

> The typical large business 20 years hence will have fewer than half the levels of management of its counterpart today, and no more than a third the managers. In its structure, and in its management problems and concerns, it will bear little resemblance to the typical manufacturing concern, circa 1950, which our textbooks still consider the norm. . . . The typical business will be knowledge-based, an organization composed largely of specialists who direct and discipline their own performance through organized feedback from colleagues, customers and headquarters.

Organizations of the future will be information-based. They will require more specialists than the command-and-control organizations we are used to. The number of management levels and the number of managers can be sharply cut. The trend towards flatter, leaner organizations is already here. But it will accelerate in the future and this means that many ideas developed in the 1950s, '60s, and '70s about organization structures, job design, motivating techniques, remuneration policies, management development, and industrial relations will become increasingly irrelevant. They are being replaced by a more flexible approach which treats organizational members more as individuals who get their satisfaction from opportunities to use and develop their skills in a more fluid, 'organic' environment, who are rewarded according to their individual contribution, who are less concerned about careers within a job hierarchy, who accept that traditional methods of managing are no longer appropriate, and who can tolerate a little ambiguity about where they are going because they know that their skills are in demand and that, in any case, they have the capacity to make and enjoy their own future, in or out of work.

The future of work

The future of work is clearly a function of the changes in the economy and organizations mentioned above. High levels of unemployment, caused by increases in the labour supply and by the dual effects of new technology and the recession, seem inevitable in the medium term. Skill shortages still exist, but the unemployed will continue to be those who are poorly qualified or those whose skills have become obsolete.

Handy[3] has stated that future developments in the nature of work will include:

- many more people than at present not working in an organization — an increase in outworkers and subcontracting facilitated by information technology in the shape of computer networks and electronic mail;
- shorter working hours;
- fewer mammoth bureaucracies, more federal organizations and more small businesses;
- more requirements for specialists and professionals in organizations;
- more importance given to the informal, uncounted economy of the home and the community;
- a manufacturing sector that is smaller in terms of people but larger in terms of output;

- a smaller working population and a larger dependent population;
- a greatly increased demand for education, often provided by distance learning;
- new forms of social organization to complement the employment organization.

Trends in personnel management

Personnel management will have to adjust itself to tomorrow's world. Tyson and Fell[4] have suggested that already the personnel function is being 'redefined and expanded from the role of being a control-orientated supplier of labour to an overall human resource planning, development and utilization agency'.

The particular areas of personnel management that will be affected by these changes are:

- *Organization planning.* The old principles of organization — span of control, unity of command, and the role of line and staff — which were based on the organization of the Roman Catholic Church or the Army, no longer apply. Organization design will be governed by information technology. There will be a continuous attack on unnecessary layers of management. Managers will be expected to use the instant information available to them, and to exploit their capacity to communicate numbers of data immediately to any quarter of the globe in order that they can concentrate on their roles as leaders and coordinators of much larger teams than they could handle before.
- *Commitment and motivation.* The importance of shared values will become increasingly recognized. The emphasis will be on gaining commitment by using the 'hearts and minds' approach. The 'flower people' idea, generated in the 1960s, that organizations exist to make people happy will finally vanish. Organizations exist to get work done, but job satisfaction is created by providing challenging and rewarding work. Good performance produces job satisfaction, not the other way round.
- *Job design.* Autonomy based on the use of information technology will increase, whether it be individuals working in what Alvin Toffler calls their 'electronic cottages' or autonomous working groups. High-performance work design will become the most frequently used job design technique. This approach will stress the performance requirements of jobs in terms of objectives, targets and standards, and jobs will be designed round individuals or autonomous working groups, with these requirements uppermost in people's minds. Job enrichment, with its implication that jobs exist only to enrich the lives of

people rather than that people exist in organizations to do jobs, will no longer be fashionable. High-performance design should provide all the challenge and opportunity required to meet the needs of employees for growth and achievement.

- *Human resource planning.* A strategic view of personnel management will become the rule rather than, as tends to be the case now, the exception. People will increasingly be regarded as *the* key resource for which investment plans have to be made which are fully integrated with the longer-term strategies of the business.
- *Recruitment.* Personnel specifications in the new organizations will place greater emphasis on adaptability and the need to 'fit' the corporate culture. Pre-employment education will have to be broad and should develop a range of basic skills in order that trainees have a good foundation upon which they can build quickly. Aptitude, attainment, interest and personality tests will become even more sophisticated and will increasingly be used to match people to appropriate jobs. Career guidance will also become more effective in order that school and university leavers will have a better chance of setting off in the right direction.
- *Employment.* More use will be made of contract staff and outworkers. Job sharing may not expand as quickly as some people have believed, but working hours will be more flexible to meet both operational and individual needs. Terms and conditions of employment will almost universally be harmonized. Single status will be the norm.
- *Work.* The move towards multiskilling will accelerate. Flexibility at work will be all-important and employees will have to be able to adapt themselves more quickly to technological change.
- *Database management.* Computerized personnel information systems will use personnel databases more comprehensively for decision support, as in the areas of human resource planning (with the help of models) and competence modelling. Expert systems will be developed to store and manipulate, and to present managers with the information they need to know for organization and job design, performance management, reward management, and career planning.
- *Reward management.* The rigid, multigraded salary structure with fixed increments will be a thing of the past. Pay will be fixed individually in relation to contribution and the market value of the employee. Payment will be for performance and skill rather than simply for 'being there'. Payment-by-results schemes will still have a valid role in spite of the criticisms that have been levelled at them over the years. But the schemes will be designed more carefully to fit the situation, using the

contingency approach. And they will be adaptable to changes in technology, work methods, and work mix. Benefits will be distributed equally to all employees in line with the principle of harmonization. The tax advantages provided by company cars will disappear and the reward system will depend on money alone to recognize different levels of contribution and achievement.

- *Performance management.* Systems for assessing and improving performance will concentrate on measuring and developing all round excellence. The highest ratings will be given to those who can make things happen, manage change and adjust rapidly to new challenges and opportunities. Performance improvement programmes will be designed not only to increase productivity but also to encourage flexibility and the acquisition of new skills.
- *Training.* More sophisticated techniques will be devised to identify training needs, set training objectives, use a wider range of training methods (for example, computer-based training and distance learning) and evaluate the impact of training more thoroughly.
- *Career management.* The traditional idea of a career developing through the successive levels of a management hierarchy will largely disappear. Dual career ladders will become common, allowing top specialists to advance just as far and as fast, if not faster, than their managerial colleagues. The equally traditional idea of one career will also vanish. People will have to be prepared to change direction at least once, possibly two or three times, during their working life. New methods of career management such as coaching, counselling and mentoring will replace the concept of management development with that of manager development.
- *Employee relations.* Although some trade unions are unlikely to abandon their traditional ways, 'new style' agreements, with their emphasis on single-status, single-union organizations and their belief in conjunctive rather than disjunctive bargaining, will help to achieve the replacement of industrial action (properly, industrial inaction) by industrial harmony. Management will recognize generally that it has the *duty* to manage, not the right to manage, and 'mutuality' in the form of joint involvement in problem solving and decision making will prevail.

The trade unions will still have a role to play in looking after the collective interests of their members and in protecting their rights. But individualism in employee relations will become more important as a result of the changing nature of organizations and work.

Human resource management

All these changes serve to reinforce the need to adopt the human resource management approach. In the words of Tyson and Fell:[5]

> A human resources management philosophy comes about in an organization . . . with the perception that labour is not an expense of doing business, but that people are the only resource capable of turning inanimate factors of production into wealth. People provide the source of creative energy in any direction the organization dictates and fosters.

Human resource management is an attitude of mind rather than a substantially new set of techniques for personnel managers to use. The attitude required is a belief in the importance of people as a key resource and a determination to integrate the management of that resource with the strategic planning processes of the organization. This approach provides the basis for developing personnel strategies and policies which fit or are contingent on the circumstances of the enterprise and meet organizational needs. The effectiveness and value of the contribution of the personnel function to organizational success depends upon its ability to adopt and implement this approach to the management of human resources.

References

1. Curnow, B 'Trends in human resource management', *Human Resources*, Spring 1991.
2. Drucker, P 'The coming of the new organization', *Harvard Business Review*, January–February 1988.
3. Handy, C *The Future of Work*. Blackwell, Oxford, 1984.
4. Tyson, S and Fell, A *Evaluating the Personnel Function*. Hutchinson, London, 1986.
5. Ibid.

Appendices

Appendix A

Personnel Policies

Statement of overall personnel policy

1. The firm recognizes that its prime resource is its staff. It is upon their commitment and effort that the firm depends for its continued prosperity and growth. The principles which govern the application of the firm's personnel policies are set out below.

Equity

2. Employees are treated fairly and justly and an even-handed approach is adopted. This is applied by:
   (a) rewarding staff according to their contribution;
   (b) providing equal opportunities for employment and promotion;
   (c) applying the principles of natural justice when dealing with issues concerning individuals.

Involvement and participation

3. Staff are regarded as partners in the enterprise. They are involved in decisions affecting them and are encouraged to contribute their skills and knowledge to improving performance.

Communication

4. The firm adopts an open approach which discloses and communicates information to help staff to understand the economics of the business and how they can contribute to increasing its prosperity.

Management style

5. It is expected that managers will exercise effective leadership, but the firm encourages a democratic management style. Managers are both approachable and visible. The emphasis is on teamwork and cooperation. An atmosphere of mutual trust is fostered.

Consideration

6. It is accepted that to obtain the best performance and support from staff consideration should be given to them as individuals when making decisions which affect their prospects, security and job satisfaction.

Social responsibility

7. Care is taken for the welfare of staff — serving and retired — and support and encouragement are provided where hardship occurs.

Quality of working life

8. The firm endeavours to provide agreeable working conditions for its staff and to enrich jobs wherever possible to add interest and increase involvement. The firm is fully conscious of the need to maintain a healthy and safe work environment and systems of work.

Continuous training and development

9. The firm requires staff to be fully trained for their jobs in order to ensure that the firm's activities are carried out expertly.

10. The development of the abilities of staff to their full potential is a continuous process to which all managers are expected to contribute.

Opportunity

11. Staff will be given every opportunity to advance their careers in the firm. As far as possible, promotion will be from within the firm.

Performance

12. The firm expects a high level of performance from its staff.

Employment policy

Human resource planning

1. The firm is committed to planning ahead in order to maximize the opportunities for employees to develop their careers within the firm and to minimize the possibility of redundancies.

Quality staff

2. The firm deliberately sets out to recruit and develop good-quality staff who have the ability to meet the high standards of performance that will be expected of them.

Promotion

3. The policy of the firm is to promote from within wherever possible, and, to this end, when appropriate, vacancies will be advertised internally. Employees will not be held back from promotion by their managers.

4. It is recognized, however, that it may sometimes be necessary to replace staff or fill new jobs by recruiting from outside the firm when there are no suitable staff available. It must also be appreciated that a vigorous organization needs 'new blood' from time to time.

Equal opportunity

5. The firm is an equal opportunity employer. A separate document sets out this policy in more detail.

Redundancy

6. The firm will use its best endeavours to avoid involuntary redundancy through its human resource planning, redeployment, and retraining procedures.

7. However, should redundancy be absolutely unavoidable, the firm will give the maximum amount of warning possible and will provide help in obtaining suitable alternative work.

Discipline

8. Employees have the right to know the company's rules of conduct and what could happen if they are infringed. In handling disciplinary cases, the firm will treat employees in accordance with the principles of natural justice, which are the following:

   (a)   the employee should be informed clearly of the nature of the complaint;
   (b)   the employee should be given the chance to explain;
   (c)   the employee should be given the opportunity to improve, except in particularly gross cases of incapability or misconduct;
   (d)   the employee should be warned of the consequences if specific improvements do not take place;
   (e)   the manager's decision to take disciplinary action should be based on sufficient evidence;
   (f)   the manager should take any mitigating factors into account;
   (g)   the disciplinary action should be appropriate to the nature of the offence or misbehaviour;
   (h)   the employee should have the right to appeal against disciplinary action.

Grievances

9. Employees have the right to raise any grievance with their managers and can, if they wish, be accompanied by another employee of the firm to act as their representative. Appeals can be made to a higher level if employees are not satisfied that their grievance has been dealt with adequately.

Equal opportunity policy

1. The firm is an equal opportunity employer. This means that the firm does not permit discrimination of any kind against any person on grounds of:

   (a)   colour;
   (b)   creed or religion;

(c)   race or ethnic origins;

(d)   nationality or national origin;

(e)   sex;

(f)   marital status;

(g)   disability.

2.   Direct discrimination is defined as treating a person less favourably than others are, or would be, treated in the same or similar circumstances.

3.   Indirect discrimination occurs when a requirement or condition is applied which, whether intentional or not, adversely affects a considerably larger proportion of people of one race, sex or marital status than another and cannot be justified on grounds other than race, sex or marital status.

4.   The firm regards discrimination, as defined in paras 2 and 3 above, as gross misconduct, and any employee of the firm who discriminates against any other person will be liable to instant dismissal.

5.   The firm will ensure that equal opportunity principles are applied in all its personnel policies and, in particular, in the procedures relating to the recruitment, training, development and promotion of staff. In applying the policy to the disabled, the proviso is that the disability does not prevent the function of the job from being carried out.

Human resource development policy

Preamble

The firm recognizes that the future prosperity of the firm largely depends on the knowledge, skills, expertise and motivation of its human resources.

Aims

The aim of the human resource development programmes of the firm is to provide the firm with the quality of human resources it needs — now and in the future — by:

(a)   training employees to achieve maximum effectiveness in the shortest possible time;

(b)   developing a multiskilled workforce capable of operating flexibly and responding rapidly to changes in business and organizational needs or skill requirements;

(c)   improving performance in employees' present jobs;

(d)   ensuring that the best use is made of the natural abilities of employees by developing their skills and capacities for the benefit of the organization and their future career;

(e)   developing commitment to the firm by:

      (i)   using the process of training to increase pride in the firm and its products and to inculcate the core values of the firm, especially those concerned with the pursuit of excellence, professionalism, entrepreneurship, market and customer orientation and the belief in an open and democratic management style;

      (ii)   ensuring that all employees are aware of the opportunities presented to them by the firm's training policies and programmes.

Policies for achieving the aims

1.   Development and training is a continuous and systematic process. All training is based

on the identification of relevant training needs for the enterprise as a whole, the functions within the firm and individual employees.

2. The relevance of training is directly proportional to the extent to which it contributes to achieving the strategic objectives of the firm.

3. The best training takes place in the 'real' situation, ie in the normal course of work through training on the job, coaching, counselling and self-managed projects. This means that line managers have the main responsibility for training their staff, with the support and guidance of the human resource development function within the personnel department.

4. The best form of development is self-development and the firm's training policies are designed to help staff to improve their own performance and to develop their own skills and knowledge. The system of accountable management plays an important part in the process.

5. It follows from points (3) and (4) above that the principal method by which managers and staff can be equipped to do their jobs and to develop their potential is by ensuring that they have the right variety of experience, in good time during their careers. This experience can and should be supplemented, but never replaced, by courses carefully timed and designed to meet particular needs.

6. To ensure that development and training programmes make a proper contribution to improving the firm's performance, a continuous process of evaluation takes place, on the basis of which changes are made to increase relevance and effectiveness.

Pay policy

Staff should correctly be rewarded in relation to:

1. The contribution they are expected to make towards achieving the firm's objectives.

2. The results they achieve — in accordance with the principle of paying for performance.

3. The performance of the firm.

4. The value placed on comparable jobs within the firm.

5. The value placed on comparable jobs in other companies, ie market rates.

6. The differentials required between levels of responsibility in order to:

    (a)   recognize seniority;
    (b)   provide incentives for career progression within the firm;
    (c)   reflect the skills and qualifications needed in different jobs.

7. The economic and commercial environment as it affects the firm and its staff.

Involvement and participation policy

Aims

1. The aims of the firm concerning involvement and participation policy are as follows:

    (a)   to generate the commitment of all employees to the success of the enterprise.

(b)   to enable the firm better to meet the needs of its customers and adapt to changing market requirements, and hence to maintain its future prospects and the prospects of those who work in it.

(c)   to help the organization to improve performance and productivity and adopt new methods of working to match new technology, drawing on the resources of knowledge and practical skills of all its employees.

(d)   to improve the satisfaction employees get from their work.

(e)   to provide all employees with the opportunity to influence and be involved in decisions which are likely to affect their interests.

Principles

2.   The principles of the involvement and participation policies of the firm are as follows:

(a)   *Management must lead* — senior management must provide the lead, and managers at all levels be involved in the action necessary to establish and maintain effective participation. Participation is not to be expected to occur or develop of its own accord.

(b)   *All employees are included* — all employees, including managers, should have the opportunity to participate, and the success of the participation policy will depend on their widespread response. For this they must know that their views are sought and taken into account by management. This will depend largely on individual employees' relationships with their own supervisors and managers, and the extent to which they are involved in the way objectives are set and achieved in their own work area.

(c)   *Education and training* — employees and their representatives, as well as managers, will need appropriate education and training so as to be able to fulfil their participation role in a constructive manner in the interests of the organization and all its employees. Management will provide the resources to do this.

(d)   *The role of employee representatives* — employee representatives have a key role to play in implementing the participation policies by their involvement in staff or works councils and through the operation of the normal representational system.

(e)   *The role of management* — management has the duty to manage the enterprise to satisfy the requirements of its owners, the demands of its customers and the needs of its employees. Whatever arrangements and procedures for involvement and participation may be established, managers remain responsible for making business and organization decisions falling within the area of their own accountability and for communicating such decisions, with relevant background information, to employees.

(f)   *The role of communications* — an open policy of communications about business plans (subject to confidentiality), programmes and performance is an essential part of the process of involvement and participation.

Communications policy

1.   The firm believes that it is essential that its staff are informed on the progress, policies, plans and financial state of the firm.

2.   The firm recognizes its staff as partners in the business and as such will encourage them to make their opinions known on issues which affect them directly.

3. In pursuing an effective communication policy, the firm aims to help staff achieve a better understanding of the firm's objectives and policies and to gain their commitment to them.

4. It is recognized that:

   (a) it is important to create a climate within the firm which is conducive to effective communication.

   (b) communication is a two-way process and management has the responsibility of ensuring that staff are able to communicate their views as well as to communicate to them.

   (c) in certain cases, however, there may be a need to preserve confidentiality, which could impose constraints upon communication.

5. The communication policy is closely linked to the firm's policies on involvement and participation and on employee relations.

Employee relations policy

1. The firm will strive to ensure that it maintains good relations with its staff in order to protect the interests of both parties.

2. In its dealings with staff representatives or other representative bodies, the firm will be frank and fair and aim to create an atmosphere of mutual trust, credibility, and consistency.

3. The firm is committed to involvement, participation, and open communication to build and maintain a cooperative climate within the firm. Its approach in these areas is set out in more detail in the separate policies for involvement and participation and for communications.

4. The firm recognizes that there will be issues which concern staff collectively, and its staff council system is designed to provide a medium for the exchange of views on these issues and the resolution of any problems.

New technology policy

1. The firm is committed to the introduction of new technology wherever this is cost-effective, ie in general benefits the firm and provides an appropriate return on investments, and in particular furthers the firm's need to improve profitability, productivity or the level of customer service.

2. The firm appreciates that the introduction of new technology is a matter of concern to its staff from the point of view of changes in work and skill requirements and future security of employment.

3. Recognizing this concern, the firm undertakes to consult with staff on programmes for developing new technology. The reasons for introducing it will be explained as well as its benefits.

4. The consultation process will include discussions on the implications of new technology to staff. Joint consideration will be given to training or retraining needs and policies for redeployment where this is necessary.

5.   The firm will use its best endeavours to avoid involuntary redundancy as a result of new technology. To this end, it undertakes to plan its introduction well ahead and to take full account during this planning process of the implications for staff. If, as a result of these plans, any surpluses are forecast, steps will be taken to absorb these so far as possible by redeployment, retraining or natural wastage.

Health and safety policy

Overall policy

1.   The firm regards the promotion of industrial safety and hygiene within its business as an essential part of its responsibilities. Furthermore, it regards the promotion of health and safety matters as a mutual objective of every manager and employee.

2.   It is, therefore, the firm's policy to do all that is reasonably practical to prevent personal injury and damage to property and to protect everyone from foreseeable work hazards, including the public in so far as they come into contact with the firm or its products.

The responsibility of management

3.   The responsibility of management is to:

   (a)   provide and maintain safe and healthy working conditions at each of its locations, in accordance with the relevant statutory requirements;

   (b)   provide safety training for all employees;

   (c)   provide all safety devices and protective equipment required by statute and supervise their use;

   (d)   ensure that articles and substances purchased for use at work have been so designed and constructed as to be safe and without risk to health, and that full information is made available by the suppliers where additional safety precautions are required;

   (e)   maintain a constant and continuing attention to all aspects of safety by:

      (i)   making regular location safety inspections;

      (ii)   seeking and stimulating consultation and contributions from employees on safety matters;

      (iii) ensuring that each location is given adequate health and safety cover by a person well versed in safety requirements relating to the firm's activities;

      (iv)   ensuring that all means of access and of egress are known to persons either on or using the premises;

      (v)   setting up safety committees consisting of management and staff representatives which meet regularly;

      (vi)   providing and maintaining a place of work that is, as far as is reasonably practical, safe, without risks to health, and with adequate facilities for the welfare of all employees.

The responsibility of employees

4.   All employees have the responsibility:

   (a)   to take reasonable care of the health and safety of themselves and of all persons they come into contact with at work;

(b) to cooperate with managers to enable them to carry out their statutory duties with the object of raising and maintaining a high standard of safety and health at work;

(c) report all incidents that have led, or may lead, to injury;

(d) cooperate in the investigation of accidents with the object of introducing measures to prevent a recurrence.

Appendix B

Statement of Core Values

The core values of the firm are as follows:

1. *Excellence* — anything we do well now we can do better.

2. *Profitable growth* — this is the profitable expansion of the business to generate the return our owners want on their investment and to ensure the continued prosperity and security of our employees.

3. *Enterprise* — we thrive by innovation, by creativity, and by seizing opportunities whenever they arise.

4. *Customer service* — we depend on our customers, and maintaining and improving levels of service to them is a continuing priority.

5. *Reward* — achievement brings reward to everyone involved in the firm.

6. *Teamwork* — we rely on teamwork to get results.

7. *Professionalism* — the effective and dedicated use and development of skills is a prime requirement.

8. *Productivity through people* — higher productivity and profitability are achieved by effective leadership and the development of a committed and well-trained workforce.

9. *Partnership* — all employees are treated as partners in the enterprise, to be involved in matters that affect them and to be told the results and future plans.

10. *People* — employees are treated fairly and as responsible human beings. They are given the opportunity to develop their skills and careers, and the firm is constantly aware of the need to improve the quality of their working life.

Appendix C

Example of a Statement of Accountabilities for a Personnel Manager

Overall accountability

To contribute to the achievement of the personnel objectives and strategies of the firm by:

(a) preparing and managing programmes for obtaining, maintaining, motivating, and developing the firm's human resources;
(b) providing the personnel services required;
(c) advising and assisting management in the preparation and implementation of the firm's personnel policies.

Specific accountabilities

Organization development

1. Contributes to the development of an effective organization by advising on the design of jobs and by preparing and introducing organization development programmes.

Performance indicators

Organization development

1. Performance is up to standard if:
   (a) jobs are designed to meet management requirements;
   (b) agreed organization development programmes are implemented within predetermined budgets and time-scales which meet their objectives of improving performance and teamwork and helping to manage change.

Human resource planning

2. Prepares, in the light of the firm's corporate strategies:
   (a) forecasts of human resource requirements;
   (b) plans for the acquisition, retention and motivation of employees.

Human resource planning

2. Performance is up to standard if:
   (a) corporate plans are analysed and used to provide the basis for the realistic anticipation of the firm's future human resource requirements;
   (b) a proactive approach is used in making proposals to management on how human resource management programmes can help to achieve their objectives for improving organizational and operational performance;
   (c) reactions to proposals from senior managers for improvements in the use and motivation of human resources are prompt, convincing and, ultimately, effective;
   (d) human resource acquisition, retention and motivation plans achieve the objectives set for them.

Employment

3. Provides the advice and administrative services in the fields of recruitment and employment practices needed to satisfy the requirements for human resources of the firm as a whole and of its individual managers.

4. Provides guidance, administrative services and, as required, technical direction in all areas where the firm has legal and social obligations towards its employees (eg health and safety).

Employment

3. Performance is up to standard if recruitment systems and standards are laid down and monitored in a way which ensures that management requirements are satisfied efficiently.

4. Performance is up to standard if statutory obligations affecting employment are fulfilled in order that the firm is not held liable for any transgressions, and procedures are operated which achieve the firm's personnel policies concerning social responsibility, health and safety.

Human resource development

5. Administers the performance management procedures (system of accountable management) at levels up to and including senior management.

Human resource development

5. Performance is up to standard if the system of accountable management is implemented in accordance with agreed objectives and programmes.

6. Plans and implements relevant training and development programmes designed to improve performance and develop potential.

6. Performance is up to standard if training and development programmes are prepared and implemented which satisfy identified needs within agreed budgets.

Reward management

7. Advises, in the light of the firm's pay policy, on pay systems, reward management procedures and pay levels and ensures that the systems and procedures are administered effectively.

Reward management

7. Performance is up to standard if reward management systems are operated which:
   (a) are in line with the firm's pay policies;
   (b) are cost-effective in that they satisfy requirements to attract, retain and motivate staff within agreed cost parameters.

Employee relations

8. Provides advice and services on day-to-day employee relations issues and on programmes for involvement participation and communications within the framework of employee relations strategies and policies.

Employee relations

8. Performance is up to standard if:
   (a) day-to-day issues with employees and their representatives are resolved without dissent or disruption;
   (b) the firm's policies and programmes for involvement, participation and communications are maintained and implemented according to plan and in a way which satisfies corporate objectives for increasing the motivation and commitment of employees.

Appendix D

Job Description — Personnel Director

Overall purpose

To advise on human resource strategies and personnel policies and ensure that the personnel function provides the support required to implement them.

Principal accountabilities

1. Participates as a member of the Executive Board in formulating corporate strategies, policies, plans and budgets and in monitoring the firm's performance so as to ensure that the corporate mission and goals are achieved.

2. Advises the chief executive and colleagues on the personnel and employee relations policies required by the firm in all areas of human resource management in order to uphold core values and fulfil social responsibilities.

3. Formulates and implements overall human resource strategies and specific plans derived from agreed corporate strategies to ensure that the human resources needed by the firm are available as required, in terms of both quality and quantity.

4. Advises on the development of organizational structures and processes and on the management of change in order to maximize organizational effectiveness.

5. Plans and directs human resource development, performance management and career management programmes designed to improve individual and organizational effectiveness and to give employees the best opportunities to develop their abilities and careers in the firm.

6. Develops reward management and remuneration (including pensions) policies and systems which attract, retain and motivate staff; are internally equitable as well as externally competitive; and operate cost-effectively.

7. Advises on employee relations and communication strategies and policies designed to maximize involvement and commitment while minimizing conflict.

Appendix E

Job Description — Personnel Officer

Job title: Personnel Officer

Responsible to: Personnel Manager (Service Departments)

Responsible to job holder: Secretary (half-time)

Job description

Nature and scope

The Personnel Officer is based in the London office of the company where approximately 400 staff are employed in the marketing, sales, advertising and public relations functions. The job holder is responsible to the Personnel Manager (Service Departments), based at the headquarters of the company in Birmingham. The Personnel Officer is concerned with the recruitment of clerical, secretarial, administrative and junior professional staff, of whom there are about 320. The Personnel Manager deals with more senior staff. Labour turnover is high (20 per cent), and 60 to 70 selections are handled each year. The Personnel Officer prepares job descriptions, agrees salaries, advertises, sifts applicants and carries out initial interviews. The job holder can reject unsuitable candidates, but the final selection is always made by the manager. There is a detailed personnel manual and salary grading scheme which has to be followed. In conjunction with the Training Manager, the job holder organizes induction programmes for new staff.

In addition to recruitment, the job holder is secretary of the job evaluation panel, which is chaired by the Personnel Manager (a points evaluation scheme is used). He/she conducts the job analyses for clerical, administrative and junior professional staff. The job holder also takes part in the evaluation of these staff.

The job holder's other duties include advising on disciplinary cases to ensure that the proper procedure is carried out. He/she drafts written warnings (two last year) and agrees that they should be issued, but does not deal with dismissals — these are dealt with by the Personnel Manager. The Personnel Officer advises on handling equal opportunity and maternity issues and grievances (about 12 cases a year) and is also available to counsel junior staff on work-related problems (one or two cases a week). Inevitably, the job holder is also involved in personal problems.

The Personnel Officer provides administrative support to the annual salary review but is not involved in deciding increases. He/she ensures that his/her secretary inputs personnel data to the computerized record system and does this him/herself when necessary.

Overall purpose

To provide personnel services (recruitment, job evaluation and general advice) for all clerical, secretarial, administrative and junior professional staff in the London office.

Principal accountabilities

1. Provides advice and services on the recruitment and selection of clerical, secretarial, administrative and junior professional staff.
2. Organizes induction training programmes in conjunction with the Training Manager.
3. Acts as secretary to the job evaluation panel.
4. Analyses jobs and prepares job descriptions for evaluation purposes.
5. Advises on handling disciplinary matters up to the stage of a formal written warning.
6. Advises on other employment matters, including equal opportunity, maternity leave and the handling of grievances.
7. Counsels junior staff on work-related problems.
8. Provides administrative support in conducting the annual salary review.
9. Ensures that data on personnel are input to the company computerized personnel record system.

Job analysis

Knowledge and skills

Needs to understand fully the company's selection and job evaluation procedures. Should have a good working knowledge of employment legislation, particularly that concerned with discipline, equal opportunities and maternity leave.

The skills needed include interviewing, drafting job advertisements, job analysis, counselling and instructing. Also needs to be able to handle the computerized record system.

Ideally, the Personnel Officer should be a member of the Institute of Personnel Management, having taken either a full-time, one-year course or a part-time course extending over three to four years. But the necessary knowledge and skills could be obtained by a combination of work experience and training, although it is unlikely that the maturity and skills would be acquired by anyone with less than five years' experience in administration involving extensive dealings with people.

Responsibility

The job holder can make a quite significant impact on the effectiveness of the London office by his/her contribution to maintaining morale and obtaining high-quality staff. Errors can have a damaging effect on efficiency or staff relations, but they are fairly easy to detect. The job holder controls a secretary (part-time) but no other resource of any significance.

Decisions

The job holder operates in a separate unit and his/her boss is based 100 miles away. He/she frequently has to make instant decisions within her range of responsibility. He/she is working within well-defined guide lines (administrative and legal), but, because he/she is handling people issues, she often has to use his/her discretion in interpreting how a particular guideline should apply and advise accordingly. It should be remembered, however, that the ultimate decision on personnel matters rests with the line manager, although the Personnel Officer is responsible for providing firm advice if a legal or policy issue is involved and, at his/her discretion, can refer the matter to the Personnel Manager.

Complexity

The complexity of the job arises from the constant stream of people the job holder has to see and the variety of problems (recruitment, job evaluation, employment) he/she has to deal with during the day. However, the job holder is exercising on a consistent basis a fairly limited range of skills (interpersonal and administrative).

Contacts

The job holder is constantly dealing with management at all levels and is expected to provide advice as well as services. He/she is also involved in counselling staff, often on sensitive issues. External contacts include employment agencies and the advertising agency of the company.

Appendix F

Corporate Culture Check-list

Analysis

Mission

1. Has the mission of the organization been defined and communicated to all concerned?

Norms

2. What are the norms of the organization (ie how people behave or are expected to behave) under such headings as:

   (a) the work ethic;
   (b) status;
   (c) ambition;
   (d) performance;
   (e) exercise of power;
   (f) playing politics;
   (g) managerial behaviour;
   (h) formality/informality;
   (i) openness;
   (j) trust;
   (k) interpersonal relations.

Values

3. What are the core values of the organization (ie what is believed to be important) under such headings as:

   (a) balance between needs of organization and staff;
   (b) care and consideration for people;
   (c) care for customers and clients;
   (d) competitiveness;
   (e) cost control;
   (f) enterprise;

(g)   equity in the treatment of staff;
(h)   excellence;
(i)   flexibility;
(j)   growth;
(k)   innovation;
(l)   market/customer orientation;
(m)   performance orientation;
(n)   provision of opportunity for employees;
(o)   quality;
(p)   social responsibility.

4.   To what extent have these values been defined and communicated to employees?
5.   What action has been taken by management to ensure that the values have been put into practice?

Organization climate

6.   To what extent can the climate of the organization (its working atmosphere) be described as:

(a)   action-orientated;
(b)   bureaucratic;
(c)   cooperative;
(d)   formal;
(e)   friendly;
(f)   hierarchical;
(g)   innovative;
(h)   open (communicative);
(i)   people-orientated;
(j)   political;
(k)   proactive;
(l)   reactive;
(m)   relaxed;
(n)   results-orientated;
(o)   status conscious;
(p)   stressful;
(q)   task-orientated.

Management style

7.   To what extent are managers:

(a)   autocratic, ie using authority to compel people to do what they are told; or democratic, ie encouraging people to participate in decision making;
(b)   task-centred or people-centred;
(c)   distant and cold or approachable and friendly;
(d)   hard or soft on people?

Diagnosis

8.   To what extent, and in what ways, are the norms, values, climate, and management

style of the organization functional or dysfunctional, ie how far do they support or inhibit the achievement of objectives?

9. To what extent are management and staff generally satisfied with the norms, values, etc?

10. How receptive is top management to any need for cultural change?

Appendix G

Quality Assurance — BS 5750

The BS (British Standard) 5750 series provides the national standards which tell suppliers and manufacturers what is required of a quality system. Its main provisions are summarized below.

1. A senior manager with the necessary authority must clearly be responsible for quality, with the task of coordinating and monitoring the quality system and seeing that prompt and effective action is taken to ensure that requirements of BS 5750 are met.
2. The nature and degree of organization, structure, resources, responsibilities, procedures and processes affecting quality must be documented.
3. The quality system must be planned and developed to take account of all other functions such as customer liaison, manufacturing, purchasing, subcontracting, training and installation.
4. Quality planning must identify the need for updating quality control techniques, ensuring that there are equipment and personnel capable of carrying out plans and providing for adequate quality records.
5. There must be carefully planned and documented control of design and development planning, with assignment of activities to qualified staff with adequate resources, control of interfaces between different disciplines and organizations, and documentation of design input requirements and design output.
6. A coordinated system should be established which will ensure the provision of all appropriate documents covering planning, design, packaging, manufacture and inspection of products, as well as procedures which describe how functions shall be controlled, and where and when control should be exercised.
7. Control in writing should be provided of purchased products and services, purchasing data, inspection and verification of purchased products, and the quality system to be applied (as appropriate) by the suppliers.
8. Procedures and work instructions, including all customer specifications, should be defined in a simple form which covers every phase of manufacture, assembly and installation.
9. Procedures should be set up for inspection and tests to be performed on incoming goods, taking account of the documented evidence of conformance provided with the goods.

10. Procedures and records covering the control, calibration and inspection of measuring and test equipment should be defined.
11. Written control procedures should be defined in order to establish quickly at all times whether a product has:

    (a)   not been inspected;
    (b)   been inspected and approved;
    (c)   been inspected and rejected

12. Systems for prompt and effective corrective action should be set up where non-conformance has been found.
13. Written instructions and procedures should exist on the way a product is handled, stored and protected in the process and as it moves through the plant.
14. Retailed records are required showing that customer quality requirements are being met, including data such as audit reports on the quality assurance system, results of inspections and tests, calibration of test and measuring equipment, and corrective action.
15. Effective internal quality audit systems should be set up and monitored by management.
16. Provision of training, and records of training and achievements of competence are necessary.
17. Clear statistical procedures for monitoring quality standards should exist.

Appendix H

Job Analysis Check-list: Office Staff

The following are examples of the questions that might be asked in analysing an office job. The questions would not necessarily be put in exactly these words or in this order, and it would be necessary to ask a number of supplementary questions to clarify replies.

Job title
1. What is the title of the job?

Responsible to
2. To whom are you directly responsible?

Responsible for
3. Are there any staff directly responsible to you? If so, describe briefly the main purpose of the jobs of each of your immediate subordinates.
4. Have your immediate subordinates any staff responsible to them? If so, what is the total number of staff under your control?

Main purpose of job
5. What is the main purpose of your job, ie what, in general terms, are you supposed to do?
6. How does your job fit in with the work of your section or department as a whole?
7. How can the results you achieve in the job be measured or assessed?

Main tasks
8. What tasks or duties do you carry out? Describe them either in chronological order (that is, the order in which you do them during the day or week), in order of importance, or in order of frequency.
9. Where does your work come from? eg:

    (a)   from outside the organization by post or telephone;
    (b)   from another department or section;
    (c)   from your superior;
    (d)   from colleagues.

10. Where does your completed work go?

Volume

11.   How often, and in what quantities, is your work received, eg does it reach you as a single item, in batches, or continuously?

12.   For each of your main tasks or group of tasks:

    (a)   How often has the work to be done — continuously, daily, weekly, monthly, or intermittently?

    (b)What is the volume of work you are expected to complete per hour, day, or week, as appropriate?

    (c)   Approximately how long does it take to complete the work?

Forms and equipment

13.   Do you have to complete or maintain any forms or records? If so, give examples and describe how they are completed.

14.   Do you use any machines or equipment? If so, give details of the machines used and how often you use them.

Contacts

15.   To what extent does your work bring you into contact with:

    (a)   members of other departments?

    (b)   other organizations?

    (c)   members of the public?

In each case, indicate the frequency of the contacts and describe what they are about.

Discretion

16.   Is the way you do your work laid down in a procedure manual or in any other written instructions? If so, give details.

17.   To what extent are you able to vary:

    (a)   the methods of work you use?

    (b)   the order in which you carry out your tasks?

18.   Whom would you go to if you were in difficulties over an aspect of your work?

Checking

19.   Who checks your work and how frequently?

    (b)   How is your work checked?

Supervision received

21.   On what matters and how frequently do you receive direct instructions from your supervisor or manager?

22.   What matters have to be referred by you to your supervisor or manager, either for him or her to deal with or to obtain approval for an action you propose to take?

23.   How often do you have to refer matters to your supervisor or manager?

Supervision given

24.   What authority have you got in respect of your subordinates to:

    (a)   assign work;

(b) check work;
(c) correct and discipline;
(d) deal with grievances;
(e) recommend appointments, salary increases, transfers, promotions, discharges;
(f) assess their performance.

Working conditions
25. What are the conditions under which you carry out your work?
26. What qualifications and experience do you think are necessary to carry out your work?
27. What specific training is needed to carry out your work?
28. How long did it take you to learn to do the work?

Job Description — Works Manager

Job title: Works Manager

Overall purpose

To achieve agreed budgets, quality standards, and delivery requirements by the efficient control of manufacturing operations, by developing and maintaining good industrial relations, and by ensuring that the staff work together as a team.

Principal accountabilities

1. Formulates manufacturing plans and budgets in line with estimated market requirements and ensures that production capacity, equipment, and labour are available to achieve agreed output and foreseeable additional demands.
2. Works with company engineering research and development services to develop improved production methods and techniques.
3. Controls production in order to ensure economic loading on the works and to progress availability of supplies.
4. Schedules and controls production to meet programmed delivery dates and optimize wastage, down time and stock levels.
5. Monitors production and unit costs to achieve agreed productivity and cost per unit of output targets.
6. Implements total quality management programmes to achieve company quality targets and standards.
7. Maintains in good order the works and the equipment in it.
8. Ensures that healthy and safe systems of work are maintained and that all possible steps are taken to prevent accidents and minimize hazards to occupational health.
9. Recruits, trains and develops the people required, both in number and quality, to meet present and future needs.
10. Builds effective teams, develops motivation and commitment and maintains sound labour relations and morale.

Appendix K

Person Specification — Works Manager

1.	Physical characteristics	Essential	• Fit; • Able to work long hours in fairly demanding conditions;
2.	Attainments	Essential	• Time-served apprenticeship; • HNC or equivalent;
		Desirable	• Graduate apprenticeship; • Degree in production engineering;
3.	Intelligence	Essential	• Top third of population;
4.	Special aptitudes/ knowledge	Essential	• Comprehensive knowledge of production planning and control techniques in a high-tech environment; • Evidence of well-developed leadership and team-building skills; • A practised and successful negotiator;
		Desirable	• Experience in the application of modern capacity and aggregate planning and resource allocation techniques;
5.	Interests	Desirable	• Practical interests (getting things done); • Interested in keeping up-to-date with relevant management techniques; • A self-developer;
6.	Disposition	Essential	• Self-starter; • Accepts, indeed seeks, responsibility gladly; • Capable of withstanding pressure;
7.	Circumstances	Desirable	• Willing to travel within reason.

Application Form

A, B, C & Co Ltd

SURNAME	FIRST NAMES
ADDRESS	MAIDEN NAME (IF APPLICABLE)
	DATE OF BIRTH
	COUNTRY OF BIRTH
TELEPHONE (HOME)	MARITAL STATUS
TELEPHONE (WORK)	NUMBER OF CHILDREN
POSITION APPLIED FOR	
WHERE DID YOU LEARN OF THIS VACANCY?	

EDUCATION AND TRAINING
QUALIFICATIONS

What academic and/or professional qualifications do you hold?
(Use initials to indicate this eg CSE, 'O' Level, BSc, ACA etc)

SECONDARY EDUCATION

Dates		Name of school or college	Give details of major subjects studied, examinations taken and results
From	To		

EDUCATION BEYOND SECONDARY LEVEL

Dates		Name of college/university or other institution (Indicate if part-time or by home study)	Give details of major subjects studied, examinations taken and results
From	To		

TRAINING

Give details of any specialized training received and/or courses attended

OTHER SKILLS

Other qualifications and skills (including languages, current driving licence, keyboard skills, etc)

EMPLOYMENT HISTORY

Give details here of all positions held since completing your full-time education. Start with your present or most recent position and work back.

Dates		Name of employer, address and nature of business. Include any service with the Armed Forces.	Position and duties	Starting and leaving salary and any other benefits	Reason for leaving or wanting to leave
from	to				

INTERESTS

Please describe your leisure interests.

ADDITIONAL INFORMATION AND COMMENTS

Do you have any permanent or persistent health problems? Please give details.

Have you ever worked for A, B, C & Co Ltd? Please give details.

Please state salary required.

When would you be able to start work, if you were offered a position?

Please give the names and addresses of *two* persons who are in a position to comment on your professional/work ability. (References will not be taken up without your knowledge.)

Name _____   Name _____

Address _____   Address _____

_____   _____

_____ Telephone no. _____   _____ Telephone no. _____

Position _____   Position _____

Add any comments you wish to make to support your application.

I confirm that the information given on this application form is correct.

Signature of applicant _____ Date _____

Appendix M

Guidelines on Setting Objectives

An objective is a statement of what an individual is expected to achieve on a continuing and progressive basis or over a specific period of time.

Types of objectives

Objectives can be expressed in any of the following ways:

1. Targets or budgets which state in quantified terms the results to be achieved over a period of time, eg the job holder is expected to generate x income, or process all transactions within 24 hours, or operate within a budget of y;
2. Tasks or projects which define a particular task or project which has to be completed by a specified date.
3. Performance standards which describe the observable behaviour which indicates that the job has been well done, eg 'performance is up to standard if the job holder deals promptly, politely and helpfully with all enquiries'.

Guidelines on setting objectives

4. Objectives should be defined for each of the individual's key result areas. There are two types of objectives:

   (a) Continuing objectives which are incorporated in the definition of a key result area if that indicates clearly what the individual is expected to achieve on a continuing basis. For example, 'dispatches the warehouse planned output so that all items are removed by carriers on the same day they are packed' is a continuing objective because it contains within it a precise definition of the target to be achieved.
   (b) Shorter-term or specific objectives which define, in terms of targets, standards, or projects to be completed, the outputs required within a key results area, over a specified period. For example, a key result area definition which states that the job holder 'schedules production in order to meet laid-down output and delivery targets' defines a continuing objective in non-specific terms. The specific objective would set out the actual output and delivery targets to be achieved over the review period or refer to a document which specifies them.

5. Objectives should be agreed by the manager and the individual.

6. It should be possible to measure or assess the extent to which objectives have been achieved. This means defining 'performance indicators or criteria'. These will indicate what measures are to be used (eg targets, budgets, or 'deliverables' as defined in a project or task brief, performance specifications or performance standards). The manager and the individual should agree what these measures are and establish where the information required is to be obtained and how.

7. Arrangements should be made on how to monitor performance as compared with objectives during the review period.

Planning for the achievement of objectives

When objectives have been agreed, the manager and the individual should discuss how the latter will satisfactorily achieve his or her objectives. For some objectives, little or no discussion will be necessary because the individual is quite clearly capable of meeting them. In other cases, however, the discussion can review what the individual will need to do (including the acquisition of enhanced skills or additional knowledge) and any help that the manager or other people in the organization can provide.

Appendix N

Performance Management Forms

N1   Personal preparation form
N2   Manager's preparation form
N3   Performance review and agreement form

N1: Performance Management — Personal Preparation Form

Name: *Job title:*

Department: *Date:*

Purpose of performance management

The purpose of performance management is to provide opportunities for you and your manager to discuss matters relating to your job in order to help you to develop your performance and your career.

Purpose of the personal preparation form

The purpose of the personal preparation form is to prepare you for the performance management review meeting with your manager. Would you please consider:

- what you would like to talk about in the meeting;
- how you have got on since the last review period in relation to the objectives agreed at the previous review meeting;
- how you are getting on with satisfying the development needs also agreed at the last meeting;
- any problems you have encountered in achieving objectives or meeting development needs and your ideas about resolving them;
- any ways in which you think your abilities can be better used in the future;
- any areas of skill or knowledge which you would like to develop;
- suitable objectives for the next period.

This form is for your own use and need not be shown to your manager. However, it might be helpful if your manager has time to think about any matters you want to raise so that full consideration can be given to them at the meeting. The rest of this form consists of questions for you to answer covering the points listed above. If there is insufficient space for your answers, use additional sheets of paper.

    The rest of this form contains a number of questions for you to answer.

Performance Management
Personal Preparation Form (part 1)

---

1. Please list the tasks (the most important aspects of your job) for which you are responsible.

2. Please write down what you think are the main things you are aiming to achieve (your objectives) in carrying out your key tasks.

3. What do you think have been your main achievements over the last six months?

4. Have you met any problems in carrying out your work? If so, what sort of problems and what do you think should be done about them?

Performance Management
Personal Preparation Form (part 2)

---

5. Do you believe that the best use is being made of your skills and abilities? If not, what needs to be done?

---

6. Where would you like to go from here? ie what further experience or additional responsibilities would you like and what direction would you like your future career to take?

---

7. What further development or training would you like to help you to do even better in your job and/or to further your career?

N2: Performance Management — Manager's Preparation Form

Manager's Name: *Date:*

Name of individual to be reviewed:

Review period:

Purpose of the manager's preparation form

The purpose of this form is to help you prepare for the performance review meeting with individual members of your staff. Would you please consider:

- what you would like to talk about in the meeting;
- how the individual performed during the review period in relation to the objectives agreed at the last meeting;
- the progress made in satisfying the development and training needs identified at the last meeting;
- any problems that the individual has met in carrying out his or her job and how they might be resolved;
- any future development or training needs for the individual;
- what you have done or could do to help the individual perform better and develop his or her career;
- suitable objectives for the next period.

The rest of this form consists of questions for you to answer covering the points listed above.

Appendix N

Performance Management
Manager's Preparation Form (part 1)

1. Please refer to any existing job description and decide if it needs amending. If there is no job description, please draft one. List the key tasks (principal accountabilities) you have established for discussion with the individual.

2. Consider and list the objectives you would like to discuss with the individual with regard to each of the principal accountabilities. Indicate also your views on how achievements can be measured or assessed (performance criteria).

Performance Management
Manager's Preparation Form (part 2)

3. Consider the individual's performance over the last twelve months to identify achievements or any problems met in carrying out the work.

4. Think about the individual's skills and abilities. Are you satisfied that the best use is being made of them?

5. What is the individual's potential for promotion or to take on higher levels of responsibility?

6. What sort of development or training does the individual need to fit him or her for promotion and/or improve performance?

Appendix N

N3: Performance Management — Personal Review and Agreement Form

Name: *Job title:*

Reviewing Manager: *Period of review:*

Purpose

The purpose of the performance management form is to record the discussion during the review meeting of the individual's performance in the review period and the agreement reached on future objectives and development needs.

The meeting refers to the preparation forms completed by the manager and the individual. Although it includes a discussion of past performance, it is essentially a forward-looking process.

Content

The performance management form consists of three sections:

1. the review section, which records the discussion between the manager and the individual;
2. the performance agreement section, which records the agreements reached on:

    (a) objectives;
    (b) action plans;
    (c) development and training needs for the next period;

3. the comments section, in which the reviewing manager, the individual, and the reviewing manager's manager record any points they wish to make about the outcome of the performance review and agreement.

Performance Management
Performance Review

Section 1

The manager should record the outcome of the discussion with the individual on the latter's performance in achieving the objectives and meeting the development and training needs recorded in the performance agreement reached during the last review.

---

1. *Achievement of objectives* — comment on whether objectives were achieved, partly achieved, or not achieved and the factors which are agreed to have affected performance.

---

2. *Action plans* — comment on the progress made in completing agreed action plans.

---

3. *Meeting development needs* — comment on the development and training programmes completed during the period and their effectiveness.

Appendix N

Performance Management
Performance Agreement (part 1)

Section 2

1. *Objectives for the next review period* — indicate how performance will be measured (performance measures).

2. *Agreed action plans for next review period.*

Performance Management
Performance Agreement (part 2)

3. *Development needs* — what does the individual need to do to develop his or her abilities? How will the manager help?

4. *Training needs* — what training course(s) is (are) required to enhance skills and knowledge or develop potential?

Appendix N

Performance Management
Comments on Performance Review and Agreement

Section 3

Comments of reviewing manager:

Signature   Date

Comments of individual:

Signature   Date

Comments of reviewing manager's manager:

Signature   Date

Appendix P

Training Techniques

The training techniques analysed in this appendix are classified into three groups according to where they are generally used:

1. *on-the-job techniques* — demonstration, coaching, do-it-yourself training, job rotation/planned experience;
2. *on-the-job or off-the-job techniques* — action learning, job (skill) instruction, question and answer, assignments, projects, guided reading, computer-based training, instructional systems development, interactive video, video;
3. *off-the-job techniques* — lecture, talk, discussion, 'discovery' method, programmed learning, case study, role-playing, simulation, group exercises, group dynamics (team-building), distance learning.

On-the-job techniques

Demonstration

Demonstration is the technique of telling or showing trainees how to do a job and then allowing them to get on with it. It is the most commonly used — and abused — training method. It is direct and the trainee is actively engaged. Reinforcement or feedback can be good, if the supervisor, trainer, or colleague (that well-known character, Nellie, by whom the trainee sits) does it properly by clearly defining what results have been achieved and how they can be improved. But demonstration in its typically crude form does not provide a structured learning system where trainees understand the sequence of training they are following and can proceed by deliberate steps along the learning curve. This is more likely to happen if job (skill) instruction techniques are used, as described later.

Coaching

Coaching is a personal, on-the-job technique designed to develop individual skills, knowledge and attitudes. The term is usually reserved for management or supervisory training where informal but planned encounters take place between managers and subordinates.

The agenda for such meetings may be based on a performance review system which includes some elements of management by objectives or target setting. This would identify strengths to be developed or weaknesses in performance to be overcome, and the counselling sessions that should be part of the performance review process would indicate career development needs and the additional knowledge or skills that can be acquired on the job.

Coaching is even more effective if it can take place informally as part of the normal process of management. This type of coaching consists of:

- making subordinates aware of how they are managing by, for example, asking questions on how well they have thought through what they are doing;
- controlled delegation;
- using whatever situations arise as teaching opportunities;
- setting individual projects and assignments;
- spending time in looking at higher-level problems as well as discussing the immediate job.

Coaching may be informal, but it has to be planned. It is not simply going, from time to time, to see what subordinates are doing and advising them on how to do it better. Nor is it occasionally telling subordinates where they have gone wrong and throwing in a lecture for good measure. As far as possible, coaching should take place within the framework of a general plan of the areas and direction in which the subordinate should be developed.

Coaching should provide motivation, structure and effective feedback, if the coacher is skilled, dedicated and able to develop mutual confidence. Its success depends on a clear definition of work and training objectives, and this can be a time-consuming process; ultimately, success depends upon managers and supervisors recognizing that it is one of their key responsibilities, and they should be encouraged and trained to do it.

Do-it-yourself training

Do-it-yourself training aims to apply the principles of the discovery method (see below) to training on the job. The principle behind it is that people learn and retain more if they find out for themselves, as long as they are given direction on what to look for and help in finding it.

Do-it-yourself training operates by:

- starting from a definition of what someone needs to know and do to perform a job;
- establishing where the information required is available;
- giving trainees an outline of the information they have to obtain and where and from whom to get it. They may be given questions to answer or mini-projects to complete;
- briefing those concerned (mainly the trainee's boss and colleagues, but also people in other departments) on the help they should give the trainee;
- preparing a timetable for the learning programme;
- arranging for someone (the trainee's boss or the executive responsible for training) to monitor progress. This should include periodic meetings to check on what has been learned and to provide extra encouragement and guidance.

It is not quite as simple as it may appear to implement do-it-yourself training techniques. They must still be based upon job analysis leading to a full understanding of the knowledge and skills required to do the job. Trainees should be given careful guidance on how to set about getting the information required, and they must be motivated to understand the reasons for getting this information and how they will benefit.

The managers or supervisors of those under training should be prepared to spend time and trouble helping and coaching their staff. And it is not always easy to persuade busy people to do this, as every training officer knows. The only way is to convince them that this approach produces better results more quickly and cheaply than other methods. They have to be persuaded that the technique will have a measurably beneficial effect on the performance of the individuals concerned and on the performance of the department as a whole. Training managers have to be salesmen — they have to demonstrate the benefits of the product rather than describe its inherent features.

The only other drawback to do-it-yourself training is that it is more applicable to the development of knowledge than skills. It is therefore more likely to be useful for managers, supervisors, and administrative staff than for training machine operators or those in occupations where manual skills are of primary importance. None the less, do-it-yourself training, as an embodiment of the voluntary spirit as well as a practical application of learning theory, can play an important part in a training programme, especially when shortage of funds precludes any more elaborate approach.

Job rotation/planned experience

Job rotation aims to broaden experience by moving people from job to job or department to department. It can be an inefficient and frustrating method of acquiring additional knowledge and skills unless it is carefully planned and controlled. What has sometimes been referred to as the 'Cook's tour' method of moving trainees (usually management trainees) from department to department has incurred much justified criticism because of the time wasted by trainees in departments where no one knew what to do with them or cared.

It may be better to use the term 'planned sequence of experience' rather than 'job rotation' to emphasize that the experience should be programmed to satisfy a training specification for acquiring knowledge and skills in different departments and occupations. It can be argued in support of job rotation that if it is by experience that adults learn, then that experience should be planned.

Success in using this method depends on designing a programme which sets down what trainees are expected to learn in each department or job in which they gain experience. There must also be a suitable person available to see that trainees are given the right experience or opportunity to learn, and arrangements must be made to check progress. For apprentices, this will mean the use of training supervisors within departments to see that the training syllabus is followed, and the use of logbooks to record what experience has been gained. The syllabus within a department should include specific assignments or projects. A good way of stimulating trainees to find out for themselves is to provide them with a list of questions to answer. It is essential, however, to follow up each segment of experience to check what has been learnt and, if necessary, modify the programme.

On- or off-the-job techniques

Action learning

Action learning, as developed by Revans, is a method of helping managers develop their talents by exposing them to real problems. They are required to analyse them, formulate recommendations, and then, instead of being satisfied with a report, take action. It accords with the belief that managers learn best by doing rather than being taught.

This approach conforms to the principle on which all good training should be based — ie it is problem-based and action-orientated. It recognizes that the most perplexing task managers face is how to achieve change — how to persuade their colleagues and others to commit themselves to a different way of doing things. An action-learning programme therefore concentrates on developing the skills which managers need to take action effectively, without ignoring the need for knowledge of relevant techniques.

The concept of action learning is based on six assumptions:

1. Experienced managers have a huge curiosity to know how other managers work.
2. We learn not as much when we are motivated to learn, as when we are motivated to learn something.
3. Learning about oneself is threatening and is resisted if it tends to change one's self-image. However, it is possible to reduce the external threat to a level which no longer acts as a total barrier to learning about oneself.
4. People learn only when they do something, and they learn more the more responsible they feel the task to be.
5. Learning is deepest when it involves the whole person — mind, values, body, emotions.
6. The learner knows better than anyone else what he has learned. Nobody else has much chance of knowing.

A typical action learning programme brings together a group, or 'set', of four or five managers to solve the problem. They help and learn from each other, but an external consultant, or 'set adviser', sits in with them regularly. The project may last several months, and the set meets frequently, possibly one day a week. The adviser helps the members of the set to learn from one another and clarifies the process of action learning. This process involves change embedded in the web of relationships called the 'client system'. The web comprises at least three separate networks; the power network, the information network, and the motivational network (this is what Revans means by 'who can, who knows, and who cares'). The forces for change are already there within the client system and it is the adviser's role to point out the dynamics of this system as the work of diagnosis and implementation proceeds.

The group or set has to manage the project like any other project, deciding on objectives, planning resources, initiating action and monitoring progress. But all the time, with the help of their adviser, they are learning about the management processes involved as they actually happen.

Job instruction

Job instruction techniques should be based on skills analysis and learning theory as discussed in Chapters 16 and 20. The sequence of instruction should follow four stages:

- preparation;
- presentation — explanation and demonstration;
- practice and testing;
- follow-up.

Preparation for each instruction period means that the instructor must have a plan for presenting the subject matter and using appropriate teaching methods, visual aids and demonstration aids. It also means preparing trainees for the instruction that is to follow. They should want to learn. They must perceive that the learning will be relevant and useful to them personally. They should be encouraged to take pride in their job and to appreciate the satisfaction that comes from skilled performance.

Presentation should consist of a combination of telling and showing — explanation and demonstration.

Explanation should be as simple and direct as possible: the trainer explains briefly the ground to be covered and what to look for. He or she makes the maximum use of films, charts, diagrams, and other visual aids. The aim should be to teach first things first and then proceed from the known to the unknown, the simple to the complex, the concrete to the abstract, the general to the particular, the observation to reasoning, and the whole to the parts and back to the whole again.

Demonstration is an essential stage in instruction, especially when the skill to be learned is mainly a doing skill. Demonstration takes place in three stages:

1. The complete operation is shown at normal speed to show the trainee how the task should be carried out eventually.
2. The operation is demonstrated slowly and in correct sequence, element by element, to indicate clearly what is done and the order in which each task is carried out.
3. The operation is demonstrated again slowly, at least two or three times, to stress the how, when and why of successive movements.

Practice consists of the learner's imitating the instructor and then constantly repeating the operation under guidance. The aim is to reach the target level of performance for each element of the total task, but the instructor must constantly strive to develop coordinaed and integrated performance; that is, the smooth combination of the separate elements of the task into a whole job pattern.

Follow up continues during the training period for all the time required by the learner to reach a level of performance equal to that of the normal experienced worker in terms of quality, speed, and attention to safety. During the follow-up stage, the learner will continue to need help with particularly difficult tasks or to overcome temporary set-backs which result in a deterioration of performance. The instructor may have to repeat the presentation for the elements and supervise practice more closely until the trainee regains confidence or masters the task.

Job instruction guidelines

These are the most important guidelines to follow in giving job instruction:

*   Keep instruction and practice within reasonable time limits to avoid boredom and fatigue.
*   Arrange demonstration and practice such that trainees can experience some success early in training, thus maintaining interest and providing incentive.
*   Ensure that trainees know how they are getting on, but present feedback in an encouraging and constructive way.
*   Provide useful and productive tasks to do.
*   Recognize that all learners do not develop at the same rate.
*   Provide ample opportunity for practice in order that trainees can become used to carrying out the job at the experienced worker's standard of quality and speed and in complete safety.

Question and answer

The question and answer technique consists of an exchange between trainer and trainees to test understanding, stimulate thought or extend learning. It may take place during a job instruction programme or as part of a discussion period on a formal management course. It can be used to increase involvement, to check progress, and to explore attitudes to learning. Considerable skill is required to use this method. The question should be open — they should not lead to 'yes'/'no' answers, but they should also be clear and concise. They should always be asked in an encouraging and supportive manner.

Assignments

Assignments are a specific task or investigation which trainees do at the request of their trainer or manger. The assignment may be used as a test at the end of a training session, and, as long as it is realistic, it should help to transfer learning to the work situation. The trainer may still have to provide some guidance to trainees to ensure that the latter do not lose confidence if they meet difficulties in completing the task.

Assignments may also be given by managers to their subordinates as a means of extending their experience. They should be linked to a coaching programme in order that the lessons from the assignment are fully absorbed.

Projects

Projects are broader studies or tasks which trainees are asked to complete, often with only very generalized guidelines from their trainer or manager. They encourage initiative in seeking and analysing information, in originating ideas, and in preparing and presenting the results of the project. For apprentices, especially students and graduates, the project can be a practical exercise in which the trainees are required to design, manufacture, and test a piece of equipment. Projects for managers may consist of an investigation into a company policy issue or an operating problem.

Like assignments, projects give trainees or managers an opportunity to test their learning and extend their experience, although the scope of the study is likely to be wider, and the project is often carried out by a group of people.

Guided reading

Knowledge can be increased by giving trainees books, hand-outs, or company literature and asking them to read and comment on them. Guided reading may take place before a course when the members are asked to read 'precourse' literature. They seldom do. Or it may be given during a training course and used as reinforcement. The beautiful hand-outs that lecturers prepare are often allowed to gather dust when the course is over. They can be far more effective if they are distributed at appropriate points during or immediately after the lecture and those attending are required to discuss specific questions arising from them.

Reading as part of a development programme may be a valuable way of broadening knowledge as long as the material is seen by the trainee as relevant and there is follow-up to ensure that learning has taken place. The best way is to ask trainees to read a handbook or one or two chapters from a longer text and then come back to the trainer or their manager to discuss the relevance of the material and how they can use their knowledge.

Computer-based training

Computers can be used for training in the following ways:

1. To simulate actual situations in order that trainees can 'learn by doing'. For example, technicians can be trained in troubleshooting and repairing electronic circuitry by

looking at circuit diagrams displayed on the screen and using a light pen to measure voltage at different points in the circuit. When faults are diagnosed, 'repairs' are effected by means of a light pen, this time employed as a soldering iron.

2. To extend programmed learning texts to provide diagrammatic and pictorial displays in colour and to allow more interaction between the trainee and the information presented on the screen.

3. To provide a database for information which trainees can access through a computer terminal.

4. To measure the performances of trainees against predefined criteria.

5. To provide tests or exercises for trainees. The technique of *adaptive testing* uses a program containing a large number of items designed to test trainees' comprehension of certain principles. But it is not necessary for them to work through all of them or even to satisfy them sequentially in order to demonstrate their understanding. Their responses to a limited number of questions will show whether or not they have grasped the appropriate concepts, given training objectives. The process of testing can thus be speeded up considerably and prove less frustrating for the trainee.

Instructional systems developmentt

Instructional systems development (ISD) techniques, as developed by the American armed services, are used to provide a coordinated approach to the training system as a whole. They tabulate the steps required at each stage of the training process to provide training guides to line managers as well as to professional trainers.

The sequence of stages in the ISD approach are as follows:

1. *Analysis* — training needs are determined for the requirements of each task or job. Performance criteria and learning objectives are established, the latter defining what trainees have to be able to do to meet the experienced worker's standard.

2. *Design* — the structure and sequence of training required to meet performance criteria and learning objectives are defined and tests or other methods of evaluating training are devised.

3. *Development* — learning media and methods are selected and training materials prepared to add to the basic design in order to prepare the full instructional plan.

4. *Implementation* — the instructional plan is put into effect.

5. *Control* — training is evaluated and the system modified as necessary.

Interactive video

Interactive video is based on the fusion of two powerful training technologies — computer-based training and video — combined such that the sum is greater than the parts.

Computer-based training (CBT) is individualized and interactive. It is able to accommodate each trainee's needs and pace with the software. Video is effective when realistic sound and pictures are essential and a moving camera angle can compensate for the flatness of the screen, helping to portray three-dimensional reality. But video is limited as a training medium. It cannot be individualized. Watching video is a passive activity and the sequence of instruction is always linear.

Interactive video offers the trainer the best of both worlds. It is individualistic, interactive, and random-access, like CBT, but interactive video can also present, like video, realistic still or moving pictures without sound.

Interactive video is expensive, but its benefits are considerable in a number of different applications, such as:

- *Distance learning* — where trainees are widely scattered.
- *When trainees have learning difficulties* — many people, especially those without much formal education, find it difficult to absorb information from large blocks of text. As long as the interactive video programme is carefully constructed on the basis of a thorough task and skills analysis, and is designed to meet the requirements of learning theory, it will be an effective way of helping people to take in and use complex instructions.
- *Where there is a scarce training resource* — this might include skilled trainers or the real equipment that a trainee must operate, such as a robot system or an aircraft.
- *Where interpersonal skills are important* — interactive video is much better than print or CBT in improving interpersonal skills such as interviewing, dealing with difficult customers, counselling, or handling people problems.
- *When training time is at a premium* — interactive video can cut the time required to achieve learning objectives.

Video

While the printed word is often limited as a medium, the ability of video to present information visually is an obvious aid to training where there is a shortage of good trainers to get the message across. Videos can be used to present prepared material in the same way as films. They are most effective if they are backed up by a trainer's guide which ensures that the passive nature of screen-watching is followed up by active learning.

With the help of video cameras, video can provide instant feedback when training is taking place in such interactive skills as interviewing, counselling, selling, running meetings, and instructing.

Off-the-job techniques

Lecture

A lecture is a talk with little or no participation except a question-and-answer session at the end. It is used to transfer information to an audience with controlled content and timing. When the audience is large, there may be no alternative to a 'straight lecture' if there is no scope to break it up into discussion groups.

The effectiveness of a lecture depends on the ability of the speaker to present material with judicious use of visual aids. But there are several limits on the amount an inert audience can absorb. However effective the speaker, it is unlikely that more than 20 per cent of what was said will be remembered at the end of the day. And after a week, all will be forgotten unless the listeners have put some of their learning into practice. For maximum effectiveness, the lecture must never be longer than 30 or 40 minutes; it must not contain too much information (if the speaker can convey three new ideas which more than one-half of the audience understands and remembers, the lecture will have been successful); it must reinforce learning with appropriate visual aids (but not too many); and it must clearly indicate the action that should be taken to make use of the material.

Talk

A talk is a less formal lecture for a small group of not more than 20 people, with plenty of time for discussion. The encouragement of participation and interest means that more learning is likely to be retained than in a lecture, but the discussion may be dominated by the more articulate and confident members of the group unless carefully controlled.

Discussion

The objectives of using discussion techniques are to:

- get the audience to participate actively in learning;
- give people an opportunity of learning from the experience of others;
- help people to gain understanding of other points of view;
- develop powers of self-expression.

The aim of the trainer should be to guide the group's thinking. He or she may, therefore, be more concerned with shaping attitudes than imparting new knowledge. The trainer has unobtrusively to stimulate people to talk, guide the discussion along predetermined lines (there must be a plan and an ultimate objective), summarize the discussion from time to time, and sum up at the end.

The following techniques should be used to get active participation:

- Ask for contributions by direct questions.
- Use open-ended questions which will stimulate thought.
- Check understanding; make sure that everyone is following the argument.
- Encourage participation by providing support rather than cricitism.
- Prevent domination by individual members of the group by bringing in other people and asking cross-reference questions.
- Avoid dominating the group yourself. The leader's job is to guide the discussion, maintain control and summarize from time to time. If necessary, 'reflect' opinions expressed by individuals back to the group to make sure they find the answer for themselves. The leader's job is to help them reach a conclusion, not to do it for them.
- Maintain control — ensure that the discussion is progressing along the right lines towards a firm conclusion.

Discovery method

The discovery method is a style of teaching that allows pupils to learn by finding out principles and relationships for themselves. The essence of the method is that the training designer thinks out the progression of problems which the trainee is required to solve, relates this progression to the capacity of the trainee, and ensures that learning is based on intrinsic rather that extrinsic factors. In other words, trainees do not need to rely on previous knowledge and experience, nor do they depend on outside assistance (ie extrinsic factors). The learning, however, is not a random process. The trainee progresses through a series of planned steps, using the intrinsic information provided at each stage.

The discovery method is a demanding one to develop properly. It goes deeper than skills analysis, which simply lists all that has to be learned. Instead, it first identifies the crucial concepts and removes all the non-essentials in order that the training material can be appreciated in its simplest form. The next stage is the most difficult: the training designer has to get inside the learning situation to decide what are the principal obstacles to understanding and to find out why trainees have problems in learning. The next stage is to design a discovery programme specially for the needs of a group of trainees.

The best results from discovery training techniques are achieved with middle-aged and older leaners and on tasks that demand the development of concepts and understanding. The method has three main advantages:

1. *Motivation* — adults are more motivated towards discovery learning because they are involved from the start and involved on their own terms.
2. *Control* — the discovery method reveals the trainee's progress and level of understanding to the instructor and enables easier control to be exercised over performance.
3. *Retention* — learning from experience is easier for adults than learning from words; there is no stress on memorizing; hence, this sort of learning is remembered.

The main disadvantage of the discovery method is that it has to be specially designed for limited groups. A further disadvantage is that its benefits are not as evident in the short term as are those of more conventionally based training schemes. But where real understanding and retention of knowledge about the whole job is required for older trainees or people undergoing retraining, the discovery method has a lot to offer.

Programmed learning

Programmed learning, as originally developed, consisted of a text which progressively feeds information to trainees. After each piece of information, questions are posed which the trainee should answer correctly before moving on.

The basic principles of programmed learning were as follows:

*   The subject matter is presented in small units called frames.
*   Each frame requires a response from the trainee, who is thus actively involved in the learning process.
*   Trainees are told if their answer is correct at once. This rapid feedback gives immediate reinforcement to trainees or immediately corrects a misunderstanding.
*   The units of information are arranged in correct subject matter sequence and pose increasingly difficult questions. This means that the designer has had to analyse the learning steps required with great care.
*   Trainees work independently and at their own pace. Thus, they work as quickly or as slowly as they like.

Programmed instruction is an essential feature of computer-based training. It is primarily a method of systematic presentation which relies a great deal on the self-motivation of the trainee. In its usual form, it is quite different from discovery learning, which is more concerned with skills than knowledge and allows trainees greater scope to find out for themselves.

Programmed texts may result in an over-mechanical learning process and this could hinder retention. But there are considerable advantages in using this method in conjunction with others as a means of ensuring that trainees are ready, willing, and able to deal with the material confronting them and to take an active part in learning.

Case study

A case study is a history or description of an event or set of circumstances which is analysed by trainees in order to diagnose the causes of a problem and work out how to solve it. Case studies are mainly used in courses for managers and supervisors because they are based on the belief that managerial competence and understanding can best be achieved through the study and discussion of real events.

Case studies should aim to promote enquiry, the exchange of ideas, and the analysis of experience in order that the trainees can discover underlying principles which the case study is designed to illustrate. They are not light relief. Nor are they a means of lightening the load on the instructor. Trainers have to work hard to define the learning points that must come out of each case, and they must work even harder to ensure that these points do emerge.

The danger of case studies is that they are often perceived by trainees to be irrelevant to their needs, even if based on fact. Consequently, the analysis is superficial and the situation is unrealistic. It is the trainer's job to avoid these dangers by ensuring that the participants are not allowed to get away with half-baked comments. Trainers have to challenge assumptions and force people to justify their reasoning. Above all, they have to seize every chance to draw out the principles they want to illustrate from the discussion and to get the group to see how these are relevant to their own working situation.

Role-playing

In role-playing, the participants act out a situation by assuming the roles of the characters involved. The situation will be one in which there is interaction between two people or within a group. It should be specially prepared with briefs written for each participant explaining the situation and, broadly, their role in it. Alternatively, role-playing could emerge naturally from a case study when the trainees are asked to test their solution by playing the parts of those concerned.

Role-playing is used to give managers, supervisors or sales representatives practice in dealing with face-to-face situations such as interviewing, counselling, coaching, dealing with a grievance, sellilng, leading a group or running a meeting. It develops interactive skills and gives people insight into the way in which people behave and feel.

The technique of 'role reversal', in which a pair playing, say, a manager and a supervisor run through the case and then exchange roles and repeat it, gives extra insight into the feelings involved and the skills required.

Role-playing enables trainees to get expert advice and constructive criticism from the trainer and their colleagues in a 'protected' training situation. It can help to increase confidence as well as developing skills in handling people. The main difficulties are either that trainees are embarrassed or that they do not take the exercise seriously and overplay their parts.

Simulation

Simulation is a training technique which combines case studies and role playing to obtain the maximum amount of realism in classroom training. The aim is to facilitate the transfer of what has been learned off the job to on-the-job behaviour by reproducing, in the training room, situations which are as close as possible to real life. Trainees are thus given the opportunity to practise behaviour in conditions identical to or at least very similar to those they will meet when they complete the course.

Group exercises

In a group exercise the trainees examine problems and develop solutions to them as a group. The problem may be a case study or it could be a problem entirely unrelated to everyday work. The aims of an exercise of this kind are to give members practice in working together and to obtain insight into the way in which groups behave and arrive at decisions.

Group exercises can be used as part of a team-building programme and to develop interactive skills. They can be combined with other techniques such as the discovery method to enable participants to work out for themselves the techniques and skills they need to use.

For example, a course for managers in a large firm of chartered accountants dealt with problem solving in the following steps:

1. The course was divided into three groups of six, all sitting in the same room.
2. Each group was given three linguistic/mathematical problems to solve and was then asked to discuss how the problem should be tackled.
3. Each group was then asked to develop a better problem-solving method which could be used in future.
4. Further exercises were given to the groups for them to test out their problem-solving method — the exercises were again abstract problems, unrelated to work. Managers were selected in each group to act as observers and to give feedback to the other members on how they behaved and how effective their problem-solving method was.
5. After each exercise, the observers from each group were asked to summarize their observations to the whole course, and a general discussion took place on the lessons learnt.
6. The groups were then asked to get together and work out between them a problem-solving method incorporating the best elements of the three group methods. Again, observers were appointed to report on how effectively this negotiating exercise was conducted.
7. The jointly agreed problem-solving method was tested on further case studies, which became progressively more realistic. Some of these were developed into role-playing exercises, each designed to illustrate the use of management skills such as working in groups, leadership, delegation, coaching, appraising performance, and handling disciplinary problems.

Group exercises may be introduced as part of a formal, off-the-job management or supervisory training course. They are also an essential element in an organization development programme, as described in Chapter 4. Group exercises use many of the principles of group dynamics training, as discussed below, and may constitute a major part of a group dynamics course.

Group dynamics

Group dynamics training is largely based on the work of Kurt Lewin and the Research Centre for Group Dynamics at MIT in 1946. It has three interconnected and often overlapping aims: first, to improve the effectiveness with which groups operate (team building); second, to increase self-understanding and awareness of social processes; and, third, to develop interactive skills which will enable people to function more effectively in groups. Group training can also help in modifying individual attitudes and values.

Group dynamics programmes may emphasize one of these aims more than the others, and they come in a number of forms. The basic variety is 'T-group' training, but this approach can be modified for use in courses primarily designed to improve interactive skills. There are also various packaged group dynamics courses, of which the best known are Blake's Managerial Grid and Coverdale Training.

T-group training

'T-group' stands for 'training group', which is not a very helpful description. It is also referred to as 'sensitivity training', 'group dynamics', and 'group relations training'. T-group has three aims:

1. to increase *sensitivity* — the ability to perceive accurately how others are reacting to one's behaviour;
2. to increase *diagnostic ability* — the ability to perceive accurately the state of relationships between others;
3. to increase *action skill* — the ability to carry out skilfully the behaviour required by the situation.

In a T-group, trainers explain the aims of the programme and may encourage discussion and contribute their own reactions. But they do not take a strong lead, and the group is largely left to its own devices to develop a structure which takes account of the goals of both the members of the group and the trainer, and provides a climate in which the group are sufficiently trusting of one another to discuss their own behaviour. They do this by giving feedback or expressing their reactions to one another. Members may not always accept comments about themselves, but as the T-group develops they will increasingly understand how some aspects of their behaviour are hidden from them, and they will, therefore, be well on the way to an increase in sensitivity, diagnostic ability, and action skill.

The design of a T-group 'laboratory' may include short inputs from trainers to clarify problems of group behaviour; intergroup exercises to extent T-group learning to problems of representation, negotiation, and conflict management; and application groups in which members get together to decide how they can best transfer what they have learned to their actual job behaviour. As much opportunity as possible is given to members to test out and develop their own behavioural (interactive) skills — seeking or giving information, enlisting support, persuading, and commanding.

Follow-up studies have noted three principal areas of change following the attendance of trainees at an external T-group laboratory:

1. increased openness, receptivity, and tolerance of differences;
2. increased operational skill in interpersonal relations, with overtones of increased capacity for collaboration;
3. improved understanding and diagnostic awareness of self, others, and interactive processes in groups.

T-groups have been attacked because of the possibility of negative or detrimental effects. But none of the follow-up studies have detected any significant problems. A more valid basis for doubt is that it has been difficult to prove that they have been cost-effective for organizations who have used them in-company or have strongly supported external programmes.

This criticism could be levelled at any other form of group training or, indeed, most off-the-job training. The degree to which it can be invalidated will depend on the effectiveness of the training design and of the trainer.

T-group laboratories in their purest form are unlikely ever to become a major part of company training programmes, but the group dynamics approach has valid uses in the modified forms described below.

Interactive skills training

Interactive skills training is defined by Rackham *et al* as: 'any form of training which aims to increase the effectiveness of an individual's interaction with others'. It has the following features:

- It is based on the assumption that the primary limitation on supervisory or managerial effectiveness lies not within each job boundary, but on the interface between jobs.
- There are no preconceived rules about how people should interact. It is assumed that the way interaction happens is dependent upon the situation and the people in it — this is what has to be analysed and used as a basis for the programme.
- The training takes place through groups, enabling people to practise interactive skills — such skills can only be acquired through practice.
- Participants have to receive controlled and systematic feedback on their performance — this was achieved by using specially developed techniques of behaviour analysis..
- The analysis of behaviour was used to structure groups to avoid the restrictions on behaviour change which might result from relying on arbitrarily composed groups.

A typical design for an interactive skills programme as developed by Rackman *et al* consists of three stages:

1. *The diagnostic stage*, in which the groups undertake a wide range of activities. These are designed to provide reliable behaviour samples which the trainer records and analyses.
2. *The formal feedback stage*, in which the trainer gives groups and individuals feedback on their interactive performance during the diagnostic phase.
3. *The practice, monitoring, feedback stage*, in which the group undertakes further activities to develop and practise new behaviour patterns and receives feedback from the trainer to gauge the success of attempts at behaviour change.

Coverdale Training

Coverdale Training is a more structured form of interactive skills training which is described as: 'a system of planned experience, by which people may begin to discover for themselves certain lessons — and then go on learning from their subsequent experience'. The four main characteristics or principles of Coverdale Training are that:

- managers learn by doing — practising the skills they need to get things done;
- the training is centred on practical tasks — tasks which are actually performed rather than just talked about;
- managers learn a systematic approach to getting things done;
- learning takes place in groups.

Managerial Grid

The Managerial Grid training, as developed by Blake *et al*,[2] consists of a simple diagnostic framework provided to members to aid them in describing one another's behaviour. The basic philosophy of grid training is that the task of the individual manager is to achieve production through people. In achieving this task, the manager has to show concern both for productivity and people.

Blake *et al* suggest that managers can be characterized by their location on a two-dimensional grid — the Managerial Grid — one axis of which is labelled concern for production and the other concern for people. Each axis is a scale with nine points, and thus the location of a manager on the grid can be specified by two coordinates. Five principal managerial styles are described in Blake's grid:

1,1   *Impoverished management* — exertion of minimum offer to accomplish the work required to maintain membership of the organization.

9,1   *Task management* — where a person is high in task efficiency but low in human satisfaction.

1,9   *Country club management* — high human satisfaction but low work tempo.

5,5   *Middle of the road management* — adequate task performance while maintaining morale at a satisfactory level.

9,9   *Team management* — high task achievement from committed people. Production is achieved by the integration of task and human requirements into a unified system.

A grid seminar is used to teach participants to see their managerial style. Trainees are first familiarized with grid language and theory, and they then work in groups through a series of exercises and case problems which allow individuals to exhibit their management style. This behaviour then becomes the object of feedback. Trainees acquire skills in the perception of their own and other people's style of behaviour, and the aim is to move them towards the 9,9 region of the grid.

Grid training consists of a series of seminars intended to develop the application of the message throughout the organization. In this respect, it is a type of organization development 'intervention' designed to increase organizational effectiveness rather than to concentrate on the improvement of individual interactive skills.

The grid has sound theoretical foundations, being based on a number of research studies. It recognizes the importance of developing an appropriate management style to obtain results by the effort and commitment of work groups. It has plenty of face validity — ex-grid trainees usually speak highly of it — but research studies are only partially conclusive on its overall effectiveness.

Distance learning

Distance learning enables trainees to learn, often in their own time and at home, from instructional material prepared and sometimes presented elsewhere.

The most familiar method of distance learning is the correspondence course. This is normally conducted by post and thus suffers from a time lag between the student's sending in work and receiving it back marked by the tutor. These delays could be protracted, which is a disadvantage when what is really required to enable learning to take place is a dialogue between pupil and teacher. Success in taking a correspondence course relies on the tenacity of the student as well as the quality of instruction and the speed with which correspondence is turned round.

In the UK, the Open University provides a highly developed form of distance learning with some elements of the correspondence course, but a lot is added to this basic approach by the use of television, radio, and video as well as highly sophisticated teaching texts which often rely on the discovery method or a form of programmed learning. Computer-based training techniques are also used, and there is the opportunity to be exposed directly to the Open University tutors at summer schools.

The recently introduced Open Tech programme aims to widen training and retraining opportunities for adults, with particular reference to technical, supervisory, and managerial skills. Training is open to everyone, and learning can take place at home, at work, or at an educational or training establishment.

Appendix P

Workshops

Definition
A workshop is a specially assembled group of people who, with the help of a facilitator, jointly examine organization issues and/or review their effectiveness as a team in order to develop agreed courses of action to which they will be fully committed.

Purpose
The purpose of a workshop is to draw out objectives, perceptions, attitudes and knowledge in order to produce either (or both):

- a strategy or action plan to meet specific requirements to which the members of the workshop are fully committed;
- a strengthened management team.

Uses
Apart from providing a means of gathering information for analytical and diagnostic purposes, workshops can be used in one or more of the following ways:

- to prepare or review jointly statements of the organization's mission, strategies and core values;
- to examine jointly organization issues or problems and agree plans of action, which might include the development of new strategies, systems, policies or procedures;
- to launch a project;
- to improve organizational processes — teamwork and interpersonal skills;
- to develop the competences (skills and knowledge) required to plan and implement change, in general or in particular directions.

Approach to planning workshops
One of the facilitator's key roles is to manage expectations. He or she has to:

- minimize the possibility of surprises;
- be prepared for any eventuality.

This requires thorough preparation in the form of:

- advance soundings;
- ample material.

Preparation — advance soundings
The key to a successful workshop is the preparation. It is essential to go into the workshop with maximum clarity between the facilitator and all the participants about:

- the purpose and expected outcome of the workshop;
- the role of the facilitator;
- the contribution required from the team members;
- the attitudes (including antipathies) of team members towards a workshop;
- the balance between instruction, participative training and open-ended discussion.

Preparation: material
It is advisable to have enough material to keep the workshop members busy in the event

935

that they are unforthcoming. It is also necessary to guess what possible alternative directions from those planned the workshop may take, and to be prepared for them. For both reasons, it is usually necessary to take two or three times more material than you will use.

The kinds of material used in workshops are:

- discussion groups, around an agreed topic;
- games or exercises, using prepared material;
- case studies, usually written around a specific company case;
- mini-presentations (inputs from the facilitator, which should be as brief and to the point as possible — the facilitator is there to initiate discussion, not provide solutions);
- team/style/behaviour analysis tools.

Conducting a workshop

The introductory session in a workshop is critical to its success. The members of the workshop must know why they are there, what is going to happen to them, and how the workshop will be conducted (structured but participative and flexible). It is often helpful at this stage to ask workshop members about their expectations of what they will get out of it. The resulting list can be used as a point of reference throughout the workshop and will indicate any changes in subject matter or emphasis.

A workshop may be highly structured, with specified activities and supporting material for each session. Or it may be open-ended, with little clear expectation of what will happen from hour to hour. In practice, even an open-ended workshop should have some structure which has been advertised in advance, if only to offer comfort to participants, most of whom feel less threatened if there is a visible programme. Make the event as highly structured as you possibly can, but be prepared to modify or abandon the planned timetable if necessary.

Concluding a workshop

The workshop should be concluded with a 'wrap-up' session in which the group summarizes the decisions made or lessons learnt and agrees on future action. The action may be taken by the team as a whole or it may be allocated to specially created task forces or project teams. Members of the workshop may be asked to prepare a specific action plan (an 'agenda for change') and present it to a member of top management (preferably the chief executive).

Arrangements should also be made to monitor progress in implementing agreed actions and, to this end, follow-up sessions of the workshop may be programmed. The facilitator has a key role in helping the group to reach consensus in this final session and in guiding them towards reaching a firm conclusion about what they do next as a team.

References

1. Rackham, N, Honey, P, and Colbert, M *Developing Interactive Skills*. Wellens Publishing, Northampton, 1967.
2. Blake, R, Mouton, J, Barnes, J, and Greiner, L E 'Breakthrough in Organizational Development', *Harvard Business Review*, Vol. 42, 1964, pp. 133–5.

Appendix Q

Procedural Agreements

A procedure is an established way of carrying out some piece of business. The aim of a procedure agreement is to ensure that the business conducted between management and union is carried out in an orderly, consistent and generally accepted manner.

Procedural agreements have evolved as a method of exercising joint regulation over matters that affect the interests of both the company and its employees. A procedural relationship is established between an employer and a trade union as soon as the union's right to represent the interests of its membership has been recognized. When that right includes the settlement of terms and conditions of employment by negotiation the active continuity of the relationship is maintained as adjustments are made to meet constantly changing circumstances. The procedural aspects of an act of recognition establishing negotiating rights are usually concerned with defining the area in which the union's representative capacity is acknowledged, indicating the subjects which are brought within the scope of negotiation, the steps by which agreement is to be sought and the procedure to be followed if there is failure to agree.

Procedural agreements may contain the following sections:

1. A preamble defining the objectives of the agreement.
2. A statement that the union is recognized as a representative body with negotiating rights.
3. A statement of general principles, which will include a commitment to use the procedure (a no-strike clause) and may additionally include a *status quo* clause which restricts the ability of management to introduce changes outside negotiated or customary practice.
4. A statement of the facilities granted to unions, including the rights of shop stewards and the right to hold meetings.
5. Provision for joint negotiating committees (in some agreements).
6. The negotiating or disputes procedure.
7. Provision for terminating the agreement.

Preamble — objectives

The objectives of the agreement should be stated in the preamble, for example:

> To use the processes of negotiation to achieve results beneficial to the company and the employees.

To provide a framework which will enable discussions to take place at all levels on ways of continuing the development of good industrial relations in the company.

To provide an arrangement through which matters of concern to both employers and management can be discussed and negotiated at an appropriate level.

To provide a means of negotiation and consultation on all matters directly and indirectly affecting the company's employees with the objective of achieving sound and constructive relations between the management and the employees.

Union recognition

The recognition section should confirm the right of the signatory union or unions to represent specific categories of employees within an agreed bargaining unit. The rights may be defined as being:

To represent and to negotiate wages and conditions of employment on behalf of its members who are employed by the company.

Reference may also be made in this section to union membership. A general phrase would be used such as:

The company and the union recognize that it is in the interests of good industrial relations that all employees in agreed bargaining units should become and remain members of the union.

This reference to union membership could be accompanied by an undertaking from the company to encourage employees to join the union. It could be further developed into a closed shop agreement, although those words would never be used, by a statement to the effect that all existing employees in the defined bargaining unit should become members of the union within, say, four weeks of the date of the agreement unless they have genuine religious objections. The agreement could go on to state that all new employees should join the unions within, say, two weeks of starting with the company. In the more extreme cases, where a pre-entry closed shop is in force, the agreement would state that the company undertakes only to engage men or women who are already members of the union, unless they have genuine religious objections. Reference might be made in these circumstances to the payment by those with religious objections of the equivalent of the union dues to a charity agreed with the union.

General principles

The statement of general principles should indicate how the parties to the agreement are going to work together to achieve its objectives. The following points should be included:

- A statement of common purpose — 'The company and the union have a common objective in using the processes of negotiation and consultation to achieve results beneficial to both parties'.
- A definition of the role of the unions as recognized by management — 'The company recognizes that effective industrial relations are best realized through fully representative unions capable of authoritative negotiation'.
- A definition of the role of management as recognized by the unions — 'The unions for their part recognize that management has the prime responsibility to manage the undertaking in order to achieve its objectives efficiently'.
- An undertaking not to take industrial action until the agreed procedures are exhausted (a commitment to use procedure or no-strike clause) — 'The company and the unions agree that mutually satisfactory conditions are best achieved through the process of

negotiation. The company therefore agrees to refrain from lock-out, and the union from stoppage of work or other restrictions on production until the procedure for resolving disputes prescribed in this agreement (and the national agreement) has been exhausted'.

- An undertaking may be included not to change the *status quo* without prior consultation — 'Prior consultation will take place before any change in working practices or methods of payment is implemented. Should the change result in a dispute between the management and the unions, the practice should revert to what it was prior to the dispute and the change shall only be made subsequently should it be agreed through the negotiating procedure'.

Union facilities

The agreement on union facilities should cover the following three areas:

1. *Rights and duties of shop stewards* — it is necessary to define:
   - The right of employees to elect shop stewards — 'Employees of the company who are members of the union will elect representatives to act on their behalf in accordance with this agreement'.
   - What a shop steward is — 'For the purpose of this agreement a shop steward is an accredited representative of the union who has been recognized by the company'.
   - Eligibility — the agreement may define a minimum length of service before becoming eligible for election as a steward. It may also state that the company will recognize shop stewards elected in accordance with the agreed procedure but reserves the right, after consultation with the district or regional union organizer, to withhold or withdraw recognition from any particular individual.
   - The number of shop stewards — 'The company and the union will agree the number of shop stewards to be elected each year and the areas of production or groups of people whom they will represent'.
   - Election arrangements — 'Elections by secret ballot may be held at a mutually convenient time and the company will assist in providing ballot facilities if required'.
   - Notification arrangements — 'When a shop steward has been elected the company will be notified officially by the union'.
   - Provision for a senior shop steward — 'The shop stewards may elect a senior shop steward'.
   - The duties of shop stewards — 'Shop stewards will act in accordance with agreements between the union and the company, so far as these affect the relations between the company and its employees. They will be subject to the control of the union in trade union matters'.
   - Facilities for shop stewards — 'Facilities will be afforded to shop stewards by the company to carry out their functions within the framework of this agreement to deal with questions and problems in the department or section represented by the shop steward'.
   - Arrangements for shop stewards leaving work and holding meetings and discussions — 'A shop steward wishing to leave his work to investigate a grievance, contact a union official, meet other shop stewards or carry out any other union business will first obtain the permission of his foreman or other person in authority. Should he wish to visit a department other than the one for

which he is the elected representative, he will also obtain permission of the foreman or other person in authority in that department or section. Such permission will not unreasonably be withheld'.

- The basis upon which shop stewards are paid while carrying out their duties — 'Shop stewards will suffer no financial loss through the discharge of their duties as shop stewards'.
- Training arrangements — 'The parties agree on the need to provide suitable training for shop stewards to achieve the skills required to carry out their duties'.
- Protection of employment rights — 'Action taken by shop stewards in good faith in pursuance of their duties, shall not in any way affect their employment with the company'.
- Arrangements for transferring or dismissing shop stewards — 'Before a shop steward is transferred from a department or section he represents, and before he is dismissed from the company, the transfer or dismissal will be brought to the notice of the branch secretary by management'.

2. *Union meetings and communication facilities* — for which the agreement should define:
   - Arrangements for meetings between the company and the union — 'Meetings between representatives of the company and the union will normally be held during working hours and on the company's premises'.
   - Arrangements for union meetings — 'The company recognizes that on certain occasions union meetings can with advantage be held on the company's premises outside working hours. Permission to hold such meetings should be obtained in advance from the company'.
   - The use of notice-boards by unions — 'The union will be allowed the reasonable use of company notice-boards for union announcements'.

3. *The collection of union dues* — the agreement may specify a 'check-off' arrangement for the company to collect union dues — 'It is agreed that a check-off system will operate whereby the company agrees to deduct union dues (but not entrance fees or special levies) from the wages of union members and to pay them to the union. This will only apply to employees who have previously authorized the deductions in writing'.

Joint negotiating committee

Provision for a joint negotiating committee is not a necessary part of a procedural agreement. Many, if not most, companies would prefer to avoid formalizing negotiating arrangements in this way. A joint negotiating committee, however, is sometimes set up when a large company agrees that terms and conditions of employment should be determined by collective bargaining within the company or plant, and prefers to regularize negotiating procedures rather than engage in a series of *ad hoc* trials of strength.

The terms of reference of a company joint negotiating committee should cover the following points:

1. *Objective.* To provide the means of negotiation and consultation on all matters directly and indirectly affecting the hourly paid employees in the company's establishment.
2. *Terms of reference*
   (a) To negotiate company-wide wage systems, hours of work, overtime rates and other conditions of employment.
   (b) To provide a means of joint consultation on production, safety, welfare matters and on general company problems.

(c) To review the operation of domestic disputes and disciplinary procedures and to decide on any changes necessary.

3. *Composition*
   (a) Number of shop stewards and management representatives.
   (b) Constituencies of shop steward members.
   (c) Method of election of accredited shop stewards.

4. *Officers.* Chairman and secretary of management and union sides.

5. *Meetings.* Arrangements for regular ordinary meetings and extraordinary meetings (when agreed by both chairmen).

6. *Agenda.* Arrangements for placing items on the agenda and raising additional items.

7. *Minutes.* Arrangements for chairmen to agree minutes and for distributing same.

8. *Failure to agree.* Procedure to be followed if the committee fails to agree. This could include bringing in full-time union officials and employer's officials for a works conference and, if this fails, progression through the normal negotiating procedure for the industry or some form of conciliation process. In Britain this could be provided by the Advisory, Conciliation and Arbitration Service (ACAS).

Disputes procedure

A domestic disputes procedure should describe each of the stages for dealing with disputes in the company from when an issue is first raised on the shop floor until, assuming it is not settled at an earlier stage, it is either referred to outside conciliation or is dealt with in accordance with the agreed procedure for avoiding disputes in the industry. A disputes procedure of this nature is, in effect, a grievance procedure for employees who are members of a union.

The domestic procedure should state the principle that no strike or lockout should take place until the procedure has been exhausted, unless this has already been stated as a general principle in the procedural agreement. Time limits should be given for moving from one stage to the next of the procedure in the event of a failure to agree.

The following is an example of a typical staged disputes procedure in a medium sized plant where there is no national agreement.

Domestic disputes procedure

Stage 1

1. All queries and grievances should in the first place be raised by the employee with his foreman. If the employee chooses to approach the shop steward in the first instance concerning the matter, they may subsequently jointly discuss it with the foreman, or the shop steward may raise the matter on the employee's behalf with the foreman. (The latter sentence goes further than many procedures which lay down that the shop steward should only become involved on individual issues if the employee has failed to get satisfaction. In practice, however, shop stewards do become involved in the first instance and it is realistic to allow for this in the procedure.)

2. If the issue affects a group of union members in the same department or section, the shop steward raises the matter with the foreman.

3. The foreman will do his best to resolve the issue and give an answer within *three* working days of the matter being raised with him. However, if the issue is one on which he cannot give a decision he will immediately refer the matter to stage 2 of the procedure.

Stage 2

4. If the employee or shop steward is not satisfied with the answer provided by the foreman, the latter will refer the issue to the departmental manager who will discuss the matter with the shop steward. The departmental manager may ask the personnel manager to attend this meeting and the shop steward may be accompanied by the senior shop steward of his union.
5. The departmental manager, following discussions with the personnel manager, will give his answer within *three* working days of the matter being raised with him (ie within six working days of the matter being raised initially).

Stage 3

6. If the shop steward is not satisfied with the answer given by the departmental manager, the departmental manager will refer the matter to the works manager who, together with the personnel manager, will discuss the matter with the shop steward and the senior shop steward.
7. The works manager will give his answer within *three* working days of the matter being raised with him (ie within nine working days of the matter being raised initially).

Stage 4

8. If the union is dissatisfied with the answer provided by the works manager a conference should be held to discuss the matter within the company at which a director of the company, other appropriate members of management, the senior shop steward and, if required, the district officer of the union will be present.

Stage 5

9. If a mutually satisfactory agreement is not reached in stage 4 the matter will be referred to conciliation and, if that fails, arbitration. The means of conciliation or arbitration will be agreed between the company and the district officer of the union.
10. The recommendations of the concilication body, or the decision of the arbitration body, will not be regarded as final and binding on either the company or the union. However, both parties will use these findings as a basis for further negotiation.

General

11. No lockout, stoppage of work or other unauthorized action will take place as a result of any complaint, grievance or dispute in which the company and union members are concerned. Any such action before the procedure has been exhausted will be a breach of this agreemeent.

Records

12. Records will be maintained by company foremen or managers of the details of the complaint and decisions made at each stage of the procedure. Copies of the records will be given to shop stewards or union officials concerned.

Appendix Q
Disciplinary procedure

It is normal to include a disciplinary procedure in a formal procedural agreement. The points that should be covered and an example of a procedure are given in Chapter 37 and Appendix S.

Termination of the agreement

It is usual in Britain not to specify a terminal date for the procedural agreement but to state that it would be subject to, say, six months' notice of termination from either side.

Redundancy procedures

It is not common practice for redundancy procedures to be incorporated in a procedural agreement, mainly because it is difficult to obtain complete agreement in advance on the precise criteria for redundancy and the compensation to be offered. Such procedures are often discussed separately and informal agreement reached that they should be used as guidelines for action in the event of redundancy. The points that should be covered in redundancy procedures are considered in Chapter 37 and Appendix T.

Appendix R

Grievance Procedure

Policy

1. It is the policy of the company that members of the staff should:
    (a) be given a fair hearing by their immediate supervisor or manager concerning any grievances they may wish to raise;
    (b) have the right to appeal to a more senior manager against a decision made by their supervisor or manager;
    (c) have the right to be accompanied by a fellow employee of their own choice, when raising a grievance or appealing against a decision.

The aim of the procedure is to settle the grievance as nearly as possible to its point of origin,

Procedure

2. The main stages through which a grievance may be raised are as follows:
    (a) The employee raises the matter with his or her immediate supervisor or manager and may be accompanied by a fellow employee of his or her own choice.
    (b) If the employee is not satisfied with the decision, the employee requests a meeting with a member of management who is more senior than the supervisor or manager who initially heard the grievance. This meeting takes place within five working days of the request and is attended by the manager, the manager responsible for personnel, the employee appealing against the decision, and, if desired, his or her representative. The manager responsible for personnel records the result of the meeting in writing and issues copies to all concerned.
    (c) If the employee is still not satisfied with the decision, he or she may appeal to the appropriate director. The meeting to hear this appeal is held within five working days of the request and is attended by the director, the manager responsible for personnel, the employee making the appeal, and, if desired, his or her representative. The manager responsible for personnel records the result of this meeting in writing and issues copies to all concerned.

Appendix S

Disciplinary Procedure

Policy

1. It is the policy of the company that if disciplinary action has to be taken against employees it should:
   (a) be undertaken only in cases where good reason and clear evidence exists;
   (b) be appropriate to the nature of the offence that has been committed.
   (c) be demonstrably fair and consistent with previous action in similar circumstances;
   (d) take place only when employees are aware of the standards that are expected of them or the rules with which they are required to conform.
   (e) allow employees the right to be represented by a shop steward or colleague during any formal proceedings;
   (f) allow employees the right of appeal against any disciplinary action.

Rules

2. The company is responsible for ensuring that up-to-date rules are published and available to all employees.

Procedure

Informal warning

3. A verbal or informal warning is given to the employee in the first instance or instances of minor offences. The warning is administered by the employee's immediate supervisor or manager.

Formal warning

4. A written formal warning is given to the employee in the first instance of more serious offences or after repeated instances of minor offences. The warning is administered by the employee's immediate supervisor — it states the exact nature of the offence and specifies any future disciplinary action which will be taken against the employee if the offence is repeated within a specified time limit. A copy of the written warning is placed in the employee's personnel record file but is destroyed 12 months after the date

on which it was given, if the intervening service has been satisfactory. The employee is required to read and sign the formal warning and has the right to appeal to higher management if he thinks the warning is unjustified.

Further disciplinary action

5. If, despite previous warnings, an employee still fails to reach the required standards in a reasonable period of time, it may become necessary to consider further disciplinary action. The action taken may be up to three days' suspension without pay, or dismissal. In either case the departmental manager should discuss the matter with the personnel manager before taking action. Staff below the rank of departmental manager may only recommend disciplinary action to higher management, except when their manager is not present (for example, on night-shift), when they may suspend the employee for up to one day pending an inquiry on the following day. Disciplinary action should not be confirmed until the appeal procedure (paragraphs 7 and 8) has been carried out.

Summary dismissal

6. An employee may be summarily dismissed (ie given instant dismissal without notice) only in the event of gross misconduct, as defined in company rules. Only departmental managers and above can recommend summary dismissal, and the action should not be finalized until the case has been discussed with the personnel manager and the appeal procedure has been carried out.

Appeals

7. In all circumstances, an employee may appeal against suspension, dismissal with notice, or summary dismissal. The appeal is conducted by a member of management who is more senior than the manager who initially administered the disciplinary action. The personnel manager should also be present at the hearing. If he or she wishes, the employee may be represented at the appeal by a fellow employee of his or her own choice. Appeal against summary dismissal or suspension should be heard immediately. Appeals against dismissal with notice should be held within two days. No disciplinary action which is subject to appeal is confirmed until the outcome of the appeal.

8. If an appeal against dismissal (but not suspension) is rejected at this level, the employee has the right to appeal to the chief executive. The manager responsible for personnel and, if required, the employee's representative should be present at this appeal.

Appendix T

Redundancy Procedure

Definition

1. Redundancy is defined as the situation in which management decides that an employee or employees are surplus to requirements in a particular occupation and cannot be offered suitable alternative work.

2. Employees may be surplus to requirements because changes in the economic circumstances of the company mean that fewer employees are required, or because changes in methods of working mean that a job no longer exists in its previous form. An employee who is given notice because he or she is unsuitable or inefficient is not regarded as redundant and would be dealt with in accordance with the usual disciplinary procedure.

Objectives

3. The objectives of the procedure are to ensure that:
   (a) employees who may be affected by the discontinuance of their work are given fair and equitable treatment;
   (b) the minimum disruption is caused to employees and the company;
   (c) as far as possible, changes are effected with the complete understanding and agreement of the unions and employees concerned.

Principles

4. The principles governing the procedure are as follows:
   (a) The trade unions concerned will be informed as soon as the possibility of redundancy occurs.
   (b) Every attempt will be made to:
      (i) absorb redundancy by the natural wastage of employees;
      (ii) find suitable alternative employment within the company for employees who might be affected, and provide training if this is necessary;
      (iii) give individuals reasonable warning of pending redundancy in addition to the statutory period of notice.
   (c) If alternative employment in the company is not available and more than one

individual is affected, the factors to be taken into consideration in deciding who should be made redundant will include:

(i) length of service with the company;
(ii) age (especially those who could be retired early);
(iii) effective value to the company;
(iv) opportunites for alternative employment elsewhere.

The first three of these factors should normally be regarded as the most important; other things being equal, however, length of service should be the determining factor.

Procedure

5. The procedure for dealing with employees who are surplus to requirements is set out below.

Review of manpower requirements

6. Management will continuously keep under review possible future developments which might affect the number of employees required, and will prepare overall plans for dealing with possible redundancies.

Measures to avoid redundancies

7. If the likelihood of redundancy is foreseen, the company will inform the union(s), explaining the reasons, and in consultation with the union(s) will give consideration to taking appropriate measures to prevent redundancy.
8. Departmental managers will be warned by the management of future developments which might affect them in order that detailed plans can be made for running down staff, retraining, or transfers.
9. Departmental managers will be expected to keep under review the work situation in their departments in order that contingency plans can be prepared and the manager responsible for personnel warned of any likely surpluses.

Consultation on redundancies

10. If all measures to avoid redundancy fail, the company will consult the union(s) at the earliest opportunity in order to reach agreement.

Selection of redundant employees

11. In the event of impending redundancy, the individuals who might be surplus to requirements should be selected by the departmental manager with the advice of the manager responsible for personnel on the principles that should be adopted.
12. The manager responsible for personnel should explore the possibilities of transferring affected staff to alternative work.
13. The manager responsible for personnel should inform management of proposed action (either redundancy or transfer) to obtain approval.
14. The union(s) will be informed of the numbers affected but not of individual names.
15. The departmental manager and the manager responsible for personnel will jointly

interview the employees affected either to offer a transfer or, if a suitable alternative is not available, to inform them they will be redundant. At this interview, full information should be available to give to the employee on, as appropriate:

(a) the reasons for being surplus;

(b) the alternative jobs that are available;

(c) the date when the employee will become surplus (that is, the period of notice);

(d) the entitlement to redundancy pay;

(e) the employee's right to appeal to an appropriate director;

(f) the help the company will provide.

16. An appropriate director will hear any appeals with the manager responsible for personnel.

17. The manager responsible for personnel will ensure that all the required administrative arrangements are made.

18. If the union(s) have any points to raise about the selection of employees or the actions taken by the company, these should be discussed in the first place with the manager responsible for personnel. If the results of these discussions are unsatisfactory, a meeting will be arranged with an appropriate director.

Alternative work within the company

19. If an employee is offered and accepts suitable alternative work within the company, it will take affect without a break from the previous employment and will be confirmed in writing. If the offer is refused, the employee may forfeit his or her redundancy payment.

Alternative employment

20. Employees for whom no suitable work is available in the company will be given reasonable opportunities to look for alternative employment.

Promotion Policy and Procedure

Policy

1. The promotion policy of the company is based on three main principles:
   (a) whenever possible, vacancies shall be filled by the most effective people available from within the company, subject to the right of the company to recruit from outside if there are no suitable internal candidates;
   (b) the excellence of an employee's performance in his or her present job in the company of the absence of a suitable replacement shall not be a valid reason for refusing promotion to a suitable post, provided that the procedure set out below is complied with;
   (c) promotion is not affected by race, creed, sex or marital status.

Procedure

1. When a vacancy arises, the head of the department concerned shall obtain the necessary authority, according to company regulations, and notify the personnel department, which will be responsible for submitting suitable candidates. The departmental manager has the final decision in accepting or rejecting a candidate.
2. Except for the circumstances set out in paragraph 5, the personnel department shall advertise supervisory, managerial, or specialist posts in grades C and above (works) and grades 3 and above (staff) on company notice-boards for at least three days.
3. The personnel department, with the agreement of the departmental head, can advertise the vacancy concurrently outside the company.
4. Applications from employees should be sent to the personnel department, which will carry out the following actions:
   (a) notify departmental managers of the departments in which candidates are employed;
   (b) notify the application to the manager of the department in which the vacancy occurs;
   (c) notify candidates whether or not they are required for interview;
   (d) notify candidates of the result of the interview.
5. Internal advertising can be dispensed with where management considers that:

(a) there is a natural successor (who may have been specially trained to fill the vacancy); or

(b) because of unusual requirements there is no suitable candidate within the company; or

(c) the vacancy can be filled by the transfer of an employee of equivalent grade.

6. Where departmental managers feel that the loss of an employee to another department would vitally affect the efficiency of their departments, they can appeal to the personnel manager against a transfer, provided that:

(a) the employee has served fewer than 12 months in his or her present occupation and grade; or

(b) the rate of transfer from the department of employees of similar grade has exceeded 1 per cent per calendar month over the previous six months.

If the personnel manager is unable to resolve the matter, the appeal should be submitted to an appropriate director.

7. Except in the event of a successful appeal against a transfer on the grounds stated in paragraph 6, no employee shall be refused a transfer within a reasonable time by his departmental manager. The date of the transfer should be determined between his or her present and future departmental managers. A failure to agree on a suitable date should be referred to the personnel manager for resolution or, if that fails, for reference to an appropriate director.

Subject Index

absence control 838–9
absenteeism 812–13
ACAS 97, 549, 671, 694
accidents
   identifying causes 761–2
   prevention 760–61
   reports 765–7
   safety inspections 763–5
   system of work factors 761–2
Advisory, Conciliation and Arbitration
   Services, see ACAS
achievement-motivation 465
achievement needs 157, 159
action learning 437, 460, 463, 922–3
action research 257
activities 228–9, 230
added value 499, 614, 865
advertising 357–462
affiliation needs 159, 176
age 95, 813
ageing 132–3
agencies, recruitment 360
aggression 136
Ahmedabad study 190, 215, 216
AIDS 95, 817–18
Allied Dunbar 199
ambiguity
   causes of 63
   coping with 63–4
   in line and staff jobs 64
   and management 51
   and personnel managers 112–13
   role ambiguity 62, 137, 140
   and stress 137
American Telephone and Telegraph
   (AT&T) 244
annual hours 322
Apple Computer 251

application form 363, 902–5
apprenticeship 441, 442–3
aptitude tests 372
artefacts 200
assessment centres
   advantages and disadvantages 392–3
   aims of 380
   assessment forms 385–90
   assessment instruments 384–5
   definition of 380
   development 381–92
   introduction 392
   methods of assessment 383–4
   potential assessment 482
assignments 925
attainment tests 372, 450–51
attendance management 811–13
attitude surveys
   assessing results 173, 175
   methods of conducting 172–3, 174
   reason for 142
   uses of 135–6, 171
attitudes 135–6, 142, 166, 422
attribute requirements 478
attribution theory 129, 134, 141–2
attrition, salary 659, 833
authority, 209
autonomous work groups 186, 246, 697,
   863

Bales interaction process analysis 448
bargaining
   pendulum 80
   single-table 80
   single-union 80
base rates 603
behaviour at work 144
behavioural science

Author Index

Author Index